The Wisdom Of
Orison Swett Marden Vol. II
by Orison Swett Marden

Pushing to the Front
Stories from Life

Start Publishing PD LLC
Copyright © 2024 by Start Publishing PD LLC

All rights reserved, including the right to reproduce this book or portions thereof in any form whatsoever.

Start Publishing PD is a registered trademark of Start Publishing PD LLC
Manufactured in the United States of America

Cover art: Shutterstock/Taisiya Kozorez

Cover design: Jennifer Do

10 9 8 7 6 5 4 3 2 1

ISBN 979-8-8809-2291-8

Pushing to the Front

Table of Contents:

Foreward 5
The Man and the Opportunity 7
Wanted—a Man 18
Boys with No Chance 22
The Country Boy 39
Opportunities Where You Are 46
Possibilities in Spare Moments 52
How Poor Boys and Girls Go to College 58
Your Opportunity Confronts You—what Will You Do with It? 69
Round Boys in Square Holes 77
What Career? 84
Choosing a Vocation 92
Concentrated Energy 101
The Triumphs of Enthusiasm 108
"On Time," Or, the Triumph of Promptness 117
What a Good Appearance Will Do 124
Personality as a Success Asset 131
If You Can Talk Well 139
A Fortune in Good Manners 148
Self-Consciousness and Timidity Foes to Success 162
Tact or Common Sense 166
Enamored of Accuracy 174
Do it to a Finish 183
The Reward of Persistence 196
Nerve—Grip, Pluck 205
Clear Grit 210
Success under Difficulties 218
Uses of Obstacles 224
Decision 233
Observation as a Success Factor 240
Self-Help 245

The Self-Improvement Habit	255
Raising of Values	262
Self Improvement Through Public Speaking	266
The Triumphs of the Common Virtues	274
Getting Aroused	280
The Man With an Idea	284
Dare	292
The Will and the Way	304
One Unwavering Aim	313
Work and Wait	322
The Might of Little Things	331
The Salary You Do Not Find in Your Pay Envelope	339
Expect Great Things of Yourself	349
The Next Time You Think You Are a Failure	357
Stand for Something	364
Nature's Little Bill	370
Habit—the Servant,—the Master	380
The Cigarette	388
The Power of Purity	398
The Habit of Happiness	409
Put Beauty into Your Life	417
Education by Absorption	426
The Power of Suggestion	431
The Curse of Worry	439
Take a Pleasant Thought to Bed with You	444
The Conquest of Poverty	449
A New Way of Bringing up Children	455
The Home as a School of Good Manners	465
Mother	467
Why So Many Married Women Deteriorate	476
Thrift	485
A College Education at Home	493
Discrimination in Reading	502
Reading a Spur to Ambition	508
Why Some Succeed and Others Fail	518
Rich Without Money	527

Foreword

This revised and greatly enlarged edition of "Pushing to the Front" is the outgrowth of an almost world-wide demand for an extension of the idea which made the original small volume such an ambition-arousing, energizing, inspiring force.

It is doubtful whether any other book, outside of the Bible, has been the turning-point in more lives.

It has sent thousands of youths, with renewed determination, back to school or college, back to all sorts of vocations which they had abandoned in moments of discouragement. It has kept scores of business men from failure after they had given up all hope.

It has helped multitudes of poor boys and girls to pay their way through college who had never thought a liberal education possible.

The author has received thousands of letters from people in nearly all parts of the world telling how the book has aroused their ambition, changed their ideals and aims, and has spurred them to the successful undertaking of what they before had thought impossible.

The book has been translated into many foreign languages. In Japan and several other countries it is used extensively in the public schools. Distinguished educators in many parts of the world have recommended its use in schools as a civilization-builder.

Crowned heads, presidents of republics, distinguished members of the British and other parliaments, members of the United States Supreme Court, noted authors, scholars, and eminent people in many parts of the world, have eulogized this book and have thanked the author for giving it to the world.

This volume is full of the most fascinating romances of achievement under difficulties, of obscure beginnings and triumphant endings, of stirring stories of struggles and triumphs. It gives inspiring stories of men and women who have brought great things to pass. It gives numerous examples of the triumph of mediocrity, showing how those of ordinary ability have succeeded by the use of ordinary means. It shows how invalids and cripples even have triumphed by perseverance and will over seemingly insuperable difficulties.

The book tells how men and women have seized common occasions and made them great; it tells of those of average ability who have succeeded by the use of ordinary means, by dint of indomitable will and inflexible purpose. It tells how poverty and hardship have rocked the cradle of the giants of the race. The book points out that most people do not utilize a large part of their effort because their mental attitude does not correspond with their endeavor, so that although working for one thing, they are really expecting something else; and it is what we expect that we tend to get.

No man can become prosperous while he really expects or half expects to remain poor, for holding the poverty thought, keeping in touch with poverty-producing conditions, discourages prosperity.

Before a man can lift himself he must lift his thoughts. When we shall have learned to master our thought habits, to keep our minds open to the great divine inflow of life force, we shall have learned the truths of human endowment, human possibility.

The book points out the fact that what is called success may be failure; that when men love money so much that they sacrifice their friendships, their families, their home life, sacrifice position, honor, health, everything for the dollar, their life is a failure, although they may have accumulated money. It shows how men have become rich at the price of their ideals, their character, at the cost of everything noblest, best, and truest in life. It preaches the larger doctrine of equality; the equality of will and purpose which paves a clear path even to the Presidential chair for a Lincoln or a Garfield, for any one who will pay the price of study and struggle. Men who feel themselves badly handicapped, crippled by their lack of early education, will find in these pages great encouragement to broaden their horizon, and will get a practical, helpful, sensible education in their odd moments and half-holidays.

Dr. Marden, in "Pushing to the Front," shows that the average of the leaders are not above the average of ability. They are ordinary people, but of extraordinary persistence and perseverance. It is a storehouse of noble incentive, a treasury of precious sayings. There is inspiration and encouragement and helpfulness on every page. It teaches the doctrine that no limits can be placed on one's career if he has once learned the alphabet and has push; that there are no barriers that can say to aspiring talent, "Thus far, and no farther." Encouragement is its keynote; it aims to arouse to honorable exertion those who are drifting without aim, to awaken dormant ambitions in those who have grown discouraged in the struggle for success.

The Man and the Opportunity

No man is born into this world whose work is not born with Him.—Lowell

Things don't turn up in this world until somebody turns them Up.—Garfield

Vigilance in watching opportunity; tact and daring in seizing upon opportunity; force and persistence in crowding opportunity to its utmost of possible achievement—these are the martial virtues which must command success.—Austin Phelps
"I will find a way or make one."
There never was a day that did not bring its own opportunity for doing good that never could have been done before, and never can be again.—W. H. Burleigh

"Are you in earnest? Seize this very minute; What you can do, or dream you can, *begin* it."

"If we succeed, what will the world say?" asked Captain Berry in delight, when Nelson had explained his carefully formed plan before the battle of the Nile.

"There is no if in the case," replied Nelson. "That we shall succeed is certain. Who may live to tell the tale is a very different question." Then, as his captains rose from the council to go to their respective ships, he added: "Before this time to-morrow I shall have gained a peerage or Westminster Abbey." His quick eye and daring spirit saw an opportunity of glorious victory where others saw only probable defeat.

"Is it *possible* to cross the path?" asked Napoleon of the engineers who had been sent to explore the dreaded pass of St. Bernard. "Perhaps," was the hesitating reply, "it is within the limits of *possibility*."

"Forward then," said the Little Corporal, without heeding their account of apparently insurmountable difficulties. England and Austria laughed in scorn at the idea of transporting across the Alps, where "no wheel had ever rolled, or by any possibility could roll," an army of sixty thousand men, with ponderous artillery, tons of cannon balls and baggage, and all the bulky munitions of war. But the besieged Massena was starving in Genoa, and the victorious Austrians thundered at the gates of Nice, and Napoleon was not the man to fail his former comrades in their hour of peril.

When this "impossible" deed was accomplished, some saw that it might have been done long before. Others excused themselves from encountering such gigantic obstacles by calling them insuperable. Many a commander had possessed the necessary supplies, tools, and rugged soldiers, but lacked the grit and resolution of Bonaparte, who did not shrink from mere difficulties, however great, but out of his very need made and mastered his opportunity.

Grant at New Orleans had just been seriously injured by a fall from his horse, when he received orders to take command at Chattanooga, so sorely beset by the Confederates that its surrender seemed only a question of a few days; for the hills around were all aglow by night with the camp-fires of the enemy, and supplies had been cut off. Though in great pain, he immediately gave directions for his removal to the new scene of action.

On transports up the Mississippi, the Ohio, and one of its tributaries; on a litter borne by horses for many miles through the wilderness; and into the city at last on the shoulders of four men, he was taken to Chattanooga. Things assumed a different aspect immediately. *A master* had arrived who was *equal to the situation*. The army felt the grip of his power. Before he could mount his horse he ordered an advance, and although the enemy contested the ground inch by inch, the surrounding hills were soon held by Union soldiers.

Were these things the result of chance, or were they compelled by the indominable determination of the injured General?

Did things *adjust themselves* when Horatius with two companions held ninety thousand Tuscans at bay until the bridge across the Tiber had been destroyed?—when Leonidas at Thermopylae checked the mighty march of Xerxes?—when Themistocles, off the coast of Greece, shattered the Persian's Armada?—when Caesar, finding his army hard pressed, seized spear and buckler, fought while he reorganized his men, and snatched victory from defeat?—when Winkelried gathered to his heart a sheaf of Austrian spears, thus opening a path through which his comrades pressed to freedom?—when for years Napoleon did not lose a single battle in which he was personally engaged?—when Wellington fought in many climes without ever being conquered?—when Ney, on a hundred fields, changed apparent disaster into brilliant triumph?—when Perry left the disabled *Lawrence*, rowed to the *Niagara*, and silenced the British guns? when Sheridan arrived from Winchester just as the Union retreat was becoming a rout, and turned the tide by riding along the line?—when Sherman, though sorely pressed, signaled his men to hold the fort, and they, knowing that their leader was coming, held it?

History furnishes thousands of examples of men who have seized occasions to accomplish results deemed impossible by those less resolute. Prompt decision and whole-souled action sweep the world before them.

True, there has been but one Napoleon; but, on the other hand, the Alps that oppose the progress of the average American youth are not as high or dangerous as the summits crossed by the great Corsican.

Don't wait for extraordinary opportunities. *Seize common occasions and make them great.*

On the morning of September 6, 1838, a young woman in the Longstone Lighthouse, between England and Scotland, was awakened by shrieks of agony rising above the roar of wind and wave. A storm of unwonted fury was raging, and her parents could not hear the cries; but a telescope showed nine human beings clinging to the windlass of a wrecked vessel whose bow was hanging on the rocks half a mile away. "We can do nothing," said William Darling, the light-keeper. "Ah, yes, we must go to the rescue," exclaimed his daughter, pleading tearfully with both father and mother, until the former replied: "Very well, Grace, I will let you persuade me, though it is against my better judgment." Like a feather in a whirlwind the little boat was tossed on the tumultuous sea, but, borne on the blast that swept the cruel surge, the shrieks of those shipwrecked sailors seemed to change her weak sinews into cords of steel. Strength hitherto unsuspected came from somewhere, and the heroic girl pulled one oar in even time with her father. At length the nine were safely on board. "God bless you; but ye're a bonny English lass," said one poor fellow, as he looked wonderingly upon this marvelous girl, who that day had done a deed which added more to England's glory than the exploits of many of her monarchs.

"If you will let me try, I think I can make something that will do," said a boy who had been employed as a scullion at the mansion of Signer Faliero, as the story is told by George Cary Eggleston. A large company had been invited to a banquet, and just before the hour the confectioner, who had been making a large ornament for the table, sent word that he had spoiled the piece. "You!" exclaimed the head servant, in astonishment; "and who are you?" "I am Antonio Canova, the grandson of Pisano, the stone-cutter," replied the pale-faced little fellow.

"And pray, what can you do?" asked the major-domo. "I can make you something that will do for the middle of the table, if you'll let me try." The servant was at his wits' end, so he told Antonio to go ahead and see what he could do. Calling for some butter, the scullion quickly molded a large crouching lion, which the admiring major-domo placed upon the table.

Dinner was announced, and many of the most noted merchants, princes, and noblemen of Venice were ushered into the dining-room. Among them were skilled critics of art work. When their eyes fell upon the butter lion, they forgot the purpose for which they had come in their wonder at such a work of genius. They looked at the lion long and carefully, and asked Signer Faliero what great sculptor had been persuaded to waste his skill upon such a temporary material. Faliero could not tell; so he asked the head servant, who brought Antonio before the company.

When the distinguished guests learned that the lion had been made in a short time by a scullion, the dinner was turned into a feast in his honor.

The rich host declared that he would pay the boy's expenses under the best masters, and he kept his word. Antonio was not spoiled by his good fortune, but remained at heart the same simple, earnest, faithful boy who had tried so hard to become a good stone-cutter in the shop of Pisano. Some may not have heard how the boy Antonio took advantage of this first great opportunity; but all know of Canova, one of the greatest sculptors of all time.

Weak men wait for opportunities, strong men make them.

"The best men," says E. H. Chapin, "are not those who have waited for chances but who have taken them; besieged the chance; conquered the chance; and made chance the servitor."

There may not be one chance in a million that you will ever receive unusual aid; but opportunities are often presented which you can improve to good advantage, if you will only *act*.

The lack of opportunity is ever the excuse of a weak, vacillating mind. Opportunities! Every life is full of them. Every lesson in school or college is an opportunity. Every examination is a chance in life. Every patient is an opportunity. Every newspaper article is an opportunity. Every client is an opportunity. Every sermon is an opportunity. Every business transaction is an opportunity,—an opportunity to be polite,—an opportunity to be manly,—an opportunity to be honest,—an opportunity to make friends. Every proof of confidence in you is a great opportunity. Every responsibility thrust upon your strength and your honor is priceless. Existence is the privilege of effort, and when that privilege is met like a man, opportunities to succeed along the line of your aptitude will come faster than you can use them. If a slave like Fred Douglass, who did not even own his body, can elevate himself into an orator, editor, statesman, what ought the poorest white boy to do, who is rich in opportunities compared with Douglass?

It is the idle man, not the great worker, who is always complaining that he has no time or opportunity. Some young men will make more out of the odds and ends of opportunities which many carelessly throw away than other will get out of a whole life-time. Like bees, they extract honey from every flower. Every person they meet, every circumstance of the day, adds something to their store of useful knowledge or personal power.

"There is nobody whom Fortune does not visit once in his life," says a cardinal; "but when she finds he is not ready to receive her, she goes in at the door and out at the window."

Cornelius Vanderbilt saw his opportunity in the steamboat, and determined to identify himself with steam navigation. To the surprise of all his friends, he abandoned his prosperous business and took command of one of the first steamboats launched, at a salary of one thousand dollars a year. Livingston and Fulton had acquired the sole right to navigate New York waters by steam, but Vanderbilt thought the law unconstitutional, and defied it until it was repealed. He soon became a steamboat owner.

When the government was paying a large subsidy for carrying the European mails, he offered to carry them free and give better service. His offer was accepted, and in this way he soon built up an enormous freight and passenger traffic.

Foreseeing the great future of railroads in a country like ours, he plunged into railroad enterprises with all his might, laying the foundation for the vast Vanderbilt system of to-day.

Young Philip Armour joined the long caravan of Forty-Niners, and crossed the "Great American Desert" with all his possessions in a prairie schooner drawn by mules. Hard work and steady gains carefully saved in the mines enabled him to start, six years later, in the grain and warehouse business in Milwaukee. In nine years he made five hundred thousand dollars. But he saw his great opportunity in Grant's order, "On to Richmond." One morning in 1864 he knocked at the door of Plankinton, partner in his venture as a pork packer. "I am going to take the next train to New York," said he, "to sell pork 'short.' Grant and Sherman have the rebellion by the throat, and pork will go down to twelve dollars a barrel." This was his opportunity. He went to New York and offered pork in large quantities at forty dollars per barrel. It was eagerly taken. The shrewd Wall Street speculators laughed at the young Westerner, and told him pork would go to sixty dollars, for the war was not nearly over. Mr. Armour, however, kept on selling, Grant continued to advance. Richmond fell, pork fell with it to twelve dollars a barrel, and Mr. Armour cleared two millions of dollars.

John D. Rockefeller saw his opportunity in petroleum. He could see a large population in this country with very poor lights. Petroleum was plentiful, but the refining process was so crude that the product was inferior, and not wholly safe. Here was Rockefeller's chance. Taking into partnership Samuel Andrews, the porter in a machine shop where both men had worked, he started a single barrel "still" in 1870, using an improved process discovered by his partner. They made a superior grade of oil and prospered rapidly. They admitted a third partner, Mr. Flagler, but Andrews soon became dissatisfied. "What will you take for your interest?" asked Rockefeller. Andrews wrote carelessly on a piece of paper, "One million dollars." Within twenty-four hours Mr. Rockefeller handed him the amount, saying, "Cheaper at one million than ten." In twenty years the business of the little refinery, scarcely worth one thousand dollars for building and apparatus, had grown into the Standard Oil Trust, capitalized at ninety millions of dollars, with stock quoted at 170, giving a market value of one hundred and fifty millions.

These are illustrations of seizing opportunity for the purpose of making money. But fortunately there is a new generation of electricians, of engineers, of scholars, of artists, of authors, and of poets, who find opportunities, thick as thistles, for doing something *nobler than merely amassing riches*. Wealth is not an end to strive for, but an opportunity; not the climax of a man's career, but an incident.

Mrs. Elizabeth Fry, a Quaker lady, saw her opportunity in the prisons of England. From three hundred to four hundred half-naked women, as late as 1813, would often be huddled in a single ward of Newgate, London, awaiting trial. They had neither beds nor bedding, but women, old and young, and little girls, slept in filth and rags on the floor. No one seemed to care for them, and the Government merely furnished food to keep them alive. Mrs. Fry visited Newgate, calmed the howling mob, and told them she wished to establish a school for the young women and the girls, and asked them to select a schoolmistress from their own number. They were amazed, but chose a young woman who had been committed for stealing a watch. In three months these "wild beasts," as they were sometimes called, became harmless and kind. The reform spread until the Government legalized the system, and good women throughout Great Britain became interested in the work of educating and clothing these outcasts. Fourscore years have passed, and her plan has been adopted throughout the civilized world.

A boy in England had been run over by a car, and the bright blood spurted from a severed artery. No one seemed to know what to do until another boy, Astley Cooper, took his handkerchief and stopped the bleeding by pressure above the wound. The praise which he received for thus saving the boy's life encouraging him to become a surgeon, the foremost of his day.

"The time comes to the young surgeon," says Arnold, "when, after long waiting, and patient study and experiment, he is suddenly confronted with his first critical operation. The great surgeon is away. Time is pressing. Life and death hang in the balance. Is he equal to the emergency? Can he fill the great surgeon's place, and do his work? If he can, he is the one of all others who is wanted. *His opportunity confronts him*. He and it are face to face. Shall he confess his ignorance and inability, or step into fame and fortune? It is for him to say."

Are you prepared for a great opportunity?

"Hawthorne dined one day with Longfellow," said James T. Fields, "and brought a friend, with him from Salem. After dinner the friend said, 'I have been trying to persuade Hawthorne to write a story based upon a legend of Acadia, and still current there,—the legend of a girl who, in the dispersion of the Acadians, was separated from her lover, and passed her life in waiting and seeking for him, and only found him dying in a hospital when both were old.' Longfellow wondered that the legend did not strike the fancy of Hawthorne, and he said to him, 'If you have really made up your mind not to use it for a story, will you let me have it for a poem?' To this Hawthorne consented, and promised, moreover, not to treat the subject in prose till Longfellow had seen what he could do with it in verse.

Longfellow seized his opportunity and gave to the world 'Evangeline, or the Exile of the Acadians.'"

Open eyes will discover opportunities everywhere; open ears will never fail to detect the cries of those who are perishing for assistance; open hearts will never want for worthy objects upon which to bestow their gifts; open hands will never lack for noble work to do.

Everybody had noticed the overflow when a solid is immersed in a vessel filled with water, although no one had made use of his knowledge that the body displaces its exact bulk of liquid; but when Archimedes observed the fact, he perceived therein an easy method of finding the cubical contents of objects, however irregular in shape.

Everybody knew how steadily a suspended weight, when moved, sways back and forth until friction and the resistance of the air bring it to rest, yet no one considered this information of the slightest practical importance; but the boy Galileo, as he watched a lamp left swinging by accident in the cathedral at Pisa, saw in the regularity of those oscillations the useful principle of the pendulum. Even the iron doors of a prison were not enough to shut him out from research. He experimented with the straw of his cell, and learned valuable lessons about the relative strength of tubes and rods of equal diameters.

For ages astronomers had been familiar with the rings of Saturn, and regarded them merely as curious exceptions to the supposed law of planetary formation; but Laplace saw that, instead of being exceptions, they are the sole remaining visible evidences of certain stages in the invariable process of star manufacture, and from their mute testimony he added a valuable chapter to the scientific history of Creation.

There was not a sailor in Europe who had not wondered what might lie beyond the Western Ocean, but it remained for Columbus to steer boldly out into an unknown sea and discover a new world.

Innumerable apples had fallen from trees, often hitting heedless men on the head as if to set them thinking, but Newton was the first to realize that they fall to the earth by the same law which holds the planets in their courses and prevents the momentum of all the atoms in the universe from hurling them wildly back to chaos.

Lightning had dazzled the eyes, and thunder had jarred the ears of men since the days of Adam, in the vain attempt to call their attention to the all-pervading and tremendous energy of electricity; but the discharges of Heaven's artillery were seen and heard only by the eye and ear of terror until Franklin, by a simple experiment, proved that lightning is but one manifestation of a resistless yet controllable force, abundant as air and water.

Like many others, these men are considered great, simply because they improved opportunities common to the whole human race. Read the story of any successful man and mark its moral, told thousands of years ago by Solomon: "Seest thou a man diligent in his business? he shall stand before kings." This proverb is well illustrated by the career of the industrious Franklin, for he stood before five kings and dined with two.

He who improves an opportunity sows a seed which will yield fruit in opportunity for himself and others. Every one who has labored honestly in the past has aided to place knowledge and comfort within the reach of a constantly increasing number.

Avenues greater in number, wider in extent, easier of access than ever before existed, stand open to the sober, frugal, energetic and able mechanic, to the educated youth, to the office boy and to the clerk—avenues through which they can reap greater successes than ever before within the reach of these classes in the history of the world. A little while ago there were only three or four professions—now there are fifty. And of trades, where there was one, there are a hundred now.

"What is its name?" asked a visitor in a studio, when shown, among many gods, one whose face was concealed by hair, and which had wings on its feet. "Opportunity," replied the sculptor. "Why is its face hidden?" "Because men seldom know him when he comes to them." "Why has he wings on his feet?" "Because he is soon gone, and once gone, cannot be overtaken."

"Opportunity has hair in front," says a Latin author; "behind she is bald; if you seize her by the forelock, you may hold her, but, if suffered to escape, not Jupiter himself can catch her again."

But what is the best opportunity to him who cannot or will not use it?

"It was my lot," said a shipmaster, "to fall in with the ill-fated steamer *Central America*. The night was closing in, the sea rolling high; but I hailed the crippled steamer and asked if they needed help. 'I am in a sinking condition,' cried Captain Herndon. 'Had you not better send your passengers on board directly?' I asked. 'Will you not lay by me until morning?' replied Captain Herndon. 'I will try,' I answered 'but had you not better send your passengers on board *now*?' 'Lay by me till morning,' again shouted Captain Herndon.

"I tried to lay by him, but at night, such was the heavy roll of the sea, I could not keep my position, and I never saw the steamer again. In an hour and a half after he said, 'Lay by me till morning,' his vessel, with its living freight, went down. The captain and crew and most of the passengers found a grave in the deep."

Captain Herndon appreciated the value of the opportunity he had neglected when it was beyond his reach, but of what avail was the bitterness of his self-reproach when his last moments came? How many lives were sacrificed to his unintelligent hopefulness and indecision! Like him the feeble, the sluggish, and the purposeless too often see no meaning in the happiest occasions, until too late they learn the old lesson that the mill can never grind with the water which has passed.

Such people are always a little too late or a little too early in everything they attempt. "They have three hands apiece," said John B. Gough; "a right hand, a left hand, and a little behindhand." As boys, they were late for school, and unpunctual in their home duties. That is the way the habit is acquired; and now, when responsibility claims them, they think that if they had only gone yesterday they would have obtained the situation, or they can probably get one to-morrow. They remember plenty of chances to make money, or know how to make it some other time than now; they see how to improve themselves or help others in the future, but perceive no opportunity in the present. They cannot *seize their opportunity*.

Joe Stoker, rear brakeman on the — accommodation train, was exceedingly popular with all the railroad men. The passengers liked him, too, for he was eager to please and always ready to answer questions. But he did not realize the full responsibility of his position. He "took the world easy," and occasionally tippled; and if any one remonstrated, he would give one of his brightest smiles, and reply, in such a good-natured way that the friend would think he had over-estimated the danger: "Thank you. I'm all right. Don't you worry."

One evening there was a heavy snowstorm, and his train was delayed. Joe complained of extra duties because of the storm, and slyly sipped occasional draughts from a flat bottle. Soon he became quite jolly; but the conductor and engineer of the train were both vigilant and anxious.

Between two stations the train came to a quick halt. The engine had blown out its cylinder head, and an express was due in a few minutes upon the same track. The conductor hurried to the rear car, and ordered Joe back with a red light. The brakeman laughed and said:

"There's no hurry. Wait till I get my overcoat."

The conductor answered gravely, "Don't stop a minute, Joe. The express is due."

"All right," said Joe, smilingly. The conductor then hurried forward to the engine.

But the brakeman did not go at once. He stopped to put on his overcoat. Then he took another sip from the flat bottle to keep the cold out. Then he slowly grasped the lantern and, whistling, moved leisurely down the track.

He had not gone ten paces before he heard the puffing of the express. Then he ran for the curve, but it was too late. In a horrible minute the engine of the express had telescoped the standing train, and the shrieks of the mangled passengers mingled with the hissing escape of steam.

Later on, when they asked for Joe, he had disappeared; but the next day he was found in a barn, delirious, swinging an empty lantern in front of an imaginary train, and crying, "Oh, that I had!"

He was taken home, and afterwards to an asylum, and there is no sadder sound in that sad place than the unceasing moan, "Oh, that I had! Oh, that I had!" of the unfortunate brakeman, whose criminal indulgence brought disaster to many lives.

"Oh, that I had!" or "Oh, that I had not!" is the silent cry of many a man who would give life itself for the opportunity to go back and retrieve some long-past error.

"There are moments," says Dean Alford, "which are worth more than years. We cannot help it. There is no proportion between spaces of time in importance nor in value. A stray, unthought-of five minutes may contain the event of a life. And this all-important moment—who can tell when it will be upon us?"

"What we call a turning-point," says Arnold, "is simply an occasion which sums up and brings to a result previous training. Accidental circumstances are nothing except to men who have been trained to take advantage of them."

The trouble with us is that we are ever looking for a princely chance of acquiring riches, or fame, or worth. We are dazzled by what Emerson calls the "shallow Americanism" of the day. We are expecting mastery without apprenticeship, knowledge without study, and riches by credit.

Young men and women, why stand ye here all the day idle? Was the land all occupied before you were born? Has the earth ceased to yield its increase? Are the seats all taken? the positions all filled? the chances all gone? Are the resources of your country fully developed? Are the secrets of nature all mastered? Is there no way in which you can utilize these passing moments to improve yourself or benefit others? Is the competition of modern existence so fierce that you must be content simply to gain an honest living? Have you received the gift of life in this progressive age, wherein all the experience of the past is garnered for your inspiration, merely that you may increase by one the sum total of purely animal existence?

Born in an age and country in which knowledge and opportunity abound as never before, how can you sit with folded hands, asking God's aid in work for which He has already given you the necessary faculties and strength? Even when the Chosen People supposed their progress checked by the Red Sea, and their leader paused for Divine help, the Lord said, "Wherefore criest thou unto me? Speak unto the children of Israel, *that they go forward.*"

With the world full of work that needs to be done; with human nature so constituted that often a pleasant word or a trifling assistance may stem the tide of disaster for some fellow man, or clear his path to success; with our own faculties so arranged that in honest, earnest, persistent endeavor we find our highest good; and with countless noble examples to encourage us to dare and to do, each moment brings us to the threshold of some new opportunity.

Don't *wait* for your opportunity. *Make it,*—make it as the shepherd-boy Ferguson made his when he calculated the distances of the stars with a handful of glass beads on a string. Make it as George Stephenson made his when he mastered the rules of mathematics with a bit of chalk on the grimy sides of the coal wagons in the mines. Make it, as Napoleon made his in a hundred "impossible" situations. Make it, as *all leaders of men*, in war and in peace, have made their chances of success. Golden opportunities are nothing to laziness, but industry makes the commonest chances golden.

"There is a tide in the affairs of men, Which, taken at the flood, leads on to fortune;

    Omitted, all the voyage of their life
    Is bound in shallows and in miseries;
    And we must take the current when it serves,
    Or lose our ventures."
    "'Tis never offered twice; seize, then, the hour
    When fortune smiles, and duty points the way;
    Nor shrink aside to 'scape the specter fear,
    Nor pause, though pleasure beckon from her bower;
    But bravely bear thee onward to the goal."

Wanted—A Man

*"Wanted; men:
Not systems fit and wise,
Not faiths with rigid eyes,
Not wealth in mountain piles,
Not power with gracious smiles,
Not even the potent pen;
Wanted; men."*

All the world cries, Where is the man who will save us? We want a man! Don't look so far for this man. You have him at hand. This man,—it is you, it is I, it is each one of us! . . . How to constitute one's self a man? Nothing harder, if one knows not how to will it; nothing easier, if one wills it.—Alexandre Dumas

Diogenes sought with a lantern at noontide in ancient Athens for a perfectly honest man, and sought in vain. In the market place he once cried aloud, "Hear me, O men"; and, when a crowd collected around him, he said scornfully: "I called for men, not pygmies."

Over the door of every profession, every occupation, every calling, the world has a standing advertisement: "Wanted—A Man."

Wanted, a man who will not lose his individuality in a crowd, a man who has the courage of his convictions, who is not afraid to say "No," though all the world say "Yes."

Wanted, a man who, though he is dominated by a mighty purpose, will not permit one great faculty to dwarf, cripple, warp, or mutilate his manhood; who will not allow the over-development of one faculty to stunt or paralyze his other faculties.

Wanted, a man who is larger than his calling, who considers it a low estimate of his occupation to value it merely as a means of getting a living. Wanted, a man who sees self-development, education and culture, discipline and drill, character and manhood, in his occupation.

A thousand pulpits vacant in a single religious denomination, a thousand preachers standing idle in the market place, while a thousand church committees scour the land for men to fill those same vacant pulpits, and scour in vain, is a sufficient indication, in one direction at least, of the largeness of the opportunities of the age, and also of the crying need of good men.

Wanted, a man of courage who is not a coward in any part of his nature.

Wanted, a man who is well balanced, who is not cursed with some little defect of weakness which cripples his usefulness and neutralizes his powers.

Wanted, a man who is symmetrical, and not one-sided in his development, who has not sent all the energies of his being into one narrow specialty and allowed all the other branches of his life to wither and die. Wanted, a man who is broad, who does not take half views of things; a man who mixes common sense with his theories, who does not let a college education spoil him for practical, every-day life; a man who prefers substance to show, and one who regards his good name as a priceless treasure.

Wanted, a man "who, no stunted ascetic, is full of life and fire, but whose passions are trained to heed a strong will, the servant of a tender conscience; who has learned to love all beauty, whether of nature or of art, to hate all vileness, and to respect others as himself."

The world wants a man who is educated all over; whose nerves are brought to their acutest sensibility; whose brain is cultured, keen, incisive, broad; whose hands are deft; whose eyes are alert, sensitive, microscopic; whose heart is tender, magnanimous, true.

The whole world is looking for such a man. Although there are millions out of employment, yet it is almost impossible to find just the right man in almost any department of life, and yet everywhere we see the advertisement: "Wanted—A Man."

Rousseau, in his celebrated essay on education, says; "According to the order of nature, men being equal, their common vocation is the profession of humanity; and whoever is well educated to discharge the duty of a man can not be badly prepared to fill any of those offices that have a relation to him. It matters little to me whether my pupil be designed for the army, the pulpit, or the bar. Nature has destined us to the offices of human life antecedent to our destination concerning society. To live is the profession I would teach him. When I have done with him, it is true he will be neither a soldier, a lawyer, nor a divine. *Let him first be a man*; Fortune may remove him from one rank to another as she pleases, he will be always found in his place."

A little, short doctor of divinity in a large Baptist convention stood on a step and said he thanked God he was a Baptist. The audience could not hear and called "Louder." "Get up higher," some one said. "I can't," he replied. "To be a Baptist is as high as one can get." But there is something higher than being a Baptist, and that is being a *man*.

As Emerson says, Talleyrand's question is ever the main one; not, is he rich? is he committed? is he well-meaning? has he this or that faculty? is he of the movement? is he of the establishment? but is he anybody? does he stand for something? He must be good of his kind. That is all that Talleyrand, all that the common sense of mankind asks.

When Garfield as a boy was asked what he meant to be he answered: "First of all, I must make myself a man; if I do not succeed in that, I can succeed in nothing."

Montaigne says our work is not to train a soul by itself alone, nor a body by itself alone, but to train a man.

One great need for the world to-day is for men and women who are good animals. To endure the strain of our concentrated civilization, the coming man and woman must have good bodies and an excess of animal spirits.

What more glorious than a magnificent manhood, animated with the bounding spirits of overflowing health?

It is a sad sight to see thousands of students graduated every year from our grand institutions whose object is to make stalwart, independent, self-supporting men, turned out into the world saplings instead of stalwart oaks, "memory-glands" instead of brainy men, helpless instead of self-supporting, sickly instead of robust, weak instead of strong, leaning instead of erect. "So many promising youths, and never a finished man!"

The character sympathizes with and unconsciously takes on the nature of the body. A peevish, snarling, ailing man can not develop the vigor and strength of character which is possible to a healthy, robust, cheerful man. There is an inherent love in the human mind for *wholeness*, a demand that man shall come up to the highest standard; and there is an inherent protest or contempt for preventable deficiency. Nature, too, demands that man be ever at the top of his condition.

As we stand upon the seashore while the tide is coming in, one wave reaches up the beach far higher than any previous one, then recedes, and for some time none that follows comes up to its mark, but after a while the whole sea is there and beyond it. So now and then there comes a man head and shoulders above his fellow men, showing that Nature has not lost her ideal, and after a while even the average man will overtop the highest wave of manhood yet given to the world.

Apelles hunted over Greece for many years, studying the fairest points of beautiful women, getting here an eye, there a forehead and there a nose, here a grace and there a turn of beauty, for his famous portrait of a perfect woman which enchanted the world. So the coming man will be a composite, many in one. He will absorb into himself not the weakness, not the follies, but the strength and the virtues of other types of men. He will be a man raised to the highest power. He will be a self-centered, equipoised, and ever master of himself. His sensibility will not be deadened or blunted by violation of Nature's laws. His whole character will be impressionable, and will respond to the most delicate touches of Nature.

The first requisite of all education and discipline should be man-timber. Tough timber must come from well grown, sturdy trees. Such wood can be turned into a mast, can be fashioned into a piano or an exquisite carving. But it must become timber first. Time and patience develop the sapling into the tree. So through discipline, education, experience, the sapling child is developed into hardy mental, moral, physical man-timber.

If the youth should start out with the fixed determination that every statement he makes shall be the exact truth; that every promise he makes shall be redeemed to the letter; that every appointment shall be kept with the strictest faithfulness and with full regard for other men's time; if he should hold his reputation as a priceless treasure, feel that the eyes of the world are upon him that he must not deviate a hair's breadth from the truth and right; if he should take such a stand at the outset, he would, like George Peabody, come to have almost unlimited credit and the confidence of everybody who knows him.

What are palaces and equipages; what though a man could cover a continent with his title-deeds, or an ocean with his commerce; compared with conscious rectitude, with a face that never turns pale at the accuser's voice, with a bosom that never throbs with fear of exposure, with a heart that might be turned inside out and disclose no stain of dishonor? To have done no man a wrong; to have put your signature to no paper to which the purest angel in heaven might not have been an attesting witness; to walk and live, unseduced, within arm's length of what is not your own, with nothing between your desire and its gratification but the invisible law of rectitude;—*this is to be a man.*

Man is the only great thing in the universe. All the ages have been trying to produce a perfect model. Only one complete man has yet evolved. The best of us are but prophesies of what is to come.

> What constitutes a state?
> Not high-raised battlement or labored mound,
> Thick wall or moated gate;
> Not cities proud with spires and turrets crowned;
> Not bays and broad-armed ports,
> Where, laughing at the storm, rich navies ride;
> Not starred and spangled courts,
> Where low-browed baseness wafts perfume to pride.
> No: men, high-minded men,
> With powers as far above dull brutes endued
> In forest, brake, or den,
> As beasts excel cold rocks and brambles rude,—
> Men who their duties know,
> But know their rights, and knowing, dare maintain,
> Prevent the long-aimed blow,
> And crush the tyrant while they rend the chain. —William Jones

> God give us men. A time like this demands
> Strong minds, great hearts, true faith and ready hands:
> Men whom the lust of office does not kill;
> Men whom the spoils of office cannot buy;
> Men who possess opinions and a will;
> Men who have honor—men who will not lie;
> Men who can stand before a demagogue
> And scorn his treacherous flatteries without winking;
> Tall men sun-crowned, who live above the fog
> In public duty, and in private thinking. —Anon

BOYS WITH NO CHANCE

In the blackest soils grow the fairest flowers, and the loftiest and strongest trees spring heavenward among the rocks.—J. G. Holland

Poverty is very terrible, and sometimes kills the very soul within us, but it is the north wind that lashes men into Vikings; it is the soft, luscious south wind which lulls them to lotus Dreams.—Ouida

Poverty is the sixth Sense.—German Proverb

It is not every calamity that is a curse, and early adversity is often a blessing. Surmounted difficulties not only teach, but hearten us in our future struggles.—Sharpe

There can be no doubt that the captains of industry to-day, using that term in its broadest sense, are men who began life as poor boys.—Seth Low
'Tis a common proof, That lowliness is young ambition's ladder!—Shakespeare

"I am a child of the court," said a pretty little girl at a children's party in Denmark; "*my* father is Groom of the Chambers, which is a very high office. And those whose names end with 'sen,'" she added, "can never be anything at all. We must put our arms akimbo, and make the elbows quite pointed, so as to keep these 'sen' people at a great distance."

"But my papa can buy a hundred dollars' worth of bonbons, and give them away to children," angrily exclaimed the daughter of the rich merchant Peter*sen*. "Can your papa do that?"

"Yes," chimed in the daughter of an editor, "my papa can put your papa and everybody's papa into the newspaper. All sorts of people are afraid of him, my papa says, for he can do as he likes with the paper."

"Oh, if I could be one of them!" thought a little boy peeping through the crack of the door, by permission of the cook for whom he had been turning the spit. But no, *his* parents had not even a penny to spare, and his name ended in "sen."

Years afterwards when the children of the party had become men and women, some of them went to see a splendid house, filled with all kinds of beautiful and valuable objects. There they met the owner, once the very boy who thought it so great a privilege to peep at them through a crack in the door as they played. He had become the great sculptor Thorwald*sen*.

This sketch is adapted from a story by a poor Danish cobbler's son, another whose name did not keep him from becoming famous,—Hans Christian Ander*sen*.

"There is no fear of my starving, father," said the deaf boy, Kitto, begging to be taken from the poorhouse and allowed to struggle for an education; "we are in the midst of plenty, and I know how to prevent hunger. The Hottentots subsist a long time on nothing but a little gum; they also, when hungry, tie a ligature around their bodies. Cannot I do so, too? The hedges furnish blackberries and nuts, and the fields, turnips; a hayrick will make an excellent bed."

The poor deaf boy with a drunken father, who was thought capable of nothing better than making shoes as a pauper, became one of the greatest Biblical scholars in the world. His first book was written in the workhouse.

Creon was a Greek slave, as a writer tells the story in Kate Field's "Washington," but he was also a slave of the Genius of Art. Beauty was his god, and he worshiped it with rapt adoration. It was after the repulse of the great Persian invader, and a law was in force that under penalty of death no one should espouse art except freemen. When the law was enacted he was engaged upon a group for which he hoped some day to receive the commendation of Phidias, the greatest sculptor living, and even the praise of Pericles.

What was to be done? Into the marble block before him Creon had put his head, his heart, his soul, his life. On his knees, from day to day, he had prayed for fresh inspiration, new skill. He believed, gratefully and proudly, that Apollo, answering his prayers, had directed his hand and had breathed into the figures the life that seemed to animate them; but now,—now, all the gods seemed to have deserted him.

Cleone, his devoted sister, felt the blow as deeply as her brother. "O Aphrodite!" she prayed, "immortal Aphrodite, high enthroned child of Zeus, my queen, my goddess, my patron, at whose shrine I have daily laid my offerings, to be now my friend, the friend of my brother!"

Then to her brother she said: "O Creon, go to the cellar beneath our house. It is dark, but I will furnish light and food. Continue your work; the gods will befriend us."

To the cellar Creon went, and guarded and attended by his sister, day and night, he proceeded with his glorious but dangerous task.

About this time all Greece was invited to Athens to behold an exhibit of works of art. The display took place in the Agora. Pericles presided. At his side was Aspasia. Phidias, Socrates, Sophocles, and other renowned men stood near him.

The works of the great masters were there. But one group, far more beautiful than the rest,—a group that Apollo himself must have chiseled,—challenged universal attention, exciting at the same time no little envy among rival artists.

"Who is the sculptor of this group?" None could tell. Heralds repeated the question, but there was no answer. "A mystery, then! Can it be the work of a slave?" Amid great commotion a beautiful maiden with disarranged dress, disheveled hair, a determined expression in her eyes, and with closed lips, was dragged into the Agora. "This woman," cried the officers, "this woman knows the sculptor; we are sure of it; but she will not tell his name."

Cleone was questioned, but was silent. She was informed of the penalty of her conduct, but her lips remained closed. "Then," said Pericles, "the law is imperative, and I am the minister of the law. Take the maid to the dungeon."

As he spoke a youth with flowing hair, emaciated, but with black eyes that beamed with the flashing light of genius, rushed forward, and flinging himself before him exclaimed: "O Pericles, forgive and save the maid! She is my sister. I am the culprit. The group is the work of my hands, the hands of a slave."

The indignant crowd interrupted him and cried, "To the dungeon, to the dungeon with the slave." "As I live, no!" said Pericles, rising. "Behold that group! Apollo decides by it that there is something higher in Greece than an unjust law. The highest purpose of law should be the development of the beautiful. If Athens lives in the memory and affections of men, it is her devotion to art that will immortalize her. Not to the dungeon, but to my side bring the youth."

And there, in the presence of the assembled multitude, Aspasia placed the crown of olives, which she held in her hands, on the brow of Creon; and at the same time, amid universal plaudits, she tenderly kissed Creon's affectionate and devoted sister.

The Athenians erected a statue to Aesop, who was born a slave, that men might know that the way to honor is open to all. In Greece, wealth and immortality were the sure reward of the man who could distinguish himself in art, literature, or war. No other country ever did so much to encourage and inspire struggling merit.

"I was born in poverty," said Vice-President Henry Wilson. "Want sat by my cradle. I know what it is to ask a mother for bread when she has none to give. I left my home at ten years of age, and served an apprenticeship of eleven years, receiving a month's schooling each year, and, at the end of eleven years of hard work, a yoke of oxen and six sheep, which brought me eighty-four dollars. I never spent the sum of one dollar for pleasure, counting every penny from the time I was born till I was twenty one years of age. I know what it is to travel weary miles and ask my fellow men to give me leave to toil. . . . In the first month after I was twenty-one years of age, I went into the woods, drove a team, and cut mill-logs. I rose in the morning before daylight and worked hard till after dark, and received the magnificent sum of six dollars for the month's work! Each of these dollars looked as large to me as the moon looks to-night."

Mr. Wilson determined never to lose an opportunity for self-culture or self-advancement. Few men knew so well the value of spare moments. *He seized them as though they were gold* and would not let one pass until he had wrung from it every possibility. He managed to read a thousand good books before he was twenty-one—what a lesson for boys on a farm! When he left the farm he started on foot for Natick, Mass., over one hundred miles distant, to learn the cobbler's trade. He went through Boston that he might see Bunker Hill monument and other historical landmarks. The whole trip cost him but one dollar and six cents. In a year he was the head of a debating club at Natick. Before eight years had passed, he made his great speech against slavery, in the Massachusetts Legislature. Twelve years later he stood shoulder to shoulder with the polished Sumner in Congress. With him, *every occasion was a great occasion*. He ground every circumstance of his life into material for success.

"Don't go about the town any longer in that outlandish rig. Let me give you an order on the store. Dress up a little, Horace." Horace Greeley looked down on his clothes as if he had never before noticed how seedy they were, and replied: "You see Mr. Sterrett, my father is on a new place, and I want to help him all I can." He had spent but six dollars for personal expenses in seven months, and was to receive one hundred and thirty-five from Judge J. M. Sterret of the Erie "Gazette" for substitute work. He retained but fifteen dollars and gave the rest to his father, with whom he had moved from Vermont to Western Pennsylvania, and for whom he had camped out many a night to guard the sheep from wolves. He was nearly twenty-one; and, although tall and gawky, with tow-colored hair, a pale face and whining voice, he resolved to seek his fortune in New York City. Slinging his bundle of clothes on a stick over his shoulder, he walked sixty miles through the woods to Buffalo, rode on a canal boat to Albany, descended the Hudson in a barge, and reached New York, just as the sun was rising, August 18, 1831.

He found board over a saloon at two dollars and a half a week. His journey of six hundred miles had cost him but five dollars. For days Horace wandered up and down the streets, going into scores of buildings and asking if they wanted "a hand"; but "no" was the invariable reply. His quaint appearance led many to think he was an escaped apprentice. One Sunday at his boarding-place he heard that printers were wanted at "West's Printing-office." He was at the door at five o'clock Monday morning, and asked the foreman for a job at seven. The latter had no idea that a country greenhorn could set type for the Polyglot Testament on which help was needed, but said: "Fix up a case for him and we'll see if he *can* do anything." When the proprietor came in, he objected to the new-comer and told the foreman to let him go when his first day's work was done. That night Horace showed a proof of the largest and most correct day's work that had then been done.

In ten years he was a partner in a small printing-office. He founded the "New Yorker," the best weekly paper in the United States, but it was not profitable. When Harrison was nominated for President in 1840, Greeley started "The Log-Cabin," which reached the then fabulous circulation of ninety thousand. But on this paper at a penny per copy he made no money. His next venture was "The New York Tribune," price one cent. To start it he borrowed a thousand dollars and printed five thousand copies of the first number. It was difficult to give them all away. He began with six hundred subscribers, and increased the list to eleven thousand in six weeks. The demand for the "Tribune" grew faster than new machinery could be obtained to print it. It was a paper whose editor, whatever his mistakes, always tried to be right.

James Gordon Bennett had made a failure of his "New York Courier" in 1825, of the "Globe" in 1832, and of the "Pennsylvanian" a little later, and was only known as a clever writer for the press, who had saved a few hundred dollars by hard labor and strict economy for fourteen years. In 1835 he asked Horace Greeley to join him in starting a new daily paper, the "New York Herald." Greeley declined, but recommended two young printers, who formed partnership with Bennett, and the "Herald" was started on May 6, 1835, with a cash capital to pay expenses for *ten days*. Bennet hired a small cellar in Wall Street, furnished it with a chair and a desk composed of a plank supported by two barrels; and there, doing all the work except the printing, began the work of making a really great daily newspaper, a thing then unknown in America, as all its predecessors were party organs. Steadily the young man struggled towards his ideal, giving the news, fresh and crisp, from an ever-widening area, until his paper was famous for giving the current history of the world as fully and quickly as any competitor, and often much more thoroughly and far more promptly. Neither labor nor expense was spared in obtaining prompt and reliable information on every topic of general interest. It was an up-hill job, but its completion was finally marked by the opening at the corner of Broadway and Ann Street of the most complete newspaper establishment then known.

One of the first things to attract the attention on entering George W. Childs' private office in Philadelphia was this motto, which was the key-note of the success of a boy who started with "no chance": "Nihil sine labore." It was his early ambition to own the "Philadelphia Ledger" and the great building in which it was published; but how could a poor boy working for $2.00 a week ever hope to own such a great paper? However, he had great determination and indomitable energy; and as soon as he had saved a few hundred dollars as a clerk in a bookstore, he began business as a publisher. He made "great hits" in some of the works he published, such as "Kane's Arctic Expedition." He had a keen sense of what would please the public, and there seemed no end to his industry.

In spite of the fact that the "Ledger" was losing money every day, his friends could not dissuade him from buying it, and in 1864 the dreams of his boyhood found fulfilment. He doubled the subscription price, lowered the advertising rates, to the astonishment of everybody, and the paper entered upon a career of remarkable prosperity, the profits sometimes amounting to over four hundred thousand dollars a year. He always refused to lower the wages of his employees even when every other establishment in Philadelphia was doing so.

At a banquet in Lyons, nearly a century and a half ago, a discussion arose in regard to the meaning of a painting representing some scene in the mythology or history of Greece. Seeing that the discussion was growing warm, the host turned to one of the waiters and asked him to explain the picture. Greatly to the surprise of the company, the servant gave a clear concise account of the whole subject, so plain and convincing that it at once settled the dispute.

"In what school have you studied, Monsieur?" asked one of the guests, addressing the waiter with great respect. "I have studied in many schools, Monseigneur," replied the young servant: "but the school in which I studied longest and learned most is the school of adversity." Well had he profited by poverty's lessons; for, although then but a poor waiter, all Europe soon rang with the fame of the writings of the greatest genius of his age and country, Jean Jacques Rousseau.

The smooth sand beach of Lake Erie constituted the foolscap on which, for want of other material, P. R. Spencer, a barefoot boy with no chance, perfected the essential principles of the Spencerian system of penmanship, the most beautiful exposition of graphic art.

For eight years William Cobbett had followed the plow, when he ran away to London, copied law papers for eight or nine months, and then enlisted in an infantry regiment. During his first year of soldier life he subscribed to a circulating library at Chatham, read every book in it, and began to study.

"I learned grammar when I was a private soldier on the pay of sixpence a day. The edge of my berth, or that of the guard-bed, was my seat to study in; my knapsack was my bookcase; a bit of board lying on my lap was my writing-table, and the task did not demand anything like a year of my life. I had no money to purchase candles or oil; in winter it was rarely that I could get any evening light but that of the fire, and only my turn, even, of that. To buy a pen or a sheet of paper I was compelled to forego some portion of my food, though in a state of half starvation. I had no moment of time that I could call my own, and I had to read and write amidst the talking, laughing, singing, whistling, and bawling of at least half a score of the most thoughtless of men, and that, too, in the hours of their freedom from all control. Think not lightly of the *farthing* I had to give, now and then, for pen, ink, or paper. That farthing was, alas! a great sum to me. I was as tall as I am now, and I had great health and great exercise. The whole of the money not expended for us at market was *twopence a week* for each man. I remember, and well I may! that upon one occasion I had, after all absolutely necessary expenses, made shift to have a half-penny in reserve, which I had destined for the purpose of a red herring in the morning, but so hungry as to be hardly able to endure life, when I pulled off my clothes at night, I found that I had lost my half-penny. I buried my head in the miserable sheet and rug, and cried like a child."

But Cobbett made even his poverty and hard circumstances serve his all-absorbing passion for knowledge and success. "If I," said he, "under such circumstances could encounter and overcome this task, is there, can there be in the whole world, a youth to find any excuse for its non-performance?"

Humphrey Davy had but a slender chance to acquire great scientific knowledge, yet he had true mettle in him, and he made even old pans, kettles, and bottles contribute to his success, as he experimented and studied in the attic of the apothecary-store where he worked.

"Many a farmer's son," says Thurlow Weed, "has found the best opportunities for mental improvement in his intervals of leisure while tending 'sap-bush.' Such, at any rate, was my own experience. At night you had only to feed the kettles and keep up the fires, the sap having been gathered and the wood cut before dark. During the day we would always lay in a good stock of 'fat-pine,' by the light of which, blazing bright before the sugar-house, I passed many a delightful night in reading. I remember in this way to have a history of the French Revolution, and to have obtained a better and more enduring knowledge of its events and horrors and of the actors in that great national tragedy than I have received from all subsequent reading. I remember, also, how happy I was in being able to borrow the books of a Mr. Keyes, after a two-mile tramp through the snow, shoeless, my feet swaddled in remnants of rag carpet."

"May I have a holiday to-morrow, father?" asked Theodore Parker one August afternoon. The poor Lexington millwright looked in surprise at his youngest son, for it was a busy time, but he saw from the boy's earnest face that he had no ordinary object in view, and granted the request. Theodore rose very early the next morning, walked through the dust ten miles to Harvard College, and presented himself for a candidate for admission. He had been unable to attend school regularly since he was eight years old, but he had managed to go three months each winter, and had reviewed his lessons again and again as he followed the plow or worked at other tasks. All his odd moments had been hoarded, too, for reading useful books, which he borrowed. One book he could not borrow, but he felt that he must have it; so on summer mornings he rose long before the sun and picked bushel after bushel of berries, which he sent to Boston, and so got the money to buy that coveted Latin dictionary.

"Well done, my boy!" said the millwright, when his son came home late at night and told of his successful examination; "but, Theodore, I cannot afford to keep you there!" "True, father," said Theodore, "I am not going to stay there; I shall study at home, at odd times, and thus prepare myself for a final examination, which will give me a diploma." He did this; and, by teaching school as he grew older, got money to study for two years at Harvard, where he was graduated with honor. Years after, when, as the trusted friend and adviser of Seward, Chase, Sumner, Garrison, Horace Mann, and Wendell Phillips, his influence for good was felt in the hearts of all his countrymen, it was a pleasure for him to recall his early struggles and triumphs among the rocks and bushes of Lexington.

"The proudest moment of my life," said Elihu Burritt, "was when I had first gained the full meaning of the first fifteen lines of Homer's Iliad." Elihu Burritt's father died when he was sixteen, and Elihu was apprenticed to a blacksmith in his native village of New Britain, Conn. He had to work at the forge for ten or twelve hours a day; but while blowing the bellows, he would solve mentally difficult problems in arithmetic. In a diary kept at Worcester, whither he went some ten years later to enjoy its library privileges, are such entries as these,—"Monday, June 18, headache, 40 pages Cuvier's 'Theory of the Earth,' 64 pages French, 11 hours' forging. Tuesday, June 19, 60 lines Hebrew, 30 Danish, 10 lines Bohemian, 9 lines Polish, 15 names of stars, 10 hours' forging. Wednesday, June 20, 25 lines Hebrew, 8 lines Syriac, 11 hours' forging." He mastered 18 languages and 32 dialects. He became eminent as the "Learned Blacksmith," and for his noble work in the service of humanity. Edward Everett said of the manner in which this boy with no chance acquired great learning: "It is enough to make one who has good opportunities for education hang his head in shame."

The barefoot Christine Nilsson in remote Sweden had little chance, but she won the admiration of the world for her wondrous power of song, combined with rare womanly grace.

"Let me say in regard to your adverse worldly circumstances," says Dr. Talmage to young men, "that you are on a level now with those who are finally to succeed. Mark my words, and think of it thirty years from now. You will find that those who are then the millionaires of this country, who are the orators of the country, who are the poets of the country, who are the strong merchants of the country, who are the great philanthropists of the country,—mightiest in the church and state,—are now on a level with you, not an inch above you, and in straightened circumstances.

"No outfit, no capital to start with? Young man, go down to the library and get some books, and read of what wonderful mechanism God gave you in your hand, in your foot, in your eye, in your ear, and then ask some doctor to take you into the dissecting-room and illustrate to you what you have read about, and never again commit the blasphemy of saying you have no capital to start with. *Equipped? Why, the poorest young man is equipped as only the God of the whole universe could afford to equip him.*"

A newsboy is not a very promising candidate for success or honors in any line of life. A young man can't set out in life with much less chance than when he starts his "daily" for a living. Yet the man who more than any other is responsible for the industrial regeneration of this continent started in life as a newsboy on the Grand Trunk Railway. Thomas Alva Edison was then about fifteen years of age. He had already begun to dabble in chemistry, and had fitted up a small itinerant laboratory. One day, as he was performing some occult experiment, the train rounded a curve, and the bottle of sulphuric acid broke. There followed a series of unearthly odors and unnatural complications. The conductor, who had suffered long and patiently, promptly ejected the youthful devotee, and in the process of the scientist's expulsion added a resounding box upon the ear.

Edison passed through one dramatic situation after another—always mastering it—until he attained at an early age the scientific throne of the world. When recently asked the secret of his success, he said he had always been a total abstainer and singularly moderate in everything but work.

Daniel Manning who was President Cleveland's first campaign manager and afterwards Secretary of the Treasury, started out as a newsboy with apparently the world against him. So did Thurlow Weed; so did David B. Hill. New York seems to have been prolific in enterprising newsboys.

What nonsense for two uneducated and unknown youths who met in a cheap boarding-house in Boston to array themselves against an institution whose roots were embedded in the very constitution of our country, and which was upheld by scholars, statesmen, churches, wealth, and aristocracy, without distinction of creed or politics! What chance had they against the prejudices and sentiment of a nation? But these young men were fired by a lofty purpose, and they were thoroughly in earnest. One of them, Benjamin Lundy, had already started in Ohio a paper called "The Genius of Universal Liberty," and had carried the entire edition home on his back from the printing-office, twenty miles, every month. He had walked four hundred miles on his way to Tennessee to increase his subscription list. He was no ordinary young man.

With William Lloyd Garrison, he started to prosecute his work more earnestly in Baltimore. The sight of the slave-pens along the principal streets; of vessel-loads of unfortunates torn from home and family and sent to Southern ports; the heartrending scenes at the auction blocks, made an impression on Garrison never to be forgotten; and the young man whose mother was too poor to send him to school, although she early taught him to hate oppression, resolved to devote his life to secure the freedom of these poor wretches.

In the first issue of his paper, Garrison urged an immediate emancipation, and called down upon his head the wrath of the entire community. He was arrested and sent to jail. John G. Whittier, a noble friend in the North, was so touched at the news that, being too poor to furnish the money himself, he wrote to Henry Clay, begging him to release Garrison by paying the fine. After forty-nine days of imprisonment he was set free. Wendell Phillips said of him, "He was imprisoned for his opinion when he was twenty-four. He had confronted a nation in the bloom of his youth."

In Boston, with no money, friends, or influence, in a little upstairs room, Garrison started the "Liberator." Read the declaration of this poor young man with "no chance," in the very first issue: "I will be as harsh as truth, as uncompromising as justice. I am in earnest. I will not equivocate, I will not excuse; I will not retreat a single inch, and I will be heard." What audacity for a young man, with the world against him!

Hon. Robert Y. Hayne, of South Carolina, wrote to Otis, mayor of Boston, that some one had sent him a copy of the "Liberator," and asked him to ascertain the name of the publisher. Otis replied that he had found a poor young man printing "this insignificant sheet in an obscure hole, his only auxiliary a negro boy, his supporters a few persons of all colors and little influence."

But this poor young man, eating, sleeping, and printing in this "obscure hole," had set the world to thinking, and must be suppressed. The Vigilance Association of South Carolina offered a reward of fifteen hundred dollars for the arrest and prosecution of any one detected circulating the "Liberator." The Governors of one or two States set a price on the editor's head. The legislature of Georgia offered a reward of five thousand dollars for his arrest and conviction.

Garrison and his coadjutors were denounced everywhere. A clergyman named Lovejoy was killed by a mob in Illinois for espousing the cause, while defending his printing-press, and in the old "Cradle of American Liberty" the wealth, power, and culture of Massachusetts arrayed itself against the "Abolitionists" so outrageously, that a mere spectator, a young lawyer of great promise, asked to be lifted upon the high platform, and replied in such a speech as was never before heard in Faneuil Hall. "When I heard the gentleman lay down the principles which place the murderers of Lovejoy at Alton side by side with Otis and Hancock, with Quincy and Adams," said Wendell Phillips, pointing to their portraits on the walls. "I thought those pictured lips would have broken into voice to rebuke the recreant American, the slanderer of the dead. For the sentiments that he has uttered, on soil consecrated by the prayers of the Puritans and the blood of patriots. the earth should have yawned and swallowed him up."

The whole nation was wrought to fever heat.

Between the Northern pioneers and Southern chivalry the struggle was long and fierce, even in far California. The drama culminated in the shock of civil war. When the war was ended, and, after thirty-five years of untiring, heroic conflict, Garrison was invited as the nation's guest, by President Lincoln, to see the stars and stripes unfurled once more above Fort Sumter, an emancipated slave delivered the address of welcome, and his two daughters, no longer chattels in appreciation presented Garrison with a beautiful wreath of flowers.

About this time Richard Cobden, another powerful friend of the oppressed, died in London.

His father had died leaving nine children almost penniless. The boy earned his living by watching a neighbor's sheep, but had no chance to attend school until he was ten years old. He was sent to a boarding-school, where he was abused, half starved, and allowed to write home only once in three months. At fifteen he entered his uncle's store in London as a clerk. He learned French by rising early and studying while his companions slept. He was soon sent out in a gig as a commercial traveler.

He called upon John Bright to enlist his aid in fighting the terrible "Corn-Laws" which were taking bread from the poor and giving it to the rich. He found Mr. Bright in great grief, for his wife was lying dead in the house.

"There are thousands of homes in England at this moment," said Richard Cobden, "where wives, mothers, and children are dying of hunger. Now, when the first paroxysm of grief is passed, I would advise you to come with me, and we will never rest until the Corn-Laws are repealed." Cobden could no longer see the poor man's bread stopped at the Custom-House and taxed for the benefit of the landlord and farmer, and he threw his whole soul into this great reform. "This is not a party question," said he, "for men of all parties are united upon it. It is a pantry question,—a question between the working millions and the aristocracy." They formed the "Anti-Corn-Law League," which, aided by the Irish famine,—for it was hunger that at last ate through those stone walls of protection,—secured the repeal of the law in 1846. Mr. Bright said: "There is not in Great Britain a poor man's home that has not a bigger, better, and cheaper loaf through Richard Cobden's labors."

John Bright himself was the son of a poor working man, and in those days the doors of the higher schools were closed to such as he; but the great Quaker heart of this resolute youth was touched with pity for the millions of England's and Ireland's poor, starving under the Corn-Laws. During the frightful famine, which cut off two millions of Ireland's population in a year, John Bright was more powerful than all the nobility of England. The whole aristocracy trembled before his invincible logic, his mighty eloquence, and his commanding character. Except possibly Cobden, no other man did so much to give the laborer a shorter day, a cheaper loaf, an added shilling.

Over a stable in London lived a poor boy named Michael Faraday, who carried newspapers about the streets to loan to customers for a penny apiece. He was apprenticed for seven years to a bookbinder and bookseller. When binding the Encyclopaedia Britannica, his eyes caught the article on electricity, and he could not rest until he had read it. He procured a glass vial, an old pan, and a few simple articles, and began to experiment. A customer became interested in the boy, and took him to hear Sir Humphry Davy lecture on chemistry. He summoned courage to write the great scientist and sent the notes he had taken of his lecture. One night, not long after, just as Michael was about to retire, Sir Humphry Davy's carriage stopped at his humble lodging, and a servant handed him a written invitation to call upon the great lecturer the next morning. Michael could scarcely trust his eyes as he read the note. In the morning he called as requested, and was engaged to clean instruments and take them to and from the lecture-room. He watched eagerly every movement of Davy, as with a glass mask over his face, he developed his safety-lamp and experimented with dangerous explosives. Michael studied and experimented, too, and it was not long before this poor boy with no chance was invited to lecture before the great philosophical society.

He was appointed professor at the Royal Academy of Woolwich, and became the wonder of the age in science. Tyndall said of him, "He is the greatest experimental philosopher the world has ever seen." When Sir Humphry Davy was asked what was his greatest discovery, he replied "Michael Faraday."

"What has been done can be done again," said the boy with no chance, Disraeli, who become Lord Beaconsfield, England's great Prime Minister. "I am not a slave, I am not a captive, and by energy I can overcome greater obstacles." Jewish blood flowed in his veins and everything seemed against him, but he remembered the example of Joseph, who became Prime Minister of Egypt four thousand years before, and that of Daniel, who was Prime Minister to the greatest despot of the world five centuries before the birth of Christ. He pushed his way up through the lower classes, up through the middle classes, up through the upper classes, until he stood a master, self-poised upon the topmost round of political and social power. Rebuffed, scorned, ridiculed, hissed down in the House of Commons, he simply said, "The time will come when you will hear me." The time did come, and the boy with no chance but a determined will swayed the scepter of England for a quarter of a century.

Henry Clay, the "mill-boy of the slashes," was one of seven children of a widow too poor to send him to any but a common country school, where he was drilled only in the "three R's." But he used every spare moment to study without a teacher, and in after years he was a king among self-made men. The boy who had learned to speak in a barn, with only a cow and a horse for an audience, became one of the greatest of American orators and statesmen.

See Kepler struggling with poverty and hardship, his books burned in public by order of the state, his library locked up by the Jesuits, and himself exiled by public clamor. For seventeen years he works calmly upon the demonstration of the great principles that planets revolve in ellipses, with the sun at one focus; that a line connecting the center of the earth with the center of the sun passes over equal spaces in equal times, and that the squares of the times of revolution of the planets above the sun are proportioned to the cubes by their mean distances from the sun. This boy with no chance became one of the world's greatest astronomers.

"When I found that I was black," said Alexandre Dumas, "I resolved to live as if I were white, and so force men to look below my skin."

How slender seemed the chance of James Sharples, the celebrated blacksmith artist of England! He was very poor, but he often rose at three o'clock to copy books he could not buy. He would walk eighteen miles to Manchester and back after a hard day's work to buy a shilling's worth of artist's materials. He would ask for the heaviest work in the blacksmith shop, because it took a longer time to heat at the forge, and he could thus have many spare minutes to study the precious book, which he propped up against the chimney. He was a great miser of spare moments and used every one as though he might never see another. He devoted his leisure hours for five years to that wonderful production, "The Forge," copies of which are to be seen in many a home.

What chance had Galileo to win renown in physics or astronomy, when his parents compelled him to go to a medical school? Yet while Venice slept, he stood in the tower of St. Mark's Cathedral and discovered the satellites of Jupiter and the phases of Venus, through a telescope made with his own hands. When compelled on bended knee to publicly renounce his heretical doctrine that the earth moves around the sun, all the terrors of the Inquisition could not keep this feeble man of threescore years and ten from muttering to himself, "Yet it does move." When thrown into prison, so great was his eagerness for scientific research that he proved by a straws in his cell that a hollow tube is relatively much stronger than a solid rod of the same size. Even when totally blind, he kept constantly at work.

Imagine the surprise of the Royal Society of England when the poor unknown Herschel sent in the report of his discovery of the star Georgium Sidus, its orbit and rate of motion; and of the rings and satellites of Saturn. The boy with no chance, who had played the oboe for his meals, had with his own hands made the telescope through which he discovered facts unknown to the best-equipped astronomers of his day. He had ground two hundred specula before he could get one perfect.

George Stephenson was one of eight children whose parents were so poor that all lived in a single room. George had to watch cows for a neighbor, but he managed to get time to make engines of clay, with hemlock sticks for pipes. At seventeen he had charge of an engine, with his father for fireman. He could neither read nor write, but the engine was his teacher, and he a faithful student. While the other hands were playing games or loafing in liquor shops during the holidays, George was taking his machine to pieces, cleaning it, studying it, and making experiments in engines. When he had become famous as a great inventor of improvements in engines, those who had loafed and played called him lucky.

Without a charm of face or figure, Charlotte Cushman resolved to place herself in the front rank as an actress, even in such characters as Rosalind and Queen Katherine. The star actress was unable to perform, and Miss Cushman, her understudy, took her place. That night she held her audience with such grasp of intellect and iron will that it forgot the absence of mere dimpled feminine grace. Although poor, friendless, and unknown before, when the curtain fell upon her first performance at the London theater, her reputation was made. In after years, when physicians told her she had a terrible, incurable disease, she flinched not a particle, but quietly said, "I have learned to live with my trouble."

A poor colored woman in a log-cabin in the South had three boys, but could afford only one pair of trousers for the three. She was so anxious to give them an education that she sent them to school by turns. The teacher, a Northern girl, noticed that each boy came to school only one day out of three, and that all wore the same pantaloons. The poor mother educated her boys as best she could. One became a professor in a Southern college, another a physician, and the third a clergyman. What a lesson for boys who plead "no chance" as an excuse for wasted lives!

Sam Cunard, the whittling Scotch lad of Glasgow, wrought many odd inventions with brain and jack-knife, but they brought neither honor nor profit until he was consulted by Burns & McIvor, who wished to increase their facilities for carrying foreign mails. The model of a steamship which Sam whittled out for them was carefully copied for the first vessel of the great Cunard Line, and became the standard type for all the magnificent ships since constructed by the firm.

The new Testament and the speller were Cornelius Vanderbilt's only books at school, but he learned to read, write, and cipher a little. He wished to buy a boat, but had no money. To discourage him from following the sea, his mother told him if he would plow, harrow, and plant with corn, before the twenty-seventh day of the month, ten acres of rough, hard, stony land, the worst on his father's farm, she would lend him the amount he wished. Before the appointed time the work was done, and well done. On his seventeenth birthday he bought the boat, but on his way home it struck a sunken wreck and sank just as he reached shallow water.

But Cornelius Vanderbilt was not the boy to give up. He at once began again, and in three years saved three thousand dollars. He often worked all night, and soon had far the largest patronage of any boatman in the harbor. During the War of 1812 he was awarded the Government contract to carry provisions to the military stations near the metropolis. He fulfilled his contract by night so that he might run his ferry-boat between New York and Brooklyn by day.

The boy who gave his parents all his day earnings and had half of what he got at night, was worth thirty thousand dollars at thirty-five, and when he died, at an advanced age, he left to his thirteen children one of the largest fortunes in America.

Lord Eldon might well have pleaded "no chance" when a boy, for he was too poor to go to school or even to buy books. But no; he had grit and determination, and was bound to make his way in the world. He rose at four o'clock in the morning and copied law books which he borrowed, the voluminous "Coke upon Littleton" among others. He was so eager to study that sometimes he would keep it up until his brain refused to work, when he would tie a wet towel about his head to enable him to keep awake and to study. His first year's practice brought him but nine shillings, yet he was bound not to give up.

When Eldon was leaving the chamber the Solicitor tapped him on the shoulder and said, "Young man, your bread and butter's cut for life." The boy with "no chance" became Lord Chancellor of England, and one of the greatest lawyers of his age.

Stephen Girard had "no chance." He left his home in France when ten years old, and came to America as a cabin boy. His great ambition was to get on and succeed at any cost. There was no work, however hard and disagreeable, that he would not undertake. Midas like, he turned to gold everything he touched, and became one of the wealthiest merchants of Philadelphia. His abnormal love of money cannot be commended, but his thoroughness in all he did, his public spirit at times of national need, and willingness to risk his life to save strangers sick with the deadly yellow fever, are traits of character well worthy of imitation.

John Wanamaker walked four miles to Philadelphia every day, and worked in a bookstore for one dollar and twenty-five cents a week. He next worked in a clothing store at an advance of twenty-five cents a week. From this he went up and up until he became one of the greatest living merchants. He was appointed Postmaster-General by President Harrison in 1889, and in that capacity showed great executive ability.

Prejudice against her race and sex did not deter the colored girl, Edmonia Lewis, from struggling upward to honor and fame as a sculptor.

Fred Douglass started in life with less than nothing, for he did not own his own body, and he was pledged before his birth to pay his master's debts. To reach the starting-point of the poorest white boy, he had to climb as far as the distance which the latter must ascend if he would become President of the United States. He saw his mother but two or three times, and then in the night, when she would walk twelve miles to be with him an hour, returning in time to go into the field at dawn. He had no chance to study, for he had no teacher, and the rules of the plantation forbade slaves to learn to read and write. But somehow, unnoticed by his master, he managed to learn the alphabet from scraps of paper and patent medicine almanacs, and then no limits could be placed to his career. He put to shame thousands of white boys. He fled from slavery at twenty-one, went North, and worked as a stevedore in New York and New Bedford. At Nantucket he was given an opportunity to speak at an anti-slavery meeting, and made so favorable an impression that he was made agent of the Anti-Slavery Society of Massachusetts. While traveling from place to place to lecture, he would study with all his might. He was sent to Europe to lecture, and won the friendship of several Englishmen, who gave him $750, with which he purchased his freedom. He edited a paper in Rochester, N. Y., and afterwards conducted the "New Era" in Washington. For several years he was Marshal of the District of Columbia.

Henry E. Dixey, the well-known actor, began his career upon the stage in the humble part of the hind legs of a cow.

P. T. Barnum rode a horse for ten cents a day.

It was a boy born in a log-cabin, without schooling, or books, or teacher, or ordinary opportunities, who won the admiration of mankind by his homely practical wisdom while President during our Civil War, and who emancipated four million slaves.

Behold this long, lank, awkward youth, felling trees on the little claim, building his homely log-cabin, without floor or windows, teaching himself arithmetic and grammar in the evening by the light of the fireplace. In his eagerness to know the contents of Blackstone's Commentaries, he walked forty-four miles to procure the precious volumes, and read one hundred pages while returning. Abraham Lincoln inherited no opportunities, and acquired nothing by luck. His good fortune consisted simply of untiring perseverance and a right heart.

In another log-cabin, in the backwoods of Ohio, a poor widow is holding a boy eighteen months old, and wondering if she will be able to keep the wolf from her little ones. The boy grows, and in a few years we find him chopping wood and tilling the little clearing in the forest, to help his mother. Every spare hour is spent in studying the books he has borrowed, but cannot buy. At sixteen he gladly accepts a chance to drive mules on a canal towpath. Soon he applies for a chance to sweep floors and ring the bell of an academy, to pay his way while studying there.

His first term at Geauga Seminary cost him but seventeen dollars. When he returned the next term he had but a sixpence in his pocket, and this he put into the contribution box at church the next day. He engaged board, washing, fuel, and light of a carpenter at one dollar and six cents a week, with the privilege of working at night and on Saturdays all the time he could spare. He had arrived on a Saturday and planed fifty-one boards that day, for which he received one dollar and two cents. When the term closed, he had paid all expenses and had three dollars over. The following winter he taught school at twelve dollars a month and "board around." In the spring he had forty-eight dollars, and when he returned to school he boarded himself at an expense of thirty-one cents a week.

Soon we find him in Williams College, where in two years he is graduated with honors. He reaches the State Senate at twenty-six and Congress at thirty-three. Twenty-seven years from the time he applied for a chance to ring the bell at Hiram College, James A. Garfield became President of the United States. The inspiration of such an example is worth more to the young men of America than all the wealth of the Astors, the Vanderbilts, and the Goulds.

Among the world's greatest heroes and benefactors are many others whose cradles were rocked by want in lowly cottages, and who buffeted the billows of fate without dependence, save upon the mercy of God and their own energies.

"The little gray cabin appears to be the birthplace of all your great men," said an English author who had been looking over a book of biographies of eminent Americans.

With five chances on each hand and one unwavering aim, no boy, however poor, need despair. There is bread and success for every youth under the American flag who has energy and ability to seize his opportunity. It matters not whether the boy is born in a log-cabin or in a mansion; if he is dominated by a resolute purpose and upholds himself, neither men nor demons can keep him down.

The Country Boy

The Napoleonic wars so drained the flower of French manhood that even to-day the physical stature of the average Frenchman is nearly half an inch below what it was at the beginning of Napoleon's reign.

The country in America to-day is constantly paying a similar tribute to the city in the sacrifice of its best blood, its best brain, the finest physical and mental fiber in the world. This great stream of superb country manhood, which is ever flowing cityward, is rapidly deteriorated by the softening, emasculating influences of the city, until the superior virility, stamina and sturdy qualities entirely disappear in two or three generations of city life. Our city civilization is always in a process of decay, and would, in a few generations, become emasculated and effeminate were it not for the pure, crystal stream of country youth flowing steadily into and purifying the muddy, devitalized stream of city life. It would soon become so foul and degenerate as to threaten the physical and moral health of city dwellers.

One of our great men says that one of the most unfortunate phases of modern civilization is the drift away from the farm, the drift of country youth to the city which has an indescribable fascination for him. His vivid imagination clothes it with Arabian Nights possibilities and joys. The country seems tame and commonplace after his first dream of the city. To him it is synonymous with opportunity, with power, with pleasure. He can not rid himself of its fascination until he tastes its emptiness. He can not know the worth of the country and how to appreciate the glory of its disadvantages and opportunities until he has seen the sham and shallowness of the city.

One of the greatest boons that can ever come to a human being is to be born on a farm and reared in the country. Self-reliance and grit are oftenest country-bred. The country boy is constantly thrown upon his own resources, forced to think for himself, and this calls out his ingenuity and inventiveness. He develops better all-round judgment and a more level head than the city boy. His muscles are harder, his flesh firmer, and his brain-fiber partakes of the same superior quality.

The very granite hills, the mountains, the valleys, the brooks, the miracle of the growing crops are every moment registering their mighty potencies in his constitution, putting iron into his blood and stamina into his character, all of which will help to make him a giant when he comes to compete with the city-bred youth.

The sturdy, vigorous, hardy qualities, the stamina, the brawn, the grit which characterize men who do great things in this world, are, as a rule, country bred. If power is not absorbed from the soil, it certainly comes from very near it. There seems to be a close connection between robust character and the soil, the hills, mountains and valleys, the pure air and sunshine. There is a very appreciable difference between the physical stamina, the brain vigor, the solidity and the reliability of country-bred men and that of those in the city.

The average country-bred youth has a better foundation for success-building, has greater courage, more moral stamina. He has not become weakened and softened by the superficial ornamental, decorative influences of city life. And there is a reason for all this. We are largely copies of our environment. We are under the perpetual influence of the suggestion of our surroundings. The city-bred youth sees and hears almost nothing that is natural, aside from the faces and forms of human beings. Nearly everything that confronts him from morning till night is artificial, man-made. He sees hardly anything that God made, that imparts solidity, strength and power, as do the natural objects in the country. How can a man build up a solid, substantial character when his eyes and ears bring him only sights and sounds of artificial things? A vast sea of business blocks, sky-scrapers and asphalt pavements does not generate character-building material.

Just as sculpture was once carried to such an extreme that pillars and beams were often so weakened by the extravagant carvings as to threaten the safety of the structure, so the timber in country boys and girls, when brought to the city, is often overcarved and adorned at the cost of strength, robustness and vigor.

In other words, virility, forcefulness, physical and mental stamina reach their maximum in those who live close to the soil. The moment a man becomes artificial in his living, takes on artificial conditions, he begins to deteriorate, to soften.

Much of what we call the best society in our cities is often in an advanced process of decay. The muscles may be a little more delicate but they are softer; the skin may be a little fairer, but it is not so healthy; the thought a little more supple, but less vigorous. The whole tendency of life in big cities is toward deterioration. City people rarely live really normal lives. It is not natural for human beings to live far from the soil. It is Mother Earth and country life that give vitality, stamina, courage and all the qualities which make for manhood and womanhood. What we get from the country is solid, substantial, enduring, reliable. What comes from the artificial conditions of the city is weakening, enervating, softening.

The country youth, on the other hand, is in the midst of a perpetual miracle. He can not open his eyes without seeing a more magnificent painting than a Raphael or a Michael Angelo could have created in a lifetime. And this magnificent panorama is changing every instant.

There is a miracle going on in every growing blade of grass and flower. Is it not wonderful to watch the chemical processes in nature's laboratory, mixing and flinging out to the world the gorgeous colorings and marvelous perfumes of the rose and wild flower! No city youth was ever in such a marvelous kindergarten, where perpetual creation is going on in such a vast multitude of forms.

The city youth has too many things to divert his attention. Such a multiplicity of objects appeals to him that he is often superficial; he lacks depth; his mind is perpetually drawn away from his subject, and he lacks continuity of thought and application. His reading is comparatively superficial. He glances through many papers; magazines and periodicals and gives no real thought to any. His evenings are much more broken up than those of the country boy, who, having very little diversion after supper, can read continuously for an entire evening on one subject. The country boy does not read as many books as the city boy, but, as a rule, he reads them with much better results.

The dearth of great libraries, books and periodicals is one reason why the country boy makes the most of good books and articles, often reading them over and over again, while the city youth, in the midst of newspapers and libraries, sees so many books that in most instances he cares very little for them, and will often read the best literature without absorbing any of it.

The fact is that there is such a diversity of attractions and distractions, of temptation and amusement in the city, that unless a youth is made of unusual stuff he will yield to the persuasion of the moment and follow the line of least resistance. It is hard for the city-bred youth to resist the multiplicity of allurements and pleasures that bid for his attention, to deny himself and turn a deaf ear to the appeals of his associates and tie himself down to self-improvement while those around him are having a good time.

These exciting, diverting, tempting conditions of city life are not conducive to generating the great master purpose, the one unwavering life aim, which we often see so marked in the young man from the country. Nor do city-bred youths store up anything like the reserve power, the cumulative force, the stamina, which are developed in the simple life of the soil.

For one thing, the country boy is constantly developing his muscular system. His health is better. He gets more exercise, more time to think and to reflect; hence, he is not so superficial as the city boy. His perceptions are not so quick, he is not so rapid in his movements, his thought action is slower and he does not have as much polish, it is true, but he is better balanced generally. He has been forced to do a great variety of work and this has developed corresponding mental qualities.

The drudgery of the farm, the chores which we hated as boys, the rocks which we despised, we have found were the very things which educated us, which developed our power and made us practical. The farm is a great gymnasium, a superb manual training school, nature's kindergarten, constantly calling upon the youth's self-reliance and inventiveness. He must make the implements and toys which he can not afford to buy or procure. He must run, adjust and repair all sorts of machinery and farm utensils. His ingenuity and inventiveness are constantly exercised. If the wagon or plow breaks down it must be repaired on the spot, often without the proper tools. This training develops instinctive courage, strong success qualities, and makes him a resourceful man.

Is it any wonder that the boy so trained in self-reliance, so superbly equipped with physical and mental stamina, should take such pre-eminence, should be in such demand when he comes to the city? Is it any wonder that he is always in evidence in great emergencies and crises? Just stand a stamina-filled, self-reliant country boy beside a pale, soft, stamina-less, washed-out city youth. Is it any wonder that the country-bred boy is nearly always the leader; that he heads the banks, the great mercantile houses? It is this peculiar, indescribable something; this superior stamina and mental caliber, that makes the stuff that rises to the top in all vocations.

There is a peculiar quality of superiority which comes from dealing with *realities* that we do not find in the superficial city conditions. The life-giving oxygen, breathed in great inspirations through constant muscular effort, develops in the country boy much greater lung power than is developed in the city youth, and his outdoor work tends to build up a robust constitution. Plowing, hoeing, mowing, everything he does on the farm gives him vigor and strength. His muscles are harder, his flesh firmer, and his brain-fiber partakes of the same superior quality. He is constantly bottling up forces, storing up energy in his brain and muscles which later may be powerful factors in shaping the nation's destiny or which may furnish backbone to keep the ship of state from floundering on the rocks. This marvelous reserve power which he stores up in the country will come out in the successful banker, statesman, lawyer, merchant, or business man.

Self-reliance and grit are oftenest country-bred. The country boy is constantly thrown upon his own resources; he is forced to think for himself, and this calls out his ingenuity and makes him self-reliant and strong. It has been found that the use of tools in our manual training schools develops the brain, strengthens the deficient faculties and brings out latent powers. The farm-reared boy is in the best manual training school in the world and is constantly forced to plan things, make things; he is always using tools. This is one of the reasons why he usually develops better all-round judgment and a more level head than the city boy.

It is human nature to exaggerate the value of things beyond our reach. People save money for years in order to go to Europe to visit the great art centers and see the famous masterpieces, when they have really never seen the marvelous pictures painted by the Divine Artist and spread in the landscape, in the sunset, in the glory of flowers and plant life, right at their very doors.

What a perpetual inspiration, what marvels of beauty, what miracles of coloring are spread everywhere in nature, confronting us on every hand! We see them almost every day of our lives and they become so common that they make no impression upon us. Think of the difference between what a Ruskin sees in a landscape and the impression conveyed to his brain, and what is seen by the ordinary mind, the ordinary person who has little or no imagination and whose esthetic faculties have scarcely been developed!

We are immersed in a wilderness of mysteries and marvelous beauties. Miracles innumerable in grass and flower and fruit are performed right before our eyes. How marvelous is Nature's growing of fruit, for example! How she packs the concentrated sunshine and delicious juices into the cans that she makes as she goes along, cans exactly the right size, without a particle of waste, leakage or evaporation, with no noise of factories, no hammering of tins! The miracles are wrought in a silent laboratory; not a sound is heard, and yet what marvels of skill, deliciousness and beauty?

What interrogation points, what wonderful mysteries, what wit-sharpeners are ever before the farmer boy, whichever way he turns! Where does all this tremendous increase of corn, wheat, fruit and vegetables come from? There seems to be no loss to the soil, and yet, what a marvelous growth in everything! Life, life, more life on every hand! Wherever he goes he treads on chemical forces which produce greater marvels than are described in the Arabian Nights. The trees, the brooks, the mountains, the hills, the valleys, the sunsets, the growing animals on the farm, are all mysteries that set him thinking and to wondering at the creative processes which are working on every hand.

Then again, the delicious freedom of it all, as contrasted with the cramped, artificial life in the city! Everything in the country tends to set the boy thinking, to call out his dormant powers and develop his latent forces. And what health there is in it all! How hearty and natural he is in comparison with the city boy, who is tempted to turn night into day, to live an artificial, purposeless life.

The very temptation in the city to turn night into day is of itself health-undermining, stamina-dissipating and character-weakening.

While the city youth is wasting his precious energy capital in late hours, pleasure seeking, and often dissipation, the country youth is storing up power and vitality; he is being recharged with physical force by natural, refreshing sleep, away from the distracting influence and enervating excitement of city life. The country youth does not learn to judge people by the false standards of wealth and social standing. He is not inculcated with snobbish ideas. Everything in the great farm kindergarten teaches him sincerity, simplicity and honesty.

The time was when the boy who gave no signs of genius or unusual ability was consigned to the farm, and the brilliant boy was sent to college or to the city to make a career for himself. But we are now beginning to see that man has made a botch of farming only because he looked upon it as a sort of humdrum occupation; as a means provided by nature for living-getting for those who were not good for much else. Farming was considered by many people as a sort of degrading occupation desirable only for those who lacked the brains and education to go into a profession or some of the more refined callings. But the searchlight of science has revealed in it possibilities hitherto undreamed of. We are commencing to realize that it takes a high order of ability and education to bring out the fullest possibilities of the soil; that it requires fine-grained sympathetic talent. We are now finding that agriculture is as great a science as astronomy, and that ignorant men have been getting an indifferent living from their farms simply because they did not know how to mix brains with the soil.

The science of agriculture is fast becoming appreciated and is more and more regarded as a high and noble calling, a dignified profession. Think of what it means to go into partnership with the Creator in bringing out larger, grander products from the soil; to be able to co-operate with that divine creative force, and even to vary the size, the beauty, the perfume of flowers; to enlarge, modify and change the flavor of fruits and vegetables to our liking!

Think what it must mean to be a magician in the whole vegetable kingdom, like Luther Burbank, changing colors, flavors, perfumes, species! Almost anything is possible when one knows enough and has heart and sympathy enough to enter into partnership with the great creative force in nature. Mr. Burbank says that the time will come when man will be able to do almost anything he wishes in the vegetable kingdom; will be able to produce at will any shade or color he wishes, and almost any flavor in any fruit; that the size of all fruits and vegetables and flowers is just a matter of sufficient understanding, and that Nature will give us almost anything when we know enough to treat her intelligently, wisely and sympathetically.

The history of most great men shows that there is a disadvantage in having too many advantages.

Who can tell what the consequences would have been had Lincoln been born in New York and educated at Harvard? If he had been reared in the midst of great libraries, brought up in an atmosphere of books, of only a small fraction of which he could get even a superficial knowledge, would he have had that insatiable hunger which prompted him to walk twenty miles in order to borrow Blackstone's "Commentaries" and to read one hundred pages on the way home?

[Illustration: House in which Abraham Lincoln was born]

What was there in that rude frontier forest, where this poor boy scarcely ever saw any one who knew anything of books, to rouse his ambition and to stimulate him to self-education? Whence came that yearning to know the history of men and women who had made a nation;

to know the history of his country? Whence came that passion to devour the dry statutes of Indiana, as a young girl would devour a love story? Whence came that all-absorbing ambition to be somebody in the world; to serve his country with no selfish ambition? Had his father been rich and well-educated instead of a poor man who could neither read nor write and who was generally of a shiftless and roving disposition, there is no likelihood that Lincoln would ever have become the powerful man he was.

Had he not felt that imperious "must" calling him, the prod of necessity spurring him on, whence would have come the motive which led him to struggle for self-development, self-unfoldment? If he had been born and educated in luxury, his character would probably have been soft and flabby in comparison with what it was.

Where in all the annals of history is there another record of one born of such poor parentage and reared in such a wretched environment, who ever rose to such eminence? Imagine a boy of to-day, so hungry for an education that he would walk nine miles a day to attend a rude frontier school in a log cabin! What would the city boys of to-day, who do not want to walk even a few blocks to school, think of a youth who would do what Lincoln did to overcome his handicap?

Opportunities Where You Are

*To each man's life there comes a time supreme;
One day, one night, one morning, or one noon,
One freighted hour, one moment opportune,
One rift through which sublime fulfillments gleam,
One space when fate goes tiding with the stream,
One Once, in balance 'twixt Too Late, Too Soon,
And ready for the passing instant's boon
To tip in favor the uncertain beam.
Ah, happy he who, knowing how to wait,
Knows also how to watch and work and stand
On Life's broad deck alert, and at the prow
To seize the passing moment, big with fate,
From Opportunity's extended hand,
When the great clock of destiny strikes Now! —Mary A. Townsend*

What is opportunity to a man who can't use it? An unfecundated egg, which the waves of time wash away into non-entity.—George Eliot

The secret of success in life is for a man to be ready for his opportunity when it comes.— Disraeli

"There are no longer any good chances for young men," complained a youthful law student to Daniel Webster. "There is always room at the top," replied the great statesman and jurist.

No chance, no opportunities, in a land where thousands of poor boys become rich men, where newsboys go to Congress, and where those born in the lowest stations attain the highest positions? The world is all gates, all opportunities to him who will use them. But, like Bunyan's Pilgrim in the dungeon of Giant Despair's castle, who had the key of deliverance all the time with him but had forgotten it, we fail to rely wholly upon the ability to advance all that is good for us which has been given to the weakest as well as the strongest. We depend too much upon outside assistance.

"We look too high
For things close by."

A Baltimore lady lost a valuable diamond bracelet at a ball, and supposed that it was stolen from the pocket of her cloak. Years afterward she washed the steps of the Peabody Institute, pondering how to get money to buy food. She cut up an old, worn-out, ragged cloak to make a hood, when lo! in the lining of the cloak she discovered the diamond bracelet. During all her poverty she was worth $3500, but did not know it.

Many of us who think we are poor are rich in opportunities, if we could only see them, in possibilities all about us, in faculties worth more than diamond bracelets. In our large Eastern cities it has been found that at least ninety-four out of every hundred found their first fortune at home, or near at hand, and in meeting common every-day wants. It is a sorry day for a young man who can not see any opportunities where he is, but thinks he can do better somewhere else. Some Brazilian shepherds organized a party to go to California to dig gold, and took along a handful of translucent pebbles to play checkers with on the voyage. After arriving in San Francisco, and after they had thrown most of the pebbles away, they discovered that they were diamonds. They hastened back to Brazil, only to find that the mines from which the pebbles had been gathered had been taken up by other prospectors and sold to the government.

The richest gold and silver mine in Nevada was sold by the owner for $42, to get money to pay his passage to other mines, where he thought he could get rich. Professor Agassiz once told the Harvard students of a farmer who owned a farm of hundreds of acres of unprofitable woods and rocks, and concluded to sell out and get into a more profitable business. He decided to go into the coal-oil business; he studied coal measures and coal-oil deposits, and experimented for a long time. He sold his farm for $200, and engaged in his new business two hundred miles away. Only a short time after, the man who bought his farm discovered upon it a great flood of coal-oil, which the farmer had previously ignorantly tried to drain off.

Hundreds of years ago there lived near the shore of the river Indus a Persian by the name of Ali Hafed. He lived in a cottage on the river bank, from which he could get a grand view of the beautiful country stretching away to the sea. He had a wife and children; an extensive farm, fields of grain, gardens of flowers, orchards of fruit, and miles of forest. He had plenty of money and everything that heart could wish. He was contented and happy. One evening a priest of Buddha visited him, and, sitting before the fire, explained to him how the world was made, and how the first beams of sunlight condensed on the earth's surface into diamonds.

The old priest told that a drop of sunlight the size of his thumb was worth more than large mines of copper, silver, or gold; that with one of them he could buy many farms like his; that with a handful he could buy a province, and with a mine of diamonds he could purchase a kingdom. Ali Hafed listened, and was no longer a rich man. He had been touched with discontent, and with that all wealth vanishes. Early the next morning he woke the priest who had been the cause of his unhappiness, and anxiously asked him where he could find a mine of diamonds. "What do you want of diamonds?" asked the astonished priest. "I want to be rich and place my children on thrones." "All you have to do is to go and search until you find them," said the priest. "But where shall I go?" asked the poor farmer. "Go anywhere, north, south, east, or west." "How shall I know when I have found the place?" "When you find a river running over white sands between high mountain ranges, in those white sands you will find diamonds," answered the priest.

The discontented man sold the farm for what he could get, left his family with a neighbor, took the money he had at interest, and went to search for the coveted treasure. Over the mountains of Arabia, through Palestine and Egypt, he wandered for years, but found no diamonds. When his money was all gone and starvation stared him in the face, ashamed of his folly and of his rags, poor Ali Hafed threw himself into the tide and was drowned. The man who bought his farm was a contented man, who made the most of his surroundings, and did not believe in going away from home to hunt for diamonds or success. While his camel was drinking in the garden one day, he noticed a flash of light from the white sands of the brook. He picked up a pebble, and pleased with its brilliant hues took it into the house, put it on the shelf near the fireplace, and forgot all about it.

The old priest of Buddha who had filled Ali Hafed with the fatal discontent called one day upon the new owner of the farm. He had no sooner entered the room than his eye caught that flash of light from the stone. "Here's a diamond! here's a diamond!" he shouted in great excitement. "Has Ali Hafed returned?" "No," said the farmer, "nor is that a diamond. That is but a stone." They went into the garden and stirred up the white sand with their fingers, and behold, other diamonds more beautiful than the first gleamed out of it. So the famous diamond beds of Golconda were discovered. Had Ali Hafed been content to remain at home, and dug in his own garden, instead of going abroad in search for wealth, he would have been one of the richest men in the world, for the entire farm abounded in the richest of gems.

You have your own special place and work. Find it, fill it. Scarcely a boy or girl will read these lines but has much better opportunity to win success than Garfield, Wilson, Franklin, Lincoln, Harriet Beecher Stowe, Frances Willard, and thousands of others had. But to succeed you must be prepared to seize and improve the opportunity when it comes. Remember that four things come not back: the spoken word, the sped arrow, the past life, and the neglected opportunity.

It is one of the paradoxes of civilization that the more opportunities are utilized, the more new ones are thereby created. New openings are as easy to find as ever to those who do their best; although it is not so easy as formerly to obtain great distinction in the old lines, because the standard has advanced so much, and competition has so greatly increased. "The world is no longer clay," said Emerson, "but rather iron in the hands of its workers, and men have got to hammer out a place for themselves by steady and rugged blows."

Thousands of men have made fortunes out of trifles which others pass by. As the bee gets honey from the same flower from which the spider gets poison, so some men will get a fortune out of the commonest and meanest things, as scraps of leather, cotton waste, slag, iron filings, from which others get only poverty and failure. There is scarcely a thing which contributes to the welfare and comfort of humanity, scarcely an article of household furniture, a kitchen utensil, an article of clothing or of food, that is not capable of an improvement in which there may be a fortune.

Opportunities? They are all around us. Forces of nature plead to be used in the service of man, as lightning for ages tried to attract his attention to the great force of electricity, which would do his drudgery and leave him to develop the God-given powers within him. There is power lying latent everywhere waiting for the observant eye to discover it.

First find out what the world needs and then supply the want. An invention to make smoke go the wrong way in a chimney might be a very ingenious thing, but it would be of no use to humanity. The patent office at Washington is full of wonderful devices of ingenious mechanism, but not one in hundreds is of use to the inventor or to the world. And yet how many families have been impoverished, and have struggled for years amid want and woe, while the father has been working on useless inventions. A. T. Stewart, as a boy, lost eighty-seven cents, when his capital was one dollar and a half, in buying buttons and thread which shoppers did not call for. After that he made it a rule never to buy anything which the public did not want, and so prospered.

An observing man, the eyelets of whose shoes pulled out, but who could not afford to get another pair, said to himself, "I will make a metallic lacing hook, which can be riveted into the leather." He was then so poor that he had to borrow a sickle to cut grass in front of his hired tenement. He became a very rich man.

An observing barber in Newark, N. J., thought he could make an improvement on shears for cutting hair, invented clippers, and became rich. A Maine man was called in from the hayfield to wash clothes for his invalid wife. He had never realized what it was to wash before. Finding the method slow and laborious, he invented the washing machine, and made a fortune. A man who was suffering terribly with toothache felt sure there must be some way of filling teeth which would prevent their aching and he invented the method of gold filling for teeth.

The great things of the world have not been done by men of large means. Ericsson began the construction of the screw propellers in a bathroom. The cotton-gin was first manufactured in a log cabin. John Harrison, the great inventor of the marine chronometer, began his career in the loft of an old barn. Parts of the first steamboat ever run in America were set up in the vestry of a church in Philadelphia by Fitch. McCormick began to make his famous reaper in a grist-mill. The first model dry-dock was made in an attic. Clark, the founder of Clark University of Worcester, Mass., began his great fortune by making toy wagons in a horse shed. Farquhar made umbrellas in his sitting-room, with his daughter's help, until he sold enough to hire a loft. Edison began his experiments in a baggage car on the Grand Trunk Railroad when a newsboy.

Michael Angelo found a piece of discarded Carrara marble among waste rubbish beside a street in Florence, which some unskilful workman had cut, hacked, spoiled, and thrown away. No doubt many artists had noticed the fine quality of the marble, and regretted that it should have been spoiled. But Michael Angelo still saw an angel in the ruin, and with his chisel and mallet he called out from it one of the finest pieces of statuary in Italy, the young David.

Patrick Henry was called a lazy boy, a good-for-nothing farmer, and he failed as a merchant. He was always dreaming of some far-off greatness, and never thought he could be a hero among the corn and tobacco and saddlebags of Virginia. He studied law for six weeks; when he put out his shingle. People thought he would fail, but in his first case he showed that he had a wonderful power of oratory. It then first dawned upon him that he could be a hero in Virginia. From the time the Stamp Act was passed and Henry was elected to the Virginia House of Burgesses, and he had introduced his famous resolution against the unjust taxation of the American colonies, he rose steadily until he became one of the brilliant orators of America. In one of his first speeches upon this resolution he uttered these words, which were prophetic of his power and courage: "Caesar had his Brutus, Charles the First his Cromwell, and George the Third—may profit by their example. If this be treason, make the most of it."

The great natural philosopher, Faraday, who was the son of a blacksmith, wrote, when a young man, to Humphry Davy, asking for employment at the Royal Institution. Davy consulted a friend on the matter. "Here is a letter from a young man named Faraday; he has been attending my lectures, and wants me to give him employment at the Royal Institution—what can I do?" "Do? put him to washing bottles; if he is good for anything he will do it directly; if he refuses he is good for nothing." But the boy who could experiment in the attic of an apothecary shop with an old pan and glass vials during every moment he could snatch from his work saw an opportunity in washing bottles, which led to a professorship at the Royal Academy at Woolwich. Tyndall said of this boy with no chance, "He is the greatest experimental philosopher the world has ever seen." He became the wonder of his age in science.

There is a legend of an artist who long sought for a piece of sandalwood, out of which to carve a Madonna. He was about to give up in despair, leaving the vision of his life unrealized, when in a dream he was bidden to carve his Madonna from a block of oak wood which was destined for the fire. He obeyed, and produced a masterpiece from a log of common firewood. Many of us lose great opportunities in life by waiting to find sandalwood for our carvings, when they really lie hidden in the common logs that we burn. One man goes through life without seeing chances for doing anything great, while another close beside him snatches from the same circumstances and privileges opportunities for achieving grand results.

Opportunities? They are everywhere. "America is another name for opportunities. Our whole history appears like a last effort of divine Providence in behalf of the human race." Never before were there such grand openings, such chances, such opportunities. Especially is this true for girls and young women. A new era is dawning for them. Hundreds of occupations and professions, which were closed to them only a few years ago, are now inviting them to enter.

We can not all of us perhaps make great discoveries like Newton, Faraday, Edison, and Thompson, or paint immortal pictures like an Angelo or a Raphael. But we can all of us make our lives sublime, by *seizing common occasions and making them great.* What chance had the young girl, Grace Darling, to distinguish herself, living on those barren lighthouse rocks alone with her aged parents? But while her brothers and sisters, who moved to the cities to win wealth and fame, are not known to the world, she became more famous than a princess. This poor girl did not need to go to London to see the nobility; they came to the lighthouse to see her. Right at home she had won fame which the regal heirs might envy, and a name which will never perish from the earth. She did not wander away into dreamy distance for fame and fortune, but did her best where duty had placed her.

If you want to get rich, study yourself and your own wants. You will find that millions have the same wants. The safest business is always connected with man's prime necessities. He must have clothing and dwelling; he must eat. He wants comforts, facilities of all kinds for pleasure, education, and culture. Any man who can supply a great want of humanity, improve any methods which men use, supply any demand of comfort, or contribute in any way to their well-being, can make a fortune.

"The golden opportunity Is never offered twice; seize then the hour When Fortune smiles and Duty points the way."

Why thus longing, thus forever sighing, For the far-off, unattained and dim, While the beautiful, all around thee lying Offers up its low, perpetual hymn? —Harriet Winslow

Possibilities in Spare Moments

Dost thou love life? Then do not squander time, for that is the stuff life is made of.—Franklin

Eternity itself cannot restore the loss struck from the minute.—Ancient Poet

Periunt et imputantur,—the hours perish and are laid to our charge.—Inscription on a Dial at Oxford

I wasted time, and now doth time waste me.—Shakespeare

Believe me when I tell you that thrift of time will repay you in after life with a usury of profit beyond your most sanguine dreams, and that waste of it will make you dwindle alike in intellectual and moral stature beyond your darkest reckoning.—Gladstone

Lost! Somewhere between sunrise and sunset, two golden hours, each set with sixty diamond minutes. No reward is offered, for they are gone forever.—Horace Mann

"What is the price of that book?" at length asked a man who had been dawdling for an hour in the front store of Benjamin Franklin's newspaper establishment. "One dollar," replied the clerk. "One dollar," echoed the lounger; "can't you take less than that?" "One dollar is the price," was the answer.

The would-be purchaser looked over the books on sale a while longer, and then inquired: "Is Mr. Franklin in?" "Yes," said the clerk, "he is very busy in the press-room." "Well, I want to see him," persisted the man. The proprietor was called, and the stranger asked: "What is the lowest, Mr. Franklin, that you can take for that book?" "One dollar and a quarter," was the prompt rejoinder. "One dollar and a quarter! Why, your clerk asked me only a dollar just now." "True," said Franklin, "and I could have better afforded to take a dollar than to leave my work."

The man seemed surprised; but, wishing to end a parley of his own seeking, he demanded: "Well, come now, tell me your lowest price for this book." "One dollar and a half," replied Franklin. "A dollar and a half! Why, you offered it yourself for a dollar and a quarter." "Yes," said Franklin coolly, "and I could better have taken that price then than a dollar and a half now."

The man silently laid the money on the counter, took his book, and left the store, having received a salutary lesson from a master in the art of transmuting time, at will, into either wealth or wisdom.

Time-wasters are everywhere.

On the floor of the gold-working room, in the United States Mint at Philadelphia, there is a wooden lattice-work which is taken up when the floor is swept, and the fine particles of gold-dust, thousands of dollars' yearly, are thus saved. So every successful man has a kind of network to catch "the raspings and parings of existence, those leavings of days and wee bits of hours" which most people sweep into the waste of life. He who hoards and turns to account all odd minutes, half hours, unexpected holidays, gaps "between times," and chasms of waiting for unpunctual persons, achieves results which astonish those who have not mastered this most valuable secret.

"All that I have accomplished, expect to, or hope to accomplish," said Elihu Burritt, "has been and will be by that plodding, patient, persevering process of accretion which builds the ant-heap—particle by particle, thought by thought, fact by fact. And if ever I was actuated by ambition, its highest and warmest aspiration reached no further than the hope to set before the young men of my country an example in employing those invaluable fragments of time called moments."

"I have been wondering how Ned contrived to monopolize all the talents of the family," said a brother, found in a brown study after listening to one of Burke's speeches in Parliament; "but then I remember; when we were at play, he was always at work."

The days come to us like friends in disguise, bringing priceless gifts from an unseen hand; but, if we do not use them, they are borne silently away, never to return. Each successive morning new gifts are brought, but if we failed to accept those that were brought yesterday and the day before, we become less and less able to turn them to account, until the ability to appreciate and utilize them is exhausted. Wisely was it said that lost wealth may be regained by industry and economy, lost knowledge by study, lost health by temperance and medicine, but lost time is gone forever.

"Oh, it's only five minutes or ten minutes till mealtime; there's no time to do anything now," is one of the commonest expressions heard in the family. But what monuments have been built up by poor boys with no chance, out of broken fragments of time which many of us throw away! The very hours you have wasted, if improved, might have insured your success.

Marion Harland has accomplished wonders, and she has been able to do this by economizing the minutes to shape her novels and newspaper articles, when her children were in bed and whenever she could get a spare minute. Though she has done so much, yet all her life has been subject to interruptions which would have discouraged most women from attempting anything outside their regular family duties. She has glorified the commonplace as few other women have done. Harriet Beecher Stowe, too, wrote her great masterpiece, "Uncle Tom's Cabin," in the midst of pressing household cares. Beecher read Froude's "England" a little each day while he had to wait for dinner. Longfellow translated the "Inferno" by snatches of ten minutes a day, while waiting for his coffee to boil, persisting for years until the work was done.

Hugh Miller, while working hard as a stone-mason, found time to read scientific books, and write the lessons learned from the blocks of stone he handled.

Madame de Genlis, when companion of the future Queen of France, composed several of her charming volumes while waiting for the princess to whom she gave her daily lessons. Burns wrote many of his most beautiful poems while working on a farm. The author of "Paradise Lost" was a teacher, Secretary of the Commonwealth, Secretary of the Lord Protector, and had to write his sublime poetry whenever he could snatch a few minutes from a busy life. John Stuart Mill did much of his best work as a writer while a clerk in the East India House. Galileo was a surgeon, yet to the improvement of his spare moments the world owes some of its greatest discoveries.

If a genius like Gladstone carried through life a little book in his pocket lest an unexpected spare moment slip from his grasp, what should we of common abilities not resort to, to save the precious moments from oblivion? What a rebuke is such a life to the thousands of young men and women who throw away whole months and even years of that which the "Grand Old Man" hoarded up even to the smallest fragments! Many a great man has snatched his reputation from odd bits of time which others, who wonder at their failure to get on, throw away. In Dante's time nearly every literary man in Italy was a hard-working merchant, physician, statesman, judge, or soldier.

While Michael Faraday was employed binding books, he devoted all his leisure to experiments. At one time he wrote to a friend, "Time is all I require. Oh, that I could purchase at a cheap rate some of our modern gentlemen's spare hours—nay, days."

Oh, the power of ceaseless industry to perform miracles!

Alexander von Humboldt's days were so occupied with his business that he had to pursue his scientific labors in the night or early morning, while others were asleep.

One hour a day withdrawn from frivolous pursuits and profitably employed would enable any man of ordinary capacity to master a complete science. One hour a day would in ten years make an ignorant man a well-informed man. It would earn enough to pay for two daily and two weekly papers, two leading magazines, and at least a dozen good books. In an hour a day a boy or girl could read twenty pages thoughtfully—over seven thousand pages, or eighteen large volumes in a year. An hour a day might make all the difference between bare existence and useful, happy living. An hour a day might make—nay, has made—an unknown man a famous one, a useless man a benefactor to his race. Consider, then, the mighty possibilities of two—four—yes, six hours a day that are, on the average, thrown away by young men and women in the restless desire for fun and diversion!

Every young man should have a hobby to occupy his leisure hours, something useful to which he can turn with delight. It might be in line with his work or otherwise, only *his heart must be in it.*

If one chooses wisely, the study, research, and occupation that a hobby confers will broaden character and transform the home.

"He has nothing to prevent him but too much idleness, which, I have observed," says Burke, "fills up a man's time much more completely and leaves him less his own master, than any sort of employment whatsoever."

Some boys will pick up a good education in the odds and ends of time which others carelessly throw away, as one man saves a fortune by small economies which others disdain to practise. What young man is too busy to get an hour a day for self-improvement? Charles C. Frost, the celebrated shoemaker of Vermont, resolved to devote one hour a day to study. He became one of the most noted mathematicians in the United States, and also gained an enviable reputation in other departments of knowledge. John Hunter, like Napoleon, allowed himself but four hours of sleep. It took Professor Owen ten years to arrange and classify the specimens in Comparative Anatomy, over twenty-four thousand in number, which Hunter's industry had collected. What a record for a boy who began his studies while working as a carpenter!

John Q. Adams complained bitterly when robbed of his time by those who had no right to it. An Italian scholar put over his door the inscription: "Whoever tarries here must join in my labors." Carlyle, Tennyson, Browning, and Dickens signed a remonstrance against organ-grinders who disturbed their work.

Many of the greatest men of history earned their fame outside of their regular occupations in odd bits of time which most people squander. Spenser made his reputation in his spare time while Secretary to the Lord Deputy of Ireland. Sir John Lubbock's fame rests on his prehistoric studies, prosecuted outside of his busy banking-hours. Southey, seldom idle for a minute, wrote a hundred volumes. Hawthorne's notebook shows that he never let a chance thought or circumstance escape him. Franklin was a tireless worker. He crowded his meals and sleep into as small compass as possible so that he might gain time for study. When a child, he became impatient of his father's long grace at table, and asked him if he could not say grace over a whole cask once for all, and save time. He wrote some of his best productions on shipboard, such as his "Improvement of Navigation" and "Smoky Chimneys."

What a lesson there is in Raphael's brief thirty-seven years to those who plead "no time" as an excuse for wasted lives!

Great men have ever been misers of moments. Cicero said: "What others give to public shows and entertainments, nay, even to mental and bodily rest, I give to the study of philosophy." Lord Bacon's fame springs from the work of his leisure hours while Chancellor of England. During an interview with a great monarch, Goethe suddenly excused himself, went into an adjoining room and wrote down a thought for his "Faust," lest it should be forgotten. Sir Humphry Davy achieved eminence in spare moments in an attic of an apothecary's shop. Pope would often rise in the night to write out thoughts that would not come during the busy day. Grote wrote his matchless "History of Greece" during the hours of leisure snatched from his duties as a banker.

George Stephenson seized the moments as though they were gold. He educated himself and did much of his best work during his spare moments. He learned arithmetic during the night shifts when he was an engineer. Mozart would not allow a moment to slip by unimproved. He would not stop his work long enough to sleep, and would sometimes write two whole nights and a day without intermission. He wrote his famous "Requiem" on his death-bed.

Caesar said: "Under my tent in the fiercest struggle of war I have always found time to think of many other things." He was once shipwrecked, and had to swim ashore; but he carried with him the manuscript of his "Commentaries," upon which he was at work when the ship went down.

Dr. Mason Good translated "Lucretius" while riding to visit his patients in London. Dr. Darwin composed most of his works by writing his thoughts on scraps of paper wherever he happened to be. Watt learned chemistry and mathematics while working at his trade of a mathematical instrument-maker. Henry Kirke White learned Greek while walking to and from the lawyer's office where he was studying. Dr. Burney learned Italian and French on horseback. Matthew Hale wrote his "Contemplations" while traveling on his circuit as judge.

The present time is the raw material out of which we make whatever we will. Do not brood over the past, or dream of the future, but seize the instant and *get your lesson from the hour*. The man is yet unborn who rightly measures and fully realizes the value of an hour. As Fenelon says, God never gives but one moment at a time, and does not give a second until he withdraws the first.

Lord Brougham could not bear to lose a moment, yet he was so systematic that he always seemed to have more leisure than many who did not accomplish a tithe of what he did. He achieved distinction in politics, law, science, and literature.

Dr. Johnson wrote "Rasselas" in the evenings of a single week, in order to meet the expenses of his mother's funeral.

Lincoln studied law during his spare hours while surveying, and learned the common branches unaided while tending store. Mrs. Somerville learned botany and astronomy and wrote books while her neighbors were gossiping and idling. At eighty she published "Molecular and Microscopical Science."

The worst of a lost hour is not so much in the wasted time as in the wasted power. Idleness rusts the nerves and makes the muscles creak. Work has system, laziness has none.

President Quincy never went to bed until he had laid his plans for the next day.

Dalton's industry was the passion of his life. He made and recorded over two hundred thousand meteorological observations.

In factories for making cloth a single broken thread ruins a whole web; it is traced back to the girl who made the blunder and the loss is deducted from her wages. But who shall pay for the broken threads in life's great web? We cannot throw back and forth an empty shuttle; threads of some kind follow every movement as we weave the web of our fate. It may be a shoddy thread of wasted hours or lost opportunities that will mar the fabric and mortify the workman forever; or it may be a golden thread which will add to its beauty and luster. We cannot stop the shuttle or pull out the unfortunate thread which stretches across the fabric, a perpetual witness of our folly.

No one is anxious about a young man while he is busy in useful work. But where does he eat his lunch at noon? Where does he go when he leaves his boarding-house at night? What does he do after supper? Where does he spend his Sundays and holidays? The way he uses his spare moments reveals his character. The great majority of youths who go to the bad are ruined after supper. Most of those who climb upward to honor and fame devote their evenings to study or work or the society of those who can help and improve them. Each evening is a crisis in the career of a young man. There is a deep significance in the lines of Whittier:—

This day we fashion Destiny, our web of Fate we spin;
This day for all hereafter choose we holiness or sin.

Time is money. We should not be stingy or mean with it, but we should not throw away an hour any more than we would throw away a dollar-bill. Waste of time means waste of energy, waste of vitality, waste of character in dissipation. It means the waste of opportunities which will never come back. Beware how you kill time, for all your future lives in it.

"And it is left for each," says Edward Everett, "by the cultivation of every talent, by watching with an eagle's eye for every chance of improvement, by redeeming time, defying temptation, and scorning sensual pleasure, to make himself useful, honored, and happy."

How Poor Boys and Girls Go to College

"Can I afford to go to college?" asks many an American youth who has hardly a dollar to his name and who knows that a college course means years of sacrifice and struggle.

It seems a great hardship, indeed, for a young man with an ambition to do something in the world to be compelled to pay his own way through school and college by hard work. But history shows us that the men who have led in the van of human progress have been, as a rule, self-educated, self-made.

The average boy of to-day who wishes to obtain a liberal education has a better chance by a hundredfold than had Daniel Webster or James A. Garfield. There is scarcely one in good health who reads these lines but can be assured that if he will he may. Here, as elsewhere, the will can usually make the way, and never before was there so many avenues of resource open to the strong will, the inflexible purpose, as there are to-day—at this hour and this moment.

"Of the five thousand persons—students,—directly connected with Harvard University," writes a graduate, "five hundred are students entirely or almost entirely dependent upon their own resources. They are not a poverty-stricken lot, however, for half of them make an income above the average allowance of boys in smaller colleges. From $700 to $1,000 are by no means exceptional yearly earnings of a student who is capable of doing newspaper work or tutoring,—branches of employment that pay well at Harvard.

"There are some men that make much more. A classmate of the writer entered college with about twenty-five dollars. As a freshman he had a hard struggle. In his junior year, however, he prospered and in his last ten months of undergraduate work he cleared above his college expenses, which were none too low, upward of $3,000.

"He made his money by advertising schemes and other publishing ventures. A few months after graduation he married. He is now living comfortably in Cambridge."

A son of poor parents, living in Springfield, New York, worked his way through an academy. This only whetted his appetite for knowledge, and he determined to advance, relying wholly on himself for success. Accordingly, he proceeded to Schenectady, and arranged with a professor of Union College to pay for his tuition by working. He rented a small room, which served for study and home, the expense of his bread-and-milk diet never exceeding fifty cents a week. After graduation, he turned his attention to civil engineering, and, later, to the construction of iron bridges of his own design. He procured many valuable patents, and amassed a fortune. His life was a success, the foundation being self-reliance and integrity.

Albert J. Beveridge, the junior United States Senator from Indiana, entered college with no other capital than fifty dollars loaned to him by a friend. He served as steward of a college club, and added to his original fund of fifty dollars by taking the freshman essay prize of twenty-five dollars. When summer came, he returned to work in the harvest fields and broke the wheat-cutting records of the county. He carried his books with him morning, noon and night, and studied persistently. When he returned to college he began to be recognized as an exceptional man. He had shaped his course and worked to it.

The president of his class at Columbia University recently earned the money to pay for his course by selling agricultural implements. One of his classmates, by the savings of two years' work as a farm laborer, and money earned by tutoring, writing, and copying done after study hours, not only paid his way through college, but helped to support his aged parents. He believed that he could afford a college training and he got it.

At Chicago University many hundreds of plucky young men are working their way. The ways of earning money are various, depending upon the opportunities for work, and the student's ability and adaptability. To be a correspondent of city daily papers is the most coveted occupation, but only a few can obtain such positions. Some dozen or more teach night school. Several teach in the public schools in the daytime, and do their university work in the afternoons and evenings, so as to take their degrees. Scores carry daily papers, by which they earn two and one-half to three and one-half dollars a week; but, as this does not pay expenses, they add other employments. A few find evening work in the city library. Some attend to lawns in summer and furnaces in winter; by having several of each to care for, they earn from five to ten dollars a week. Many are waiters at clubs and restaurants. Some solicit advertisements. The divinity students, after the first year, preach in small towns. Several are tutors. Two young men made twelve hundred dollars apiece, in this way, in one year. One student is a member of a city orchestra, earning twelve dollars a week. A few serve in the university postoffice, and receive twenty cents an hour.

A representative American college president recently said: "I regard it as, on the whole, a distinct advantage that a student should have to pay his own way in part as a condition of obtaining a college education. It gives a reality and vigor to one's work which is less likely to be obtained by those who are carried through college. I do not regard it, however, as desirable that one should have to work his own way entirely, as the tax upon strength and time is likely to be such as to interfere with scholarship and to undermine health."

Circumstances have rarely favored great men. A lowly beginning is no bar to a great career. The boy who works his way through college may have a hard time of it, but he will learn how to work his way in life, and will often take higher rank in school, and in after life, than his classmate who is the son of a millionaire. It is the son and daughter of the farmer, the mechanic and the operative, the great average class of our country, whose funds are small and opportunities few, that the republic will depend on most for good citizenship and brains in the future. The problem of securing a good education, where means are limited and time short, is of great importance both to the individual and the nation. Encouragement and useful hints are offered by the experience of many bright young people who have worked their way to diplomas worthily bestowed.

Gaius B. Frost was graduated at the Brattleboro, Vt., High School, taught district schools six terms, and entered Dartmouth College with just money enough to pay the first necessary expenses. He worked in gardens and as a janitor for some time. During his course he taught six terms as principal of a high school, and one year as assistant superintendent in the Essex County Truant School, at Lawrence, Mass., pushed a rolling chair at the Columbian Exposition, Chicago, was porter one season at Oak Hill House, Littleton, N. H., and canvassed for a publishing house one summer in Maine. None of his fellow-students did more to secure an education.

Isaac J. Cox of Philadelphia worked his way through Kimball Academy, Meriden, N. H., and through Dartmouth College, doing many kinds of work. There was no honest work within the limits of his ability that he would not undertake to pay his way. He served summers as waiter in a White Mountain hotel, finally becoming head-waiter. Like Mr. Frost, he ranked well in his classes, and is a young man of solid character and distinguished attainments.

For four years Richard Weil was noted as the great prize winner of Columbia College, and for "turning his time, attention and energy to any work that would bring remuneration." He would do any honest work that would bring cash,—and every cent of this money as well as every hour not spent in sleep throughout the four years of his college course was devoted to getting his education.

All these and many more from the ranks of the bright and well-trained young men who have been graduated from the colleges and universities of the country in recent years believed—sincerely, doggedly believed—that a college training was something that they must have. The question of whether or not they could afford it does not appear to have occasioned much hesitancy on their part. It is evident that they did not for one instant think that they could not afford to go to college.

In an investigation conducted to ascertain exact figures and facts which a poor boy must meet in working his way through college, it was found that, in a list of forty-five representative colleges and universities, having a student population of somewhat over forty thousand, the average expense per year is three hundred and four dollars; the average maximum expense, five hundred and twenty-nine dollars. In some of the smaller colleges the minimum expense per year is from seventy-five dollars to one hundred and ten dollars. There are many who get along on an expenditure of from one hundred and fifty dollars to two hundred dollars per year, while the maximum expense rises in but few instances above one thousand dollars.

In Western and Southern colleges the averages are lower. For example, eighteen well-known Western colleges and universities have a general average expense of two hundred and forty-two dollars per year, while fourteen as well-known Eastern institutions give an average expense of four hundred and forty-four dollars.

Statistics of expense, and the opportunities for self-help, at some of the best known Eastern institutions are full of interest:

Amherst makes a free gift of the tuition to prospective ministers; has one hundred tuition scholarships for other students of good character, habits, and standing; has some free rooms; makes loans at low rates; students have chances to earn money at tutoring, table-waiting, shorthand, care of buildings, newspaper correspondence, agencies for laundries, sale of books, etc. Five hundred dollars a year will defray all necessary expenses.

Bowdoin has nearly a hundred scholarships, fifty dollars to seventy-five dollars a year: "no limits placed on habits or social privileges of recipients;" students getting employment in the library or laboratories can earn about one-fourth of their expenses; these will be, for the college year, three hundred dollars to four hundred dollars.

Brown University has over a hundred tuition scholarships and a loan fund; often remits room rent in return for services about the college buildings; requires studiousness and economy in the case of assisted students. Many students earn money in various ways. The average yearly expenditure is five hundred dollars.

The cost at Columbia University averages five hundred and forty-seven dollars, the lowest being three hundred and eighty-seven dollars. A great many students who know how to get on in a great city work their way through Columbia.

Cornell University gives free tuition and free rooms to seniors and juniors of good standing in their studies and of good habits. It has thirty-six two-year scholarships (two hundred dollars), for freshmen, won by success in competitive examination. It has also five hundred and twelve state tuition scholarships. Many students support themselves in part by waiting on table, by shorthand, newspaper work, etc. The average yearly expenditure per student is five hundred dollars.

Dartmouth has some three hundred scholarships; those above fifty dollars conditioned on class rank; some rooms at nominal rent; requirements, economy and total abstinence; work of one sort or another to be had by needy students; a few get through on less than two hundred and fifty dollars a year; the average expenditure is about four hundred dollars.

Harvard has about two hundred and seventy-five scholarships, sixty dollars to four hundred dollars apiece, large beneficiary and loan funds, distributed or loaned in sums of forty dollars to two hundred and fifty dollars to needy and promising under-graduates; freshmen (usually) barred; a faculty employment committee; some students earning money as stenographers, typewriters, reporters, private tutors, clerks, canvassers, and singers; yearly expenditure (exclusive of clothes, washing, books, and stationery, laboratory charges, membership in societies, subscriptions and service), three hundred and fifty-eight dollars to one thousand and thirty-five dollars.

The University of Pennsylvania in a recent year gave three hundred and fifteen students forty-three thousand, two hundred and forty-two dollars in free scholarships and fellowships; no requirements except good standing. No money loaned, no free rooms. Many students support themselves in part, and a few wholly. The average expenditure per year, exclusive of clothes, railway fares, etc., is four hundred and fifty dollars.

Wesleyan University remits tuition wholly or in part to two-thirds of its under-graduates. Loan funds are available. "Beneficiaries must be frugal in habits, total abstainers, and maintain good standing and conduct." Many students are self-supporting, thirty-five per cent of the whole undergraduate body earning money. The yearly expenditure is three hundred and twenty-five dollars.

Yale is pretty well off now for fellowships and prizes; remits all but forty dollars of term bills, in case of worthy students, regular in attendance and studious; many such students earning money for themselves; average yearly expenditure, about six hundred dollars.

There is a splendid chance for girls at some of the soundest and best known girls' colleges in the United States.

The number of girls in the University of Michigan who are paying their own way is large. "Most of them," says Dr. Eliza M. Mosher, woman's dean of the college, "have earned the money by teaching. It is not unusual for students to come here for two years and go away for a time, in order to earn money to complete the course. Some of our most worthy graduates have done this. Some lighten their expenses by waiting on tables in boarding-houses, thus paying for their board. Others get room and board in the homes of professors by giving, daily, three hours of service about the house. A few take care of children, two or three hours a day, in the families of the faculty. One young woman, who is especially brave and in good earnest, worked as a chambermaid on a lake steamer last year and hurried away this year to do the same. It is her aim to earn one hundred dollars. With this sum, and a chance to pay for room and board by giving service, she will pay the coming year's expenses. Because it is especially difficult to obtain good servants in this inland town, there are a few people who are glad to give the college girls such employment."

"It is my opinion," said Miss Mary E. Woolley, president of Mount Holyoke College, "that, if a girl with average intelligence and energy wishes a college education, she can obtain it. As far as I know, the girls who have earned money to pay their way through college, at least in part, have accomplished it by tutoring, typewriting or stenography. Some of them earn pin-money while in college by tutoring, typewriting, sewing, summer work in libraries and offices, and in various little ways such as putting up lunches, taking care of rooms, executing commissions, and newspaper work. There are not many opportunities at Mount Holyoke to earn large amounts of money, but pin-money may be acquired in many little ways by a girl of ingenuity."

The system of compulsory domestic service obtaining now at Mount Holyoke—whereby, in return for thirty, or at the most, fifty minutes a day of light household labor, every student reduces her college expenses by a hundred dollars or a hundred and fifty,—was formerly in use at Wellesley; now, however, it is confined there to a few cottages. It has no foothold at Bryn Mawr, Smith and Vassar, or at the affiliated colleges, Barnard and Radcliffe.

At city colleges, like the last two mentioned, board and lodging cost more than in the country; and in general it is more difficult for a girl to pay any large part of her expenses through her own efforts and carry on her college work at the same time.

A number of girls in Barnard are, however, paying for their clothes, books, car fares, etc., by doing what work they can find. Tutoring in Barnard is seldom available for the undergraduates, because the lists are always full of experienced teachers, who can be engaged by the hour. Typewriting is one of the favorite resources. One student has done particularly well as agent for a firm that makes college caps and gowns. Another girl, a Russian Jewess, from the lower East Side, New York, runs a little "sweat shop," where she keeps a number of women busy making women's wrappers and children's dresses. She has paid all the expenses of her education in this way.

"Do any of your students work their way through?" was asked of a Bryn Mawr authority.

"Some,—to a certain extent," was the reply; "but not many. The lowest entire expenses of a year, are between four hundred and five hundred and fifty dollars. This amount includes positively everything. Two girls may pay part of their expenses by taking charge of the library, and by selling stationery; another, by distributing the mail, and others by 'tutoring'. Those who 'tutor' receive a dollar, a dollar and a half, and sometimes a very good one receives two dollars and a half, a lesson. But to earn all of one's way in a college year, and at the same time to keep up in all the studies, is almost impossible, and is not often done. Yet several are able to pay half their way."

A similar question put to a Vassar student brought the following response:

"Why, yes, I know a girl who has a sign on the door of her room,—'Dresses pressed,'—and she earns a good deal of money, too. Of course, there are many wealthy girls here who are always having something like that done, and who are willing to pay well for it. And so this girl makes a large sum of money, evenings and Saturdays.

"There are other girls who are agents for two of the great manufacturers of chocolate creams.

"The girl that plays the piano for the exercises in the gymnasium is paid for that, and some of the girls paint and make fancy articles, which they sell here, or send to the stores in New York, to be sold. Some of them write for the newspapers and magazines, too, and still others have pupils in music, etc., in Poughkeepsie. Yes, there are a great many girls who manage to pay most of their expenses."

Typewriting, tutoring, assistance rendered in library or laboratory or office, furnish help to many a girl who wishes to help herself, in nearly every college. Beside these standard employments, teaching in evening schools occasionally offers a good opportunity for steady eking out of means.

In many colleges there is opportunity for a girl with taste and cunning fingers to act as a dressmaker, repairer, and general refurnisher to students with generous allowances. Orders for gymnasium suits and swimming suits mean good profits. The reign of the shirt-waist has been a boon to many, for the well-dressed girl was never known to have enough pretty ones, and by a judicious display of attractive samples she is easily tempted to enlarge her supply. Then, too, any girl who is at all deft in the art of sewing can make a shirt-waist without a professional knowledge of cutting and fitting.

No boy or girl in America to-day who has good health, good morals and good grit need despair of getting a college education unless there are extremely unusual reasons against the undertaking.

West of the Alleghanies a college education is accessible to all classes. In most of the state universities tuition is free. In Kansas, for example, board and a room can be had for twelve dollars a month; the college fees are five dollars a year, while the average expenditure of the students does not exceed two hundred dollars per annum. In Ohio, the state university has abolished all tuition fees, and most of the denominational colleges demand fees even lower than were customary in New England half a century ago. Partly by reason of the cheapness of a college education in Ohio, that state now sends more students to college than all of New England. Yet if the total cost is less in the West, on the other hand, the opportunities for self-help are correspondingly more in the East. Every young man or woman should weigh the matter well before concluding that a college education is out of the question.

Former President Tucker of Dartmouth says: "The student who works his way may do it with ease and profit; or he may be seriously handicapped both by his necessities and the time he is obliged to bestow on outside matters. I have seen the sons of rich men lead in scholarship, and the sons of poor men. Poverty under most of the conditions in which we find it in colleges is a spur. Dartmouth College, I think, furnishes a good example. The greater part of its patronage is from poor men. Without examining the statistics, I should say, from facts that have fallen under my observation, that a larger percentage of Dartmouth men have risen to distinction than those of almost any other American college."

The opportunities of to-day are tenfold what they were half a century ago. Former President Schurman of Cornell says of his early life: "At the age of thirteen I left home. I hadn't definite plans as to my future. I merely wanted to get into a village, and to earn some money.

"My father got me a place in the nearest town,—Summerside,—a village of about one thousand inhabitants. For my first year's work I was to receive thirty dollars and my board. Think of that, young men of to-day! Thirty dollars a year for working from seven in the morning until ten at night! But I was glad to get the place. It was a start in the world, and the little village was like a city to my country eyes.

"From the time I began working in the store until to-day, I have always supported myself, and during all the years of my boyhood I never received a penny that I did not earn myself. At the end of my first year, I went to a larger store in the same town, where I was to receive sixty dollars a year and my board. My salary was doubled; I was getting on swimmingly.

"I kept this place for two years, and then I gave it up, against the wishes of my employer, because I had made up my mind that I wanted to get a better education. I determined to go to college.

"I did not know how I was going to do this, except that it must be by my own efforts. I had saved about eighty dollars from my store-keeping, and that was all the money I had in the world.

"When I told my employer of my plan, he tried to dissuade me from it. He pointed out the difficulties in the way of my going to college, and offered to double my pay if I would stay in the store.

"That was the turning-point in my life. In one side was the certainty of one hundred and twenty dollars a year, and the prospect of promotion as fast as I deserved it. Remember what one hundred and twenty dollars meant on Prince Edward Island, and to me, a poor boy who had never possessed such a sum in his life. On the other side was my hope of obtaining an education. I knew that it involved hard work and self-denial, and there was the possibility of failure in the end. But my mind was made up. I would not turn back. I need not say that I do not regret that early decision, although I think that I should have made a successful storekeeper.

"With my capital of eighty dollars, I began to attend the village high school, to get my preparation for college. I had only one year to do it in. My money would not last longer than that. I recited in Latin, Greek, and algebra, all on the same day, and for the next forty weeks I studied harder than I ever had before or have since. At the end of the year I entered the competitive examination for a scholarship in Prince of Wales College, at Charlottetown, on the Island. I had small hope of winning it, my preparation had been so hasty and incomplete. But when the result was announced, I found that I had not only won the scholarship from my county, but stood first of all the competitors on the Island.

"The scholarship I had won amounted to only sixty dollars a year. It seems little enough, but I can say now, after nearly thirty years, that the winning of it was the greatest success I ever have had. I have had other rewards, which, to most persons, would seem immeasurably greater, but with this difference: that first success was essential; without it I could not have gone on. The others I could have done without, if it had been necessary."

For two years young Schurman attended Prince of Wales College. He lived on his scholarship and what he could earn by keeping books for one of the town storekeepers, spending less than one hundred dollars during the entire college year. Afterward, he taught a country school for a year, and then went to Acadia College in Nova Scotia to complete his course.

One of Mr. Schurman's fellow-students in Acadia says that he was remarkable chiefly for taking every prize to which he was eligible. In his senior year, he learned of a scholarship in the University of London offered for competition by the students of Canadian colleges. The scholarship paid five hundred dollars a year for three years. The young student in Acadia was ambitious to continue his studies in England, and saw in this offer his opportunity. He tried the examination and won the prize, in competition with the brightest students in the larger Canadian colleges.

During the three years in the University of London, Mr. Schurman became deeply interested in the study of philosophy, and decided that he had found in it his life-work. He was eager to go to Germany to study under the great leaders of philosophic thought. A way was opened for him, through the offer of the Hibbard Society, in London, of a traveling fellowship with two thousand dollars a year. The honor men of the great English Universities like Oxford and Cambridge were among the competitors, but the poor country boy from Prince Edward Island was again successful, greatly to the surprise of the others.

At the end of his course in Germany, Mr. Schurman, then a Doctor of Philosophy, returned to Acadia College to become a teacher there. Soon afterward, he was called to Dalhousie University, at Halifax, Nova Scotia.

In 1886, when a chair of philosophy was established at Cornell, President White, who had once met the brilliant young Canadian, called him to that position. Two years later, Dr. Schurman became dean of the Sage School of Philosophy at Cornell; and, in 1892, when the president's chair became vacant, he was placed at the head of the great university. At that time he was only thirty-eight years of age.

A well-known graduate of Amherst college gives the following figures, which to the boy who earnestly wants to go to college are of the most pertinent interest:

"I entered college with $8.42 in my pocket. During the year I earned $60; received from the college a scholarship of $60, and an additional gift of $20; borrowed $190. My current expenses during my freshman year were $4.50 per week. Besides this I spent $10.55 for books; $23.45 for clothing; $10.57 for voluntary subscriptions; $15 for railroad fares; $8.24 for sundries.

"During the next summer I earned $100. I waited on table at a $4 boarding-house all of my sophomore year, and earned half board, retaining my old room at $1 per week. The expenses of the sophomore year were $394.50. I earned during the year, including board, $87.20; received a scholarship of $70, and gifts amounting to $12.50, and borrowed $150, with all of which I just covered expenses.

"In my junior year I engaged a nice furnished room at $60 per year, which I agreed to pay for by work about the house. By clerical work, etc., I earned $37; also earned full board waiting upon table; received $70 for a scholarship; $55 from gifts; borrowed $70, which squared my accounts for the year, excepting $40 due on tuition. The expenses for the year, including, of course, the full value of board, room, and tuition, were $478.76.

"During the following summer I earned $40. Throughout the senior year I retained the same room, under the same conditions as the previous year. I waited on table all the year, and received full board; earned by clerical work, tutoring, etc., $40; borrowed $40; secured a scholarship of $70; took a prize of $25; received a gift of $35. The expenses of the senior year, $496.64 were necessarily heavier than these of previous years. But having secured a good position as teacher for the coming year, I was permitted to give my note for the amount I could not raise, and so was enabled to graduate without financial embarrassment.

"The total expense for the course was about $1,708; of which (counting scholarships as earnings) I earned $1,157."

Twenty-five of the young men graduated at Yale not long ago paid their way entirely throughout their courses. It seemed as if they left untried no avenue for earning money. Tutoring, copying, newspaper work, and positions as clerks were well-occupied fields; and painters, drummers, founders, machinists, bicycle agents, and mail carriers were numbered among the twenty-five.

In a certain district in Boston there are ten thousand students. Many of them come from the country and from factory towns. A large number come from the farms of the West. Many of these students are paying for their education by money earned by their own hands. It is said that unearned money does not enrich. The money that a student earns for his own education does enrich his life. It is true gold.

Every young man or woman should weigh the matter well before concluding that a college education is out of the question.

If Henry Wilson, working early and late on a farm with scarcely any opportunities to go to school, bound out until he was twenty-one for only a yoke of oxen and six sheep, could manage to read a thousand good books before his time had expired; if the slave Frederick Douglass, on a plantation where it was almost a crime to teach a slave to read, could manage from scraps of paper, posters on barns, and old almanacs, to learn the alphabet and lift himself to eminence; if the poor deaf boy Kitto, who made shoes in an alms-house, could become the greatest Biblical scholar of his age, where is the boy or girl to-day, under the American flag, who cannot get a fair education and escape the many disadvantages of ignorance?

"If a man empties his purse into his head," says Franklin, "no man can take it away from him. An investment in knowledge always pays the best interest."

Your Opportunity Confronts You—what Will You Do with It?

Never before was the opportunity of the educated man so great as to-day. Never before was there such a demand for the trained man, *the man who can do a thing superbly well*. At the door of every vocation is a sign out, "Wanted—a man." No matter how many millions are out of employment, the whole world is hunting for a man who can do things; a trained thinker who can do whatever he undertakes a little better than it has ever before been done. Everywhere it is the educated, the trained man, the man whose natural ability has been enlarged, enhanced one hundredfold by superior training, that is wanted.

On all sides we see men with small minds, but who are well educated, pushing ahead of those who have greater capabilities, but who are only half educated. A one-talent man, superbly trained, often gets the place when a man with many untrained or half-trained talents loses it. Never was ignorance placed at such a disadvantage as to-day.

While the opportunities awaiting the educated man, the college graduate, on his entrance into practical life were never before so great and so numerous as to-day, so also the dangers and temptations which beset him were never before so great, so numerous, so insidious.

All education which does not elevate, refine, and ennoble its recipient is a curse instead of a blessing. A liberal education only renders a rascal more dishonest, more dangerous. *Educated rascality is infinitely more of a menace to society than ignorant rascality.*

Every year, thousands of young men and young women graduate full of ambition and hope, full of expectancy, go out from the schools, the colleges, and the universities, with their diplomas, to face for the first time the practical world.

There is nothing else, perhaps, which the graduate needs to be cautioned against more than the money madness which has seized the American people, for nothing else is more fatal to the development of the higher, finer instincts and nobler desires.

Wealth with us multiplies a man's power so tremendously that everything gravitates toward it. A man's genius, art, what he stands for, is measured largely by how many dollars it will bring. "How much can I get for my picture?" "How much royalty for my book?" "How much can I get out of my specialty, my profession, my business?" "How can I make the most money?" or "How can I get rich?" is the great interrogation of the century. How will the graduate, the trained young man or woman answer it?

The dollar stands out so strongly in all the undertakings of life that the ideal is often lowered or lost, the artistic suffers, the soul's wings are weighted down with gold. The commercial spirit tends to drag everything down to its dead, sordid level. It is the subtle menace which threatens to poison the graduate's ambition. *Whichever way you turn, the dollar-mark will swing info your vision.* The money-god, which nearly everybody worships in some form or other, will tempt you on every hand.

Never before was such pressure brought to bear on the trained youth to sell his brains, to coin his ability into dollars, to prostitute his education, as to-day. The commercial prizes held up to him are so dazzling, so astounding, that it takes a strong, vigorous character to resist their temptation, even when the call in one to do something which bears little relation to money-making speaks very loudly.

The song of the money-siren to-day is so persistent, so entrancing, so overwhelming that it often drowns the still small voice which bids one follow the call that runs in his blood, that is indicated in the very structure in his brain.

Tens of thousands of young people just out of school and college stand tiptoe on the threshold of active life, with high ideals and glorious visions, full of hope and big with promise, but many of them will very quickly catch the money contagion; the fatal germ will spread through their whole natures, inoculating their ambition with its vicious virus, and, after a few years, their fair college vision will fade, their yearnings for something higher will gradually die and be replaced by material, sordid, selfish ideals.

The most unfortunate day in a youth's career is that one on which his ideals begin to grow dim and his high standards begin to drop; that day on which is born in him the selfish, money-making germ, which so often warps and wrenches the whole nature out of its legitimate orbit.

You will need to be constantly on your guard to resist the attack of this germ. After you graduate and go out into the world, powerful influences will be operative in your life, tending to deteriorate your standards, lower your ideals, and encoarsen you generally.

When you plunge into the swim of things, you will be constantly thrown into contact with those of lower ideals, who are actuated only by sordid, selfish aims. Then dies the man, the woman in you, unless you are made of superior stuff.

What a contrast that high and noble thing which the college diploma stands for presents to that which many owners of the diploma stand for a quarter of a century later! It is often difficult to recognize any relationship between the two.

American-Indian graduates, who are so transformed by the inspiring, uplifting influences of the schools and colleges which are educating them that they are scarcely recognizable by their own tribes when they return home, very quickly begin to change under the deteriorating influences operating upon them when they leave college. They soon begin to shed their polish, their fine manners, their improved language, and general culture; the Indian blanket replaces their modern dress, and they gradually drift back into their former barbarism. They become Indians again.

The influences that will surround you when you leave college or your special training school will be as potent to drag you down as those that cause the young Indian to revert to barbarism. The shock you will receive in dropping from the atmosphere of high ideals and beautiful promise in which you have lived for four years to that of a very practical, cold, sordid materiality will be a severe test to your character, your manhood.

But the graduate whose training, whose education counts for anything ought to be able to resist the shock, to withstand all temptations.

The educated man ought to be able to do something better, something higher than merely to put money in his purse. Money-making can not compare with man-making. There is something infinitely better than to be a millionaire of money, and that is to be a millionaire of brains, of culture, of helpfulness to one's fellows, a millionaire of character—a gentleman.

Whatever degrees you carry from school or college, whatever distinction you may acquire in your career, no title will ever mean quite so much, will ever be quite so noble, as that of gentleman.

"A keen and sure sense of honor," says Ex-President Eliot, of Harvard University, "is the finest result of college life." The graduate who has not acquired this keen and sure sense of honor, this thing that stamps the gentleman, misses the best thing that a college education can impart.

Your future, fortunate graduate, like a great block of pure white marble, stands untouched before you. You hold the chisel and mallet—your ability, your education—in your hands. There is something in the block for you, and it lives in your ideal. Shall it be angel or devil? What are your ideals, as you stand tiptoe on the threshold of active life? Will you smite the block and shatter it into an unshapely or hideous piece; or will you call out a statue of usefulness, of grace and beauty, a statue which will tell the unborn generations the story of a noble life?

Great advantages bring great responsibilities. You can not divorce them. A liberal education greatly increases a man's obligations. There is coupled with it a responsibility which you can not shirk without paying the penalty in a shriveled soul, a stunted mentality, a warped conscience, and a narrow field of usefulness. It is more of a disgrace for a college graduate to grovel, to stoop to mean, low practises, than for a man who has not had a liberal education. The educated man has gotten a glimpse of power, of grander things, and he is expected to look up, not down, to aspire, not to grovel.

We cannot help feeling that it is worse for a man to go wrong who has had all the benefits of a liberal education, than it is for one who has not had glimpses of higher things, who has not had similar advantages, because where much is given, much is expected. The world has a right to expect that wherever there is an educated, trained man people should be able to say of him as Lincoln said of Walt Whitman, "There goes a man."

The world has a right to expect that the graduate, having once faced the light and felt its power, will not turn his back on it; that he will not disgrace his *alma mater* which has given him his superior chance in life and opened wide for him the door of opportunity. It has a right to expect that a man who has learned how to use skilfully the tools of life, will be an artist and not an artisan; that he will not stop growing. Society has a right to look to the collegian to be a refining, uplifting force in his community, an inspiration to those who have not had his priceless chance; it is justified in expecting that he will raise the standard of intelligence in his community; that he will illustrate in his personality, his finer culture, the possible glory of life. It has a right to expect that he will not be a victim of the narrowing, cramping influence of avarice; that he will not be a slave of the dollar or stoop to a greedy, grasping career: that he will be free from the sordidness which often characterizes the rich ignoramus.

If you have the ability and have been given superior opportunities, it simply means that you have a great commission to do something out of the ordinary for your fellows; a special message for humanity.

If the torch of learning has been put in your hand, its significance is that you should light up the way for the less fortunate.

If you have received a message which carries freedom for people enslaved by ignorance and bigotry, you have no right to suppress it. Your education means an increased obligation to live your life up to the level of your gift, your superior opportunity. Your duty is to deliver your message to the world with all the manliness, vigor, and force you possess.

What shall we think of a man who has been endowed with godlike gifts, who has had the inestimable advantage of a liberal education, who has ability to ameliorate the hard conditions of his fellows, to help to emancipate them from ignorance and drudgery; what shall we think of this man, so divinely endowed, so superbly equipped, who, instead of using his education to lift his fellow men, uses it to demoralize, to drag them down; who employs his talents in the book he writes, in the picture he paints, in his business, whatever it may be, to mislead, to demoralize, to debauch; who uses his light as a decoy to lure his fellows on the rocks and reefs, instead of as a beacon to guide them into port?

We imprison the burglar for breaking into our houses and stealing, but what shall we do with the educated rascal who uses his trained mind and all his gifts to ruin the very people who look up to him as a guide?

"The greatest thing you can do is to be what you ought to be."

A great man has said that no man will be content to live a half life when he has once discovered it is a half life, because the other half, the higher half, will haunt him. Your superior training has given you a glimpse of the higher life. Never lose sight of your college vision. Do not permit yourself to be influenced by the maxims of a low, sordid prudence, which will be dinned into your ears wherever you go. Regard the very suggestion that you shall coin your education, your high ideals into dollars; that you lower your standards, prostitute your education by the practise of low-down, sordid methods, as an insult.

Say to yourself, *"If the highest thing in me will not bring success, surely the lowest, the worst, cannot."*

The mission of the trained man is to show the world a higher, finer type of manhood.

The world has a right to expect better results from the work of the educated man; something finer, of a higher grade, and better quality, than from the man who lacks early training, the man who has discovered only a small part of himself. "Pretty good," "Fairly good," applied either to character or to work are bad mottoes for an educated man. You should be able to demonstrate that the man with a diploma has learned to use the tools of life skilfully; has learned how to focus his faculties so that he can bring the whole man to his task, and not a part of himself. Low ideals, slipshod work, aimless, systemless, half-hearted endeavors, should have no place in your program.

It is a disgrace for a man with a liberal education to botch his work, demoralize his ideals, discredit his teachers, dishonor the institution which has given him his chance to be a superior man.

"Keep your eye on the model, don't watch your hands," is the injunction of a great master as he walks up and down among his pupils, criticizing their work. The trouble with most of us is that we do not keep our eyes on the model; we lose our earlier vision. A liberal education ought to broaden a man's mind so that he will be able to keep his eye always on the model, the perfect ideal of his work, uninfluenced by the thousand and one petty annoyances, bickerings, misunderstandings, and discords which destroy much of the efficiency of narrower, less cultivated minds.

The graduate ought to be able to rise above these things so that he can use all his brain power and energy and fling the weight of his entire being into work that is worth while.

After the withdrawal of a play that has been only a short time on the stage, we often read this comment, "An artistic success, but a financial failure." While an education should develop all that is highest and best in a man, it should also make him a practical man, not a financial failure. Be sure that you possess your knowledge, that your knowledge does not possess you.

The mere possession of a diploma will only hold you up to ridicule, will only make you more conspicuous as a failure, if you cannot bring your education to a focus and utilize it in a practical way.

Knowledge is power only when it can be made available, practical.

Only what you can use of your education will benefit you or the world.

The great question which confronts you in the practical world is "What can you do with what you know?" Can you transmute your knowledge into power? Your ability to read your Latin diploma is not a test of true education; a stuffed memory does not make an educated man. The knowledge that can be utilized, that can be translated into power, constitutes the only education worthy of the name. There are thousands of college-bred men in this country, who are loaded down with knowledge that they have never been able to utilize, to make available for working purposes. There is a great difference between absorbing knowledge, making a sponge of one's brain, and transmuting every bit of knowledge into power, into working capital.

As the silkworm transmutes the mulberry leaf into satin, so you should transmute your knowledge into practical wisdom.

There is no situation in life in which the beneficent influence of a well-assimilated education will not make itself felt.

The college man *ought* to be a superb figure anywhere. The consciousness of being well educated should put one at ease in any society. The knowledge that one's mentality has been broadened out by college training, that one has discovered his possibilities, not only adds wonderfully to one's happiness, but also increases one's self-confidence immeasurably, and *self-confidence is the lever that moves the world*. On every hand we see men of good ability who feel crippled all their lives and are often mortified, by having to confess, by the poverty of their language, their sordid ideals, their narrow outlook on life, that they are not educated. The superbly trained man can go through the world with his head up and feel conscious that he is not likely to play the ignoramus in any company, or be mortified or pained by ignorance of matters which every well-informed person is supposed to know. This assurance of knowledge multiplies self-confidence and gives infinite satisfaction.

In other words, a liberal education makes a man think a little more of himself, feel a little surer of himself, have more faith in himself, because he has discovered himself. There is also great satisfaction in the knowledge that one has not neglected the unfoldment and expansion of his mind, that he has not let the impressionable years of youth go by unimproved.

But the best thing you carry from your *alma mater* is not what you there prized most, not your knowledge of the sciences, languages, literature, art; it is something infinitely more sacred, of greater value than all these, and that is *your aroused ambition, your discovery of yourself, of your powers, of your possibilities; your resolution to be a little more of a man, to play a manly part in life, to do the greatest, grandest thing possible to you*. This will mean infinitely more to you than all you have learned from books or lectures.

The most precious thing of all, however, if you have made the most of your chance, is the uplift, encouragement, inspiration, which you have absorbed from your teachers, from your associations; this is the embodiment of the college spirit, the spirit of your *alma mater*; it is that which should make you reach up as well as on, which should make you aspire instead of grovel—look up, instead of down.

The graduate should regard his education as a sacred trust. He should look upon it as a power to be used, not alone for his advancement, or for his own selfish ends, but for the betterment of all mankind. As a matter of fact, things are so arranged in this world that no one can use his divine gift for himself alone and get the best out of it. To try to keep it would be as foolish as for the farmer to hoard his seed corn in a bin instead of giving it to the earth, for fear he would never get it back.

The man who withholds the giving of himself to the world, does it at his peril, at the cost of mental and moral penury.

The way to get the most out of ourselves, or out of life, is not to try to *sell* ourselves for the highest possible price but to *give* ourselves, not stingily, meanly, but *royally, magnanimously, to our fellows*. If the rosebud should try to retain all of its sweetness and beauty locked within its petals and refuse to give it out, it would be lost. It is only by flinging them out to the world that their fullest development is possible. The man who tries to keep his education, his superior advantages for himself, who is always looking out for the main chance, only shrivels, and strangles the very faculties he would develop.

The trouble with most of us is that, in our efforts to sell ourselves for selfish ends or for the most dollars, we impoverish our own lives, stifle our better natures.

The graduate should show the world that he has something in him too sacred to be tampered with, something marked "not for sale," a sacred something that bribery cannot touch, that influence cannot buy. You should so conduct yourself that every one will see that there is something in you that would repel as an insult the very suggestion that you could be bought or bribed, or influenced to stoop to anything low or questionable.

The college man who is cursed with commonness, who gropes along in mediocrity, who lives a shiftless, selfish life, and does not lift up his head and show that he has made the most of his great privileges disgraces the institution that gave him his chance.

You have not learned the best lesson from your school or college if you have not discovered the secret of making life a glory instead of a sordid grind. When you leave your *alma mater*, my young friend, whatever your vocation, do not allow all that is finest within you, your high ideals and noble purposes to be suffocated, strangled, in the everlasting scramble for the dollar. Put beauty into your life, do not let your esthetic faculties, your aspiring instincts, be atrophied in your efforts to make a living. Do not, as thousands of graduates do, sacrifice your social instincts, your friendships, your good name, for power or position.

Whether you make money or lose it, never sell your divine heritage, your good name, for a mess of pottage. Whatever you do, be larger than your vocation; never let it be said of you that you succeeded in your vocation, but failed as a man.

When William Story, the sculptor, was asked to make a speech at the unveiling of his great statue of George Peabody, in London, he simply pointed to the statue and said, "*That is my speech.*"

So conduct yourself that your life shall need no eulogy in words. Let it be its own eulogy, let your success tell to the world the story of a noble career. However much money you may accumulate, carry your greatest wealth with you, in *a clean record, an unsullied reputation.* Then you will not need houses or lands or stocks or bonds to testify to a rich life.

Never before did an opportunity to render such great service to mankind confront the educated youth as confronts you to-day. *What Will You Do with It?*

Round Boys in Square Holes

The high prize of life, the crowning fortune of a man, is to be born with a bias to some pursuit, which finds him in employment and happiness.—Emerson

There is hardly a poet, artist, philosopher, or man of science mentioned in the history of the human intellect, whose genius was not opposed by parents, guardians, or teachers. In these cases Nature seems to have triumphed by direct interposition; to have insisted on her darlings having their rights, and encouraged disobedience, secrecy, falsehood, even flight from home and occasional vagabondism, rather than the world should lose what it cost her so much pains to produce.—E. P. Whipple

I hear a voice you cannot hear,
Which says, I must not stay;
I see a hand you cannot see,
Which beckons me away. —Tickell.

"James Watt, I never saw such an idle young fellow as you are," said his grandmother; "do take a book and employ yourself usefully. For the last half-hour you have not spoken a single word. Do you know what you have been doing all this time? Why, you have taken off and replaced, and taken off again, the teapot lid, and you have held alternately in the steam, first a saucer and then a spoon, and you have busied yourself in examining and, collecting together the little drops formed by the condensation of the steam on the surface of the china and the silver. Now, are you not ashamed to waste your time in this disgraceful manner?"

The world has certainly gained much through the old lady's failure to tell James how he could employ his time to better advantage!

"But I'm good for something," pleaded a young man whom a merchant was about to discharge for his bluntness. "You are good for nothing as a salesman," said his employer. "I am sure I can be useful," said the youth. "How? Tell me how." "I don't know, sir, I don't know." "Nor do I," said the merchant, laughing at the earnestness of his clerk. "Only don't put me away, sir, don't put me away. Try me at something besides selling. I cannot sell; I know I cannot sell." "I know that, too," said the principal; "that is what is wrong." "But I can make myself useful somehow," persisted the young man; "I know I can." He was placed in the counting-house, where his aptitude for figures soon showed itself, and in a few years he became not only chief cashier in the large store, but an eminent accountant.

You cannot look into a cradle and read the secret message traced by a divine hand and wrapped up in that bit of clay, any more than you can see the North Star in the magnetic needle. God has loaded the needle of that young life so it will point to the star of its own destiny; and though you may pull it around by artificial advice and unnatural education, and compel it to point to the star which presides over poetry, art, law, medicine, or whatever your own pet calling is until you have wasted years of a precious life, yet, when once free, the needle flies back to its own star.

"Rue it as he may, repent it as he often does," says Robert Waters, "the man of genius is drawn by an irresistible impulse to the occupation for which he was created. No matter by what difficulties surrounded, no matter how unpromising the prospect, this occupation is the only one which he will pursue with interest and pleasure. When his efforts fail to procure means of subsistence, and he finds himself poor and neglected, he may, like Burns, often look back with a sigh and think how much better off he would be had he pursued some other occupation, but he will stick to his favorite pursuit nevertheless."

Civilization will mark its highest tide when every man has chosen his proper work. No man can be ideally successful until he has found his place. Like a locomotive, he is strong on the track, but weak anywhere else. "Like a boat on a river," says Emerson, "every boy runs against obstructions on every side but one. On that side all obstruction is taken away, and he sweeps serenely over a deepening channel into an infinite sea."

Only a Dickens can write the history of "Boy Slavery," of boys whose aspirations and longings have been silenced forever by ignorant parents; of boys persecuted as lazy, stupid, or fickle, simply because they were out of their places; of square boys forced into round holes, and oppressed because they did not fit; of boys compelled to pore over dry theological books when the voice within continually cried "Law," "Medicine," "Art," "Science," or "Business"; of boys tortured because they were not enthusiastic in employments which they loathed, and against which every fiber of their being was uttering perpetual protest.

It is often a narrow selfishness in a father which leads him to wish his son a reproduction of himself. "You are trying to make that boy another you. One is enough," said Emerson. John Jacob Astor's father wished his son to be his successor as a butcher, but the instinct of commercial enterprise was too strong in the future merchant.

Nature never duplicates men. She breaks the pattern at every birth. The magic combination is never used but once. Frederick the Great was terribly abused because he had a passion for art and music and did not care for military drill. His father hated the fine arts and imprisoned him. He even contemplated killing his son, but his own death placed Frederick on the throne at the age of twenty-eight. This boy, who, because he loved art and music, was thought good for nothing, made Prussia one of the greatest nations of Europe.

How stupid and clumsy is the blinking eagle at perch, but how keen his glance, how steady and true his curves, when turning his powerful wing against the clear blue sky!

Ignorant parents compelled the boy Arkwright to become a barber's apprentice, but Nature had locked up in his brain a cunning device destined to bless humanity and to do the drudgery of millions of England's poor; so he must needs say "hands off" even to his parents, as Christ said to his mother, "Wist ye not that I must be about my Father's business?"

Galileo was set apart for a physician, but when compelled to study anatomy and physiology, he would hide his Euclid and Archimedes and stealthily work out the abstruse problems. He was only eighteen when he discovered the principle of the pendulum in a lamp left swinging in the cathedral at Pisa. He invented both the microscope and telescope, enlarging knowledge of the vast and minute alike.

The parents of Michael Angelo had declared that no son of theirs should ever follow the discreditable profession of an artist, and even punished him for covering the walls and furniture with sketches; but the fire burning in his breast was kindled by the Divine Artist, and would not let him rest until he had immortalized himself in the architecture of St. Peter's, in the marble of his Moses, and on the walls of the Sistine Chapel.

Pascal's father determined that his son should teach the dead languages, but the voice of mathematics drowned every other call, haunting the boy until he laid aside his grammar for Euclid.

The father of Joshua Reynolds rebuked his son for drawing pictures, and wrote on one: "Done by Joshua out of pure idleness." Yet this "idle boy" became one of the founders of the Royal Academy.

Turner was intended for a barber in Maiden Lane, but became the greatest landscape-painter of modern times.

Claude Lorraine, the painter, was apprenticed to a pastry-cook; Molière, the author, to an upholsterer; and Guido, the famous painter of Aurora, was sent to a music school.

Schiller was sent to study surgery in the military school at Stuttgart, but in secret he produced his first play, "The Robbers," the first performance of which he had to witness in disguise. The irksomeness of his prison-like school so galled him, and his longing for authorship so allured him, that he ventured, penniless, into the inhospitable world of letters. A kind lady aided him, and soon he produced the two splendid dramas which made him immortal.

The physician Handel wished his son to become a lawyer, and so tried to discourage his fondness for music. But the boy got an old spinet and practiced on it secretly in a hayloft. When the doctor visited a brother in the service of the Duke of Weisenfelds, he took his son with him. The boy wandered unobserved to the organ in a chapel, and soon had a private concert under full blast. The duke happened to hear the performance, and wondered who could possibly combine so much melody with so much evident unfamiliarity with the instrument. The boy was brought before him, and the duke, instead of blaming him for disturbing the organ, praised his performance, and persuaded Dr. Handel to let his son follow his bent.

Daniel Defoe had been a trader, a soldier, a merchant, a secretary, a factory manager, a commissioner's accountant, an envoy, and an author of several indifferent books, before he wrote his masterpiece, "Robinson Crusoe."

Wilson, the ornithologist, failed in five different professions before he found his place.

Erskine spent four years in the navy, and then, in the hope of more rapid promotion, joined the army. After serving more than two years, he one day, out of curiosity, attended a court, in the town where his regiment was quartered. The presiding judge, an acquaintance, invited Erskine to sit near him, and said that the pleaders at the bar were among the most eminent lawyers of Great Britain. Erskine took their measure as they spoke, and believed he could excel them. He at once began the study of law, in which he eventually soon stood alone as the greatest forensic orator of his country.

A. T. Stewart studied for the ministry, and became a teacher, before he drifted into his proper calling as a merchant, through the accident of having lent money to a friend. The latter, with failure imminent, insisted that his creditor should take the shop as the only means of securing the money.

"Jonathan," said Mr. Chase, when his son told of having nearly fitted himself for college, "thou shalt go down to the machine-shop on Monday morning." It was many years before Jonathan escaped from the shop, to work his way up to the position of a man of great influence as a United States Senator from Rhode Island.

It has been well said that if God should commission two angels, one to sweep a street crossing, and the other to rule an empire, they could not be induced to exchange callings. Not less true is it that he who feels that God has given him a particular work to do can be happy only when earnestly engaged in its performance. Happy the youth who finds the place which his dreams have pictured! If he does not fill that place, he will not fill any to the satisfaction of himself or others. Nature never lets a man rest until he has found his place. She haunts him and drives him until all his faculties give their consent and he falls into his proper niche. A parent might just as well decide that the magnetic needle will point to Venus or Jupiter without trying it, as to decide what profession his son shall adopt.

What a ridiculous exhibition a great truck-horse would make on the race-track; yet this is no more incongruous than the popular idea that law, medicine, and theology are the only desirable professions. How ridiculous, too, for fifty-two per cent. of our American college graduates to study law! How many young men become poor clergymen by trying to imitate their fathers who were good ones; of poor doctors and lawyers for the same reason! The country is full of men who are out of place, "disappointed, soured, ruined, out of office, out of money, out of credit, out of courage, out at elbows, out in the cold." The fact is, nearly every college graduate who succeeds in the true sense of the word, prepares himself in school, but makes himself after he is graduated. The best thing his teachers have taught him is *how* to study. The moment he is beyond the college walls he ceases to use books and helps which do not feed him, and seizes upon those that do.

We must not jump to the conclusion that because a man has not succeeded in what he has really tried to do with all his might, he cannot succeed at anything. Look at a fish floundering on the sand as though he would tear himself to pieces. But look again: a huge wave breaks higher up the beach and covers the unfortunate creature. The moment his fins feel the water, he is himself again, and darts like a flash through the waves. His fins mean something now, while before they beat the air and earth in vain, a hindrance instead of a help.

If you fail after doing your level best, examine the work attempted, and see if it really be in the line of your bent or power of achievement. Cowper failed as a lawyer. He was so timid that he could not plead a case, but he wrote some of our finest poems. Molière found that he was not adapted to the work of a lawyer, but he left a great name in literature. Voltaire and Petrarch abandoned the law, the former choosing philosophy, the latter, poetry. Cromwell was a farmer until forty years old.

Very few of us, before we reach our teens, show great genius or even remarkable talent for any line of work or study. The great majority of boys and girls, even when given all the latitude and longitude heart could desire, find it very difficult before their fifteenth or even before their twentieth year to decide what to do for a living. Each knocks at the portals of the mind, demanding a wonderful aptitude for some definite line of work, but it is not there. That is no reason why the duty at hand should be put off, or why the labor that naturally falls to one's lot should not be done well. Samuel Smiles was trained to a profession which was not to his taste, yet he practiced it so faithfully that it helped him to authorship, for which he was well fitted.

Fidelity to the work or everyday duties at hand, and a genuine feeling of responsibility to our parents or employers, ourselves, and our God, will eventually bring most of us into the right niches at the proper time.

Garfield would not have become President if he had not previously been a zealous teacher, a responsible soldier, a conscientious statesman. Neither Lincoln nor Grant started as a baby with a precocity for the White House, or an irresistible genius for ruling men. So no one should be disappointed because he was not endowed with tremendous gifts in the cradle. His business is to do the best he can wherever his lot may be cast, and advance at every honorable opportunity in the direction towards which the inward monitor points. Let duty be the guiding-star, and success will surely be the crown, to the full measure of one's ability and industry.

What career? What shall my life's work be?

If instinct and heart ask for carpentry, be a carpenter; if for medicine, be a physician. With a firm choice and earnest work, a young man or woman cannot help but succeed. But if there be no instinct, or if it be weak or faint, one should choose cautiously along the line of his best adaptability and opportunity. No one need doubt that the world has use for him. True success lies in acting well your part, and this every one can do. Better be a first-rate hod-carrier than a second-rate anything.

The world has been very kind to many who were once known as dunces or blockheads, after they have become very successful; but it was very cross to them while they were struggling through discouragement and misinterpretation. Give every boy and girl a fair chance and reasonable encouragement, and do not condemn them because of even a large degree of downright stupidity; for many so-called good-for-nothing boys, blockheads, numskulls, dullards, or dunces, were only boys out of their places, round boys forced into square holes.

Wellington was considered a dunce by his mother. At Eton he was called dull, idle, slow, and was about the last boy in school of whom anything was expected. He showed no talent, and had no desire to enter the army. His industry and perseverance were his only redeeming characteristics in the eyes of his parents and teachers. But at forty-six he had defeated the greatest general living, except himself.

Goldsmith was the laughing-stock of his schoolmasters. He was graduated "Wooden Spoon," a college name for a dunce. He tried to enter a class in surgery, but was rejected. He was driven to literature. Goldsmith found himself totally unfit for the duties of a physician; but who else could have written the "Vicar of Wakefield" or the "Deserted Village"? Dr. Johnson found him very poor and about to be arrested for debt. He made Goldsmith give him the manuscript of the "Vicar of Wakefield," sold it to the publishers, and paid the debt. This manuscript made its author famous.

Robert Clive bore the name of "dunce" and "reprobate" at school, but at thirty two, with three thousand men, he defeated fifty thousand at Plassey and laid the foundation of the British Empire in India. Sir Walter Scott was called a blockhead by his teacher. When Byron happened to get ahead of his class, the master would say: "Now, Jordie, let me see how soon you will be at the foot again."

Young Linnaeus was called by his teachers almost a blockhead. Not finding him fit for the church, his parents sent him to college to study medicine. But the silent teacher within, greater and wiser than all others, led him to the fields; and neither sickness, misfortune, nor poverty could drive him from the study of botany, the choice of his heart, and he became the greatest botanist of his age.

Richard B. Sheridan's mother tried in vain to teach him the most elementary studies. The mother's death aroused slumbering talents, as has happened in hundreds of cases, and he became one of the most brilliant men of his age.

Samuel Drew was one of the dullest and most listless boys in his neighborhood, yet after an accident by which he nearly lost his life, and after the death of his brother, he became so studious and industrious that he could not bear to lose a moment. He read at every meal, using all the time he could get for self-improvement. He said that Paine's "Age of Reason" made him an author, for it was by his attempt to refute its arguments that he was first known as a strong, vigorous writer.

It has been well said that no man ever made an ill figure who understood his own talents, nor a good one who mistook them.

What Career?

Brutes find out where their talents lie;
A bear will not attempt to fly,
A foundered horse will oft debate
Before he tries a five-barred gate.
A dog by instinct turns aside
Who sees the ditch too deep and wide.
But man we find the only creature
Who, led by folly, combats nature;
Who, when she loudly cries—Forbear!
With obstinacy fixes there;
And where his genius least inclines,
Absurdly bends his whole designs. —Swift

The crowning fortune of a man is to be born to some pursuit which finds him in employment and happiness, whether it be to make baskets, or broadswords, or canals, or statues, or songs.—Emerson

Whatever you are by nature, keep to it; never desert your line of talent. Be what nature intended you for, and you will succeed; be anything else, and you will be ten thousand times worse than nothing.—Sydney Smith

"Every man has got a Fort," said Artemus Ward. "It's some men's fort to do one thing, and some other men's fort to do another, while there is numeris shiftless critters goin' round loose whose fort is not to do nothin'.

"Twice I've endevered to do things which they wasn't my Fort. The first time was when I undertook to lick a owdashus cuss who cut a hole in my tent and krawld threw. Sez I, 'My jentle sir, go out, or I shall fall onto you putty hevy.' Sez he, 'Wade in, Old Wax Figgers,' whereupon I went for him, but he cawt me powerful on the hed and knockt me threw the tent into a cow pastur. He pursood the attack and flung me into a mud puddle. As I aroze and rung out my drencht garmints, I concluded fitin was n't my fort.

"I'le now rize the curtain upon seen 2nd. It is rarely seldom that I seek consolation in the Flowin Bole. But in a certain town in Injianny in the Faul of 18—, my orgin grinder got sick with the fever and died. I never felt so ashamed in my life, and I thought I'd hist in a few swallers of suthin strengthnin. Konsequents was, I histed so much I didn't zackly know whereabouts I was. I turned my livin' wild beasts of Pray loose into the streets, and split all my wax-works.

"I then Bet I cood play hoss. So I hitched myself to a kanawl bote, there bein' two other hosses behind and anuther ahead of me. But the hosses bein' onused to such a arrangemunt, begun to kick and squeal and rair up. Konsequents was, I was kicked vilently in the stummuck and back, and presently, I found myself in the kanawl with the other hosses, kikin and yellin like a tribe of Cusscaroorus savajis. I was rescood, and as I was bein carried to the tavern on a hemlock bored I sed in a feeble voice, 'Boys, playin' hoss isn't my Fort.'

"*Moral: Never don't do nothin' which isn't your Fort, for ef you do you'll find yourself splashin' round in the kanawl, figuratively speakin.*"

The following advertisement, which appeared day after day in a Western paper, did not bring a single reply:—

"Wanted.—Situation by a Practical Printer, who is competent to take charge of any department in a printing and publishing house. Would accept a professorship in any of the academies. Has no objection to teach ornamental painting and penmanship, geometry, trigonometry, and many other sciences. Has had some experience as a lay preacher. Would have no objection to form a small class of young ladies and gentlemen to instruct them in the higher branches. To a dentist or chiropodist he would be invaluable; or he would cheerfully accept a position as bass or tenor singer in a choir."

At length there appeared this addition to the notice:—

"P. S. Will accept an offer to saw and split wood at less than the usual rates." This secured a situation at once, and the advertisement was seen no more.

Your talent is your *call*. Your legitimate destiny speaks in your character. If you have found your place, your occupation has the consent of every faculty of your being.

If possible, choose that occupation which focuses the largest amount of your experience and tastes. You will then not only have a congenial vocation, but also will utilize largely your skill and business knowledge, which is your true capital.

Follow your bent. You cannot long fight successfully against your aspirations. Parents, friends, or misfortune may stifle and suppress the longings of the heart, by compelling you to perform unwelcome tasks; but, like a volcano, the inner fire will burst the crusts which confine it and will pour forth its pent-up genius in eloquence, in song, in art, or in some favorite industry. Beware of "a talent which you cannot hope to practice in perfection." Nature hates all botched and half-finished work, and will pronounce her curse upon it.

Better be the Napoleon of bootblacks, or the Alexander of chimney-sweeps, let us say with Matthew Arnold, than a shallow-brained attorney who, like necessity, knows no law.

Half the world seems to have found uncongenial occupation, as though the human race had been shaken up together and exchanged places in the operation. A servant girl is trying to teach, and a natural teacher is tending store. Good farmers are murdering the law, while Choates and Websters are running down farms, each tortured by the consciousness of unfulfilled destiny. Boys are pining in factories who should be wrestling with Greek and Latin, and hundreds are chafing beneath unnatural loads in college who should be on the farm or before the mast. Artists are spreading "daubs" on canvas who should be whitewashing board fences. Behind counters stand clerks who hate the yard-stick and neglect their work to dream of other occupations. A good shoemaker writes a few verses for the village paper, his friends call him a poet, and the last, with which he is familiar, is abandoned for the pen, which he uses awkwardly. Other shoemakers are cobbling in Congress, while statesmen are pounding shoe-lasts. Laymen are murdering sermons while Beechers and Whitefields are failing as merchants, and people are wondering what can be the cause of empty pews. A boy who is always making something with tools is railroaded through the university and started on the road to inferiority in one of the "three honorable professions." Real surgeons are handling the meat-saw and cleaver, while butchers are amputating human limbs. How fortunate that—

"There's a divinity that shapes our ends, *Rough-hew them how we will.*"
"He that hath a trade," says Franklin, "hath an estate; and he that hath a calling hath a place of profit and honor. A plowman on his legs is higher than a gentleman on his knees."

A man's business does more to make him than anything else. It hardens his muscles, strengthens his body, quickens his blood, sharpens his mind, corrects his judgment, wakes up his inventive genius, puts his wits to work, starts him on the race of life, arouses his ambition, makes him feel that he is a man and must fill a man's shoes, do a man's work, bear a man's part in life, and show himself a man in that part. No man feels himself a man who is not doing a man's business. A man without employment is not a man. He does not prove by his works that he is a man. A hundred and fifty pounds of bone and muscle do not make a man. A good cranium full of brains is not a man. The bone and muscle and brain must know how to do a man's work, think a man's thoughts, mark out a man's path, and bear a man's weight of character and duty before they constitute a man.

Go-at-it-iveness is the first requisite for success. Stick-to-it-iveness is the second. Under ordinary circumstances, and with practical common sense to guide him, one who has these requisites will not fail.

Don't wait for a higher position or a larger salary. Enlarge the position you already occupy; put originality of method into it. Fill it as it never was filled before. Be more prompt, more energetic, more thorough, more polite than your predecessor or fellow workmen. Study your business, devise new modes of operation, be able to give your employer points. The art lies not in giving satisfaction merely, not in simply filling your place, but in doing better than was expected, in surprising your employer; and the reward will be a better place and a larger salary.

When out of work, take the first respectable job that offers, heeding not the disproportion between your faculties and your task. If you put your manhood into your labor, you will soon be given something better to do.

This question of a right aim in life has become exceedingly perplexing in our complicated age. It is not a difficult problem to solve when one is the son of a Zulu or the daughter of a Bedouin. The condition of the savage hardly admits of but one choice; but as one rises higher in the scale of civilization and creeps nearer to the great centers of activity, the difficulty of a correct decision increases with its importance. In proportion as one is hard pressed in competition is it of the sternest necessity for him to choose the right aim, so as to be able to throw the whole of his energy and enthusiasm into the struggle for success. The dissipation of strength or hope is fatal to prosperity even in the most attractive field.

Gladstone says there is a limit to the work that can be got out of a human body, or a human brain, and he is a wise man who wastes no energy on pursuits for which he is not fitted.

"Blessed is he who has found his work," says Carlyle. "Let him ask no other blessedness. He has a work—a life purpose; he has found it, and will follow it."

In choosing an occupation, do not ask yourself how you can make the most money or gain the most notoriety, but choose that work which will call out all your powers and develop your manhood into the greatest strength and symmetry. Not money, not notoriety, not fame even, but power is what you want. Manhood is greater than wealth, grander than fame. Character is greater than any career. Each faculty must be educated, and any deficiency in its training will appear in whatever you do. The hand must be educated to be graceful, steady, and strong. The eye must be educated to be alert, discriminating, and microscopic. The heart must be educated to be tender, sympathetic, and true. The memory must be drilled for years in accuracy, retention, and comprehensiveness. The world does not demand that you be a lawyer, minister, doctor, farmer, scientist, or merchant; it does not dictate what you shall do, but it does require that you be a master in whatever you undertake. If you are a master in your line, the world will applaud you and all doors will fly open to you. But it condemns all botches, abortions, and failures.

"Whoever is well educated to discharge the duty of a man," says Rousseau, "cannot be badly prepared to fill any of those offices that have relation to him. It matters little to me whether my pupils be designed for the army, the pulpit, or the bar. Nature has destined us to the offices of human life antecedent to our destination concerning society. To live is the profession I would teach him. When I have done with him, it is true he will be neither a soldier, a lawyer, nor a divine. Let him first be a man.

Fortune may remove him from one rank to another as she pleases; he will be always found in his place."

In the great race of life common sense has the right of way. Wealth, a diploma, a pedigree, talent, genius, without tact and common sense, cut but a small figure. The incapables and the impracticables, though loaded with diplomas and degrees, are left behind. Not what do you know, or *who are* you, but *what* are you, *what can you do*, is the interrogation of the century.

George Herbert has well said: "What we are is much more to us than what we do." An aim that carries in it the least element of doubt as to its justice or honor or right should be abandoned at once. The art of dishing up the wrong so as to make it look and taste like the right has never been more extensively cultivated than in our day. It is a curious fact that reason will, on pressure, overcome a man's instinct of right. An eminent scientist has said that a man could soon reason himself out of the instinct of decency if he would only take pains and work hard enough. So when a doubtful but attractive future is placed before one, there is a great temptation to juggle with the wrong until it seems the right. Yet any aim that is immoral carries in itself the germ of certain failure, in the real sense of the word—failure that is physical and spiritual.

There is no doubt that every person has a special adaptation for his own peculiar part in life. A very few—geniuses, we call them—have this marked in an unusual degree, and very early in life.

Madame de Staël was engrossed in political philosophy at an age when other girls are dressing dolls. Mozart, when but four years old, played the clavichord and composed minuets and other pieces still extant. The little Chalmers, with solemn air and earnest gestures, would preach often from a stool in the nursery. Goethe wrote tragedies at twelve, and Grotius published an able philosophical work before he was fifteen. Pope "lisped in numbers." Chatterton wrote good poems at eleven, and Cowley published a volume of poetry in his sixteenth year. Thomas Lawrence and Benjamin West drew likenesses almost as soon as they could walk. Liszt played in public at twelve. Canova made models in clay while a mere child. Bacon exposed the defects of Aristotle's philosophy when but sixteen. Napoleon was at the head of armies when throwing snowballs at Brienne.

All these showed their bent while young, and followed it in active life. But precocity is not common, and, except in rare cases, we must discover the bias in our natures, and not wait for the proclivity to make itself manifest. When found, it is worth more to us than a vein of gold.

"*I* do not forbid you to preach," said a Bishop to a young clergyman, "but nature does."

Lowell said: "It is the vain endeavor to make ourselves what we are not that has strewn history with so many broken purposes, and lives left in the rough."

You have not found your place until all your faculties are roused, and your whole nature consents and approves of the work you are doing; not until you are so enthusiastic in it that you take it to bed with you. You may be forced to drudge at uncongenial toil for a time, but emancipate yourself as soon as possible. Carey, the "Consecrated Cobbler," before he went as a missionary said: "My business is to preach the gospel. I cobble shoes to pay expenses."

If your vocation be only a humble one, elevate it with more manhood than others put into it. Put into it brains and heart and energy and economy. Broaden it by originality of methods. Extend it by enterprise and industry. Study it as you would a profession. Learn everything that is to be known about it. Concentrate your faculties upon it, for the greatest achievements are reserved for the man of single aim, in whom no rival powers divide the empire of the soul. *Better adorn your own than seek another's place.*

Go to the bottom of your business if you would climb to the top. Nothing is small which concerns your business. Master every detail. This was the secret of A. T. Stewart's and of John Jacob Astor's great success. They knew everything about their business.

As love is the only excuse for marriage, and the only thing which will carry one safely through the troubles and vexations of married life, so love for an occupation is the only thing which will carry one safely and surely through the troubles which overwhelm ninety-five out of every one hundred who choose the life of a merchant, and very many in every other career.

A famous Englishman said to his nephew, "Don't choose medicine, for we have never had a murderer in our family, and the chances are that in your ignorance you may kill a patient; as to the law, no prudent man is willing to risk his life or his fortune to a young lawyer, who has not only no experience, but is generally too conceited to know the risks he incurs for his client, who alone is the loser; therefore, as the mistakes of a clergyman in doctrine or advice to his parishioners cannot be clearly determined in this world, I advise you by all means to enter the church."

"I felt that I was in the world to do something, and thought I must," said Whittier, thus giving the secret of his great power. It is the man who must enter law, literature, medicine, the ministry, or any other of the overstocked professions, who will succeed. His certain call, that is his love for it, and his fidelity to it, are the imperious factors of his career. If a man enters a profession simply because his grandfather made a great name in it, or his mother wants him to, with no love or adaptability for it, it were far better for him to be a motor-man on an electric car at a dollar and seventy-five cents a day. In the humbler work his intelligence may make him a leader; in the other career he might do as much harm as a bowlder rolled from its place upon a railroad track, a menace to the next express.

Only a few years ago marriage was the only "sphere" open to girls, and the single woman had to face the disapproval of her friends. Lessing said: "The woman who thinks is like a man who puts on rouge, ridiculous." Not many years have elapsed since the ambitious woman who ventured to study or write would keep a bit of embroidery at hand to throw over her book or manuscript when callers entered. Dr. Gregory said to his daughters: "If you happen to have any learning, keep it a profound secret from the men, who generally look with a jealous and malignant eye on a woman of great parts and a cultivated understanding." Women who wrote books in those days would deny the charge as though a public disgrace.

All this has changed, and what a change it is! As Frances Willard said, the greatest discovery of the century is the discovery of woman. We have emancipated her, and are opening countless opportunities for our girls outside of marriage. Formerly only a boy could choose a career; now his sister can do the same. This freedom is one of the greatest glories of the twentieth century. But with freedom comes responsibility, and under these changed conditions every girl should have a definite aim.

Dr. Hall says that the world has urgent need of "girls who are mother's right hand, girls who can cuddle the little ones next best to mamma, and smooth out the tangles in the domestic skein when thing's get twisted; girls whom father takes comfort in for something better than beauty, and the big brothers are proud of for something that outranks the ability to dance or shine in society. Next, we want girls of sense,—girls who have a standard of their own, regardless of conventionalities, and are independent enough to live up to it; girls who simply won't wear a trailing dress on the street to gather up microbes and all sorts of defilement; girls who don't wear a high hat to the theater, or lacerate their feet and endanger their health with high heels and corsets; girls who will wear what is pretty and becoming and snap their fingers at the dictates of fashion when fashion is horrid and silly. And we want good girls,—girls who are sweet, right straight out from the heart to the lips; innocent and pure and simple girls, with less knowledge of sin and duplicity and evil-doing at twenty than the pert little schoolgirl of ten has all too often. And we want careful girls and prudent girls, who think enough of the generous father who toils to maintain them in comfort, and of the gentle mother who denies herself much that they may have so many pretty things, to count the cost and draw the line between the essentials and non-essentials; girls who strive to save and not to spend; girls who are unselfish and eager to be a joy and a comfort in the home rather than an expense and a useless burden. We want girls with hearts,—girls who are full of tenderness and sympathy, with tears that flow for other people's ills, and smiles that light outward their own beautiful thoughts. We have lots of clever girls, and brilliant girls, and witty girls. Give us a consignment of jolly girls, warm-hearted and impulsive girls; kind and entertaining to their own folks, and with little desire to shine in the garish world. With a few such girls scattered around, life would freshen up for all of us, as the weather does under the spell of summer showers."

"They talk about a woman's sphere,
As though it had a limit;
There's not a place in earth or heaven,
There's not a task to mankind given,
There's not a blessing or a woe,
There's not a whisper, Yes or No,
There's not a life, or death, or birth,
That has a feather's weight of worth,
Without a woman in it."

"Do that which is assigned you," says Emerson, "and you cannot hope too much or dare too much. There is at this moment for you an utterance brave and grand as that of the colossal chisel of Phidias, or trowel of the Egyptians, or the pen of Moses or Dante, but different from all these."

"The best way for a young man to begin, who is without friends or influence," said Russell Sage, "is, first, by getting a position; second, keeping his mouth shut; third, observing; fourth, being faithful; fifth, making his employer think he would be lost in a fog without him; and sixth, being polite."

"Close application, integrity, attention to details, discreet advertising," are given as the four steps to success by John Wanamaker, whose motto is, "Do the next thing."

Whatever you do in life, be greater than your calling. Most people look upon an occupation or calling as a mere expedient for earning a living. What a mean, narrow view to take of what was intended for the great school of life, the great man developer, the character-builder; that which should broaden, deepen, heighten, and round out into symmetry, harmony, and beauty all the God-given faculties within us! How we shrink from the task and evade the lessons which were intended for the unfolding of life's great possibilities into usefulness and power, as the sun unfolds into beauty and fragrance the petals of the flower!

I am glad to think
I am not bound to make the world go round;
But only to discover and to do,
With cheerful heart, the work that God appoints. —Jean Ingelow.

"'What shall I do to be forever known?'
Thy duty ever!
'This did full many who yet sleep all unknown,'—
Oh, never, never!
Think'st thou, perchance, that they remain unknown
Whom thou know'st not?
By angel trumps in heaven their praise is blown,
Divine their lot."

Choosing a Vocation

Be what nature intended you for, and you will succeed; be anything else, and you will be ten thousand times worse than nothing.—Sydney Smith

"Many a man pays for his success with a slice of his constitution."

No man struggles perpetually and victoriously against his own character; and one of the first principles of success in life is so to regulate our career as rather to turn our physical constitution and natural inclinations to good account than to endeavor to counteract the one or oppose the other.—Bulwer

He that hath a trade hath an estate.—Franklin

Nature fits all her children with something to do.—Lowell

As occupations and professions have a powerful influence upon the length of human life, the youth should first ascertain whether the vocation he thinks of choosing is a healthy one. Statesmen, judges, and clergymen are noted for their longevity. They are not swept into the great business vortex, where the friction and raspings of sharp competition whittle life away at a fearful rate. Astronomers, who contemplate vast systems, moving through enormous distances, are exceptionally long lived,—as Herschel and Humboldt. Philosophers, scientists, and mathematicians, as Galileo, Bacon, Newton, Euler, Dalton, in fact, those who have dwelt upon the exact sciences, seem to have escaped many of the ills from which humanity suffers. Great students of natural history have also, as a rule, lived long and happy lives. Of fourteen members of a noted historical society in England, who died in 1870, two were over ninety, five over eighty, and two over seventy.

The occupation of the mind has a great influence upon the health of the body.

There is no employment so dangerous and destructive to life but plenty of human beings can be found to engage in it. Of all the instances that can be given of recklessness of life, there is none which exceeds that of the workmen employed in what is called dry-pointing—the grinding of needles and of table forks. The fine steel dust which they breathe brings on a painful disease, of which they are almost sure to die before they are forty. Yet not only are men tempted by high wages to engage in this employment, but they resist to the utmost all contrivances devised for diminishing the danger, through fear that such things would cause more workmen to offer themselves and thus lower wages. Many physicians have investigated the effects of work in the numerous match factories in

France upon the health of the employees, and all agree that rapid destruction of the teeth, decay or necrosis of the jawbone, bronchitis, and other diseases result.

We will probably find more old men on farms than elsewhere. There are many reasons why farmers should live longer than persons residing in cities or than those engaged in other occupations. Aside from the purer air, the outdoor exercise, both conducive to a good appetite and sound sleep, which comparatively few in cities enjoy, they are free from the friction, harassing cares, anxieties, and the keen competition incident to city life. On the other hand, there are some great drawbacks and some enemies to longevity, even on the farm. Man does not live by bread alone. The mind is by far the greatest factor in maintaining the body in a healthy condition. The social life of the city, the great opportunities afforded the mind for feeding upon libraries and lectures, great sermons, and constant association with other minds, the great variety of amusements compensate largely for the loss of many of the advantages of farm life. In spite of the great temperance and immunity from things which corrode, whittle, and rasp away life in the cities, farmers in many places do not live so long as scientists and some other professional men.

There is no doubt that aspiration and success tend to prolong life. Prosperity tends to longevity, if we do not wear life away or burn it out in the feverish pursuit of wealth. Thomas W. Higginson made a list of thirty of the most noted preachers of the last century, and found that their average length of life was sixty-nine years.

Among miners in some sections over six hundred out of a thousand die from consumption. In the prisons of Europe, where the fatal effects of bad air and filth are shown, over sixty-one per cent. of the deaths are from tuberculosis. In Bavarian monasteries, fifty per cent. of those who enter in good health die of consumption, and in the Prussian prisons it is almost the same. The effect of bad air, filth, and bad food is shown by the fact that the death-rate among these classes, between the ages of twenty and forty, is five times that of the general population of the same age. In New York City, over one-fifth of all the deaths of persons over twenty are from this cause. In large cities in Europe the percentage is often still greater. Of one thousand deaths from all causes, on the average, one hundred and three farmers die of pulmonary tuberculosis, one hundred and eight fishermen, one hundred and twenty-one gardeners, one hundred and twenty-two farm laborers, one hundred and sixty-seven grocers, two hundred and nine tailors, three hundred and one dry-goods dealers, and four hundred and sixty-one compositors,—nearly one-half.

According to a long series of investigations by Drs. Benoysten and Lombard into occupations or trades where workers must inhale dust, it appears that mineral dust is the most detrimental to health, animal dust ranking next, and vegetable dust third.

In choosing an occupation, cleanliness, pure air, sunlight, and freedom from corroding dust and poisonous gases are of the greatest importance. A man who would sell a year of his life for any amount of money would be considered insane, and yet we deliberately choose occupations and vocations which statistics and physicians tell us will be practically sure to cut off from five to twenty-five, thirty, or even forty years of our lives, and are seemingly perfectly indifferent to our fate.

There is danger in a calling which requires great expenditure of vitality at long, irregular intervals. He who is not regularly, or systematically employed incurs perpetual risk. "Of the thirty-two all-round athletes in a New York club not long ago," said a physician, "three are dead of consumption, five have to wear trusses, four or five are lop-shouldered, and three have catarrh and partial deafness." Dr. Patten, chief surgeon at the National Soldiers' Home at Dayton, Ohio, says that "of the five thousand soldiers in that institution fully eighty per cent. are suffering from heart disease in one form or another, due to the forced physical exertions of the campaigns."

Man's faculties and functions are so interrelated that whatever affects one affects all. Athletes who over-develop the muscular system do so at the expense of the physical, mental, and moral well-being. It is a law of nature that the overdevelopment of any function or faculty, forcing or straining it, tends not only to ruin it, but also to cause injurious reactions on every other faculty and function.

Vigorous thought must come from a fresh brain. We cannot expect nerve, snap, robustness and vigor, sprightliness and elasticity, in the speech, in the book, or in the essay, from an exhausted, jaded brain. The brain is one of the last organs of the body to reach maturity (at about the age of twenty-eight), and should never be overworked, especially in youth. The whole future of a man is often ruined by over-straining the brain in school.

Brain-workers cannot do good, effective work in one line many hours a day. When the brain is weary, when it begins to lose its elasticity and freshness, there will be the same lack of tonicity and strength in the brain product. Some men often do a vast amount of literary work in entirely different lines during their spare hours.

Cessation of brain activity does not necessarily constitute brain rest, as most great thinkers know. The men who accomplish the most brain-work, sooner or later—usually later, unfortunately—learn to give rest to one set of faculties and use another, as interest begins to flag and a sense of weariness comes. In this way they have been enabled to astonish the world by their mental achievements, which is very largely a matter of skill in exercising alternate sets of faculties, allowing rest to some while giving healthy exercise to others. The continual use of one set of faculties by an ambitious worker will soon bring him to grief. No set of brain cells can possibly set free more brain force in the combustion of thought than is stored up in them. The tired brain must have rest, or nervous exhaustion, brain fever, or even softening of the brain is liable to follow.

As a rule, physical vigor is the condition of a great career. What would Gladstone have accomplished with a weak, puny physique? He addresses an audience at Corfu in Greek, and another at Florence in Italian. A little later he converses at ease with Bismarck in German, or talks fluent French in Paris, or piles up argument on argument in English for hours in Parliament. There are families that have "clutched success and kept it through generations from the simple fact of a splendid physical organization handed down from one generation to another."

All occupations that enervate, paralyze, or destroy body or soul should be avoided. Our manufacturing interests too often give little thought to the employed; the article to be made is generally the only object considered. They do not care if a man spends the whole of his life upon the head of a pin, or in making a screw in a watch factory. They take no notice of the occupations that ruin, or the phosphorus, the dust, the arsenic that destroys the health, that shortens the lives of many workers; of the cramped condition of the body which creates deformity.

The moment we compel those we employ to do work that demoralizes them or does not tend to elevate or lift them, we are forcing them into service worse than useless. "If we induce painters to work in fading colors, or architects with rotten stone, or contractors to construct buildings with imperfect materials, we are forcing our Michael Angelos to carve in snow."

Ruskin says that the tendency of the age is to expend its genius in perishable art, *as if it were a triumph to burn its thoughts away in bonfires*. Is the work you compel others to do useful to yourself and to society? If you employ a seamstress to make four or five or six beautiful flounces for your ball dress, flounces which will only clothe yourself, and which you will wear at only one ball, you are employing your money selfishly. Do not confuse covetousness with benevolence, nor cheat yourself into thinking that all the finery you can wear is so much put into the hungry mouths of those beneath you. It is what those who stand shivering on the street, forming a line to see you step out of your carriage, know it to be. These fine dresses do not mean that so much has been put into their mouths, but *that so much has been taken out of their mouths*.

Select a clean, useful, honorable occupation. If there is any doubt on this point, abandon it at once, for *familiarity with a bad business will make it seem good*. Choose a business that has expansiveness in it. Some kinds of business not even a J. Pierpont Morgan could make respectable. Choose an occupation which will develop you; which will elevate you; which will give you a chance for self-improvement and promotion. You may not make quite so much money, but you will be more of a man, and *manhood is above all riches, overtops all titles, and character is greater than any career*. If possible avoid occupations which compel you to work in a cramped position, or where you must work at night and on Sundays.

Don't try to justify yourself on the ground that somebody must do this kind of work. Let "somebody," not yourself, take the responsibility. Aside from the right and wrong of the thing, it is injurious to the health to work seven days in the week, to work at night when Nature intended you to sleep, or to sleep in the daytime when she intended you to work.

Many a man has dwarfed his manhood, cramped his intellect, crushed his aspiration, blunted his finer sensibilities, in some mean, narrow occupation just because there was money in it.

"Study yourself," says Longfellow, "and most of all, note well wherein kind nature meant you to excel."

Dr. Matthews says that "to no other cause, perhaps, is failure in life so frequently to be traced as to a mistaken calling." We can often find out by hard knocks and repeated failures what we can not do before what we can do. This negative process of eliminating the doubtful chances is often the only way of attaining to the positive conclusion.

How many men have been made ridiculous for life by choosing law or medicine or theology, simply because they are "honorable professions"! These men might have been respectable farmers or merchants, but are "nobodies" in such vocations. The very glory of the profession which they thought would make them shining lights simply renders more conspicuous their incapacity.

Thousands of youths receive an education that fits them for a profession which they have not the means or inclination to follow, and that unfits them for the conditions of life to which they were born. Unsuccessful students with a smattering of everything are raised as much above their original condition as if they were successful. A large portion of Paris cabmen are unsuccessful students in theology and other professions and also unfrocked priests. They are very bad cabmen.

> "Tompkins forsakes his last and awl
> For literary squabbles;
> Styles himself poet; but his trade
> Remains the same,—he cobbles."

Don't choose a profession or occupation because your father, or uncle, or brother is in it. Don't choose a business because you inherit it, or because parents or friends want you to follow it. Don't choose it because others have made fortunes in it. Don't choose it because it is considered the "proper thing" and a "genteel" business. The mania for a "genteel" occupation, for a "soft job" which eliminates drudgery, thorns, hardships, and all disagreeable things, and one which can be learned with very little effort, ruins many a youth.

When we try to do that for which we are unfitted we are not working along the line of our strength, but of our weakness; our will power and enthusiasm become demoralized; we do half work, botched work, lose confidence in ourselves, and conclude that we are dunces because we cannot accomplish what others do; the whole tone of life is demoralized and lowered because we are out of place.

How it shortens the road to success to make a wise choice of one's occupation early, to be started on the road of a proper career while young, full of hope, while the animal spirits are high, and enthusiasm is vigorous; to feel that every step we take, that every day's work we do, that every blow we strike helps to broaden, deepen, and enrich life!

Those who fail are, as a rule, those who are out of their places. *A man out of his place is but half a man; his very nature is perverted.* He is working against his nature, rowing against the current. When his strength is exhausted he will float down the stream. A man can not succeed when his whole nature is entering its perpetual protest against his occupation. To succeed, his vocation must have the consent of all his faculties; they must be in harmony with his purpose.

Has a young man a right to choose an occupation which will only call into play his lower and inferior qualities, as cunning, deceit, letting all his nobler qualities shrivel and die? Has he a right to select a vocation that will develop only the beast within him instead of the man? which will call out the bulldog qualities only, the qualities which overreach and grasp, the qualities which get and never give, which develop long-headedness only, while his higher self atrophies?

The best way to choose an occupation is to ask yourself the question, "What would my government do with me if it were to consider scientifically my qualifications and adaptations, and place me to the best possible advantage for all the people?" The Norwegian precept is a good one: "Give thyself wholly to thy fellow-men; they will give thee back soon enough." We can do the most possible for ourselves when we are in a position where we can do the most possible for others. *We are doing the most for ourselves and for others when we are in a position which calls into play in the highest possible way the greatest number of our best faculties; in other words, we are succeeding best for ourselves when we are succeeding best for others.*

The time will come when there will be institutions for determining the natural bent of the boy and girl; where men of large experience and close observation will study the natural inclination of the youth, help him to find where his greatest strength lies and how to use it to the best advantage. Even if we take for granted what is not true, that every youth will sooner or later discover the line of his greatest strength so that he may get his living by his strong points rather than by his weak ones, the discovery is often made so late in life that great success is practically impossible. Such institutions would help boys and girls to start in their proper careers early in life; and *an early choice shortens the way.* Can anything be more important to human beings than a start in life in the right direction, where even small effort will count for more in the race than the greatest effort—and a life of drudgery—in the wrong direction? A man is seldom unsuccessful, unhappy, or vicious when he is in his place.

After once choosing your occupation, however, never look backward; stick to it with all the tenacity you can muster. Let nothing tempt you or swerve you a hair's breadth from your aim, and you will win. Do not let the thorns which appear in every vocation, or temporary despondency or disappointment, shake your purpose. You will never succeed while smarting under the drudgery of your occupation, if you are constantly haunted with the idea that you could succeed better in something else. Great tenacity of purpose is the only thing that will carry you over the hard places which appear in every career to ultimate triumph. This determination, or fixity of purpose, has a great moral bearing upon our success, for it leads others to feel confidence in us, and this is everything. It gives credit and moral support in a thousand ways. People always believe in a man with a fixed purpose, and will help him twice as quickly as one who is loosely or indifferently attached to his vocation, and liable at any time to make a change, or to fail. Everybody knows that determined men are not likely to fail. They carry in their very pluck, grit, and determination the conviction and assurance of success.

The world does not dictate *what* you shall do, but it does demand that you do *something*, and that you shall be a king in your line. There is no grander sight than that of a young man or woman in the right place struggling with might and main to make the most of the stuff at command, determined that not a faculty or power shall run to waste. Not money, not position, but power is what we want; and character is greater than any occupation or profession.

"Do not, I beseech you," said Garfield, "be content to enter on any business that does not require and compel constant intellectual growth." Choose an occupation that is refining and elevating; an occupation that you will be proud of; an occupation that will give you time for self-culture and self-elevation; an occupation that will enlarge and expand your manhood and make you a better citizen, a better man.

Power and constant growth toward a higher life are the great end of human existence. Your calling should be the great school of life, the great man-developer, character-builder, that which should broaden, deepen, and round out into symmetry, harmony, and beauty, all the God-given faculties within you.

But whatever you do be greater than your calling; let your manhood overtop your position, your wealth, your occupation, your title. A man must work hard and study hard to counteract the narrowing, hardening tendency of his occupation. Said Goldsmith,—

Burke, born for the universe, narrowed his mind,
And to party gave up what was meant for mankind.

"Constant engagement in traffic and barter has no elevating influence," says Lyndall. "The endeavor to obtain the upper hand of those with whom we have to deal, to make good bargains, the higgling and scheming, and the thousand petty artifices, which in these days of stern competition are unscrupulously resorted to, tend to narrow the sphere and to lessen the strength of the intellect, and, at the same time, the delicacy of the moral sense."

Choose upward, study the men in the vocation you think of adopting. Does it elevate those who follow it? Are they broad, liberal, intelligent men? Or have they become mere appendages of their profession, living in a rut with no standing in the community, and of no use to it? Don't think you will be the great exception, and can enter a questionable vocation without becoming a creature of it. In spite of all your determination and will power to the contrary, your occupation, from the very law of association and habit, will seize you as in a vise, will mold you, shape you, fashion you, and stamp its inevitable impress upon you. How frequently do we see bright, open-hearted, generous young men come out of college with high hopes and lofty aims, enter a doubtful vocation, and in a few years return to college commencement so changed that they are scarcely recognized. The once broad, noble features have become contracted and narrowed. The man has become grasping, avaricious, stingy, mean, hard. Is it possible, we ask, that a few years could so change a magnanimous and generous youth?

Go to the bottom if you would get to the top. Be master of your calling in all its details. Nothing is small which concerns your business.

Thousands of men who have been failures in life have done drudgery enough in half a dozen different occupations to have enabled them to reach great success, if their efforts had all been expended in one direction. That mechanic is a failure who starts out to build an engine, but does not *quite* accomplish it, and shifts into some other occupation where perhaps he will almost succeed, but stops just short of the point of proficiency in his acquisition and so fails again. The world is full of people who are "almost a success." They stop just this side of success. Their courage oozes out just before they become expert. How many of us have acquisitions which remain permanently unavailable because not carried quite to the point of skill? How many people "almost know a language or two," which they can neither write nor speak; a science or two whose elements they have not quite acquired; an art or two partially mastered, but which they can not practice with satisfaction or profit! The habit of desultoriness, which has been acquired by allowing yourself to abandon a half-finished work, more than balances any little skill gained in one vocation which might possibly be of use later.

Beware of that frequently fatal gift, versatility. Many a person misses being a great man by splitting into two middling ones. Universality is the *ignis fatuus* which has deluded to ruin many a promising mind. In attempting to gain a knowledge of half a hundred subjects it has mastered none. "The jack-of-all-trades," says one of the foremost manufacturers of this country, "had a chance in my generation. In this he has none."

"The measure of a man's learning will be the amount of his voluntary ignorance," said Thoreau. If we go into a factory where the mariner's compass is made we can see the needles before they are magnetized, they will point in any direction. But when they have been applied to the magnet and received its peculiar power, from that moment they point to the north, and are true to the pole ever after. So man never points steadily in any direction until he has been polarized by a great master purpose.

Give your life, your energy, your enthusiasm, all to the highest work of which you are capable. Canon Farrar said, "There is only one real failure in life possible, and that is, not to be true to the best one knows."

"'What must I do to be forever known?' Thy duty ever."
Who does the best his circumstance allows,
Does well, acts nobly, angels could do no more. —Young

"Whoever can make two ears of corn, two blades of grass to grow upon a spot of ground where only one grew before," says Swift, "would deserve better of mankind and do more essential service to his country than the whole race of politicians put together."

Concentrated Energy

This one thing I do.—St. Paul

The one prudence in life is concentration; the one evil is dissipation; and it makes no difference whether our dissipations are coarse or fine . . . Everything is good which takes away one plaything and delusion more, and sends us home to add one stroke of faithful work.— Emerson

The man who seeks one thing in life, and but one,
May hope to achieve it before life be done;
But he who seeks all things, wherever he goes,
Only reaps from the hopes which around him he sows,
A harvest of barren regrets. —Owen Meredith

The longer I live, the more deeply am I convinced that that which makes the difference between one man and another—between the weak and powerful, the great and insignificant, is energy—invincible determination—a purpose once formed, and then death or victory.—Fowell Buxton

"There was not enough room for us all in Frankfort," said Nathan Mayer Rothschild, in speaking of himself and his four brothers. "I dealt in English goods. One great trader came there, who had the market to himself: he was quite the great man, and did us a favor if he sold us goods. Somehow I offended him, and he refused to show me his patterns. This was on a Tuesday. I said to my father, 'I will go to England.' On Thursday I started. The nearer I got to England, the cheaper goods were. As soon as I got to Manchester, I laid out all my money, things were so cheap, and I made a good profit."

"I hope," said a listener, "that your children are not too fond of money and business to the exclusion of more important things. I am sure you would not wish that."

"I am sure I would wish that," said Rothschild; "I wish them to give mind, and soul, and heart, and body, and everything to business; that is the way to be happy." "Stick to one business, young man," he added, addressing a young brewer; "stick to your brewery, and you may be the great brewer of London. But be a brewer, and a banker, and a merchant, and a manufacturer, and you will soon be in the Gazette."

Not many things indifferently, but one thing supremely, is the demand of the hour. He who scatters his efforts in this intense, concentrated age, cannot hope to succeed.

"Goods removed, messages taken, carpets beaten, and poetry composed on any subject," was the sign of a man in London who was not very successful at any of these lines of work, and reminds one of Monsieur Kenard, of Paris, "a public scribe, who digests accounts, explains the language of flowers, and sells fried potatoes."

The great difference between those who succeed and those who fail does not consist in the amount of work done by each, but in the amount of intelligent work. Many of those who fail most ignominiously do enough to achieve grand success; but they labor at haphazard, building up with one hand only to tear down with the other. They do not grasp circumstances and change them into opportunities. They have no faculty of turning honest defeats into telling victories. With ability enough, and time in abundance,—the warp and woof of success,—they are forever throwing back and forth an empty shuttle, and the real web of life is never woven.

If you ask one of them to state his aim and purpose in life, he will say: "I hardly know yet for what I am best adapted, but I am a thorough believer in genuine hard work, and I am determined to dig early and late all my life, and I know I shall come across something—either gold, silver, or at least iron." I say most emphatically, no. Would an intelligent man dig up a whole continent to find its veins of silver and gold? The man who is forever looking about to see what he can find never finds anything. If we look for nothing in particular, we find just that and no more. We find what we seek with all our heart. The bee is not the only insect that visits the flower, but it is the only one that carries honey away. It matters not how rich the materials we have gleaned from the years of our study and toil in youth, if we go out into life with no well-defined idea of our future work, there is no happy conjunction of circumstances that will arrange them into an imposing structure, and give it magnificent proportions.

"What a immense power over the life," says Elizabeth Stuart Phelps Ward, "is the power of possessing distinct aims. The voice, the dress, the look, the very motions of a person, define and alter when he or she begins to live for a reason. I fancy that I can select, in a crowded street, the busy, blessed women who support themselves. They carry themselves with an air of conscious self-respect and self-content, which a shabby alpaca cannot hide, nor a bonnet of silk enhance, nor even sickness nor exhaustion quite drag out."

It is said that the wind never blows fair for that sailor who knows not to what port he is bound.

"The weakest living creature," says Carlyle, "by concentrating his powers on a single object, can accomplish something; whereas the strongest, by dispersing his over many, may fail to accomplish anything. The drop, by continually falling, bores its passage through the hardest rock. The hasty torrent rushes over it with hideous uproar and leaves no trace behind."

"When I was young I used to think it was thunder that killed men," said a shrewd preacher; "but as I grew older, I found it was lightning. So I resolved to thunder less, and lighten more."

The man who knows one thing, and can do it better than anybody else, even if it only be the art of raising turnips, receives the crown he merits. If he raises the best turnips by reason of concentrating all his energy to that end, he is a benefactor to the race, and is recognized as such.

If a salamander be cut in two, the front part will run forward and the other backward. Such is the progress of him who divides his purpose. Success is jealous of scattered energies.

No one can pursue a worthy object steadily and persistently with all the powers of his mind, and yet make his life a failure. You can't throw a tallow candle through the side of a tent, but you can shoot it through an oak board. Melt a charge of shot into a bullet, and it can be fired through the bodies of four men. Focus the rays of the sun in winter, and you can kindle a fire with ease.

The giants of the race have been men of concentration, who have struck sledgehammer blows in one place until they have accomplished their purpose. The successful men of to-day are men of one overmastering idea, one unwavering aim, men of single and intense purpose. "Scatteration" is the curse of American business life. Too many are like Douglas Jerrold's friend, who could converse in twenty-four languages, but had no ideas to express in any one of them.

"The only valuable kind of study," said Sydney Smith, "is to read so heartily that dinner-time comes two hours before you expected it; to sit with your Livy before you and hear the geese cackling that saved the Capitol, and to see with your own eyes the Carthaginian sutlers gathering up the rings of the Roman knights after the battle of Cannae, and heaping them into bushels, and to be so intimately present at the actions you are reading of, that when anybody knocks at the door it will take you two or three seconds to determine whether you are in your own study or on the plains of Lombardy, looking at Hannibal's weather-beaten face and admiring the splendor of his single eye."

"The one serviceable, safe, certain, remunerative, attainable quality in every study and pursuit is the quality of attention," said Charles Dickens. "My own invention, or imagination, such as it is, I can most truthfully assure you, would never have served me as it has, but for the habit of commonplace, humble, patient, daily, toiling, drudging attention." When asked on another occasion the secret of his success, he said: "I never put one hand to anything on which I could throw my whole self." "Be a whole man at everything," wrote Joseph Gurney to his son, "a whole man at study, in work, and in play."

Don't dally with your purpose.

"I go at what I am about," said Charles Kingsley, "as if there was nothing else in the world for the time being. That's the secret of all hard-working men; but most of them can't carry it into their amusements."

Many a man fails to become a great man by splitting into several small ones, choosing to be a tolerable Jack-of-all-trades rather than to be an unrivaled specialist.

"Many persons seeing me so much engaged in active life," said Edward Bulwer Lytton, "and as much about the world as if I had never been a student, have said to me, 'When do you get time to write all your books? How on earth do you contrive to do so much work?' I shall surprise you by the answer I made. The answer is this—'I contrive to do so much by never doing too much at a time. A man to get through work well must not overwork himself; or, if he do too much to-day, the reaction of fatigue will come, and he will be obliged to do too little to-morrow. Now, since I began really and earnestly to study, which was not till I had left college and was actually in the world, I may perhaps say that I have gone through as large a course of general reading as most men of my time. I have traveled much and I have seen much; I have mixed much in politics, and in the various business of life; and in addition to all this, I have published somewhere about sixty volumes, some upon subjects requiring much special research. And what time do you think, as a general rule, I have devoted to study, to reading and writing? Not more than three hours a day; and, when Parliament is sitting, not always that. But then, during these three hours, I have given my whole attention to what I was about.'"

S. T. Coleridge possessed marvelous powers of mind, but he had no definite purpose; he lived in an atmosphere of mental dissipation which consumed his energy, exhausted his stamina, and his life was in many respects a miserable failure. He lived in dreams and died in reverie. He was continually forming plans and resolutions, but to the day of his death they remained simply resolutions and plans.

He was always just going to do something, but never did it. "Coleridge is dead," wrote Charles Lamb to a friend, "and is said to have left behind him above forty thousand treatises on metaphysics and divinity—not one of them complete!"

Every great man has become great, every successful man has succeeded, in proportion as he has confined his powers to one particular channel.

Hogarth would rivet his attention upon a face and study it until it was photographed upon his memory, when he could reproduce it at will. He studied and examined each object as eagerly as though he would never have a chance to see it again, and this habit of close observation enabled him to develop his work with marvelous detail. The very modes of thought of the time in which he lived were reflected from his works. He was not a man of great education or culture, except in his power of observation.

With an immense procession passing up Broadway, the streets lined with people, and bands playing lustily, Horace Greeley would sit upon the steps of the Astor House, use the top of his hat for a desk, and write an editorial for the "New York Tribune" which would be quoted far and wide.

Offended by a pungent article, a gentleman called at the "Tribune" office and inquired for the editor. He was shown into a little seven-by-nine sanctum, where Greeley, with his head close down to his paper, sat scribbling away at a two-forty rate. The angry man began by asking if this was Mr. Greeley. "Yes, sir; what do you want?" said the editor quickly, without once looking up from his paper. The irate visitor then began using his tongue, with no regard for the rules of propriety, good breeding, or reason. Meantime Mr. Greeley continued to write. Page after page was dashed off in the most impetuous style, with no change of features and without his paying the slightest attention to the visitor. Finally, after about twenty minutes of the most impassioned abuse ever poured out in an editor's office, the angry man became disgusted, and abruptly turned to walk out of the room. Then, for the first time, Mr. Greeley quickly looked up, rose from his chair, and slapping the gentleman familiarly on his shoulder, in a pleasant tone of voice said: "Don't go, friend; sit down, sit down, and free your mind; it will do you good,—you will feel better for it. Besides, it helps me to think what I am to write about. Don't go."

One unwavering aim has ever characterized successful men.

"Daniel Webster," said Sydney Smith, "struck me much like a steam-engine in trousers."

As Adams suggests, Lord Brougham, like Canning, had too many talents; and, though as a lawyer he gained the most splendid prize of his profession, the Lord Chancellorship of England, and merited the applause of scientific men for his investigations in science, yet his life on the whole was a failure. He was "everything by turns and nothing long." With all his magnificent abilities he left no permanent mark on history or literature, and actually outlived his own fame.

Miss Martineau says, "Lord Brougham was at his chateau at Cannes when the daguerreotype process first came into vogue. An artist undertook to take a view of the chateau with a group of guests on the balcony. His Lordship was, asked to keep perfectly still for five seconds, and he promised that he would not stir, but alas,—he moved. The consequence was that there was a blur where Lord Brougham should have been.

"There is something," continued Miss Martineau, "very typical in this. In the picture of our century, as taken from the life by history, this very man should have been the central figure. But, owing to his want of steadfastness, there will be forever a blur where Lord Brougham should have been. How many lives are blurs for want of concentration and steadfastness of purpose!"

Fowell Buxton attributed his success to ordinary means and extraordinary application, and being a whole man to one thing at a time.

It is ever the unwavering pursuit of a single aim that wins. "*Non multa, sed multum*"—not many things, but much, was Coke's motto.

It is the almost invisible point of a needle, the keen, slender edge of a razor or an ax, that opens the way for the bulk that follows. Without point or edge the bulk would be useless. It is the man of one line of work, the sharp-edged man, who cuts his way through obstacles and achieves brilliant success. While we should shun that narrow devotion to one idea which prevents the harmonious development of our powers, we should avoid on the other hand the extreme versatility of one of whom W. M. Praed says:—

> His talk is like a stream which runs
> With rapid change from rocks to roses,
> It slips from politics to puns,
> It glides from Mahomet to Moses:
> Beginning with the laws that keep
> The planets in their radiant courses,
> And ending with some precept deep
> For skinning eels or shoeing horses.

If you can get a child learning to walk to fix his eyes on any object, he will generally navigate to that point without capsizing, but distract his attention and down he goes.

The young man seeking a position to-day is not asked what college he came from or who his ancestors were. "*What can you do?*" is the great question. It is special training that is wanted. Most of the men at the head of great firms and great enterprises have been promoted step by step from the bottom.

"I know that he can toil terribly," said Cecil of Walter Raleigh, in explanation of the latter's success.

As a rule, what the heart longs for the head and the hands may attain. The currents of knowledge, of wealth, of success, are as certain and fixed as the tides of the sea. In all great successes we can trace the power of concentration, riveting every faculty upon one unwavering aim; perseverance in the pursuit of an undertaking in spite of every difficulty; and courage which enables one to bear up under all trials, disappointments, and temptations.

Chemists tell us that there is power enough in a single acre of grass to drive all the mills and steam-cars in the world, could we but concentrate it upon the piston-rod of a steam-engine. But it is at rest, and so, in the light of science, it is comparatively valueless.

Dr. Mathews says that the man who scatters himself upon many objects soon loses his energy, and with his energy his enthusiasm.

"Never study on speculation," says Waters; "all such study is vain. Form a plan; have an object; then work for it, learn all you can about it, and you will be sure to succeed. What I mean by studying on speculation is that aimless learning of things because they may be useful some day; which is like the conduct of the woman who bought at auction a brass door-plate with the name of Thompson on it, thinking it might be useful some day!"

Definiteness of aim is characteristic of all true art. He is not the greatest painter who crowds the greatest number of ideas upon a single canvas, giving all the figures equal prominence. He is the genuine artist who makes the greatest variety express the greatest unity, who develops the leading idea in the central figure, and makes all the subordinate figures, lights, and shades point to that center and find expression there. So in every well-balanced life, no matter how versatile in endowments or how broad in culture, there is one grand central purpose, in which all the subordinate powers of the soul are brought to a focus, and where they will find fit expression. In nature we see no waste of energy, nothing left to chance. Since the shuttle of creation shot for the first time through chaos, design has marked the course of every golden thread. Every leaf, every flower, every crystal, every atom even, has a purpose stamped upon it which unmistakably points to the crowning summit of all creation—man.

Young men are often told to aim high, but we must aim at what we would hit. A general purpose is not enough. The arrow shot from the bow does not wander around to see what it can hit on its way, but flies straight to the mark. The magnetic needle does not point to all the lights in the heavens to see which it likes best. They all attract it. The sun dazzles, the meteor beckons, the stars twinkle to it, and try to win its affections; but the needle, true to its instinct, and with a finger that never errs in sunshine or in storm, points steadily to the North Star; for, while all the other stars must course with untiring tread around their great centers through all the ages, the North Star, alone, distant beyond human comprehension, moves with stately sweep on its circuit of more than 25,000 years, for all practical purposes of man stationary, not only for a day, but for a century. So all along the path of life other luminaries will beckon to lead us from our cherished aim—from the course of truth and duty; but let no moons which shine with borrowed light, no meteors which dazzle, but never guide, turn the needle of our purpose from the North Star of its hope.

The Triumphs of Enthusiasm

The labor we delight in physics pain.—Shakespeare

The only conclusive evidence of a man's sincerity is that he gives himself for a principle. Words, money, all things else are comparatively easy to give away; but when a man makes a gift of his daily life and practise, it is plain that the truth, whatever it may be, has taken possession of him.—Lowell

Let us beware of losing our enthusiasm. Let us ever glory in something, and strive to retain our admiration for all that would ennoble, and our interest in all that would enrich and beautify our life.—Phillips Brooks

In the Galérie des Beaux Arts in Paris is a beautiful statue conceived by a sculptor who was so poor that he lived and worked in a small garret. When his clay model was nearly done, a heavy frost fell upon the city. He knew that if the water in the interstices of the clay should freeze, the beautiful lines would be distorted. So he wrapped his bedclothes around the clay image. In the morning he was found dead, but his idea was saved, and other hands gave it enduring form in marble.

"I do not know how it is with others when speaking on an important question," said Henry Clay; "but on such occasions I seem to be unconscious of the external world. Wholly engrossed by the subject before me, I lose all sense of personal identity, of time, or of surrounding objects."

"A bank never becomes very successful," says a noted financier, "until it gets a president who takes it to bed with him." Enthusiasm gives the otherwise dry and uninteresting subject or occupation a new meaning.

As the young lover has finer sense and more acute vision and sees in the object of his affections a hundred virtues and charms invisible to all other eyes, so a man permeated with enthusiasm has his power of perception heightened and his vision magnified until he sees beauty and charms others cannot discern which compensate for drudgery, privations, hardships, and even persecution. Dickens says he was haunted, possessed, spirit-driven by the plots and characters in his stories which would not let him sleep or rest until he had committed them to paper. On one sketch he shut himself up for a month, and when he came out he looked as haggard as a murderer. His characters haunted him day and night.

"Herr Capellmeister, I should like to compose something; how shall I begin?" asked a youth of twelve who had played with great skill on the piano. "Pooh, pooh," replied Mozart, "you must wait." "But you began when you were younger than I am," said the boy. "Yes, so I did," said the great composer, "but I never asked anything about it. When one has the spirit of a composer, he writes because he can't help it."

Gladstone said that what is really desired is to light up the spirit that is within a boy. In some sense and in some degree, in some effectual degree, there is in every boy the material of good work in the world; in every boy, not only in those who are brilliant, not only in those who are quick, but in those who are stolid, and even in those who are dull, or who seem to be dull. If they have only the good will, the dulness will day by day clear away and vanish completely under the influence of the good will.

Gerster, an unknown Hungarian, made fame and fortune sure the first night she appeared in opera. Her enthusiasm almost hypnotized her auditors. In less than a week she had become popular and independent. Her soul was smitten with a passion for growth, and all the powers of heart and mind she possessed were enthusiastically devoted to self-improvement.

All great works of art have been produced when the artist was intoxicated with the passion for beauty and form which would not let him rest until his thought was expressed in marble or on canvas.

"Well, I've worked hard enough for it," said Malibran when a critic expressed his admiration of her D in alt, reached by running up three octaves from low D; "I've been chasing it for a month. I pursued it everywhere,—when I was dressing, when I was doing my hair; and at last I found it on the toe of a shoe that I was putting on."

"Every great and commanding moment in the annals of the world," says Emerson, "is the triumph of some enthusiasm. The victories of the Arabs after Mahomet, who, in a few years, from a small and mean beginning, established a larger empire than that of Rome, is an example. They did they knew not what. The naked Derar, horsed on an idea, was found an overmatch for a troop of cavalry. The women fought like men and conquered the Roman men. They were miserably equipped, miserably fed, but they were temperance troops. There was neither brandy nor flesh needed to feed them. They conquered Asia and Africa and Spain on barley. The Caliph Omar's walking-stick struck more terror into those who saw it than another man's sword."

It was enthusiasm that enabled Napoleon to make a campaign in two weeks that would have taken another a year to accomplish. "These Frenchmen are not men, they fly," said the Austrians in consternation. In fifteen days Napoleon, in his first Italian campaign, had gained six victories, taken twenty-one standards, fifty-five pieces of cannon, had captured fifteen thousand prisoners, and had conquered Piedmont.

After this astonishing avalanche a discomfited Austrian general said: "This young commander knows nothing whatever about the art of war. He is a perfect ignoramus. There is no doing anything with him." But his soldiers followed their "Little Corporal" with an enthusiasm which knew no defeat or disaster.

"There are important cases," says A. H. K. Boyd, "in which the difference between half a heart and a whole heart makes just the difference between signal defeat and a splendid victory."

"Should I die this minute," said Nelson at an important crisis, "want of frigates would be found written on my heart."

The simple, innocent Maid of Orleans with her sacred sword, her consecrated banner, and her belief in her great mission, sent a thrill of enthusiasm through the whole French army such as neither king nor statesmen could produce. Her zeal carried everything before it. Oh! what a great work each one could perform in this world if he only knew his power! But, like a bitted horse, man does not realize his strength until he has once run away with himself.

"Underneath is laid the builder of this church and city, Christopher Wren, who lived more than ninety years, not for himself, but for the public good. Reader, if you seek his monument, look around!" Turn where you will in London, you find noble monuments of the genius of a man who never received instruction from an architect. He built fifty-five churches in the city and thirty-six halls. "I would give my skin for the architect's design of the Louvre," said he, when in Paris to get ideas for the restoration of St. Paul's Cathedral in London. His rare skill is shown in the palaces of Hampton Court and Kensington, in Temple Bar, Drury Lane Theater, the Royal Exchange, and the great Monument. He changed Greenwich palace into a sailor's retreat, and built churches and colleges at Oxford. He also planned for the rebuilding of London after the great fire, but those in authority would not adopt his splendid idea. He worked thirty-five years upon his master-piece, St. Paul's Cathedral. Although he lived so long, and was exceedingly healthy in later life, he was so delicate as a child that he was a constant source of anxiety to his parents. His great enthusiasm alone seemed to give strength to his body.

Indifference never leads armies that conquer, never models statues that live, nor breathes sublime music, nor harnesses the forces of nature, nor rears impressive architecture, nor moves the soul with poetry, nor the world with heroic philanthropies. Enthusiasm, as Charles Bell says of the hand, wrought the statue of Memnon and hung the brazen gates of Thebes. It fixed the mariner's trembling needle upon its axis, and first heaved the tremendous bar of the printing-press. It opened the tubes for Galileo, until world after world swept before his vision, and it reefed the high topsail that rustled over Columbus in the morning breezes of the Bahamas. It has held the sword with which freedom has fought her battles, and poised the axe of the dauntless woodman as he opened the paths of civilization, and turned the mystic leaves upon which Milton and Shakespeare inscribed their burning thoughts.

Horace Greeley said that the best product of labor is the high-minded workman with an enthusiasm for his work.

"The best method is obtained by earnestness," said Salvini. "If you can impress people with the conviction that you feel what you say, they will pardon many shortcomings. And above all, study, study, study! All the genius in the world will not help you along with any art, unless you become a hard student. It has taken me years to master a single part."

There is a "go," a zeal, a furore, almost a fanaticism for one's ideals or calling, that is peculiar to our American temperament and life. You do not find this in tropical countries. It did not exist fifty years ago. It could not be found then even on the London Exchange. But the influence of the United States and of Australia, where, if a person is to succeed, he must be on the jump with all the ardor of his being, has finally extended until what used to be the peculiar strength of a few great minds has now become characteristic of the leading nations. Enthusiasm is the being awake; it is the tingling of every fiber of one's being to do the work that one's heart desires. Enthusiasm made Victor Hugo lock up his clothes while writing "Notre Dame," that he might not leave the work until it was finished. The great actor Garrick well illustrated it when asked by an unsuccessful preacher the secret of his power over audiences: "You speak of eternal verities and what you know to be true as if you hardly believed what you were saying yourself, whereas I utter what I know to be unreal and untrue as if I did believe it in my very soul."

"When he comes into a room, every man feels as if he had taken a tonic and had a new lease of life," said a man when asked the reason for his selection, after he, with two companions, had written upon a slip of paper the name of the most agreeable companion he had ever met. "He is an eager, vivid fellow, full of joy, bubbling over with spirits. His sympathies are quick as an electric flash."

"He throws himself into the occasion, whatever it may be, with his whole heart," said the second, in praise of the man of his choice.

"He makes the best of everything," said the third, speaking of his own most cherished acquaintance.

The three were traveling correspondents of great English journals, who had visited every quarter of the world and talked with all kinds of men. The papers were examined and all were found to contain the name of a prominent lawyer in Melbourne, Australia.

"If it were not for respect for human opinions," said Madame de Staël to M. Mole, "I would not open my window to see the Bay of Naples for the first time, while I would go five hundred leagues to talk with a man of genius whom I had not seen."

Enthusiasm is that secret and harmonious spirit which hovers over the production of genius, throwing the reader of a book, or the spectator of a statue, into the very ideal presence whence these works have originated.

"One moonlight evening in winter," writes the biographer of Beethoven, "we were walking through a narrow street of Bonn. 'Hush!' exclaimed the great composer, suddenly pausing before a little, mean dwelling, 'what sound is that? It is from my Sonata in F. Hark! how well it is played!'

"In the midst of the finale there was a break, and a sobbing voice cried: 'I cannot play any more. It is so beautiful; it is utterly beyond my power to do it justice. Oh, what would I not give to go to the concert at Cologne!' 'Ah! my sister,' said a second voice; 'why create regrets when there is no remedy? We can scarcely pay our rent.' 'You are right,' said the first speaker, 'and yet I wish for once in my life to hear some really good music. But it is of no use.'

"'Let us go in,' said Beethoven. 'Go in!' I remonstrated; 'what should we go in for?' 'I will play to her,' replied my companion in an excited tone; 'here is feeling,—genius,—understanding! I will play to her, and she will understand it. Pardon me,' he continued, as he opened the door and saw a young man sitting by a table, mending shoes, and a young girl leaning sorrowfully upon an old-fashioned piano; 'I heard music and was tempted to enter. I am a musician. I—I also overheard something of what you said. You wish to hear—that is, you would like—that is—shall I play for you?'

"'Thank you,' said the shoemaker, 'but our piano is so wretched, and we have no music.'

"'No music!' exclaimed the composer; 'how, then, does the young lady—I—I entreat your pardon,' he added, stammering as he saw that the girl was blind; 'I had not perceived before. Then you play by ear? But where do you hear the music, since you frequent no concerts?'

"'We lived at Bruhl for two years; and, while there, I used to hear a lady practicing near us. During the summer evenings her windows were generally open, and I walked to and fro outside to listen to her.'

"Beethoven seated himself at the piano. Never, during all the years I knew him, did I hear him play better than to that blind girl and her brother. Even the old instrument seemed inspired. The young man and woman sat as if entranced by the magical, sweet sounds that flowed out upon the air in rhythmical swell and cadence, until, suddenly, the flame of the single candle wavered, sank, flickered, and went out. The shutters were thrown open, admitting a flood of brilliant moonlight, but the player paused, as if lost in thought.

"'Wonderful man!' said the shoemaker in a low tone; 'who and what are you?'

"'Listen!' replied the master, and he played the opening bars of the Sonata in F. 'Then you are Beethoven!' burst from the young people in delighted recognition. 'Oh, play to us once more,' they added, as he rose to go,—'only once more!'

"'I will improvise a sonata to the moonlight,' said he, gazing thoughtfully upon the liquid stars shining so softly out of the depths of a cloudless winter sky. Then he played a sad and infinitely lovely movement, which crept gently over the instrument, like the calm flow of moonlight over the earth. This was followed by a wild, elfin passage in triple time—a sort of grotesque interlude, like the dance of fairies upon the lawn. Then came a swift agitated ending—a breathless, hurrying, trembling movement, descriptive of flight, and uncertainty, and vague impulsive terror, which carried us away on its rustling wings, and left us all in emotion and wonder. 'Farewell to you,' he said, as he rose and turned toward the door. 'You will come again?' asked the host and hostess in a breath. 'Yes, yes,' said Beethoven hurriedly, 'I will come again, and give the young lady some lessons. Farewell!' Then to me he added: 'Let us make haste back, that I may write out that sonata while I can yet remember it.' We did return in haste, and not until long past the dawn of day did he rise from his table with the full score of the Moonlight Sonata in his hand."

Michael Angelo studied anatomy twelve years, nearly ruining his health, but this course determined his style, his practice, and his glory. He drew his figures in skeleton, added muscles, fat, and skin successively, and then draped them. He made every tool he used in sculpture, such as files, chisels, and pincers. In painting he prepared all his own colors, and would not let servants or students even mix them.

Raphael's enthusiasm inspired every artist in Italy, and his modest, charming manners disarmed envy and jealousy. He has been called the only distinguished man who lived and died without an enemy or detractor. Again and again poor Bunyan might have had his liberty; but not the separation from his poor blind daughter Mary, which he said was like pulling the flesh from his bones; not the need of a poor family dependent upon him; not the love of liberty nor the spur of ambition could induce him to forego his plain preaching in public places. He had so forgotten his early education that his wife had to teach him again to read and write. It was the enthusiasm of conviction which enabled this poor, ignorant, despised Bedford tinker to write his immortal allegory with such fascination that a whole world has read it.

Only thoughts that breathe in words that burn can kindle the spark slumbering in the heart of another.

Rare consecration to a great enterprise is found in the work of the late Francis Parkman. While a student at Harvard he determined to write the history of the French and English in North America. With a steadiness and devotion seldom equaled he gave his life, his fortune, his all to this one great object. Although he had, while among the Dakota Indians, collecting material for his history, ruined his health and could not use his eyes more than five minutes at a time for fifty years, he did not swerve a hair's breadth from the high purpose formed in his youth, until he gave to the world the best history upon this subject ever written.

After Lincoln had walked six miles to borrow a grammar, he returned home and burned one shaving after another while he studied the precious prize.

Gilbert Becket, an English Crusader, was taken prisoner and became a slave in the palace of a Saracen prince, where he not only gained the confidence of his master, but also the love of his master's fair daughter. By and by he escaped and returned to England, but the devoted girl determined to follow him. She knew but two words of the English language—*London* and *Gilbert*; but by repeating the first she obtained passage in a vessel to the great metropolis, and then she went from street to street pronouncing the other—"Gilbert." At last she came to the street on which Gilbert lived in prosperity. The unusual crowd drew the family to the window, when Gilbert himself saw and recognized her, and took to his arms and home his far-come princess with her solitary fond word.

The most irresistible charm of youth is its bubbling enthusiasm. Youth sees no darkness ahead,—no defile that has no outlet,—it forgets that there is such a thing as failure in the world, and believes that mankind has been waiting all these centuries for him to come and be the liberator of truth and energy and beauty.

Of what use was it to forbid the boy Handel to touch a musical instrument, or to forbid him going to school, lest he learn the gamut? He stole midnight interviews with a dumb spinet in a secret attic. The boy Bach copied whole books of studies by moonlight, for want of a candle churlishly denied. Nor was he disheartened when these copies were taken from him. The painter West began in a garret, and plundered the family cat for bristles to make his brushes.

It is the enthusiasm of youth which cuts the Gordian knot age cannot untie. "People smile at the enthusiasm of youth," says Charles Kingsley; "that enthusiasm which they themselves secretly look back to with a sigh, perhaps unconscious that it is partly their own fault that they ever lost it."

How much the world owes to the enthusiasm of Dante!

Tennyson wrote his first volume at eighteen, and at nineteen gained a medal at Cambridge.

"The most beautiful works of all art were done in youth," says Ruskin. "Almost everything that is great has been done by youth," wrote Disraeli. "The world's interests are, under God, in the hands of the young," says Dr. Trumbull.

It was the youth Hercules that performed the Twelve Labors. Enthusiastic youth faces the sun, it shadows all behind it. The heart rules youth; the head, manhood. Alexander was a mere youth when he rolled back the Asiatic hordes that threatened to overwhelm European civilization almost at its birth. Napoleon had conquered Italy at twenty-five. Byron and Raphael died at thirty-seven, an age which has been fatal to many a genius, and Poe lived but a few months longer. Romulus founded Rome at twenty. Pitt and Bolingbroke were ministers almost before they were men. Gladstone was in Parliament in early manhood. Newton made some of his greatest discoveries before he was twenty-five. Keats died at twenty-five, Shelley at twenty-nine. Luther was a triumphant reformer at twenty-five. It is said that no English poet ever equaled Chatterton at twenty-one. Whitefield and Wesley began their great revival as students at Oxford, and the former had made his influence felt throughout England before he was twenty-four. Victor Hugo wrote a tragedy at fifteen, and had taken three prizes at the Academy and gained the title of Master before he was twenty.

Many of the world's greatest geniuses never saw forty years. Never before has the young man, who is driven by his enthusiasm, had such an opportunity as he has to-day. It is the age of young men and young women. Their ardor is their crown, before which the languid and the passive bow.

But if enthusiasm is irresistible in youth, how much more so is it when carried into old age! Gladstone at eighty had ten times the weight and power that any man of twenty-five would have with the same ideals. The glory of age is only the glory of its enthusiasm, and the respect paid to white hairs is reverence to a heart fervent, in spite of the torpid influence of an enfeebled body. The "Odyssey" was the creation of a blind old man, but that old man was Homer.

The contagious zeal of an old man, Peter the Hermit, rolled the chivalry of Europe upon the ranks of Islam.

Dandolo, the Doge of Venice, won battles at ninety-four, and refused a crown at ninety-six. Wellington planned and superintended fortifications at eighty. Bacon and Humboldt were enthusiastic students to the last gasp. Wise old Montaigne was shrewd in his gray-beard wisdom and loving life, even in the midst of his fits of gout and colic.

Dr. Johnson's best work, "The Lives of the Poets," was written when he was seventy-eight. Defoe was fifty-eight when he published "Robinson Crusoe." Newton wrote new briefs to his "Principia" at eighty-three. Plato died writing, at eighty-one. Tom Scott began the study of Hebrew at eighty-six. Galileo was nearly seventy when he wrote on the laws of motion. James Watt learned German at eighty-five. Mrs. Somerville finished her "Molecular and Microscopic Science" at eighty-nine. Humboldt completed his "Cosmos" at ninety, a month before his death. Burke was thirty-five before he obtained a seat in Parliament, yet he made the world feel his character. Unknown at forty, Grant was one of the most famous generals in history at forty-two. Eli Whitney was twenty-three when he decided to prepare for college, and thirty when he graduated from Yale; yet his cotton-gin opened a great industrial future for the Southern States. What a power was Bismarck at eighty! Lord Palmerston was an "Old Boy" to the last. He became Prime Minister of England the second time at seventy-five, and died Prime Minister at eighty-one. Galileo at seventy-seven, blind and feeble, was working every day, adapting the principle of the pendulum to clocks. George Stephenson did not learn to read and write until he had reached manhood. Some of Longfellow's, Whittier's, and Tennyson's best work was done after they were seventy.

At sixty-three Dryden began the translation of the "Aeneid." Robert Hall learned Italian when past sixty, that he might read Dante in the original. Noah Webster studied seventeen languages after he was fifty. Cicero said well that men are like wine: age sours the bad and improves the good.

With enthusiasm we may retain the youth of the spirit until the hair is silvered, even as the Gulf Stream softens the rigors of northern Europe.

"How ages thine heart,—towards youth? If not, doubt thy fitness for thy work."

"On Time," or, the Triumph of Promptness

"On the great clock of time there is but one Word—now."

Note the sublime precision that leads the earth over a circuit of five hundred millions of miles back to the solstice at the appointed moment without the loss of one second,—no, not the millionth part of a second,—for ages and ages of which it traveled that imperiled road.—Edward Everett

"Who cannot but see oftentimes how strange the threads of our destiny run? Oft it is only for a moment the favorable instant is presented. We miss it, and months and years are lost."
By the street of by and by one arrives at the house of never.—Cervantes

"Lose this day by loitering—'t will be the same story tomorrow, and the next more dilatory."
Let's take the instant by the forward top.—Shakespeare

"Haste, post, haste! Haste for thy life!" was frequently written upon messages in the days of Henry VIII of England, with a picture of a courier swinging from a gibbet. Post-offices were unknown, and letters were carried by government messengers subject to hanging if they delayed upon the road.

Even in the old, slow days of stage-coaches, when it took a month of dangerous traveling to accomplish the distance we can now span in a few hours, unnecessary delay was a crime. One of the greatest gains civilization has made is in measuring and utilizing time. We can do as much in an hour to-day as they could in twenty hours a hundred years ago.

"Delays have dangerous ends." Caesar's delay to read a message cost him his life when he reached the senate house. Colonel Rahl, the Hessian commander at Trenton, was playing cards when a messenger brought a letter stating that Washington was crossing the Delaware. He put the letter in his pocket without reading it until the game was finished, when he rallied his men only to die just before his troops were taken prisoners. Only a few minutes' delay, but he lost honor, liberty, life!

Success is the child of two very plain parents—punctuality and accuracy. There are critical moments in every successful life when if the mind hesitate or a nerve flinch all will be lost.

"Immediately on receiving your proclamation," wrote Governor Andrew of Massachusetts to President Lincoln on May 3, 1861, "we took up the war, and have carried on our part of it, in the spirit in which we believe the Administration and the American people intend to act, namely, as if there were not an inch of red tape in the world." He had received a telegram for troops from Washington on Monday, April 15; at nine o'clock the next Sunday he said: "All the regiments demanded from Massachusetts are already either in Washington, or in Fortress Monroe, or on their way to the defence of the Capitol."

"The only question which I can entertain," he said, "is what to do; and when that question is answered, the other is, what next to do."

"The whole period of youth," said Ruskin, "is one essentially of formation, edification, instruction. There is not an hour of it but is trembling with destinies—not a moment of which, once passed, the appointed work can ever be done again, or the neglected blow struck on the cold iron."

Napoleon laid great stress upon that "supreme moment," that "nick of time" which occurs in every battle, to take advantage of which means victory, and to lose in hesitation means disaster. He said that he beat the Austrians because they did not know the value of five minutes; and it has been said that among the trifles that conspired to defeat him at Waterloo, the loss of a few moments by himself and Grouchy on the fatal morning was the most significant. Blucher was on time, and Grouchy was late. It was enough to send Napoleon to St. Helena, and to change the destiny of millions.

It is a well-known truism that has almost been elevated to the dignity of a maxim, that what may be done at any time will be done at no time.

The African Association of London wanted to send Ledyard, the traveler, to Africa, and asked when he would be ready to go. "To-morrow morning," was the reply. John Jervis, afterwards Earl St. Vincent, was asked when he could join his ship, and replied, "Directly." Colin Campbell, appointed commander of the army in India, and asked when he could set out, replied without hesitation, "To-morrow."

The energy wasted in postponing until to-morrow a duty of to-day would often do the work. How much harder and more disagreeable, too, it is to do work which has been put off! What would have been done at the time with pleasure or even enthusiasm, after it has been delayed for days and weeks, becomes drudgery. Letters can never be answered so easily as when first received. Many large firms make it a rule never to allow a letter to lie unanswered overnight.

Promptness takes the drudgery out of an occupation. Putting off usually means leaving off, and going to do becomes going undone. Doing a deed is like sowing a seed: if not done at just the right time it will be forever out of season. The summer of eternity will not be long enough to bring to maturity the fruit of a delayed action. If a star or planet were delayed one second, it might throw the whole universe out of harmony.

"There is no moment like the present," said Maria Edgeworth; "not only so, there is no moment at all, no instant force and energy, but in the present. The man who will not execute his resolutions when they are fresh upon him can have no hopes from them afterward. They will be dissipated, lost in the hurry and scurry of the world, or sunk in the slough of indolence."

Cobbett said he owed his success to being "always ready" more than to all his natural abilities combined.

"To this quality I owed my extraordinary promotion in the army," said he. "If I had to mount guard at ten, I was ready at nine; never did any man or anything wait one minute for me."

"How," asked a man of Sir Walter Raleigh, "do you accomplish so much, and in so short a time?" "When I have anything to do, I go and do it," was the reply. The man who always acts promptly, even if he makes occasional mistakes, will succeed when a procrastinator, even if he have the better judgment, will fail.

When asked how he managed to accomplish so much work, and at the same time attend to his social duties, a French statesman replied, "I do it simply by never postponing till to-morrow what should be done to-day." It was said of an unsuccessful public man that he used to reverse this process, his favorite maxim being "never to do to-day what might be postponed till to-morrow." How many men have dawdled away their success and allowed companions and relatives to steal it away five minutes at a time!

"To-morrow, didst thou say?" asked Cotton. "Go to—I will not hear of it. To-morrow! 'tis a sharper who stakes his penury against thy plenty—who takes thy ready cash and pays thee naught but wishes, hopes, and promises, the currency of idiots. *To-morrow*! it is a period nowhere to be found in all the hoary registers of time, unless perchance in the fool's calendar. Wisdom disclaims the word, nor holds society with those that own it. 'Tis fancy's child, and folly is its father; wrought of such stuffs as dreams are; and baseless as the fantastic visions of the evening." Oh, how many a wreck on the road to success could say: "I have spent all my life in pursuit of to-morrow, being assured that to-morrow has some vast benefit or other in store for me."

"But his resolutions remained unshaken," Charles Reade continues in his story of Noah Skinner, the defaulting clerk, who had been overcome by a sleepy languor after deciding to make restitution; "by and by, waking up from a sort of heavy doze, he took, as it were, a last look at the receipts, and murmured, 'My head, how heavy it feels!' But presently he roused himself, full of his penitent resolutions, and murmured again, brokenly, 'I'll take it to—Pembroke—Street to—morrow; to—morrow.' The morrow found him, and so did the detectives, dead."

"To-morrow." It is the devil's motto. All history is strewn with its brilliant victims, the wrecks of half-finished plans and unexecuted resolutions. It is the favorite refuge of sloth and incompetency.

"Strike while the iron is hot," and "Make hay while the sun shines," are golden maxims.

Very few people recognize the hour when laziness begins to set in. Some people it attacks after dinner; some after lunch; and some after seven o'clock in the evening. There is in every person's life a crucial hour in the day, which must be employed instead of wasted if the day is to be saved. With most people the early morning hour becomes the test of the day's success.

A person was once extolling the skill and courage of Mayenne in Henry's presence. "You are right," said Henry, "he is a great captain, but I have always five hours' start of him." Henry rose at four in the morning, and Mayenne at about ten. This made all the difference between them. Indecision becomes a disease and procrastination is its forerunner. There is only one known remedy for the victims of indecision, and that is prompt decision. Otherwise the disease is fatal to all success or achievement. He who hesitates is lost.

A noted writer says that a bed is a bundle of paradoxes. We go to it with reluctance, yet we quit it with regret. We make up our minds every night to leave it early, but we make up our bodies every morning to keep it late.

Yet most of those who have become eminent have been early risers. Peter the Great always rose before daylight. "I am," said he, "for making my life as long as possible, and therefore sleep as little as possible." Alfred the Great rose before daylight. In the hours of early morning Columbus planned his voyage to America, and Napoleon his greatest campaigns. Copernicus was an early riser, as were most of the famous astronomers of ancient and modern times. Bryant rose at five, Bancroft at dawn, and nearly all our leading authors in the early morning. Washington, Jefferson, Webster, Clay, and Calhoun were all early risers.

Daniel Webster used often to answer twenty to thirty letters before breakfast.

Walter Scott was a very punctual man. This was the secret of his enormous achievements. He rose at five. By breakfast-time he had, as he used to say, broken the neck of the day's work. Writing to a youth who had obtained a situation and asked him for advice, he gave this counsel: "Beware of stumbling over a propensity which easily besets you from not having your time fully employed—I mean what the women call dawdling. Do instantly whatever is to be done, and take the hours of recreation after business, never before it."

Not too much can be said about the value of the habit of rising early. Eight hours is enough sleep for any man. Very frequently seven hours is plenty. After the eighth hour in bed, if a man is able, it is his business to get up, dress quickly, and go to work.

"A singular mischance has happened to some of our friends," said Hamilton. "At the instant when He ushered them into existence, God gave them a work to do, and He also gave them a competence of time; so much that if they began at the right moment, and wrought with sufficient vigor, their time and their work would end together. But a good many years ago a strange misfortune befell them. A fragment of their allotted time was lost. They cannot tell what became of it, but sure enough, it has dropped out of existence; for just like two measuring-lines laid alongside, the one an inch shorter than the other, their work and their time run parallel, but the work is always ten minutes in advance of the time. They are not irregular. They are never too soon. Their letters are posted the very minute after the mail is closed. They arrive at the wharf just in time to see the steamboat off, they come in sight of the terminus precisely as the station gates are closing. They do not break any engagement or neglect any duty; but they systematically go about it too late, and usually too late by about the same fatal interval."

Some one has said that "promptness is a contagious inspiration." Whether it be an inspiration, or an acquirement, it is one of the practical virtues of civilization.

There is one thing that is almost as sacred as the marriage relation,—that is, an appointment. A man who fails to meet his appointment, unless he has a good reason, is practically a liar, and the world treats him as such.

"If a man has no regard for the time of other men," said Horace Greeley, "why should he have for their money? What is the difference between taking a man's hour and taking his five dollars? There are many men to whom each hour of the business day is worth more than five dollars."

When President Washington dined at four, new members of Congress invited to dine at the White House would sometimes arrive late, and be mortified to find the President eating. "My cook," Washington would say, "never asks if the visitors have arrived, but if the hour has arrived."

When his secretary excused the lateness of his attendance by saying that his watch was too slow, Washington replied, "Then you must get a new watch, or I another secretary."

Franklin said to a servant who was always late, but always ready with an excuse, "I have generally found that the man who is good at an excuse is good for nothing else."

Napoleon once invited his marshals to dine with him, but, as they did not arrive at the moment appointed, he began to eat without them. They came in just as he was rising from the table. "Gentlemen," said he, "it is now past dinner, and we will immediately proceed to business."

Blücher was one of the promptest men that ever lived. He was called "Marshal Forward."

John Quincy Adams was never known to be behind time. The Speaker of the House of Representatives knew when to call the House to order by seeing Mr. Adams coming to his seat. Once a member said that it was time to begin. "No," said another, "Mr. Adams is not in his seat." It was found that the clock was three minutes fast, and prompt to the minute, Mr. Adams arrived.

Webster was never late at a recitation in school or college. In court, in congress, in society, he was equally punctual. Amid the cares and distractions of a singularly busy life, Horace Greeley managed to be on time for every appointment. Many a trenchant paragraph for the "Tribune" was written while the editor was waiting for men of leisure, tardy at some meeting.

Punctuality is the soul of business, as brevity is of wit.

During the first seven years of his mercantile career, Amos Lawrence did not permit a bill to remain unsettled over Sunday. Punctuality is said to be the politeness of princes. Some men are always running to catch up with their business: they are always in a hurry, and give you the impression that they are late for a train. They lack method, and seldom accomplish much. Every business man knows that there are moments on which hang the destiny of years. If you arrive a few moments late at the bank, your paper may be protested and your credit ruined.

One of the best things about school and college life is that the bell which strikes the hour for rising, for recitations, or for lectures, teaches habits of promptness. Every young man should have a watch which is a good timekeeper; one that is *nearly* right encourages bad habits, and is an expensive investment at any price.

"Oh, how I do appreciate a boy who is always on time!" says H. C. Brown. "How quickly you learn to depend on him, and how soon you find yourself intrusting him with weightier matters! The boy who has acquired a reputation for punctuality has made the first contribution to the capital that in after years makes his success a certainty."

Promptness is the mother of confidence and gives credit. It is the best possible proof that our own affairs are well ordered and well conducted, and gives others confidence in our ability. The man who is punctual, as a rule, will keep his word, and may be depended upon.

A conductor's watch is behind time, and a terrible railway collision occurs. A leading firm with enormous assets becomes bankrupt, simply because an agent is tardy in transmitting available funds, as ordered. An innocent man is hanged because the messenger bearing a reprieve should have arrived five minutes earlier. A man is stopped five minutes to hear a trivial story and misses a train or steamer by one minute.

Grant decided to enlist the moment that he learned of the fall of Sumter. When Buckner sent him a flag of truce at Fort Donelson, asking for the appointment of commissioners to consider terms of capitulation, he promptly replied: "No terms except an unconditional and immediate surrender can be accepted. I propose to move immediately upon your works." Buckner replied that circumstances compelled him "to accept the ungenerous and unchivalrous terms which you propose."

The man who, like Napoleon, can on the instant seize the most important thing and sacrifice the others, is sure to win.

Many a wasted life dates its ruin from a lost five minutes. "Too late" can be read between the lines on the tombstone of many a man who has failed. A few minutes often makes all the difference between victory and defeat, success and failure.

What a Good Appearance Will Do

Let thy attire be comely but not costly.—Livy

*Costly thy habit as thy purse can buy,
But not expressed in fancy; rich not gaudy;
For the apparel oft proclaims the man. —Shakespeare*

I hold that gentleman to be the best dressed whose dress no one observes.— Anthony Trollope

As a general thing an individual who is neat in his person is neat in his morals.—H. W. Shaw

There are two chief factors in good appearance; cleanliness of body and comeliness of attire. Usually these go together, neatness of attire indicating a sanitary care of the person, while outward slovenliness suggests a carelessness for appearance that probably goes deeper than the clothes covering the body.

We express ourselves first of all in our bodies. The outer condition of the body is accepted as the symbol of the inner. If it is unlovely, or repulsive, through sheer neglect or indifference, we conclude that the mind corresponds with it. As a rule, the conclusion is a just one. High ideals and strong, clean, wholesome lives and work are incompatible with low standards of personal cleanliness. A young man who neglects his bath will neglect his mind; he will quickly deteriorate in every way. A young woman who ceases to care for her appearance in minutest detail will soon cease to please. She will fall little by little until she degenerates into an ambitionless slattern.

It is not to be wondered at that the Talmud places cleanliness next to godliness. I should place it nearer still, for I believe that absolute cleanliness *is* godliness. Cleanliness or purity of soul and body raises man to the highest estate. Without this he is nothing but a brute.

There is a very close connection between a fine, strong, clean physique and a fine, strong, clean character. A man who allows himself to become careless in regard to the one will, in spite of himself, fall away in the other.

But self-interest clamors as loudly as esthetic or moral considerations for the fulfilment of the laws of cleanliness. Every day we see people receiving "demerits" for failure to live up to them. I can recall instances of capable stenographers who forfeited their positions because they did not keep their finger nails clean. An honest, intelligent man whom I know lost his place in a large publishing firm because he was careless about shaving and brushing his teeth. The other day a lady remarked that she went into a store to buy some ribbons, but when she saw the salesgirl's hands she changed her mind and made her purchase elsewhere. "Dainty ribbons," she said, "could not be handled by such soiled fingers without losing some of their freshness." Of course, it will not be long until that girl's employer will discover that she is not advancing his business, and then,—well, the law will work inexorably.

The first point to be emphasized in the making of a good appearance is the necessity of frequent bathing. A daily bath insures a clean, wholesome condition of the skin, without which health is impossible.

Next in importance to the bath is the proper care of the hair, the hands, and the teeth. This requires little more than a small amount of time and the use of soap and water.

The hair, of course, should be combed and brushed regularly every day. If it is naturally oily, it should be washed thoroughly every two weeks with a good reliable scalp soap and warm water, to which a very little ammonia may be added. If the hair is dry or lacking in oily matter, it should not be washed oftener than once a month and the ammonia may be omitted. Manicure sets are so cheap that they are within the reach of almost everyone. If you can not afford to buy a whole set, you can buy a file (you can get one as low as ten cents), and keep your nails smooth and clean. Keeping the teeth in good condition is a very simple matter, yet perhaps more people sin in this particular point of cleanliness than in any other. I know young men, and young women, too, who dress very well and seem to take considerable pride in their personal appearance, yet neglect their teeth. They do not realize that there could hardly be a worse blot on one's appearance than dirty or decaying teeth, or the absence of one or two in front. Nothing can be more offensive in man or woman than a foul breath, and no one can have neglected teeth without reaping this consequence. We all know how disagreeable it is to be anywhere near a person whose breath is bad. It is positively disgusting. No employer wants a clerk, or stenographer, or other employee about him who contaminates the atmosphere. Nor does he, if he is at all particular, want one whose appearance is marred by a lack of one or two front teeth. Many an applicant has been denied the position he sought because of bad teeth.

For those who have to make their way in the world, the best counsel on the subject of clothes may be summed up in this short sentence, "Let thy attire be comely, but not costly." Simplicity in dress is its greatest charm, and in these days, when there is such an infinite variety of tasteful but inexpensive fabrics to choose from, the majority can afford to be well dressed. But no one need blush for a shabby suit, if circumstances prevent his having a better one. You will be more respected by yourself and every one else with an old coat on your back that has been paid for than a new one that has not. It is not the shabbiness that is unavoidable, but the slovenliness that is avoidable, that the world frowns upon. No one, no matter how poor he may be, will be excused for wearing a dirty coat, a crumpled collar, or muddy shoes. If you are dressed according to your means, no matter how poorly, you are appropriately dressed. The consciousness of making the best appearance you possibly can, of always being scrupulously neat and clean, and of maintaining your self-respect and integrity at all costs, will sustain you under the most adverse circumstances, and give you a dignity, strength, and magnetic forcefulness that will command the respect and admiration of others.

Herbert H. Vreeland, who rose in a short time from a section hand on the Long Island Railroad to the presidency of all the surface railways in New York City, should be a practical authority on this subject. In the course of an address on how to attain success, he said:—

"Clothes don't make the man, but good clothes have got many a man a good job. If you have twenty-five dollars, and want a job, it is better to spend twenty dollars for a suit of clothes, four dollars for shoes, and the rest for a shave, a hair-cut, and a clean collar, and walk to the place, than go with the money in the pockets of a dingy suit."

Most large business houses make it a rule not to employ anyone who looks seedy, or slovenly, or who does not make a good appearance when he applies for a position. The man who hires all the salespeople for one of the largest retail stores in Chicago says:

"While the routine of application is in every case strictly adhered to, the fact remains that the most important element in an applicant's chance for a trial is his personality."

It does not matter how much merit or ability an applicant for a position may possess, he can not afford to be careless of his personal appearance. Diamonds in the rough of infinitely greater value than the polished glass of some of those who get positions may, occasionally, be rejected. Applicants whose good appearance helped them to secure a place may often be very superficial in comparison with some who were rejected in their favor and may not have half their merit; but having secured it, they may keep it, though not possessing half the ability of the boy or girl who was turned away.

That the same rule that governs employers in America holds in England, is evidenced by the "London Draper's Record." It says:—

"Wherever a marked personal care is exhibited for the cleanliness of the person and for neatness in dress, there is also almost always found extra carefulness as regards the finish of work done. Work people whose personal habits are slovenly produce slovenly work; those who are careful of their own appearance are equally careful of the looks of the work they turn out. And probably what is true of the workroom is equally true of the region behind the counter. Is it not a fact that the smart saleswoman is usually rather particular about her dress, is averse to wearing dingy collars, frayed cuffs; and faded ties? The truth of the matter seems to be that extra care as regards personal habits and general appearance is, as a rule, indicative of a certain alertness of mind, which shows itself antagonistic to slovenliness of all kinds."

No young man or woman who wishes to retain that most potent factor of the successful life, self-respect, can afford to be negligent in the matter of dress, for "the character is subdued to what it is clothed in." As the consciousness of being well dressed tends to grace and ease of manner, so shabby, ill-fitting, or soiled attire makes one feel awkward and constrained, lacking in dignity and importance. Our clothes unmistakably affect our feelings, and self respect, as anyone knows who has experienced the sensation—and who has not?—that comes from being attired in new and becoming raiment. Poor, ill-fitting, or soiled garments are detrimental to morals and manners. "The consciousness of clean linen," says Elizabeth Stuart Phelps, "is in and of itself a source of moral strength, second only to that of a clean conscience. A well-ironed collar or a fresh glove has carried many a man through an emergency in which a wrinkle or a rip would have defeated him."

The importance of attending to little details—the perfection of which really constitutes the well-dressed man or woman—is well illustrated by this story of a young woman's failure to secure a desirable position. One of those large-souled women of wealth, in which our generation is rich, had established an industrial school for girls in which they received a good English education and were trained to be self-supporting. She needed the services of a superintendent and teacher, and considered herself fortunate when the trustees of the institution recommended to her a young woman whose tact, knowledge, perfect manners, and general fitness for the position they extolled in the highest terms. The young woman was invited by the founder of the school to call on her at once. Apparently she possessed all the required qualifications; and yet, without assigning any reason, Mrs. V. absolutely refused to give her a trial. Long afterward, when questioned by a friend as to the cause of her seemingly inexplicable conduct in refusing to engage so competent a teacher, she replied: "It was a trifle, but a trifle in which, as in an Egyptian hieroglyphic, lay a volume of meaning. The young woman came to me fashionably and expensively dressed, but with torn and soiled gloves, and half of the buttons off her shoes. A slovenly woman is not a fit guide for any young girl." Probably the applicant never knew why she did not obtain the position, for she was undoubtedly well qualified to fill it in every respect, except in this seemingly unimportant matter of attention to the little details of dress.

From every point of view it pays well to dress well. The knowledge that we are becomingly clothed acts like a mental tonic. Very few men or women are so strong and so perfectly poised as to be unaffected by their surroundings. If you lie around half-dressed, without making your toilet, and with your room all in disorder, taking it easy because you do not expect or wish to see anybody, you will find yourself very quickly taking on the mood of your attire and environment. Your mind will slip down; it will refuse to exert itself; it will become as slovenly, slipshod, and inactive as your body. On the other hand, if, when you have an attack of the "blues," when you feel half sick and not able to work, instead of lying around the house in your old wrapper or dressing gown, you take a good bath,—a Turkish bath, if you can afford it,—put on your best clothes, and make your toilet as carefully as if you were going to a fashionable reception, you will feel like a new person. Nine times out of ten, before you have finished dressing your "blues" and your half-sick feeling will have vanished like a bad dream, and your whole outlook on life will have changed.

By emphasizing the importance of dress I do not mean that you should be like Beau Brummel, the English fop, who spent four thousand dollars a year at his tailor's alone, and who used to take hours to tie his cravat. An undue love of dress is worse than a total disregard of it, and they love dress too much who "go in debt" for it, who make it their chief object in life, to the neglect of their most sacred duty to themselves and others, or who, like Beau Brummel, devote most of their waking hours to its study. But I do claim, in view of its effect on ourselves and on those with whom we come in contact, that it is a duty, as well as the truest economy, to dress as well and becomingly as our position requires and our means will allow.

Many young men and women make the mistake of thinking that "well dressed" necessarily means being expensively dressed, and, with this erroneous idea in mind, they fall into as great a pitfall as those who think clothes are of no importance. They devote the time that should be given to the culture of head and heart to studying their toilets, and planning how they can buy, out of their limited salaries, this or that expensive hat, or tie or coat, which they see exhibited in some fashionable store. If they can not by any possibility afford the coveted article, they buy some cheap, tawdry imitation, the effect of which is only to make them look ridiculous. Young men of this stamp wear cheap rings, vermilion-tinted ties, and broad checks, and almost invariably they occupy cheap positions. Like the dandy, whom Carlyle describes as "a clothes-wearing man,—a man whose trade, office and existence consists in the wearing of clothes,—every faculty of whose soul, spirit, person and purse is heroically consecrated to this one object," they live to dress, and have no time to devote to self-culture or to fitting themselves for higher positions.

The overdressed young woman is merely the feminine of the overdressed young man. The manners of both seem to have a subtle connection with their clothes. They are loud, flashy, vulgar. Their style of dress bespeaks a type of character even more objectionable than that of the slovenly, untidily dressed person. The world accepts the truth announced by Shakespeare that "the apparel oft proclaims the man"; and the man and the woman, too, are frequently condemned by the very garb which they think makes them so irresistible. At first sight, it may seem hasty or superficial to judge men or women by their clothes, but experience has proved, again and again, that they do, as a rule, measure the sense and self-respect of the wearer; and aspirants to success should be as careful in choosing their dress as their companions, for the old adage: "Tell me thy company and I will tell thee what thou art," is offset by this wise saying of some philosopher of the commonplace: "Show me all the dresses a woman has worn in the course of her life, and I will write you her biography."

"How exquisitely absurd it is," says Sydney Smith, "to teach a girl that beauty is of no value, dress of no use. Beauty is of value. Her whole prospect and happiness in life may often depend upon a new gown or a becoming bonnet. If she has five grains of common sense, she will find this out. The great thing is to teach her their proper value."

It is true that clothes do not make the man, but they have a much larger influence on man's life than we are wont to attribute to them. Prentice Mulford declares dress to be one of the avenues for the spiritualization of the race. This is not an extravagant statement, when we remember what an effect clothes have in inciting to personal cleanliness. Let a woman, for instance, don an old soiled or worn wrapper, and it will have the effect of making her indifferent as to whether her hair is frowsy or in curl papers. It does not matter whether her face or hands are clean or not, or what sort of slipshod shoes she wears, for "anything," she argues, "is good enough to go with this old wrapper." Her walk, her manner, the general trend of her feelings, will in some subtle way be dominated by the old wrapper. Suppose she changes,—puts on a dainty muslin garment instead; how different her looks and acts! Her hair must be becomingly arranged, so as not to be at odds with her dress. Her face and hands and finger nails must be spotless as the muslin which surrounds them. The down-at-heel old shoes are exchanged for suitable slippers. Her mind runs along new channels. She has much more respect for the wearer of the new, clean wrapper than for the wearer of the old, soiled one. "Would you change the current of your thoughts? Change your raiment, and you will at once feel the effect." Even so great an authority as Buffon, the naturalist and philosopher, testifies to the influence of dress on thought. He declared himself utterly incapable of thinking to good purpose except in full court dress. This he always put on before entering his study, not even omitting his sword.

There is something about ill-fitting, unbecoming, or shabby apparel which not only robs one of self-respect, but also of comfort and power. Good clothes give ease of manner, and make one talk well. The consciousness of being well dressed gives a grace and ease of manner that even religion will not bestow, while inferiority of garb often induces restraint.

One can not but feel that God is a lover of appropriate dress. He has put robes of beauty and glory upon all His works. Every flower is dressed in richness; every field blushes beneath a mantle of beauty; every star is veiled in brightness; every bird is clothed in the habiliments of the most exquisite taste. And surely He is pleased when we provide a beautiful setting for the greatest of His handiworks.

Personality as a Success Asset

There is something about one's personality which eludes the photographer, which the painter can not reproduce, which the sculptor can not chisel. This subtle something which every one feels, but which no one can describe, which no biographer ever put down in a book, has a great deal to do with one's success in life.

It is this indescribable quality, which some persons have in a remarkable degree, which sets an audience wild at the mention of the name of a Blaine or a Lincoln,—which makes people applaud beyond the bounds of enthusiasm. It was this peculiar atmosphere which made Clay the idol of his constituents. Although, perhaps, Calhoun was a greater man, he never aroused any such enthusiasm as "the mill-boy of the slashes." Webster and Sumner were great men, but they did not arouse a tithe of the spontaneous enthusiasm evoked by men like Blaine and Clay.

A historian says that, in measuring Kossuth's influence over the masses, "we must first reckon with the orator's physical bulk, and then carry the measuring line above his atmosphere." If we had discernment fine enough and tests delicate enough, we could not only measure the personal atmosphere of individuals, but could also make more accurate estimates concerning the future possibilities of schoolmates and young friends. We are often misled as to the position they are going to occupy from the fact that we are apt to take account merely of their ability, and do not reckon this personal atmosphere or magnetic power as a part of their success-capital. Yet this individual atmosphere has quite as much to do with one's advancement as brain-power or education. Indeed, we constantly see men of mediocre ability but with fine personal presence, superb manner, and magnetic qualities, being rapidly advanced over the heads of those who are infinitely their superiors in mental endowments.

A good illustration of the influence of personal atmosphere is found in the orator who carries his audience with him like a whirlwind, while he is delivering his speech, and yet so little of this personal element adheres to his cold words in print that those who read them are scarcely moved at all. The influence of such speakers depends almost wholly upon their presence,—the atmosphere that emanates from them. They are much larger than anything they say or do.

Certain personalities are greater than mere physical beauty and more powerful than learning. Charm of personality is a divine gift that sways the strongest characters, and sometimes even controls the destinies of nations.

We are unconsciously influenced by people who possess this magnetic power. The moment we come into their presence we have a sense of enlargement. They unlock within us possibilities of which we previously had no conception. Our horizon broadens; we feel a new power stirring through all our being; we experience a sense of relief, as if a great weight which long had pressed upon us had been removed.

We can converse with such people in a way that astonishes us, although meeting them, perhaps, for the first time. We express ourselves more clearly and eloquently than we believed we could. They draw out the best that is in us; they introduce us, as it were, to our larger, better selves. With their presence, impulses and longings come thronging to our minds which never stirred us before. All at once life takes on a higher and nobler meaning, and we are fired with a desire to do more than we have ever before done, and to be more than we have been in the past.

A few minutes before, perhaps, we were sad and discouraged, when, suddenly, the flashlight of a potent personality of this kind has opened a rift in our lives and revealed to us hidden capabilities. Sadness gives place to joy, despair to hope, and disheartenment to encouragement. We have been touched to finer issues; we have caught a glimpse of higher ideals; and, for the moment, at least, have been transformed. The old commonplace life, with its absence of purpose and endeavor, has dropped out of sight, and we resolve, with better heart and newer hope, to struggle to make permanently ours the forces and potentialities that have been revealed to us.

Even a momentary contact with a character of this kind seems to double our mental and soul powers, as two great dynamos double the current which passes over the wire, and we are loath to leave the magical presence lest we lose our new-born power.

On the other hand, we frequently meet people who make us shrivel and shrink into ourselves. The moment they come near us we experience a cold chill, as if a blast of winter had struck us in midsummer. A blighting, narrowing sensation, which seems to make us suddenly smaller, passes over us. We feel a decided loss of power, of possibility. We could no more smile in their presence than we could laugh while at a funeral. Their gloomy miasmatic atmosphere chills all our natural impulses. In their presence there is no possibility of expansion for us. As a dark cloud suddenly obscures the brightness of a smiling summer sky, their shadows are cast upon us and fill us with vague, undefinable uneasiness.

We instinctively feel that such people have no sympathy with our aspirations, and our natural prompting is to guard closely any expression of our hopes and ambitions. When they are near us our laudable purposes and desires shrink into insignificance and mere foolishness; the charm of sentiment vanishes and life seems to lose color and zest. The effect of their presence is paralyzing, and we hasten from it as soon as possible.

If we study these two types of personality, we shall find that the chief difference between them is that the first loves his kind, and the latter does not. Of course, that rare charm of manner which captivates all those who come within the sphere of its influence, and that strong personal magnetism which inclines all hearts toward its fortunate possessor, are largely natural gifts. But we shall find that the man who practises unselfishness, who is genuinely interested in the welfare of others, who feels it a privilege to have the power to do a fellow-creature a kindness,—even though polished manners and a gracious presence may be conspicuous by their absence,—will be an elevating influence wherever he goes. He will bring encouragement to and uplift every life that touches his. He will be trusted and loved by all who come in contact with him. This type of personality we may all cultivate if we will.

Magnetic personality is intangible. This mysterious something, which we sometimes call individuality, is often more powerful than the ability which can be measured, or the qualities that can be rated.

Many women are endowed with this magnetic quality, which is entirely independent of personal beauty. It is often possessed in a high degree by very plain women. This was notably the case with some of the women who ruled in the French *salons* more absolutely than the king on his throne.

At a social gathering, when conversation drags, and interest is at a low ebb, the entrance of some bright woman with a magnetic personality instantly changes the whole situation. She may not be handsome, but everybody is attracted; it is a privilege to speak to her.

People who possess this rare quality are frequently ignorant of the source of their power. They simply know they have it, but can not locate or describe it. While it is, like poetry, music, or art, a gift of nature, born in one, it can be cultivated to a certain extent.

Much of the charm of a magnetic personality comes from a fine, cultivated manner. Tact, also, is a very important element,—next to a fine manner, perhaps the most important. One must know exactly what to do, and be able to do just the right thing at the proper time. Good judgment and common sense are indispensable to those who are trying to acquire this magic power. Good taste is also one of the elements of personal charm. You can not offend the tastes of others without hurting their sensibilities.

One of the greatest investments one can make is that of attaining a gracious manner, cordiality of bearing, generosity of feeling,—the delightful art of pleasing. It is infinitely better than money capital, for all doors fly open to sunny, pleasing personalities. They are more than welcome; they are sought for everywhere.

Many a youth owes his promotion or his first start in life to the disposition to be accommodating, to help along wherever he could. This was one of Lincoln's chief characteristics; he had a passion for helping people, for making himself agreeable under all circumstances. Mr. Herndon, his law partner, says: "When the Rutledge Tavern, where Lincoln boarded, was crowded, he would often give up his bed, and sleep on the counter in his store with a roll of calico for his pillow. Somehow everybody in trouble turned to him for help." This generous desire to assist others and to return kindnesses especially endeared Lincoln to the people.

The power to please is a tremendous asset. What can be more valuable than a personality which always attracts, never repels? It is not only valuable in business, but also in every field of life. It makes statesmen and politicians, it brings clients to the lawyer, and patients to the physician. It is worth everything to the clergyman. No matter what career you enter, you can not overestimate the importance of cultivating that charm of manner, those personal qualities, which attract people to you. They will take the place of capital, or influence. They are often a substitute for a large amount of hard work.

Some men attract business, customers, clients, patients, as naturally as magnets attract particles of steel. Everything seems to point their way, for the same reason that the steel particles point toward the magnet,—because they are attracted.

Such men are business magnets. Business moves toward them, even when they do not apparently make half so much effort to get it as the less successful. Their friends call them "lucky dogs." But if we analyze these men closely, we find that they have attractive qualities. There is usually some charm of personality about them that wins all hearts.

Many successful business and professional men would be surprised, if they should analyze their success, to find what a large percentage of it is due to their habitual courtesy and other popular qualities. Had it not been for these, their sagacity, long-headedness, and business training would not, perhaps, have amounted to half so much; for, no matter how able a man may be, if his coarse, rude manners drive away clients, patients, or customers, if his personality repels, he will always be placed at a disadvantage.

It pays to cultivate popularity. It doubles success possibilities, develops manhood, and builds up character. To be popular, one must strangle selfishness, he must keep back his bad tendencies, he must be polite, gentlemanly, agreeable, and companionable. In trying to be popular, he is on the road to success and happiness as well. The ability to cultivate friends is a powerful aid to success. It is capital which will stand by one when panics come, when banks fail, when business concerns go to the wall. How many men have been able to start again after having everything swept away by fire or flood, or some other disaster, just because they had cultivated popular qualities, because they had learned the art of being agreeable, of making friends and holding them with hooks of steel! People are influenced powerfully by their friendships, by their likes and dislikes, and a popular business or professional man has every advantage in the world over a cold, indifferent man, for customers, clients, or patients will flock to him.

Cultivate the art of being agreeable. It will help you to self-expression as nothing else will; it will call out your success qualities; it will broaden your sympathies. It is difficult to conceive of any more delightful birthright than to be born with this personal charm, and yet it is comparatively easy to cultivate, because it is made up of so many other qualities, all of which are cultivatable.

I never knew a thoroughly unselfish person who was not an attractive person. No person who is always thinking of himself and trying to figure out how he can get some advantage from everybody else will ever be attractive. We are naturally disgusted with people who are trying to get everything for themselves and never think of anybody else.

The secret of pleasing is in being pleasant yourself, in being interesting. If you would be agreeable, you must be magnanimous. The narrow, stingy soul is not lovable. People shrink from such a character. There must be heartiness in the expression, in the smile, in the hand-shake, in the cordiality, which is unmistakable. The hardest natures can not resist these qualities any more than the eyes can resist the sun. If you radiate sweetness and light, people will love to get near you, for we are all looking for the sunlight, trying to get away from the shadows.

It is unfortunate that these things are not taught more in the home and in the school; for our success and happiness depend largely upon them. Many of us are no better than uneducated heathens. We may know enough, but we give ourselves out stingily and we live narrow and reserved lives, when we should be broad, generous, sympathetic, and magnanimous.

Popular people, those with great personal charm, take infinite pains to cultivate all the little graces and qualities which go to make up popularity. If people who are naturally unsocial would only spend as much time and take as much pains as people who are social favorites in making themselves popular, they would accomplish wonders.

Everybody is attracted by lovable qualities and is repelled by the unlovely wherever found. The whole principle of an attractive personality lives in this sentence. A fine manner pleases; a coarse, brutal manner repels. We cannot help being attracted to one who is always trying to help us,—who gives us his sympathy, who is always trying to make us comfortable and to give us every advantage he can. On the other hand, we are repelled by people who are always trying to get something out of us, who elbow their way in front of us, to get the best seat in a car or a hall, who are always looking for the easiest chair, or for the choicest bits at the table, who are always wanting to be waited on first at the restaurant or hotel, regardless of others.

The ability to bring the best that is in you to the man you are trying to reach, to make a good impression at the very first meeting, to approach a prospective customer as though you had known him for years without offending his taste, without raising the least prejudice, but getting his sympathy and good will, is a great accomplishment, and this is what commands a great salary.

There is a charm in a gracious personality from which it is very hard to get away. It is difficult to snub the man who possesses it. There is something about him which arrests your prejudice, and no matter how busy or how worried you may be, or how much you may dislike to be interrupted, somehow you haven't the heart to turn away the man with a pleasing personality.

Who has not felt his power multiplied many times, his intellect sharpened, and a keener edge put on all of his faculties, when coming into contact with a strong personality which has called forth hidden powers which he never before dreamed he possessed, so that he could say things and do things impossible to him when alone? The power of the orator, which he flings back to his listeners, he first draws from his audience, but he could never get it from the separate individuals any more than the chemist could get the full power from chemicals standing in separate bottles in his laboratory. It is in contact and combination only that new creations, new forces, are developed.

We little realize what a large part of our achievement is due to others working through us, to their sharpening our faculties, radiating hope, encouragement, and helpfulness into our lives, and sustaining and inspiring us mentally.

We are apt to overestimate the value of an education from books alone. A large part of the value of a college education comes from the social intercourse of the students, the reenforcement, the buttressing of character by association. Their faculties are sharpened and polished by the attrition of mind with mind, and the pitting of brain against brain, which stimulate ambition, brighten the ideals, and open up new hopes and possibilities. Book knowledge is valuable, but the knowledge which comes from mind intercourse is invaluable.

Two substances totally unlike, but having a chemical affinity for each other, may produce a third infinitely stronger than either, or even both of those which unite. Two people with a strong affinity often call into activity in each other a power which neither dreamed he possessed before. Many an author owes his greatest book, his cleverest saying to a friend who has aroused in him latent powers which otherwise might have remained dormant. Artists have been touched by the power of inspiration through a masterpiece, or by some one they happened to meet who saw in them what no one else had ever seen,—the power to do an immortal thing.

The man who mixes with his fellows is ever on a voyage of discovery, finding new islands of power in himself which would have remained forever hidden but for association with others. Everybody he meets has some secret for him, if he can only extract it, something which he never knew before, something which will help him on his way, something which will enrich his life. No man finds himself alone. Others are his discoverers.

It is astonishing how much you can learn from people in social intercourse when you know how to look at them rightly. But it is a fact that you can only get a great deal out of them by giving them a great deal of yourself. The more you radiate yourself, the more magnanimous you are, the more generous of yourself, the more you fling yourself out to them without reserve, the more you will get back.

You must give much in order to get much. The current will not set toward you until it goes out from you. About all you get from others is a reflex of the currents from yourself. The more generously you give, the more you get in return. You will not receive if you give out stingily, narrowly, meanly. You must give of yourself in a whole-hearted, generous way, or you will receive only stingy rivulets, when you might have had great rivers and torrents of blessings.

A man who might have been symmetrical, well-rounded, had he availed himself of every opportunity of touching life along all sides, remains a pygmy in everything except his own little specialty, because he did not cultivate his social side.

It is always a mistake to miss an opportunity of meeting with our kind, and especially of mixing with those above us, because we can always carry away something of value. It is through social intercourse that our rough corners are rubbed off, that we become polished and attractive.

If you go into social life with a determination to give it something, to make it a school for self-improvement, for calling out your best social qualities, for developing the latent brain cells, which have remained dormant for the lack of exercise, you will not find society either a bore or unprofitable. But you must give it something, or you will not get anything.

When you learn to look upon every one you meet as holding a treasure, something which will enrich your life, which will enlarge and broaden your experience, and make you more of a man, you will not think the time in the drawing-room wasted.

The man who is determined to get on will look upon every experience as an educator, as a culture chisel, which will make his life a little more shapely and attractive.

Frankness of manner is one of the most delightful of traits in young or old. Everybody admires the open-hearted, the people who have nothing to conceal, and who do not try to cover up their faults and weaknesses. They are, as a rule, large-hearted and magnanimous. They inspire love and confidence, and, by their very frankness and simplicity, invite the same qualities in others.

Secretiveness repels as much as frankness attracts. There is something about the very inclination to conceal or cover up which arouses suspicion and distrust. We cannot have the same confidence in people who possess this trait, no matter how good they may seem to be, as in frank, sunny natures. Dealing with these secretive people is like traveling on a stage coach on a dark night. There is always a feeling of uncertainty. We may come out all right, but there is a lurking fear of some pitfall or unknown danger ahead of us. We are uncomfortable because of the uncertainties. They may be all right, and may deal squarely with us, but we are not sure and can not trust them. No matter how polite or gracious a secretive person may be, we can never rid ourselves of the feeling that there is a motive behind his graciousness, and that he has an ulterior purpose in view. He is always more or less of an enigma, because he goes through life wearing a mask. He endeavors to hide every trait that is not favorable to himself. Never, if he can help it, do we get a glimpse of the real man.

How different the man who comes out in the open, who has no secrets, who reveals his heart to us, and who is frank, broad and liberal! How quickly he wins our confidence! How we all like and trust him! We forgive him for many a slip or weakness, because he is always ready to confess his faults, and to make amends for them. It he has bad qualities, they are always in sight, and we are ready to make allowances for them. His heart is sound and true, his sympathies are broad and active. The very qualities he possesses—frankness and simplicity,—are conducive to the growth of the highest manhood and womanhood.

In the Black Hills of South Dakota there lived a humble, ignorant miner, who won the love and good will of everyone. "You can't 'elp likin' 'im," said an English miner, and when asked why the miners and the people in the town couldn't help liking him, he answered. "Because he has a 'eart in 'im; he's a man. He always 'elps the boys when in trouble. You never go to 'im for nothin'."

Bright, handsome young men, graduates of Eastern colleges, were there seeking their fortune; a great many able, strong men drawn there from different parts of the country by the gold fever; but none of them held the public confidence like this poor man. He could scarcely write his name, and knew nothing of the usages of polite society, yet he so intrenched himself in the hearts in his community that no other man, however educated or cultured, had the slightest chance of being elected to any office of prominence while "Ike" was around.

He was elected mayor of his town, and sent to the legislature, although he could not speak a grammatical sentence. It was all because he had a heart in him; he was a man.

If You Can Talk Well

When Charles W. Eliot was president of Harvard, he said, "I recognize but one mental acquisition as an essential part of the education of a lady or gentleman, namely, an accurate and refined use of the mother-tongue."

Sir Walter Scott defined "a good conversationalist" as "one who has ideas, who reads, thinks, listens, and who has therefore something to say."

There is no other one thing which enables us to make so good an impression, especially upon those who do not know us thoroughly, as the ability to converse well.

To be a good conversationalist, able to interest people, to rivet their attention, to draw them to you naturally, by the very superiority of your conversational ability, is to be the possessor of a very great accomplishment, one which is superior to all others. It not only helps you to make a good impression upon strangers, it also helps you to make and keep friends. It opens doors and softens hearts. It makes you interesting in all sorts of company. It helps you to get on in the world. It sends you clients, patients, customers. It helps you into the best society, even though you are poor.

A man who can talk well, who has the art of putting things in an attractive way, who can interest others immediately by his power of speech, has a very great advantage over one who may know more than he, but who cannot express himself with ease or eloquence.

No matter how expert you may be in any other art or accomplishment, you cannot use your expertness always and everywhere as you can the power to converse well. If you are a musician, no matter how talented you may be, or how many years you may have spent in perfecting yourself in your specialty, or how much it may have cost you, only comparatively few people can ever hear or appreciate your music.

You may be a fine singer, and yet travel around the world without having an opportunity of showing your accomplishment, or without anyone guessing your specialty. But wherever you go and in whatever society you are, no matter what your station in life may be, you talk.

You may be a painter, you may have spent years with great masters, and yet, unless you have very marked ability so that your pictures are hung in the salons or in the great art galleries, comparatively few people will ever see them. But if you are an artist in conversation, everyone who comes in contact with you will see your life-picture, which you have been painting ever since you began to talk. Everyone knows whether you are an artist or a bungler.

In fact, you may have a great many accomplishments which people occasionally see or enjoy, and you may have a very beautiful home and a lot of property which comparatively few people ever know about; but if you are a good converser, everyone with whom you talk will feel the influence of your skill and charm.

A noted society leader, who has been very successful in the launching of *débutantes* in society, always gives this advice to her *protégés*, "Talk, talk. It does not matter much what you say, but chatter away lightly and gayly. Nothing embarrasses and bores the average man so much as a girl who has to be entertained."

There is a helpful suggestion in this advice. The way to learn to talk is to talk. The temptation for people who are unaccustomed to society, and who feel diffident, is to say nothing themselves and listen to what others say.

Good talkers are always sought after in society. Everybody wants to invite Mrs. So-and-So to dinners or receptions because she is such a good talker. She entertains. She may have many defects, but people enjoy her society because she can talk well.

Conversation, if used as an educator, is a tremendous power developer; but talking without thinking, without an effort to express oneself with clearness, conciseness, or efficiency, mere chattering, or gossiping, the average society small talk, will never get hold of the best thing in a man. It lies too deep for such superficial effort.

Thousands of young people who envy such of their mates as are getting on faster than they are keep on wasting their precious evenings and their half-holidays, saying nothing but the most frivolous, frothy, senseless things—things which do not rise to the level of humor, but the foolish, silly talk which demoralizes one's ambition, lowers one's ideals and all the standards of life, because it begets habits of superficial and senseless thinking. On the streets, on the cars, and in public places, loud, coarse voices are heard in light, flippant, slipshod speech, in coarse slang expressions. "You're talking through your hat"; "Search me"; "You just bet"; "Well, that's the limit"; "I hate that man; he gets on my nerves," and a score of other such vulgarities we often hear.

Nothing else will indicate your fineness or coarseness of culture, your breeding or lack of it, so quickly as your conversation. It will tell your whole life's story. What you say, and how you say it, will betray all your secrets, will give the world your true measure.

There is no accomplishment, no attainment which you can use so constantly and effectively, which will give so much pleasure to your friends, as fine conversation. There is no doubt that the gift of language was intended to be a much greater accomplishment than the majority of us have ever made of it.

Most of us are bunglers in our conversation, because we do not make an art of it; we do not take the trouble or pains to learn to talk well. We do not read enough or think enough. Most of us express ourselves in sloppy, slipshod English, because it is so much easier to do so than it is to think before we speak, to make an effort to express ourselves with elegance, ease, and power.

Poor conversers excuse themselves for not trying to improve by saying that "good talkers are born, not made." We might as well say that good lawyers, good physicians, or good merchants are born, not made. None of them would ever get very far without hard work. This is the price of all achievement that is of value.

Many a man owes his advancement very largely to his ability to converse well. The ability to interest people in your conversation, to hold them, is a great power. The man who has a bungling expression, who knows a thing, but never can put it in logical, interesting, or commanding language, is always placed at a great disadvantage.

I know a business man who has cultivated the art of conversation to such an extent that it is a great treat to listen to him. His language flows with such liquid, limpid beauty, his words are chosen with such exquisite delicacy, taste, and accuracy, there is such a refinement in his diction that he charms everyone who hears him speak. All his life he has been a reader of the finest prose and poetry, and has cultivated conversation as a fine art.

You may think you are poor and have no chance in life. You may be situated so that others are dependent upon you, and you may not be able to go to school or college, or to study music or art, as you long to; you may be tied down to an iron environment; you may be tortured with an unsatisfied, disappointed ambition; and yet you can become an interesting talker, because in every sentence you utter you can practise the best form of expression. Every book you read, every person with whom you converse, who uses good English, can help you.

Few people think very much about how they are going to express themselves. They use the first words that come to them. They do not think of forming a sentence so that it will have beauty, brevity, transparency, power. The words flow from their lips helter-skelter, with little thought of arrangement or order.

Now and then we meet a real artist in conversation, and it is such a treat and delight that we wonder why the most of us should be such bunglers in our conversation, that we should make such a botch of the medium of communication between human beings, when it is capable of being made the art of arts.

I have met a dozen persons in my lifetime who have given me such a glimpse of its superb possibilities that it has made all other arts seem comparatively unimportant to me.

I was once a visitor at Wendell Phillips's home in Boston, and the music of his voice, the liquid charm of his words, the purity, the transparency of his diction, the profundity of his knowledge, the fascination of his personality, and his marvelous art of putting things, I shall never forget. He sat down on the sofa beside me and talked as he would to an old schoolmate, and it seemed to me that I had never heard such exquisite and polished English. I have met several English people who possessed that marvelous power of "soul in conversation which charms all who come under its spell."

Mrs. Mary A. Livermore, Julia Ward Howe, and Elizabeth S. P. Ward, had this wonderful conversational charm, as has ex-President Eliot of Harvard.

The quality of the conversation is everything. We all know people who use the choicest language and express their thoughts in fluent, liquid diction, who impress us by the wonderful flow of their conversation; but that is all there is to it. They do not impress us with their thoughts; they do not stimulate us to action. We do not feel any more determined to do something in the world, to be somebody, after we have heard them talk than we felt before.

We know other people who talk very little, but whose words are so full of meat and stimulating brain force that we feel ourselves multiplied many times by the power they have injected into us.

In olden times the art of conversation reached a much higher standard than that of to-day. The deterioration is due to the complete revolution in the conditions of modern civilization. Formerly people had almost no other way of communicating their thoughts than by speech. Knowledge of all kinds was disseminated almost wholly through the spoken word. There were no great daily newspapers, no magazines or periodicals of any kind.

The great discoveries of vast wealth in the precious minerals, the new world opened up by inventions and discoveries, and the great impetus to ambition have changed all this. In this lightning-express age, in these strenuous times, when everybody has the mania to attain wealth and position, we no longer have time to reflect with deliberation, and to develop our powers of conversation. In these great newspaper and periodical days, when everybody can get for one or a few cents the news and information which it has cost thousands of dollars to collect, everybody sits behind the morning sheet or is buried in a book or magazine. There is no longer the same need of communicating thought by the spoken word.

Oratory is becoming a lost art for the same reason. Printing has become so cheap that even the poorest homes can get more reading for a few dollars than kings and noblemen could afford in the Middle Ages.

It is a rare thing to find a polished conversationalist to-day. So rare is it to hear one speaking exquisite English, and using a superb diction, that it is indeed a luxury.

Good reading, however, will not only broaden the mind and give new ideas, but it will also increase one's vocabulary, and that is a great aid to conversation. Many people have good thoughts and ideas, but they cannot express them because of the poverty of their vocabulary. They have not words enough to clothe their ideas and make them attractive. They talk around in a circle, repeat and repeat, because, when they want a particular word to convey their exact meaning, they cannot find it.

If you are ambitious to talk well, you must be as much as possible in the society of well-bred, cultured people. If you seclude yourself, though you are a college graduate, you will be a poor converser.

We all sympathize with people, especially the timid and shy, who have that awful feeling of repression and stifling of thought, when they make an effort to say something and cannot. Timid young people often suffer keenly in this way in attempting to declaim at school or college. But many a great orator went through the same sort of experience, when he first attempted to speak in public and was often deeply humiliated by his blunders and failures. There is no other way, however, to become an orator or a good conversationalist than by constantly trying to express oneself efficiently and elegantly.

If you find that your ideas fly from you when you attempt to express them, that you stammer and flounder about for words which you are unable to find, you may be sure that every honest effort you make, even if you fail in your attempt, will make it all the easier for you to speak well the next time. It is remarkable, if one keeps on trying, how quickly he will conquer his awkwardness and self-consciousness, and will gain ease of manner and facility of expression.

Everywhere we see people placed at a tremendous disadvantage because they have never learned the art of putting their ideas into interesting, telling language. We see brainy men at public gatherings, when momentous questions are being discussed, sit silent, unable to tell what they know, when they are infinitely better informed than those who are making a great deal of display of oratory or smooth talk.

People with a lot of ability, who know a great deal, often appear like a set of dummies in company, while some superficial, shallow-brained person holds the attention of those present simply because he can tell what he knows in an interesting way. They are constantly humiliated and embarrassed when away from those who happen to know their real worth, because they can not carry on an intelligent conversation upon any topic. There are hundreds of these silent people at our national capital—many of them wives of husbands who have suddenly and unexpectedly come into political prominence.

Many people—and this is especially true of scholars—seem to think that the great *desideratum* in life is to get as much valuable information into the head as possible. But it is just as important to know how to give out knowledge in a palatable manner as to acquire it. You may be a profound scholar, you may be well read in history and in politics, you may be wonderfully well-posted in science, literature, and art, and yet, if your knowledge is locked up within you, you will always be placed at a great disadvantage.

Locked-up ability may give the individual some satisfaction, but it must be exhibited, expressed in some attractive way, before the world will appreciate it or give credit for it. It does not matter how valuable the rough diamond may be, no explaining, no describing its marvels of beauty within, and its great value, would avail; nobody would appreciate it until it was ground and polished and the light let into its depths to reveal its hidden brilliancy. Conversation is to the man what the cutting of the diamond is to the stone. The grinding does not add anything to the diamond. It merely reveals its wealth.

How little parents realize the harm they are doing their children by allowing them to grow up ignorant of or indifferent to the marvelous possibilities in the art of conversation! In the majority of homes, children are allowed to mangle the English language in a most painful way.

Nothing else will develop the brain and character more than the constant effort to talk well, intelligently, interestingly, upon all sorts of topics. There is a splendid discipline in the constant effort to express one's thoughts in clear language and in an interesting manner. We know people who are such superb conversers that no one would ever dream that they have not had the advantages of the higher schools. Many a college graduate has been silenced and put to shame by people who have never even been to a high school, but who have cultivated the art of self-expression.

The school and the college employ the student comparatively a few hours a day for a few years; conversation is a training in a perpetual school. Many get the best part of their education in this school.

Conversation is a great ability discoverer, a great revealer of possibilities and resources. It stimulates thought wonderfully. We think more of ourselves if we can talk well, if we can interest and hold others. The power to do so increases our self-respect, our self-confidence.

No man knows what he really possesses until he makes his best effort to express to others what is in him. Then the avenues of the mind fly open, the faculties are on the alert. Every good converser has felt a power come to him from the listener which he never felt before, and which often stimulates and inspires to fresh endeavor. The mingling of thought with thought, the contact of mind with mind, develops new powers, as the mixing of two chemicals often produces a new third substance.

To converse well one must listen well also—hold oneself in a receptive attitude.

We are not only poor conversationalists, but we are poor listeners as well. We are too impatient to listen. Instead of being attentive and eager to drink in the story or the information, we have not enough respect for the talker to keep quiet. We look about impatiently, perhaps snap our watch, play a tattoo with our fingers on a chair or a table, hitch about as if we were bored and were anxious to get away, and interrupt the speaker before he reaches his conclusion. In fact, we are such an impatient people that we have no time for anything excepting to push ahead, to elbow our way through the crowd to get the position or the money we desire. Our life is feverish and unnatural. We have no time to develop charm of manner, or elegance of diction. "We are too intense for epigram or repartee. We lack time."

Nervous impatience is a conspicuous characteristic of the American people. Everything bores us which does not bring us more business, or more money, or which does not help us to attain the position for which we are striving. Instead of enjoying our friends, we are inclined to look upon them as so many rungs in a ladder, and to value them in proportion as they furnish readers for our books, send us patients, clients, customers or show their ability to give us a boost for political position.

Before these days of hurry and drive, before this age of excitement, it was considered one of the greatest luxuries possible to be a listener in a group surrounding an intelligent talker. It was better than most modern lectures, than anything one could find in a book; for there was a touch of personality, a charm of style, a magnetism which held, a superb personality which fascinated. For the hungry soul, yearning for an education, to drink in knowledge from those wise lips was to be fed with a royal feast indeed.

But to-day everything is "touch and go." We have no time to stop on the street and give a decent salutation. It is: "How do?" or "Morning," accompanied by a sharp nod of the head, instead of by a graceful bow. We have no time for the graces and the charms. Everything must give way to the material.

We have no time for the development of a fine manner; the charm of the days of chivalry and leisure has almost vanished from our civilization. A new type of individual has sprung up. We work like Trojans during the day, and then rush to a theater or other place of amusement in the evening. We have no time to make our own amusement or to develop the faculty of humor and fun-making as people used to do. We pay people for doing that while we sit and laugh. We are like some college boys, who depend upon tutors to carry them through their examinations—they expect to buy their education ready-made.

Life is becoming so artificial, so forced, so diverse from naturalness, we drive our human engines at such a fearful speed, that our finer life is crushed out. Spontaneity and humor, and the possibility of a fine culture and a superb charm of personality in us are almost impossible and extremely rare.

One cause for our conversational decline is a lack of sympathy. We are too selfish, too busily engaged in our own welfare, and wrapped up in our own little world, too intent upon our own self-promotion to be interested in others. No one can make a good conversationalist who is not sympathetic. You must be able to enter into another's life, to live it with the other person, to be a good listener or a good talker.

Walter Besant used to tell of a clever woman who had a great reputation as a conversationalist, though she talked very little. She had such a cordial, sympathetic manner that she helped the timid and the shy to say their best things, and made them feel at home. She dissipated their fears, and they could say things to her which they could not say to anyone else. People thought her an interesting conversationalist because she had this ability to call out the best in others.

If you would make yourself agreeable you must be able to enter into the life of the people you are conversing with, and you must touch them along the lines of their interest. No matter how much you may know about a subject, if it does not happen to interest those to whom you are talking your efforts will be largely lost.

It is pitiable, sometimes, to see men standing around at the average reception or club gathering, dumb, almost helpless, and powerless to enter heartily into the conversation because they are in a subjective mood. They are thinking, thinking, thinking business, business, business; thinking how they can get on a little faster—get more business, more clients, more patients, or more readers for their books—or a better house to live in; how they can make more show. They do not enter heartily into the lives of others, or abandon themselves to the occasion enough to make good talkers. They are cold and reserved, distant, because their minds are somewhere else, their affections on themselves and their own affairs. There are only two things that interest them; business and their own little world. If you talk about these things, they are interested at once; but they do not care a snap about your affairs, how you get on, or what your ambition is, or how they can help you. Our conversation will never reach a high standard while we live in such a feverish, selfish, and unsympathetic state.

Great conversationalists have always been very tactful—interesting without offending. It does not do to stab people if you would interest them, nor to drag out their family skeletons. Some people have the peculiar quality of touching the best that is in us; others stir up the bad. Every time they come into our presence they irritate us. Others allay all that is disagreeable. They never touch our sensitive spots, and they call out all that is spontaneous and sweet and beautiful.

Lincoln was master of the art of making himself interesting to everybody he met. He put people at ease with his stories and jokes, and made them feel so completely at home in his presence that they opened up their mental treasures to him without reserve. Strangers were always glad to talk with him because he was so cordial and quaint, and always gave more than he got.

A sense of humor such as Lincoln had is, of course, a great addition to one's conversational power. But not everyone can be funny; and, if you lack the sense of humor, you will make yourself ludicrous by attempting to be funny.

A good conversationalist, however, is not too serious. He does not deal too much with facts, no matter how important. Facts, statistics, weary. Vivacity is absolutely necessary. Heavy conversation bores; too light, disgusts.

Therefore, to be a good conversationalist you must be spontaneous, buoyant, natural, sympathetic, and must show a spirit of good will. You must feel a spirit of helpfulness, and must enter heart and soul into things which interest others. You must get the attention of people and hold it by interesting them, and you can only interest them by a warm sympathy—a real friendly sympathy. If you are cold, distant, and unsympathetic you can not hold their attention.

You must be broad, tolerant. A narrow stingy soul never talks well. A man who is always violating your sense of taste, of justice, and of fairness, never interests you. You lock tight all the approaches to your inner self, every avenue is closed to him. Your magnetism and your helpfulness are thus cut off, and the conversation is perfunctory, mechanical, and without life or feeling.

You must bring your listener close to you, must open your heart wide, and exhibit a broad free nature, and an open mind. You must be responsive, so that he will throw wide open every avenue of his nature and give you free access to his heart of hearts.

If a man is a success anywhere, it ought to be in his personality, in his power to express himself in strong, effective, interesting language. He should not be obliged to give a stranger an inventory of his possessions in order to show that he has achieved something. A greater wealth should flow from his lips, and express itself in his manner.

No amount of natural ability or education or good clothes, no amount of money, will make you appear well if you use poor English.

A Fortune in Good Manners

Give a boy address and accomplishments, and you give him the mastery of palaces and fortunes wherever he goes; he has not the trouble of earning or owning them; they solicit him to enter and possess.—Emerson

With hat in hand, one gets on in the world.— German Proverb

What thou wilt,
Thou must rather enforce it with thy smile,
Than hew to it with thy sword. —Shakespeare

Politeness has been compared to an air cushion, which, although there is apparently nothing in it, eases our jolts wonderfully.—George L. Carey.

Birth's gude, but breedin's better.— Scotch Proverb

Conduct is three fourths of life.—Matthew Arnold

"Why the doose de 'e 'old 'is 'ead down like that?" asked a cockney sergeant-major angrily, when a worthy fellow soldier wished to be reinstated in a position from which he had been dismissed. "Has 'e 's been han hofficer 'e bought to know 'ow to be'ave 'isself better. What use 'ud 'e be has a non-commissioned hofficer hif 'e didn't dare look 'is men in the face? Hif a man wants to be a soldier, hi say, let 'im cock 'is chin hup, switch 'is stick abart a bit, an give a crack hover the 'ead to hanybody who comes foolin' round 'im, helse 'e might just has well be a Methodist parson."

The English is somewhat rude, but it expresses pretty forcibly the fact that a good bearing is indispensable to success as a soldier. Mien and manner have much to do with our influence and reputation in any walk of life.

"Don't you wish you had my power?" asked the East Wind of the Zephyr. "Why, when I start they hail me by storm signals all along the coast. I can twist off a ship's mast as easily as you can waft thistledown. With one sweep of my wing I strew the coast from Labrador to Cape Horn with shattered ship timber. I can lift and have often lifted the Atlantic. I am the terror of all invalids, and to keep me from piercing to the very marrow of their bones, men cut down forests for their fires and explore the mines of continents for coal to feed their furnaces. Under my breath the nations crouch in sepulchers. Don't you wish you had my power?"

Zephyr made no reply, but floated from out the bowers of the sky, and all the rivers and lakes and seas, all the forests and fields, all the beasts and birds and men smiled at its coming. Gardens bloomed, orchards ripened, silver wheat-fields turned to gold, fleecy clouds went sailing in the lofty heaven, the pinions of birds and the sails of vessels were gently wafted onward, and health and happiness were everywhere. The foliage and flowers and fruits and harvests, the warmth and sparkle and gladness and beauty and life were the only answer Zephyr gave to the insolent question of the proud but pitiless East Wind.

The story goes that Queen Victoria once expressed herself to her husband in rather a despotic tone, and Prince Albert, whose manly self-respect was smarting at her words, sought the seclusion of his own apartment, closing and locking the door. In about five minutes some one knocked.

"Who is it?" inquired the Prince.

"It is I. Open to the Queen of England!" haughtily responded her Majesty. There was no reply. After a long interval there came a gentle tapping and the low spoken words: "It is I, Victoria, your wife." Is it necessary to add that the door was opened, or that the disagreement was at an end? It is said that civility is to a man what beauty is to a woman: it creates an instantaneous impression in his behalf.

The monk Basle, according to a quaint old legend, died while under the ban of excommunication by the pope, and was sent in charge of an angel to find his proper place in the nether world. But his genial disposition and great conversational powers won friends wherever he went. The fallen angels adopted his manner, and even the good angels went a long way to see him and live with him. He was removed to the lowest depths of Hades, but with the same result. His inborn politeness and kindness of heart were irresistible, and he seemed to change the hell into a heaven. At length the angel returned with the monk, saying that no place could be found in which to punish him. He still remained the same Basle. So his sentence was revoked, and he was sent to Heaven and canonized as a saint.

The Duke of Marlborough "wrote English badly and spelled it worse," yet he swayed the destinies of empires. The charm of his manner was irresistible and influenced all Europe. His fascinating smile and winning speech disarmed the fiercest hatred and made friends of the bitterest enemies.

A gentleman took his daughter of sixteen to Richmond to witness the trial of his bitter personal enemy, Aaron Burr, whom he regarded as an arch-traitor. But she was so fascinated by Burr's charming manner that she sat with his friends. Her father took her from the courtroom, and locked her up, but she was so overcome by the fine manner of the accused that she believed in his innocence and prayed for his acquittal. "To this day," said she fifty years afterwards, "I feel the magic of his wonderful deportment."

Madame Récamier was so charming that when she passed around the box at the Church St. Roche in Paris, twenty thousand francs were put into it. At the great reception to Napoleon on his return from Italy, the crowd caught sight of this fascinating woman and almost forgot to look at the great hero.

"Please, Madame," whispered a servant to Madame de Maintenon at dinner, "one anecdote more, for there is no roast to-day." She was so fascinating in manner and speech that her guests appeared to overlook all the little discomforts of life.

According to St. Beuve, the privileged circle at Coppet after making an excursion returned from Chambéry in two coaches. Those arriving in the first coach had a rueful experience to relate—a terrific thunder-storm, shocking roads, and danger and gloom to the whole company. The party in the second coach heard their story with surprise; of thunder-storm, of steeps, of mud, of danger, they knew nothing; no, they had forgotten earth, and breathed a purer air; such a conversation between Madame de Staël and Madame Récamier and Benjamin Constant and Schlegel! they were all in a state of delight. The intoxication of the conversation had made them insensible to all notice of weather or rough roads. "If I were Queen," said Madame Tesse, "I should command Madame de Staël to talk to me every day." "When she had passed," as Longfellow wrote of Evangeline, "it seemed like the ceasing of exquisite music."

Madame de Staël was anything but beautiful, but she possessed that indefinable something before which mere conventional beauty cowers, commonplace and ashamed. Her hold upon the minds of men was wonderful. They were the creatures of her will, and she shaped careers as if she were omnipotent. Even the Emperor Napoleon feared her influence over his people so much that he destroyed her writings and banished her from France.

In the words of Whittier it could be said of her as might be said of any woman:—

Our homes are cheerier for her sake,
Our door-yards brighter blooming,
And all about the social air
Is sweeter for her coming.

A guest for two weeks at the house of Arthur M. Cavanaugh, M. P., who was without arms or legs, was very desirous of knowing how he fed himself; but the conversation and manner of the host were so charming that the visitor was scarcely conscious of his deformity.

"When Dickens entered a room," said one who knew him well, "it was like the sudden kindling of a big fire, by which every one was warmed."

It is said that when Goethe entered a restaurant people would lay down their knives and forks to admire him.

Philip of Macedon, after hearing the report of Demosthenes' famous oration, said: "Had I been there he would have persuaded me to take up arms against myself."

Henry Clay was so graceful and impressive in his manner that a Pennsylvania tavern-keeper tried to induce him to get out of the stage-coach in which they were riding, and make a speech to himself and his wife.

"I don't think much of Choate's spread-eagle talk," said a simple-minded member of a jury that had given five successive verdicts to the great advocate; "but I call him a very lucky lawyer, for there was not one of those five cases that came before us where he wasn't on the right side." His manner as well as his logic was irresistible.

When Edward Everett took a professor's chair at Harvard after five years of study in Europe, he was almost worshiped by the students. His manner seemed touched by that exquisite grace seldom found except in women of rare culture. His great popularity lay in a magical atmosphere which every one felt, but no one could describe, and which never left him.

A New York lady had just taken her seat in a car on a train bound for Philadelphia, when a somewhat stout man sitting just ahead of her lighted a cigar. She coughed and moved uneasily; but the hints had no effect, so she said tartly: "You probably are a foreigner, and do not know that there is a smoking-car attached to the train. Smoking is not permitted here." The man made no reply, but threw his cigar from the window. What has her astonishment when the conductor told her, a moment later, that she had entered the private car of General Grant. She withdrew in confusion, but the same fine courtesy which led him to give up his cigar was shown again as he spared her the mortification of even a questioning glance, still less of a look of amusement, although she watched his dumb, immovable figure with apprehension until she reached the door.

Julian Ralph, after telegraphing an account of President Arthur's fishing-trip to the Thousand Islands, returned to his hotel at two o'clock in the morning, to find all the doors locked. With two friends who had accompanied him, he battered at a side door to wake the servants, but what was his chagrin when the door was opened by the President of the United States!

"Why, that's all right," said Mr. Arthur when Mr. Ralph asked his pardon. "You wouldn't have got in till morning if I had not come. No one is up in the house but me. I could have sent my colored boy, but he had fallen asleep and I hated to wake him."

The late King Edward, when Prince of Wales, the first gentleman in Europe, invited an eminent man to dine with him. When coffee was served, the guest, to the consternation of the others, drank from his saucer. An open titter of amusement went round the table. The Prince, quickly noting the cause of the untimely amusement, gravely emptied his cup into his saucer and drank after the manner of his guest. Silent and abashed, the other members of the princely household took the rebuke and did the same.

Queen Victoria sent for Carlyle, who was a Scotch peasant, offering him the title of nobleman, which he declined, feeling that he had always been a nobleman in his own right. He understood so little of the manners at court that, when presented to the Queen, after speaking to her a few minutes, being tired, he said, "Let us sit down, madam;" whereat the courtiers were ready to faint. But she was great enough, and gave a gesture that seated all her puppets in a moment. The Queen's courteous suspension of the rules of etiquette, and what it may have cost her, can be better understood from what an acquaintance of Carlyle said of him when he saw him for the first time. "His presence, in some unaccountable manner, rasped the nerves. I expected to meet a rare being, and I left him feeling as if I had drunk sour wine, or had had an attack of seasickness."

Some persons wield a scepter before which others seem to bow in glad obedience. But whence do they obtain such magic power? What is the secret of that almost hypnotic influence over people which we would give anything to possess?

Courtesy is not always found in high places. Even royal courts furnish many examples of bad manners. At an entertainment given years ago by Prince Edward and the Princess of Wales, to which only the very cream of the cream of society was admitted, there was such pushing and struggling to see the Princess, who was then but lately married, that, as she passed through the reception rooms, a bust of the Princess Royal was thrown from its pedestal and damaged, and the pedestal upset; and the ladies, in their eagerness to see the Princess, actually stood upon it.

When Catherine of Russia gave receptions to her nobles, she published the following rules of etiquette upon cards: "Gentlemen will not get drunk before the feast is ended. Noblemen are forbidden to strike their wives in company. Ladies of the court must not wash out their mouths in the drinking-glasses, or wipe their faces on the damask, or pick their teeth with forks." But to-day the nobles of Russia have no superiors in manners.

Etiquette originally meant the ticket or tag tied to a bag to indicate its contents. If a bag had this ticket it was not examined. From this the word passed to cards upon which were printed certain rules to be observed by guests. These rules were "the ticket" or the etiquette. To be "the ticket," or, as it was sometimes expressed, to act or talk by the card, became the thing with the better classes.

It was fortunate for Napoleon that he married Josephine before he was made commander-in-chief of the armies of Italy. Her fascinating manners and her wonderful powers of persuasion were more influential than the loyalty of any dozen men in France in attaching to him the adherents who would promote his interests. Josephine was to the drawing-room and the salon what Napoleon was to the field—a preeminent leader. The secret of her personality that made her the Empress not only of the hearts of the Frenchmen, but also of the nations her husband conquered, has been beautifully told by herself. "There is only one occasion," she said to a friend, "in which I would voluntarily use the words, 'I *will!*'—namely, when I would say, 'I will that all around me be happy.'"

"It was only a glad 'good-morning,'
As she passed along the way,
But it spread the morning's glory
Over the livelong day."

A fine manner more than compensates for all the defects of nature. The most fascinating person is always the one of most winning manners, not the one of greatest physical beauty. The Greeks thought beauty was a proof of the peculiar favor of the gods, and considered that beauty only worth adorning and transmitting which was unmarred by outward manifestations of hard and haughty feeling. According to their ideal, beauty must be the expression of attractive qualities within—such as cheerfulness, benignity, contentment, charity, and love.

Mirabeau was one of the ugliest men in France. It was said he had "the face of a tiger pitted by smallpox," but the charm of his manner was almost irresistible.

Beauty of life and character, as in art, has no sharp angles. Its lines seem continuous, so gently does curve melt into curve. It is sharp angles that keep many souls from being beautiful that are almost so. Our good is less good when it is abrupt, rude, ill timed, or ill placed. Many a man and woman might double their influence and success by a kindly courtesy and a fine manner.

Tradition tells us that before Apelles painted his wonderful Goddess of Beauty which enchanted all Greece, he traveled for years observing fair women, that he might embody in his matchless Venus a combination of the loveliest found in all. So the good-mannered study, observe, and adopt all that is finest and most worthy of imitation in every cultured person they meet.

Throw a bone to a dog, said a shrewd observer, and he will run off with it in his mouth, but with no vibration in his tail. Call the dog to you, pat him on the head, let him take the bone from your hand, and his tail will wag with gratitude. The dog recognizes the good deed and the gracious manner of doing it. Those who throw their good deeds should not expect them to be caught with a thankful smile.

"Ask a person at Rome to show you the road," said Dr. Guthrie of Edinburgh, "and he will always give you a civil and polite answer; but ask any person a question for that purpose in this country (Scotland), and he will say, 'Follow your nose and you will find it.' But the blame is with the upper classes; and the reason why, in this country, the lower classes are not polite is because the upper classes are not polite. I remember how astonished I was the first time I was in Paris. I spent the first night with a banker, who took me to a pension, or, as we call it, a boarding-house. When we got there, a servant girl came to the door, and the banker took off his hat, and bowed to the servant girl, and called her mademoiselle, as though she were a lady. Now, the reason why the lower classes there are so polite is because the upper classes are polite and civil to them."

A fine courtesy is a fortune in itself. The good-mannered can do without riches, for they have passports everywhere. All doors fly open to them, and they enter without money and without price. They can enjoy nearly everything without the trouble of buying or owning. They are as welcome in every household as the sunshine; and why not? for they carry light, sunshine, and joy everywhere. They disarm jealousy and envy, for they bear good will to everybody. Bees will not sting a man smeared with honey.

"A man's own good breeding," says Chesterfield, "is the best security against other people's ill manners. It carries along with it a dignity that is respected by the most petulant. Ill breeding invites and authorizes the familiarity of the most timid. No man ever said a pert thing to the Duke of Marlborough, or a civil one to Sir Robert Walpole."

The true gentleman cannot harbor those qualities which excite the antagonism of others, as revenge, hatred, malice, envy, or jealousy, for these poison the sources of spiritual life and shrivel the soul. Generosity of heart and a genial good will towards all are absolutely essential to him who would possess fine manners. Here is a man who is cross, crabbed, moody, sullen, silent, sulky, stingy, and mean with his family and servants. He refuses his wife a little money to buy a needed dress, and accuses her of extravagance that would ruin a millionaire. Suddenly the bell rings. Some neighbors call: what a change! The bear of a moment ago is as docile as a lamb. As by magic he becomes talkative, polite, generous. After the callers have gone, his little girl begs her father to keep on his "company manners" for a little while, but the sullen mood returns and his courtesy vanishes as quickly as it came. He is the same disagreeable, contemptible, crabbed bear as before the arrival of his guests.

What friend of the great Dr. Johnson did not feel mortified and pained to see him eat like an Esquimau, and to hear him call men "liars" because they did not agree with him? He was called the "Ursa Major," or Great Bear.

Benjamin Rush said that when Goldsmith at a banquet in London asked a question about "the American Indians," Dr. Johnson exclaimed: "There is not an Indian in North America foolish enough to ask such a question." "Sir," replied Goldsmith, "there is not a savage in America rude enough to make such a speech to a gentleman."

After Stephen A. Douglas had been abused in the Senate he rose and said: "What no gentleman should say no gentleman need answer."

Aristotle thus described a real gentleman more than two thousand years ago: "The magnanimous man will behave with moderation under both good fortune and bad. He will not allow himself to be exalted; he will not allow himself to be abased. He will neither be delighted with success, nor grieved with failure. He will never choose danger, nor seek it. He is not given to talk about himself or others. He does not care that he himself should be praised, nor that other people should be blamed."

A gentleman is just a gentle man: no more, no less; a diamond polished that was first a diamond in the rough. A gentleman is gentle, modest, courteous, slow to take offense, and never giving it. He is slow to surmise evil, as he never thinks it. He subjects his appetites, refines his tastes, subdues his feelings, controls his speech, and deems every other person as good as himself. A gentleman, like porcelain-ware, must be painted before he is glazed. There can be no change after it is burned in, and all that is put on afterwards will wash off. He who has lost all but retains his courage, cheerfulness, hope, virtue, and self-respect, is a true gentleman, and is rich still.

"You replace Dr. Franklin, I hear," said the French Minister, Count de Vergennes, to Mr. Jefferson, who had been sent to Paris to relieve our most popular representative. "I succeed him; no man can replace him," was the felicitous reply of the man who became highly esteemed by the most polite court in Europe.

"You should not have returned their salute," said the master of ceremonies, when Clement XIV bowed to the ambassadors who had bowed in congratulating him upon his election. "Oh, I beg your pardon," replied Clement. "I have not been pope long enough to forget good manners."

Cowper says:—

A modest, sensible, and well-bred man
Would not insult me, and no other can.

"I never listen to calumnies," said Montesquieu, "because if they are untrue I run the risk of being deceived, and if they are true, of hating people not worth thinking about."

"I think," says Emerson, "Hans Andersen's story of the cobweb cloth woven so fine that it was invisible—woven for the king's garment—must mean manners, which do really clothe a princely nature."

No one can fully estimate how great a factor in life is the possession of good manners, or timely thoughtfulness with human sympathy behind it. They are the kindly fruit of a refined nature, and are the open sesame to the best of society. Manners are what vex or soothe, exalt or debase, barbarize or refine us by a constant, steady, uniform, invincible operation like that of the air we breathe. Even power itself has not half the might of gentleness, that subtle oil which lubricates our relations with each other, and enables the machinery of society to perform its functions without friction.

"Have you not seen in the woods, in a late autumn morning," asks Emerson, "a poor fungus, or mushroom,—a plant without any solidity, nay, that seemed nothing but a soft mush or jelly,—by its constant, total, and inconceivably gentle pushing, manage to break its way up through the frosty ground, and actually to lift a hard crust on its head? It is the symbol of the power of kindness."

"There is no policy like politeness," says Magoon; "since *a good manner often succeeds where the best tongue has failed.*" The art of pleasing is the art of rising in the world.

The politest people in the world, it is said, are the Jews. In all ages they have been maltreated and reviled, and despoiled of their civil privileges and their social rights; yet are they everywhere polite and affable. They indulge in few or no recriminations; are faithful to old associations; more considerate of the prejudices of others than others are of theirs; not more worldly-minded and money-loving than people generally are; and, everything considered, they surpass all nations in courtesy, affability, and forbearance.

"Men, like bullets," says Richter, "go farthest when they are smoothest."

Napoleon was much displeased on hearing that Josephine had permitted General Lorges, a young and handsome man, to sit beside her on the sofa. Josephine explained that, instead of its being General Lorges, it was one of the aged generals of his army, entirely unused to the customs of courts. She was unwilling to wound the feelings of the honest old soldier, and so allowed him to retain his seat. Napoleon commended her highly for her courtesy.

President Jefferson was one day riding with his grandson, when they met a slave, who took off his hat and bowed. The President returned the salutation by raising his hat, but the grandson ignored the civility of the negro. "Thomas," said the grandfather, "do you permit a slave to be more of a gentleman than yourself?"

"Lincoln was the first great man I talked with freely in the United States," said Fred Douglass, "who in no single instance reminded me of the difference between himself and me, of the difference in color."

"Eat at your own table," says Confucius, "as you would eat at the table of the king." If parents were not careless about the manners of their children at home, they would seldom be shocked or embarrassed at their behavior abroad.

James Russell Lowell was as courteous to a beggar as to a lord, and was once observed holding a long conversation in Italian with an organ-grinder whom he was questioning about scenes in Italy with which they were each familiar.

In hastily turning the corner of a crooked street in London, a young lady ran with great force against a ragged beggar-boy and almost knocked him down. Stopping as soon as she could, she turned around and said very kindly: "I beg your pardon, my little fellow; I am very sorry that I ran against you." The astonished boy looked at her a moment, and then, taking off about three quarters of a cap, made a low bow and said, while a broad, pleasant smile overspread his face: "You have my parding, miss, and welcome,—and welcome; and the next time you run ag'in' me, you can knock me clean down and I won't say a word." After the lady had passed on, he said to a companion: "I say, Jim, it's the first time I ever had anybody ask my parding, and it kind o' took me off my feet."

"Respect the burden, madame, respect the burden," said Napoleon, as he courteously stepped aside at St. Helena to make way for a laborer bending under a heavy load, while his companion seemed inclined to keep the narrow path.

A Washington politician went to visit Daniel Webster at Marshfield, Mass., and, in taking a short cut to the house, came to a stream which he could not cross. Calling to a rough-looking farmer near by, he offered a quarter to be carried to the other side. The farmer took the politician on his broad shoulders and landed him safely, but would not take the quarter. The old rustic presented himself at the house a few minutes later, and to the great surprise and chagrin of the visitor was introduced as Mr. Webster.

Garrison was as polite to the furious mob that tore his clothes from his back and dragged him through the streets as he could have been to a king. He was one of the serenest souls that ever lived. Christ was courteous, even to His persecutors, and in terrible agony on the cross, He cried: "Father, forgive them, for they know not what they do." St. Paul's speech before Agrippa is a model of dignified courtesy, as well as of persuasive eloquence.

Good manners often prove a fortune to a young man. Mr. Butler, a merchant in Providence, R. I., had once closed his store and was on his way home when he met a little girl who wanted a spool of thread. He went back, opened the store, and got the thread. This little incident was talked of all about the city and brought him hundreds of customers. He became very wealthy, largely because of his courtesy.

Ross Winans of Baltimore owed his great success and fortune largely to his courtesy to two foreign strangers. Although his was but a fourth-rate factory, his great politeness in explaining the minutest details to his visitors was in such marked contrast with the limited attention they had received in large establishments that it won their esteem. The strangers were Russians sent by their Czar, who later invited Mr. Winans to establish locomotive works in Russia. He did so, and soon his profits resulting from his politeness were more than $100,000 a year.

A poor curate saw a crowd of rough boys and men laughing and making fun of two aged spinsters dressed in antiquated costume. The ladies were embarrassed and did not dare enter the church. The curate pushed through the crowd, conducted them up the central aisle, and amid the titter of the congregation, gave them choice seats. These old ladies although strangers to him, at their death left the gentle curate a large fortune. Courtesy pays.

Not long ago a lady met the late President Humphrey of Amherst College, and she was so much pleased with his great politeness that she gave a generous donation to the college.

"Why did our friend never succeed in business?" asked a man returning to New York after years of absence; "he had sufficient capital, a thorough knowledge of his business, and exceptional shrewdness and sagacity." "He was sour and morose," was the reply; "he always suspected his employees of cheating him, and was discourteous to his customers. Hence, no man ever put good will or energy into work done for him, and his patrons went to shops where they were sure of civility."

Some men almost work their hands off and deny themselves many of the common comforts of life in their earnest efforts to succeed, and yet render success impossible by their cross-grained ungentlemanliness. They repel patronage, and, naturally, business which might easily be theirs goes to others who are really less deserving but more companionable.

Bad manners often neutralize even honesty, industry, and the greatest energy; while agreeable manners win in spite of other defects. Take two men possessing equal advantages in every other respect; if one be gentlemanly, kind, obliging, and conciliating, and the other disobliging, rude, harsh, and insolent, the former will become rich while the boorish one will starve.

A fine illustration of the business value of good manners is found in the Bon Marché, an enormous establishment in Paris where thousands of clerks are employed, and where almost everything is kept for sale. The two distinguishing characteristics of the house are one low price to all, and extreme courtesy. Mere politeness is not enough; the employees must try in every possible way to please and to make customers feel at home. Something more must be done than is done in other stores, so that every visitor will remember the Bon Marché with pleasure. By this course the business has been developed until it is said to be the largest of the kind in the world.

"Thank you, my dear; please call again," spoken to a little beggar-girl who bought a pennyworth of snuff proved a profitable advertisement and made Lundy Foote a millionaire.

Many persons of real refinement are thought to be stiff, proud, reserved, and haughty who are not, but are merely diffident and shy.

It is a curious fact that diffidence often betrays us into discourtesies which our hearts abhor, and which cause us intense mortification and embarrassment. Excessive shyness must be overcome as an obstacle to perfect manners. It is peculiar to the Anglo-Saxon and the Teutonic races, and has frequently been a barrier to the highest culture. It is a disease of the finest organizations and the highest types of humanity. It never attacks the coarse and vulgar.

Sir Isaac Newton was the shyest man of his age. He did not acknowledge his great discovery for years just for fear of attracting attention to himself. He would not allow his name to be used in connection with his theory of the moon's motion, for fear it would increase the acquaintances he would have to meet. George Washington was awkward and shy and had the air of a countryman. Archbishop Whately was so shy that he would escape notice whenever it was possible. At last he determined to give up trying to cure his shyness; "for why," he asked, "should I endure this torture all my life?" when, to his surprise, it almost entirely disappeared. Elihu Burritt was so shy that he would hide in the cellar when his parents had company.

Practice on the stage or lecture platform does not always eradicate shyness. David Garrick, the great actor, was once summoned to testify in court; and, though he had acted for thirty years with marked self-possession, he was so confused and embarrassed that the judge dismissed him. John B. Gough said that he could not rid himself of his early diffidence and shrinking from public notice. He said that he never went on the platform without fear and trembling, and would often be covered with cold perspiration.

There are many worthy people who are brave on the street, who would walk up to a cannon's mouth in battle, but who are cowards in the drawing-room, and dare not express an opinion in the social circle. They feel conscious of a subtle tyranny in society's code, which locks their lips and ties their tongues. Addison was one of the purest writers of English and a perfect master of the pen, but he could scarcely utter a dozen words in conversation without being embarrassed. Shakespeare was very shy. He retired from London at forty, and did not try to publish or preserve one of his plays. He took second or third-rate parts on account of his diffidence.

Generally shyness comes from a person thinking too much about himself—which in itself is a breach of good breeding—and wondering what other people think about him.

"I was once very shy," said Sydney Smith, "but it was not long before I made two very useful discoveries; first, that all mankind were not solely employed in observing me; and next, that shamming was of no use; that the world was very clear-sighted, and soon estimated a man at his true value. This cured me."

What a misfortune it is to go through life apparently encased in ice, yet all the while full of kindly, cordial feeling for one's fellow men! Shy people are always distrustful of their powers and look upon their lack of confidence as a weakness or lack of ability, when it may indicate quite the reverse. By teaching children early the arts of social life, such as boxing, horseback riding, dancing, elocution, and similar accomplishments, we may do much to overcome the sense of shyness.

Shy people should dress well. Good clothes give ease of manner, and unlock the tongue. The consciousness of being well dressed gives a grace and ease of manner that even religion will not bestow, while inferiority of garb often induces restraint. As peculiarities in apparel are sure to attract attention, it is well to avoid bright colors and fashionable extremes, and wear plain, well-fitting garments of as good material as the purse will afford.

Beauty in dress is a good thing, rail at it who may. But it is a lower beauty, for which a higher beauty should not be sacrificed. They love dress too much who give it their first thought, their best time, or all their money; who for it neglect the culture of the mind or heart, or the claims of others on their service; who care more for dress than for their character; who are troubled more by an unfashionable garment than by a neglected duty.

When Ezekiel Whitman, a prominent lawyer and graduate of Harvard, was elected to the Massachusetts legislature, he came to Boston from his farm in countryman's dress, and went to a hotel in Boston. He entered the parlor and sat down, when he overheard the remark between some ladies and gentlemen: "Ah, here comes a real homespun countryman. Here's fun." They asked him all sorts of queer questions, tending to throw ridicule upon him, when he arose and said, "Ladies and gentlemen, permit me to wish you health and happiness, and may you grow better and wiser in advancing years, bearing in mind that outward appearances are deceitful. You mistook me, from my dress, for a country booby; while I, from the same superficial cause, thought you were ladies and gentlemen. The mistake has been mutual." Just then Governor Caleb Strong entered and called to Mr. Whitman, who, turning to the dumfounded company, said: "I wish you a very good evening."

"In civilized society," says Johnson, "external advantages make us more respected. A man with a good coat upon his back meets with a better reception than he who has a bad one."

One cannot but feel that God is a lover of the beautiful. He has put robes of beauty and glory upon all his works. Every flower is dressed in richness; every field blushes beneath a mantle of beauty; every star is veiled in brightness; every bird is clothed in the habiliments of the most exquisite taste.

Some people look upon polished manners as a kind of affectation. They claim admiration for plain, solid, square, rugged characters. They might as well say that they prefer square, plain, unornamented houses made from square blocks of stone. St. Peter's is none the less strong and solid because of its elegant columns and the magnificent sweep of its arches, its carved and fretted marbles of matchless hues.

Our manners, like our characters, are always under inspection. Every time we go into society we must step on the scales of each person's opinion, and the loss or gain from our last weight is carefully noted. Each mentally asks, "Is this person going up or down? Through how many grades has he passed?" For example, young Brown enters a drawing-room. All present weigh him in their judgment and silently say, "This young man is gaining; he is more careful, thoughtful, polite, considerate, straightforward, industrious." Besides him stands young Jones. It is evident that he is losing ground rapidly. He is careless, indifferent, rough, does not look you in the eye, is mean, stingy, snaps at the servants, yet is over-polite to strangers.

And so we go through life, tagged with these invisible labels by all who know us. I sometimes think it would be a great advantage if one could read these ratings of his associates. We cannot long deceive the world, for that other self, who ever stands in the shadow of ourselves holding the scales of justice, that telltale in the soul, rushes to the eye or into the manner and betrays us.

But manners, while they are the garb of the gentleman, do not constitute or finally determine his character. Mere politeness can never be a substitute for moral excellence, any more than the bark can take the place of the heart of the oak. It may well indicate the kind of wood below, but not always whether it be sound or decayed. Etiquette is but a substitute for good manners and is often but their mere counterfeit.

Sincerity is the highest quality of good manners.

The following recipe is recommended to those who wish to acquire genuine good manners:—

Of Unselfishness, three drachms;
Of the tincture of Good Cheer, one ounce;
Of Essence of Heart's-Ease, three drachms;
Of the Extract of the Rose of Sharon, four ounces;
Of the Oil of Charity, three drachms, and no scruples;
Of the Infusion of Common Sense and Tact, one ounce;
Of the Spirit of Love, two ounces.

The Mixture to be taken whenever there is the slightest symptom of selfishness, exclusiveness, meanness, or I-am-better-than-you-ness.

Pattern after Him who gave the Golden Rule, and who was the first true gentleman that ever breathed.

Self-Consciousness and Timidity Foes to Success

Timid, shy people are morbidly self-conscious; they think too much about themselves. Their thoughts are always turned inward; they are always analyzing, dissecting themselves, wondering how they appear and what people think of them. If these people could only forget themselves and think of others, they would be surprised to see what freedom, ease, and grace they would gain; what success in life they would achieve.

Timidity, shyness, and self-consciousness belong to the same family. We usually find all where we find any one of these qualities, and they are all enemies of peace of mind, happiness, and achievement. No one has ever done a great thing while his mind was centered upon himself. We must lose ourselves before we can find ourselves. Self analysis is valuable only to learn our strength; fatal, if we dwell upon our weaknesses.

Thousands of young people are held back from undertaking what they long to do, and are kept from trying to make real their great life-dreams, because they are afraid to jostle with the world. They shrink from exposing their sore spots and sensitive points, which smart from the lightest touch. Their super-sensitiveness makes cowards of them.

Over-sensitiveness, whether in man or woman, is really an exaggerated form of self-consciousness. It is far removed from conceit or self-esteem, yet it causes one's personality to overshadow everything else. A sensitive person feels that, whatever he does, wherever he goes, or whatever he says, he is the center of observation. He imagines that people are criticizing his movements, making fun at his expense, or analyzing his character, when they are probably not thinking of him at all. He does not realize that other people are too busy and too much interested in themselves and other things to devote to him any of their time beyond what is absolutely necessary. When he thinks they are aiming remarks at him, putting slights upon him, or trying to hold him up to the ridicule of others, they may not be even conscious of his presence.

Morbid sensitiveness requires heroic treatment. A sufferer who wishes to overcome it must take himself in hand as determinedly as he would if he wished to get control of a quick temper, or to rid himself of a habit of lying, or stealing, or drinking, or any other defect which prevented his being a whole man.

"What shall I do to get rid of it?" asks a victim. Think less of yourself and more of others. Mingle freely with people. Become interested in things outside of yourself. Do not brood over what is said to you, or analyze every simple remark until you magnify it into something of the greatest importance. Do not have such a low and unjust estimate of people as to think they are bent on nothing but hurting the feelings of others, and depreciating and making light of them on every possible occasion. A man who appreciates himself at his true value, and who gives his neighbors credit for being at least as good as he is, cannot be a victim of over-sensitiveness.

One of the best schools for a sensitive boy is a large business house in which he will be thrown among strangers who will not handle him with gloves. In such an environment he will soon learn that everyone has all he can do to attend to his own business. He will realize that he must be a man and give and take with the others, or get out. He will be ashamed to play "cry baby" every time he feels hurt, but will make up his mind to grin and bear it. Working in competition with other people, and seeing that exactly the same treatment is given to those above him as to himself, takes the nonsense out of him. He begins to see that the world is too busy to bother itself especially about him, and that, even when people look at him, they are not usually thinking of him.

A college course is of inestimable value to a boy or girl of over-refined sensibilities. Oftentimes, when boys enter college as freshmen, they are so touchy that their sense of honor is constantly being hurt and their pride stung by the unconscious thrusts of classmates and companions. But after they have been in college a term, and have been knocked about and handled in a rough but good-humored manner by youths of their own age, they realize that it would be the most foolish thing in the world to betray resentment. If one shows that he is hurt, he knows that he will be called the class booby, and teased unmercifully, so he is simply forced to drop his foolish sensitiveness.

Thousands of people are out of positions, and cannot keep places when they get them, because of this weakness. Many a good business man has been kept back, or even ruined, by his quickness to take offense, or to resent a fancied slight. There is many a clergyman, well educated and able, who is so sensitive that he can not keep a pastorate long. From his distorted viewpoint some brother or sister in the church is always hurting him, saying and thinking unkind things, or throwing out hints and suggestions calculated to injure him in the eyes of the congregation.

Many schoolteachers are great sufferers from over-sensitiveness. Remarks of parents, or school committees, or little bits of gossip which are reported to them make them feel as if people were sticking pins in them, metaphorically speaking, all the time. Writers, authors, and other people with artistic temperaments, are usually very sensitive. I have in mind a very strong, vigorous editorial writer who is so prone to take offense that he can not hold a position either on a magazine or a daily paper. He is cut to the very quick by the slightest criticism, and regards every suggestion for the improvement of his work as a personal affront. He always carries about an injured air, a feeling that he has been imposed upon, which greatly detracts from an otherwise agreeable personality.

The great majority of people, no matter how rough in manner or bearing, are kind-hearted, and would much rather help than hinder a fellowbeing, but they have all they can do to attend to their own affairs, and have no time to spend in minutely analyzing the nature and feeling of those whom they meet in the course of their daily business. In the busy world of affairs, it is give and take, touch and go, and those who expect to get on must rid themselves of all morbid sensitiveness. If they do not, they doom themselves to unhappiness and failure.

Self-consciousness is a foe to greatness in every line of endeavor. No one ever does a really great thing until he feels that he is a part of something greater than himself, until he surrenders to that greater principle.

Some of our best writers never found themselves, never touched their power, until they forgot their rules for construction, their grammar, their rhetorical arrangement, by losing themselves in their subject. Then they found their style.

It is when a writer is so completely carried away with his subject that he cannot help writing, that he writes naturally. He shows what his real style is.

No orator has ever electrified an audience while he was thinking of his style or was conscious of his rhetoric, or trying to apply the conventional rules of oratory. It is when the orator's soul is on fire with his theme, and he forgets his audience, forgets everything but his subject, that he really does a great thing.

No painter ever did a great masterpiece when trying to keep all the rules of his profession, the laws of drawing, of perspective, the science of color, in his mind. Everything must be swallowed up in his zeal, fused in the fire of his genius,—then, and then only, can he really create.

No singer ever captivated her audience until she forgot herself, until she was lost in her song.

Could anything be more foolish and short-sighted than to allow a morbid sensitiveness to interfere with one's advancement in life?

I know a young lady with a superb mind and a fine personality, capable of filling a superior position, who has been kept in a very ordinary situation for years simply because of her morbid sensitiveness.

She takes it for granted that if any criticism is made in the department where she works, it is intended for her, and she "flies off the handle" over every little remark that she can possibly twist into a reflection upon herself.

The result is that she makes it so unpleasant for her employers that they do not promote her. And she can not understand why she does not get on faster.

No one wishes to employ anyone who is so sensitive that he is obliged to be on his guard every moment lest he wound him or touch a sore spot. It makes an employer very uncomfortable to feel that those about him are carrying around an injured air a large part of the time, so that he never quite knows whether they are in sympathy with him or not. If anything has gone wrong in his business and he feels vexed, he knows that he is liable to give offense to these people without ever intending it.

A man wants to feel that his employees understand him, and that they take into consideration the thousand and one little vexations and happenings which are extremely trying, and that if he does not happen to approach them with a smiling face, with consideration and friendliness in his words or commands, they will not take offense. They will think of his troubles, not their own, if they are wise: they will forget self, and contribute their zeal to the greater good.

Tact or Common Sense

"Who is stronger than thou?" asked Braham; and Force replied "Address."—Victor Hugo

Address makes opportunities; the want of it gives them.— Bovee

*He'll suit his bearing to the hour,
Laugh, listen, learn, or teach. —Eliza Cook*

A man who knows the world will not only make the most of everything he does know, but of many things he does not know; and will gain more credit by his adroit mode of hiding his ignorance, than the pedant by his awkward attempt to exhibit his erudition.—Colton

The art of using moderate abilities to advantage wins praise, and often acquires more reputation than actual brilliancy.—Rochefoucauld

*"Tact clinches the bargain,
Sails out of the bay,
Gets the vote in the Senate,
Spite of Webster or Clay."*

"I never will surrender to a nigger," said a Confederate officer, when a colored soldier chased and caught him. "Berry sorry, massa," said the negro, leveling his rifle; "must kill you den; hain't time to go back and git a white man." The officer surrendered.

"When God endowed human beings with brains," says Montesquieu, "he did not intend to guarantee them."

When Abraham Lincoln was running for the legislature the first time, on the platform of the improvement of the Sangamon River, he went to secure the votes of thirty men who were cradling a wheatfield. They asked no questions about internal improvements, but only seemed curious to know whether he had muscle enough to represent them in the legislature. Lincoln took up a cradle and led the gang around the field. The whole thirty voted for him.

"I do not know how it is," said Napoleon in surprise to his cook, "but at whatever hour I call for my breakfast my chicken is always ready and always in good condition." This seemed to him the more strange because sometimes he would breakfast at eight and at other times as late as eleven. "Sire," said the cook, "the reason is, that every quarter of an hour I put a fresh chicken down to roast, so that your Majesty is sure always to have it at perfection."

Talent in this age is no match for tact. We see its failure everywhere. Tact will manipulate one talent so as to get more out of it in a lifetime than ten talents will accomplish without it. "Talent lies abed till noon; tact is up at six." Talent is power, tact is skill. Talent knows what to do, tact knows how to do it.

"Talent is something, but tact is everything. It is not a sixth sense, but it is like the life of all the five. It is the open eye, the quick ear, the judging taste, the keen smell, and lively touch; it is the interpreter of all riddles, the surmounter of all difficulties, the remover of all obstacles."

The world is full of theoretical, one-sided, impractical men, who have turned all the energies of their lives into one faculty until they have developed, not a full-orbed, symmetrical man, but a monstrosity, while all their other faculties have atrophied and died. We often call these one-sided men geniuses, and the world excuses their impractical and almost idiotic conduct in most matters, because they can perform one kind of work that no one else can do as well. A merchant is excused if he is a giant in merchandise, though he may be an imbecile in the drawing-room. Adam Smith could teach the world economy in his "Wealth of Nations," but he could not manage the finances of his own household.

Many great men are very impractical even in the ordinary affairs of life. Isaac Newton could read the secret of creation; but, tired of rising from his chair to open the door for a cat and her kitten, he had two holes cut through the panels for them to pass at will, a large hole for the cat, and a small one for the kitten. Beethoven was a great musician, but he sent three hundred florins to pay for six shirts and half a dozen handkerchiefs. He paid his tailor as large a sum in advance, and yet he was so poor at times that he had only a biscuit and a glass of water for dinner. He did not know enough of business to cut the coupon from a bond when he wanted money, but sold the whole instrument. Dean Swift nearly starved in a country parish where his more practical classmate Stafford became rich. One of Napoleon's marshals understood military tactics as well as his chief, but he did not know men so well, and lacked the other's skill and tact. Napoleon might fall; but, like a cat, he would fall upon his feet.

For his argument in the Florida Case, a fee of one thousand dollars in crisp new bills of large denomination was handed to Daniel Webster as he sat reading in his library. The next day he wished to use some of the money, but could not find any of the bills. Years afterward, as he turned the page of a book, he found a bank-bill without a crease in it. On turning the next leaf he found another, and so on until he took the whole amount lost from the places where he had deposited them thoughtlessly, as he read. Learning of a new issue of gold pieces at the Treasury, he directed his secretary, Charles Lanman, to obtain several hundred dollars' worth. A day or two after he put his hand in his pocket for one, but they were all gone. Webster was at first puzzled, but on reflection remembered that he had given them away, one by one, to friends who seemed to appreciate their beauty.

A professor in mathematics in a New England college, a "book-worm," was asked by his wife to bring home some coffee. "How much will you have?" asked the merchant. "Well, I declare, my wife did not say, but I guess a bushel will do."

Many a great man has been so absent-minded at times as to seem devoid of common-sense.

"The professor is not at home," said his servant who looked out of a window in the dark and failed to recognize Lessing when the latter knocked at his own door in a fit of absent-mindedness. "Oh, very well," replied Lessing. "No matter, I'll call at another time."

Louis Philippe said he was the only sovereign in Europe fit to govern, for he could black his own boots. The world is full of men and women apparently splendidly endowed and highly educated, yet who can scarcely get a living.

Not long ago three college graduates were found working on a sheep farm in Australia, one from Oxford, one from Cambridge, and the other from a German University,—college men tending brutes! Trained to lead men, they drove sheep. The owner of the farm was an ignorant, coarse sheep-raiser. He knew nothing of books or theories, but he knew sheep. His three hired graduates could speak foreign languages and discuss theories of political economy and philosophy, but he could make money. He could talk about nothing but sheep and farm; but he had made a fortune, while the college men could scarcely get a living. Even the University could not supply common sense. It was "culture against ignorance; the college against the ranch; and the ranch beat every time."

Do not expect too much from books. Bacon said that studies "teach not their own use, but that there is a practical wisdom without them, won by observation." The use of books must be found outside their own lids. It was said of a great French scholar: "He was drowned in his talents." Over-culture, without practical experience, weakens a man, and unfits him for real life. Book education alone tends to make a man too critical, too self-conscious, timid, distrustful of his abilities, too fine for the mechanical drudgery of practical life, too highly polished, and too finely cultured for every day use.

The culture of books and colleges refines, yet it is often but an ethical culture, and is gained at the cost of vigor and rugged strength. Book culture alone tends to paralyze the practical faculties. The bookworm loses his individuality; his head is filled with theories and saturated with other men's thoughts. The stamina of the vigorous mind he brought from the farm has evaporated in college; and when he graduates, he is astonished to find that he has lost the power to grapple with men and things, and is therefore out-stripped in the race of life by the boy who has had no chance, but who, in the fierce struggle for existence, has developed hard common sense and practical wisdom. The college graduate often mistakes his crutches for strength. He inhabits an ideal realm where common sense rarely dwells. The world cares little for his theories or his encyclopaedic knowledge. The cry of the age is for practical men.

"We have been among you several weeks," said Columbus to the Indian chiefs; "and, although at first you treated us like friends, you are now jealous of us and are trying to drive us away. You brought us food in plenty every morning, but now you bring very little and the amount is less with each succeeding day. The Great Spirit is angry with you for not doing as you agreed in bringing us provisions. To show his anger he will cause the sun to be in darkness." He knew that there was to be an eclipse of the sun, and told the day and hour it would occur, but the Indians did not believe him, and continued to reduce the supply of food.

On the appointed day the sun rose without a cloud, and the Indians shook their heads, beginning to show signs of open hostility as the hours passed without a shadow on the face of the sun. But at length a dark spot was seen on one margin; and, as it became larger, the natives grew frantic and fell prostrate before Columbus to entreat for help. He retired to his tent, promising to save them, if possible. About the time for the eclipse to pass away, he came out and said that the Great Spirit had pardoned them, and would soon drive away the monster from the sun if they would never offend him again. They readily promised, and when the sun had passed out of the shadow they leaped and danced and sang for joy. Thereafter the Spaniards had all the provisions they needed.

"Common sense," said Wendell Phillips, "bows to the inevitable and makes use of it."

When Caesar stumbled in landing on the beach of Britain, he instantly grasped a handful of sand and held it aloft as a signal of triumph, hiding forever from his followers the ill omen of his threatened fall.

Goethe, speaking of some comparisons that had been instituted between himself and Shakespeare, said: "Shakespeare always hits the right nail on the head at once; but I have to stop and think which is the right nail, before I hit."

It has been said that a few pebbles from a brook in the sling of a David who knows how to send them to the mark are more effective than a Goliath's spear and a Goliath's strength with a Goliath's clumsiness.

"Get ready for the redskins!" shouted an excited man as he galloped up to the log-cabin of the Moore family in Ohio many years ago; "and give me a fresh horse as soon as you can. They killed a family down the river last night, and nobody knows where they'll turn up next!"

"What shall we do?" asked Mrs. Moore, with a pale face. "My husband went away yesterday to buy our winter supplies, and will not be back until morning."

"Husband away? Whew! that's bad! Well, shut up as tight as you can. Cover up your fire, and don't strike a light to-night." Then springing upon the horse the boys had brought, he galloped away to warn other settlers.

Mrs. Moore carried the younger children to the loft of the cabin, and left Obed and Joe to watch, reluctantly yielding the post of danger to them at their urgent request. "They're coming, Joe!" whispered Obed early in the evening, as he saw several shadows moving across the fields. "Stand by that window with the axe, while I get the rifle pointed at this one." Opening the bullet-pouch, he took out a ball, but nearly fainted as he found it was too large for the rifle. His father had taken the wrong pouch. Obed felt around to see if there were any smaller balls in the cupboard, and almost stumbled over a very large pumpkin, one of the two which he and Joe had been using to make Jack-o'-lanterns when the messenger alarmed them. Pulling off his coat, he flung it over the vegetable lantern, made to imitate a gigantic grinning face, with open eyes, nose, and mouth, and with a live coal from the ashes he lighted the candle inside. "They'll sound the war-whoop in a minute, if I give them time," he whispered, as he raised the covered lantern to the window. "Now for it!" he added, pulling the coat away. An unearthly yell greeted the appearance of the grinning monster, and the Indians fled wildly to the woods. "Quick, Joe! Light up the other one! Don't you see that's what scar't 'em so?" demanded Obed; and at the appearance of the second fiery face the savages gave a final yell and vanished in the forest. Mr. Moore and daylight came together, but the Indians did not return.

Thurlow Weed earned his first quarter by carrying a trunk on his back from a sloop in New York harbor to a Broad Street hotel. He had very few chances such as are now open to the humblest boy, but he had tact and intuition. He could read men as an open book, and mold them to his will. He was unselfish. By three presidents whom his tact and shrewdness had helped to elect he was offered the English mission and scores of other important positions, but he invariably declined.

Lincoln selected Weed to attempt the reconciliation of the "New York Herald," which had a large circulation in Europe, and was creating a dangerous public sentiment abroad and at home by its articles in sympathy with the Confederacy. Though Weed and Bennett had not spoken to each other before for thirty years, the very next day after their interview the "Herald" became a strong Union paper. Weed was then sent to Europe to counteract the pernicious influence of secession agents. The emperor of France favored the South. He was very indignant because Charleston harbor had been blockaded, thus shutting off French manufacturers from large supplies of cotton. But Weed's rare tact modified his views, and induced him to change to friendliness the tone of a hostile speech prepared for delivery to the National Assembly. England was working night and day preparing for war when Weed arrived upon the scene, and soon changed largely the current of public sentiment. On his return to America the city of New York extended public thanks to him for his inestimable services. He was equally successful in business, and acquired a fortune of a million dollars.

"Tell me the breadth of this stream," said Napoleon to his chief engineer, as they came to a bridgeless river which the army had to cross. "Sire, I cannot. My scientific instruments are with the army, and we are ten miles ahead of it."

"Measure the width of this stream instantly."—"Sire, be reasonable!"—"Ascertain at once the width of this river, or you shall be deposed."

The engineer drew the cap-piece of his helmet down until the edge seemed just in line between his eye and the opposite bank; then, holding himself carefully erect, he turned on his heel and noticed where the edge seemed to touch the bank on which he stood, which was on the same level as the other. He paced the distance to the point last noted, and said: "This is the approximate width of the stream." He was promoted.

"Mr. Webster," said the mayor of a Western city, when it was learned that the great statesman, although weary with travel, would be delayed for an hour by a failure to make close connections, "allow me to introduce you to Mr. James, one of our most distinguished citizens." "How do you do, Mr. James?" asked Webster mechanically, as he glanced at a thousand people waiting to take his hand. "The truth is, Mr. Webster," replied Mr. James in a most lugubrious tone, "I am not very well." "I hope nothing serious is the matter," thundered the godlike Daniel, in a tone of anxious concern. "Well, I don't know that, Mr. Webster. I think it's rheumatiz, but my wife— "Mr. Webster, this is Mr. Smith," broke in the mayor, leaving poor Mr. James to enjoy his bad health in the pitiless solitude of a crowd. His total want of tact had made him ridiculous.

"Address yourself to the jury, sir," said a judge to a witness who insisted upon imparting his testimony in a confidential tone to the court direct. The man did not understand and continued as before. "Speak to the jury, sir, the men sitting behind you on the raised benches." Turning, the witness bowed low in awkward suavity, and said, "Good-morning, gentlemen."

"What are these?" asked Napoleon, pointing to twelve silver statues in a cathedral. "The twelve Apostles," was the reply. "Take them down," said Napoleon, "melt them, coin them into money, and let them go about doing good, as their Master did."

"I don't think the Proverbs of Solomon show very great wisdom," said a student at Brown University; "I could make as good ones myself." "Very well," replied President Wayland, "bring in two to-morrow morning." He did not bring them.

"Will you lecture for us for fame?" was the telegram young Henry Ward Beecher received from a Young Men's Christian Association in the West.

"Yes, F. A. M. E. Fifty and my expenses," was the answer the shrewd young preacher sent back.

Montaigne tells of a monarch who, on the sudden death of an only child, showed his resentment against Providence by abolishing the Christian religion throughout his dominions for a fortnight.

The triumphs of tact, or common sense, over talent and genius, are seen everywhere. Walpole was an ignorant man, and Charlemagne could hardly write his name so that it could be deciphered; but these giants knew men and things, and possessed that practical wisdom and tact which have ever moved the world.

Tact, like Alexander, cuts the knots it cannot untie, and leads its forces to glorious victory. A practical man not only sees, but seizes the opportunity. There is a certain getting-on quality difficult to describe, but which is the great winner of the prizes of life. Napoleon could do anything in the art of war with his own hands, even to the making of gunpowder. Paul was all things to all men, that he might save some. The palm is among the hardest and least yielding of all woods, yet rather than be deprived of the rays of the life-giving sun in the dense forests of South America, it is said to turn into a creeper, and climb the nearest trunk to the light.

A farmer who could not get a living sold one half of his farm to a young man who made enough money on the half to pay for it and buy the rest. "You have not tact," was his reply, when the old man asked how one could succeed so well where the other had failed.

According to an old custom a Cape Cod minister was called upon in April to make a prayer over a piece of land. "No," said he, when shown the land, "this does not need a prayer; it needs manure."

To see a man as he is you must turn him round and round until you get him at the right angle. Place him in a good light, as you would a picture. The excellences and defects will appear if you get the right angle. How our old schoolmates have changed places in the ranking of actual life! The boy who led his class and was the envy of all has been distanced by the poor dunce who was called slow and stupid, but who had a sort of dull energy in him which enabled him to get on in the world. The class leader had only a theoretical knowledge, and could not cope with the stern realities of the age. Even genius, however rapid its flight, must not omit a single essential detail, and must be willing to work like a horse.

Shakespeare had marvelous tact; he worked everything into his plays. He ground up the king and his vassal, the fool and the fop, the prince and the peasant, the black and the white, the pure and the impure, the simple and the profound, passions and characters, honor and dishonor,—everything within the sweep of his vision he ground up into paint and spread it upon his mighty canvas.

Some people show want of tact in resenting every slight or petty insult, however unworthy their notice. Others make Don Quixote's mistake of fighting a windmill by engaging in controversies with public speakers and editors, who are sure to have the advantage of the final word. One of the greatest elements of strength in the character of Washington was found in his forbearance when unjustly attacked or ridiculed.

Artemus Ward touches this bubble with a pretty sharp-pointed pen.

"It was in a surtin town in Virginny, the Muther of Presidents and things, that I was shaimfully aboozed by a editor in human form. He set my Show up steep, and kalled me the urbane and gentlemunly manager, but when I, fur the purpuss of showin' fair play all round, went to anuther offiss to get my handbills printed, what duz this pussillanermus editor do but change his toon and abooze me like a injun. He sed my wax-wurks was a humbug, and called me a horey-heded itinerent vagabone. I thort at fust Ide pollish him orf ar-lar Beneki Boy, but on reflectin' that he cood pollish me much wuss in his paper, I giv it up; and I wood here take occashun to advise people when they run agin, as they sumtimes will, these miserable papers, to not pay no attenshun to um. Abuv all, don't assault a editer of this kind. It only gives him a notorosity, which is jist what he wants, and don't do you no more good than it would to jump into enny other mudpuddle. Editors are generally fine men, but there must be black sheep in every flock."

John Jacob Astor had practical talent in a remarkable degree. During a storm at sea, on his voyage to America, the other passengers ran about the deck in despair, expecting every minute to go down; but young Astor went below and coolly put on his best suit of clothes, saying that if the ship should founder and he should happen to be rescued, he would at least save his best suit of clothes.

"Their trading talent is bringing the Jews to the front in America as well as in Europe," said a traveler to one of that race; "and it has gained for them an ascendency, at least in certain branches of trade, from which nothing will ever displace them."

"Dey are coming to de vront, most zairtainly," replied his companion; "but vy do you shpeak of deir drading dalent all de time?"

"But don't you regard it as a talent?"

"A dalent? No! It is chenius. I vill dell you what is de difference, in drade, between dalent and chenius. Ven one goes into a man's shtore and manaches to seel him vat he vonts, dat is dalent; but ven annoder man goes into dat man's shtore and sells him vot he don't vont, dat is chenius; and dat is de chenius vot my race has got."

Enamored of Accuracy

"Antonio Stradivari has an eye That winces at false work and loves the true."

Accuracy is the twin brother of honesty.—C. Simmons

Genius is the infinite art of taking pains.—Carlyle

I hate a thing done by halves. If it be right, do it boldly; if it be wrong, leave it undone.—Gilpin

If I were a cobbler, it would be my pride
The best of all cobblers to be;
If I were a tinker, no tinker beside
Should mend an old kettle like me. —Old Song

If a man can write a better book, preach a better sermon, or make a better mouse-trap than his neighbor, though he build his house in the woods, the world will make a beaten path to his door.—Emerson

"Sir, it is a watch which I have made and regulated myself," said George Graham of London to a customer who asked how far he could depend upon its keeping correct time; "take it with you wherever you please. If after seven years you come back to see me, and can tell me there has been a difference of five minutes, I will return you your money." Seven years later the gentleman returned from India. "Sir," said he, "I bring you back your watch."

"I remember our conditions," said Graham. "Let me see the watch. Well, what do you complain of?" "Why," said the man, "I have had it seven years, and there is a difference of more than five minutes."

"Indeed! In that case I return you your money." "I would not part with my watch," said the man, "for ten times the sum I paid for it." "And I would not break my word for any consideration," replied Graham; so he paid the money and took the watch, which he used as a regulator.

He learned his trade of Tampion, the most exquisite mechanic in London, if not in the world, whose name on a timepiece was considered proof positive of its excellence. When a person once asked him to repair a watch upon which his name was fraudulently engraved, Tampion smashed it with a hammer, and handed the astonished customer one of his own master-pieces, saying, "Sir, here is a watch of my making."

Graham invented the "compensating mercury pendulum," the "dead escapement," and the "orrery," none of which have been much improved since. The clock which he made for Greenwich Observatory has been running one hundred and fifty years, yet it needs regulating but once in fifteen months. Tampion and Graham lie in Westminster Abbey, because of the accuracy of their work.

To insure safety, a navigator must know how far he is from the equator, north or south, and how far east or west of some known point, as Greenwich, Paris, or Washington. He could be sure of this knowledge when the sun is shining, if he could have an absolutely accurate timekeeper; but such a thing has not yet been made. In the sixteenth century Spain offered a prize of a thousand crowns for the discovery of an approximately correct method of determining longitude. About two hundred years later the English government offered 5,000 pounds for a chronometer by which a ship six months from home could get her longitude within sixty miles; 7,500 pounds if within forty miles; 10,000 pounds if within thirty miles; and in another clause 20,000 pounds for correctness within thirty miles, a careless repetition.

The watchmakers of the world contested for the prizes, but 1761 came, and they had not been awarded. In that year John Harrison asked for a test of his chronometer. In a trip of one hundred and forty-seven days from Portsmouth to Jamaica and back, it varied less than two minutes, and only four seconds on the outward voyage. In a round trip of one hundred and fifty-six days to Barbadoes, the variation was only fifteen seconds. The 20,000 pounds was paid to the man who had worked and experimented for forty years, and whose hand was as exquisitely delicate in its movement as the mechanism of his chronometer.

"Make me as good a hammer as you know how," said a carpenter to the blacksmith in a New York village before the first railroad was built; "six of us have come to work on the new church, and I've left mine at home." "As good a one as I know how?" asked David Maydole, doubtfully, "but perhaps you don't want to pay for as good a one as I know how to make." "Yes, I do," said the carpenter, "I want a good hammer."

It was indeed a good hammer that he received, the best, probably, that had ever been made. By means of a longer hole than usual, David had wedged the handle in its place so that the head could not fly off, a wonderful improvement in the eyes of the carpenter, who boasted of his prize to his companions. They all came to the shop next day, and each ordered just such a hammer. When the contractor saw the tools, he ordered two for himself, asking that they be made a little better than those of his men. "I can't make any better ones," said Maydole; "when I make a thing, I make it as well as I can, no matter whom it is for."

The storekeeper soon ordered two dozen, a supply unheard of in his previous business career. A New York dealer in tools came to the village to sell his wares, and bought all the storekeeper had, and left a standing order for all the blacksmith could make. David might have grown very wealthy by making goods of the standard already attained; but throughout his long and successful life he never ceased to study still further to perfect his hammers in the minutest detail. They were usually sold without any warrant of excellence, the word "Maydole" stamped on the head being universally considered a guaranty of the best article the world could produce.

Character is power, and is the best advertisement in the world.

"We have no secret," said the manager of an iron works employing thousands of men. "We always try to beat our last batch of rails. That is all the secret we've got, and we don't care who knows it."

"I don't try to see how cheap a machine I can produce, but how good a machine," said the late John C. Whitin, of Northbridge, Mass., to a customer who complained of the high price of some cotton machinery. Business men soon learned what this meant; and when there was occasion to advertise any machinery for sale, New England cotton manufacturers were accustomed to state the number of years it had been in use and add, as an all-sufficient guaranty of Northbridge products, "Whitin make."

"Madam," said the sculptor H. K. Brown, as he admired a statue in alabaster made by a youth in his teens, "this boy has something in him." It was the figure of an Irishman who worked for the Ward family in Brooklyn years ago, and gave with minutest fidelity not merely the man's features and expression, but even the patches in his trousers, the rent in his coat, and the creases in his narrow-brimmed stove-pipe hat. Mr. Brown saw the statue at the house of a lady living at Newburgh-on-the-Hudson. Six years later he invited her brother, J. Q. A. Ward, to become a pupil in his studio. To-day the name of Ward is that of the most prosperous of all Americans sculptors.

"Paint me just as I am, warts and all," said Oliver Cromwell to the artist who, thinking to please the great man, had omitted a mole.

"I can remember when you blacked my father's shoes," said one member of the House of Commons to another in the heat of debate. "True enough," was the prompt reply, "but did I not black them well?"

"It is easy to tell good indigo," said an old lady. "Just take a lump and put it into water, and if it is good, it will either sink or swim, I am not sure which; but never mind, you can try it for yourself."

John B. Gough told of a colored preacher who, wishing his congregation to fresco the recess back of the pulpit, suddenly closed his Bible and said, "There, my bredren, de Gospel will not be dispensed with any more from dis pulpit till de collection am sufficient to fricassee dis abscess."

When troubled with deafness, Wellington consulted a celebrated physician, who put strong caustic into his ear, causing an inflammation which threatened his life. The doctor apologized, expressed great regrets, and said that the blunder would ruin him. "No," said Wellington, "I will never mention it." "But you will allow me to attend you, so that people will not withdraw their confidence?" "No," said the Iron Duke, "that would be lying."

"Father," said a boy, "I saw an immense number of dogs—five hundred, I am sure—in our street, last night." "Surely not so many," said the father. "Well, there were one hundred, I'm quite sure." "It could not be," said the father; "I don't think there are a hundred dogs in our village." "Well, sir, it could not be less than ten: this I am quite certain of." "I will not believe you saw ten even," said the father; "for you spoke as confidently of seeing five hundred as of seeing this smaller number. You have contradicted yourself twice already, and now I cannot believe you." "Well, sir," said the disconcerted boy, "I saw at least our Dash and another one."

We condemn the boy for exaggerating in order to tell a wonderful story; but how much more truthful are they who "never saw it rain so before," or who call day after day the hottest of the summer or the coldest of the winter?

There is nothing which all mankind venerate and admire so much as simple truth, exempt from artifice, duplicity, and design. It exhibits at once a strength of character and integrity of purpose in which all are willing to confide.

To say nice things merely to avoid giving offense; to keep silent rather than speak the truth; to equivocate, to evade, to dodge, to say what is expedient rather than what is truthful; to shirk the truth; to face both ways; to exaggerate; to seem to concur with another's opinions when you do not; to deceive by a glance of the eye, a nod of the head, a smile, a gesture; to lack sincerity; to assume to know or think or feel what you do not—all these are but various manifestations of hollowness and falsehood resulting from want of accuracy.

We find no lying, no inaccuracy, no slipshod business in nature. Roses blossom and crystals form with the same precision of tint and angle to-day as in Eden on the morning of creation. The rose in the queen's garden is not more beautiful, more fragrant, more exquisitely perfect, than that which blooms and blushes unheeded amid the fern-decked brush by the roadside, or in some far-off glen where no human eye ever sees it. The crystal found deep in the earth is constructed with the same fidelity as that formed above ground. Even the tiny snowflake whose destiny is to become an apparently insignificant and a wholly unnoticed part of an enormous bank, assumes its shape of ethereal beauty as faithfully as though preparing for some grand exhibition. Planets rush with dizzy sweep through almost limitless courses, yet return to equinox or solstice at the appointed second, their very movement being "the uniform manifestation of the will of God."

The marvelous resources and growth of America have developed an unfortunate tendency to overstate, overdraw, and exaggerate. It seems strange that there should be so strong a temptation to exaggerate in a country where the truth is more wonderful than fiction. The positive is stronger than the superlative, but we ignore this fact in our speech. Indeed, it is really difficult to ascertain the exact truth in America. How many American fortunes are built on misrepresentation that is needless, for nothing else is half so strong as truth.

"Does the devil lie?" was asked of Sir Thomas Browne. "No, for then even he could not exist." Truth is necessary to permanency.

In Siberia a traveler found men who could see the satellites of Jupiter with the naked eye. These men have made little advance in civilization, yet they are far superior to us in their accuracy of vision. It is a curious fact that not a single astronomical discovery of importance has been made through a large telescope, the men who have advanced our knowledge of that science the most working with ordinary instruments backed by most accurately trained minds and eyes.

A double convex lens three feet in diameter is worth $60,000. Its adjustment is so delicate that the human hand is the only instrument thus far known suitable for giving the final polish, and one sweep of the hand more than is needed, Alvan Clark says, would impair the correctness of the glass. During the test of the great glass which he made for Russia, the workmen turned it a little with their hands. "Wait, boys, let it cool before making another trial," said Clark; "the poise is so delicate that the heat from your hands affects it."

Mr. Clark's love of accuracy has made his name a synonym of exactness the world over.

"No, I can't do it, it is impossible," said Webster, when urged to speak on a question soon to come up, toward the close of a Congressional session. "I am so pressed with other duties that I haven't time to prepare myself to speak upon that theme." "Ah, but, Mr. Webster, you always speak well upon any subject. You never fail." "But that's the very reason," said the orator, "because I never allow myself to speak upon any subject without first making that subject thoroughly my own. I haven't time to do that in this instance. Hence I must refuse."

Rufus Choate would plead before a shoemaker justice of the peace in a petty case with all the fervor and careful attention to detail with which he addressed the United States Supreme Court.

"Whatever is right to do," said an eminent writer, "should be done with our best care, strength, and faithfulness of purpose; we have no scales by which we can weigh our faithfulness to duties, or determine their relative importance in God's eyes. That which seems a trifle to us may be the secret spring which shall move the issues of life and death."

"There goes a man that has been in hell," the Florentines would say when Dante passed, so realistic seemed to them his description of the nether world.

"There is only one real failure in life possible," said Canon Farrar; "and that is, not to be true to the best one knows."

"It is quite astonishing," Grove said of Beethoven, "to find the length of time during which some of the best known instrumental melodies remained in his thoughts till they were finally used, or the crude, vague, commonplace shape in which they were first written down. The more they are elaborated, the more fresh and spontaneous they become."

Leonardo da Vinci would walk across Milan to change a single tint or the slightest detail in his famous picture of the Last Supper. "Every line was then written twice over by Pope," said his publisher Dodsley, of manuscript brought to be copied. Gibbon wrote his memoir nine times, and the first chapters of his history eighteen times. Of one of his works Montesquieu said to a friend: "You will read it in a few hours, but I assure you it has cost me so much labor that it has whitened my hair." He had made it his study by day and his dream by night, the alpha and omega of his aims and objects. "He who does not write as well as he can on every occasion," said George Ripley, "will soon form the habit of not writing well on any occasion."

An accomplished entomologist thought he would perfect his knowledge by a few lessons under Professor Agassiz. The latter handed him a dead fish and told him to use his eyes. Two hours later he examined his new pupil, but soon remarked, "You haven't really looked at the fish yet. You'll have to try again." After a second examination he shook his head, saying, "You do not show that you can use your eyes." This roused the pupil to earnest effort, and he became so interested in things he had never noticed before that he did not see Agassiz when he came for the third examination. "That will do," said the great scientist. "I now see that you can use your eyes."

Reynolds said he could go on retouching a picture forever.

The captain of a Nantucket whaler told the man at the wheel to steer by the North Star, but was awakened towards morning by a request for another star to steer by, as they had "sailed by the other."

Stephen Girard was precision itself. He did not allow those in his employ to deviate in the slightest degree from his iron-clad orders. He believed that no great success is possible without the most rigid accuracy in everything. He did not vary from a promise in the slightest degree. People knew that his word was not "pretty good," but *absolutely* good. He left nothing to chance. Every detail of business was calculated and planned to a nicety. He was as exact and precise even in the smallest trifles as Napoleon; yet his brother merchants attributed his superior success to good luck.

In 1805 Napoleon broke up the great camp he had formed on the shores of the English Channel, and gave orders for his mighty host to defile toward the Danube. Vast and various as were the projects fermenting in his brain, however, he did not content himself with giving the order, and leaving the elaboration of its details to his lieutenants. To details and minutiae which inferior captains would have deemed too microscopic for their notice, he gave such exhaustive attention that before the bugle had sounded for the march he had planned the exact route which every regiment was to follow, the exact day and hour it was to leave that station, and the precise moment when it was to reach its destination. These details, so thoroughly premeditated, were carried out to the letter, and the result of that memorable march was the victory of Austerlitz, which sealed the fate of Europe for ten years.

When a noted French preacher speaks in Notre Dame, the scholars of Paris throng the cathedral to hear his fascinating, eloquent, polished discourses. This brilliant finish is the result of most patient work, as he delivers but five or six sermons a year.

When Sir Walter Scott visited a ruined castle about which he wished to write, he wrote in a notebook the separate names of grasses and wild flowers growing near, saying that only by such means can a writer be natural.

The historian, Macaulay, never allowed a sentence to stand until it was as good as he could make it.

Besides his scrapbooks, Garfield had a large case of some fifty pigeonholes, labeled "Anecdotes," "Electoral Laws and Commissions," "French Spoliation," "General Politics," "Geneva Award," "Parliamentary Decisions," "Public Men," "State Politics," "Tariff," "The Press," "United States History," etc.; every valuable hint he could get being preserved in the cold exactness of black and white. When he chose to make careful preparation on a subject, no other speaker could command so great an array of facts. Accurate people are methodical people, and method means character.

"Am offered 10,000 bushels wheat on your account at $1.00. Shall I buy, or is it too high?" telegraphed a San Francisco merchant to one in Sacramento. "No price too high," came back over the wire instead of "No. Price too high," as was intended. The omission of a period cost the Sacramento dealer $1,000. How many thousands have lost their wealth or lives, and how many frightful accidents have occurred through carelessness in sending messages!

"The accurate boy is always the favored one," said President Tuttle. "Those who employ men do not wish to be on the constant lookout, as though they were rogues or fools. If a carpenter must stand at his journeyman's elbow to be sure his work is right, or if a cashier must run over his bookkeeper's columns, he might as well do the work himself as employ another to do it in that way; and it is very certain that the employer will get rid of such a blunderer as soon as he can."

"If you make a good pin," said a successful manufacturer, "you will earn more than if you make a bad steam-engine."

"There are women," said Fields, "whose stitches always come out, and the buttons they sew on fly off on the mildest provocation; there are other women who use the same needle and thread, and you may tug away at their work on your coat, or waistcoat, and you can't start a button in a generation."

"Carelessness," "indifference," "slouchiness," "slipshod financiering," could truthfully be written over the graves of thousands who have failed in life. How many clerks, cashiers, clergymen, editors, and professors in colleges have lost position and prestige by carelessness and inaccuracy!

"You would be the greatest man of your age, Grattan," said Curran, "if you would buy a few yards of red tape and tie up your bills and papers." Curran realized that methodical people are accurate, and, as a rule, successful.

Bergh tells of a man beginning business who opened and shut his shop regularly at the same hour every day for weeks, without selling two cents' worth, yet whose application attracted attention and paved the way to fortune.

A. T. Stewart was extremely systematic and precise in all his transactions. Method ruled in every department of his store, and for every delinquency a penalty was rigidly enforced. His eye was upon his business in all its ramifications; he mastered every detail and worked hard.

From the time Jonas Chickering began to work for a piano-maker, he was noted for the pains and care with which he did everything. To him there were no trifles in the manufacturing of pianos. Neither time nor labor was of any account to him, compared with accuracy and knowledge. He soon made pianos in a factory of his own. He determined to make an instrument yielding the fullest and richest volume of melody with the least exertion to the player, withstanding atmospheric changes, and preserving its purity and truthfulness of tone. He resolved that each piano should be an improvement upon the one which preceded it; perfection was his aim. To the end of his life he gave the finishing touch to each of his instruments, and would trust it to no one else. He permitted no irregularity in workmanship or sales, and was characterized by simplicity, transparency, and straightforwardness.

He distanced all competitors. Chickering's name was such a power that one piano-maker had his name changed to Chickering by the Massachusetts legislature, and put it on his pianos; but Jonas Chickering sent a petition to the legislature, and the name was changed back. Character has a commercial as well as an ethical value.

Joseph M. W. Turner was intended by his father for a barber, but he showed such a taste for drawing that a reluctant permission was given for him to follow art as a profession. He soon became skilful, but as he lacked means he took anything to do that came in his way, frequently illustrating guide-books and almanacs. But although the pay was very small the work was never careless. His labor was worth several times what he received for it, but the price was increased and work of higher grade given him simply because men seek the services of those who are known to be faithful, and employ them in as lofty work as they seem able to do. And so he toiled upward until he began to employ himself, his work sure of a market at some price, and the price increasing as other men began to get glimpses of the transcendent art revealed in his paintings, an art not fully comprehended even in our day. He surpassed the acknowledged masters in various fields of landscape work, and left matchless studies of natural scenery in lines never before attempted. What Shakespeare is in literature, Turner is in his special field, the greatest name on record.

The demand for perfection in the nature of Wendell Phillips was wonderful. Every word must exactly express the shade of his thought; every phrase must be of due length and cadence; every sentence must be perfectly balanced before it left his lips. Exact precision characterized his style. He was easily the first forensic orator America has produced. The rhythmical fulness and poise of his periods are remarkable.

Alexandre Dumas prepared his manuscript with the greatest care. When consulted by a friend whose article had been rejected by several publishers, he advised him to have it handsomely copied by a professional penman, and then change the title. The advice was taken, and the article eagerly accepted by one of the very publishers who had refused it before. Many able essays have been rejected because of poor penmanship. We must strive after accuracy as we would after wisdom, or hidden treasure or anything we would attain. Determine to form exact business habits. Avoid slipshod financiering as you would the plague. Careless and indifferent habits would soon ruin a millionaire. Nearly every very successful man is accurate and painstaking. Accuracy means character, and character is power.

Do it to a Finish

Years ago a relief lifeboat at New London sprung a leak, and while being repaired a hammer was found in the bottom that had been left there by the builders thirteen years before. From the constant motion of the boat the hammer had worn through the planking, clear down to the plating.

Not long since, it was discovered that a girl had served twenty years for a twenty months' sentence, in a southern prison, because of the mistake of a court clerk who wrote "years" instead of "months" in the record of the prisoner's sentence.

The history of the human race is full of the most horrible tragedies caused by carelessness and the inexcusable blunders of those who never formed the habit of accuracy, of thoroughness, of doing things to a finish.

Multitudes of people have lost an eye, a leg, or an arm, or are otherwise maimed, because dishonest workmen wrought deception into the articles they manufactured, slighted their work, covered up defects and weak places with paint and varnish.

How many have lost their lives because of dishonest work, carelessness, criminal blundering in railroad construction? Think of the tragedies caused by lies packed in car-wheels, locomotives, steamboat boilers, and engines; lies in defective rails, ties, or switches; lies in dishonest labor put into manufactured material by workmen who said it was good enough for the meager wages they got! Because people were not conscientious in their work there were flaws in the steel, which caused the rail or pillar to snap, the locomotive or other machinery to break. The steel shaft broke in mid-ocean, and the lives of a thousand passengers were jeopardized because of somebody's carelessness.

Even before they are completed, buildings often fall and bury the workmen under their ruins, because somebody was careless, dishonest—either employer or employee—and worked lies, deceptions, into the building.

The majority of railroad wrecks, of disasters on land and sea, which cause so much misery and cost so many lives, are the result of carelessness, thoughtlessness, or half-done, botched, blundering work. They are the evil fruit of the low ideals of slovenly, careless, indifferent workers.

Everywhere over this broad earth we see the tragic results of botched work. Wooden legs, armless sleeves, numberless graves, fatherless and motherless homes everywhere speak of somebody's carelessness, somebody's blunders, somebody's habit of inaccuracy. The worst crimes are not punishable by law. Carelessness, slipshodness, lack of thoroughness, are crimes against self, against humanity, that often do more harm than the crimes that make the perpetrator an outcast from society. Where a tiny flaw or the slightest defect may cost a precious life, carelessness is as much a crime as deliberate criminality.

If everybody put his conscience into his work, did it to a complete finish, it would not only reduce the loss of human life, the mangling and maiming of men and women, to a fraction of what it is at present, but it would also give us a higher quality of manhood and womanhood.

Most young people think too much of quantity, and too little of quality in their work. They try to do too much, and do not do it well. They do not realize that the education, the comfort, the satisfaction, the general improvement, and bracing up of the whole man that comes from doing one thing absolutely right, from putting the trade-mark of one's character on it, far outweighs the value that attaches to the doing of a thousand botched or slipshod jobs.

We are so constituted that the quality which we put into our life-work affects everything else in our lives, and tends to bring our whole conduct to the same level. The entire person takes on the characteristics of one's usual way of doing things. The habit of precision and accuracy strengthens the mentality, improves the whole character.

On the contrary, doing things in a loose-jointed, slipshod, careless manner deteriorates the whole mentality, demoralizes the mental processes, and pulls down the whole life.

Every half-done or slovenly job that goes out of your hands leaves its trace of demoralization behind. After slighting your work, after doing a poor job, you are not quite the same man you were before. You are not so likely to try to keep up the standard of your work, not so likely to regard your word as sacred as before.

The mental and moral effect of half doing, or carelessly doing things; its power to drag down, to demoralize, can hardly be estimated because the processes are so gradual, so subtle. No one can respect himself who habitually botches his work, and when self-respect drops, confidence goes with it; and when confidence and self-respect have gone, excellence is impossible.

It is astonishing how completely a slovenly habit will gradually, insidiously fasten itself upon the individual and so change his whole mental attitude as to thwart absolutely his life-purpose, even when he may think he is doing his best to carry it out.

I know a man who was extremely ambitious to do something very distinctive and who had the ability to do it. When he started on his career he was very exact and painstaking. He demanded the best of himself—would not accept his second best in anything. The thought of slighting his work was painful to him, but his mental processes have so deteriorated, and he has become so demoralized by the habit which, after a while, grew upon him, of accepting his second-best, that he now slights his work without a protest, seemingly without being conscious of it. He is to-day doing quite ordinary things, without apparent mortification or sense of humiliation, and the tragedy of it all is, *he does not know why he has failed*!

One's ambition and ideals need constant watching and cultivation in order to keep up to the standards. Many people are so constituted that their ambition wanes and their ideals drop when they are alone, or with careless, indifferent people. They require the constant assistance, suggestion, prodding, or example of others to keep them up to standard.

How quickly a youth of high ideals, who has been well trained in thoroughness, often deteriorates when he leaves home and goes to work for an employer with inferior ideals and slipshod methods!

The introduction of inferiority into our work is like introducing subtle poison into the system. It paralyzes the normal functions. Inferiority is an infection which, like leaven, affects the entire system. It dulls ideals, palsies the aspiring faculty, stupefies the ambition, and causes deterioration all along the line.

The human mechanism is so constituted that whatever goes wrong in one part affects the whole structure. There is a very intimate relation between the quality of the work and the quality of the character. Did you ever notice the rapid decline in a young man's character when he began to slight his work, to shirk, to slip in rotten hours, rotten service?

If you should ask the inmates of our penitentiaries what had caused their ruin, many of them could trace the first signs of deterioration to shirking, clipping their hours, deceiving their employers—to indifferent, dishonest work.

We were made to be honest. Honesty is our normal expression, and any departure from it demoralizes and taints the whole character. Honesty means integrity in everything. It not only means reliability in your word, but also carefulness, accuracy, honesty in your work. It does not mean that if only you will not lie with your lips you may lie and defraud in the quality of your work. Honesty means wholeness, completeness; it means truth in everything—in deed and in word. Merely not to steal another's money or goods is not all there is to honesty. You must not steal another's time, you must not steal his goods or ruin his property by half finishing or botching your work, by blundering through carelessness or indifference. Your contract with your employer means that you will give him your best, and not your second-best.

"What a fool you are," said one workman to another, "to take so much pains with that job, when you don't get much pay for it. 'Get the most money for the least work,' is my rule, and I get twice as much money as you do."

"That may be," replied the other, "but I shall like myself better, I shall think more of myself, and that is more important to me than money."

You will like yourself better when you have the approval of your conscience. That will be worth more to you than any amount of money you can pocket through fraudulent, skimped, or botched work. Nothing else can give you the glow of satisfaction, the electric thrill and uplift which come from a superbly-done job. Perfect work harmonizes with the very principles of our being, because we were made for perfection. It fits our very natures.

Some one has said: "It is a race between negligence and ignorance as to which can make the more trouble."

Many a young man is being kept down by what probably seems a small thing to him—negligence, lack of accuracy. He never quite finishes anything he undertakes; he can not be depended upon to do anything quite right; his work always needs looking over by some one else. Hundreds of clerks and book-keepers are getting small salaries in poor positions today because they have never learned to do things absolutely right.

A prominent business man says that the carelessness, inaccuracy, and blundering of employees cost Chicago one million dollars a day. The manager of a large house in that city, says that he has to station pickets here and there throughout the establishment in order to neutralize the evils of inaccuracy and the blundering habit. One of John Wanamaker's partners says that unnecessary blunders and mistakes cost that firm twenty-five thousand dollars a year. The dead letter department of the Post Office in Washington received in one year seven million pieces of undelivered mail. Of these more than eighty thousand bore no address whatever. A great many of them were from business houses. Are the clerks who are responsible for this carelessness likely to win promotion?

Many an employee who would be shocked at the thought of telling his employer a lie with his lips is lying every day in the quality of his work, in his dishonest service, in the rotten hours he is slipping into it, in shirking, in his indifference to his employer's interests. It is just as dishonest to express deception in poor work, in shirking, as to express it with the lips, yet I have known office-boys, who could not be induced to tell their employer a direct lie, to steal his time when on an errand, to hide away during working hours to smoke a cigarette or take a nap, not realizing, perhaps, that lies can be acted as well as told and that acting a lie may be even worse than telling one.

The man who botches his work, who lies or cheats in the goods he sells or manufactures, is dishonest with himself as well as with his fellow men, and must pay the price in loss of self-respect, loss of character, of standing in his community.

Yet on every side we see all sorts of things selling for a song because the maker put no character, no thought into them. Articles of clothing that look stylish and attractive when first worn, very quickly get out of shape, and hang and look like old, much-worn garments. Buttons fly off, seams give way at the slightest strain, dropped stitches are everywhere in evidence, and often the entire article goes to pieces before it is worn half a dozen times.

Everywhere we see furniture which looks all right, but which in reality is full of blemishes and weaknesses, covered up with paint and varnish. Glue starts at joints, chairs and bedsteads break down at the slightest provocation, castors come off, handles pull out, many things "go to pieces" altogether, even while practically new.

"Made to sell, not for service," would be a good label for the great mass of manufactured articles in our markets to-day.

It is difficult to find anything that is well and honestly made, that has character, individuality and thoroughness wrought into it. Most things are just thrown together. This slipshod, dishonest manufacturing is so general that concerns which turn out products based upon honesty and truth often win for themselves a world-wide reputation and command the highest prices.

There is no other advertisement like a good reputation. Some of the world's greatest manufacturers have regarded their reputation as their most precious possession, and under no circumstances would they allow their names to be put on an imperfect article. Vast sums of money are often paid for the use of a name, because of its great reputation for integrity and square dealing.

There was a time when the names of Graham and Tampion on timepieces were guarantees of the most exquisite workmanship and of unquestioned integrity. Strangers from any part of the world could send their purchase money and order goods from those manufacturers without a doubt that they would be squarely dealt with.

Tampion and Graham lie in Westminster Abbey because of the accuracy of their work—because they refused to manufacture and sell lies.

When you finish a thing you ought to be able to say to yourself: "There, I am willing to stand for that piece of work. It is not pretty well done; it is done as well as I can do it; done to a complete finish. I will stand for that. I am willing to be judged by it."

Never be satisfied with "fairly good," "pretty good," "good enough." Accept nothing short of your best. Put such a quality into your work that anyone who comes across anything you have ever done will see character in it, individuality in it, your trade-mark of superiority upon it. Your reputation is at stake in everything you do, and your reputation is your capital. You cannot afford to do a poor job, to let botched work or anything that is inferior go out of your hands. Every bit of your work, no matter how unimportant or trivial it may seem, should bear your trade-mark of excellence; you should regard every task that goes through your hands, every piece of work you touch, as Tampion regarded every watch that went out of his shop. It must be the very best you can do, the best that human skill can produce.

It is just the little difference between the good and the best that makes the difference between the artist and the artisan. It is just the little touches after the average man would quit that make the master's fame.

Regard your work as Stradivarius regarded his violins, which he "made for eternity," and not one of which was ever known to come to pieces or break. Stradivarius did not need any patent on his violins, for no other violin maker would pay such a price for excellence as he paid; would take such pains to put his stamp of superiority upon his instrument. Every "Stradivarius" now in existence is worth from three to ten thousand dollars, or several times its weight in gold.

Think of the value such a reputation for thoroughness as that of Stradivarius or Tampion, such a passion to give quality to your work, would give you! There is nothing like being enamored of accuracy, being grounded in thoroughness as a life-principle, of always striving for excellence.

No other characteristic makes such a strong impression upon an employer as the habit of painstaking, carefulness, accuracy. He knows that if a youth puts his conscience into his work from principle, not from the standpoint of salary or what he can get for it, but because there is something in him which refuses to accept anything from himself but the best, that he is honest and made of good material.

I have known many instances where advancement hinged upon the little overplus of interest, of painstaking an employee put into his work, on his doing a little better than was expected of him. Employers do not say all they think, but they detect very quickly the earmarks of superiority. They keep their eye on the employee who has the stamp of excellence upon him, who takes pains with his work, who does it to a finish. They know he has a future.

John D. Rockefeller, Jr., says that the "secret of success is to do the common duty uncommonly well." The majority of young people do not see that the steps which lead to the position above them are constructed, little by little, by the faithful performance of the common, humble, every-day duties of the position they are now filling. The thing which you are now doing will unlock or bar the door to promotion.

Many employees are looking for some great thing to happen that will give them an opportunity to show their mettle. "What can there be," they say to themselves, "in this dry routine, in doing these common, ordinary things, to help me along?" But it is the youth who sees a great opportunity hidden in just these simple services, who sees a very uncommon chance in a common situation, a humble position, who gets on in the world. It is doing things a little better than those about you do them; being a little neater, a little quicker, a little more accurate, a little more observant; it is ingenuity in finding new and more progressive ways of doing old things; it is being a little more polite, a little more obliging, a little more tactful, a little more cheerful, optimistic, a little more energetic, helpful, than those about you that attracts the attention of your employer and other employers also.

Many a boy is marked for a higher position by his employer long before he is aware of it himself. It may be months, or it may be a year before the opening comes, but when it does come the one who has appreciated the infinite difference between "good" and "better," between "fairly good" and "excellent," between what others call "good" and the best that can be done, will be likely to get the place.

If there is that in your nature which demands the best and will take nothing less; if you insist on keeping up your standards in everything you do, you will achieve distinction in some line provided you have the persistence and determination to follow your ideal.

But if you are satisfied with the cheap and shoddy, the botched and slovenly, if you are not particular about quality in your work, or in your environment, or in your personal habits, then you must expect to take second place, to fall back to the rear of the procession.

People who have accomplished work worth while have had a very high sense of the way to do things. They have not been content with mediocrity. They have not confined themselves to the beaten tracks; they have never been satisfied to do things just as others do them, but always a little better. They always pushed things that came to their hands a little higher up, a little farther on. It is this little higher up, this little farther on, that counts in the quality of life's work. It is the constant effort to be first-class in everything one attempts that conquers the heights of excellence.

It is said that Daniel Webster made the best chowder in his state on the principle that he would not be second-class in anything. This is a good resolution with which to start out in your career; never to be second-class in anything. No matter what you do, try to do it as well as it can be done. Have nothing to do with the inferior. Do your best in everything; deal with the best; choose the best; live up to your best.

Everywhere we see mediocre or second-class men—perpetual clerks who will never get away from the yardstick; mechanics who will never be anything but bunglers, all sorts of people who will never rise above mediocrity, who will always fill very ordinary positions because they do not take pains, do not put conscience into their work, do not try to be first-class.

Aside from the lack of desire or effort to be first-class, there are other things that help to make second-class men. Dissipation, bad habits, neglect of health, failure to get an education, all make second-class men. A man weakened by dissipation, whose understanding has been dulled, whose growth has been stunted by self-indulgences, is a second-class man, if, indeed, he is not third-class. A man who, through his amusements in his hours of leisure, exhausts his strength and vitality, vitiates his blood, wears his nerves till his limbs tremble like leaves in the wind, is only half a man, and could in no sense be called first-class.

Everybody knows the things that make for second-class characteristics. Boys imitate older boys and smoke cigarettes in order to be "smart." Then they keep on smoking because they have created an appetite as unnatural as it is harmful. Men get drunk for all sorts of reasons; but, whatever the reason, they cannot remain first-class men and drink. Dissipation in other forms is pursued because of pleasure to be derived, but the surest consequence is that of becoming second-class, below the standard of the best men for any purpose.

Every fault you allow to become a habit, to get control over you, helps to make you second-class, and puts you at a disadvantage in the race for honor, position, wealth, and happiness. Carelessness as to health fills the ranks of the inferior. The submerged classes that the economists talk about are those that are below the high-water mark of the best manhood and womanhood. Sometimes they are second-rate or third-rate people because those who are responsible for their being and their care during their minor years were so before them, but more and more is it becoming one's own fault if, all through life, he remains second-class. Education of some sort, and even a pretty good sort, is possible to practically everyone in our land. Failure to get the best education available, whether it be in books or in business training, is sure to relegate one to the ranks of the second-class.

There is no excuse for incompetence in this age of opportunity; no excuse for being second-class when it is possible to be first-class, and when first-class is in demand everywhere.

Second-class things are wanted only when first-class can't be had. You wear first-class clothes if you can pay for them, eat first-class butter, first-class meat, and first-class bread, or, if you don't, you wish you could. Second-class men are no more wanted than any other second-class commodity. They are taken and used when the better article is scarce or is too high-priced for the occasion. For work that really amounts to anything, first-class men are wanted. If you make yourself first-class in anything, no matter what your condition or circumstances, no matter what your race or color, you will be in demand. If you are a king in your calling, no matter how humble it may be, nothing can keep you from success.

The world does not demand that you be a physician, a lawyer, a farmer, or a merchant; but it does demand that whatever you do undertake, you will do it right, will do it with all your might and with all the ability you possess. It demands that you be a master in your line.

When Daniel Webster, who had the best brain of his time, was asked to make a speech on some question at the close of a Congressional session, he replied: "I never allow myself to speak on any subject until I have made it my own. I haven't time to do that in this case, hence, I must refuse to speak on the subject."

Dickens would never consent to read before an audience until he had thoroughly prepared his selection.

Balzac, the great French novelist, sometimes worked a week on a single page.

Macready, when playing before scant audiences in country theaters in England, Ireland, and Scotland, always played as if he were before the most brilliant audiences in the great metropolises of the world.

Thoroughness characterizes all successful men. Genius is the art of taking infinite pains. The trouble with many Americans is that they seem to think they can put any sort of poor, slipshod, half-done work into their careers and get first-class products. They do not realize that all great achievement has been characterized by extreme care, infinite painstaking, even to the minutest detail. No youth can ever hope to accomplish much who does not have thoroughness and accuracy indelibly fixed in his life-habit. Slipshodness, inaccuracy, the habit of half doing things, would ruin the career of a youth with a Napoleon's mind.

If we were to examine a list of the men who have left their mark on the world, we should find that, as a rule, it is not composed of those who were brilliant in youth, or who gave great promise at the outset of their careers, but rather of the plodding young men who, if they have not dazzled by their brilliancy, have had the power of a day's work in them, who could stay by a task until it was done, and well done; who have had grit, persistence, common sense, and honesty.

The thorough boys are the boys that are heard from, and usually from posts far higher up than those filled by the boys who were too "smart" to be thorough. One such boy is Elihu Root, now United States Senator. When he was a boy in the grammar school at Clinton, New York, he made up his mind that anything he had to study he would keep at until he mastered it. Although not considered one of the "bright" boys of the school, his teacher soon found that when Elihu professed to know anything he knew it through and through. He was fond of hard problems requiring application and patience. Sometimes the other boys called him a plodder, but Elihu would only smile pleasantly, for he knew what he was about. On winter evenings, while the other boys were out skating, Elihu frequently remained in his room with his arithmetic or algebra. Mr. Root recently said that if his close application to problems in his boyhood did nothing else for him, it made him careful about jumping at conclusions. To every problem there was only one answer, and patience was the price to be paid for it. Carrying the principle of "doing everything to a finish" into the law, he became one of the most noted members of the New York bar, intrusted with vast interests, and then a member of the President's cabinet.

William Ellery Channing, the great New England divine, who in his youth was hardly able to buy the clothes he needed, had a passion for self-improvement. "I wanted to make the most of myself," he says; "I was not satisfied with knowing things superficially and by halves, but tried to get comprehensive views of what I studied."

The quality which, more than any other, has helped to raise the German people to their present commanding position in the world, is their thoroughness. It is giving young Germans a great advantage over both English and American youths. Every employer is looking for thoroughness, and German employees, owing to their preeminence in this respect, the superiority of their training, and the completeness of their preparation for business, are in great demand to-day in England, especially in banks and large mercantile houses.

As a rule, a German who expects to engage in business takes a four years' course in some commercial school, and after graduation serves three years' apprenticeship without pay, to his chosen business.

Thoroughness and reliability, the German's characteristics, are increasing the power of Germany throughout the civilized world.

Our great lack is want of thoroughness. How seldom you find a young man or woman who is willing to prepare for his life-work! A little education is all they want, a little smattering of books, and then they are ready for business.

"Can't wait," "haven't time to be thorough," is characteristic of our country, and is written on everything—on commerce, on schools, on society, on churches. We can't wait for a high-school, seminary, or college education. The boy can't wait to become a youth, nor the youth to become a man. Young men rush into business with no great reserve of education or drill; of course, they do poor, feverish work, and break down in middle life, while many die of old age in the forties.

Perhaps there is no other country in the world where so much poor work is done as in America. Half-trained medical students perform bungling operations, and butcher their patients, because they are not willing to take time for thorough preparation. Half-trained lawyers stumble through their cases, and make their clients pay for experience which the law school should have given. Half-trained clergymen bungle away in the pulpit, and disgust their intelligent and cultured parishioners. Many an American youth is willing to stumble through life half prepared for his work, and then blame society because he is a failure.

A young man, armed with letters of introduction from prominent men, one day presented himself before Chief Engineer Parsons, of the Rapid Transit Commission of New York as a candidate for a position. "What can you do? Have you any specialty?" asked Mr. Parsons. "I can do almost anything," answered the young man. "Well," remarked the Chief Engineer, rising to end the interview, "I have no use for anyone who can 'almost' do anything. I prefer someone who can actually do one thing thoroughly."

There is a great crowd of human beings just outside the door of proficiency. They can half do a great many things, but can't do any one thing well, to a finish. They have acquisitions which remain permanently unavailable because they were not carried quite to the point of skill; they stopped just short of efficiency. How many people almost know a language or two, which they can neither write nor speak; a science or two, whose elements they have not fully mastered; an art or two, which they can not practise with satisfaction or profit!

The Patent Office at Washington contains hundreds,—yes, thousands,—of inventions which are useless simply because they are not quite practical, because the men who started them lacked the staying quality, the education, or the ability necessary to carry them to the point of practicability.

The world is full of half-finished work,—failures which require only a little more persistence, a little finer mechanical training, a little better education, to make them useful to civilization. Think what a loss it would be if such men as Edison and Bell had not come to the front and carried to a successful termination the half-finished work of others!

Make it a life-rule to give your best to whatever passes through your hands. Stamp it with your manhood. Let superiority be your trade-mark, let it characterize everything you touch. This is what every employer is looking for. It indicates the best kind of brain; it is the best substitute for genius; it is better capital than cash; it is a better promoter than friends, or "pulls" with the influential.

A successful manufacturer says: "If you make a good pin, you will earn more money than if you make a bad steam engine." "If a man can write a better book, preach a better sermon, or make a better mousetrap than his neighbor," says Emerson, "though he build his house in the woods, the world will make a path to his door."

Never allow yourself to dwell too much upon what you are getting for your work. You have something of infinitely greater importance, greater value, at stake. Your honor, your whole career, your future success, will be affected by the way you do your work, by the conscience or lack of it which you put into your job. Character, manhood and womanhood are at stake, compared with which salary is nothing.

Everything you do is a part of your career. If any work that goes out of your hands is skimped, shirked, bungled, or botched, your character will suffer. If your work is badly done; if it goes to pieces; if there is shoddy or sham in it; if there is dishonesty in it, there is shoddy, sham, dishonesty in your character. We are all of a piece. We cannot have an honest character, a complete, untarnished career, when we are constantly slipping rotten hours, defective material and slipshod service into our work.

The man who has dealt in shams and inferiority, who has botched his work all his life, must be conscious that he has not been a real man; he can not help feeling that his career has been a botched one.

To spend a life buying and selling lies, dealing in cheap, shoddy shams, or botching one's work, is demoralizing to every element of nobility.

Beecher said he was never again quite the same man after reading Ruskin. You are never again quite the same man after doing a poor job, after botching your work. You cannot be just to yourself and unjust to the man you are working for in the quality of your work, for, if you slight your work, you not only strike a fatal blow at your efficiency, but also smirch your character. If you would be a full man, a complete man, a just man, you must be honest to the core in the quality of your work.

No one can be really happy who does not believe in his own honesty. We are so constituted that every departure from the right, from principle, causes loss of self-respect, and makes us unhappy.

Every time we obey the inward law of doing right we hear an inward approval, the amen of the soul, and every time we disobey it, a protest or condemnation.

There is everything in holding a high ideal of your work, for whatever model the mind holds, the life copies. Whatever your vocation, let quality be your life-slogan.

A famous artist said he would never allow himself to look at an inferior drawing or painting, to do anything that was low or demoralizing, lest familiarity with it should taint his own ideal and thus be communicated to his brush.

Many excuse poor, slipshod work on the plea of lack of time. But in the ordinary situations of life there is plenty of time to do everything as it ought to be done.

There is an indescribable superiority added to the character and fiber of the man who always and everywhere puts quality into his work. There is a sense of wholeness, of satisfaction, of happiness, in his life which is never felt by the man who does not do his level best every time. He is not haunted by the ghosts or tail ends of half-finished tasks, of skipped problems; is not kept awake by a troubled conscience.

When we are trying with all our might to do our level best, our whole nature improves. Everything looks down when we are going down hill. Aspiration lifts the life; groveling lowers it.

Don't think you will never hear from a half-finished job, a neglected or botched piece of work. It will never die. It will bob up farther along in your career at the most unexpected moments, in the most embarrassing situations. It will be sure to mortify you when you least expect it. Like Banquo's ghost, it will arise at the most unexpected moments to mar your happiness. A single broken thread in a web of cloth is traced back to the girl who neglected her work in the factory, and the amount of damage is deducted from her wages.

Thousands of people are held back all their lives and obliged to accept inferior positions because they cannot entirely overcome the handicap of slipshod habits formed early in life, habits of inaccuracy, of slovenliness, of skipping difficult problems in school, of slurring their work, shirking, or half doing it. "Oh, that's good enough, what's the use of being so awfully particular?" has been the beginning of a life-long handicap in many a career.

I was much impressed by this motto, which I saw recently in a great establishment, *"Where Only the Best Is Good Enough."* What a life-motto this would be! How it would revolutionize civilization if everyone were to adopt it and use it; to resolve that, whatever they did only the best they could do would be good enough, would satisfy them!

Adopt this motto as yours. Hang it up in your bedroom, in your office or place of business, put it into your pocket-book, weave it into the texture of everything you do, and your life-work will be what every one's should be—A Masterpiece

The Reward of Persistence

Every noble work is at first impossible.—Carlyle

Victory belongs to the most persevering.—Napoleon

Success in most things depends on knowing how long it takes to succeed.—Montesquieu

Perpetual pushing and assurance put a difficulty out of countenance, and make a seeming impossibility give way.—Jeremy Collier

"Unstable as water, thou shalt not excel."
The nerve that never relaxes, the eye that never blanches, the thought that never wanders, these are the masters of victory.—Burke

"The pit rose at me!" exclaimed Edmund Kean in a wild tumult of emotion, as he rushed home to his trembling wife. "Mary, you shall ride in your carriage yet, and Charles shall go to Eton!" He had been so terribly in earnest with the study of his profession that he had at length made a mark on his generation. He was a little dark man with a voice naturally harsh, but he determined, when young, to play the character of Sir Giles Overreach, in Massinger's drama, as no other man had ever played it. By a persistency that nothing seemed able to daunt, he so trained himself to play the character that his success, when it did come, was overwhelming, and all London was at his feet.

"I am sorry to say that I don't think this is in your line," said Woodfall the reporter, after Sheridan had made his first speech in Parliament. "You would better have stuck to your former pursuits." With head on his hand Sheridan mused for a time, then looked up and said, "It is in me, and it shall come out of me." From the same man came that harangue against Warren Hastings which the orator Fox called the best speech ever made in the House of Commons.

"I had no other books than heaven and earth, which are open to all," said Bernard Palissy, who left his home in the south of France in 1828, at the age of eighteen. Though only a glass-painter, he had the soul of an artist. The sight of an elegant Italian cup disturbed his whole existence and from that moment the determination to discover the enamel with which it was glazed possessed him like a passion. For months and years he tried all kinds of experiments to learn the materials of which the enamel was compounded. He built a furnace, which was a failure, and then a second, burning so much wood, spoiling so many drugs and pots of common earthenware, and losing so much time, that poverty stared him in the face, and he was forced, from lack of ability to buy fuel, to try his experiments in a common furnace. Flat failure was the result, but he decided on the spot to begin all over again, and soon had three hundred pieces baking, one of which came out covered with beautiful enamel.

To perfect his invention he next built a glass-furnace, carrying the bricks on his back. At length the time came for a trial; but, though he kept the heat up six days, his enamel would not melt. His money was all gone, but he borrowed some, and bought more pots and wood, and tried to get a better flux. When next he lighted his fire, he attained no result until his fuel was gone. Tearing off the palings of his garden fence, he fed them to the flames, but in vain. His furniture followed to no purpose. The shelves of his pantry were then broken up and thrown into the furnace; and the great burst of heat melted the enamel. The grand secret was learned. Persistence had triumphed again.

"If you work hard two weeks without selling a book," wrote a publisher to an agent, "you will make a success of it."

"Know thy work and do it," said Carlyle; "and work at it like a Hercules."

"Whoever is resolved to excel in painting, or, indeed, in any other art," said Reynolds, "must bring all his mind to bear upon that one object from the moment that he rises till he goes to bed."

"I have no secret but hard work," said Turner, the painter.

"The man who is perpetually hesitating which of two things he will do first," said William Wirt, "will do neither. The man who resolves, but suffers his resolution to be changed by the first counter-suggestion of a friend—who fluctuates from opinion to opinion, from plan to plan, and veers like a weather-cock to every point of the compass, with every breath of caprice that blows,—can never accomplish anything great or useful. Instead of being progressive in anything, he will be at best stationary, and, more probably, retrograde in all."

Perseverance built the pyramids on Egypt's plains, erected the gorgeous temple at Jerusalem, inclosed in adamant the Chinese Empire, scaled the stormy, cloud-capped Alps, opened a highway through the watery wilderness of the Atlantic, leveled the forests of the new world, and reared in its stead a community of states and nations. Perseverance has wrought from the marble block the exquisite creations of genius, painted on canvas the gorgeous mimicry of nature, and engraved on a metallic surface the viewless substance of the shadow. Perseverance has put in motion millions of spindles, winged as many flying shuttles, harnessed thousands of iron steeds to as many freighted cars, and set them flying from town to town and nation to nation, tunneled mountains of granite, and annihilated space with the lightning's speed. It has whitened the waters of the world with the sails of a hundred nations, navigated every sea and explored every land. It has reduced nature in her thousand forms to as many sciences, taught her laws, prophesied her future movements, measured her untrodden spaces, counted her myriad hosts of worlds, and computed their distances, dimensions, and velocities.

The slow penny is surer than the quick dollar. The slow trotter will out-travel the fleet racer. Genius darts, flutters, and tires; but perseverance wears and wins. The all-day horse wins the race. The afternoon-man wears off the laurels. The last blow drives home the nail.

"Are your discoveries often brilliant intuitions?" asked a reporter of Thomas A. Edison. "Do they come to you while you are lying awake nights?"

"I never did anything worth doing by accident," was the reply, "nor did any of my inventions come indirectly through accident, except the phonograph. No, when I have fully decided that a result is worth getting I go ahead on it and make trial after trial until it comes. I have always kept strictly within the lines of commercially useful inventions. I have never had any time to put on electrical wonders, valuable simply as novelties to catch the popular fancy. *I like it*," continued the great inventor. "I don't know any other reason. Anything I have begun is always on my mind, and I am not easy while away from it until it is finished."

A man who thus gives himself wholly to his work is certain to accomplish something; and if he have ability and common sense, his success will be great.

How Bulwer wrestled with the fates to change his apparent destiny! His first novel was a failure; his early poems were failures; and his youthful speeches provoked the ridicule of his opponents. But he fought his way to eminence through ridicule and defeat.

Gibbon worked twenty years on his "Decline and Fall of the Roman Empire." Noah Webster spent thirty-six years on his dictionary. What a sublime patience he showed in devoting a life to the collection and definition of words! George Bancroft spent twenty-six years on his "History of the United States." Newton rewrote his "Chronology of Ancient Nations" fifteen times. Titian wrote to Charles V.: "I send your majesty the Last Supper, after working on it almost daily for seven years." He worked on his Pietro Martyn eight years. George Stephenson was fifteen years perfecting his locomotive; Watt, twenty years on his condensing engine. Harvey labored eight long years before he published his discovery of the circulation of the blood. He was then called a crack-brained impostor by his fellow physicians. Amid abuse and ridicule he waited twenty-five years before his great discovery was recognized by the profession.

Newton discovered the law of gravitation before he was twenty-one, but one slight error in a measurement of the earth's circumference interfered with a demonstration of the correctness of his theory. Twenty years later he corrected the error, and showed that the planets roll in their orbits as a result of the same law which brings an apple to the ground.

Sothern, the great actor, said that the early part of his theatrical career was spent in getting dismissed for incompetency.

"Never depend upon your genius," said John Ruskin, in the words of Joshua Reynolds; "if you have talent, industry will improve it; if you have none, industry will supply the deficiency."

Savages believe that when they conquer an enemy, his spirit enters into them, and fights for them ever afterwards. So the spirit of our conquests enters us, and helps us to win the next victory.

Blücher may have been routed at Ligny yesterday, but to-day you hear the thunder of his guns at Waterloo hurling dismay and death among his former conquerors.

Opposing circumstances create strength. Opposition gives us greater power of resistance. To overcome one barrier gives us greater ability to overcome the next.

In February, 1492, a poor gray-haired man, his head bowed with discouragement almost to the back of his mule, rode slowly out through the beautiful gateway of the Alhambra. From boyhood he had been haunted with the idea that the earth is round. He believed that the piece of carved wood picked up four hundred miles at sea and the bodies of two men unlike any other human beings known, found on the shores of Portugal, had drifted from unknown lands in the west. But his last hope of obtaining aid for a voyage of discovery had failed. King John of Portugal, while pretending to think of helping him, had sent out secretly an expedition of his own.

He had begged bread, drawn maps and charts to keep from starving; he had lost his wife; his friends had called him crazy, and forsaken him. The council of wise men called by Ferdinand and Isabella ridiculed his theory of reaching the east by sailing west.

"But the sun and moon are round," said Columbus, "why not the earth?"

"If the earth is a ball, what holds it up?" asked the wise men.

"What holds the sun and moon up?" inquired Columbus.

"But how can men walk with their heads hanging down, and their feet up, like flies on a ceiling?" asked a learned doctor; "how can trees grow with their roots in the air?"

"The water would run out of the ponds and we should fall off," said another philosopher.

"This doctrine is contrary to the Bible, which says, 'The heavens are stretched out like a tent:'—of course it is flat; it is rank heresy to say it is round," said a priest.

Columbus left the Alhambra in despair, intending to offer his services to Charles VII., but he heard a voice calling his name. An old friend had told Isabella that it would add great renown to her reign at a trifling expense if what the sailor believed should prove true. "It shall be done," said Isabella, "I will pledge my jewels to raise the money. Call him back."

Columbus turned and with him turned the world. Not a sailor would go voluntarily; so the king and queen compelled them. Three days out, in his vessels scarcely larger than fishing-schooners, the *Pinta* floated a signal of distress for a broken rudder. Terror seized the sailors, but Columbus calmed their fears with pictures of gold and precious stones from India. Two hundred miles west of the Canaries, the compass ceased to point to the North Star. The sailors are ready to mutiny, but he tells them the North Star is not exactly north. Twenty-three hundred miles from home, though he tells them it is but seventeen hundred, a bush with berries floats by, land birds fly near, and they pick up a piece of wood curiously carved. On October 12, Columbus raised the banner of Castile over the western world.

"How hard I worked at that tremendous shorthand, and all improvement appertaining to it," said Dickens. "I will only add to what I have already written of my perseverance at this time of my life, and of a patient and continuous energy which then began to be matured."

Cyrus W. Field had retired from business with a large fortune when he became possessed with the idea that by means of a cable laid upon the bottom of the Atlantic Ocean, telegraphic communication could be established between Europe and America. He plunged into the undertaking with all the force of his being. The preliminary work included the construction of a telegraph line one thousand miles long, from New York to St. John's, Newfoundland. Through four hundred miles of almost unbroken forest they had to build a road as well as a telegraph line across Newfoundland. Another stretch of one hundred and forty miles across the island of Cape Breton involved a great deal of labor, as did the laying of a cable across the St. Lawrence.

By hard work he secured aid for his company from the British government, but in Congress he encountered such bitter opposition from a powerful lobby that his measure only had a majority of one in the Senate. The cable was loaded upon the *Agamemnon*, the flag ship of the British fleet at Sebastopol, and upon the *Niagara*, a magnificent new frigate of the United States Navy; but, when five miles of cable had been paid out, it caught in the machinery and parted. On the second trial, when two hundred miles at sea, the electric current was suddenly lost, and men paced the decks nervously and sadly, as if in the presence of death. Just as Mr. Field was about to give the order to cut the cable, the current returned as quickly and mysteriously as it had disappeared. The following night, when the ship was moving but four miles an hour and the cable running out at the rate of six miles, the brakes were applied too suddenly just as the steamer gave a heavy lurch, breaking the cable.

Field was not the man to give up. Seven hundred miles more of cable were ordered, and a man of great skill was set to work to devise a better machine for paying out the long line. American and British inventors united in making a machine. At length in mid-ocean the two halves of the cable were spliced and the steamers began to separate, the one headed for Ireland, the other for Newfoundland, each running out the precious thread, which, it was hoped, would bind two continents together. Before the vessels were three miles apart, the cable parted. Again it was spliced, but when the ships were eighty miles apart, the current was lost. A third time the cable was spliced and about two hundred miles paid out, when it parted some twenty feet from the *Agamemnon*, and the vessels returned to the coast of Ireland.

Directors were disheartened, the public skeptical, capitalists were shy, and but for the indomitable energy and persuasiveness of Mr. Field, who worked day and night almost without food or sleep, the whole project would have been abandoned. Finally a third attempt was made, with such success that the whole cable was laid without a break, and several messages were flashed through nearly seven hundred leagues of ocean, when suddenly the current ceased.

Faith now seemed dead except in the breast of Cyrus W. Field, and one or two friends, yet with such persistence did they work that they persuaded men to furnish capital for yet another trial even against what seemed their better judgment. A new and superior cable was loaded upon the *Great Eastern*, which steamed slowly out to sea, paying out as she advanced. Everything worked to a charm until within six hundred miles of Newfoundland, when the cable snapped and sank. After several attempts to raise it, the enterprise was abandoned for a year.

Not discouraged by all these difficulties, Mr. Field went to work with a will, organized a new company, and made a new cable far superior to anything before used, and on July 13, 1866, was begun the trial which ended with the following message sent to New York:—

"*Heart's Content*, July 27.
"We arrived here at nine o'clock this morning. All well. Thank God! the cable is laid and is in perfect working order.
"Cyrus W. Field."

The old cable was picked up, spliced, and continued to Newfoundland, and the two are still working, with good prospects for usefulness for many years.

In Revelation we read: "He that overcometh, I will give him to sit down with me on my throne."

Successful men, it is said, owe more to their perseverance than to their natural powers, their friends, or the favorable circumstances around them. Genius will falter by the side of labor, great powers will yield to great industry. Talent is desirable, but perseverance is more so.

"How long did it take you to learn to play?" asked a young man of Geradini. "Twelve hours a day for twenty years," replied the great violinist. Lyman Beecher when asked how long it took him to write his celebrated sermon on the "Government of God," replied, "About forty years."

A Chinese student, discouraged by repeated failures, had thrown away his book in despair, when he saw a poor woman rubbing an iron bar on a stone to make a needle. This example of patience sent him back to his studies with a new determination, and he became one of the three greatest scholars of China.

Malibran said: "If I neglect my practice a day, I see the difference in my execution; if for two days, my friends see it; and if for a week, all the world knows my failure." Constant, persistent struggle she found to be the price of her marvelous power.

When an East India boy is learning archery, he is compelled to practise three months drawing the string to his ear before he is allowed to touch an arrow.

Benjamin Franklin had this tenacity of purpose in a wonderful degree. When he started in the printing business in Philadelphia, he carried his material through the streets on a wheelbarrow. He hired one room for his office, work-room, and sleeping-room. He found a formidable rival in the city and invited him to his room. Pointing to a piece of bread from which he had just eaten his dinner, he said: "Unless you can live cheaper than I can you can not starve me out."

All are familiar with the misfortune of Carlyle while writing his "History of the French Revolution." After the first volume was ready for the press, he loaned the manuscript to a neighbor who left it lying on the floor, and the servant girl took it to kindle the fire. It was a bitter disappointment, but Carlyle was not the man to give up. After many months of poring over hundreds of volumes of authorities and scores of manuscripts, he reproduced that which had burned in a few minutes.

Audubon, the naturalist, had spent two years with his gun and note-book in the forests of America, making drawings of birds. He nailed them all up securely in a box and went off on a vacation. When he returned he opened the box only to find a nest of Norwegian rats in his beautiful drawings. Every one was ruined. It was a terrible disappointment, but Audubon took his gun and note-book and started for the forest. He reproduced his drawings, and they were even better than the first.

When Dickens was asked to read one of his selections in public he replied that he had not time, for he was in the habit of reading the same piece every day for six months before reading it in public. "My own invention," he says, "such as it is, I assure you, would never have served me as it has but for the habit of commonplace, humble, patient, toiling attention."

Addison amassed three volumes of manuscript before he began the "Spectator."

Everyone admires a determined, persistent man. Marcus Morton ran sixteen times for governor of Massachusetts. At last his opponents voted for him from admiration of his pluck, and he was elected by a majority of one! Such persistence always triumphs.

Webster declared that when a pupil at Phillips Exeter Academy he never could declaim before the school. He said he committed piece after piece and rehearsed them in his room, but when he heard his name called in the academy and all eyes turned towards him the room became dark and everything he ever knew fled from his brain; but he became the great orator of America. Indeed, it is doubtful whether Demosthenes himself surpassed his great reply to Hayne in the United States Senate. Webster's tenacity was illustrated by a circumstance which occurred in the academy. The principal punished him for shooting pigeons by compelling him to commit one hundred lines of Vergil. He knew the principal was to take a certain train that afternoon, so he went to his room and learned seven hundred lines. He went to recite them to the principal just before train time. After repeating the hundred lines he continued until he had recited two hundred. The principal anxiously looked at his watch and grew nervous, but Webster kept right on. The principal finally stopped him and asked him how many more he had learned. "About five hundred more," said Webster, continuing to recite.

"You can have the rest of the day for pigeon-shooting," said the principal.

Great writers have ever been noted for their tenacity of purpose. Their works have not been flung off from minds aglow with genius, but have been elaborated and elaborated into grace and beauty, until every trace of their efforts has been obliterated.

Bishop Butler worked twenty years incessantly on his "Analogy," and even then was so dissatisfied that he wanted to burn it. Rousseau says he obtained the ease and grace of his style only by ceaseless inquietude, by endless blotches and erasures. Vergil worked eleven years on the Aeneid. The note-books of great men like Hawthorne and Emerson are tell-tales of the enormous drudgery, of the years put into a book which may be read in an hour. Montesquieu was twenty-five years writing his "Esprit des Lois," yet you can read it in sixty minutes. Adam Smith spent ten years on his "Wealth of Nations." A rival playwright once laughed at Euripides for spending three days on three lines, when he had written five hundred lines. "But your five hundred lines in three days will be dead and forgotten, while my three lines will live forever," he replied.

Ariosto wrote his "Description of a Tempest" in sixteen different ways. He spent ten years on his "Orlando Furioso," and only sold one hundred copies at fifteen pence each. The proof of Burke's "Letters to a Noble Lord" (one of the sublimest things in all literature) went back to the publisher so changed and blotted with corrections that the printer absolutely refused to correct it, and it was entirely reset. Adam Tucker spent eighteen years on the "Light of Nature." Thoreau's New England pastoral, "A Week on the Concord and Merrimac Rivers," was an entire failure. Seven hundred of the one thousand copies printed were returned from the publishers. Thoreau wrote in his diary: "I have some nine hundred volumes in my library, seven hundred of which I wrote myself." Yet he took up his pen with as much determination as ever.

The rolling stone gathers no moss. The persistent tortoise outruns the swift but fickle hare. An hour a day for twelve years more than equals the time given to study in a four years' course at a high school. The reading and re-reading of a single volume has been the making of many a man. "Patience," says Bulwer "is the courage of the conqueror; it is the virtue *par excellence*, of Man against Destiny—of the One against the World, and of the Soul against Matter. Therefore, this is the courage of the Gospel; and its importance in a social view—its importance to races and institutions—cannot be too earnestly inculcated."

Want of constancy is the cause of many a failure, making the millionaire of to-day a beggar to-morrow. Show me a really great triumph that is not the reward of persistence. One of the paintings which made Titian famous was on his easel eight years; another, seven. How came popular writers famous? By writing for years without any pay at all; by writing hundreds of pages as mere practise-work; by working like galley-slaves at literature for half a lifetime with no other compensation than—fame.

"Never despair," says Burke; "but if you do, work on in despair."

The head of the god Hercules is represented as covered with a lion's skin with claws joined under the chin, to show that when we have conquered our misfortunes, they become our helpers. Oh, the glory of an unconquerable will!

Nerve—Grip, Pluck

"Never give up; for the wisest is boldest,
Knowing that Providence mingles the cup;
And of all maxims, the best, as the oldest,
Is the stern watchword of 'Never give up!'"
Be firm; one constant element of luck
Is genuine, solid, old Teutonic pluck.
Stick to your aim; the mongrel's hold will slip,
But only crowbars loose the bulldog's grip;
Small though he looks, the jaw that never yields
Drags down the bellowing monarch of the fields! —Holmes

"Soldiers, you are Frenchmen," said Napoleon, coolly walking among his disaffected generals when they threatened his life in the Egyptian campaign; "you are too many to assassinate, and too few to intimidate me." "How brave he is!" exclaimed the ringleader, as he withdrew, completely cowed.

"General Taylor never surrenders," said old "Rough and Ready" at Buena Vista, when Santa Anna with 20,000 men offered him a chance to save his 4,000 soldiers by capitulation. The battle was long and desperate, but at length the Mexicans were glad to avoid further defeat by flight. When Lincoln was asked how Grant impressed him as a general, he replied, "The greatest thing about him is cool persistency of purpose. He has the grip of a bulldog; when he once gets his teeth in, nothing can shake him off." It was "On to Richmond," and "I propose to fight it out on this line if it takes all summer," that settled the fate of the Rebellion.

"My sword is too short," said a Spartan youth to his father. "Add a step to it, then," was the only reply.

It is said that the snapping-turtle will not release his grip, even after his head is cut off. He is resolved, if he dies, to die hard. It is just such grit that enables men to succeed, for what is called luck is generally the prerogative of valiant souls. It is the final effort that brings victory. It is the last pull of the oar, with clenched teeth and knit muscles, that shows what Oxford boatmen call "the beefiness of the fellow."

After Grant's defeat at the first battle of Shiloh, nearly every newspaper of both parties in the North, almost every member of Congress, and public sentiment everywhere demanded his removal. Friends of the President pleaded with him to give the command to some one else, for his own sake as well as for the good of the country. Lincoln listened for hours one night, speaking only at rare intervals to tell a pithy story, until the clock struck one. Then, after a long silence, he said: "I can't spare this man. He fights." It was Lincoln's marvelous insight and sagacity that saved Grant from the storm of popular passion, and gave us the greatest hero of the Civil War.

It is this keeping right on that wins in the battle of life.

Grant never looked backward. Once, after several days of hard fighting without definite result, he called a council of war. One general described the route by which he would retreat, another thought it better to retire by a different road, and general after general told how he would withdraw, or fall back, or seek a more favorable position in the rear. At length all eyes were turned upon Grant, who had been a silent listener for hours. He rose, took a bundle of papers from an inside pocket, handed one to each general, and said: "Gentlemen, at dawn you will execute those orders." Every paper gave definite directions for an advance, and with the morning sun the army moved forward to victory.

Massena's army of 18,000 men in Genoa had been reduced by fighting and famine to 8,000. They had killed and captured more than 15,000 Austrians, but their provisions were completely exhausted; starvation stared them in the face; the enemy outnumbered them four to one, and they seemed at the mercy of their opponents. General Ott demanded a discretionary surrender, but Massena replied: "My soldiers must be allowed to march out with colors flying, and arms and baggage; not as prisoners of war, but free to fight when and where we please. If you do not grant this, I will sally forth from Genoa sword in hand. With eight thousand famished men I will attack your camp, and I will fight till I cut my way through it." Ott knew the temper of the great soldier, and agreed to accept the terms if he would surrender himself, or if he would depart by sea so as not to be quickly joined by reinforcements. Massena's only reply was: "Take my terms, or I will cut my way through your army." Ott at last agreed, when Massena said: "I give you notice that ere fifteen days are passed I shall be once more in Genoa," and he kept his word.

Napoleon said of this man, who was orphaned in infancy and cast upon the world to make his own way in life: "When defeated, Massena was always ready to fight a battle over again, as though he had been the conqueror."

"The battle is completely lost," said Desaix, looking at his watch, when consulted by Napoleon at Marengo; "but it is only two o'clock, and we shall have time to gain another." He then made his famous cavalry charge, and won the field, although a few minutes before the French soldiers all along the line were momentarily expecting an order to retreat.

"Well," said Barnum to a friend in 1841, "I am going to buy the American Museum." "Buy it!" exclaimed the astonished friend, who knew that the showman had not a dollar; "what do you intend buying it with?" "Brass," was the prompt reply, "for silver and gold have I none."

Everyone interested in public entertainments in New York knew Barnum, and knew the condition of his pocket; but Francis Olmstead, who owned the Museum building, consulted numerous references all telling of "a good showman, who would do as he agreed," and accepted a proposition to give security for the purchaser. Mr. Olmstead was to appoint a money-taker at the door, and credit Barnum towards the purchase with all above expenses and an allowance of fifty dollars per month to support his wife and three children. Mrs. Barnum assented to the arrangement, and offered to cut down the household expenses to a little more than a dollar a day. Six months later Mr. Olmstead entered the ticket-office at noon, and found Barnum eating for dinner a few slices of bread and some corned beef. "Is this the way you eat your dinner?" he asked.

"I have not eaten a warm dinner since I bought the Museum, except on the Sabbath; and I intend never to eat another until I get out of debt." "Ah! you are safe, and will pay for the Museum before the year is out," said Mr. Olmstead, slapping the young man approvingly on the shoulder. He was right, for in less than a year Barnum had paid every cent out of the profits of the establishment.

"Hard pounding, gentlemen," said Wellington at Waterloo to his officers, "but we will see who can pound the longest."

"It is very kind of them to 'sand' our letters for us," said young Junot coolly, as an Austrian shell scattered earth over the dispatch he was writing at the dictation of his commander-in-chief. The remark attracted Napoleon's attention and led to the promotion of the scrivener.

"There is room enough up higher," said Webster to a young man hesitating to study law because the profession was so crowded. This is true in every department of activity. The young man who succeeds must hold his ground and push hard. Whoever attempts to pass through the door to success will find it labeled, "Push."

There is another big word in the English language: the perfection of grit is the power of saying "No," with emphasis that can not be mistaken. Learn to meet hard times with a harder will, and more determined pluck. The nature which is all pine and straw is of no use in times of trial, we must have some oak and iron in us. The goddess of fame or of fortune has been won by many a poor boy who had no friends, no backing, or anything but pure grit and invincible purpose.

A good character, good habits, and *iron industry* are impregnable to the assaults of the ill luck that fools are dreaming of. There is no luck, for all practical purposes, to him who is not striving, and whose senses are not all eagerly attent. What are called accidental discoveries are almost invariably made by those who are looking for something. A man incurs about as much risk of being struck by lightning as by accidental luck. There is, perhaps, an element of luck in the amount of success which crowns the efforts of different men; but even here it will usually be found that the sagacity with which the efforts are directed and the energy with which they are prosecuted measure pretty accurately the luck contained in the results achieved. Apparent exceptions will be found to relate almost wholly to single undertakings, while in the long run the rule will hold good. Two pearl-divers, equally expert, dive together and work with equal energy. One brings up a pearl, while the other returns empty-handed. But let both persevere and at the end of five, ten, or twenty years it will be found that they succeeded almost in exact proportion to their skill and industry.

"Varied experience of men has led me, the longer I live," says Huxley, "to set less value on mere cleverness; to attach more and more importance to industry and physical endurance. Indeed, I am much disposed to think that endurance is the most valuable quality of all; for industry, as the desire to work hard, does not come to much if a feeble frame is unable to respond to the desire. No life is wasted unless it ends in sloth, dishonesty, or cowardice. No success is worthy of the name unless it is won by honest industry and brave breasting of the waves of fortune."

Has luck ever made a fool speak words of wisdom; an ignoramus utter lectures on science; a dolt write an Odyssey, an Aeneid, a Paradise Lost, or a Hamlet; a loafer become a Girard or Astor, a Rothschild, Stewart, Vanderbilt, Field, Gould, or Rockefeller; a coward win at Yorktown, Wagram, Waterloo, or Richmond; a careless stonecutter carve an Apollo, a Minerva, a Venus de Medici, or a Greek Slave? Does luck raise rich crops on the land of the sluggard, weeds and brambles on that of the industrious farmer? Does luck make the drunkard sleek and attractive, and his home cheerful, while the temperate man looks haggard and suffers want and misery? Does luck starve honest labor, and pamper idleness? Does luck put common sense at a discount, folly at a premium? Does it cast intelligence into the gutter, and raise ignorance to the skies? Does it imprison virtue, and laud vice? Did luck give Watt his engine, Franklin his captive lightning, Whitney his cotton-gin, Fulton his steamboat, Morse his telegraph, Blanchard his lathe, Howe his sewing-machine, Goodyear his rubber, Bell his telephone, Edison his phonograph?

If you are told of the man who, worn out by a painful disorder, tried to commit suicide, but only opened an internal tumor, effecting a cure; of the Persian condemned to lose his tongue, on whom a bungling operation merely removed an impediment of speech; of a painter who produced an effect long desired by throwing his brush at a picture in rage and despair; of a musician who, after repeated failures in trying to imitate a storm at sea, obtained the result desired by angrily running his hands together from the extremities of the keyboard,—bear in mind that even this "luck" came to men as the result of action, not inaction.

"Luck is ever waiting for something to turn up," says Cobden; "labor, with keen eyes and strong will, will turn up something. Luck lies in bed, and wishes the postman would bring him the news of a legacy; labor turns out at six o'clock, and with busy pen or ringing hammer lays the foundation of a competence. Luck whines; labor whistles. Luck relies on chance; labor, on character."

Stick to the thing and carry it through. *Believe you were made for the place you fill*, and that no one else can fill it as well. Put forth your whole energies. Be awake, electrify yourself; go forth to the task. Only once learn to carry a thing through in all its completeness and proportion, and you will become a hero. You will think better of yourself; others will think better of you. The world in its very heart admires the stern, determined doer.

"I like the man who faces what he must
With step triumphant and a heart of cheer;
Who fights the daily battle without fear;
Sees his hopes fail, yet keeps unfaltering trust
That God is God; that somehow, true and just,
His plans work out for mortals; not a tear
Is shed when fortune, which the world holds dear,
Falls from his grasp; better, with love, a crust
Than living in dishonor; envies not,
Nor loses faith in man; but does his best,
Nor even murmurs at his humbler lot;
But with a smile and words of hope, gives zest
To every toiler; he alone is great,
Who by a life heroic conquers fate."

Clear Grit

*Let fortune empty her whole quiver on me,
I have a soul that, like an ample shield,
Can take in all, and verge enough for more. —Dryden*

*There's a brave fellow! There's a man of pluck!
A man who's not afraid to say his say,
Though a whole town's against him. —Longfellow*

Our greatest glory is not in never falling, but in rising every time we fall.—Goldsmith

The barriers are not yet erected which shall say to aspiring talent, "Thus far and no farther."—Beethoven

"Friends and comrades," said Pizarro, as he turned toward the south, after tracing with his sword upon the sand a line from east to west, "on that side are toil, hunger, nakedness, the drenching storm, desertion, and death; on this side, ease and pleasure. There lies Peru with its riches: here, Panama and its poverty. Choose, each man, what best becomes a brave Castilian. For my part, I go to the south." So saying, he crossed the line and was followed by thirteen Spaniards in armor. Thus, on the little island of Gallo in the Pacific, when his men were clamoring to return to Panama, did Pizarro and his few volunteers resolve to stake their lives upon the success of a desperate crusade against the powerful empire of the Incas. At the time they had not even a vessel to transport them to the country they wished to conquer. Is it necessary to add that all difficulties yielded at last to such resolute determination?

"Perseverance is a Roman virtue,
That wins each godlike act, and plucks success
E'en from the spear-proof crest of rugged danger."

"When you get into a tight place and everything goes against you, till it seems as if you could not hold on a minute longer," said Harriet Beecher Stowe, "never give up then, for that's just the place and time that the tide'll turn."

Charles Sumner said "three things are necessary to a strong character: First, backbone; second, backbone; third, backbone."

While digging among the ruins of Pompeii, which was buried by the dust and ashes from an eruption of Vesuvius A. D. 79, the workmen found the skeleton of a Roman soldier in the sentry-box at one of the city's gates. He might have found safety under sheltering rocks close by; but, in the face of certain death, he had remained at his post, a mute witness to the thorough discipline, the ceaseless vigilance and fidelity which made the Roman legionaries masters of the known world.

The world admires the man who never flinches from unexpected difficulties, who calmly, patiently, and courageously grapples with his fate; who dies, if need be, at his post.

"Clear grit" always commands respect. It is that quality which achieves, and everybody admires achievement. In the strife of parties and principles, backbone without brains will carry against brains without backbone. You can not, by tying an opinion to a man's tongue, make him the representative of that opinion; at the close of any battle for principles, his name will be found neither among the dead nor among the wounded, but among the missing.

The "London Times" was an insignificant sheet published by Mr. Walter and was steadily losing money. John Walter, Jr., then only twenty-seven years old, begged his father to give him full control of the paper. After many misgivings, the father finally consented. The young journalist began to remodel the establishment and to introduce new ideas everywhere. The paper had not attempted to mold public opinion, and had had no individuality or character of its own. The audacious young editor boldly attacked every wrong, even the government, whenever he thought it corrupt. Thereupon the public customs, printing, and the government advertisements were withdrawn. The father was in utter dismay. His son, he was sure, would ruin the paper and himself. But no remonstrance could swerve the son from his purpose to give the world a great journal which should have weight, character, individuality, and independence.

The public soon saw that a new power stood behind the "Times"; that its articles meant business; that new life and new blood and new ideas had been infused into the insignificant sheet; that a man with brains and push and tenacity of purpose stood at the helm,—a man who could make a way when he could not find one. Among other new features foreign dispatches were introduced, and they appeared in the "Times" several days before their appearance in the government organs. The "leading article" also was introduced to stay. The aggressive editor antagonized the government, and his foreign dispatches were all stopped at the outposts, while the ministerial journalists were allowed to proceed. But nothing could daunt this resolute young spirit. At enormous expense he employed special couriers. Every obstacle put in his way, and all opposition from the government, only added to his determination to succeed. Enterprise, push, grit were behind the "Times," and nothing could stay its progress. Young Walter was the soul of the paper, and his personality pervaded every detail. In those days only three hundred copies of the paper could be struck off in an hour by the best presses, and Walter had duplicate and even triplicate types set. Then he set his brain to work, and finally the Walter Press, throwing off 17,000 copies per hour, both sides printed, was the result. It was the 29th of November, 1814, that the first steam printed paper was given to the world.

"Mean natures always feel a sort of terror before great natures, and many a base thought has been unuttered, many a sneaking vote withheld, through the fear inspired by the rebuking presence of one noble man." As a rule, pure grit, character, has the right of way. In the presence of men permeated with grit and sound in character, meanness and baseness slink out of sight. Mean men are uncomfortable, dishonesty trembles, hypocrisy is uncertain.

Lincoln, being asked by an anxious visitor what he would do after three or four years if the rebellion were not subdued, replied: "Oh, there is no alternative but to keep pegging away."

"It is in me and it shall come out," said Sheridan, when told that he would never make an orator as he had failed in his first speech in Parliament. He became known as one of the foremost orators of his day.

When a boy Henry Clay was very bashful and diffident, and scarcely dared recite before his class at school, but he determined to become an orator. So he committed speeches and recited them in the cornfields, or in the barn with the horse and cows for an audience.

If impossibilities ever exist, popularly speaking, they ought to have been found somewhere between the birth and death of Kitto, that deaf pauper and master of Oriental learning. But Kitto did not find them there. In the presence of his decision and imperial energy they melted away. He begged his father to take him out of the poorhouse, even if he had to subsist like the Hottentots. He told him that he would sell his books and pawn his handkerchief, by which he thought he could raise about twelve shillings. He said he could live upon blackberries, nuts, and field turnips, and was willing to sleep on a hayrick. Here was real grit. What were impossibilities to such a resolute, indomitable will?

Grit is a permanent, solid quality, which enters into the very structure, the very tissues of the constitution.

Many of our generals in the Civil War exhibited heroism; they were "plucky," and often displayed great determination, but Grant had pure "grit" in the most concentrated form. He could not be moved from his base; he was self-centered, immovable. "If you try to wheedle out of him his plans for a campaign, he stolidly smokes; if you call him an imbecile and a blunderer, he blandly lights another cigar; if you praise him as the greatest general living, he placidly returns the puff from his regalia; and if you tell him he should run for the presidency, it does not disturb the equanimity with which he inhales and exhales the unsubstantial vapor which typifies the politician's promises. While you are wondering what kind of creature this man without a tongue is, you are suddenly electrified with the news of some splendid victory; proving that behind the cigar, and behind the face discharged of all telltale expression, is the best brain to plan and the strongest heart to dare among the generals of the Republic."

Lincoln had pure "grit." When the illustrated papers everywhere were caricaturing him, when no epithet seemed too harsh to heap upon him, when his methods were criticized by his own party, and the generals in the war were denouncing his "foolish" confidence in Grant, and delegations were waiting upon him to ask for that general's removal, the great President sat with crossed legs, and was reminded of a story.

Lincoln and Grant both had that rare nerve which cares not for ridicule, is not swerved by public clamor, can bear abuse and hatred. There is a mighty force in truth, and in the sublime conviction and supreme self-confidence behind it; in the knowledge that truth is mighty, and the conviction and confidence that it will prevail.

Pure grit is that element of character which enables a man to clutch his aim with an iron grip, and keep the needle of his purpose pointing to the star of his hope. Through sunshine and storm, through hurricane and tempest, through sleet and rain, with a leaky ship, with a crew in mutiny, it perseveres; in fact, nothing but death can subdue it, and it dies still struggling.

The man of grit carries in his very presence a power which controls and commands. He is spared the necessity of declaring himself, for his grit speaks in his every act. It does not come by fits and starts, it is a part of his life. It inspires a sublime audacity and a heroic courage. Many of the failures of life are due to the want of grit or business nerve. It is unfortunate for a young man to start out in business life with a weak, yielding disposition, with no resolution or backbone to mark his own course and stick to it; with no ability to say "No" with an emphasis, obliging this man by investing in hopeless speculation, and, rather than offend a friend, indorsing a questionable note.

A little boy was asked how he learned to skate. "Oh, by getting up every time I fell down," he replied.

Whipple tells a story of Masséna which illustrates the masterful purpose that plucks victory out of the jaws of defeat. "After the defeat at Essling, the success of Napoleon's attempt to withdraw his beaten army depended on the character of Masséna, to whom the Emperor dispatched a messenger, telling him to keep his position for two hours longer at Aspern. This order, couched in the form of a request, required almost an impossibility; but Napoleon knew the indomitable tenacity of the man to whom he gave it. The messenger found Masséna seated on a heap of rubbish, his eyes bloodshot, his frame weakened by his unparalleled exertions during a contest of forty hours, and his whole appearance indicating a physical state better befitting the hospital than the field. But that steadfast soul seemed altogether unaffected by bodily prostration. Half dead as he was with fatigue, he rose painfully and said courageously, 'Tell the Emperor that I will hold out for two hours.' And he kept his word."

"Often defeated in battle," said Macaulay of Alexander the Great, "he was always successful in war."

In the battle of Marengo, the Austrians considered the day won. The French army was inferior in numbers, and had given way. The Austrian army extended its wings on the right and on the left, to follow up the French. Then, though the French themselves thought that the battle was lost, and the Austrians were confident it was won, Napoleon gave the command to charge; and, the trumpet's blast being given, the Old Guard charged down into the weakened center of the enemy, cut it in two, rolled the two wings up on either side, and the battle was won for France.

Once when Marshal Ney was going into battle, looking down at his knees which were smiting together, he said, "You may well shake; you would shake worse yet if you knew where I am going to take you."

It is victory after victory with the soldier, lesson after lesson with the scholar, blow after blow with the laborer, crop after crop with the farmer, picture after picture with the painter, and mile after mile with the traveler, that secures what all so much Desire—*success*.

A promising Harvard student was stricken with paralysis of both legs. Physicians said there was no hope for him. The lad determined to continue his college studies. The examiners heard him at his bedside, and in four years he took his degree. He resolved to make a critical study of Dante, to do which he had to learn Italian and German. He persevered in spite of repeated attacks of illness and partial loss of sight. He was competing for the university prize. Think of the paralytic lad, helpless in bed, competing for a prize, fighting death inch by inch! What a lesson! Before his manuscript was published or the prize awarded, the brave student died, but his work was successful.

Congressman William W. Crapo, while working his way through college, being too poor to buy a dictionary, actually copied one, walking from his home in the village of Dartmouth, Mass., to New Bedford to replenish his store of words and definitions from the town library.

Oh, the triumphs of this indomitable spirit of the conqueror! This it was that enabled Franklin to dine on a small loaf in the printing-office with a book in his hand. It helped Locke to live on bread and water in a Dutch garret. It enabled Gideon Lee to go barefoot in the snow, half starved and thinly clad. It sustained Lincoln and Garfield on their hard journeys from the log cabin to the White House.

President Chadbourne put grit in place of his lost lung, and worked thirty-five years after his funeral had been planned.

Henry Fawcett put grit in place of eyesight, and became the greatest Postmaster-General England ever had.

Prescott also put grit in place of eyesight, and became one of America's greatest historians. Francis Parkman put grit in place of health and eyesight, and became the greatest historian of America in his line. Thousands of men have put grit in place of health, eyes, ears, hands, legs and yet have achieved marvelous success. Indeed, most of the great things of the world have been accomplished by grit and pluck. You can not keep a man down who has these qualities. He will make stepping-stones out of his stumbling-blocks, and lift himself to success.

At fifty, Barnum was a ruined man, owing thousands more than he possessed, yet he resolutely resumed business once more, fairly wringing success from adverse fortune, and paying his notes at the same time. Again and again he was ruined; but phoenix-like, he rose repeatedly from the ashes of his misfortune each time more determined than before.

"It is all very well," said Charles J. Fox, "to tell me that a young man has distinguished himself by a brilliant first speech. He may go on, or he may be satisfied with his first triumph; but show me a young man who has not succeeded at first, and nevertheless has gone on, and I will back that young man to do better than most of those who have succeeded at the first trial."

Cobden broke down completely the first time he appeared on a platform in Manchester, and the chairman apologized for him. But he did not give up speaking till every poor man in England had a larger, better, and cheaper loaf.

See young Disraeli, sprung from a hated and persecuted race; without opportunity, pushing his way up through the middle classes, up through the upper classes, until he stands self-poised upon the topmost round of political and social power. Scoffed, ridiculed, rebuffed, hissed from the House of Commons, he simply says, "The time will come when you will hear me." The time did come, and the boy with no chance swayed the scepter of England for a quarter of a century.

One of the most remarkable examples in history is Disraeli, forcing his leadership upon that very party whose prejudices were deepest against his race, and which had an utter contempt for self-made men and interlopers. Imagine England's surprise when she awoke to find this insignificant Hebrew actually Chancellor of the Exchequer! He was easily master of all the tortures supplied by the armory of rhetoric; he could exhaust the resources of the bitterest invective; he could sting Gladstone out of his self-control; he was absolute master of himself and his situation. You could see that this young man intended to make his way in the world. Determined audacity was in his very face. Handsome, with the hated Hebrew blood in his veins, after three defeats in parliamentary elections he was not the least daunted, for he knew his day would come. Lord Melbourne, the great Prime Minister, when this gay young fop was introduced to him, asked him what he wished to be. "Prime Minister of England," was his audacious reply.

William H. Seward was given a thousand dollars by his father with which to go to college; this was all he was to have. The son returned at the end of the freshman year with extravagant habits and no money. His father refused to give him more, and told him he could not stay at home.

When the youth found the props all taken out from under him, and that he must now sink or swim, he left home moneyless, returned to college, graduated at the head of his class, studied law, was elected Governor of New York, and became Lincoln's great Secretary of State during the Civil War.

Garfield said, "If the power to do hard work is not talent, it is the best possible substitute for it." The triumph of industry and grit over low birth and iron fortune in America, the land of opportunity, ought to be sufficient to put to shame all grumblers over their hard fortune and those who attempt to excuse aimless, shiftless, successless men because they have no chance.

During a winter in the War of 1812, General Jackson's troops, unprovided for and starving, became mutinous and were going home. But the general set the example of living on acorns; and then he rode before the rebellious line and threatened with instant death the first mutineer that should try to leave.

The race is not always to the swift, the battle is not always to the strong. Horses are sometimes weighted or hampered in the race, and this is taken into account in the result. So in the race of life the distance alone does not determine the prize. We must take into consideration the hindrances, the weights we have carried, the disadvantages of education, of breeding, of training, of surroundings, of circumstances. How many young men are weighted down with debt, with poverty, with the support of invalid parents or brothers and sisters, or friends? How many are fettered with ignorance, hampered by inhospitable surroundings, with the opposition of parents who do not understand them? How many a round boy is hindered in the race by being forced into a square hole? How many youths are delayed in their course because nobody believes in them, because nobody encourages them, because they get no sympathy and are forever tortured for not doing that against which every fiber of their being protests, and every drop of their blood rebels? How many men have to feel their way to the goal through the blindness of ignorance and lack of experience? How many go bungling along from the lack of early discipline and drill in the vocation they have chosen? How many have to hobble along on crutches because they were never taught to help themselves, but have been accustomed to lean upon a father's wealth or a mother's indulgence? How many are weakened for the journey of life by self-indulgence, by dissipation, by "life-sappers"; how many are crippled by disease, by a weak constitution, by impaired eyesight or hearing?

When the prizes of life shall be finally awarded, the distance we have run, the weights we have carried, the handicaps, will all be taken into account. Not the distance we have run, but the obstacles we have overcome, the disadvantages under which we have made the race, will decide the prizes. The poor wretch who has plodded along against unknown temptations, the poor woman who has buried her sorrows in her silent heart and sewed her weary way through life, those who have suffered abuse in silence, and who have been unrecognized or despised by their fellow-runners, will often receive the greater prize.

"The wise and active conquer difficulties, By daring to attempt them; sloth and folly Shiver and sink at sight of toil and hazard, And make the impossibility they fear."

"I can't, it is impossible," said a foiled lieutenant, to Alexander. "Begone," shouted the conquering Macedonian, "there is nothing impossible to him who will try."

Were I called upon to express in a word the secret of so many failures among those who started out in life with high hopes, I should say unhesitatingly, they lacked will-power. They could not half will. What is a man without a will? He is like an engine without steam, a mere sport of chance, to be tossed about hither and thither, always at the mercy of those who have wills. I should call the strength of will the test of a young man's possibilities. Can he will strong enough, and hold whatever he undertakes with an iron grip? It is the iron grip that takes the strong hold on life. What chance is there in this crowding, pushing, selfish, greedy world, where everything is pusher or pushed, for a young man with no will, no grip on life? "The truest wisdom," said Napoleon, "is a resolute determination." An iron will without principle might produce a Napoleon; but with character it would make a Wellington or a Grant, untarnished by ambition or avarice.

"The undivided will
'T is that compels the elements and wrings
A human music from the indifferent air."

Success under Difficulties

Victories that are easy are cheap. Those only are worth having which come as the result of hard fighting.— Beecher

Little minds are tamed and subdued by misfortunes; but great minds rise above them.—Washington Irving

"I have here three teams that I want to get over to Staten Island," said a boy of twelve one day in 1806 to the innkeeper at South Amboy, N. J. "If you will put us across, I'll leave with you one of my horses in pawn, and if I don't send you back six dollars within forty-eight hours you may keep the horse."

The innkeeper asked the reason for this novel proposition, and learned that the lad's father had contracted to get the cargo of a vessel stranded near Sandy Hook, and take it to New York in lighters. The boy had been sent with three wagons, six horses, and three men, to carry the cargo across a sand-spit to the lighters. The work accomplished, he had started with only six dollars to travel a long distance home over the Jersey sands, and reached South Amboy penniless. "I'll do it," said the innkeeper, as he looked into the bright honest eyes of the boy. The horse was soon redeemed.

"My son," said this same boy's mother, on the first of May, 1810, when he asked her to lend him one hundred dollars to buy a boat, having imbibed a strong liking for the sea; "on the twenty-seventh of this month you will be sixteen years old. If, by that time, you will plow, harrow, and plant with corn the eight-acre lot, I will advance you the money." The field was rough and stony, but the work was done in time, and well done. From this small beginning Cornelius Vanderbilt laid the foundation of a colossal fortune.

In 1818 Vanderbilt owned two or three of the finest coasting schooners in New York harbor, and had a capital of nine thousand dollars. Seeing that steam-vessels would soon win supremacy over those carrying sails only, he gave up his fine business to become the captain of a steamboat at one thousand dollars a year. For twelve years he ran between New York City and New Brunswick, N. J. In 1829 he began business as a steamboat owner, in the face of opposition so bitter that he lost his last dollar. But the tide turned, and he prospered so rapidly that he at length owned over a hundred steamboats. He early identified himself with the growing railroad interests of the country, and became the richest man of his day in America.

Barnum began the race of business life barefoot, for at the age of fifteen he was obliged to buy on credit the shoes he wore at his father's funeral.

He was a remarkable example of success under difficulties. There was no keeping him down; no opposition daunted him.

"Eloquence must have been born with you," said a friend to J. P. Curran. "Indeed, my dear sir, it was not," replied the orator; "it was born some three and twenty years and some months after me." Speaking of his first attempt at a debating club, he said: "I stood up, trembling through every fiber; but remembering that in this I was but imitating Tully, I took courage and had actually proceeded almost as far as 'Mr. Chairman,' when, to my astonishment and terror, I perceived that every eye was turned on me. There were only six or seven present, and the room could not have contained as many more; yet was it, to my panic-stricken imagination, as if I were the central object in nature, and assembled millions were gazing upon me in breathless expectation. I became dismayed and dumb. My friends cried, 'Hear him!' but there was nothing to hear." He was nicknamed "Orator Mum," and well did he deserve the title until he ventured to stare in astonishment at a speaker who was "culminating chronology by the most preposterous anachronisms." "I doubt not," said the annoyed speaker, "that 'Orator Mum' possesses wonderful talents for eloquence, but I would recommend him to show it in future by some more popular method than his silence." Stung by the taunt, Curran rose and gave the man a "piece of his mind," speaking fluently in his anger. Encouraged by this success, he took great pains to become a good speaker. He corrected his habit of stuttering by reading favorite passages aloud every day slowly and distinctly, and spoke at every opportunity.

Bunyan wrote his "Pilgrim's Progress" on the untwisted papers which were used to cork the bottles of milk brought for his meals. Gifford wrote his first copy of a mathematical work, when a cobbler's apprentice, on small scraps of leather; and Rittenhouse, the astronomer, first calculated eclipses on his plow handle.

David Livingstone at ten years of age was put into a cotton factory near Glasgow. Out of his first week's wages he bought a Latin grammar, and studied in the night schools for years. He would sit up and study till midnight unless his mother drove him to bed, notwithstanding he had to be at the factory at six in the morning. He mastered Vergil and Horace in this way, and read extensively, besides studying botany. So eager for knowledge was he, that he would place his book before him on the spinning-jenny, and amid the deafening roar of machinery would pore over its pages.

"All the performances of human art, at which we look with praise and wonder," says Johnson, "are instances of the resistless force of perseverance: it is by this that the quarry becomes a pyramid, and that distant countries are united with canals. If a man was to compare the effect of a single stroke of the pickax, or of one impression of the spade, with the general design and last result, he would be overwhelmed by the sense of their disproportion; yet those petty operations, incessantly continued, in time surmount the greatest difficulties, and mountains are leveled, and oceans bounded, by the slender force of human beings."

Great men never wait for opportunities; they make them. Nor do they wait for facilities or favoring circumstances; they seize upon whatever is at hand, work out their problem, and master the situation. A young man determined and willing will find a way or make one. A Franklin does not require elaborate apparatus; he can bring electricity from the clouds with a common kite.

Great men have found no royal road to their triumph. It is always the old route, by way of industry and perseverance.

The farmer boy, Elihu B. Washburn, taught school at ten dollars per month, and early learned the lesson that it takes one hundred cents to make a dollar. In after years he fought "steals" in Congress, until he was called the "Watchdog of the Treasury."

When Elias Howe, harassed by want and woe, was in London completing his first sewing-machine, he had frequently to borrow money to live on. He bought beans and cooked them himself. He also borrowed money to send his wife back to America. He sold his first machine for five pounds, although it was worth fifty, and then he pawned his letters patent to pay his expenses home.

The boy Arkwright begins barbering in a cellar, but dies worth a million and a half. The world treated his novelties just as it treats everybody's novelties—made infinite objection, mustered all the impediments, but he snapped his fingers at their objections, and lived to become honored and wealthy.

There is scarcely a great truth or doctrine but has had to fight its way to public recognition in the face of detraction, calumny, and persecution.

Nearly every great discovery or invention that has blessed mankind has had to fight its way to recognition, even against the opposition of the most progressive men.

William H. Prescott was a remarkable example of what a boy with "no chance" can do. While at college, he lost one eye by a hard piece of bread thrown during a "biscuit battle," and the other eye became almost useless. But the boy would not lead a useless life. He set his heart upon being a historian, and turned all his energies in that direction. By the aid of others' eyes, he spent ten years studying before he even decided upon a particular theme for his first book. Then he spent ten years more, poring over old archives and manuscripts, before he published his "Ferdinand and Isabella." What a lesson in his life for young men! What a rebuke to those who have thrown away their opportunities and wasted their lives!

"Galileo with an opera-glass," said Emerson, "discovered a more splendid series of celestial phenomena than any one since with the great telescopes. Columbus found the new world in an undecked boat."

Surroundings which men call unfavorable can not prevent the unfolding of your powers. From among the rock-ribbed hills of New Hampshire sprang the greatest of American orators and statesmen, Daniel Webster. From the crowded ranks of toil, and homes to which luxury is a stranger, have often come the leaders and benefactors of our race.

Where shall we find an illustration more impressive than in Abraham Lincoln, whose life, career, and death might be chanted by a Greek chorus as at once the prelude and the epilogue of the most imperial theme of modern times? Born as lowly as the Son of God, in a hovel; of what real parentage we know not; reared in penury, squalor, with no gleam of light, nor fair surrounding; a young manhood vexed by weird dreams and visions; with scarcely a natural grace; singularly awkward, ungainly even among the uncouth about him: it was reserved for this remarkable character, late in life, to be snatched from obscurity, raised to supreme command at a supreme moment, and intrusted with the destiny of a nation. The great leaders of his party were made to stand aside; the most experienced and accomplished men of the day, men like Seward, and Chase, and Sumner, statesmen famous and trained, were sent to the rear, while this strange figure was brought by unseen hands to the front, and given the reins of power.

There is no open door to the temple of success. Everyone who enters makes his own door, which closes behind him to all others, not even permitting his own children to pass.

Not in the brilliant salon, not in the tapestried library, not in ease and competence, is genius born and nurtured; but often in adversity and destitution, amidst the harassing cares of a straitened household, in bare and fireless garrets. Amid scenes unpropitious, repulsive, wretched, have men labored, studied, and trained themselves, until they have at last emanated from the gloom of that obscurity the shining lights of their times; have become the companions of kings, the guides and teachers of their kind, and exercised an influence upon the thought of the world amounting to a species of intellectual legislation.

"What does he know," said a sage, "who has not suffered?" Schiller produced his greatest tragedies in the midst of physical suffering almost amounting to torture. Handel was never greater than when, warned by palsy of the approach of death, and struggling with distress and suffering, he sat down to compose the great works which have made his name immortal in music. Mozart composed his great operas, and last of all his "Requiem," when oppressed by debt and struggling with a fatal disease. Beethoven produced his greatest works amidst gloomy sorrow, when oppressed by almost total deafness.

Perhaps no one ever battled harder to overcome obstacles which would have disheartened most men than Demosthenes. He had such a weak voice, and such an impediment in his speech, and was so short of breath, that he could scarcely get through a single sentence without stopping to rest. All his first attempts were nearly drowned by the hisses, jeers, and scoffs of his audiences. His first effort that met with success was against his guardian, who had defrauded him, and whom he compelled to refund a part of his fortune. He was so discouraged by his defeats that he determined to give up forever all attempts at oratory. One of his auditors, however, believed the young man had something in him, and encouraged him to persevere. He accordingly appeared again in public, but was hissed down as before. As he withdrew, hanging his head in great confusion, a noted actor, Satyrus, encouraged him still further to try to overcome his impediment. He stammered so much that he could not pronounce some of the letters at all, and his breath would give out before he could get through a sentence. Finally, he determined to be an orator at any cost. He went to the seashore and practised amid the roar of the breakers with small pebbles in his mouth, in order to overcome his stammering, and at the same time accustom himself to the hisses and tumults of his audience. He overcame his short breath by practising while running up steep and difficult places on the shore. His awkward gestures were also corrected by long and determined drill before a mirror.

Columbus was dismissed as a fool from court after court, but he pushed his suit against an incredulous and ridiculing world. Rebuffed by kings, scorned by queens, he did not swerve a hair's breadth from the overmastering purpose which dominated his soul. The words "New World" were graven upon his heart; and reputation, ease, pleasure, position, life itself if need be, must be sacrificed. Threats, ridicule, ostracism, storms, leaky vessels, mutiny of sailors, could not shake his mighty purpose.

You can not keep a determined man from success. Place stumbling-blocks in his way and he takes them for stepping-stones, and on them will climb to greatness. Take away his money, and he makes spurs of his poverty to urge him on. Cripple him, and he writes the Waverley Novels.

All that is great and noble and true in the history of the world is the result of infinite painstaking, perpetual plodding, of common every-day industry.

Roger Bacon, one of the profoundest thinkers the world has produced, was terribly persecuted for his studies in natural philosophy, yet he persevered and won success. He was accused of dealing in magic, his books were burned in public, and he was kept in prison for ten years. Even our own revered Washington was mobbed in the streets because he would not pander to the clamor of the people and reject the treaty which Mr. Jay had arranged with Great Britain. But he remained firm, and the people adopted his opinion. The Duke of Wellington was mobbed in the streets of London and his windows were broken while his wife lay dead in the house; but the "Iron Duke" never faltered in his course, or swerved a hair's breadth from his purpose.

William Phipps, when a young man, heard some sailors on the street, in Boston, talking about a Spanish ship wrecked off the Bahama Islands, which was supposed to have money on board. Young Phipps determined to find it. He set out at once, and, after many hardships, discovered the lost treasure. He then heard of another ship, which had been wrecked off Port De La Plata many years before. He set sail for England and importuned Charles II for aid. To his delight the king fitted up the ship *Rose Algier* for him. He searched and searched for a long time in vain, and at length had to return to England to repair his vessel. James II was then on the throne, and Phipps had to wait for four years before he could raise money to return. His crew mutinied and threatened to throw him overboard, but he turned the ship's guns on them. One day an Indian diver went down for a curious sea plant and saw several cannon lying on the bottom. They proved to belong to the wreck. He had nothing but dim traditions to guide him, but he returned to England with $1,500,000.

A constant struggle, a ceaseless battle to win success in spite of every barrier, is the price of all great achievements.

The man who has not fought his way up to his own loaf, and does not bear the scar of desperate conflict, does not know the highest meaning of success.

The money acquired by those who have thus struggled upward to success is not their only, or indeed their chief reward. When, after years of toil, of opposition, of ridicule, of repeated failure, Cyrus W. Field placed his hand upon the telegraph instrument ticking a message under the sea, think you that the electric thrill passed no further than the tips of his fingers? When Thomas A. Edison demonstrated that the electric light had at last been developed into a commercial success, do you suppose those bright rays failed to illuminate the inmost recesses of his soul?

Uses of Obstacles

Nature, when she adds difficulties, adds brains.—Emerson

Many men owe the grandeur of their lives to their tremendous difficulties.—Spurgeon

The good are better made by ill,
As odors crushed are sweeter still. —Rogers

Though losses and crosses be lessons right severe,
There's wit there ye'll get there, ye'll find no other where. —Burns

"Adversity is the prosperity of the great."
"Kites rise against, not with, the wind."

"Many and many a time since," said Harriet Martineau, referring to her father's failure in business, "have we said that, but for that loss of money, we might have lived on in the ordinary provincial method of ladies with small means, sewing and economizing and growing narrower every year; whereas, by being thrown, while it was yet time, on our own resources, we have worked hard and usefully, won friends, reputation, and independence, seen the world abundantly, abroad and at home; in short, have truly lived instead of vegetating."

Two of the three greatest epic poets of the world were blind,—Homer and Milton; while the third, Dante, was in his later years nearly, if not altogether, blind. It almost seems as though some great characters had been physically crippled in certain respects so that they would not dissipate their energy, but concentrate it all in one direction.

A distinguished investigator in science said that when he encountered an apparently insuperable obstacle, he usually found himself upon the brink of some discovery.

"Returned with thanks" has made many an author. Failure often leads a man to success by arousing his latent energy, by firing a dormant purpose, by awakening powers which were sleeping. Men of mettle turn disappointments into helps as the oyster turns into pearl the sand which annoys it.

"Let the adverse breath of criticism be to you only what the blast of the storm wind is to the eagle,—a force against him that lifts him higher."

A kite would not fly unless it had a string tying it down. It is just so in life. The man who is tied down by half a dozen blooming responsibilities and their mother will make a higher and stronger flight than the bachelor who, having nothing to keep him steady, is always floundering in the mud.

When Napoleon's school companions made sport of him on account of his humble origin and poverty he devoted himself entirely to books, and, quickly rising above them in scholarship, commanded their respect. Soon he was regarded as the brightest ornament of the class.

"To make his way at the bar," said an eminent jurist, "a young man must live like a hermit and work like a horse. There is nothing that does a young lawyer so much good as to be half starved."

Thousands of men of great native ability have been lost to the world because they have not had to wrestle with obstacles, and to struggle under difficulties sufficient to stimulate into activity their dormant powers. No effort is too dear which helps us along the line of our proper career.

Poverty and obscurity of origin may impede our progress, but it is only like the obstruction of ice or débris in the river temporarily forcing the water into eddies, where it accumulates strength and a mighty reserve which ultimately sweeps the obstruction impetuously to the sea. Poverty and obscurity are not insurmountable obstacles, but they often act as a stimulus to the naturally indolent, and develop a firmer fiber of mind, a stronger muscle and stamina of body.

If the germ of the seed has to struggle to push its way up through the stones and hard sod, to fight its way up to sunlight and air, and then to wrestle with storm and tempest, with snow and frost, the fiber of its timber will be all the tougher and stronger.

There is good philosophy in the injunction to love our enemies, for they are often our best friends in disguise. They tell us the truth when friends flatter. Their biting sarcasm and scathing rebuke are mirrors which reveal us to ourselves. These unkind stings and thrusts are often spurs which urge us on to grander success and nobler endeavor. Friends cover our faults and rarely rebuke; enemies drag out to the light all our weaknesses without mercy. We dread these thrusts and exposures as we do the surgeon's knife, but are the better for them. They reach depths before untouched, and we are led to resolve to redeem ourselves from scorn and inferiority.

We are the victors of our opponents. They have developed in us the very power by which we overcome them. Without their opposition we could never have braced and anchored and fortified ourselves, as the oak is braced and anchored for its thousand battles with the tempests. Our trials, our sorrows, and our griefs develop us in a similar way.

The man who has triumphed over difficulties bears the signs of victory in his face. An air of triumph is seen in every movement.

John Calvin, who made a theology for the seventeenth and eighteenth centuries, was tortured with disease for many years, and so was Robert Hall. The great men who have lifted the world to a higher level were not developed in easy circumstances, but were rocked in the cradle of difficulties and pillowed on hardships.

"The gods look on no grander sight than an honest man struggling with adversity."

"Then I must learn to sing better," said Anaximander, when told that the very boys laughed at his singing.

Strong characters, like the palm-tree, seem to thrive best when most abused. Men who have stood up bravely under great misfortune for years are often unable to bear prosperity. Their good fortune takes the spring out of their energy, as the torrid zone enervates races accustomed to a vigorous climate. Some people never come to themselves until baffled, rebuffed, thwarted, defeated, crushed, in the opinion of those around them. Trials unlock their virtues; defeat is the threshold of their victory.

It is defeat that turns bone to flint; it is defeat that turns gristle to muscle; it is defeat that makes men invincible; it is defeat that has made those heroic natures that are now in the ascendency, and that has given the sweet law of liberty instead of the bitter law of oppression.

Difficulties call out great qualities, and make greatness possible. How many centuries of peace would have developed a Grant? Few knew Lincoln until the great weight of the war showed his character. A century of peace would never have produced a Bismarck. Perhaps Phillips and Garrison would never have been known to history had it not been for slavery.

"Will he not make a great painter?" was asked in regard to an artist fresh from his Italian tour. "No, never," replied Northcote. "Why not?" "Because he has an income of six thousand pounds a year." In the sunshine of wealth a man is, as a rule, warped too much to become an artist of high merit. He should have some great thwarting difficulty to struggle against. A drenching shower of adversity would straighten his fibers out again.

The best tools receive their temper from fire, their edge from grinding; the noblest characters are developed in a similar way. The harder the diamond, the more brilliant the luster, and the greater the friction necessary to bring it out. Only its own dust is hard enough to make this most precious stone reveal its full beauty.

The spark in the flint would sleep forever but for friction; the fire in man would never blaze but for antagonism.

Suddenly, with much jarring and jolting, an electric car came to a standstill just in front of a heavy truck that was headed in an opposite direction. The huge truck wheels were sliding uselessly round on the car tracks that were wet and slippery from rain. All the urging of the teamster and the straining of the horses were in vain,—until the motorman quietly tossed a shovelful of sand on the track under the heavy wheels, and then the truck lumbered on its way. "Friction is a very good thing," remarked a passenger.

The philosopher Kant observed that a dove, inasmuch as the only obstacle it has to overcome is the resistance of the air, might suppose that if only the air were out of the way it could fly with greater rapidity and ease. Yet if the air were withdrawn, and the bird should try to fly in a vacuum, it would fall instantly to the ground, unable to fly at all. The very element that offers the opposition to flying is at the same time the condition of any flight whatever.

Emergencies make giant men. But for our Civil War the names of its grand heroes would not be written among the greatest of our time.

The effort or struggle to climb to a higher place in life has strength and dignity in it, and cannot fail to leave us stronger, even though we may never reach the position we desire, or secure the prize we seek.

From an aimless, idle, and useless brain, emergencies often call out powers and virtues before unknown and unsuspected. How often we see a young man develop astounding ability and energy after the death of a parent, or the loss of a fortune, or after some other calamity has knocked the props and crutches from under him. The prison has roused the slumbering fire in many a noble mind. "Robinson Crusoe" was written in prison. The "Pilgrim's Progress" appeared in Bedford Jail, Sir Walter Raleigh wrote "The History of the World" during his imprisonment of thirteen years. Luther translated the Bible while confined in the Castle of Wartburg. For twenty years Dante worked in exile, and even under sentence of death.

Take two acorns from the same tree, as nearly alike as possible; plant one on a hill by itself, and the other in the dense forest, and watch them grow. The oak standing alone is exposed to every storm. Its roots reach out in every direction, clutching the rocks and piercing deep into the earth. Every rootlet lends itself to steady the growing giant, as if in anticipation of fierce conflict with the elements. Sometimes its upward growth seems checked for years, but all the while it has been expending its energy in pushing a root across a large rock to gain a firmer anchorage. Then it shoots proudly aloft again, prepared to defy the hurricane. The gales which sport so rudely with its wide branches find more than their match, and only serve still further to toughen every minutest fiber from pith to bark.

The acorn planted in the deep forest, on the other hand, shoots up a weak, slender sapling. Shielded by its neighbors, it feels no need of spreading its roots far and wide for support.

Take two boys, as nearly alike as possible. Place one in the country away from the hothouse culture and refinements of the city, with only the district school, the Sunday-school, and a few books. Remove wealth and props of every kind; and, if he has the right sort of material in him, he will thrive. Every obstacle overcome lends him strength for the next conflict. If he falls, he rises with more determination than before. Like a rubber ball, the harder the obstacle he meets the higher he rebounds. Obstacles and opposition are but apparatus of the gymnasium in which the fibers of his manhood are developed. He compels respect and recognition from those who have ridiculed his poverty. Put the other boy in a Vanderbilt family. Give him French and German nurses; gratify his every wish. Place him under the tutelage of great masters and send him to Harvard. Give him thousands a year for spending money, and let him travel extensively.

The two meet. The city lad is ashamed of his country brother. The plain, threadbare clothes, hard hands, tawny face, and awkward manner of the country boy make sorry contrast with the genteel appearance of the other. The poor boy bemoans his hard lot, regrets that he has "no chance in life," and envies the city youth. He thinks that it is a cruel Providence that places such a wide gulf between them.

They meet again as men, but how changed! It is as easy to distinguished the sturdy, self-made man from the one who has been propped up all his life by wealth, position, and family influence, as it is for the shipbuilder to tell the difference between the plank from the rugged mountain oak and one from the sapling of the forest.

When God wants to educate a man, he does not send him to school to the Graces, but to the Necessities. Through the pit and the dungeon Joseph came to a throne. We are not conscious of the mighty cravings of our half divine humanity; we are not aware of the God within us until some chasm yawns which must be filled, or till the rending asunder of our affections forces us to become conscious of a need. St. Paul in his Roman cell; John Huss led to the stake at Constance; Tyndale dying in his prison at Amsterdam; Milton, amid the incipient earthquake throes of revolution, teaching two little boys in Aldgate Street; David Livingstone, worn to a shadow, dying in a negro hut in Central Africa, alone—what failures they might all have seemed to themselves to be, yet what mighty purposes was God working out by their apparent humiliations!

Two highwaymen chancing once to pass a gibbet, one of them exclaimed: "What a fine profession ours would be if there were no gibbets!" "Tut, you blockhead," replied the other, "gibbets are the making of us; for, if there were no gibbets, every one would be a highwayman." Just so with every art, trade, or pursuit; it is the difficulties that scare and keep out unworthy competitors.

"Success grows out of struggles to overcome difficulties," says Smiles. "If there were no difficulties there would be no success. In this necessity for exertion we find the chief source of human advancement,—the advancement of individuals as of nations. It has led to most of the mechanical inventions and improvements of the age."

"Stick your claws into me," said Mendelssohn to his critics when entering the Birmingham orchestra. "Don't tell me what you like, but what you don't like."

John Hunter said that the art of surgery would never advance until professional men had the courage to publish their failures as well as their successes.

"Young men need to be taught not to expect a perfectly smooth and easy way to the objects of their endeavor or ambition," says Dr. Peabody. "Seldom does one reach a position with which he has reason to be satisfied without encountering difficulties and what might seem discouragements. But if they are properly met, they are not what they seem, and may prove to be helps, not hindrances. There is no more helpful and profiting exercise than surmounting obstacles."

It was in the Madrid jail that Cervantes wrote "Don Quixote." He was so poor that he could not even get paper during the last of his writing, and had to write on scraps of leather. A rich Spaniard was asked to help him, but replied: "Heaven forbid that his necessities should be relieved; it is his poverty that makes the world rich."

"He has the stuff in him to make a good musician," said Beethoven of Rossini, "if he had only been well flogged when a boy; but he is spoiled by the ease with which he composes."

We do our best while fighting desperately to attain what the heart covets.

Waters says that the struggle to obtain knowledge and to advance one's self in the world strengthens the mind, disciplines the faculties, matures the judgment, promotes self-reliance, and gives one independence of thought and force of character.

Kossuth called himself "a tempest-tossed soul, whose eyes have been sharpened by affliction."

As soon as young eagles can fly the old birds tumble them out and tear the down and feathers from their nest. The rude and rough experience of the eaglet fits him to become the bold king of birds, fierce and expert in pursuing his prey.

Boys who are bound out, crowded out, kicked out, usually "turn out," while those who do not have these disadvantages frequently fail to "come out."

"It was not the victories but the defeats of my life which have strengthened me," said the aged Sidenham Poyntz.

Almost from the dawn of history, oppression has been the lot of the Hebrews, yet they have given the world its noblest songs, its wisest proverbs, its sweetest music. With them persecution seems to bring prosperity. They thrive where others would starve. They hold the purse-strings of many nations. To them hardship has been "like spring mornings, frosty but kindly, the cold of which will kill the vermin, but will let the plant live."

In one of the battles of the Crimea a cannon-ball struck inside the fort, crashing through a beautiful garden. But from the ugly chasm there burst forth a spring of water which ever afterward flowed a living fountain. From the ugly gashes which misfortunes and sorrows make in our hearts, perennial fountains of rich experience and new joys often spring.

Don't lament and grieve over lost wealth. The Creator may see something grand and mighty which even He can not bring out as long as your wealth stands in the way. You must throw away the crutches of riches and stand upon your own feet, and develop the long unused muscles of manhood. God may see a rough diamond in you which only the hard hits of poverty can polish.

God knows where the richest melodies of our lives are, and what drill and what discipline are necessary to bring them out. The frost, the snows, the tempests, the lightnings are the rough teachers that bring the tiny acorn to the sturdy oak. Fierce winters are as necessary to it as long summers. It is its half-century's struggle with the elements for existence, wrestling with the storm, fighting for its life from the moment that it leaves the acorn until it goes into the ship, that gives it value. Without this struggle it would have been characterless, staminaless, nerveless, and its grain would have never been susceptible of high polish. The most beautiful as well as the strongest woods are found not in tropical climates, but in severe climates, where they have to fight the frosts and the winter's cold.

Many a man has never found himself until he has lost his all. Adversity stripped him only to discover him. Obstacles, hardships, are the chisel and mallet which shape the strong life into beauty. The rough ledge on the hillside complains of the drill, of the blasting which disturbs its peace of centuries: it is not pleasant to be rent with powder, to be hammered and squared by the quarryman. But look again: behold the magnificent statue, the monument, chiseled into grace and beauty, telling its grand story of valor in the public square for centuries.

The statue would have slept in the marble forever but for the blasting, the chiseling, and the polishing. The angel of our higher and nobler selves would remain forever unknown in the rough quarries of our lives but for the blastings of affliction, the chiseling of obstacles, and the sand-papering of a thousand annoyances.

Who has not observed the patience, the calm endurance, the sweet loveliness chiseled out of some rough life by the reversal of fortune or by some terrible affliction?

How many business men have made their greatest strides toward manhood, and developed their greatest virtues when reverses of fortune have swept away everything they had in the world; when disease had robbed them of all they held dear in life! Often we can not see the angel in the quarry of our lives, the statue of manhood, until the blasts of misfortune have rent the ledge, and difficulties and obstacles have squared and chiseled the granite blocks into grace and beauty.

Many a man has been ruined into salvation. The lightning which smote his dearest hopes opened up a new rift in his dark life, and gave him glimpses of himself which, until then, he had never seen. The grave buried his dearest hopes, but uncovered in his nature possibilities of patience, endurance, and hope which he never before dreamed he possessed.

"Adversity is a severe instructor," says Edmund Burke, "set over us by one who knows us better than we do ourselves, as he loves us better too. He that wrestles with us strengthens our nerves and sharpens our skill. Our antagonist is our helper. This conflict with difficulty makes us acquainted with our object, and compels us to consider it in all its relations. It will not suffer us to be superficial."

Men who have the right kind of material in them will assert their personality and rise in spite of a thousand adverse circumstances. You can not keep them down. Every obstacle seems only to add to their ability to get on.

The greatest men will ever be those who have risen from the ranks. It is said that there are ten thousand chances to one that genius, talent, and virtue shall issue from a farmhouse rather than from a palace.

Adversity exasperates fools, dejects cowards, but draws out the faculties of the wise and industrious, puts the modest to the necessity of trying their skill, awes the opulent, and makes the idle industrious. The storms of adversity, like those of the ocean, rouse the faculties, and excite the invention, prudence, skill, and fortitude of the voyager. A man upon whom continuous sunshine falls is like the earth in August: he becomes parched and dry and hard and close-grained. Men have drawn from adversity the elements of greatness.

Beethoven was almost totally deaf and burdened with sorrow when he produced his greatest works. Schiller wrote his best books in great bodily suffering. He was not free from pain for fifteen years. Milton wrote his leading productions when blind, poor, and sick. "Who best can suffer," said he, "best can do." Bunyan said that, if it were lawful, he could even pray for greater trouble, for the greater comfort's sake.

Not until the breath of the plague had blasted a hundred thousand lives, and the great fire had licked up cheap, shabby, wicked London, did she arise, phoenix-like, from her ashes and ruin, a grand and mighty city.

True salamanders live best in the furnace of persecution.

Many of our best poets

"Are cradled into poetry by wrong, And learn in suffering what they teach in song."

Byron was stung into a determination to go to the top by a scathing criticism of his first book, "Hours of Idleness," published when he was but nineteen years of age. Macaulay said, "There is scarce an instance in history of so sudden a rise to so dizzy an eminence as Byron reached." In a few years he stood by the side of such men as Scott, Southey, and Campbell, and died at thirty-seven, that age so fatal to genius. Many an orator like "stuttering Jack Curran," or "Orator Mum," as he was once called, has been spurred into eloquence by ridicule and abuse.

This is the crutch age. "Helps" and "aids" are advertised everywhere. We have institutes, colleges, universities, teachers, books, libraries, newspapers, magazines. Our thinking is done for us. Our problems are all worked out in "explanations" and "keys." Our boys are too often tutored through college with very little study. "Short roads" and "abridged methods" are characteristic of the century. Ingenious methods are used everywhere to get the drudgery out of the college course. Newspapers give us our politics, and preachers our religion. Self-help and self-reliance are getting old-fashioned. Nature, as if conscious of delayed blessings, has rushed to man's relief with her wondrous forces, and undertakes to do the world's drudgery and emancipate him from Eden's curse.

But do not misinterpret her edict. She emancipates from the lower only to call to the higher. She does not bid the world go and play while she does the work. She emancipates the muscles only to employ the brain and heart.

The most beautiful as well as the strongest characters are not developed in warm climates, where man finds his bread ready made on trees, and where exertion is a great effort, but rather in a trying climate and on a stubborn soil. It is not chance that returns to the Hindoo ryot a penny and to the American laborer a dollar for his daily toil; that makes Mexico with its mineral wealth poor, and New England with its granite and ice rich. It is rugged necessity, it is the struggle to obtain; it is poverty, the priceless spur, that develops the stamina of manhood, and calls the race out of barbarism. Intelligent labor found the world a wilderness and has made it a garden.

As the sculptor thinks only of the angel imprisoned in the marble block, so Nature cares only for the man or woman shut up in the human being. The sculptor cares nothing for the block as such; Nature has little regard for the mere lump of breathing clay. The sculptor will chip off all unnecessary material to set free the angel. Nature will chip and pound us remorselessly to bring out our possibilities. She will strip us of wealth, humble our pride, humiliate our ambition, let us down from the ladder of fame, will discipline us in a thousand ways, if she can develop a little character. Everything must give way to that.

"The hero is not fed on sweets,
Daily his own heart he eats;
Chambers of the great are jails,
And head-winds right for royal sails."
Then welcome each rebuff,
That turns earth's smoothness rough,
Each sting, that bids not sit nor stand but go. —Browning

Decision

Resolve, and thou art free.—Longfellow

The heaviest charged words in our language are those briefest ones, "yes" and "no." One stands for the surrender of the will, the other for denial; one stands for gratification, the other for character. A stout "no" means a stout character, the ready "yes" a weak one, gild it as we may.—T. T. Munger

The world is a market where everything is marked at a set price, and whatever we buy with our time, labor, or ingenuity, whether riches, ease, fame, integrity, or knowledge, we must stand by our decision, and not like children, when we have purchased one thing, repine that we do not possess another we did not buy.—Mathews

A man must master his undertaking and not let it master him. He must have the power to decide instantly on which side he is going to make his Mistakes.—P. D. Armour

When Rome was besieged by the Gauls in the time of the Republic, the Romans were so hard pressed that they consented to purchase immunity with gold. They were in the act of weighing it, a legend tells us, when Camillus appeared on the scene, threw his sword into the scales in place of the ransom, and declared that the Romans should not purchase peace, but would win it with the sword. This act of daring and prompt decision so roused the Romans that they triumphantly swept from the sacred soil the enemy of their peace.

In an emergency, the arrival of a prompt, decided, positive man, who will do something, although it may be wrong, changes the face of everything. Such a man comes upon the scene like a refreshing breeze blown down from the mountain top. He is a tonic to the hesitating, bewildered crowd.

When Antiochus Epiphanes invaded Egypt, which was then under the protection of Rome, the Romans sent an ambassador who met Antiochus near Alexandria and commanded him to withdraw. The invader gave an evasive reply. The brave Roman swept a circle around the king with his sword, and forbade his crossing the line until he had given his answer. By the prompt decision of the intrepid ambassador the invader was led to withdraw, and war was prevented. The prompt decision of the Romans won them many a battle, and made them masters of the world. All the great achievements in the history of the world are the results of quick and steadfast decision.

Men who have left their mark upon their century have been men of great and prompt decision. An undecided man, a man who is ever balancing between two opinions, forever debating which of two courses he will pursue, proclaims by his indecision that he can not control himself, that he was meant to be possessed by others; he is not a man, only a satellite. The decided man, the prompt man, does not wait for favorable circumstances; he does not submit to events; events must submit to him.

The vacillating man is ever at the mercy of the opinion of the man who talked with him last. He may see the right, but he drifts toward the wrong. If he decides upon a course he only follows it until somebody opposes it.

When Julius Caesar came to the Rubicon, which formed the boundary of Italia,—"the sacred and inviolable,"—even his great decision wavered at the thought of invading a territory which no general was allowed to enter without the permission of the Senate. But his alternative was "destroy myself, or destroy my country," and his intrepid mind did not waver long. "The die is cast," he said, as he dashed into the stream at the head of his legions. The whole history of the world was changed by that moment's decision. The man who said, "I came, I saw, I conquered," could not hesitate long. He, like Napoleon, had the power to choose one course, and sacrifice every conflicting plan on the instant. When he landed with his troops in Britain, the inhabitants resolved never to surrender. Caesar's quick mind saw that he must commit his soldiers to victory or death. In order to cut off all hope of retreat, he burned all the ships which had borne them to the shores of Britain. There was no hope of return, it was victory or death. This action was the key to the character and triumphs of this great warrior.

Satan's sublime decision in "Paradise Lost," after his hopeless banishment from heaven, excites a feeling akin to admiration. After a few moments of terrible suspense he resumes his invincible spirit and expresses that sublime line: "What matter where, if I be still the same?"

That power to decide instantly the best course to pursue, and to sacrifice every opposing motive; and, when once sacrificed, to silence them forever and not allow them continually to plead their claims and distract us from our single decided course, is one of the most potent forces in winning success. To hesitate is sometimes to be lost. In fact, the man who is forever twisting and turning, backing and filling, hesitating and dawdling, shuffling and parleying, weighing and balancing, splitting hairs over non-essentials, listening to every new motive which presents itself, will never accomplish anything. There is not positiveness enough in him; negativeness never accomplishes anything. The negative man creates no confidence, he only invites distrust. But the positive man, the decided man, is a power in the world, and stands for something. You can measure him, gauge him. You can estimate the work that his energy will accomplish. It is related of Alexander the Great that, when asked how it was that he had conquered the world, he replied, "By not wavering."

When the packet ship *Stephen Whitney* struck, at midnight, on an Irish cliff, and clung for a few moments to the cliff, all the passengers who leaped instantly upon the rock were saved. The positive step landed them in safety. Those who lingered were swept off by the returning wave, and engulfed forever.

The vacillating man is never a prompt man, and without promptness no success is possible. Great opportunities not only come seldom into the most fortunate life, but also are often quickly gone.

"A man without decision," says John Foster, "can never be said to belong to himself; since if he dared to assert that he did, the puny force of some cause, about as powerful as a spider, may make a seizure of the unhappy boaster the very next minute, and contemptuously exhibit the futility of the determination by which he was to have proved the independence of his understanding and will. He belongs to whatever can make capture of him; and one thing after another vindicates its right to him by arresting him while he is trying to go on; as twigs and chips floating near the edge of a river are intercepted by every weed and whirled into every little eddy."

The decided man not only has the advantage of the time saved from dillydallying and procrastination, but he also saves the energy and vital force which is wasted by the perplexed man who takes up every argument on one side and then on the other, and weighs them until the two sides hang in equipoise, with no prepondering motive to enable him to decide. He is in stable equilibrium, and so does not move at all of his own volition, but moves very easily at the slightest volition of another.

Yet there is not a man living who might not be a prompt and decided man if he would only learn always to act quickly. The punctual man, the decided man, can do twice as much as the undecided and dawdling man who never quite knows what he wants. Prompt decision saved Napoleon and Grant and their armies many a time when delay would have been fatal. Napoleon used to say that although a battle might last an entire day, yet it generally turned upon a few critical minutes, in which the fate of the engagement was decided. His will, which subdued nearly the whole of Europe, was as prompt and decisive in the minutest detail of command as in the greatest battle.

Decision of purpose and promptness of action enabled him to astonish the world with his marvelous successes. He seemed to be everywhere at once. What he could accomplish in a day surprised all who knew him. He seemed to electrify everybody about him. His invincible energy thrilled the whole army. He could rouse to immediate and enthusiastic action the dullest troops, and inspire with courage the most stupid men. The "ifs and buts," he said, "are at present out of season; and above all it must be done with speed." He would sit up all night if necessary, after riding thirty or forty leagues, to attend to correspondence, dispatches and, details. What a lesson to dawdling, shiftless, half-hearted men!

"The doubt of Charles V.," says Motley, "changed the destinies of the civilized world."

So powerful were President Washington's views in determining the actions of the people, that when Congress adjourned, Jefferson wrote to Monroe at Paris: "You will see by their proceedings the truth of what I always told you,—namely, that one man outweighs them all in influence, who supports his judgment against their own and that of their representatives. Republicanism resigns the vessel to the pilot."

There is no vocation or occupation which does not present many difficulties, at times almost overwhelming, and the young man who allows himself to waver every time he comes to a hard place in life will not succeed. Without decision there can be no concentration; and, to succeed, a man must concentrate.

The undecided man can not bring himself to a focus. He dissipates his energy, scatters his forces, and executes nothing. He can not hold to one thing long enough to bring success out of it. One vocation or occupation presents its rosy side to him, he feels sure it is the thing he wants to do, and, full of enthusiasm, adopts it as his life's work. But in a few days the thorns begin to appear, his enthusiasm evaporates, and he wonders why he is so foolish as to think himself fitted for that vocation. The one which his friend adopted is much better suited to him; he drops his own and adopts the other. So he vacillates through life, captured by any new occupation which happens to appeal to him as the most desirable at the time, never using his judgment or common sense, but governed by his impressions and his feelings at the moment. Such people are never led by principle. You never know where to find them; they are here to-day and there to-morrow, doing this thing and that thing, throwing away all the skill they had acquired in mastering the drudgery of the last occupation. In fact, they never go far enough in anything to get beyond the drudgery stage to the remunerative and agreeable stage, the skilful stage. They spend their lives at the beginning of occupations, which are always most agreeable. These people rarely reach the stage of competency, comfort, and contentment.

There is a legend of a powerful genius who promised a lovely maiden a gift of rare value if she would go through a field of corn, and, without pausing, going backward, or wandering hither and thither, select the largest and ripest ear. The value of the gift was to be in proportion to the size and perfection of the ear. She passed by many magnificent ones, but was so eager to get the largest and most perfect that she kept on without plucking any until the ears she passed were successively smaller and smaller and more stunted. Finally they became so small that she was ashamed to select one of them; and, not being allowed to go backward, she came out on the other side without any.

Alexander, his heart throbbing with a great purpose, conquers the world; Hannibal, impelled by his hatred to the Romans, even crosses the Alps to compass his design. While other men are bemoaning difficulties and shrinking from dangers and obstacles, and preparing expedients, the great soul, without fuss or noise, takes the step, and lo, the mountain has been leveled and the way lies open. Learn, then, to will strongly and decisively; thus fix your floating life and leave it no longer to be carried hither and thither, like a withered leaf, by every wind that blows. An undecided man is like the turnstile at a fair, which is in everybody's way but stops no one.

"The secret of the whole matter was," replied Amos Lawrence, "we had formed the habit of prompt acting, thus taking the top of the tide; while the habit of some others was to delay till about half tide, thus getting on the flats."

Most of the young men and women who are lost in our cities are ruined because of their inability to say "No" to the thousand allurements and temptations which appeal to their weak passions. If they would only show a little decision at first, one emphatic "No" might silence their solicitors forever. But they are weak, they are afraid of offending, they don't like to say "No," and thus they throw down the gauntlet and are soon on the broad road to ruin. A little resolution early in life will soon conquer the right to mind one's own business.

An old legend says that a fool and a wise man were journeying together, and came to a point where two ways opened before them,—one broad and beautiful, the other narrow and rough. The fool desired to take the pleasant way; the wise man knew that the difficult one was the shortest and safest, and so declared. But at last the urgency of the fool prevailed; they took the more inviting path, and were soon met by robbers, who seized their goods and made them captives. A little later both they and their captors were arrested by officers of the law and taken before the judge. Then the wise man pleaded that the fool was to blame because he desired to take the wrong way. The fool pleaded that he was only a fool, and no sensible man should have heeded his counsel. The judge punished them both equally. "If sinners entice thee, consent thou not."

There is no habit that so grows on the soul as irresolution. Before a man knows what he has done, he has gambled his life away, and all because he has never made up his mind what he would do with it. On many of the tombstones of those who have failed in life could be read between the lines: "He Dawdled," "Behind Time," "Procrastination," "Listlessness," "Shiftlessness," "Nervelessness," "Always Behind." Oh, the wrecks strewn along the shores of life "just behind success," "just this side of happiness," above which the words of warning are flying!

Webster said of such an undecided man that "he is like the irresolution of the sea at the turn of tide. This man neither advances nor recedes; he simply hovers." Such a man is at the mercy of any chance occurrence that may overtake him. His "days are lost lamenting o'er lost days." He has no power to seize the facts which confront him and compel them to serve him.

To indolent, shiftless, listless people life becomes a mere shuffle of expedients. They do not realize that the habit of putting everything off puts off their manhood, their capacity, their success; their contagion infects their whole neighborhood. Scott used to caution youth against the habit of dawdling, which creeps in at every crevice of unoccupied time and often ruins a bright life. "Your motto must be," he said, "*Hoc age*,"—do instantly. This is the only way to check the propensity to dawdling. How many hours have been wasted dawdling in bed, turning over and dreading to get up! Many a career has been crippled by it. Burton could not overcome this habit, and, convinced that it would ruin his success, made his servant promise before he went to bed to get him up at just such a time; the servant called, and called, and coaxed; but Burton would beg him to be left a little longer. The servant, knowing that he would lose his shilling if he did not get him up, then dashed cold water into the bed between the sheets, and Burton came out with a bound. When one asked a lazy young fellow what made him lie in bed so long, "I am employed," said he, "in hearing counsel every morning. *Industry* advises me to get up; *Sloth* to lie still; and they give me twenty reasons for and against. It is my part, as an impartial judge, to hear all that can be said on both sides, and by the time the cause is over dinner is ready."

There is no doubt that, as a rule, great decision of character is usually accompanied by great constitutional firmness. Men who have been noted for great firmness of character have usually been strong and robust. There is no quality of the mind which does not sympathize with bodily weakness, and especially is this true with the power of decision, which is usually impaired or weakened from physical suffering or any great physical debility. As a rule, it is the strong physical man who carries weight and conviction. Any bodily weakness, or lassitude, or lack of tone and vigor, is, perhaps, first felt in the weakened or debilitated power of decisions.

Nothing will give greater confidence, and bring assistance more quickly from the bank or from a friend, than the reputation of promptness. The world knows that the prompt man's bills and notes will be paid on the day, and will trust him. "Let it be your first study to teach the world that you are not wood and straw; that there is some iron in you." "Let men know that what you say you will do; that your decision, once made, is final,—no wavering; that, once resolved, you are not to be allured or intimidated."

Some minds are so constructed that they are bewildered and dazed whenever a responsibility is thrust upon them; they have a mortal dread of deciding anything. The very effort to come to immediate and unflinching decision starts up all sorts of doubts, difficulties, and fears, and they can not seem to get light enough to decide nor courage enough to attempt to remove the obstacle. They know that hesitation is fatal to enterprise, fatal to progress, fatal to success. Yet somehow they seem fated with a morbid introspection which ever holds them in suspense. They have just energy enough to weigh motives, but nothing left for the momentum of action. They analyze and analyze, deliberate, weigh, consider, ponder, but never act. How many a man can trace his downfall in life to the failure to seize his opportunity at the favorable moment, when it was within easy grasp, the nick of time, which often does not present itself but once!

It was said that Napoleon had an officer under him who understood the tactics of war better than his commander, but he lacked that power of rapid decision and powerful concentration which characterized the greatest military leaders perhaps of the world. There were several generals under Grant who were as well skilled in war tactics, knew the country as well, were better educated, but they lacked that power of decision which made unconditional surrender absolutely imperative wherever he met the foe. Grant's decision was like inexorable fate. There was no going behind it, no opening it up for reconsideration. It was his decision which voiced itself in those memorable words in the Wilderness, "I propose to fight it out on these lines if it takes all summer," and which sent back the words "unconditional surrender" to General Buckner, who asked him for conditions of capitulation, that gave the first confidence to the North that the rebellion was doomed. At last Lincoln had a general who had the power of decision, and the North breathed easy for the first time.

The man who would forge to the front in this competitive age must be a man of prompt and determined decision; like Caesar, he must burn his ships behind him, and make retreat forever impossible. When he draws his sword he must throw the scabbard away, lest in a moment of discouragement and irresolution he be tempted to sheathe it. He must nail his colors to the mast as Nelson did in battle, determined to sink with his ship if he can not conquer. Prompt decision and sublime audacity have carried many a successful man over perilous crises where deliberation would have been ruin.

"*Hoc age.*"

Observation as a Success Factor

Henry Ward Beecher was not so foolish as to think that he could get on without systematic study, and a thorough-going knowledge of the world of books. "When I first went to Brooklyn," he said, "men doubted whether I could sustain myself. I replied, 'Give me uninterrupted time till nine o'clock every morning, and I do not care what comes after.'"

He was a hard student during four hours every morning; those who saw him after that imagined that he picked up the material for his sermons on the street.

Yet having said so much, it is true that much that was most vital in his preaching he did pick up on the street.

"Where does Mr. Beecher get his sermons?" every ambitious young clergyman in the country was asking, and upon one occasion he answered: "I keep my eyes open and ask questions."

This is the secret of many a man's success,—keeping his eyes open and asking questions. Although Beecher was an omnivorous reader he did not care much for the writings of the theologians; the Christ was his great model, and he knew that He did not search the writings of the Sanhedrin for His sermons, but picked them up as He walked along the banks of the Jordan and over the hills and through the meadows and villages of Galilee. He saw that the strength of this great Master's sermons was in their utter simplicity, their naturalness.

Beecher's sermons were very simple, healthy, and strong. They pulsated with life; they had the vigor of bright red blood in them, because, like Christ's, they grew out of doors. He got them everywhere from life and nature. He picked them up in the marketplace, on Wall Street, in the stores. He got them from the brakeman, the mechanic, the blacksmith, the day laborer, the newsboy, the train conductor, the clerk, the lawyer, the physician, and the business man.

He did not watch the progress of the great human battle from his study, as many did. He went into the thick of the fight himself. He was in the smoke and din. Where the battle of life raged fiercest, there he was studying its great problems. Now it was the problem of slavery; again the problem of government, or commerce, or education,—whatever touched the lives of men. He kept his hand upon the pulse of events. He was in the swim of things. The great, busy, ambitious world was everywhere throbbing for him.

When he once got a taste of the power and helpfulness which comes from the study of real life, when he saw how much more forceful and interesting actual life stories were as they were being lived than anything he could get out of any book except the Bible, he was never again satisfied without illustrations fresh from the lives of the people he met every day.

Beecher believed a sermon a failure when it does not make a great mass of hearers go away with a new determination to make a little more of themselves, to do their work a little better, to be a little more conscientious, a little more helpful, a little more determined to do their share in the world.

This great observer was not only a student of human nature, but of all nature as well. I watched him, many a time, completely absorbed in drinking in the beauties of the marvelous landscape, gathering grandeur and sublimity from the great White Mountains, which he loved so well, and where he spent many summers.

He always preached on Sunday at the hotel where he stayed, and great crowds came from every direction to hear him. There was something in his sermons that appealed to the best in everyone who heard him. They were full of pictures of beautiful landscapes, seascapes, and entrancing sunsets. The clouds, the rain, the sunshine, and the storm were reflected in them. The flowers, the fields, the brooks, the record of creation imprinted in the rocks and the mountains were intermingled with the ferryboats, the steam-cars, orphans, calamities, accidents, all sorts of experiences and bits of life. Happiness and sunshine, birds and trees alternated with the direst poverty in the slums, people on sick beds and death beds, in hospitals and in funeral processions; life pictures of successes and failures, of the discouraged, the despondent, the cheerful, the optimist and the pessimist, passed in quick succession and stamped themselves on the brains of his eager hearers.

Wherever he went, Beecher continued his study of life through observation. Nothing else was half so interesting. To him man was the greatest study in the world. To place the right values upon men, to emphasize the right thing in them, to be able to discriminate between the genuine and the false, to be able to pierce their masks and read the real man or woman behind them, he regarded as one of a clergyman's greatest accomplishments.

Like Professor Agassiz, who could see wonders in the scale of a fish or a grain of sand, Beecher had an eye like the glass of a microscope, which reveals marvels of beauty in common things. He could see beauty and harmony where others saw only ugliness and discord, because he read the hidden meaning in things. Like Ruskin, he could see the marvelous philosophy, the Divine plan, in the lowliest object. He could feel the Divine presence in all created things.

"An exhaustive observation," says Herbert Spencer, "is an element of all great success." There is no position in life where a trained eye can not be made a great success asset.

"Let's leave it to Osler," said the physicians at a consultation where a precious life hung by a thread. Then the great Johns Hopkins professor examined the patient. He did not ask questions. His experienced eye drew a conclusion from the slightest evidence. He watched the patient closely;

his manner of breathing, the appearance of the eye,—everything was a telltale of the patient's condition, which he read as an open book. He saw symptoms which others could not see. He recommended a certain operation, which was performed, and the patient recovered. The majority of those present disagreed with him, but such was their confidence in his power to diagnose a case through symptoms and indications which escape most physicians, that they were willing to leave the whole decision to him. Professor Osler was called a living X-ray machine, with additional eyes in finger tips so familiar with the anatomy that they could detect a growth or displacement so small that it would escape ordinary notice.

The power which inheres in a trained faculty of observation is priceless. The education which Beecher got through observation, by keeping his eyes, his ears, and his mind open, meant a great deal more to him and to the world than his college education. He was not a great scholar; he did not stand nearly as high in college as some of his classmates whom he far outstripped in life, but his mind penetrated to the heart of things.

Lincoln was another remarkable example of the possibilities of an education through reflection upon what he observed. His mind stopped and questioned, and extracted the meaning of everything that came within its range. Wherever he went, there was a great interrogation point before him. Everything he saw must give up its secret before he would let it go. He had a passion for knowledge; he yearned to know the meaning of things, the philosophy underlying the common, everyday occurrences.

Ruskin says: "Hundreds of people can talk for one who can think; but thousands can think for one who can see."

I once traveled abroad with two young men, one of whom was all eyes,—nothing seemed to escape him,—and the other never saw anything. The day after leaving a city, the latter could scarcely recall anything of interest, while the former had a genius for absorbing knowledge of every kind through the eye. Things so trivial that his companion did not notice them at all, meant a great deal to him. He was a poor student, but he brought home rich treasures from over the sea. The other young man was comparatively rich, and brought home almost nothing of value.

While visiting Luther Burbank, the wizard horticulturist, in his famous garden, recently, I was much impressed by his marvelous power of seeing things. He has observed the habits of fruits and flowers to such purpose that he has performed miracles in the fields of floriculture and horticulture. Stunted and ugly flowers and fruits, under the eye of this miracle worker, become marvels of beauty.

George W. Cortelyou was a stenographer not long ago. Many people thought he would remain a stenographer, but he always kept his eyes open. He was after an opportunity. Promotion was always staring him in the face. He was always looking for the next step above him. He was a shrewd observer. But for this power of seeing things quickly, of absorbing knowledge, he would never have advanced.

The youth who would get on must keep his eyes open, his ears open, his mind open. He must be quick, alert, ready.

I know a young Turk, who has been in this country only a year, yet he speaks our language fluently. He has studied the map of our country. He knows its geography, and a great deal of our history, and much about our resources and opportunities. He said that when he landed in New York it seemed to him that he saw more opportunities in walking every block of our streets than he had ever seen in the whole of Turkey. And he could not understand the lethargy, the lack of ambition, the indifference of our young men to our marvelous possibilities.

The efficient man is always growing. He is always accumulating knowledge of every kind. He does not merely look with his eyes. He sees with them. He keeps his ears open. He keeps his mind open to all that is new and fresh and helpful.

The majority of people do not *see* things; they just *look* at them. The power of keen observation is indicative of a superior mentality; for it is the mind, not the optic nerve, that really sees.

Most people are too lazy, mentally, to see things carefully. Close observation is a powerful mental process. The mind is all the time working over the material which the eye brings it, considering, forming opinions, estimating, weighing, balancing, calculating.

Careless, indifferent observation does not go back of the eye. If the mind is not focused, the image is not clean-cut, and is not carried with force and distinctness enough to the brain to enable it to get at the truth and draw accurate conclusions.

The observing faculty is particularly susceptible to culture, and is capable of becoming a mighty power. Few people realize what a tremendous success and happiness is possible through the medium of the eye.

The telegraph, the sewing machine, the telephone, the telescope, the miracles of electricity, in fact, every great invention of the past or present, every triumph of modern labor-saving machinery, every discovery in science and art, is due to the trained power of seeing things.

The whole secret of a richly stored mind is alertness, sharp, keen attention, and thoughtfulness. Indifference, apathy, mental lassitude and laziness are fatal to all effective observation.

It does not take long to develop a habit of attention that seizes the salient points of things.

It is a splendid drill for children to send them out on the street, or out of doors anywhere, just for the purpose of finding out how many things they can see in a certain given time, and how closely they can observe them. Just the effort to try to see how much they can remember and bring back is a splendid drill. Children often become passionately fond of this exercise, and it becomes of inestimable value in their lives.

Other things equal, it is the keen observer who gets ahead. Go into a place of business with the eye of an eagle. Let nothing escape you. Ask yourself why it is that the proprietor at fifty or sixty years of age is conducting a business which a boy of eighteen or twenty ought to be able to handle better. Study his employees; analyze the situation. You will find perhaps that he never knew the value of good manners in clerks. He thought a boy, if honest, would make a good salesman; but, perhaps, by gruff, uncouth manners, he is driving out of the door customers the proprietor is trying to bring in by advertisements. You will see by his show windows, perhaps, before you go into his store, that there is no business insight, no detection of the wants of possible buyers. If you keep your eyes open, you can, in a little while, find out why this man is not a greater success. You can see that a little more knowledge of human nature would have revolutionized his whole business, multiplied the receipts tenfold in a few years. You will see that this man has not studied men. He does not know them.

No matter where you go, study the situation. Think why the man does not do better if he is not doing well, why he remains in mediocrity all his life. If he is making a remarkable success, try to find out why. Keep your eyes open, your ears open. Make deductions from what you see and hear. Trace difficulties; look up evidences of success or failure everywhere. It will be one of the greatest factors in your own success.

Self-Help

I learned that no man in God's wide earth is either willing or able to help any other man.—Pestalozzi

What I am I have made myself.— Humphry Davy

Be sure, my son, and remember that the best men always make themselves.—Patrick Henry

Hereditary bondsmen, know ye not Who would be free themselves must strike the blow? —Byron

Who waits to have his task marked out, Shall die and leave his errand unfulfilled. —Lowell

"Colonel Crockett makes room for himself!" exclaimed a backwoods congressman in answer to the exclamation of the White House usher to "Make room for Colonel Crockett!" This remarkable man was not afraid to oppose the head of a great nation. He preferred being right to being president. Though rough, uncultured, and uncouth, Crockett was a man of great courage and determination.

"Poverty is uncomfortable, as I can testify," said James A. Garfield; "but nine times out of ten the best thing that can happen to a young man is to be tossed overboard and compelled to sink or swim for himself. In all my acquaintance I have never known a man to be drowned who was worth the saving."

Garfield was the youngest member of the House of Representatives when he entered, but he had not been in his seat sixty days before his ability was recognized and his place conceded. He stepped to the front with the confidence of one who belonged there. He succeeded because all the world in concert could not have kept him in the background, and because when once in the front he played his part with an intrepidity and a commanding ease that were but the outward evidences of the immense reserves of energy on which it was in his power to draw.

"Take the place and attitude which belong to you," says Emerson, "and all men acquiesce. The world must be just. It leaves every man with profound unconcern to set his own rate."

"A person under the firm persuasion that he can command resources virtually has them," says Livy.

Richard Arkwright, the thirteenth child, in a hovel, with no education, no chance, gave his spinning model to the world, and put a scepter in England's right hand such as the queen never wielded.

Solario, a wandering gypsy tinker, fell deeply in love with the daughter of the painter Coll' Antonio del Fiore, but was told that no one but a painter as good as the father should wed the maiden. "Will you give me ten years to learn to paint, and so entitle myself to the hand of your daughter?" Consent was given, Coll' Antonio thinking that he would never be troubled further by the gypsy.

About the time that the ten years were to end the king's sister showed Coll' Antonio a Madonna and Child, which the painter extolled in terms of the highest praise. Judge of his surprise on learning that Solario was the artist. His great determination gained him his bride.

Louis Philippe said he was the only sovereign in Europe fit to govern, for he could black his own boots.

When asked to name his family coat-of-arms, a self-made President of the United States replied, "A pair of shirtsleeves."

It is not the men who have inherited most, except it be in nobility of soul and purpose, who have risen highest; but rather the men with no "start" who have won fortunes, and have made adverse circumstances a spur to goad them up the steep mount, where

"Fame's proud temple shines afar."

To such men, every possible goal is accessible, and honest ambition has no height that genius or talent may tread, which has not felt the impress of their feet.

You may leave your millions to your son, but have you really given him anything? You can not transfer the discipline, the experience, the power, which the acquisition has given you; you can not transfer the delight of achieving, the joy felt only in growth, the pride of acquisition, the character which trained habits of accuracy, method, promptness, patience, dispatch, honesty of dealing, politeness of manner have developed. You cannot transfer the skill, sagacity, prudence, foresight, which lie concealed in your wealth. It meant a great deal for you, but means nothing to your heir. In climbing to your fortune, you developed the muscle, stamina, and strength which enabled you to maintain your lofty position, to keep your millions intact. You had the power which comes only from experience, and which alone enables you to stand firm on your dizzy height. Your fortune was experience to you, joy, growth, discipline, and character; to him it will be a temptation, an anxiety, which will probably dwarf him. It was wings to you, it will be a dead weight to him; to you it was education and expansion of your highest powers; to him it may mean inaction, lethargy, indolence, weakness, ignorance. You have taken the priceless spur—necessity—away from him, the spur which has goaded man to nearly all the great achievements in the history of the world.

You thought it a kindness to deprive yourself in order that your son might begin where you left off. You thought to spare him the drudgery, the hardships, the deprivations, the lack of opportunities, the meager education, which you had on the old farm. But you have put a crutch into his hand instead of a staff; you have taken away from him the incentive to self-development, to self-elevation, to self-discipline and self-help, without which no real success, no real happiness, no great character is ever possible. His enthusiasm will evaporate, his energy will be dissipated, his ambition, not being stimulated by the struggle for self-elevation, will gradually die away. If you do everything for your son and fight his battles for him, you will have a weakling on your hands at twenty-one.

"My life is a wreck," said the dying Cyrus W. Field, "my fortune gone, my home dishonored. Oh, I was so unkind to Edward when I thought I was being kind. If I had only had firmness enough to compel my boys to earn their living, then they would have known the meaning of money." His table was covered with medals and certificates of honor from many nations, in recognition of his great work for civilization in mooring two continents side by side in thought, of the fame he had won and could never lose. But grief shook the sands of life as he thought only of the son who had brought disgrace upon a name before unsullied; the wounds were sharper than those of a serpent's tooth.

During the great financial crisis of 1857 Maria Mitchell, who was visiting England, asked an English lady what became of daughters when no property was left them. "They live on their brothers," was the reply. "But what becomes of the American daughters," asked the English lady, "when there is no money left?" "They earn it," was Miss Mitchell's reply.

Men who have been bolstered up all their lives are seldom good for anything in a crisis. When misfortune comes, they look around for somebody to lean upon. It the prop is not there, down they go. Once down, they are as helpless as capsized turtles, or unhorsed men in armor. Many a frontier boy has succeeded beyond all his expectations simply because all props were early knocked out from under him and he was obliged to stand upon his own feet.

"A man's best friends are his ten fingers," said Robert Collyer, who brought his wife to America in the steerage.

There is no manhood mill which takes in boys and turns out men. What you call "no chance" may be your only chance. Don't wait for your place to be made for you; make it yourself. Don't wait for somebody to give you a lift; lift yourself. Henry Ward Beecher did not wait for a call to a big church with a large salary. He accepted the first pastorate offered him, in a little town near Cincinnati. He became literally the light of the church, for he trimmed the lamps, kindled the fires, swept the rooms, and rang the bell. His salary was only about $200 a year,—but he knew that a fine church and great salary can not make a great man. It was work and opportunity that he wanted. He felt that if there were anything in him work would bring it out.

When Beethoven was examining the work of Moscheles, he found written at the end, "Finis, with God's help." He wrote under it, "Man, help yourself."

A young man stood listlessly watching some anglers on a bridge. He was poor and dejected. At length, approaching a basket filled with fish, he sighed, "If now I had these I would be happy. I could sell them and buy food and lodgings." "I will give you just as many and just as good," said the owner, who chanced to overhear his words, "if you will do me a trifling favor." "And what is that?" asked the other. "Only to tend this line till I come back; I wish to go on a short errand." The proposal was gladly accepted. The old man was gone so long that the young man began to get impatient. Meanwhile the fish snapped greedily at the hook, and he lost all his depression in the excitement of pulling them in. When the owner returned he had caught a large number. Counting out from them as many as were in the basket, and presenting them to the youth, the old fisherman said, "I fulfil my promise from the fish you have caught, to teach you whenever you see others earning what you need to waste no time in foolish wishing, but cast a line for yourself."

A white squall caught a party of tourists on a lake in Scotland, and threatened to capsize the boat. When it seemed that the crisis had really come, the largest and strongest man in the party, in a state of intense fear, said, "Let us pray." "No, no, my man," shouted the bluff old boatman; "*let the little man pray. You take an oar.*"

The grandest fortunes ever accumulated or possessed on earth were and are the fruit of endeavor that had no capital to begin with save energy, intellect, and the will. From Croesus down to Rockefeller the story is the same, not only in the getting of wealth, but also in the acquirement of eminence; those men have won most who relied most upon themselves.

"The male inhabitants in the Township of Loaferdom, in the County of Hatework," says a printer's squib, "found themselves laboring under great inconvenience for want of an easily traveled road between Poverty and Independence. They therefore petitioned the Powers that be to levy a tax upon the property of the entire county for the purpose of laying out a macadamized highway, broad and smooth, and all the way down hill to the latter place."

"Every one is the artificer of his own fortune," says Sallust.

Man is not merely the architect of his own fate, but he must lay the bricks himself. Bayard Taylor, at twenty-three, wrote: "I will become the sculptor of my own mind's statue." His biography shows how often the chisel and hammer were in his hands to shape himself into his ideal.

Labor is the only legal tender in the world to true success. The gods sell everything for that, nothing without it. You will never find success "marked down." The door to the temple of success is never left open. Every one who enters makes his own door, which closes behind him to all others.

Circumstances have rarely favored great men. They have fought their way to triumph over the road of difficulty and through all sorts of opposition. A lowly beginning and a humble origin are no bar to a great career. The farmer's boys fill many of the greatest places in legislatures, in business, at the bar, in pulpits, in Congress, to-day. Boys of lowly origin have made many of the greatest discoveries, are presidents of our banks, of our colleges, of our universities. Our poor boys and girls have written many of our greatest books, and have filled the highest places as teachers and journalists. Ask almost any great man in our large cities where he was born, and he will tell you it was on a farm or in a small country village. Nearly all of the great capitalists of the city came from the country.

Isaac Rich, the founder of Boston University, left Cape Cod for Boston to make his way with a capital of only four dollars. Like Horace Greeley, he could find no opening for a boy; but what of that? He made an opening. He found a board, and made it into an oyster stand on the street corner. He borrowed a wheelbarrow, and went three miles to an oyster smack, bought three bushels of oysters, and wheeled them to his stand. Soon his little savings amounted to $130, and then he bought a horse and cart.

Self-help has accomplished about all the great things of the world. How many young men falter, faint, and dally with their purpose because they have no capital to start with, and wait and wait for some good luck to give them a lift! But success is the child of drudgery and perseverance. It cannot be coaxed or bribed; pay the price and it is yours. Where is the boy to-day who has less chance to rise in the world than Elihu Burritt, apprenticed to a blacksmith, in whose shop he had to work at the forge all the daylight, and often by candle-light? Yet, he managed, by studying with a book before him at his meals, carrying it in his pocket that he might utilize every spare moment, and studying at night and holidays, to pick up an excellent education in the odds and ends of time which most boys throw away. While the rich boy and the idler were yawning and stretching and getting their eyes open, young Burritt had seized the opportunity and improved it. At thirty years of age he was master of every important language in Europe and was studying those of Asia. What chance had such a boy for distinction?

Probably not a single youth will read this book who has not a better opportunity for success. Yet he had a thirst for knowledge and a desire for self-improvement, which overcame every obstacle in his pathway.

If the youth of America who are struggling against cruel circumstances to do something and be somebody in the world could only understand that ninety per cent. of what is called genius is merely the result of persistent, determined industry, in most cases of down-right hard work, that it is the slavery to a single idea which has given to many a mediocre talent the reputation of being a genius, they would be inspired with new hope. It is interesting to note that the men who talk most about genius are the men who like to work the least. The lazier the man, the more he will have to say about great things being done by genius.

The greatest geniuses have been the greatest workers. Sheridan was considered a genius, but it was found that the "brilliants" and "off-hand sayings" with which he used to dazzle the House of Commons were elaborated, polished and repolished, and put down in his memorandum book ready for any emergency.

Genius has been well defined as the infinite capacity for taking pains. If men who have done great things could only reveal to the struggling youth of to-day how much of their reputations was due to downright hard digging and plodding, what an uplift of inspiration and encouragement they would give! How often I have wished that the discouraged, struggling youth could know of the heartaches, the headaches, the nerve-aches, the disheartening trials, the discouraged hours, the fears and despair involved in works which have gained the admiration of the world, but which have taxed the utmost powers of their authors. You can read in a few minutes or a few hours a poem or a book with only pleasure and delight, but the days and months of weary plodding over details and dreary drudgery often required to produce it would stagger belief.

The greatest works in literature have been elaborated and elaborated, line by line, paragraph by paragraph, often rewritten a dozen times. The drudgery which literary men have put into the productions which have stood the test of time is almost incredible. Lucretius worked nearly a lifetime on one poem. It completely absorbed his life. It is said that Bryant rewrote "Thanatopsis" a hundred times, and even then was not satisfied with it. John Foster would sometimes linger a week over a single sentence. He would hack, split, prune, pull up by the roots, or practise any other severity on whatever he wrote, till it gained his consent to exist. Chalmers was once asked what Foster was about in London. "Hard at it," he replied, "at the rate of a line a week."

Even Lord Bacon, one of the greatest geniuses that ever lived, at his death left large numbers of manuscripts filled with "sudden thoughts set down for use." Hume toiled thirteen hours a day on his "History of England." Lord Eldon astonished the world with his great legal learning, but when he was a student too poor to buy books, he had actually borrowed and copied many hundreds of pages of large law books. Matthew Hale for years studied law sixteen hours a day. Speaking of Fox, some one declared that he wrote "drop by drop." Rousseau says of the labor involved in his smooth and lively style: "My manuscripts, blotted, scratched, interlined, and scarcely legible, attest the trouble they cost me. There is not one of them which I have not been obliged to transcribe four or five times before it went to press . . . Some of my periods I have turned or returned in my head for five or six nights before they were fit to be put to paper."

Beethoven probably surpassed all other musicians in his painstaking fidelity and persistent application. There is scarcely a bar in his music that was not written and rewritten at least a dozen times. His favorite maxim was, "The barriers are not yet erected which can say to aspiring talent and industry 'thus far and no further.'" Gibbon wrote his autobiography nine times, and was in his study every morning, summer and winter, at six o'clock; and yet youth who waste their evenings wonder at the genius which can produce "The Decline and Fall of the Roman Empire," upon which Gibbon worked twenty years. Even Plato, one of the greatest writers that ever lived, wrote the first sentence in his "Republic" nine different ways before he was satisfied with it. Burke wrote the conclusion of his speech at the trial of Hastings sixteen times, and Butler his famous "Analogy" twenty times. It took Vergil seven years to write his Georgics, and twelve years to write the Aeneid. He was so displeased with the latter that he attempted to rise from his deathbed to commit it to the flames.

Haydn was very poor; his father was a coachman and he, friendless and lonely, married a servant girl. He was sent away from home to act as errand boy for a music teacher. He absorbed a great deal of information, but he had a hard life of persecution until he became a barber in Vienna. Here he blacked boots for an influential man, who became a friend to him. In 1798 this poor boy's oratorio, "The Creation," came upon the musical world like the rising of a new sun which never set. He was courted by princes and dined with kings and queens; his reputation was made; there was no more barbering, no more poverty. But of his eight hundred compositions, "The Creation" eclipsed them all. He died while Napoleon's guns were bombarding Vienna, some of the shot falling in his garden.

When a man like Lord Cavanagh, without arms or legs, manages to put himself into Parliament, when a man like Francis Joseph Campbell, a blind man, becomes a distinguished mathematician, a musician, and a great philanthropist, we get a hint as to what it means to make the most possible out of ourselves and our opportunities. Perhaps ninety-nine of a hundred under such unfortunate circumstances would be content to remain helpless objects of charity for life. If it is your call to acquire money power instead of brain power, to acquire business power instead of professional power, double your talent just the same, no matter what it may be.

A glover's apprentice of Glasgow, Scotland, who was too poor to afford even a candle or a fire, and who studied by the light of the shop windows in the streets, and when the shops were closed climbed the lamp-post, holding his book in one hand, and clinging to the lamp-post with the other,—this poor boy, with less chance than almost any boy in America, became the most eminent scholar of Scotland.

Francis Parkman, half blind, became one of America's greatest historians in spite of everything, because he made himself such. Personal value is a coin of one's own minting; one is taken at the worth he has put into himself. Franklin was but a poor printer's boy, whose highest luxury at one time was only a penny roll, eaten in the streets of Philadelphia.

Michael Faraday was a poor boy, son of a blacksmith, who apprenticed him at the age of thirteen to a bookbinder in London. Michael laid the foundations of his future greatness by making himself familiar with the contents of the books he bound. He remained at night, after others had gone, to read and study the precious volumes. Lord Tenterden was proud to point out to his son the shop where he had shaved for a penny. A French doctor once taunted Fléchier, Bishop of Nismes, who had been a tallow-chandler in his youth, with the meanness of his origin, to which he replied, "If you had been born in the same condition that I was, you would still have been but a maker of candles."

Edwin Chadwick, in his report to the British Parliament, stated that children, working on half time (that is, studying three hours a day and working the rest of their time out of doors), really made the greatest intellectual progress during the year. Business men have often accomplished wonders during the busiest lives by simply devoting one, two, three, or four hours daily to study or other literary work.

James Watt received only the rudiments of an education at school, for his attendance was irregular on account of delicate health. He more than made up for all deficiencies, however, by the diligence with which he pursued his studies at home. Alexander V was a beggar; he was "born mud, and died marble." William Herschel, placed at the age of fourteen as a musician in the band of the Hanoverian Guards, devoted all his leisure to philosophical studies. He acquired a large fund of general knowledge, and in astronomy, a science in which he was wholly self-instructed, his discoveries entitle him to rank with the greatest astronomers of all time.

George Washington was the son of a widow, born under the roof of a Westmoreland farmer; almost from infancy his lot had been that of an orphan. No academy had welcomed him to its shade, no college crowned him with its honors; to read, to write, to cipher—these had been his degrees in knowledge. Shakespeare learned little more than reading and writing at school, but by self-culture he made himself the great master among literary men. Burns, too, enjoyed few advantages of education, and his youth was passed in almost abject poverty.

James Ferguson, the son of a half-starved peasant, learned to read by listening to the recitations of one of his elder brothers. While a mere boy he discovered several mechanical principles, made models of mills and spinning-wheels, and by means of beads on strings worked out an excellent map of the heavens. Ferguson made remarkable things with a common penknife. How many great men have mounted the hill of knowledge by out-of-the-way paths! Gifford worked his intricate problems with a shoemaker's awl on a bit of leather. Rittenhouse first calculated eclipses on his plow-handle.

Columbus, while leading the life of a sailor, managed to become the most accomplished geographer and astronomer of his time.

When Peter the Great, a boy of seventeen, became the absolute ruler of Russia his subjects were little better than savages, and in himself even the passions and propensities of barbarism were so strong that they were frequently exhibited during his whole career. But he determined to transform himself and the Russians into civilized people. He instituted reforms with great energy, and at the age of twenty-six started on a visit to the other countries of Europe for the purpose of learning about their arts and institutions. At Saardam, Holland, he was so impressed with the sights of the great East India dockyard that he apprenticed himself to a shipbuilder, and helped to build the *St. Peter*, which he promptly purchased. Continuing his travels, after he had learned his trade, he worked in England in paper-mills, saw-mills, rope-yards, watchmakers' shops, and other manufactories, doing the work and receiving the treatment of a common laborer.

While traveling, his constant habit was to obtain as much information as he could beforehand with regard to every place he was to visit, and he would demand, "Let me see all." When setting out on his investigations, on such occasions, he carried his tablets in his hand and whatever he deemed worthy of remembrance was carefully noted down. He would often leave his carriage if he saw the country people at work by the wayside as he passed along, and not only enter into conversation with them on agricultural affairs, but also accompany them to their homes, examine their furniture, and take drawings of their implements of husbandry. Thus he obtained much minute and correct knowledge, which he would scarcely have acquired by other means, and which he afterward turned to admirable account in the improvement of his own country.

The ancients said, "Know thyself"; the twentieth century says, "Help thyself." Self-culture gives a second birth to the soul. A liberal education is a true regeneration. When a man is once liberally educated, he will generally remain a man, not shrink to a manikin, nor dwindle to a brute. But if he is not properly educated, if he has merely been crammed and stuffed through college, if he has merely a broken-down memory from trying to hold crammed facts enough to pass the examination, he will continue to shrink, shrivel, and dwindle, often below his original proportions, for he will lose both his confidence and self-respect, as his crammed facts, which never became a part of himself, evaporate from his distended memory.

Every bit of education or culture is of great advantage in the struggle for existence. The microscope does not create anything new, but it reveals marvels. To educate the eye adds to its magnifying power until it sees beauty where before it saw only ugliness. It reveals a world we never suspected, and finds the greatest beauty even in the commonest things. The eye of an Agassiz could see worlds of which the uneducated eye never dreamed. The cultured hand can do a thousand things the uneducated hand can not do. It becomes graceful, steady of nerve, strong, skilful, indeed it almost seems to think, so animated is it with intelligence. The cultured will can seize, grasp, and hold the possessor, with irresistible power and nerve, to almost superhuman effort. The educated touch can almost perform miracles. The educated taste can achieve wonders almost past belief. What a contrast between the cultured, logical, profound, masterly reason of a Gladstone and that of the hod-carrier who has never developed or educated his reason beyond what is necessary to enable him to mix mortar and carry brick!

Be careful to avoid that over-intellectual culture which is purchased at the expense of moral vigor. An observant professor of one of our colleges has remarked that "the mind may be so rounded and polished by education, and so well balanced, as not to be energetic in any one faculty. In other men not thus trained, the sense of deficiency and of the sharp, jagged corners of their knowledge leads to efforts to fill up the chasms, rendering them at last far better educated men than the polished, easy-going graduate who has just knowledge enough to prevent consciousness of his ignorance. While all the faculties of the mind should be cultivated, it is yet desirable that it should have two or three rough-hewn features of massive strength. Young men are too apt to forget the great end of life, which is to be and do, not to read and brood over what other men have been and done."

"I repeat that my object is not to give him knowledge, but to teach him how to acquire it at need," said Rousseau.

All learning is self-teaching. It is upon the working of the pupil's own mind that his progress in knowledge depends. The great business of the master is to teach the pupil to teach himself.

"Thinking, not growth, makes manhood," says Isaac Taylor. "Accustom yourself, therefore, to thinking. Set yourself to understand whatever you see or read. To join thinking with reading is one of the first maxims, and one of the easiest operations."

"How few think justly of the thinking few:
How many never think who think they do."

The Self-Improvement Habit

If you want knowledge you must toil for it.—Ruskin

We excuse our sloth under the pretext of difficulty.—Quintillian

What sculpture is to a block of marble, education is to the human soul.—Addison

A boy is better unborn than untaught.—Gascoigne

It is ignorance that wastes; it is knowledge that saves, an untaught faculty is at once quiescent and dead.— N. D. Hillis

The plea that this or that man has no time for culture will vanish as soon as we desire culture so much that we begin to examine seriously into our present use of time.— Matthew Arnold

Education, as commonly understood, is the process of developing the mind by means of books and teachers. When education has been neglected, either by reason of lack of opportunity, or because advantage was not taken of the opportunities afforded, the one remaining hope is self-improvement. Opportunities for self-improvement surround us, the helps to self-improvement are abundant, and in this day of cheap books and free libraries, there can be no good excuse for neglect to use the faculties for mental growth and development which are so abundantly supplied.

When we look at the difficulties which hindered the acquisition of knowledge fifty years to a century ago; the scarcity and the costliness of books, the value of the dimmest candle-light, the unremitting toil which left so little time for study, the physical weariness which had to be overcome to enable mental exertion in study, we may well marvel at the giants of scholarship those days of hardship produced. And when we add to educational limitations, physical disabilities, blindness, deformity, ill-health, hunger and cold, we may feel shame as we contemplate the fulness of modern opportunity and the helps and incentives to study and self-development which are so lavishly provided for our use and inspiration, and of which we make so little use.

Self-improvement implies one essential feeling: the desire for improvement. If the desire exists, then improvement is usually accomplished only by the conquest of self—the material self, which seeks pleasure and amusement. The novel, the game of cards, the billiard cue, idle whittling and story-telling will have to be eschewed, and every available moment of leisure turned to account. For all who seek self-improvement "there is a lion in the way," the lion of self-indulgence, and it is only by the conquest of this enemy that progress is assured.

Show me how a youth spends his evenings, his odd bits of time, and I will forecast his future. Does he look upon this leisure as precious, rich in possibilities, as containing golden material for his future life structure? Or does he look upon it as an opportunity for self-indulgence, for a light, flippant good time?

The way he spends his leisure will give the keynote of his life, will tell whether he is dead in earnest, or whether he looks upon it as a huge joke.

He may not be conscious of the terrible effects, the gradual deterioration of character which comes from a frivolous wasting of his evenings and half-holidays, but the character is being undermined just the same.

Young men are often surprised to find themselves dropping behind their competitors, but if they will examine themselves, they will find that they have stopped growing, because they have ceased their effort to keep abreast of the times, to be widely read, to enrich life with self culture.

It is the right use of spare moments in reading and study which qualify men for leadership. And in many historic cases the "spare" moments utilized for study were not spare in the sense of being the spare time of leisure. They were rather *spared* moments, moments spared from sleep, from meal times, from recreation.

Where is the boy to-day who has less chance to rise in the world than Elihu Burritt, apprenticed at sixteen to a blacksmith, in whose shop he had to work at the forge all the daylight, and often by candle-light? Yet he managed, by studying with a book before him at his meals, carrying it in his pocket that he might utilize every spare moment, and studying nights and holidays, to pick up an excellent education in the odds and ends of time which most boys throw away. While the rich boy and the idler were yawning and stretching and getting their eyes open, young Burritt had seized the opportunity and improved it.

He had a thirst for knowledge and a desire for self-improvement, which overcame every obstacle in his pathway. A wealthy gentleman offered to pay his expenses at Harvard. But no, Elihu said he could get his education himself, even though he had to work twelve or fourteen hours a day at the forge. Here was a determined boy. He snatched every spare moment at the anvil and forge as if it were gold. He believed, with Gladstone, that thrift of time would repay him in after years with usury, and that waste of it would make him dwindle. Think of a boy working nearly all the daylight in a blacksmith shop, and yet finding time to study seven languages in a single year.

It is not lack of ability that holds men down but lack of industry. In many cases the employee has a better brain, a better mental capacity than his employer. But he does not improve his faculties. He dulls his mind by cigarette smoking. He spends his money at the pool table, theater, or dance, and as he grows old, and the harness of perpetual service galls him, he grumbles at his lack of luck, his limited opportunity.

The number of perpetual clerks is constantly being recruited by those who did not think it worth while as boys to learn to write a good hand or to master the fundamental branches of knowledge requisite in a business career. The ignorance common among young men and young women, in factories, stores, and offices, everywhere, in fact, in this land of opportunity, where youth should be well educated, is a pitiable thing in American life. On every hand we see men and women of ability occupying inferior positions because they did not think it worth while in youth to develop their powers and to concentrate their attention on the acquisition of sufficient knowledge.

Thousands of men and women find themselves held back, handicapped for life because of the seeming trifles which they did not think it worth while to pay attention to in their early days.

Many a girl of good natural ability spends her most productive years as a cheap clerk, or in a mediocre position because she never thought it worth while to develop her mental faculties or to take advantage of opportunities within reach to fit herself for a superior position. Thousands of girls unexpectedly thrown on their own resources have been held down all their lives because of neglected tasks in youth, which at the time were dismissed with a careless "I don't think it worth while." They did not think it would pay to go to the bottom of any study at school, to learn to keep accounts accurately, or fit themselves to do anything in such a way as to be able to make a living by it. They expected to marry, and never prepared for being dependent on themselves,—a contingency against which marriage, in many instances, is no safeguard.

The trouble with most youths is that they are not willing to fling the whole weight of their being into their location. They want short hours, little work and a lot of play. They think more of leisure and pleasure than of discipline and training in their great life specialty.

Many a clerk envies his employer and wishes that he could go into business for himself, be an employer too but it is too much work to make the effort to rise above a clerkship. He likes to take life easy; and he wonders idly whether, after all, it is worth while to strain and strive and struggle and study to prepare oneself for the sake of getting up a little higher and making a little more money.

The trouble with a great many people is that they are not willing to make present sacrifices for future gain. They prefer to have a good time as they go along, rather than spend time in self-improvement. They have a sort of vague wish to do something great, but few have that intensity of longing which impels them to make the sacrifice of the present for the future. Few are willing to work underground for years laying a foundation for the life monument. They yearn for greatness, but their yearning is not the kind which is willing to pay any price in endeavor or make any sacrifice for its object.

So the majority slide along in mediocrity all their lives. They have ability for something higher up, but they have not the energy and determination to prepare for it. They do not care to make necessary effort. They prefer to take life easier and lower down rather than to struggle for something higher. They do not play the game for all they are worth.

If a man or woman has but the disposition for self-improvement and advancement he will find opportunity to rise or "what he can not find create." Here is an example from the everyday life going on around us and in which we are all taking part.

A young Irishman who had reached the age of nineteen or twenty without learning to read or write, and who left home because of the intemperance that prevailed there, learned to read a little by studying billboards, and eventually got a position as steward aboard a man-of-war. He chose that occupation and got leave to serve at the captain's table because of a great desire to learn. He kept a little tablet in his coat-pocket, and whenever he heard a new word wrote it down. One day an officer saw him writing and immediately suspected him of being a spy. When he and the other officers learned what the tablet was used for, the young man was given more opportunities to learn, and these led in time to promotion, until, finally, the sometime steward won a prominent position in the navy. Success as a naval officer prepared the way for success in other fields.

Self-help has accomplished about all the great things of the world. How many young men falter, faint, and dally with their purpose, because they have no capital to start with, and wait and wait for some good luck to give them a lift! But success is the child of drudgery and perseverance. It can not be coaxed or bribed; pay the price and it is yours.

One of the sad things about the neglected opportunities for self-improvement is that it puts people of great natural ability at a disadvantage among those who are their mental inferiors.

I know a member of one of our city legislatures, a splendid fellow, immensely popular, who has a great, generous heart and broad sympathies, but who can not open his mouth without so murdering the English language that it is really painful to listen to him.

There are a great many similar examples in Washington of men who have been elected to important positions because of their great natural ability and fine characters, but who are constantly mortified and embarrassed by their ignorance and lack of early training.

One of the most humiliating experiences that can ever come to a human being is to be conscious of possessing more than ordinary ability, and yet be tied to an inferior position because of lack of early and intelligent training commensurate with his ability. To be conscious that one has ability to realize eighty or ninety per cent of his possibilities, if he had only had the proper education and training, but because of this lack to be unable to bring out more than twenty-five per cent of it on account of ignorance, is humiliating and embarrassing. In other words, to go through life conscious that you are making a botch of your capabilities just because of lack of training, is a most depressing thing.

Nothing else outside of sin causes more sorrow than that which comes from not having prepared for the highest career possible to one. There are no bitterer regrets than those which come from being obliged to let opportunities pass by for which one never prepared himself.

I know a pitiable case of a born naturalist whose ambition was so suppressed, and whose education so neglected in youth, that later when he came to know more about natural history than almost any man of his day, he could not write a grammatical sentence, and could never make his ideas live in words, perpetuate them in books, because of his ignorance of even the rudiments of an education. His early vocabulary was so narrow and pinched, and his knowledge of his language so limited that he always seemed to be painfully struggling for words to express his thought.

Think of the suffering of this splendid man, who was conscious of possessing colossal scientific knowledge, and yet was absolutely unable to express himself grammatically!

How often stenographers are mortified by the use of some unfamiliar word or term, or quotation, because of the shallowness of their preparation!

It is not enough to be able to take dictation when ordinary letters are given, not enough to do the ordinary routine of office work. The ambitious stenographer must be prepared for the unusual demand, must have good reserves of knowledge to draw from in case of emergency.

But, if she is constantly slipping up upon her grammar, or is all at sea the moment she steps out of her ordinary routine, her employer knows that her preparation is shallow, that her education is very limited, and her prospects will be limited also.

A young lady writes me that she is so handicapped by the lack of an early education that she fairly dreads to write a letter to anyone of education or culture for fear of making ignorant mistakes in grammar and spelling. Her letter indicates that she has a great deal of natural ability. Yet she is much limited and always placed at a disadvantage because of this lack of an early education. It is difficult to conceive of a greater misfortune than always to be embarrassed and handicapped just because of the neglect of those early years.

I am often pained by letters from people, especially young people, which indicate that the writers have a great deal of natural ability, that they have splendid minds, but a large part of their ability is covered up, rendered ineffectual by their ignorance.

Many of these letters show that the writers are like diamonds in the rough, with only here and there a little facet ground off, just enough to let in the light and reveal the great hidden wealth within.

I always feel sorry for these people who have passed the school age and who will probably go through life with splendid minds handicapped by their ignorance which, even late in life, they might largely or entirely overcome.

It is such a pity that, a young man, for instance, who has the natural ability which would make him a leader among men, must, for the lack of a little training, a little preparation, work for somebody else, perhaps with but half of his ability but with a better preparation, more education.

Everywhere we see clerks, mechanics, employees in all walks of life, who cannot rise to anything like positions which correspond with their natural ability, because they have not had the education. They are ignorant. They can not write a decent letter. They murder the English language, and hence their superb ability cannot be demonstrated, and remains in mediocrity.

The parable of the talents illustrates and enforces one of nature's sternest laws: "To him that hath shall be given; from him that hath not shall be taken away even that which he hath." Scientists call this law the survival of the fittest. The fittest are those who use what they have, who gain strength by struggle, and who survive by self-development by control of their hostile or helpful environment.

The soil, the sunshine, the atmosphere are very liberal with the material for the growth of the plant or the tree, but the plant must use all it gets, it must work it up into flowers, into fruit, into leaf or fiber or something or the supply will cease. In other words, the soil will not send any more building material up the sap than is used for growth, and the faster this material is used the more rapid the growth, the more abundantly the material will come.

The same law holds good everywhere. Nature is liberal with us if we utilize what she gives us, but if we stop using it, if we do not transform what she gives us into power, if we do not do some building somewhere, if we do not transform the material which she gives us into force and utilize that force, we not only find the supply cut off, but we find that we are growing weaker, less efficient.

Everything in nature is on the move, either one way or the other. It is either going up or down. It is either advancing or retrograding; we cannot hold without using.

Nature withdraws muscle or brain if we do not use them. She withdraws skill the moment we stop drilling efficiently, the moment we stop using our power. The force is withdrawn when we cease exercising it.

A college graduate is often surprised years after he leaves the college to find that about all he has to show for his education is his diploma. The power, the efficiency which he gained there has been lost because he has not been using them. He thought at the time that everything was still fresh in his mind after his examination that this knowledge would remain with him, but it has been slipping away from him every minute since he stopped using it, and only that has remained and increased which he has used; the rest has evaporated. A great many college graduates ten years afterwards find that they have but very little left to show for their four years' course, because they have not utilized their knowledge. They have become weaklings without knowing it. They constantly say to themselves, "I have a college education, I must have some ability, I must amount to something in the world." But the college diploma has no more power to hold the knowledge you have gained in college than a piece of tissue paper over a gas jet can hold the gas in the pipe.

Everything which you do not use is constantly slipping away from you. Use it or lose it. The secret of power is use. Ability will not remain with us, force will evaporate the moment we cease to do something with it.

The tools for self-improvement are at your hand, use them. If the ax is dull the more strength must be put forth. If your opportunities are limited you must use more energy, put forth more effort. Progress may seem slow at first, but perseverance assures success. "Line upon line, and precept upon precept" is the rule of mental upbuilding and "In due time ye shall reap if ye faint not."

Raising of Values

"Destiny is not about thee, but within,— Thyself must make thyself."

"The world is no longer clay, but rather iron in the hands of its workers," says Emerson, "and men have got to hammer out a place for themselves by steady and rugged blows."

To make the most of your "stuff," be it cloth, iron, or character,—this is success. Raising common "stuff" to priceless value is great success.

The man who first takes the rough bar of wrought iron may be a blacksmith, who has only partly learned his trade, and has no ambition to rise above his anvil. He thinks that the best possible thing he can do with his bar is to make it into horseshoes, and congratulates himself upon his success. He reasons that the rough lump of iron is worth only two or three cents a pound, and that it is not worth while to spend much time or labor on it. His enormous muscles and small skill have raised the value of the iron from one dollar, perhaps, to ten dollars.

Along comes a cutler, with a little better education, a little more ambition, a little finer perception, and says to the blacksmith: "Is this all you can see in that iron? Give me a bar, and I will show you what brains and skill and hard work can make of it." He sees a little further into the rough bar. He has studied many processes of hardening and tempering; he has tools, grinding and polishing wheels, and annealing furnaces. The iron is fused, carbonized into steel, drawn out, forged, tempered, heated white-hot, plunged into cold water or oil to improve its temper, and ground and polished with great care and patience. When this work is done, he shows the astonished blacksmith two thousand dollars' worth of knife-blades where the latter only saw ten dollars' worth of crude horseshoes. The value has been greatly raised by the refining process.

"Knife-blades are all very well, if you can make nothing better," says another artisan, to whom the cutler has shown the triumph of his art, "but you haven't half brought out what is in that bar of iron. I see a higher and better use; I have made a study of iron, and know what there is in it and what can be made of it."

This artisan has a more delicate touch, a finer perception, a better training, a higher ideal, and superior determination, which enable him to look still further into the molecules of the rough bar,—past the horse-shoes, past the knife-blades,—and he turns the crude iron into the finest cambric needles, with eyes cut with microscopic exactness. The production of the invisible points requires a more delicate process, a finer grade of skill than the cutler possesses.

This feat the last workman considers marvelous, and he thinks he has exhausted the possibilities of the iron. He has multiplied many times the value of the cutler's product.

But, behold! another very skilful mechanic, with a more finely organized mind, a more delicate touch, more patience, more industry, a higher order of skill, and a better training, passes with ease by the horse-shoes, the knife-blades, and the needles, and returns the product of his bar in fine mainsprings for watches. Where the others saw horseshoes, knife-blades, or needles, worth only a few thousand dollars, his penetrating eye saw a product worth one hundred thousand dollars.

A higher artist-artisan appears, who tells us that the rough bar has not even yet found its highest expression; that he possesses the magic that can perform a still greater miracle in iron. To him, even main-springs seem coarse and clumsy. He knows that the crude iron can be manipulated and coaxed into an elasticity that can not even be imagined by one less trained in metallurgy. He knows that, if care enough be used in tempering the steel, it will not be stiff, trenchant, and merely a passive metal, but so full of its new qualities that it almost seems instinct with life.

With penetrating, almost clairvoyant vision, this artist-artisan sees how every process of mainspring making can be carried further; and how, at every stage of manufacture, more perfection can be reached; how the texture of the metal can be so much refined that even a fiber, a slender thread of it, can do marvelous work. He puts his bar through many processes of refinement and fine tempering, and, in triumph, turns his product into almost invisible coils of delicate hair-springs. After infinite toil and pain, he has made his dream true; he has raised the few dollars' worth of iron to a value of one million dollars, perhaps forty times the value of the same weight of gold.

Still another workman, whose processes are so almost infinitely delicate, whose product is so little known, by even the average educated man, that his trade is unmentioned by the makers of dictionaries and encylopedias, takes but a fragment of one of the bars of steel, and develops its higher possibilities with such marvelous accuracy, such ethereal fineness of touch, that even mainsprings and hairsprings are looked back upon as coarse, crude, and cheap. When his work is done, he shows you a few of the minutely barbed instruments used by dentists to draw out the finest branches of the dental nerves. While a pound of gold, roughly speaking, is worth about two hundred and fifty dollars, a pound of these slender, barbed filaments of steel, if a pound could be collected, might be worth hundreds of times as much.

Other experts may still further refine the product, but it will be many a day before the best will exhaust the possibilities of a metal that can be subdivided until its particles will float in the air.

It sounds magical, but the magic is only that wrought by the application of the homeliest virtues; by the training of the eye, the hand, the perception; by painstaking care, by hard work, and by determination and grit.

If a metal possessing only a few coarse material qualities is capable of such marvelous increase in value, by mixing brains with its molecules, who shall set bounds to the possibilities of the development of a human being, that wonderful compound of physical, mental, moral, and spiritual forces? Whereas, in the development of iron, a dozen processes are possible, a thousand influences may be brought to bear upon mind and character. While the iron is an inert mass acted upon by external influences only, the human being is a bundle of forces, acting and counteracting, yet all capable of control and direction by the higher self, the real, dominating personality.

The difference in human attainment is due only slightly to the original material. It is the ideal followed and unfolded, the effort made, the processes of education and experience undergone that fuse, hammer, and mold our life-bar into its ultimate development.

Life, everyday life, has counterparts of all the tortures the iron undergoes, and through them it comes to its highest expression. The blows of opposition, the struggles amid want and woe, the fiery trials of disaster and bereavement, the crushings of iron circumstances, the raspings of care and anxiety, the grinding of constant difficulties, the rebuffs that chill enthusiasm, the weariness of years of dry, dreary drudgery in education and discipline,—all these are necessary to the man who would reach the highest success.

The iron, by this manipulation, is strengthened, refined, made more elastic or more resistant, and adapted to the use each artisan dreams of. If every blow should fracture it, if every furnace should burn the life out of it, if every roller should pulverize it, of what use would it be? It has that virtue, those qualities that withstand all; that draw profit from every test, and come out triumphant in the end. In the iron the qualities are, in the main, inherent; but in ourselves they are largely matters of growth, culture, and development, and all are subject to the dominating will.

Just as each artisan sees in the crude iron some finished, refined product, so must we see in our lives glorious possibilities, if we would but realize them. If we see only horseshoes or knife-blades, all our efforts and struggles will never produce hairsprings. We must realize our own adaptability to great ends; we must resolve to struggle, to endure trials and tests, to pay the necessary price, confident that the result will pay us for our suffering, our trials, and our efforts.

Those who shrink from the forging, the rolling, and the drawing out, are the ones who fail, the "nobodies," the faulty characters, the criminals. Just as a bar of iron, if exposed to the elements, will oxidize, and become worthless, so will character deteriorate if there is no constant effort to improve its form, to increase its ductility, to temper it, or to better it in some way.

It is easy to remain a common bar of iron, or comparatively so, by becoming merely a horseshoe; but it is hard to raise your life-product to higher values.

Many of us consider our natural gift-bars poor, mean, and inadequate, compared with those of others; but, if we are willing, by patience, toil, study, and struggle, to hammer, draw out, and refine, to work on and up from clumsy horseshoes to delicate hairsprings, we can, by infinite patience and persistence, raise the value of the raw material to almost fabulous heights. It was thus that Columbus, the weaver, Franklin, the journeyman printer, Aesop, the slave, Homer, the beggar, Demosthenes, the cutler's son, Ben Jonson, the bricklayer, Cervantes, the common soldier, and Haydn, the poor wheelwright's son, developed their powers, until they towered head and shoulders above other men.

There is very little difference between the material given to a hundred average boys and girls at birth, yet one with no better means of improvement than the others, perhaps with infinitely poorer means, will raise his material in value a hundredfold, five-hundredfold, aye, a thousandfold, while the ninety-nine will wonder why their material remains so coarse and crude, and will attribute their failure to hard luck.

While one boy is regretting his want of opportunities, his lack of means to get a college education, and remains in ignorance, another with half his chances picks up a good education in the odds and ends of time which other boys throw away. From the same material, one man builds a palace and another a hovel. From the same rough piece of marble, one man calls out an angel of beauty which delights every beholder, another a hideous monster which demoralizes every one who sees it.

The extent to which you can raise the value of your life-bar depends very largely upon yourself. Whether you go upward to the mainspring or hairspring stage, depends very largely upon your ideal, your determination to be the higher thing, upon your having the grit to be hammered, to be drawn out, to be thrust from the fire into cold water or oil in order to get the proper temper.

Of course, it is hard and painful, and it takes lots of stamina to undergo the processes that produce the finest product, but would you prefer to remain a rough bar of iron or a horseshoe all your life?

Self Improvement Through Public Speaking

It does not matter whether you want to be a public speaker or not, everybody should have such complete control of himself, should be so self-centered and self-posed that he can get up in any audience, no matter how large or formidable, and express his thoughts clearly and distinctly.

Self-expression in some manner is the only means of developing mental power. It may be in music; it may be on canvas: it may be through oratory; it may come through selling goods or writing a book; but it must come through self-expression.

Self-expression in any legitimate form tends to call out what is in a man, his resourcefulness, inventiveness; but no other form of self-expression develops a man so thoroughly and so effectively, and so quickly unfolds all of his powers, as expression before an audience.

It is doubtful whether anyone can reach the highest standard of culture without studying the art of expression, especially public vocal expression. In all ages oratory has been regarded as the highest expression of human achievement. Young people, no matter what they intend to be, whether blacksmith or farmer, merchant or physician, should make it a study.

Nothing else will call out what is in a man so quickly and so effectively as the constant effort to do his best in speaking before an audience. When one undertakes to think on his feet and speak extemporaneously before the public, the power and the skill of the entire man are put to a severe test.

The writer has the advantage of being able to wait for his moods. He can write when he feels like it; and he knows that he can burn his manuscript again and again if it does not suit him. There are not a thousand eyes upon him. He does not have a great audience criticizing every sentence, weighing every thought. He does not have to step upon the scales of every listener's judgment to be weighed, as does the orator. A man may write as listlessly as he pleases, use much or little of his brain or energy, just as he chooses or feels like doing. No one is watching him. His pride and vanity are not touched, and what he writes may never be seen by anyone. Then, there is always a chance for revision. In conversation, we do not feel that so much depends upon our words; only a few persons hear them, and perhaps no one will ever think of them again. In music, whether vocal or instrumental, what one gives out is only partially one's own; the rest is the composer's.

Yet anyone who lays any claim to culture, should train himself to think on his feet, so that he can at a moment's notice rise and express himself intelligently. The occasions for little speaking are increasing enormously. A great many questions which used to be settled in the office are now discussed and settled at dinners. All sorts of business deals are now carried through at dinners. There was never before any such demand for dinner oratory as to-day.

We know men who have, by the dint of hard work and persistent grit, lifted themselves into positions of prominence, and yet they are not able to stand on their feet in public, even to make a few remarks, or scarcely to put a motion without trembling like an aspen leaf. They had plenty of opportunities when they were young, at school, in debating clubs to get rid of their self-consciousness and to acquire ease and facility in public speaking, but they always shrank from every opportunity, because they were timid, or felt that somebody else could handle the debate or questions better.

There are plenty of business men to-day who would give a great deal of money if they could only go back and improve the early opportunities for learning to think and speak on their feet which they threw away. Now they have money, they have position, but they are nobodies when called upon to speak in public. All they can do is to look foolish, blush, stammer out an apology and sit down.

Some time ago I was at a public meeting when a man who stands very high in the community, who is king in his specialty, was called upon to give his opinion upon the matter under consideration, and he got up and trembled and stammered and could scarcely say his soul was his own. He could not even make a decent appearance. He had power and a great deal of experience, but there he stood, as helpless as a child, and he felt cheap, mortified, embarrassed, and probably would have given anything if he had early in life trained himself to get himself in hand so that he could think on his feet and say with power and effectiveness that which he knew.

At the very meeting where this strong man who had the respect and confidence of everybody who knew him, and who made such a miserable failure of his attempt to give his opinion upon an important public matter on which he was well posted, being so confused and self-conscious and "stage struck" that he could say scarcely anything, a shallow-brained business man, in the same city, who hadn't a hundredth part of the other man's practical power in affairs, got up and made a brilliant speech, and strangers no doubt thought that he was much the stronger man. He had simply cultivated the ability to say his best thing on his feet, and the other man had not, and was placed at a tremendous disadvantage.

A very brilliant young man in New York who has climbed to a responsible position in a very short time, tells me that he has been surprised on several occasions when he has been called upon to speak at banquets, or on other public occasions, at the new discoveries he has made of himself of power which he never before dreamed he possessed, and he now regrets more than anything else that he has allowed so many opportunities for calling himself out to go by in the past.

The effort to express one's ideas in lucid, clean-cut, concise, telling English tends to make one's everyday language choicer and more direct, and improves one's diction generally. In this and other ways speech-making develops mental power and character. This explains the rapidity with which a young man develops in school or college when he begins to take part in public debates or in debating societies.

Every man, says Lord Chesterfield, may choose good words instead of bad ones and speak properly instead of improperly; he may have grace in his motions and gestures, and may be a very agreeable instead of disagreeable speaker if he will take care and pains.

It is a matter of painstaking and preparation. There is everything in learning what you wish to know. Your vocal culture, manner, and mental furnishing, are to be made a matter for thought and careful training. Nothing will tire an audience more quickly than monotony, everything expressed on the same dead level. There must be variety; the human mind tires very quickly without it.

This is especially true of a monotonous tone. It is a great art to be able to raise and lower the voice with sweet flowing cadences which please the ear.

Gladstone said, "Ninety-nine men in every hundred never rise above mediocrity because the training of the voice is entirely neglected and considered of no importance."

It was indeed said of a certain Duke of Devonshire that he was the only English statesman who ever took a nap during the progress of his own speech. He was a perfect genius for dry uninteresting oratory, moving forward with a monotonous droning, and pausing now and then as if refreshing himself by slumber.

In thinking on one's feet before an audience, one must think quickly, vigorously, effectively. At the same time he must speak effectively through a properly modulated voice, with proper facial and bodily expression and gesture. This requires practise in early life.

In youth the would-be orator must cultivate robust health, since force, enthusiasm, conviction, will-power are greatly affected by physical condition. One, too, must cultivate bodily posture, and have good habits at easy command. What would have been the result of Webster's reply to Hayne, the greatest oratorical effort ever made on this continent, if he had sat down in the Senate and put his feet on his desk? Think of a great singer like Nordica attempting to electrify an audience while lounging on a sofa or sitting in a slouchy position.

An early training for effective speaking will make one careful to secure a good vocabulary by good reading and a dictionary. One must know words.

There is no class of people put to such a severe test of showing what is in them as public speakers; no other men who run such a risk of exposing their weak spots, or making fools of themselves in the estimation of others, as do orators. Public speaking—thinking on one's feet—is a powerful educator except to the thick-skinned man, the man who has no sensitiveness, or who does not care for what others think of him. Nothing else so thoroughly discloses a man's weaknesses or shows up his limitations of thought, his poverty of speech, his narrow vocabulary. Nothing else is such a touchstone of the character and the extent of one's reading, the carefulness or carelessness of his observation.

Close, compact statement must be had. Learn to stop when you get through. Do not keep stringing out conversation or argument after you have made your point. You only weaken your case and prejudice people against you for your lack of tact, good judgment, or sense of proportion. Do not neutralize all the good impression you have made by talking on and on long after you have made your point.

The attempt to become a good public speaker is a great awakener of all the mental faculties. The sense of power that comes from holding attention, stirring the emotions or convincing the reason of an audience, gives self-confidence, assurance, self-reliance, arouses ambition, and tends to make one more effective in every particular. One's manhood, character, learning, judgment of his opinions—all things that go to make him what he is—are being unrolled like a panorama. Every mental faculty is quickened, every power of thought and expression spurred. Thoughts rush for utterance, words press for choice. The speaker summons all his reserves of education, of experience, of natural or acquired ability, and masses all his forces in the endeavor to capture the approval and applause of the audience.

Such an effort takes hold of the entire nature, beads the brow, fires the eye, flushes the cheek, and sends the blood surging through the veins. Dormant impulses are stirred, half-forgotten memories revived, the imagination quickened to see figures and similes that would never come to calm thought.

This forced awakening of the whole personality has effects reaching much further than the oratorical occasion. The effort to marshal all one's reserves in a logical and orderly manner, to bring to the front all the power one possesses, leaves these reserves permanently better in hand, more readily in reach.

The Debating Club is the nursery of orators. No matter how far you have to go to attend it, or how much trouble it is, or how difficult it is to get the time, the drill you will get by it is the turning point. Lincoln, Wilson, Webster, Choate, Clay, and Patrick Henry got their training in the old-fashioned Debating Society.

Do not think that because you do not know anything about parliamentary law that you should not accept the presidency of your club or debating society. This is just the place to learn, and when you have accepted the position you can post yourself on the rules, and the chances are that you will never know the rules until you are thrust into the chair where you will be obliged to give rulings. Join just as many young people's organizations—especially self-improvement organizations—as you can, and force yourself to speak every time you get a chance. If the chance does not come to you, make it. Jump to your feet and say something upon every question that is up for discussion. Do not be afraid to rise to put a motion or to second it or give your opinion upon it. Do not wait until you are better prepared. You never will be.

Every time you rise to your feet will increase your confidence, and after awhile you will form the habit of speaking until it will be as easy as anything else, and there is no one thing which will develop young people so rapidly and effectively as the debating clubs and discussions of all sorts. A vast number of our public men have owed their advance more to the old-fashioned debating societies than anything else. Here they learned confidence, self-reliance; they discovered themselves. It was here they learned not to be afraid of themselves, to express their opinions with force and independence. Nothing will call a young man out more than the struggle in a debate to hold his own. It is strong, vigorous exercise for the mind as wrestling is for the body.

Do not remain way back on the back seat. Go up front. Do not be afraid to show yourself. This shrinking into a corner and getting out of sight and avoiding publicity is fatal to self-confidence.

It is so easy and seductive, especially for boys and girls in school or college, to shrink from the public debates or speaking, on the ground that they are not quite well enough educated at present. They want to wait until they can use a little better grammar, until they have read more history and more literature, until they have gained a little more culture and ease of manner.

The way to acquire grace, ease, facility, the way to get poise and balance so that you will not feel disturbed in public gatherings, is to get the experience. Do the thing so many times that it will become second nature to you. If you have an invitation to speak, no matter how much you may shrink from it, or how timid or shy you may be, resolve that you will not let this opportunity for self-enlargement slip by you.

We know of a young man who has a great deal of natural ability for public speaking, and yet he is so timid that he always shrinks from accepting invitations to speak at banquets or in public because he is so afraid that he has not had experience enough. He lacks confidence in himself. He is so proud, and so afraid that he will make some slip which will mortify him, that he has waited and waited and waited until now he is discouraged and thinks that he will never be able to do anything in public speaking at all. He would give anything in the world if he had only accepted all of the invitations he has had, because then he would have profited by experience. It would have been a thousand times better for him to have made a mistake, or even to have broken down entirely a few times, than to have missed the scores of opportunities which would undoubtedly have made a strong public speaker of him.

What is technically called "stage fright" is very common. A college boy recited an address "to the conscript fathers." His professor asked,—"Is that the way Caesar would have spoken it?" "Yes," he replied, "if Caesar had been scared half to death, and as nervous as a cat."

An almost fatal timidity seizes on an inexperienced person, when he knows that all eyes are watching him, that everybody in his audience is trying to measure and weigh him, studying him, scrutinizing him to see how much there is in him; what he stands for, and making up their minds whether he measures more or less than they expected.

Some are constitutionally sensitive, and so afraid of being gazed at that they don't dare to open their mouths, even when a question in which they are deeply interested and on which they have strong views is being discussed. At debating clubs, meetings of literary societies, or gatherings of any kind, they sit dumb, longing, yet fearing to speak. The sound of their own voices, if they should get on their feet to make a motion or to speak in a public gathering, would paralyze them. The mere thought of asserting themselves, of putting forward their views or opinions on any subject as being worthy of attention, or as valuable as those of their companions, makes them blush and shrink more into themselves.

This timidity is often, however, not so much the fear of one's audience, as the fear lest one can make no suitable expression of his thought.

The hardest thing for the public speaker to overcome is self-consciousness. Those terrible eyes which pierce him through and through, which are measuring him, criticizing him, are very difficult to get out of one's consciousness.

But no orator can make a great impression until he gets rid of himself, until he can absolutely annihilate his self-consciousness, forget himself in his speech. While he is wondering what kind of an impression he is making, what people think of him, his power is crippled, and his speech to that extent will be mechanical, wooden.

Even a partial failure on the platform has good results, for it often arouses a determination to conquer the next time, which never leaves one. Demosthenes' heroic efforts, and Disraeli's "The time will come when you will hear me," are historic examples.

It is not the speech, but the man behind the speech, that wins a way to the front.

One man carries weight because he is himself the embodiment of power, he is himself convinced of what he says. There is nothing of the negative, the doubtful, the uncertain in his nature. He not only knows a thing, but he knows that he knows it. His opinion carries with it the entire weight of his being. The whole man gives consent to his judgment. He himself is in his conviction, in his act.

One of the most entrancing speakers I have ever listened to—a man to hear whom people would go long distances and stand for hours to get admission to the hall where he spoke—never was able to get the confidence of his audience because he lacked character. People liked to be swayed by his eloquence. There was a great charm in the cadences of his perfect sentences. But somehow they could not believe what he said.

The orator must be sincere. The public is very quick to see through shams. If the audience sees mud at the bottom of your eye, that you are not honest yourself, that you are acting, they will not take any stock in you.

It is not enough to say a pleasing thing, an interesting thing, the orator must be able to convince; and to convince others he must have strong convictions.

Great speeches have become the beacon lights of history. Those who are prepared acquire a world-wide influence when the fit occasion comes.

Very few people ever rise to their greatest possibilities or ever know their entire power unless confronted by some great occasion. We are as much amazed as others are when, in some great emergency, we out-do ourselves. Somehow the power that stands behind us in the silence, in the depths of our natures, comes to our relief, intensifies our faculties a thousandfold and enables us to do things which before we thought impossible.

It would be difficult to estimate the great part which practical drill in oratory may play in one's life.

Great occasions, when nations have been in peril, have developed and brought out some of the greatest orators of the world. Cicero, Mirabeau, Patrick Henry, Webster, and John Bright might all be called to witness to this fact.

The occasion had much to do with the greatest speech delivered in the United States Senate—Webster's reply to Hayne. Webster had no time for immediate preparation, but the occasion brought all the reserves in this giant, and he towered so far above his opponent that Hayne looked like a pygmy in comparison.

The pen has discovered many a genius, but the process is slower and less effective than the great occasion that discovers the orator. Every crisis calls out ability, previously undeveloped, and perhaps unexpected.

No orator living was ever great enough to give out the same power and force and magnetism to an empty hall, to empty seats, that he could give to an audience capable of being fired by his theme.

In the presence of the audience lies a fascination, an indefinable magnetism that stimulates all the mental faculties, and acts as a tonic and vitalizer. An orator can say before an audience what he could not possibly say before he went on the platform, just as we can often say to a friend in animated conversation things which we could not possibly say when alone. As when two chemicals are united, a new substance is formed from the combination, which did not exist in either alone, he feels surging through his brain the combined force of his audience, which he calls inspiration, a mighty power which did not exist in his own personality.

Actors tell us that there is an indescribable inspiration which comes from the orchestra, the footlights, the audience, which it is impossible to feel at a cold mechanical rehearsal. There is something in a great sea of expectant faces which awakens the ambition and arouses the reserve of power which can never be felt except before an audience. The power was there just the same before, but it was not aroused.

In the presence of the orator, the audience is absolutely in his power to do as he will. They laugh or cry as he pleases, or rise and fall at his bidding, until he releases them from the magic spell.

What is oratory but to stir the blood of all hearers, to so arouse their emotions that they can not control themselves a moment longer without taking the action to which they are impelled?

"His words are laws" may be well said of the statesmen whose orations sway the world. What art is greater than that of changing the minds of men?

Wendell Phillips so played upon the emotions, so changed the convictions of Southerners who hated him, but who were curious to listen to his oratory, that, for the time being he almost persuaded them that they were in the wrong. I have seen him when it seemed to me that he was almost godlike in his power. With the ease of a master he swayed his audience. Some who hated him in the slavery days were there, and they could not resist cheering him. He warped their own judgment and for the time took away their prejudice.

When James Russell Lowell was a student, said Wetmore Story, he and Story went to Faneuil Hall to hear Webster. They meant to hoot him for his remaining in Tyler's cabinet. It would be easy, they reasoned, to get the three thousand people to join them. When he begun, Lowell turned pale, and Story livid. His great eyes, they thought, were fixed on them. His opening words changed their scorn to admiration, and their contempt to approbation.

"He gave us a glimpse into the Holy of Holies," said another student, in relating his experience in listening to a great preacher.

Is not oratory a fine art? The well-spring of eloquence, when up-gushing as the very water of life, quenches the thirst of myriads of men, like the smitten rock of the wilderness reviving the life of desert wanderers.

The Triumphs of the Common Virtues

The talent of success is nothing more than doing what you can do well, and doing well whatever you do, without a thought of fame.—Longfellow

It is not a question of what a man knows but what use he can make of what he knows.—J. G. Holland

Seest thou a man diligent in business? He shall stand before kings.—Solomon

The most encouraging truth that can be impressed upon the mind of youth is this: "What man has done man may do." Men of great achievements are not to be set on pedestals and reverenced as exceptions to the average of humanity. Instead, these great men are to be considered as setting a standard of success for the emulation of every aspiring youth. Their example shows what can be accomplished by the practise of the common virtues,—diligence, patience, thrift, self-denial, determination, industry, and persistence.

We can best appreciate the uplifting power of these simple virtues which all may cultivate and exercise, by taking some concrete example of great success which has been achieved by patient plodding toward a definite goal. No more illustrious example of success won by the exercise of common virtues can be offered than Abraham Lincoln, rail-splitter and president.

Probably Lincoln has been the hero of more American boys during the last two generations than any other American character. Young people look upon him as a marvelous being, raised up for a divine purpose; and yet, if we analyze his character, we find it made up of the humblest virtues, the commonest qualities; the poorest boys and girls, who look upon him as a demigod, possess these qualities.

The strong thing about Lincoln was his manliness, his straightforward, downright honesty. You could depend upon him. He was ambitious to make the most of himself. He wanted to know something, to be somebody, to lift his head up from his humble environment and be of some account in the world. He simply wanted to better his condition.

It is true that he had a divine hunger for growth, a passion for a larger and completer life than that of those about him; but there is no evidence of any great genius, any marvelous powers. He was a simple man, never straining after effect.

His simplicity was his chief charm. Everybody who knew him felt that he was a man, a large-hearted, generous friend, always ready to help everybody and everything out of their troubles, whether it was a pig stuck in the mire, a poor widow in trouble, or a farmer who needed advice. He had a helpful mind, open, frank, transparent. He never covered up anything, never had secrets. The door of his heart was always open so that anyone could read his inmost thoughts.

The ability to do hard work, and to stick to it, is the right hand of genius and the best substitute for it,—in fact, that is genius.

If young people were to represent Lincoln's total success by one hundred, they would probably expect to find some brilliant faculty which would rank at least fifty per cent of the total. But I think that the verdict of history has given his honesty of purpose, his purity and unselfishness of motive as his highest attributes, and certainly these qualities are within the reach of the poorest boy and the humblest girl in America.

Suppose we rank his honesty, his integrity twenty per cent of the total, his dogged persistence, his ability for hard work ten per cent, his passion for wholeness, for completeness, for doing everything to a finish ten more, his aspiration, his longing for growth, his yearning for fulness of life ten more. The reader can see that it would be easy to make up the hundred per cent, without finding any one quality which could be called genius; that the total of his character would be made up of the sum of the commonest qualities, the most ordinary virtues within the reach of the poorest youth in the land. There is no one quality in his entire make-up so overpowering, so commanding that it could be ranked as genius.

What an inestimable blessing to the world, what an encouragement, an inspiration to poor boys and poor girls that his great achievement can be accounted for by the triumph in his character of those qualities which are beyond the reach of money, of family, of influence, but that are within the reach of the poorest and the humblest.

In a speech to the people in Colorado Mountains, Roosevelt said: "You think that my success is quite foreign to anything you can achieve. Let me assure you that the big prizes I have won are largely accidental. If I have succeeded, it is only as anyone of you can succeed, merely because I have tried to do my duty as I saw it in my home and in my business, and as a citizen.

"If when I die the ones who know me best believe that I was a thoughtful, helpful husband, a loving, wise and painstaking father, a generous, kindly neighbor and an honest citizen, that will be a far more real honor, and will prove my life to have been more successful than the fact that I have ever been president of the United States. Had a few events over which no one had control been other than they were it is quite possible I might never have held the high office I now occupy, but no train of events could accidentally make me a noble character or a faithful member of my home and community. Therefore each of you has the same chance to succeed in true success as I have had, and if my success in the end proves to have been as great as that achieved by many of the humblest of you I shall be fortunate."

McKinley did not start with great mental ability. There was nothing very surprising or startling in his career. He was not a great genius, not notable as a scholar. He did not stand very high in school; he was not a great lawyer; he did not make a great record in Congress; but he had a good, level head. He had *the best substitute for genius—the ability for hard work and persistence.* He knew how to keep plodding, how to hang on, and he knew that the only way to show what he was made of in Congress was to stick to one thing, and he made a specialty of the tariff, following the advice of a statesman friend.

The biographies of the giants of the race are often discouraging to the average poor boy, because the moment he gets the impression that the character he is reading about was a genius, the effect is largely lost upon himself, because he knows that he is not a genius, and he says to himself, "This is very interesting reading, but I can never do those things." But when he reads the life of McKinley he does not see any reason why he could not do the same things himself, because there were no great jumps, no great leaps and bounds in his life from particular ability or special opportunity. He had no very brilliant talents, but he averaged well. He had good common sense and was a hard worker. He had tact and diplomacy and made the most of every opportunity.

Nothing can keep from success the man who has iron in his blood and is determined that he will succeed. When he is confronted by barriers he leaps over them, tunnels through them, or makes a way around them. Obstacles only serve to stiffen his backbone, increase his determination, sharpen his wits and develop his innate resources. The record of human achievement is full of the truth. "There is no difficulty to him who wills."

"All the performances of human art, at which we look with praise and wonder," says Johnson, "are instances of the resistless force of perseverance."

It has been well said that from the same materials one man builds palaces, another hovels; one warehouses, another villas. Bricks and mortar are mortar and bricks until the architect makes them something else. The boulder which was an obstacle in the path of the weak becomes a stepping-stone in the pathway of the resolute. The difficulties which dishearten one man only stiffen the sinews of another, who looks on them as a sort of mental spring-board by which to vault across the gulf of failure to the sure, solid ground of full success.

One of the greatest generals on the Confederate side in the Civil War, "Stonewall" Jackson, was noted for his slowness. With this he possessed great application and dogged determination. If he undertook a task, he never let go till he had it done. So, when he went to West Point, his habitual class response was that he was too busy getting the lesson of a few days back to look at the one of the day. He kept up this steady gait, and, from the least promising "plebe," came out seventeenth in a class of seventy, distancing fifty-three who started with better attainments and better minds. His classmates used to say that, if the course was ten years instead of four, he would come out first.

The world always stands aside for the determined man. You will find no royal road to your triumph. There is no open door to the Temple of Success.

One of the commonest of common virtues is perseverance, yet it has been the open sesame of more fast locked doors of opportunity than have brilliant tributes. Every man and woman can exercise this virtue of perseverance, can refuse to stop short of the goal of ambition, can decline to turn aside in search of pleasures that do but hinder progress.

The romance of perseverance under especial difficulty is one of the most fascinating subjects in history. Tenacity of purpose has been characteristic of all characters who have left their mark on the world. Perseverance, it has been said, is the statesman's brain, the warrior's sword, the inventor's secret, the scholar's "open sesame."

Persistency is to talent what steam is to the engine. It is the driving force by which the machine accomplishes the work for which it was intended. A great deal of persistency, with a very little talent, can be counted on to go farther than a great deal of talent without persistency.

You cannot keep a determined man from success. Take away his money, and he makes spurs of his poverty to urge him on. Lock him up in a dungeon, and he writes the immortal "Pilgrim's Progress."

Stick to a thing and carry it through in all its completeness and proportion, and you will become a hero. You will think better of yourself; others will exalt you.

Thoroughness is another of the common virtues which all may cultivate. The man who puts his best into every task will leave far behind the man who lets a job go with the comment "That's good enough." Nothing is good enough unless it reflects our best.

Daniel Webster had no remarkable traits of character in his boyhood. He was sent to Phillips Exeter Academy in New Hampshire, and stayed there only a short time when a neighbor found him crying on his way home, and asked the reason. Daniel said he despaired of ever making a scholar. He said the boys made fun of him, for always being at the foot of the class, and that he had decided to give up and go home. The friend said he ought to go back, and see what hard study would do. He went back, applied himself to his studies with determination to win, and it was not long before he silenced those who had ridiculed him, by reaching the head of the class, and remaining there.

Fidelity to duty has been a distinguishing virtue in men who have risen to positions of authority and command. It has been observed that the dispatches of Napoleon rang with the word glory. Wellington's dispatches centered around the common word duty.

Nowadays people seem unwilling to tread the rough path of duty and by patience and steadfast perseverance step into the ranks of those the country delights to honor.

Every little while I get letters from young men who say, if they were positively sure that they could be a Webster in law, they would devote all their energies to study, fling their whole lives into their work; or if they could be an Edison in invention, or a great leader in medicine, or a merchant prince like Wanamaker or Marshall Field, they could work with enthusiasm and zeal and power and concentration. They would be willing to make any sacrifice, to undergo any hardship in order to achieve what these men have achieved. But many of them say they do not feel that they have the marvelous ability, the great genius, the tremendous talent exhibited by those leaders, and so they are not willing to make the great exertion.

They do not realize that success is not necessarily doing some great thing, that it is not making a tremendous strain to do something great; but that it is just honestly, earnestly living the everyday simple life. It is by the exercise of the common everyday virtues; it is by trying to do everything one does to a complete finish; it is by trying to be scrupulously honest in every transaction; it is by always ringing true in our friendships, by holding a helpful, accommodating attitude toward those about us; by trying to be the best possible citizen, a good, accommodating, helpful neighbor, a kind, encouraging father; it is by all these simple things that we attain success.

There is no great secret about success. It is just a natural persistent exercise of the commonest every-day qualities.

We have seen people in the country in the summer time trampling down the daisies and the beautiful violets, the lovely wild flowers in their efforts to get a branch of showy flowers off a large tree, which, perhaps, would not compare in beauty and delicacy and loveliness to the things they trampled under their feet in trying to procure it.

Oh, how many exquisite experiences, delightful possible joys we trample under our feet in straining after something great, in trying to do some marvelous thing that will attract attention and get our names in the papers! We trample down the finer emotions, we spoil many of the most delicious things in life in our scrambling and greed to grasp something which is unusual, something showy that we can wave before the world in order to get its applause.

In straining for effect, in the struggle to do something great and wonderful, we miss the little successes, the sum of which would make our lives sublime; and often, after all this straining and struggling for the larger, for the grander things, we miss them, and then we discover to our horror what we have missed on the way up—what sweetness, what beauty, what loveliness, what a lot of common, homely, cheering things we have lost in the useless struggle.

Great scientists tell us that the reason why the secrets of nature have been hidden from the world so long is because we are not simple enough in our methods of reasoning; that investigators are always looking for unusual phenomena, for something complicated; that the principles of nature's secrets are so extremely simple that men overlook them in their efforts to see and solve the more intricate problems.

It is most unfortunate that so many young people get the impression that success consists in doing some marvelous thing, that there must be some genius born in the man who achieves it, else he could not do such remarkable things.

Getting Aroused

"How's the boy gittin' on, Davis?" asked Farmer John Field, as he watched his son, Marshall, waiting upon a customer. "Well, John, you and I are old friends," replied Deacon Davis, as he took an apple from a barrel and handed it to Marshall's father as a peace offering; "we are old friends, and I don't want to hurt your feelin's; but I'm a blunt man, and air goin' to tell you the truth. Marshall is a good, steady boy, all right, but he wouldn't make a merchant if he stayed in my store a thousand years. He weren't cut out for a merchant. Take him back to the farm, John, and teach him how to milk cows!"

If Marshall Field had remained as clerk in Deacon Davis's store in Pittsfield, Massachusetts, where he got his first position, he could never have become one of the world's merchant princes. But when he went to Chicago and saw the marvelous examples around him of poor boys who had won success, it aroused his ambition and fired him with the determination to be a great merchant himself. "If others can do such wonderful things," he asked himself, "why cannot I?"

Of course, there was the making of a great merchant in Mr. Field from the start; but circumstances, an ambition-arousing environment, had a great deal to do with stimulating his latent energy and bringing out his reserve force. It is doubtful if he would have climbed so rapidly in any other place than Chicago. In 1856, when young Field went there, this marvelous city was just starting on its unparalleled career. It had then only about eighty-five thousand inhabitants. A few years before it had been a mere Indian trading village. But the city grew by leaps and bounds, and always beat the predictions of its most sanguine inhabitants. Success was in the air. Everybody felt that there were great possibilities there.

Many people seem to think that ambition is a quality born within us; that it is not susceptible to improvement; that it is something thrust upon us which will take care of itself. But it is a passion that responds very quickly to cultivation, and it requires constant care and education, just as the faculty for music or art does, or it will atrophy.

If we do not try to realize our ambition, it will not keep sharp and defined. Our faculties become dull and soon lose their power if they are not exercised. How can we expect our ambition to remain fresh and vigorous through years of inactivity, indolence, or indifference? If we constantly allow opportunities to slip by us without making any attempt to grasp them, our inclination will grow duller and weaker.

"What I most need," as Emerson says, "is somebody to make me do what I can." To do what I can, that is my problem; not what a Napoleon or a Lincoln could do, but what *I* can do. It makes all the difference in the world to me whether I bring out the best thing in me or the worst,—whether I utilize ten, fifteen, twenty-five, or ninety per cent of my ability.

Everywhere we see people who have reached middle life or later without being aroused. They have developed only a small percentage of their success possibilities. They are still in a dormant state. The best thing in them lies so deep that it has never been awakened. When we meet these people we feel conscious that they have a great deal of latent power that has never been exercised. Great possibilities of usefulness and of achievement are, all unconsciously, going to waste within them.

Some time ago there appeared in the newspapers an account of a girl who had reached the age of fifteen years, and yet had only attained the mental development of a small child. Only a few things interested her. She was dreamy, inactive, and indifferent to everything around her most of the time until, one day, while listening to a hand organ on the street, she suddenly awakened to full consciousness. She came to herself; her faculties were aroused, and in a few days she leaped forward years in her development. Almost in a day she passed from childhood to budding womanhood. Most of us have an enormous amount of power, of latent force, slumbering within us, as it slumbered in this girl, which could do marvels if we would only awaken it.

The judge of the municipal court in a flourishing western city, one of the most highly esteemed jurists in his state, was in middle life, before his latent power was aroused, an illiterate blacksmith. He is now sixty, the owner of the finest library in his city, with the reputation of being its best-read man, and one whose highest endeavor is to help his fellow man. What caused the revolution in his life? The hearing of a single lecture on the value of education. This was what stirred the slumbering power within him, awakened his ambition, and set his feet in the path of self-development.

I have known several men who never realized their possibilities until they reached middle life. Then they were suddenly aroused, as if from a long sleep, by reading some inspiring, stimulating book, by listening to a sermon or a lecture, or by meeting some friend,—someone with high ideals,—who understood, believed in, and encouraged them.

It will make all the difference in the world to you whether you are with people who are watching for ability in you, people who believe in, encourage, and praise you, or whether you are with those who are forever breaking your idols, blasting your hopes, and throwing cold water on your aspirations.

The chief probation officer of the children's court in New York, in his report for 1905, says: "Removing a boy or girl from improper environment is the first step in his or her reclamation." The New York Society for the Prevention of Cruelty to Children, after thirty years of investigation of cases involving the social and moral welfare of over half a million of children, has also come to the conclusion that environment is stronger than heredity.

Even the strongest of us are not beyond the reach of our environment. No matter how independent, strong-willed, and determined our nature, we are constantly being modified by our surroundings. Take the best-born child, with the greatest inherited advantages, and let it be reared by savages, and how many of its inherited tendencies will remain? If brought up from infancy in a barbarous, brutal atmosphere, it will, of course, become brutal. The story is told of a well-born child who, being lost or abandoned as an infant, was suckled by a wolf with her own young ones, and who actually took on all the characteristics of the wolf,—walked on all fours, howled like a wolf, and ate like one.

It does not take much to determine the lives of most of us. We naturally follow the examples about us, and, as a rule, we rise or fall according to the strongest current in which we live. The poet's "I am a part of all that I have met" is not a mere poetic flight of fancy; it is an absolute truth. Everything—every sermon or lecture or conversation you have heard, every person who has touched your life—has left an impress upon your character, and you are never quite the same person after the association or experience. You are a little different,—modified somewhat from what you were before,—just as Beecher was never the same man after reading Ruskin.

Some years ago a party of Russian workmen were sent to this country by a Russian firm of shipbuilders, in order that they might acquire American methods and catch the American spirit. Within six months the Russians had become almost the equals of the American artisans among whom they worked. They had developed ambition, individuality, personal initiative, and a marked degree of excellence in their work. A year after their return to their own country, the deadening, non-progressive atmosphere about them had done its work. The men had lost the desire to improve; they were again plodders, with no goal beyond the day's work. The ambition aroused by stimulating environment had sunk to sleep again.

Our Indian schools sometimes publish, side by side, photographs of the Indian youths as they come from the reservation and as they look when they are graduated,—well dressed, intelligent, with the fire of ambition in their eyes. We predict great things for them; but the majority of those who go back to their tribes, after struggling awhile to keep up their new standards, gradually drop back to their old manner of living. There are, of course, many notable exceptions, but these are strong characters, able to resist the downward-dragging tendencies about them.

If you interview the great army of failures, you will find that multitudes have failed because they never got into a stimulating, encouraging environment, because their ambition was never aroused, or because they were not strong enough to rally under depressing, discouraging, or vicious surroundings. Most of the people we find in prisons and poor-houses are pitiable examples of the influence of an environment which appealed to the worst instead of to the best in them.

Whatever you do in life, make any sacrifice necessary to keep in an ambition-arousing atmosphere, an environment that will stimulate you to self-development. Keep close to people who understand you, who believe in you, who will help you to discover yourself and encourage you to make the most of yourself. This may make all the difference to you between a grand success and a mediocre existence. Stick to those who are trying to do something and to be somebody in the world,—people of high aims, lofty ambition. Keep close to those who are dead-in-earnest. Ambition is contagious. You will catch the spirit that dominates in your environment. The success of those about you who are trying to climb upward will encourage and stimulate you to struggle harder if you have not done quite so well yourself.

There is a great power in a battery of individuals who are struggling for the achievement of high aims, a great magnetic force which will help you to attract the object of your ambition. It is very stimulating to be with people whose aspirations run parallel with your own. If you lack energy, if you are naturally lazy, indolent, or inclined to take it easy, you will be urged forward by the constant prodding of the more ambitious.

The Man With an Idea

He who wishes to fulfil his mission must be a man of one idea, that is, of one great overmastering purpose, over shadowing all his aims, and guiding and controlling his entire life.—Bate

A healthful hunger for a great idea is the beauty and blessedness of life.—Jean Ingelow

A profound conviction raises a man above the feeling of ridicule.—J. Stuart Mill

Ideas go booming through the world louder than cannon. Thoughts are mightier than armies. Principles have achieved more victories than horsemen or chariots.—W. M. Paxton

"What are you bothering yourselves with a knitting machine for?" asked Ari Davis, of Boston, a manufacturer of instruments; "why don't you make a sewing-machine?" His advice had been sought by a rich man and an inventor who had reached their wits' ends in the vain attempt to produce a device for knitting woolen goods. "I wish I could, but it can't be done." "Oh, yes it can," said Davis; "I can make one myself." "Well," the capitalist replied, "you do it, and I'll insure you an independent fortune." The words of Davis were uttered in a spirit of jest, but the novel idea found lodgment in the mind of one of the workmen who stood by, a mere youth of twenty, who was thought not capable of a serious idea.

But Elias Howe was not so rattle-headed as he seemed, and the more he reflected, the more desirable such a machine appeared to him. Four years passed, and with a wife and three children to support in a great city on a salary of nine dollars a week, the light-hearted boy had become a thoughtful, plodding man. The thought of the sewing-machine haunted him night and day, and he finally resolved to produce one.

After months wasted in the effort to work a needle pointed at both ends, with the eye in the middle, that should pass up and down through the cloth, suddenly the thought flashed through his mind that another stitch must be possible, and with almost insane devotion he worked night and day, until he had made a rough model of wood and wire that convinced him of ultimate success. In his mind's eye he saw his idea, but his own funds and those of his father, who had aided him more or less, were insufficient to embody it in a working machine. But help came from an old schoolmate, George Fisher, a coal and wood merchant of Cambridge. He agreed to board Elias and his family and furnish five hundred dollars, for which he was to have one-half of the patent, if the machine proved to be worth patenting. In May, 1845, the machine was completed, and in July Elias Howe sewed all the seams of two suits of woolen clothes, one for Mr. Fisher and the other for himself. The sewing outlasted the cloth. This machine, which is still preserved, will sew three hundred stitches a minute, and is considered more nearly perfect than any other prominent invention at its first trial. There is not one of the millions of sewing-machines now in use that does not contain some of the essential principles of this first attempt.

When it was decided to try and elevate Chicago out of the mud by raising its immense blocks up to grade, the young son of a poor mechanic, named George M. Pullman, appeared on the scene, and put in a bid for the great undertaking, and the contract was awarded to him. He not only raised the blocks, but did it in such a way that business within them was scarcely interrupted. All this time he was revolving in his mind his pet project of building a "sleeping car" which would be adopted on all railroads. He fitted up two old cars on the Chicago and Alton road with berths, and soon found they would be in demand. He then went to work on the principle that the more luxurious his cars were, the greater would be the demand for them. After spending three years in Colorado gold mines, he returned and built two cars which cost $18,000 each. Everybody laughed at "Pullman's folly." But Pullman believed that whatever relieved the tediousness of long trips would meet with speedy approval, and he had faith enough in his idea to risk his all in it.

Pullman was a great believer in the commercial value of beauty. The wonderful town which he built and which bears his name, as well as his magnificent cars, is an example of his belief in this principle. He counts it a good investment to surround his employees with comforts and beauty and good sanitary conditions, and so the town of Pullman is a model of cleanliness, order, and comfort.

It has ever been the man with an idea, which he puts into practical effect, who has changed the face of Christendom. The germ idea of the steam engine can be seen in the writings of the Greek philosophers, but it was not developed until more than two thousand years later.

It was an English blacksmith, Newcomen, with no opportunities, who in the seventeenth century conceived the idea of moving a piston by the elastic force of steam; but his engine consumed thirty pounds of coal in producing one horse power. The perfection of the modern engine is largely due to James Watt, a poor, uneducated Scotch boy, who at fifteen walked the streets of London in a vain search for work. A professor in the Glasgow University gave him the use of a room to work in, and while waiting for jobs he experimented with old vials for steam reservoirs and hollow canes for pipes, for he could not bear to waste a moment. He improved Newcomen's engine by cutting off the steam after the piston had completed a quarter or a third of its stroke, and letting the steam already in the chamber expand and drive the piston the remaining distance. This saved nearly three-fourths of the steam. Watt suffered from pinching poverty and hardships which would have disheartened ordinary men; but he was terribly in earnest, and his brave wife Margaret begged him not to mind her inconvenience, nor be discouraged. "If the engine will not work," she wrote him while struggling in London, "something else will. Never despair."

"I had gone to take a walk," said Watt, "on a fine Sabbath afternoon, and had passed the old washing-house, thinking upon the engine at the time, when the idea came into my head that, as steam is an elastic body, it would rush into a vacuum, and if a communication were made between the cylinder and an exhausted vessel, it would rush into it, and might be there condensed without cooling the cylinder." The idea was simple, but in it lay the germ of the first steam engine of much practical value. Sir James Mackintosh places this poor Scotch boy who began with only an idea "at the head of all inventors in all ages and all nations."

See George Stephenson, working in the coal pits for sixpence a day, patching the clothes and mending the boots of his fellow-workmen at night, to earn a little money to attend a night school, giving the first money he ever earned, $150, to his blind father to pay his debts. People say he is crazy; his "roaring steam engine will set the house on fire with its sparks"; "smoke will pollute the air"; "carriage makers and coachmen will starve for want of work." For three days the committee of the House of Commons plies questions to him. This was one of them: "If a cow get on the track of the engine traveling ten miles an hour, will it not be an awkward situation?" "Yes, very awkward, indeed, for the coo," replied Stephenson. A government inspector said that if a locomotive ever went ten miles an hour, he would undertake to eat a stewed engine for breakfast.

"What can be more palpably absurd and ridiculous than the prospect held out of locomotives traveling twice as fast as horses?" asked a writer in the English "Quarterly Review" for March, 1825. "We should as soon expect the people of Woolwich to suffer themselves to be fired off upon one of Congreve's rockets as to trust themselves to the mercy of such a machine, going at such a rate. We trust that Parliament will, in all the railways it may grant, *limit the speed to eight or nine miles an hour*, which we entirely agree with Mr. Sylvester is as great as can be ventured upon." This article referred to Stephenson's proposition to use his newly invented locomotive instead of horses on the Liverpool and Manchester Railroad, then in process of construction.

The company decided to lay the matter before two leading English engineers, who reported that steam would be desirable only when used in stationary engines one and a half miles apart, drawing the cars by means of ropes and pulleys. But Stephenson persuaded them to test his idea by offering a prize of about twenty-five hundred dollars for the best locomotive produced at a trial to take place October 6, 1829.

On the eventful day, thousands of spectators assembled to watch the competition of four engines, the "Novelty," the "Rocket," the "Perseverance," and the "Sanspareil." The "Perseverance" could make but six miles an hour, and so was ruled out, as the conditions called for at least ten. The "Sanspareil" made an average of fourteen miles an hour, but as it burst a water-pipe it lost its chance. The "Novelty" did splendidly, but also burst a pipe, and was crowded out, leaving the "Rocket" to carry off the honors with an average speed of fifteen miles an hour, the highest rate attained being twenty-nine. This was Stephenson's locomotive, and so fully vindicated his theory that the idea of stationary engines on a railroad was completely exploded. He had picked up the fixed engines which the genius of Watt had devised, and set them on wheels to draw men and merchandise, against the most direful predictions of the foremost engineers of his day.

In all the records of invention there is no more sad or affecting story than that of John Fitch. Poor he was in many senses, poor in appearance, poor in spirit. He was born poor, lived poor, and died poor. If there ever was a true inventor, this man was one. He was one of those eager souls that would coin their own flesh to carry their point. He only uttered the obvious truth when he said one day, in a crisis of his invention, that if he could get one hundred pounds by cutting off one of his legs he would gladly give it to the knife.

He tried in vain both in this country and in France to get money to build his steamboat. He would say: "You and I will not live to see the day, but the time will come when the steamboat will be preferred to all other modes of conveyance, when steamboats will ascend the Western rivers from New Orleans to Wheeling, and when steamboats will cross the ocean. Johnny Fitch will be forgotten, but other men will carry out his ideas and grow rich and great upon them."

Poor, ragged, forlorn, jeered at, pitied as a madman, discouraged by the great, refused by the rich, he kept on till, in 1790, he had the first vessel on the Delaware that ever answered the purpose of a steamboat. It ran six miles an hour against the tide, and eight miles with it.

At noon, on Friday, August 4, 1807, a crowd of curious people might have been seen along the wharves of the Hudson River. They had gathered to witness what they considered a ridiculous failure of a "crank" who proposed to take a party of people up the Hudson River to Albany in what he called a steam vessel named the *Clermont*. Did anybody ever hear of such a ridiculous idea as navigating against the current up the Hudson in a vessel without sails? "The thing will 'bust,'" says one; "it will burn up," says another, and "they will all be drowned," exclaims a third, as he sees vast columns of black smoke shoot up with showers of brilliant sparks. Nobody present, in all probability, ever heard of a boat going by steam. It was the opinion of everybody that the man who had tooled away his money and his time on the *Clermont* was little better than an idiot, and ought to be in an insane asylum. But the passengers go on board, the plank is pulled in, and the steam is turned on. The walking beam moves slowly up and down, and the *Clermont* floats out into the river. "It can never go up stream," the spectators persist. But it did go up stream, and the boy, who in his youth said there is nothing impossible, had scored a great triumph, and had given to the world the first steamboat that had any practical value.

Notwithstanding that Fulton had rendered such great service to humanity, a service which has revolutionized the commerce of the world, he was looked upon by many as a public enemy. Critics and cynics turned up their noses when Fulton was mentioned. The severity of the world's censure, ridicule, and detraction has usually been in proportion to the benefit the victim has conferred upon mankind.

As the *Clermont* burned pine wood, dense columns of fire and smoke belched forth from her smoke-stack while she glided triumphantly up the river, and the inhabitants along the banks were utterly unable to account for the spectacle. They rushed to the shore amazed to see a boat "on fire" go against the stream so rapidly with neither oars nor sails. The noise of her great paddle-wheels increased the wonder. Sailors forsook their vessels, and fishermen rowed home as fast as possible to get out of the way of the fire monster. The Indians were as much frightened as their predecessors were when the first ship approached their hunting-ground on Manhattan Island. The owners of sailing vessels were jealous of the *Clermont*, and tried to run her down. Others whose interests were affected denied Fulton's claim to the invention and brought suits against him. But the success of the *Clermont* soon led to the construction of other steamships all over the country. The government employed Fulton to aid in building a powerful steam frigate, which was called *Fulton the First*. He also built a diving boat for the government for the discharge of torpedoes. By this time his fame had spread all over the civilized world, and when he died, in 1815, newspapers were marked with black lines; the legislature of New York wore badges of mourning; and minute guns were fired as the long funeral procession passed to old Trinity churchyard. Very few private persons were ever honored with such a burial.

True, Dr. Lardner had "proved" to scientific men that a steamship could not cross the Atlantic, but in 1810 the *Savannah* from New York appeared off the coast of Ireland under sail and steam, having made this "impossible" passage. Those on shore thought that a fire had broken out below the decks, and a king's cutter was sent to her relief. Although the voyage was made without accident, it was nearly twenty years before it was admitted that steam navigation could be made a commercial success in ocean traffic.

As Junius Smith impatiently paced the deck of a vessel sailing from an English port to New York, on a rough and tedious voyage in 1832, he said to himself, "Why not cross the ocean regularly in steamships?" In New

York and in London a deaf ear was turned to any such nonsense. Smith's first encouragement came from George Grote, the historian and banker, who said the idea was practicable; but it was the same old story,—he would risk no money in it. At length Isaac Selby, a prominent business man of London, agreed to build a steamship of two thousand tons, the *British Queen*. An unexpected delay in fitting the engines led the projectors to charter the *Sirius*, a river steamer of seven hundred tons, and send her to New York. Learning of this, other parties started from Bristol four days later in the *Great Western*, and both vessels arrived at New York the same day. Soon after Smith made the round trip between London and New York in thirty-two days.

What a sublime picture of determination and patience was that of Charles Goodyear, of New Haven, buried in poverty and struggling with hardships for eleven long years, to make India rubber of practical use! See him in prison for debt; pawning his clothes and his wife's jewelry to get a little money to keep his children (who were obliged to gather sticks in the field for fire) from starving. Watch his sublime courage and devotion to his idea, when he had no money to bury a dead child and when his other five were near starvation; when his neighbors were harshly criticizing him for his neglect of his family and calling him insane. But, behold his vulcanized rubber; the result of that heroic struggle, applied to over five hundred uses by 100,000 employees.

What a pathetic picture was that of Palissy, plodding on through want and woe to rediscover the lost art of enameling pottery; building his furnaces with bricks carried on his back, seeing his six children die of neglect, probably of starvation, his wife in rags and despair over her husband's "folly"; despised by his neighbors for neglecting his family, worn to a skeleton himself, giving his clothes to his hired man because he could not pay him in money, hoping always, failing steadily, until at last his great work was accomplished, and he reaped his reward.

German unity was the idea engraven upon Bismarck's heart. What cared this herculean despot for the Diet chosen year after year simply to vote down every measure he proposed? He was indifferent to all opposition. He simply defied and sent home every Diet which opposed him. He could play the game alone. To make Germany the greatest power in Europe, to make William of Prussia a greater potentate than Napoleon or Alexander, was his all-absorbing purpose. It mattered not what stood in his way, whether people, Diet, or nation; all must bend to his mighty will. Germany must hold the deciding voice in the Areopagus of the world. He rode roughshod over everybody and everything that stood in his way, defiant of opposition, imperious, irrepressible!

See the great Dante in exile, condemned to be burnt alive on false charges of embezzlement. Look at his starved features, gaunt form, melancholy, a poor wanderer; but he never gave up his idea; he poured out his very soul into his immortal poem, ever believing that right would at last triumph.

Columbus was exposed to continual scoffs and indignities, being ridiculed as a mere dreamer and stigmatized as an adventurer. The very children, it is said, pointed to their foreheads as he passed, being taught to regard him as a kind of madman.

An American was once invited to dine with Oken, the famous German naturalist. To his surprise, they had neither meats nor dessert, but only baked potatoes. Oken was too great a man to apologize for their simple fare. His wife explained, however, that her husband's income was very small, and that they preferred to live simply in order that he might obtain books and instruments for his scientific researches.

Before the discovery of ether it often took a week, in some cases a month, to recover from the enormous dose, sometimes five hundred drops of laudanum, given to a patient to deaden the pain during a surgical operation. Young Dr. Morton believed that there must be some means provided by Nature to relieve human suffering during these terrible operations; but what could he do? He was not a chemist; he did not know the properties of chemical substances; he was not liberally educated.

Dr. Morton did not resort to books, however, nor did he go to scientific men for advice, but immediately began to experiment with well-known substances. He tried intoxicants even to the point of intoxication, but as soon as the instruments were applied the patient would revive. He kept on experimenting with narcotics in this manner until at last he found what he sought in ether.

What a grand idea Bishop Vincent worked out for the young world in the Chautauqua Circle, Dr. Clark in his world-wide Christian Endeavor movement, the Methodist Church in the Epworth League, Edward Everett Hale in his little bands of King's Daughters and Ten Times One is Ten! Here is Clara Barton who has created the Red Cross Society, which is loved by all nations. She noticed in our Civil War that the Confederates were shelling the hospital. She thought it the last touch of cruelty to fight what couldn't fight back, and she determined to have the barbarous custom stopped. Of course the world laughed at this poor unaided woman. But her idea has been adopted by all nations; and the enemy that aims a shot at the tent or building over which flies the white flag with the red cross has lost his last claim to human consideration.

In all ages those who have advanced the cause of humanity have been men and women "possessed," in the opinion of their neighbors. Noah in building the ark, Moses in espousing the cause of the Israelites, or Christ in living and dying to save a fallen race, incurred the pity and scorn of the rich and highly educated, in common with all great benefactors. Yet in every age and in every clime men and women have been willing to incur poverty, hardship, toil, ridicule, persecution, or even death, if thereby they might shed light or comfort upon the path which all must walk from the cradle to the grave. In fact it is doubtful whether a man can perform very great service to mankind who is not permeated with a great purpose—with an overmastering idea.

Beecher had to fight every step of the way to his triumph through obstacles which would have appalled all but the greatest characters. Oftentimes in these great battles for principle and struggles for truth, he stood almost alone fighting popular prejudice, narrowness, and bigotry, uncharitableness and envy even in his own church. But he never hesitated nor wavered when he once saw his duty. There was no shilly-shallying, no hunting for a middle ground between right and wrong, no compromise on principles. He hewed close to the chalk line and held his line plumb to truth. He never pandered for public favor nor sought applause. Duty and truth were his goal, and he went straight to his mark. Other churches did not agree with him nor his, but he was too broad for hatred, too charitable for revenge, and too magnanimous for envy.

What tale of the "Arabian Nights" equals in fascination the story of such lives as those of Franklin, of Morse, Goodyear, Howe, Edison, Bell, Beecher, Gough, Mrs. Harriet Beecher Stowe, Amos Lawrence, George Peabody, McCormick, Hoe, and scores of others, each representing some great idea embodied in earnest action, and resulting in an improvement of the physical, mental, and moral condition of those around them?

There are plenty of ideas left in the world yet. Everything has not been invented. All good things have not been done. There are thousands of abuses to rectify, and each one challenges the independent soul, armed with a new idea.

"But how shall I get ideas?" Keep your wits open! Observe! Study! But above all, Think! and when a noble image is indelibly impressed upon the mind—*Act*!

Dare

The Spartans did not inquire how many the enemy are, but where they Are.—Agis II

What's brave, what's noble, let's do it after the high Roman fashion, and make death proud to take Us.—Shakespeare

Let me die facing the Enemy.—Bayard

Who conquers me, shall find a stubborn foe.— Byron

No great deed is done By falterers who ask for certainty.— George Eliot

Fortune befriends the bold.— Dryden

To stand with a smile upon your face against a stake from which you cannot get away—that, no doubt, is heroic. But the true glory is resignation to the inevitable. To stand unchained, with perfect liberty to go away, held only by the higher claims of duty, and let the fire creep up to the heart,—this is heroism.— F. W. Robertson

"Steady, men! Every man must die where he stands!" said Colin Campbell to the Ninety-third Highlanders at Balaklava, as an overwhelming force of Russian cavalry came sweeping down. "Ay, ay, Sir Colin! we'll do that!" was the response from men, many of whom had to keep their word by thus obeying.

"Bring back the colors," shouted a captain at the battle of the Alma, when an ensign maintained his ground in front, although the men were retreating. "No," cried the ensign, "bring up the men to the colors."

"To dare, and again to dare, and without end to dare," was Danton's noble defiance to the enemies of France. "The Commons of France have resolved to deliberate," said Mirabeau to De Breze, who brought an order from the king for them to disperse, June 23, 1789. "We have heard the intentions that have been attributed to the king; and you, sir, who cannot be recognized as his organ in the National Assembly,—you, who have neither place, voice, nor right to speak,—you are not the person to bring to us a message of his. Go, say to those who sent you that we are here by the power of the people, and that we will not be driven hence, save by the power of the bayonet."

When the assembled senate of Rome begged Regulus not to return to Carthage to fulfil an illegal promise, he calmly replied: "Have you resolved to dishonor me? Torture and death are awaiting me, but what are these to the shame of an infamous act, or the wounds of a guilty mind? Slave as

I am to Carthage, I still have the spirit of a Roman. I have sworn to return. It is my duty. Let the gods take care of the rest."

The courage which Cranmer had shown since the accession of Mary gave way the moment his final doom was announced. The moral cowardice which had displayed itself in his miserable compliance with the lust and despotism of Henry VIII displayed itself again in six successive recantations by which he hoped to purchase pardon. But pardon was impossible; and Cranmer's strangely mingled nature found a power in its very weakness when he was brought into the church of St. Mary at Oxford on the 21st of March, to repeat his recantation on the way to the stake. "Now," ended his address to the hushed congregation before him,—"now I come to the great thing that troubleth my conscience more than any other thing that ever I said or did in my life, and that is the setting abroad of writings contrary to the truth; which here I now renounce and refuse as things written by a hand contrary to the truth which I thought in my heart, and written for fear of death, to save my life, if it might be. And, forasmuch as my hand offended in writing contrary to my heart, my hand therefore shall be the first punished; for if I come to the fire it shall be the first burned." "This was the hand that wrote it," he again exclaimed at the stake, "therefore it shall suffer first punishment"; and holding it steadily in the flame, "he never stirred nor cried till life was gone."

A woman's piercing shriek suddenly startled a party of surveyors at dinner in a forest of northern Virginia on a calm, sunny day in 1750. The cries were repeated in quick succession, and the men sprang through the undergrowth to learn their cause. "Oh, sir," exclaimed the woman as she caught sight of a youth of eighteen, but a man in stature and bearing; "you will surely do something for me! Make these friends release me. My boy,—my poor boy is drowning, and they will not let me go!" "It would be madness; she will jump into the river," said one of the men who was holding her; "and the rapids would dash her to pieces in a moment!" Throwing off his coat, the youth sprang to the edge of the bank, scanned for a moment the rocks and whirling currents, and then, at sight of part of the boy's dress, plunged into the roaring rapids. "Thank God, he will save my child!" cried the mother, and all rushed to the brink of the precipice; "there he is! Oh, my boy, my darling boy! How could I leave you?"

But all eyes were bent upon the youth struggling with strong heart and hope amid the dizzy sweep of the whirling currents far below. Now it seemed as if he would be dashed against a projecting rock, over which the water flew in foam, and anon a whirlpool would drag him in, from whose grasp escape would seem impossible. Twice the boy went out of sight, but he had reappeared the second time, although terribly near the most dangerous part of the river. The rush of waters here was tremendous, and no one had ever dared to approach it, even in a canoe, lest he should be dashed to pieces. The youth redoubled his exertions. Three times he was about to grasp the child, when some stronger eddy would toss it from him. One final effort he makes; the child is held aloft by his strong right arm; but a cry of horror bursts from the lips of every spectator as boy and man shoot over the falls and vanish in the seething waters below.

"There they are!" shouted the mother a moment later, in a delirium of joy. "See! they are safe! Great God, I thank Thee!" And sure enough, they emerged unharmed from the boiling vortex, and in a few minutes reached a low place in the bank and were drawn up by their friends, the boy senseless, but still alive, and the youth almost exhausted. "God will give you a reward," solemnly spoke the grateful woman. "He will do great things for you in return for this day's work, and the blessings of thousands besides mine will attend you."

The youth was George Washington.

"Your Grace has not the organ of animal courage largely developed," said a phrenologist, who was examining Wellington's head. "You are right," replied the Iron Duke, "and but for my sense of duty I should have retreated in my first fight." That first fight, on an Indian field, was one of the most terrible on record.

When General Jackson was a judge and was holding court in a small settlement, a border ruffian, a murderer and desperado, came into the court-room with brutal violence and interrupted the court. The judge ordered him to be arrested. The officer did not dare to approach him. "Call a posse," said the judge, "and arrest him." But they also shrank in fear from the ruffian. "Call me, then," said Jackson; "this court is adjourned for five minutes." He left the bench, walked straight up to the man, and with his eagle eye actually cowed the ruffian, who dropped his weapons, afterwards saying, "There was something in his eye I could not resist."

One of the last official acts of President Carnot, of France, was the sending of a medal of the French Legion of Honor to a little American girl who lives in Indiana. While a train on the Pan Handle Railroad, having on board several distinguished Frenchmen, was bound to Chicago and the World's Fair, Jennie Carey, who was then ten years old, discovered that a trestle was on fire, and that if the train, which was nearly due, entered it a dreadful wreck would take place. Thereupon she ran out upon the track to a place where she could be seen from some little distance. Then she took off her red flannel skirt and, when the train came in view, waved it back and forth across the track. It was seen, and the train stopped. On board of it were seven hundred people, many of whom must have suffered death but for Jennie's courage and presence of mind. When they returned to France, the Frenchmen brought the occurrence to the notice of President Carnot, and the result was the sending of the medal of this famous French society, the purpose of which is the honoring of bravery and merit, wherever they may be found.

It was the heroic devotion of an Indian girl that saved the life of Captain John Smith, when the powerful King Powhatan had decreed his death. Ill could the struggling colony spare him at that time.

On May 10, 1796, Napoleon carried the bridge at Lodi, in the face of the Austrian batteries. Fourteen cannon—some accounts say thirty—were trained upon the French end of the structure. Behind them were six thousand troops. Napoleon massed four thousand grenadiers at the head of the bridge, with a battalion of three hundred carbineers in front. At the tap of the drum the foremost assailants wheeled from the cover of the street wall under a terrible hail of grape and canister, and attempted to pass the gateway to the bridge. The front ranks went down like stalks of grain before a reaper; the column staggered and reeled backward, and the valiant grenadiers were appalled by the task before them. Without a word or a look of reproach, Napoleon placed himself at their head, and his aides and generals rushed to his side. Forward again, this time over heaps of dead that choked the passage, and a quick run, counted by seconds only, carried the column across two hundred yards of clear space, scarcely a shot from the Austrians taking effect beyond the point where the platoons wheeled for the first leap. So sudden and so miraculous was it all that the Austrian artillerists abandoned their guns instantly, and instead of rushing to the front and meeting the French onslaught, their supports fled in a panic. This Napoleon had counted on in making the bold attack. The contrast between Napoleon's slight figure and the massive grenadiers suggested the nickname "Little Corporal."

When Stephen of Colonna fell into the hands of base assailants, they asked him in derision, "Where is now your fortress?" "Here," was his bold reply, placing his hand upon his heart.

After the Mexican War General McClellan was employed as a topographical engineer in surveying the Pacific coast. From his headquarters at Vancouver he had gone on an exploring expedition with two companions, a soldier and a servant, when one evening he received word that the chiefs of the Columbia River tribes desired to confer with him. From the messenger's manner he suspected that the Indians meant mischief, and so he warned his companions that they must be ready to leave camp at a moment's notice.

Mounting his horse, he rode boldly into the Indian village. About thirty chiefs were holding council. McClellan was led into the circle, and placed at the right hand of Saltese. He was familiar with the Chinook jargon, and could understand every word spoken in the council. Saltese made known the grievance of the tribes. Two Indians had been captured by a party of white pioneers and hanged for theft. Retaliation for this outrage seemed imperative. The chiefs pondered long, but had little to say. McClellan had been on friendly terms with them, and was not responsible for the forest executions, but still, he was a white man, and the chiefs had vowed vengeance against the race. The council was prolonged for hours before sentence was passed, and then Saltese, in the name of the head men of the tribes, decreed that McClellan should immediately be put to death.

McClellan said nothing. He had known that argument and pleas for justice or mercy would be of no avail. He sat motionless, apparently indifferent to his fate. By his listlessness he had thrown his captors off their guard. When the sentence was passed he acted like a flash. Flinging his left arm around the neck of Saltese, he whipped out his revolver and held it close to the chief's temple. "Revoke that sentence, or I shall kill you this instant!" he cried, with his fingers clicking the trigger. "I revoke it!" exclaimed Saltese, fairly livid from fear. "I must have your word that I can leave this council in safety." "You have the word of Saltese," was the quick response.

McClellan knew how sacred was the pledge which he had received. The revolver was lowered. Saltese was released from the embrace of the strong arm. McClellan strode out of the tent with his revolver in his hand. Not a hand was raised against him. He mounted his horse and rode to his camp, where his two followers were ready to spring into the saddle and to escape from the villages. He owed his life to his quickness of perception, his courage, and to his accurate knowledge of Indian character.

In 1856, Rufus Choate spoke to an audience of nearly five thousand in Lowell, Mass., in favor of the candidacy of James Buchanan for the presidency. The floor of the great hall began to sink, settling more and more as he proceeded with his address, until a sound of cracking timber below would have precipitated a stampede with fatal results but for the coolness of B. F. Butler, who presided. Telling the people to remain quiet, he said that he would see if there were any cause for alarm. He found the supports of the floor in so bad a condition that the slightest applause would be likely to bury the audience in the ruins of the building. Returning rather leisurely to the platform, he whispered to Choate as he passed, "We shall all be in — in five minutes"; then he told the crowd that there was no immediate danger if they would slowly disperse. The post of danger, he added, was on the platform, which was most weakly supported, therefore he and those with him would be the last to leave. No doubt many lives were saved by his coolness.

Many distinguished foreign and American statesmen were present at a fashionable dinner party where wine was freely poured, but Schuyler Colfax, then vice-president of the United States, declined to drink from a proffered cup. "Colfax dares not drink," sneered a Senator who had already taken too much. "You are right," said the Vice-President, "I dare not."

When Grant was in Houston many years ago, he was given a rousing reception. Naturally hospitable, and naturally inclined to like a man of Grant's make-up, the Houstonites determined to go beyond any other Southern city in the way of a banquet and other manifestations of their good-will and hospitality. They made lavish preparations for the dinner, the committee taking great pains to have the finest wines that could be procured for the table that night. When the time came to serve the wine, the headwaiter went first to Grant. Without a word the general quietly turned down all the glasses at his plate. This movement was a great surprise to the Texans, but they were equal to the occasion. Without a single word being spoken, every man along the line of the long tables turned his glasses down, and there was not a drop of wine taken that night.

Two French officers at Waterloo were advancing to charge a greatly superior force. One, observing that the other showed signs of fear, said, "Sir, I believe you are frightened." "Yes, I am," was the reply, "and if you were half as much frightened, you would run away."

"That's a brave man," said Wellington, when he saw a soldier turn pale as he marched against a battery; "he knows his danger, and faces it."

"There are many cardinals and bishops at Worms," said a friend to Luther, "and they will burn your body to ashes as they did that of John Huss." Luther replied: "Although they should make a fire that should reach from Worms to Wittenberg, and that should flame up to heaven, in the Lord's name I would pass through it and appear before them." He said to another: "I would enter Worms though there were as many devils there as there are tiles upon the roofs of the houses." Another man said to him: "Duke George will surely arrest you." He replied: "It is my duty to go, and I will go, though it rain Duke Georges for nine days together."

A Western paper recently invited the surviving Union and Confederate officers to give an account of the bravest act observed by each during the Civil War. Colonel Thomas Wentworth Higginson said that at a dinner at Beaufort, S. C., where wine flowed freely and ribald jests were bandied, Dr. Miner, a slight, boyish fellow who did not drink, was told that he could not go until he had drunk a toast, told a story, or sung a song. He replied: "I cannot sing, but I will give a toast, although I must drink it in water. It is 'Our Mothers.'" The men were so affected and ashamed that they took him by the hand and thanked him for displaying such admirable moral courage.

It takes courage for a young man to stand firmly erect while others are bowing and fawning for praise and power. It takes courage to wear threadbare clothes while your comrades dress in broadcloth. It takes courage to remain in honest poverty when others grow rich by fraud. It takes courage to say "No" squarely when those around you say "Yes." It takes courage to do your duty in silence and obscurity while others prosper and grow famous although neglecting sacred obligations. It takes courage to unmask your true self, to show your blemishes to a condemning world, and to pass for what you really are.

It takes courage and pluck to be outvoted, beaten, laughed at, scoffed, ridiculed, derided, misunderstood, misjudged, to stand alone with all the world against you, but

"They are slaves who dare not be In the right with two or three."
"An honest man is not the worse because a dog barks at him."
We live ridiculously for fear of being thought ridiculous.
"Tis he is the coward who proves false to his vows, To his manhood, his honor, for a laugh or a sneer."

The youth who starts out by being afraid to speak what he thinks will usually end by being afraid to think what he wishes.

How we shrink from an act of our own! We live as others live. Custom or fashion, or your doctor or minister, dictates, and they in turn dare not depart from their schools. Dress, living, servants, carriages, everything must conform, or we are ostracized. Who dares conduct his household or business affairs in his own way, and snap his fingers at Dame Grundy?

It takes courage for a public man not to bend the knee to popular prejudice. It takes courage to refuse to follow custom when it is injurious to his health and morals. How much easier for a politician to prevaricate and dodge an issue than to stand squarely on his feet like a man!

As the strongest man has a weakness somewhere, so the greatest hero is a coward somewhere. Peter was courageous enough to draw his sword to defend his Master, but he could not stand the ridicule and the finger of scorn of the maidens in the high priest's hall, and he actually denied even the acquaintance of the Master he had declared he would die for.

Don't be like Uriah Heep, begging everybody's pardon for taking the liberty of being in the world. There is nothing attractive in timidity, nothing lovable in fear. Both are deformities and are repulsive. Manly courage is always dignified and graceful.

Bruno, condemned to be burned alive in Rome, said to his judge: "You are more afraid to pronounce my sentence than I am to receive it." Anne Askew, racked until her bones were dislocated, never flinched, but looked her tormentor calmly in the face and refused to adjure her faith.

"I should have thought fear would have kept you from going so far," said a relative who found the little boy Nelson wandering a long distance from home. "Fear?" said the future admiral, "I don't know him."

"To think a thing is impossible is to make it so." *Courage is victory, timidity's defeat.*

That simple shepherd-lad, David, fresh from his flocks, marching unattended and unarmed, save with his shepherd's staff and sling, to confront the colossal Goliath with his massive armor, is the sublimest audacity the world has ever seen.

"Dent, I wish you would get down and see what is the matter with that leg there," said Grant, when he and Colonel Dent were riding through the thickest of a fire that had become so concentrated and murderous that his troops had all been driven back. "I guess looking after your horse's legs can wait," said Dent; "it is simply murder for us to sit here." "All right," said Grant; "if you don't want to see to it, I will." He dismounted, untwisted a piece of telegraph wire which had begun to cut the horse's leg, examined it deliberately, and climbed into his saddle. "Dent," said he, "when you've got a horse that you think a great deal of, you should never take any chances with him. If that wire had been left there for a little time longer he would have gone dead lame, and would perhaps have been ruined for life."

Wellington said that at Waterloo the hottest of the battle raged round a farmhouse, with an orchard surrounded by a thick hedge, which was so important a point in the British position that orders were given to hold it at any hazard or sacrifice. At last the powder and ball ran short and the hedges took fire, surrounding the orchard with a wall of flame. A messenger had been sent for ammunition, and soon two loaded wagons came galloping toward the farmhouse. "The driver of the first wagon, with the reckless daring of an English boy, spurred his struggling and terrified horses through the burning heap; but the flames rose fiercely round, and caught the powder, which exploded in an instant, sending wagon, horses, and rider in fragments into the air. For a instant the driver of the second wagon paused, appalled by his comrade's fate; the next, observing that the flames, beaten back for the moment by the explosion, afforded him one desperate chance, sent his horses at the smoldering breach and, amid the deafening cheers of the garrison, landed his terrible cargo safely within. Behind him the flames closed up, and raged more fiercely than ever."

At the battle of Friedland a cannon-ball came over the heads of the French soldiers, and a young soldier instinctively dodged. Napoleon looked at him and smilingly said: "My friend, if that ball were destined for you, though you were to burrow a hundred feet under ground it would be sure to find you there."

When the mine in front of Petersburg was finished the fuse was lighted and the Union troops were drawn up ready to charge the enemy's works as soon as the explosion should make a breach. But seconds, minutes, and tens of minutes passed, without a sound from the mine, and the suspense became painful. Lieutenant Doughty and Sergeant Rees volunteered to examine the fuse. Through the long subterranean galleries they hurried in silence, not knowing but that they were advancing to a horrible death. They found the defect, fired the train anew, and soon a terrible upheaval of earth gave the signal to march to victory.

At the battle of Copenhagen, as Nelson walked the deck slippery with blood and covered with the dead, he said: "This is warm work, and this day may be the last to any of us in a moment. But, mark me, I would not be elsewhere for thousands." At the battle of Trafalgar, when he was shot and was being carried below, he covered his face, that those fighting might not know their chief had fallen.

In a skirmish at Salamanca, while the enemy's guns were pouring shot into his regiment, Sir William Napier's men became disobedient. He at once ordered a halt, and flogged four of the ringleaders under fire. The men yielded at once, and then marched three miles under a heavy cannonade as coolly as if it were a review.

Execute your resolutions immediately. Thoughts are but dreams until their effects be tried. Does competition trouble you? work away; what is your competitor but a man? *Conquer your place in the world*, for all things serve a brave soul. Combat difficulty manfully; sustain misfortune bravely; endure poverty nobly; encounter disappointment courageously. The influence of the brave man is contagious and creates an epidemic of noble zeal in all about him. Every day sends to the grave obscure men who have only remained in obscurity because their timidity has prevented them from making a first effort; and who, if they could have been induced to begin, would in all probability have gone great lengths in the career of usefulness and fame. "No great deed is done," says George Eliot, "by falterers who ask for certainty."

After the great inward struggle was over, and he had determined to remain loyal to his principles, Thomas More walked cheerfully to the block. His wife called him a fool for staying in a dark, damp, filthy prison when he might have his liberty by merely renouncing his doctrines, as some of the bishops had done. But Thomas More preferred death to dishonor.

His daughter showed the power of love to drive away fear. She remained true to her father when all others, even her mother, had forsaken him. After his head had been cut off and exhibited on a pole on London Bridge, the poor girl begged it of the authorities, and requested that it be buried in the coffin with her. Her request was granted, for her death soon occurred.

When Sir Walter Raleigh came to the scaffold he was very faint, and began his speech to the crowd by saying that during the last two days he had been visited by two ague fits. "If, therefore, you perceive any weakness in me, I beseech you ascribe it to my sickness rather than to myself." He took the ax and kissed the blade, and said to the sheriff: "'T is a sharp medicine, but a sound cure for all diseases."

Don't waste time dreaming of obstacles you may never encounter, or in crossing bridges you have not reached. To half will and to hang forever in the balance is to lose your grip on life.

Abraham Lincoln's boyhood was one long struggle with poverty, with little education, and no influential friends. When at last he had begun the practice of law, it required no little courage to cast his fortune with the weaker side in politics, and thus imperil what small reputation he had gained. Only the most sublime moral courage could have sustained him as President to hold his ground against hostile criticism and a long train of disaster; to issue the Emancipation Proclamation, to support Grant and Stanton against the clamor of the politicians and the press.

Lincoln never shrank from espousing an unpopular cause when he believed it to be right. At the time when it almost cost a young lawyer his bread and butter to defend the fugitive slave, and when other lawyers had refused, Lincoln would always plead the cause of the unfortunate whenever an opportunity presented. "Go to Lincoln," people would say, when these hounded fugitives were seeking protection; "he's not afraid of any cause, if it's right."

> Then to side with Truth is noble when we share her wretched crust,
> Ere her cause bring fame and profit, and 'tis prosperous to be just:
> Then it is the brave man chooses, while the coward stands aside,
> Doubting in his abject spirit, till his Lord is crucified. —Lowell.

As Salmon P. Chase left the court room after an impassioned plea for the runaway slave girl Matilda, a man looked at him in surprise and said: "There goes a fine young fellow who has just ruined himself." But in thus ruining himself Chase had taken the first important step in a career in which he became Governor of Ohio, United States Senator from Ohio, Secretary of the United States Treasury, and Chief Justice of the United States Supreme Court.

At the trial of William Penn for having spoken at a Quaker meeting, the recorder, not satisfied with the first verdict, said to the jury: "We will have a verdict by the help of God, or you shall starve for it." "You are Englishmen," said Penn; "mind your privileges, give not away your right." At last the jury, after two days and two nights without food, returned a verdict of "Not guilty." The recorder fined them forty marks apiece for their independence.

What cared Christ for the jeers of the crowd? The palsied hand moved, the blind saw, the leper was made whole, the dead spake, despite the ridicule and scoffs of the spectators.

What cared Wendell Phillips for rotten eggs, derisive scorn, and hisses? In him "at last the scornful world had met its match." Were Beecher and Gough to be silenced by the rude English mobs that came to extinguish them? No! they held their ground and compelled unwilling thousands to hear and to heed. Did Anna Dickinson leave the platform when the pistol bullets of the Molly Maguires flew about her head? She silenced those pistols by her courage and her arguments.

What the world wants is a Knox, who dares to preach on with a musket leveled at his head; a Garrison, who is not afraid of a jail, or a mob, or a scaffold erected in front of his door.

When General Butler was sent with nine thousand men to quell the New York riots, he arrived in advance of his troops, and found the streets thronged with an angry mob, which had already hanged several men to lamp-posts. Without waiting for his men, Butler went to the place where the crowd was most dense, overturned an ash barrel, stood upon it, and began: "Delegates from Five Points, fiends from hell, you have murdered your superiors," and the bloodstained crowd quailed before the courageous words of a single man in a city which Mayor Fernando Wood could not restrain with the aid of police and militia.

"Our enemies are before us," exclaimed the Spartans at Thermopylae. "And we are before them." was the cool reply of Leonidas. "Deliver your arms," came the message from Xerxes. "Come and take them," was the answer Leonidas sent back. A Persian soldier said: "You will not be able to see the sun for flying javelins and arrows." "Then we will fight in the shade," replied a Lacedemonian. What wonder that a handful of such men checked the march of the greatest host that ever trod the earth!

"It is impossible," said a staff officer, when Napoleon gave directions for a daring plan. "Impossible!" thundered the great commander, "*impossible is the adjective of fools!*"

The courageous man is an example to the intrepid. His influence is magnetic. Men follow him, even to the death.

Men who have dared have moved the world, often before reaching the prime of life. It is astonishing what daring to begin and perseverance have enabled even youths to achieve. Alexander, who ascended the throne at twenty, had conquered the known world before dying at thirty-three. Julius Caesar captured eight hundred cities, conquered three hundred nations, defeated three million men, became a great orator and one of the greatest statesmen known, and still was a young man. Washington was appointed adjutant-general at nineteen, was sent at twenty one as an ambassador to treat with the French, and won his first battle as a colonel at twenty-two. Lafayette was made general of the whole French Army at twenty. Charlemagne was master of France and Germany at thirty. Galileo was but eighteen when he saw the principle of the pendulum in the swing lamp in the cathedral at Pisa. Peel was in Parliament at twenty-one. Gladstone was in Parliament before he was twenty-two, and at twenty-four he was Lord of the Treasury. Elizabeth Barrett Browning was proficient in Greek and Latin at twelve; De Quincey at eleven. Robert Browning wrote at eleven poetry of no mean order. Cowley, who sleeps in Westminster Abbey, published a volume of poems at fifteen. Luther was but twenty-nine when he nailed his famous thesis to the door of the bishop and defied the pope. Nelson was a lieutenant in the British Navy before he was twenty. He was but forty-seven when he received his death wound at Trafalgar. At thirty-six, Cortez was the conqueror of Mexico; at thirty-two, Clive had established the British power in India. Hannibal, the greatest of military commanders, was only thirty when, at Cannae, he dealt an almost annihilating blow at the republic of Rome, and Napoleon was only twenty-seven when, on the plains of Italy, he outgeneraled and defeated, one after another, the veteran marshals of Austria.

Equal courage and resolution are often shown by men who have passed the allotted limit of life. Victor Hugo and Wellington were both in their prime after they had reached the age of threescore years and ten. Gladstone ruled England with a strong hand at eighty-four, and was a marvel of literary and scholarly ability.

Shakespeare says: "He is not worthy of the honeycomb that shuns the hive because the bees have stings."

"The brave man is not he who feels no fear, For that were stupid and irrational; But he whose noble soul its fear subdues And bravely dares the danger nature shrinks from."

Many a bright youth has accomplished nothing of worth to himself or the world simply because he did not dare to commence things.

Begin! Begin! Begin!!!

Whatever people may think of you, do that which you believe to be right. Be alike indifferent to censure or praise.— Pythagoras

I dare to do all that may become a man:
Who dares do more is none. — Shakespeare

For man's great actions are performed in minor struggles. There are obstinate and unknown braves who defend themselves inch by inch in the shadows against the fatal invasion of want and turpitude. There are noble and mysterious triumphs which no eye sees, no renown rewards, and no flourish of trumpets salutes. Life, misfortune, isolation, abandonment, and poverty are battlefields which have their heroes.— Victor Hugo

Quit yourselves like men.—1 SamueL IV. 9.

The Will and the Way

"I will find a way or make one."
Nothing is impossible to the man who can will.— Mirabeau

The iron will of one stout heart shall make a thousand quail:
A feeble dwarf, dauntlessly resolved, will turn the tide of battle,
And rally to a nobler strife the giants that had fled.— Tupper

In the lexicon of youth which fate reserves for a bright manhood there is no such word as fail.— Bulwer

When a firm and decisive spirit is recognized, it is curious to see how the space clears around a man and leaves him room and freedom.— John Foster

"As well can the Prince of Orange pluck the stars from the sky, as bring the ocean to the wall of Leyden for your relief," was the derisive shout of the Spanish soldiers when told that the Dutch fleet would raise that terrible four months' siege of 1574. But from the parched lips of William, tossing on his bed of fever at Rotterdam, had issued the command: "*Break down the dikes: give Holland back to ocean!*" and the people had replied: "Better a drowned land than a lost land." They began to demolish dike after dike of the strong lines, ranged one within another for fifteen miles to their city of the interior. It was an enormous task; the garrison was starving; and the besiegers laughed in scorn at the slow progress of the puny insects who sought to rule the waves of the sea. But ever, as of old, Heaven aids those who help themselves. On the first and second of October a violent equinoctial gale rolled the ocean inland, and swept the fleet on the rising waters almost to the camp of the Spaniards. The next morning the garrison sallied out to attack their enemies, but the besiegers had fled in terror under cover of the darkness. The next day the wind changed, and a counter tempest brushed the water, with the fleet upon it, from the surface of Holland. The outer dikes were replaced at once, leaving the North Sea within its old bounds. When the flowers bloomed the following spring, a joyous procession marched through the streets to found the University of Leyden, in commemoration of the wonderful deliverance of the city.

At a dinner party given in 1837, at the residence of Chancellor Kent, in New York City, some of the most distinguished men in the country were invited, and among them was a young and rather melancholy and reticent Frenchman. Professor Morse was also one of the guests, and during the evening he drew the attention of Mr. Gallatin, then a prominent statesman, to the stranger, observing that his forehead indicated a great intellect. "Yes," replied Mr. Gallatin, touching his own forehead with his finger, "there is a great deal in that head of his: but he has a strange fancy. Can you believe it? He has the idea that he will one day be the Emperor of France. Can you conceive anything more absurd than that?"

It did seem absurd, for this reserved Frenchman was then a poor adventurer, an exile from his country, without fortune or powerful connections, and yet, fourteen years later, his idea became a fact,—his dream of becoming Napoleon III. was realized. True, before he accomplished his purpose there were long, dreary years of imprisonment, exile, disaster, and patient labor and hope, but he gained his ambition at last. He was not scrupulous as to the means employed to accomplish his ends, yet he is a remarkable example of what pluck and energy can do.

When Mr. Ingram, publisher of the "Illustrated London News," began life as a newsdealer at Nottingham, England, he walked ten miles to deliver a single paper rather than disappoint a customer. Does any one wonder that such a youth succeeded? Once he rose at two o'clock in the morning and walked to London to get some papers because there was no post to bring them. He determined that his customers should not be disappointed. This is the kind of will that finds a way.

There is scarcely anything in all biography grander than the saying of young Henry Fawcett, Gladstone's last Postmaster-General, to his grief-stricken father, who had put out both his eyes by birdshot during a game hunt: "Never mind, father, blindness shall not interfere with my success in life." One of the most pathetic sights in London streets, long afterward, was Henry Fawcett, M. P., led everywhere by a faithful daughter, who acted as amanuensis as well as guide to her plucky father. Think of a young man, scarcely on the threshold of active life, suddenly losing the sight of both eyes and yet by mere pluck and almost incomprehensible tenacity of purpose, lifting himself into eminence in any direction, to say nothing of becoming one of the foremost men in a country noted for its great men!

The courageous daughter who was eyes to her father was herself a marvelous example of pluck and determination. For the first time in the history of Oxford College, which reaches back centuries, she succeeded in winning the post which had only been gained before by great men, such as Gladstone,—the post of senior wrangler. This achievement had had no parallel in history up to that date, and attracted the attention of the whole civilized world. Not only had no woman ever held this position before, but with few exceptions it had only been held by men who in after life became highly distinguished.

"Circumstances," says Milton, "have rarely favored famous men. They have fought their way to triumph through all sorts of opposing obstacles."

The true way to conquer circumstances is to be a greater circumstance yourself.

Yet, while desiring to impress in the most forcible manner possible the fact that will-power is necessary to success, and that, other things being equal, the greater the will-power, the grander and more complete the success, we can not indorse the theory that there is nothing in circumstances or environments, or that any man, simply because he has an indomitable will, may become a Bonaparte, a Pitt, a Webster, a Beecher, a Lincoln. We must temper determination with discretion, and support it with knowledge and common sense, or it will only lead us to run our heads against posts. We must not expect to overcome a stubborn fact merely by a stubborn will. We only have the right to assume that we can do anything within the limit of our utmost faculty, strength, and endurance. Obstacles permanently insurmountable bar our progress in some directions, but in any direction we may reasonably hope and attempt to go we shall find that, as a rule, they are either not insurmountable or else not permanent. The strong-willed, intelligent, persistent man will find or make a way where, in the nature of things, a way can be found or made.

Every schoolboy knows that circumstances do give clients to lawyers and patients to physicians; place ordinary clergymen in extraordinary pulpits; place sons of the rich at the head of immense corporations and large houses, when they have very ordinary ability and scarcely any experience, while poor young men with unusual ability, good education, good character, and large experience, often have to fight their way for years to obtain even very mediocre situations; that there are thousands of young men of superior ability, both in the city and in the country, who seem to be compelled by circumstances to remain in very ordinary positions for small pay, when others about them are raised by money or family influence into desirable places. In other words, we all know that the best men do not always get the best places; circumstances do have a great deal to do with our position, our salaries, our station in life.

Every one knows that there is not always a way where there is a will; that labor does not always conquer all things; that there are things impossible even to him that wills, however strongly; that one can not always make anything of himself he chooses; that there are limitations in our very natures which no amount of will-power or industry can overcome.

But while it is true that the will-power can not perform miracles, yet that it is almost omnipotent, and can perform wonders, all history goes to prove. As Shakespeare says:—

Men at some time are masters of their fates;
The fault, dear Brutus, is not in our stars,
But in ourselves, that we are underlings.

Show me a man who according to popular prejudice is a victim of bad luck, and I will show you one who has some unfortunate crooked twist of temperament that invites disaster. He is ill-tempered, conceited, or trifling; lacks character, enthusiasm, or some other requisite for success.

Disraeli said that man is not the creature of circumstances, but that circumstances are the creatures of men.

Believe in the power of will, which annihilates the sickly, sentimental doctrine of fatalism,—you must, but can't, you ought, but it is impossible.

Give me the man who faces what he must,
"Who breaks his birth's invidious bar,
And grasps the skirts of happy chance,
And breasts the blows of circumstance,
And grapples with his evil star."

The indomitable will, the inflexible purpose, will find a way or make one. There is always room for a man of force.

"He who has a firm will," says Goethe, "molds the world to himself." "People do not lack strength," says Victor Hugo, "they lack will."

"He who resolves upon any great end, by that very resolution has scaled the great barriers to it, and he who seizes the grand idea of self-cultivation, and solemnly resolves upon it, will find that idea, that resolution, burning like fire within him, and ever putting him upon his own improvement. He will find it removing difficulties, searching out, or making means; giving courage for despondency, and strength for weakness."

Nearly all great men, those who have towered high above their fellows, have been remarkable above all things else for their energy of will. Of Julius Caesar it was said by a contemporary that it was his activity and giant determination, rather than his military skill, that won his victories. The youth who starts out in life determined to make the most of his eyes and let nothing escape him which he can possibly use for his own advancement; who keeps his ears open for every sound that can help him on his way, who keeps his hands open that he may clutch every opportunity, who is ever on the alert for everything which can help him to get on in the world, who seizes every experience in life and grinds it up into paint for his great life's picture, who keeps his heart open that he may catch every noble impulse, and everything which may inspire him,—that youth will be sure to make his life successful; there are no "ifs" or "ands" about it. If he has his health, nothing can keep him from final success.

No tyranny of circumstances can permanently imprison a determined will.

The world always stands aside for the determined man.

"The general of a large army may be defeated," said Confucius, "but you can not defeat the determined mind of a peasant."

The poor, deaf pauper, Kitto, who made shoes in the almshouse, and who became the greatest of Biblical scholars, wrote in his journal, on the threshold of manhood: "I am not myself a believer in impossibilities: I think that all the fine stories about natural ability, etc., are mere rigmarole, and that every man may, according to his opportunities and industry, render himself almost anything he wishes to become."

Lincoln is probably the most remarkable example on the pages of history, showing the possibilities of our country. From the poverty in which he was born, through the rowdyism of a frontier town, the discouragement of early bankruptcy, and the fluctuations of popular politics, he rose to the championship of union and freedom.

Lincoln's will made his way. When his friends nominated him as a candidate for the legislature, his enemies made fun of him. When making his campaign speeches he wore a mixed jean coat so short that he could not sit down on it, flax and tow-linen trousers, straw hat, and pot-metal boots. He had nothing in the world but character and friends.

When his friends suggested law to him, he laughed at the idea of his being a lawyer. He said he had not brains enough. He read law barefoot under the trees, his neighbors said, and he sometimes slept on the counter in the store where he worked. He had to borrow money to buy a suit of clothes to make a respectable appearance in the legislature, and walked to take his seat at Vandalia,—one hundred miles.

See Thurlow Weed, defying poverty and wading through the snow two miles, with rags for shoes, to borrow a book to read before the sap-bush fire. See Locke, living on bread and water in a Dutch garret. See Heyne, sleeping many a night on a barn floor with only a book for his pillow. See Samuel Drew, tightening his apron string "in lieu of a dinner." History is full of such examples. He who will pay the price for victory need never fear final defeat.

Paris was in the hands of a mob, the authorities were panic-stricken, for they did not dare to trust their underlings. In came a man who said, "I know a young officer who has the courage and ability to quell this mob." "Send for him; send for him; send for him," said they. Napoleon was sent for, came, subjugated the mob, subjugated the authorities, ruled France and then conquered Europe.

Success in life is dependent largely upon the will-power, and whatever weakens or impairs it diminishes success. The will can be educated. That which most easily becomes a habit in us is the will. Learn, then, to will decisively and strongly; thus fix your floating life, and leave it no longer to be carried hither and thither, like a withered leaf, by every wind that blows. "It is not talent that men lack, it is the will to labor; it is the purpose."

It was the insatiable thirst for knowledge which held to his task, through poverty and discouragement, John Leyden, a Scotch shepherd's son. Barefoot and alone, he walked six or eight miles daily to learn to read, which was all the schooling he had. His desire for an education defied the extremest poverty, and no obstacle could turn him from his purpose. He was rich when he discovered a little bookstore, and his thirsty soul would drink in the precious treasures from its priceless volumes for hours, perfectly oblivious of the scanty meal of bread and water which awaited him at his lowly lodging. Nothing could discourage him from trying to improve himself by study. It seemed to him that an opportunity to get at books and lectures was all that any man could need. Before he was nineteen, this poor shepherd boy with no chance had astonished the professors of Edinburgh by his knowledge of Greek and Latin.

Hearing that a surgeon's assistant in the Civil Service was wanted, although he knew nothing whatever of medicine, he determined to apply for it. There were only six months before the place was to be filled, but nothing would daunt him, and he took his degree with honor. Walter Scott, who thought this one of the most remarkable illustrations of perseverance, helped to fit him out, and he sailed for India.

Webster was very poor even after he entered Dartmouth College. A friend sent him a recipe for greasing his boots. Webster wrote and thanked him, and added: "But my boots needs other doctoring, for they not only admit water, but even peas and gravel-stones." Yet he became one of the greatest men in the world. Sydney Smith said: "Webster was a living lie, because no man on earth could be as great as he looked." Carlyle said of him: "One would incline at sight to back him against the world."

What seemed to be luck followed Stephen Girard all his life. No matter what he did, it always seemed to others to turn to his account.

Being a foreigner, unable to speak English, short, stout, and with a repulsive face, blind in one eye, it was hard for him to get a start. But he was not the man to give up. He had begun as a cabin boy at thirteen, and for nine years sailed between Bordeaux and the French West Indies. He improved every leisure minute at sea, mastering the art of navigation.

At the age of eight he had first discovered that he was blind in one eye. His father, evidently thinking that he would never amount to anything, would not help him to an education beyond that of mere reading and writing, but sent his younger brothers to college. The discovery of his blindness, the neglect of his father, and the chagrin of his brothers' advancement soured his whole life.

When he began business for himself in Philadelphia, there seemed to be nothing he would not do for money. He bought and sold anything, from groceries to old junk; he bottled wine and cider, from which he made a good profit. Everything he touched prospered.

He left nothing to chance. His plans and schemes were worked out with mathematical care. His letters written to his captains in foreign ports, laying out their routes and giving detailed instructions, are models of foresight and systematic planning. He never left anything of importance to others. He was rigidly accurate in his instructions, and would not allow the slightest departure from them. He used to say that while his captains might save him money by deviating from instructions once, yet they would cause loss in ninety-nine other cases.

He never lost a ship, and many times that which brought financial ruin to many others, as the War of 1812, only increased his wealth. Everybody, especially his jealous brother merchants, attributed his great success to his luck. While undoubtedly he was fortunate in happening to be at the right place at the right time, yet he was precision, method, accuracy, energy itself. What seemed luck with him was only good judgment and promptness in seizing opportunities, and the greatest care and zeal in improving them to their utmost possibilities.

The mathematician tells you that if you throw the dice, there are thirty chances to one against your turning up a particular number, and a hundred to one against your repeating the same throw three times in succession: and so on in an augmenting ratio.

Many a young man who has read the story of John Wanamaker's romantic career has gained very little inspiration or help from it toward his own elevation and advancement, for he looks upon it as the result of good luck, chance, or fate. "What a lucky fellow," he says to himself as he reads; "what a bonanza he fell into!" But a careful analysis of Wanamaker's life only enforces the same lesson taught by the analysis of most great lives, namely, that a good mother, a good constitution, the habit of hard work, indomitable energy, determination which knows no defeat, decision which never wavers, a concentration which never scatters its forces, courage which never falters, self-mastery which can say No, and stick to it, strict integrity and downright honesty, a cheerful disposition, unbounded enthusiasm in one's calling, and a high aim and noble purpose insure a very large measure of success.

Youth should be taught that there is something in circumstances; that there is such a thing as a poor pedestrian happening to find no obstruction in his way, and reaching the goal when a better walker finds the drawbridge up, the street blockaded, and so fails to win the race; that wealth often does place unworthy sons in high positions; that family influence does gain a lawyer clients, a physician patients, an ordinary scholar a good professorship; but that, on the other hand, position, clients, patients, professorships, managers' and superintendents' positions do not necessarily constitute success. He should be taught that in the long run, as a rule, *the best man does win the best place*, and that persistent merit does succeed.

There is about as much chance of idleness and incapacity winning real success or a high position in life, as there would be in producing a "Paradise Lost" by shaking up promiscuously the separate words of

Webster's Dictionary, and letting them fall at random on the floor. Fortune smiles upon those who roll up their sleeves and put their shoulders to the wheel; upon men who are not afraid of dreary, dry, irksome drudgery, men of nerve and grit who do not turn aside for dirt and detail.

The youth should be taught that "he alone is great, who, by a life heroic, conquers fate"; that "diligence is the mother of good luck"; that nine times out of ten what we call luck or fate is but a mere bugbear of the indolent, the languid, the purposeless, the careless, the indifferent; that, as a rule, the man who fails does not see or seize his opportunity. Opportunity is coy, is swift, is gone, before the slow, the unobservant, the indolent, or the careless can seize her:—

"In idle wishes fools supinely stay:
Be there a will and wisdom finds a way."

It has been well said that the very reputation of being strong-willed, plucky, and indefatigable is of priceless value. It often cows enemies and dispels at the start opposition to one's undertakings which would otherwise be formidable.

It is astonishing what men who have come to their senses late in life have accomplished by a sudden resolution.

Arkwright was fifty years of age when he began to learn English grammar and improve his writing and spelling. Benjamin Franklin was past fifty before he began the study of science and philosophy. Milton, in his blindness, was past the age of fifty when he sat down to complete his world-known epic, and Scott at fifty-five took up his pen to redeem a liability of $600,000. "Yet I am learning," said Michael Angelo, when threescore years and ten were past, and he had long attained the highest triumphs of his art.

Even brains are second in importance to will. The vacillating man is always pushed aside in the race of life. It is only the weak and vacillating who halt before adverse circumstances and obstacles. A man with an iron will, with a determination that nothing shall check his career, is sure, if he has perseverance and grit, to succeed. We may not find time for what we would like, but what we long for and strive for with all our strength, we usually approximate, if we do not fully reach.

I wish it were possible to show the youth of America the great part that the will might play in their success in life and in their happiness as well. The achievements of will-power are simply beyond computation. Scarcely anything in reason seems impossible to the man who can will strong enough and long enough.

How often we see this illustrated in the case of a young woman who suddenly becomes conscious that she is plain and unattractive; who, by prodigious exercise of her will and untiring industry, resolves to redeem herself from obscurity and commonness; and who not only makes up for her deficiencies, but elevates herself into a prominence and importance which mere personal attractions could never have given her! Charlotte Cushman, without a charm of form or face, climbed to the very top of her profession. How many young men, stung by consciousness of physical deformity or mental deficiencies, have, by a strong, persistent exercise of will-power, raised themselves from mediocrity and placed themselves high above those who scorned them!

History is full of examples of men and women who have redeemed themselves from disgrace, poverty, and misfortune by the firm resolution of an iron will. The consciousness of being looked upon as inferior, as incapable of accomplishing what others accomplish; the sensitiveness at being considered a dunce in school, has stung many a youth into a determination which has elevated him far above those who laughed at him, as in the case of Newton, of Adam Clark, of Sheridan, Wellington, Goldsmith, Dr. Chalmers, Curran, Disraeli and hundreds of others.

It is men like Mirabeau, who "trample upon impossibilities"; like Napoleon, who do not wait for opportunities, but make them; like Grant, who has only "unconditional surrender" for the enemy, who change the very front of the world.

"I can't, it is impossible," said a foiled lieutenant to Alexander. "Be gone," shouted the conquering Macedonian, "there is nothing impossible to him who will try."

Were I called upon to express in a word the secret of so many failures among those who started out in life with high hopes, I should say unhesitatingly, they lacked will-power. They could not half will. What is a man without a will? He is like an engine without steam, a mere sport of chance, to be tossed about hither and thither, always at the mercy of those who have wills. I should call the strength of will the test of a young man's possibilities. Can he will strong enough, and hold whatever he undertakes with an iron grip? It is the iron grip that takes the strong hold on life. "The truest wisdom," said Napoleon, "is a resolute determination." An iron will without principle might produce a Napoleon; but with character it would make a Wellington or a Grant, untarnished by ambition or avarice.

"The undivided will
'Tis that compels the elements and wrings
A human music from the indifferent air."

One Unwavering Aim

*Life is an arrow—therefore you must know
What mark to aim at, how to use the bow—
Then draw it to the head and let it go.—* Henry Van Dyke

The important thing in life is to have a great aim, and to possess the aptitude and perseverance to attain it.— Goethe

"*A double-minded man is unstable in all his ways.*"
Let every one ascertain his special business and calling, and then stick to it if he would be successful.— *Franklin*

"Why do you lead such a solitary life?" asked a friend of Michael Angelo. "Art is a jealous mistress," replied the artist; "she requires the whole man." During his labors at the Sistine Chapel, according to Disraeli, he refused to meet any one, even at his own house.

"This day we sailed westward, which was our course," were the simple but grand words which Columbus wrote in his journal day after day. Hope might rise and fall, terror and dismay might seize upon the crew at the mysterious variations of the compass, but Columbus, unappalled, pushed due west and nightly added to his record the above words.

"Cut an inch deeper," said a member of the Old Guard to the surgeon probing his wound, "and you will find the Emperor,"—meaning his heart. By the marvelous power of concentrated purpose Napoleon had left his name on the very stones of the capital, had burned it indelibly into the heart of every Frenchman, and had left it written in living letters all over Europe. France to-day has not shaken off the spell of that name. In the fair city on the Seine the mystic "N" confronts you everywhere.

Oh, the power of a great purpose to work miracles! It has changed the face of the world. Napoleon knew that there were plenty of great men in France, but they did not know the might of the unwavering aim by which he was changing the destinies of Europe. He saw that what was called the "balance of power" was only an idle dream; that, unless some master-mind could be found which was a match for events, the millions would rule in anarchy. His iron will grasped the situation; and like William Pitt, he did not loiter around balancing the probabilities of failure or success, or dally with his purpose. There was no turning to the right nor to the left; no dreaming away time, nor building air-castles; but one look and purpose, forward, upward and onward, straight to his goal. His great success in war was due largely to his definiteness of aim. He always hit the bull's-eye. He was like a great burning-glass, concentrating the rays of the sun upon a single spot; he burned a hole wherever he went. After finding the weak place in the enemy's ranks, he would mass his men and hurl them like an avalanche upon the critical point, crowding volley upon volley, charge upon charge, till he made a breach. What a lesson of the power concentration there is in this man's life!

To succeed to-day a man must concentrate all the faculties of his mind upon one unwavering aim, and have a tenacity of purpose which means death or victory. Every other inclination which tempts him from his aim must be suppressed.

A man may starve on a dozen half-learned trades or occupations; he may grow rich and famous upon one trade thoroughly mastered, even though it be the humblest.

Even Gladstone, with his ponderous yet active brain, said he could not do two things at once; he threw his entire strength upon whatever he did. The intensest energy characterized everything he undertook, even his recreation. If such concentration of energy is necessary for the success of a Gladstone, what can we common mortals hope to accomplish by "scatteration"?

All great men have been noted for their power of concentration which makes them oblivious of everything outside their aim. Victor Hugo wrote his "Notre Dame" during the revolution of 1830, while the bullets were whistling across his garden. He shut himself up in one room, locking his clothes up in another, lest they should tempt him to go out into the street, and spent most of that winter wrapped in a big gray comforter, pouring his very life into his work.

Abraham Lincoln possessed such power of concentration that he could repeat quite correctly a sermon to which he had listened in his boyhood.

A New York sportsman, in answer to an advertisement, sent twenty-five cents for a sure receipt to prevent a shotgun from scattering, and received the following: "Dear Sir: To keep a gun from scattering put in but a single shot."

It is the men who do one thing in this world who come to the front. Who is the favorite actor? It is a Jefferson, who devotes a lifetime to a "Rip Van Winkle," a Booth, an Irving, a Kean, who plays one character until he can play it better than any other man living, and not the shallow players who impersonate all parts. The great man is the one who never steps outside of his specialty or dissipates his individuality. It is an Edison, a Morse, a Bell, a Howe, a Stephenson, a Watt. It is an Adam Smith, spending ten years on the "Wealth of Nations." It is a Gibbon, giving twenty years to his "Decline and Fall of the Roman Empire." It is a Hume, writing thirteen hours a day on his "History of England." It is a Webster, spending thirty-six years on his dictionary. It is a Bancroft, working twenty-six years on his "History of the United States." It is a Field, crossing the ocean fifty times to lay a cable, while the world ridicules. It is a Newton, writing his "Chronology of Ancient Nations" sixteen times.

A one-talent man who decides upon a definite object accomplishes more than a ten-talent man who scatters his energies and never knows exactly what he will do. The weakest living creature, by concentrating his powers upon one thing, can accomplish something; the strongest, by dispersing his over many, may fail to accomplish anything.

A great purpose is cumulative; and, like a great magnet, it attracts all that is kindred along the stream of life.

A Yankee can splice a rope in many different ways; an English sailor only knows one way, but that is the best one. It is the one-sided man, the sharp-eyed man, the man of single and intense purpose, the man of one idea, who cuts his way through obstacles and forges to the front. The time has gone forever when a Bacon can span universal knowledge; or when, absorbing all the knowledge of the times, a Dante can sustain arguments against fourteen disputants in the University of Paris, and conquer in them all. The day when a man can successfully drive a dozen callings abreast is a thing of the past. Concentration is the keynote of the century.

Scientists estimate that there is energy enough in less than fifty acres of sunshine to run all the machinery in the world, if it could be concentrated. But the sun might blaze out upon the earth forever without setting anything on fire; although these rays focused by a burning-glass would melt solid granite, or even change a diamond into vapor. There are plenty of men who have ability enough; the rays of their faculties, taken separately, are all right, but they are powerless to collect them, to bring them all to bear upon a single spot. Versatile men, universal geniuses, are usually weak, because they have no power to concentrate their talents upon one point, and this makes all the difference between success and failure.

Chiseled upon the tomb of a disappointed, heart-broken king, Joseph II. of Austria, in the Royal Cemetery at Vienna, a traveler tells us, is this epitaph: "Here lies a monarch who, with the best of intentions, never carried out a single plan."

Sir James Mackintosh was a man of remarkable ability. He excited in every one who knew him the greatest expectations. Many watched his career with much interest, expecting that he would dazzle the world; but there was no purpose in his life. He had intermittent attacks of enthusiasm for doing great things, but his zeal all evaporated before he could decide what to do. This fatal defect in his character kept him balancing between conflicting motives; and his whole life was almost thrown away. He lacked power to choose one object and persevere with a single aim, sacrificing every interfering inclination. He, for instance, vacillated for weeks trying to determine whether to use "usefulness" or "utility" in a composition.

One talent utilized in a single direction will do infinitely more than ten talents scattered. A thimbleful of powder behind a ball in a rifle will do more execution than a carload of powder unconfined. The rifle-barrel is the purpose that gives direct aim to the powder, which otherwise, no matter how good it might be, would be powerless. The poorest scholar in school or college often, in practical life, far outstrips the class leader or senior wrangler, simply because what little ability he has he employs for a definite object, while the other, depending upon his general ability and brilliant prospects, never concentrates his powers.

It is fashionable to ridicule the man of one idea, but the men who have changed the front of the world have been men of a single aim. No man can make his mark on this age of specialties who is not a man of one idea, one supreme air, one master passion. The man who would make himself felt on this bustling planet, who would make a breach in the compact conservatism of our civilization, must play all his guns on one point. A wavering aim, a faltering purpose, has no place in the twentieth century. "Mental shiftlessness" is the cause of many a failure. The world is full of unsuccessful men who spend their lives letting empty buckets down into empty wells.

"Mr. A. often laughs at me," said a young American chemist, "because I have but one idea. He talks about everything, aims to excel in many things; but I have learned that, if I ever wish to make a breach, I must play my guns continually upon one point." This great chemist, when an obscure schoolmaster, used to study by the light of a pine knot in a log cabin. Not many years later he was performing experiments in electro-magnetism before English earls, and subsequently he was at the head of one of the largest scientific institutes of this country. He was the late Professor Henry, of the Smithsonian Institution, Washington.

We should guard against a talent which we can not hope to practise in perfection, says Goethe. Improve it as we may, we shall always, in the end, when the merit of the matter has become apparent to us, painfully lament the loss of time and strength devoted to such botching. An old proverb says: "The master of one trade will support a wife and seven children, and the master of seven will not support himself."

It is the single aim that wins. Men with monopolizing ambitions rarely live in history. They do not focus their powers long enough to burn their names indelibly into the roll of honor. Edward Everett, even with his magnificent powers, disappointed the expectations of his friends. He spread himself over the whole field of knowledge and elegant culture; but the mention of the name of Everett does not call up any one great achievement as does that of names like Garrison and Phillips. Voltaire called the Frenchman La Harpe an oven which was always heating, but which never cooked anything. Hartley Coleridge was splendidly endowed with talent, but there was one fatal lack in his character—he had no definite purpose, and his life was a failure. Unstable as water, he could not excel. Southey, the uncle of Coleridge, says of him: "Coleridge has two left hands." He was so morbidly shy from living alone in his dreamland that he could not open a letter without trembling. He would often rally from his purposeless life, and resolve to redeem himself from the oblivion he saw staring him in the face; but, like Sir James Mackintosh, he remained a man of promise merely to the end of his life.

The man who succeeds has a program. He fires his course and adheres to it. He lays his plans and executes them. He goes straight to his goal. He is not pushed this way and that every time a difficulty is thrown in his path; if he can not get over it he goes through it. Constant and steady use of the faculties under a central purpose gives strength and power, while the use of faculties without an aim or end only weakens them. The mind must be focused on a definite end, or, like machinery without a balance-wheel, it will rack itself to pieces.

This age of concentration calls, not for educated men merely, not for talented men, not for geniuses, not for jacks-of-all-trades, but for men who are trained to do one thing as well as it can be done. Napoleon could go through the drill of his soldiers better than any one of his men.

Stick to your aim. The constant changing of one's occupation is fatal to all success. After a young man has spent five or six years in a dry goods store, he concludes that he would rather sell groceries, thereby throwing away five years of valuable experience which will be of very little use to him in the grocery business; and so he spends a large part of his life drifting around from one kind of employment to another, learning part of each but all of none, forgetting that experience is worth more to him than money and that the years devoted to learning his trade or occupation are the most valuable. Half-learned trades, no matter if a man has twenty, will never give him a good living, much less a competency, while wealth is absolutely out of the question.

How many young men fail to reach the point of efficiency in one line of work before they get discouraged and venture into something else! How easy to see the thorns in one's own profession or vocation, and only the roses in that of another! A young man in business, for instance, seeing a physician riding about town in his carriage, visiting his patients, imagines that a doctor must have an easy, ideal life, and wonders that he himself should have embarked in an occupation so full of disagreeable drudgery and hardships. He does not know of the years of dry, tedious study which the physician has consumed, the months and perhaps years of waiting for patients, the dry detail of anatomy, the endless names of drugs and technical terms.

There is a sense of great power in a vocation after a man has reached the point of efficiency in it, the point of productiveness, the point where his skill begins to tell and brings in returns. Up to this point of efficiency, while he is learning his trade, the time seems to have been almost thrown away. But he has been storing up a vast reserve of knowledge of detail, laying foundations, forming his acquaintances, gaining his reputation for truthfulness, trustworthiness, and integrity, and in establishing his credit. When he reaches this point of efficiency, all the knowledge and skill, character, influence, and credit thus gained come to his aid, and he soon finds that in what seemed almost thrown away lies the secret of his prosperity. The credit he established as a clerk, the confidence, the integrity, the friendships formed, he finds equal to a large capital when he starts out for himself and takes the highway to fortune; while the young man who half learned several trades, got discouraged and stopped just short of the point of efficiency, just this side of success, is a failure because he didn't go far enough; he did not press on to the point at which his acquisition would have been profitable.

In spite of the fact that nearly all very successful men have made a life-work of one thing, we see on every hand hundreds of young men and women flitting about from occupation to occupation, trade to trade, in one thing to-day and another to-morrow,—just as though they could go from one thing to another by turning a switch, as though they could run as well on another track as on the one they have left, regardless of the fact that no two careers have the same gage, that every man builds his own road upon which another man's engine can not run either with speed or safety. This fickleness, this disposition to shift about from one occupation to another, seems to be peculiar to American life, so much so that, when a young man meets a friend whom he has not seen for some time, the commonest question to ask is, "What are you doing now?" showing the improbability or uncertainty that he is doing to-day what he was doing when they last met.

Some people think that if they "keep everlastingly at it" they will succeed, but this is not always so. Working without a plan is as foolish as going to sea without a compass.

A ship which has broken its rudder in mid-ocean may "keep everlastingly at it," may keep on a full head of steam, driving about all the time, but it never arrives anywhere, it never reaches any port unless by accident; and if it does find a haven, its cargo may not be suited to the people, the climate, or conditions. The ship must be directed to a definite port, for which its cargo is adapted, and where there is a demand for it, and it must aim steadily for that port through sunshine and storm, through tempest and fog. So a man who would succeed must not drift about rudderless on the ocean of life. He must not only steer straight toward his destined port when the ocean is smooth, when the currents and winds serve, but he must keep his course in the very teeth of the wind and the tempest, and even when enveloped in the fogs of disappointment and mists of opposition. Atlantic liners do not stop for fogs or storms; they plow straight through the rough seas with only one thing in view, their destined port, and no matter what the weather is, no matter what obstacles they encounter, their arrival in port can be predicted to within a few hours.

On the prairies of South America there grows a flower that always inclines in the same direction. If a traveler loses his way and has neither compass nor chart, by turning to this flower he will find a guide on which he can implicitly rely; for no matter how the rains descend or the winds blow, its leaves point to the north. So there are many men whose purposes are so well known, whose aims are so constant, that no matter what difficulties they may encounter, or what opposition they may meet, you can tell almost to a certainty where they will come out. They may be delayed by head winds and counter currents, but they will *always head for the port* and will steer straight towards the harbor. You know to a certainty that whatever else they may lose, they will not lose their compass or rudder.

Whatever may happen to a man of this stamp, even though his sails may be swept away and his mast stripped to the deck, though he may be wrecked by the storms of life, the needle of his compass will still point to the North Star of his hope. Whatever comes, his life will not be purposeless. Even a wreck that makes its port is a greater success than a full-rigged ship with all its sails flying, with every mast and every rope intact, which merely drifts along into an accidental harbor.

To fix a wandering life and give it direction is not an easy task, but a life which has no definite aim is sure to be frittered away in empty and purposeless dreams. "Listless triflers," "busy idlers," "purposeless busy-bodies," are seen everywhere. A healthy, definite purpose is a remedy for a thousand ills which attend aimless lives. Discontent and dissatisfaction flee before a definite purpose. What we do begrudgingly without a purpose becomes a delight with one, and no work is well done nor healthily done which is not enthusiastically done.

Mere energy is not enough; it must be concentrated on some steady, unwavering aim. What is more common than "unsuccessful geniuses," or failures with "commanding talents"? Indeed, the term "unrewarded genius" has become a proverb. Every town has unsuccessful educated and talented men. But education is of no value, talent is worthless, unless it can do something, achieve something. Men who can do something at everything and a very little at anything are not wanted in this age.

What this age wants is young men and women who can do one thing without losing their identity or individuality, or becoming narrow, cramped, or dwarfed. Nothing can take the place of an all-absorbing purpose; education can not, genius can not, talent can not, industry can not, will-power can not. The purposeless life must ever be a failure. What good are powers, faculties, unless we can use them for a purpose? What good would a chest of tools do a carpenter unless he could use them? A college education, a head full of knowledge, are worth little to the men who cannot use them to some definite end.

The man without a purpose never leaves his mark upon the world. He has no individuality; he is absorbed in the mass, lost in the crowd, weak, wavering, and incompetent.

"Consider, my lord," said Rowland Hill to the Prime Minister of England, "that a letter to Ireland and the answer back would cost thousands upon thousands of my affectionate countrymen more than a fifth of their week's wages. If you shut the post-office to them, which you do now, you shut out warm hearts and generous affections from home, kindred, and friends." The lad learned that it cost to carry a letter from London to Edinburgh, four hundred and four miles, one eighteenth of a cent, while the government charged for a simple folded sheet of paper twenty-eight cents, and twice as much if there was the smallest inclosure. Against the opposition and contempt of the post-office department he at length carried his point, and on January 10, 1840, penny postage was established throughout Great Britain. Mr. Hill was chosen to introduce the system, at a salary of fifteen hundred pounds a year. His success was most encouraging, but at the end of two years a Tory minister dismissed him without paying for his services, as agreed. The public was indignant, and at once contributed sixty-five thousand dollars; and, at the request of Queen Victoria, Parliament voted him one hundred thousand dollars cash, together with ten thousand dollars a year for life.

It is a great purpose which gives meaning to life; it unifies all our powers, binds them together in one cable and makes strong and united what was weak, separated, scattered.

"Smatterers" are weak and superficial. Of what use is a man who knows a little of everything and not much of anything? It is the momentum of constantly repeated acts that tells the story. "Let thine eyes look straight before thee. Ponder the path of thy feet and let all thy ways be established. Turn not to the right hand nor to the left." One great secret of St. Paul's power lay in his strong purpose. Nothing could daunt, nothing intimidate him. The Roman Emperor could not muzzle him, the dungeon could not appall him, no prison suppress him, obstacles could not discourage him. "This one thing I do" was written all over his work. The quenchless zeal of his mighty purpose burned its way down through the centuries, and its contagion will never cease to fire the hearts of men.

"Try and come home somebody," said his mother to Gambetta as she sent him off to Paris to school. Poverty pinched this lad hard in his little garret study and his clothes were shabby, but what of that? He had made up his mind to get on in the world. For years he was chained to his desk and worked like a hero. At last his opportunity came. Jules Favre was to plead a great cause on a certain day; but, being ill, he chose this young man, absolutely unknown, rough and uncouth, to take his place. For many years Gambetta had been preparing for such an opportunity, and he was equal to it. He made one of the greatest speeches that up to that time had ever been made in France. That night all the papers in Paris were sounding the praises of this ragged, uncouth Bohemian, and soon all France recognized him as the Republican leader. This sudden rise was not due to luck or accident. He had been steadfastly working and fighting his way up against oppositions and poverty for just such an occasion. Had he not been equal to it, it would only have made him ridiculous. What a stride; yesterday, poor and unknown, living in a garret; today, deputy-elect, in the city of Marseilles, and the great Republican leader!

When Louis Napoleon had been defeated at Sedan and had delivered his sword to William of Prussia, and when the Prussian army was marching on Paris, the brave Gambetta went out of the besieged city in a balloon barely grazed by the Prussian guns, landed in Amiens, and by almost superhuman skill raised three armies of 800,000 men, provided for their maintenance, and directed their military operations. A German officer said: "This colossal energy is the most remarkable event of modern history, and will carry down Gambetta's name to remote posterity." This youth who was poring over his books in an attic while other youths were promenading the Champs Elysées, although but thirty-two years old, was now virtually dictator of France, and the greatest orator in the Republic. What a striking example of the great reserve of personal power, which, even in dissolute lives, is sometimes called out by a great emergency or sudden sorrow, and ever after leads the life to victory! When Gambetta found that his first speech had electrified all France, his great reserve rushed to the front; he was suddenly weaned from dissipation, and resolved to make his mark in the world. Nor did he lose his head in his quick leap into fame. He still lived in the upper room in the musty Latin Quarter, and remained a poor man, without stain of dishonor, though he might easily have made himself a millionaire. When he died the "Figaro" said, "The Republic has lost its greatest man." American boys should study this great man, for he loved our country, and took our Republic as the pattern for France.

There is no grander sight in the world than that of a young man fired with a great purpose, dominated by one unwavering aim. He is bound to win; the world stands to one side and lets him pass; it always makes way for the man with a will in him. He does not have one-half the opposition to overcome that the undecided, purposeless man has who, like driftwood, runs against all sorts of snags to which he must yield simply because he has no momentum to force them out of his way. What a sublime spectacle it is to see a youth going straight to his goal, cutting his way through difficulties, and surmounting obstacles which dishearten others, as though they were but stepping-stones! Defeat, like a gymnasium, only gives him new power; opposition only doubles his exertions; dangers only increase his courage. No matter what comes to him, sickness, poverty, disaster, he never turns his eye from his goal.

"Duos qui sequitur lepores, neutrum capit."

WORK AND WAIT

What we do upon some great occasion will probably depend on what we already are; and what we are will be the result of previous years of self-discipline.— H. P. Liddon

I consider a human soul without education like marble in a quarry, which shows none of its inherent beauties until the skill of the polisher sketches out the colors, makes the surface shine, and discovers every ornamental cloud, spot, and vein that runs throughout the body of it.— Addison

Use your gifts faithfully, and they shall be enlarged; practise what you know, and you shall attain to higher knowledge.— Arnold

Haste trips up its own heels, fetters and stops itself.— Seneca

The more you know, the more you can save yourself and that which belongs to you, and do more work with less effort.— Charles Kingsley

"I was a mere cipher in that vast sea of human enterprise," said Henry Bessemer, speaking of his arrival in London in 1831. Although but eighteen years old, and without an acquaintance in the city, he soon made work for himself by inventing a process of copying bas-reliefs on cardboard. His method was so simple that one could learn in ten minutes how to make a die from an embossed stamp for a penny. Having ascertained later that in this way the raised stamps on all official papers in England could easily be forged, he set to work and invented a perforated stamp which could not be forged nor removed from a document. At the public stamp office he was told by the chief that the government was losing 100,000 pounds a year through the custom of removing stamps from old parchments and using them again.

The chief also fully appreciated the new danger of easy counterfeiting. So he offered Bessemer a definite sum for his process of perforation, or an office for life at eight hundred pounds a year. Bessemer chose the office, and hastened to tell the good news to a young woman with whom he had agreed to share his fortune. In explaining his invention, he told how it would prevent any one from taking a valuable stamp from a document a hundred years old and using it a second time.

"Yes," said his betrothed, "I understand that; but, surely, if all stamps had a date put upon them they could not at a future time be used without detection."

This was a very short speech, and of no special importance if we omit a single word of four letters; but, like the schoolboy's pins which saved the lives of thousands of people annually by not getting swallowed, that little word, by keeping out of the ponderous minds of the British revenue officers, had for a long period saved the government the burden of caring for an additional income of 100,000 pounds a year. And the same little word, if published in its connection, would render Bessemer's perforation device of far less value than a last year's bird's nest. He felt proud of the young woman's ingenuity, and promptly suggested the improvement at the stamp office.

As a result his system of perforation was abandoned and he was deprived of his promised office, the government coolly making use from that day to this, without compensation, of the idea conveyed by that little insignificant word.

So Bessemer's financial prospects were not very encouraging; but, realizing that the best capital a young man can have is a capital wife, he at once entered into a partnership which placed at his command the combined ideas of two very level heads. The result, after years of thought and experiment, was the Bessemer process of making steel cheaply, which has revolutionized the iron industry throughout the world. His method consists simply in forcing hot air from below into several tons of melted pig-iron, so as to produce intense combustion; and then adding enough spiegel-eisen (looking-glass iron), an ore rich in carbon, to change the whole mass to steel.

He discovered this simple process only after trying in vain much more difficult and expensive methods.

"All things come round to him who will but wait."

The great lack of the age is want of thoroughness. How seldom you find a young man or woman who is willing to take time to prepare for his life work! A little education is all they want, a little smattering of books, and then they are ready for business.

"Can't wait" is characteristic of the century, and is written on everything; on commerce, on schools, on society, on churches. Can't wait for a high school, seminary, or college. The boy can't wait to become a youth, nor the youth a man. Youth rush into business with no great reserve of education or drill; of course they do poor, feverish work, and break down in middle life, and many die of old age in the forties. Everybody is in a hurry. Buildings are rushed up so quickly that they will not stand, and everything is made "to sell."

Not long ago a professor in one of our universities had a letter from a young woman in the West, asking him if he did not think she could teach elocution if she could come to the university and take twelve lessons. Our young people of to-day are not willing to lay broad, deep foundations. The weary years in preparatory school and college dishearten them. They only want a "smattering" of an education. But as Pope says,—

A little learning is a dangerous thing;
Drink deep, or taste not the Pierian spring:
There shallow draughts intoxicate the brain,
And drinking largely sobers us again.

The shifts to cover up ignorance, and "the constant trembling lest some blunder should expose one's emptiness," are pitiable. Short cuts and abridged methods are the demand of the hour. But the way to shorten the road to success is to take plenty of time to lay in your reserve power. Hard work, a definite aim, and faithfulness will shorten the way. Don't risk a life's superstructure upon a day's foundation.

Patience is Nature's motto. She works ages to bring a flower to perfection. What will she not do for the greatest of her creation? Ages and aeons are nothing to her; out of them she has been carving her great statue, a perfect man.

Johnson said a man must turn over half a library to write one book. When an authoress told Wordsworth she had spent six hours on a poem, he replied that he would have spent six weeks. Think of Bishop Hall spending thirty years on one of his works! Owens was working on the "Commentary to the Epistle to the Hebrews" for twenty years. Moore spent several weeks on one of his musical stanzas which reads as if it were a dash of genius.

Carlyle wrote with the utmost difficulty and never executed a page of his great histories till he had consulted every known authority, so that every sentence is the quintessence of many books, the product of many hours of drudging research in the great libraries. Today, "Sartor Resartus" is everywhere. You can get it for a mere trifle at almost any bookseller's, and hundreds of thousands of copies are scattered over the world. But when Carlyle brought it to London in 1851, it was refused almost contemptuously by three prominent publishers. At length he managed to get it into "Fraser's Magazine," the editor of which conveyed to the author the pleasing information that his work had been received with "unqualified disapprobation."

Henry Ward Beecher sent half a dozen articles to the publisher of a religious paper to pay for his subscription, but they were respectfully declined. The publishers of the "Atlantic Monthly" returned Miss Alcott's manuscript, suggesting that she had better stick to teaching. One of the leading magazines ridiculed Tennyson's first poems, and consigned the young poet to temporary oblivion. Only one of Ralph Waldo Emerson's books had a remunerative sale. Washington Irving was nearly seventy years old before the income from his books paid the expenses of his household.

In some respects it is very unfortunate that the old system of binding boys out to a trade has been abandoned. To-day very few boys learn any trade. They pick up what they know, as they go along, just as a student crams for a particular examination, just to "get through," without any effort to see how much he may learn on any subject.

Think of an American youth spending ten years with Da Vinci on the model of an equestrian statue that he might master the anatomy of the horse! Most young American artists would expect, in a quarter of that time, to sculpture an Apollo Belvidere.

A rich man asked Howard Burnett to do a little something for his album. Burnett complied and charged a thousand francs. "But it took you only five minutes," objected the rich man. "Yes, but it took me thirty years to learn how to do it in five minutes."

What the age wants is men who have the nerve and the grit to work and wait, whether the world applaud or hiss; a Mirabeau, who can struggle on for forty years before he has a chance to show the world his vast reserve, destined to shake an empire; a Farragut, a Von Moltke, who have the persistence to work and wait for half a century for their first great opportunities; a Grant, fighting on in heroic silence, when denounced by his brother generals and politicians everywhere; a Michael Angelo, working seven long years decorating the Sistine Chapel with his matchless "Creation" and the "Last Judgment," refusing all remuneration therefor, lest his pencil might catch the taint of avarice; a Thurlow Weed, walking two miles through the snow with rags tied around his feet for shoes, to borrow the history of the French Revolution, and eagerly devouring it before the sap-bush fire; a Milton, elaborating "Paradise Lost" in a world he could not see; a Thackeray, struggling on cheerfully after his "Vanity Fair" was refused by a dozen publishers; a Balzac, toiling and waiting in a lonely garret; men whom neither poverty, debt, nor hunger could discourage or intimidate; not daunted by privations, not hindered by discouragements. It wants men who can work and wait.

When a young lawyer Daniel Webster once looked in vain through all the law libraries near him, and then ordered at an expense of fifty dollars the necessary books, to obtain authorities and precedents in a case in which his client was a poor blacksmith. He won his case, but, on account of the poverty of his client, only charged fifteen dollars, thus losing heavily on the books bought, to say nothing of his time. Years after, as he was passing through New York City, he was consulted by Aaron Burr on an important but puzzling case then pending before the Supreme Court. He saw in a moment that it was just like the blacksmith's case, an intricate question of title, which he had solved so thoroughly that it was to him now as simple as the multiplication table. Going back to the time of Charles II he gave the law and precedents involved with such readiness and accuracy of sequence that Burr asked in great surprise if he had been consulted before in the case. "Most certainly not," he replied, "I never heard of your case till this evening." "Very well," said Burr, "proceed"; and, when he had finished, Webster received a fee that paid him liberally for all the time and trouble he had spent for his early client.

Albert Bierstadt first crossed the Rocky Mountains with a band of pioneers in 1859, making sketches for the paintings of Western scenes for which he had become famous. As he followed the trail to Pike's Peak, he gazed in wonder upon the enormous herds of buffaloes which dotted the plains as far as the eye could reach, and thought of the time when they would have disappeared before the march of civilization. The thought haunted him and found its final embodiment in "The Last of the Buffaloes" in 1890. To perfect this great work he had spent twenty years.

Everything which endures, which will stand the test of time, must have a deep, solid foundation. In Rome the foundation is often the most expensive part of an edifice, so deep must they dig to build on the living rock.

Fifty feet of Bunker Hill Monument is under ground; unseen and unappreciated by those who tread about that historic shaft, but it is this foundation, apparently thrown away, which enables it to stand upright, true to the plumb-line through all the tempests that lash its granite sides. A large part of every successful life must be spent in laying foundation stones underground. Success is the child of drudgery and perseverance and depends upon "knowing how long it takes to succeed."

Endurance is a much better test of character than any one act of heroism, however noble.

The pianist Thalberg said he never ventured to perform one of his celebrated pieces in public until he had played it at least fifteen hundred times. He laid no claim whatever to genius; he said it was all a question of hard work. The accomplishments of such industry, such perseverance, would put to shame many a man who claims genius.

Before Edmund Kean would consent to appear in that character which he acted with such consummate skill, The Gentleman Villain, he practised constantly before a glass, studying expression for a year and a half. When he appeared upon the stage, Byron, who went with Moore to see him, said he never looked upon so fearful and wicked a face. As the great actor went on to delineate the terrible consequences of sin, Byron fainted.

"For years I was in my place of business by sunrise," said a wealthy banker who had begun without a dollar; "and often I did not leave it for fifteen or eighteen hours."

Patience, it is said, changes the mulberry leaf to satin. The giant oak on the hillside was detained months or years in its upward growth while its root took a great turn around some rock, in order to gain a hold by which the tree was anchored to withstand the storms of centuries. Da Vinci spent four years on the head of Mona Lisa, perhaps the most beautiful ever painted, but he left therein an artistic thought for all time.

Said Captain Bingham: "You can have no idea of the wonderful machine that the German army is and how well it is prepared for war. A chart is made out which shows just what must be done in the case of wars with the different nations, and every officer's place in the scheme is laid out beforehand. There is a schedule of trains which will supersede all other schedules the moment war is declared, and this is so arranged that the commander of the army here could telegraph to any officer to take such a train and go to such a place at a moment's notice."

A learned clergyman was thus accosted by an illiterate preacher who despised education: "Sir, you have been to college, I presume?" "Yes, sir," was the reply. "I am thankful," said the former, "that the Lord opened my mouth without any learning." "A similar event," retorted the clergyman, "happened in Balaam's time."

A young man just graduated told the President of Trinity College that he had completed his education, and had come to say good-by. "Indeed," said the President, "I have just begun my education."

Many an extraordinary man has been made out of a very ordinary boy: but in order to accomplish this we must begin with him while he is young. It is simply astonishing what training will do for a rough, uncouth, and even dull lad, if he has good material in him, and comes under the tutelage of a skilled educator before his habits become fixed or confirmed.

Even a few weeks' or months' drill of the rawest and roughest recruits in the late Civil War so straightened and dignified stooping and uncouth soldiers, and made them manly, erect, and courteous in their bearing, that their own friends scarcely knew them. If this change is so marked in the youth who has grown to maturity, what a miracle is possible in the lad who is taken early and put under a course of drill and systematic training, both physical, mental, and moral! How often a man who is in the penitentiary, in the poorhouse, or among the tramps, or living out a miserable existence in the slums of our cities, rough, slovenly, has slumbering within the rags possibilities which would have developed him into a magnificent man, an ornament to the human race instead of a foul blot and ugly scar, had he only been fortunate enough early in life to have enjoyed the benefits of efficient and systematic training!

Laziness begins in cobwebs and ends in iron chains. Edison described his repeated efforts to make the phonograph reproduce an aspirated sound, and added: "From eighteen to twenty hours a day for the last seven months I have worked on this single word 'specia.' I said into the phonograph 'specia, specia, specia,' but the instrument responded 'pecia, pecia, pecia.' It was enough to drive one mad. But I held firm, and I have succeeded."

The road to distinction must be paved with years of self-denial and hard work.

Horace Mann, the great author of the common school system of Massachusetts, was a remarkable example of that pluck and patience which can work and wait. His only inheritance was poverty and hard work. But he had an unquenchable thirst for knowledge and a determination to get on in the world. He braided straw to earn money to buy books for which his soul thirsted.

Gladstone was bound to win. Although he had spent many years of preparation for his life work, in spite of the consciousness of marvelous natural endowments which would have been deemed sufficient by many young men, and notwithstanding he had gained the coveted prize of a seat in Parliament, yet he decided to make himself master of the situation; and amid all his public and private duties, he not only spent eleven terms more in the study of the law, but also studied Greek constantly and read every well-written book or paper he could obtain, so determined was he that his life should be rounded out to its fullest measure, and that his mind should have broad and liberal culture.

Ole Bull said: "If I practise one day, I can see the result; if I practise two days, my friends can see it; if I practise three days, the great public can see it."

The habit of seizing every bit of knowledge, no matter how insignificant it may seem at the time, every opportunity, every occasion, and grinding them all up into experience, can not be overestimated. You will find use for all of it. Webster once repeated with effect an anecdote which he had heard fourteen years before, and which he had not thought of in the meantime. It exactly fitted the occasion. "It is an ill mason that rejects any stone."

Webster was once urged to speak on a subject of great importance, but refused, saying he was very busy and had no time to master the subject. "But," replied his friend, "a very few words from you would do much to awaken public attention to it." Webster replied, "If there be so much weight in my words, it is because I do not allow myself to speak on any subject until my mind is imbued with it." On one occasion Webster made a remarkable speech before the Phi Beta Kappa Society at Harvard, when a book was presented to him; but after he had gone, his "impromptu" speech, carefully written out, was found in the book which he had forgotten to take away.

Demosthenes was once asked to speak on a great and sudden emergency, but replied, "I am not prepared." In fact, it was thought by many that Demosthenes did not possess any genius whatever, because he never allowed himself to speak on any subject without thorough preparation. In any meeting or assembly, when called upon, he would never rise, even to make remarks, it was said, without previously preparing himself.

Alexander Hamilton said, "Men give me credit for genius. All the genius I have lies just in this: when I have a subject in hand I study it profoundly. Day and night it is before me. I explore it in all its bearings. My mind becomes pervaded with it. Then the effort which I make the people are pleased to call the fruit of genius; it is the fruit of labor and thought." The law of labor is equally binding on genius and mediocrity.

Nelaton, the great surgeon, said that if he had four minutes in which to perform an operation on which a life depended, he would take one minute to consider how best to do it.

"Many men," says Longfellow, "do not allow their principles to take root, but pull them up every now and then, as children do flowers they have planted, to see if they are growing." We must not only work, but also wait.

"The spruce young spark," says Sizer, "who thinks chiefly of his mustache and boots and shiny hat, of getting along nicely and easily during the day, and talking about the theater, the opera, or a fast horse, ridiculing the faithful young fellow who came to learn the business and make a man of himself because he will not join in wasting his time in dissipation, will see the day, if his useless life is not earlier blasted by vicious indulgences, when he will be glad to accept a situation from the fellow-clerk whom he now ridicules and affects to despise, when the latter shall stand in the firm, dispensing benefits and acquiring fortune."

"I have been watching the careers of young men by the thousand in this busy city of New York for over thirty years," said Dr. Cuyler, "and I find that the chief difference between the successful and the failures lies in the single element of staying power. Permanent success is oftener won by holding on than by sudden dash, however brilliant. The easily discouraged, who are pushed back by a straw, are all the time dropping to the rear—to perish or to be carried along on the stretcher of charity. They who understand and practise Abraham Lincoln's homely maxim of 'pegging away' have achieved the solidest success."

The Duke of Wellington became so discouraged because he did not advance in the army that he applied for a much inferior position in the customs department, but was refused. Napoleon had applied for every vacant position for seven years before he was recognized, but meanwhile he studied with all his might, supplementing what was considered a thorough military education by researches and reflections which in later years enabled him easily to teach the art of war to veterans who had never dreamed of his novel combinations.

Reserves which carry us through great emergencies are the result of long working and long waiting. Dr. Collyer declares that reserves mean to a man also achievement,—"the power to do the grandest thing possible to your nature when you feel you must, or some precious thing will be lost,—to do well always, but best in the crisis on which all things turn; to stand the strain of a long fight, and still find you have something left, and so to never know you are beaten, because you never are beaten."

He only is independent in action who has been earnest and thorough in preparation and self-culture. "Not for school, but for life, we learn"; and our habits—of promptness, earnestness, and thoroughness, or of tardiness, fickleness, and superficiality—are the things acquired most readily and longest retained.

To vary the language of another, the three great essentials to success in mental and physical labor are Practice, Patience, and Perseverance, but the greatest of these is Perseverance.

"Let us, then, be up and doing,
With a heart for any fate;
Still achieving, still pursuing,
Learn to labor and to wait."

The Might of Little Things

Think naught a trifle, though it small appear;
Small sands the mountain, moments make the year,
And trifles, life.— Young

It is but the littleness of man that sees no greatness in trifles.— Wendell Phillips

He that despiseth small things shall fall by little and little.— Ecclesiasticus

The creation of a thousand forests is in one acorn.— Emerson

Men are led by trifles.— Napoleon

"A pebble on the streamlet scant Has turned the course of many a river."

"The bad thing about a little sin is that it won't stay little."

"Arletta's pretty feet, glistening in the brook, made her the mother of William the Conqueror," says Palgrave's "History of Normandy and England." "Had she not thus fascinated Duke Robert the Liberal, of Normandy, Harold would not have fallen at Hastings, no Anglo-Norman dynasty could have arisen, no British Empire."

We may tell which way the wind blew before the Deluge by marking the ripple and cupping of the rain in the petrified sand now preserved forever. We tell the very path by which gigantic creatures, whom man never saw, walked to the river's edge to find their food.

It was little Greece that rolled back the overflowing tide of Asiatic luxury and despotism, giving instead to Europe and America models of the highest political freedom yet attained, and germs of limitless mental growth. A different result at Plataea would have delayed the progress of the human race more than ten centuries.

Among the lofty Alps, it is said, the guides sometimes demand absolute silence, lest the vibration of the voice bring down an avalanche.

The power of observation in the American Indian would put many an educated man to shame. Returning home, an Indian discovered that his venison, which had been hanging up to dry, had been stolen. After careful observation he started to track the thief through the woods. Meeting a man on the route, he asked him if he had seen a little, old, white man, with a short gun, and with a small bobtailed dog. The man told him he had met such a man, but was surprised to find that the Indian had not even seen the one he described, and asked him how he could give such a minute description of the man he had never seen. "I knew the thief was a little man," said the Indian, "because he rolled up a stone to stand on in order to reach the venison; I knew he was an old man by his short steps; I knew he was a white man by his turning out his toes in walking, which an Indian never does; I knew he had a short gun by the mark it left on the tree where he had stood it up; I knew the dog was small by his tracks and short steps, and that he had a bob-tail by the mark it left in the dust where he sat."

Two drops of rain, falling side by side, were separated a few inches by a gentle breeze. Striking on opposite sides of the roof of a court-house in Wisconsin, one rolled southward through the Rock River and the Mississippi to the Gulf of Mexico; while the other entered successively the Fox River, Green Bay, Lake Michigan, the Straits of Mackinaw, Lake Huron, St. Clair River, Lake St. Clair, Detroit River, Lake Erie, Niagara River, Lake Ontario, the St. Lawrence River, and finally reached the Gulf of St. Lawrence. How slight the influence of the breeze, yet such was the formation of the continent that a trifling cause was multiplied almost beyond the power of figures to express its momentous effect upon the destinies of these companion raindrops. Who can calculate the future of the smallest trifle when a mud crack swells to an Amazon and the stealing of a penny may end on the scaffold? The act of a moment may cause a life's regret. A trigger may be pulled in an instant, but the soul returns never.

A spark falling upon some combustibles led to the invention of gunpowder. A few bits of seaweed and driftwood, floating on the waves, enabled Columbus to stay a mutiny of his sailors which threatened to prevent the discovery of a new world. There are moments in history which balance years of ordinary life. Dana could interest a class for hours on a grain of sand; and from a single bone, such as no one had ever seen before, Agassiz could deduce the entire structure and habits of an animal which no man had ever seen so accurately that subsequent discoveries of complete skeletons have not changed one of his conclusions.

A cricket once saved a military expedition from destruction. The commanding officer and hundreds of his men were going to South America on a great ship, and, through the carelessness of the watch, they would have been dashed upon a ledge of rock had it not been for a cricket which a soldier had brought on board. When the little insect scented the land, it broke its long silence by a shrill note, and thus warned them of their danger.

By gnawing through a dike, even a rat may drown a nation. A little boy in Holland saw water trickling from a small hole near the bottom of a dike. He realized that the leak would rapidly become larger if the water were not checked, so he held his hand over the hole for hours on a dark and dismal night until he could attract the attention of passers-by. His name is still held in grateful remembrance in Holland.

The beetling chalk cliffs of England were built by rhizopods, too small to be clearly seen without the aid of a magnifying-glass.

What was so unlikely as that throwing an empty wine-flask in the fire should furnish the first notion of a locomotive, or that the sickness of an Italian chemist's wife and her absurd craving for reptiles for food should begin the electric telegraph. Madame Galvani noticed the contraction of the muscles of a skinned frog which was accidentally touched at the moment her husband took a spark from an electrical machine. She gave the hint which led to the discovery of galvanic electricity, now so useful in the arts and in transmitting vocal or written language.

"The fate of a nation," says Gladstone, "has often depended upon the good or bad digestion of a fine dinner."

A stamp act to raise 60,000 pounds produced the American Revolution, a war that cost England 100,000,000 pounds. A war between France and England, costing more than a hundred thousand lives, grew out of a quarrel as to which of two vessels should first be served with water. The quarrel of two Indian boys over a grasshopper led to the "Grasshopper War." What mighty contests rise from trivial things!

A young man once went to India to seek his fortune, but, finding no opening, he went to his room, loaded his pistol, put the muzzle to his head, and pulled the trigger. But it did not go off. He went to the window to point it in another direction and try it again, resolved that if the weapon went off he would regard it as a Providence that he was spared. He pulled the trigger and it went off the first time. Trembling with excitement he resolved to hold his life sacred, to make the most of it, and never again to cheapen it. This young man became General Robert Clive, who, with but a handful of European soldiers, secured to the East India Company and afterwards to Great Britain a great and rich country with two hundred millions of people.

The cackling of a goose aroused the sentinels and saved Rome from the Gauls, and the pain from a thistle warned a Scottish army of the approach of the Danes.

Henry Ward Beecher came within one vote of being elected superintendent of a railway. If he had had that vote America would probably have lost its greatest preacher. What a little thing fixes destiny!

Trifles light as air often suggest to the thinking mind ideas which have revolutionized the world.

A famous ruby was offered to the English government. The report of the crown jeweler was that it was the finest he had ever seen or heard of, but that one of the "facets" was slightly fractured. That invisible fracture reduced the value of the ruby thousands of dollars, and it was rejected from the regalia of England.

It was a little thing for the janitor to leave a lamp swinging in the cathedral at Pisa, but in that steady swaying motion the boy Galileo saw the pendulum, and conceived the idea of thus measuring time.

"I was singing to the mouthpiece of a telephone," said Edison, "when the vibrations of my voice caused a fine steel point to pierce one of my fingers held just behind it. That set me to thinking. If I could record the motions of the point and send it over the same surface afterward, I saw no reason why the thing would not talk. I determined to make a machine that would work accurately, and gave my assistants the necessary instructions, telling them what I had discovered. That's the whole story. The phonograph is the result of the pricking of a finger."

It was a little thing for a cow to kick over a lantern left in a shanty, but it laid Chicago in ashes, and rendered homeless a hundred thousand people.

Some little weakness, some self-indulgence, a quick temper, want of decision, are little things, you say, when placed beside great abilities, but they have wrecked many a career.

The Parliament of Great Britain, the Congress of the United States, and representative governments all over the world have come from King John signing the Magna Charta.

Bentham says, "The turn of a sentence has decided many a friendship, and, for aught we know, the fate of many a kingdom." Perhaps you turned a cold shoulder but once, and made but one stinging remark, yet it may have cost you a friend forever.

The sight of a stranded cuttlefish led Cuvier to an investigation which made him one of the greatest natural historians in the world. The web of a spider suggested to Captain Brown the idea of a suspension bridge.

A missing marriage certificate kept the hod-carrier of Hugh Miller from establishing his claim to the Earldom of Crawford. The masons would call out, "John, Yearl of Crawford, bring us anither hod o' lime."

The absence of a comma in a bill which passed through Congress years ago cost our government a million dollars. A single misspelled word prevented a deserving young man from obtaining a situation as instructor in a New England college.

"I cannot see that you have made any progress since my last visit," said a gentleman to Michael Angelo. "But," said the sculptor, "I have retouched this part, polished that, softened that feature, brought out that muscle, given some expression to this lip, more energy to that limb, etc." "But they are trifles!" exclaimed the visitor. "It may be so," replied the great artist, "but trifles make perfection, and perfection is no trifle." That infinite patience which made Michael Angelo spend a week in bringing out a muscle in a statue, with more vital fidelity to truth, or Gerhard Dow a day in giving the right effect to a dewdrop on a cabbage leaf, makes all the difference between success and failure.

The cry of the infant Moses attracted the attention of Pharoah's daughter, and gave the Jews a lawgiver. A bird alighting on the bough of a tree at the mouth of the cave where Mahomet lay hid turned aside his pursuers, and gave a prophet to many nations. A flight of birds probably prevented Columbus from discovering this continent. When he was growing anxious, Martin Alonzo Pinzon persuaded him to follow a flight of parrots toward the southwest; for to the Spanish seamen of that day it was good luck to follow in the wake of a flock of birds when on a voyage of discovery. But for his change of course Columbus would have reached the coast of Florida. "Never," wrote Humboldt, "had the flight of birds more important consequences."

The children of a spectacle-maker placed two or more pairs of the spectacles before each other in play, and told their father that distant objects looked larger. From this hint came the telescope.

Every day is a little life; and our whole life but a day repeated. Those that dare lose a day are dangerously prodigal; those that dare misspend it, desperate. What is the happiness of your life made up of? Little courtesies, little kindnesses, pleasant words, genial smiles, a friendly letter, good wishes, and good deeds. One in a million—once in a lifetime—may do a heroic action.

Napoleon was a master of trifles. To details which his inferior officers thought too microscopic for their notice he gave the most exhaustive consideration. Nothing was too small for his attention. He must know all about the provisions, the horse fodder, the biscuits, the camp kettles, the shoes. When the bugle sounded for the march to battle, every officer had his orders as to the exact route which he should follow, the exact day he was to arrive at a certain station, and the exact hour he was to leave, and they were all to reach the point of destination at a precise moment. It is said that nothing could be more perfectly planned than his memorable march which led to the victory of Austerlitz, and which sealed the fate of Europe for many years. He would often charge his absent officers to send him perfectly accurate returns, even to the smallest detail. "When they are sent to me, I give up every occupation in order to read them in detail, and to observe the difference between one monthly return and another. No young girl enjoys her novel as much as I do these returns." Napoleon left nothing to chance, nothing to contingency, so far as he could possibly avoid it. Everything was planned to a nicety before he attempted to execute it.

Wellington, too, was "great in little things." He knew no such things as trifles. While other generals trusted to subordinates, he gave his personal attention to the minutest detail. The history of many a failure could be written in three words, "Lack of detail." How many a lawyer has failed from the lack of details in deeds and important papers, the lack of little words which seemed like surplusage, and which involved his clients in litigation, and often great losses! How many wills are contested from the carelessness of lawyers in the omission or shading of words, or ambiguous use of language!

Not even Helen of Troy, it is said, was beautiful enough to spare the tip of her nose; and if Cleopatra's had been an inch shorter Mark Antony might never have become infatuated with her wonderful charms, and the blemish would have changed the history of the world. Anne Boleyn's fascinating smile split the great Church of Rome in twain, and gave a nation an altered destiny. Napoleon, who feared not to attack the proudest monarchs in their capitols, shrank from the political influence of one independent woman in private life, Madame de Staël.

Cromwell was about to sail for America when a law was passed prohibiting emigration. At that time he was a profligate, having squandered all his property. But when he found that he could not leave England he reformed his life. Had he not been detained, who can tell what the history of Great Britain would have been?

From the careful and persistent accumulation of innumerable facts, each trivial in itself, but in the aggregate forming a mass of evidence, a Darwin extracts his law of evolution, and a Linnaeus constructs the science of botany. A pan of water and two thermometers were the tools by which Dr. Black discovered latent heat; and a prism, a lens, and a sheet of pasteboard enabled Newton to unfold the composition of light and the origin of colors. An eminent foreign savant called on Dr. Wollaston, and asked to be shown over those laboratories of his in which science had been enriched by so many great discoveries, when the doctor took him into a little study, and, pointing to an old tea tray on the table, on which stood a few watch glasses, test papers, a small balance, and a blow-pipe, said, "There is my laboratory." A burnt stick and a barn door served Wilkie in lieu of pencil and paper. A single potato, carried to England by Sir Walter Raleigh in the sixteenth century, has multiplied into food for millions, driving famine from Ireland again and again.

It seemed a small thing to drive William Brewster, John Robinson, and the poor people of Austerfield and Scrooby into perpetual exile, but as Pilgrims they became the founders of a mighty people.

A few immortal sentences from Garrison and Phillips, a few poems from Lowell and Whittier, and the leaven is at work which will not cease its action until the whipping-post and bodily servitude are abolished forever.

"For want of a nail the shoe was lost,
For want of a shoe the horse was lost;
For want of a horse the rider was lost, and all,"
says Poor Richard, "for want of a horseshoe nail."

A single remark dropped by an unknown person in the street led to the successful story of "The Bread-winners." A hymn chanted by the barefooted friars in the temple of Jupiter at Rome led to the famous "Decline and Fall of the Roman Empire."

"Words are things" says Byron, "and a small drop of ink, falling like dew upon a thought, produces that which makes thousands, perhaps millions, think."

"I give these books for the founding of a college in this colony"; such were the words of ten ministers who in the year 1700 assembled at the village of Branford, a few miles east of New Haven. Each of the worthy fathers deposited a few books upon the table around which they were sitting; such was the founding of Yale College.

Great men are noted for their attention to trifles. Goethe once asked a monarch to excuse him, during an interview, while he went to an adjoining room to jot down a stray thought. Hogarth would make sketches of rare faces and characteristics upon his finger-nails upon the streets. Indeed, to a truly great mind there are no little things. Trifles light as air suggest to the keen observer the solution of mighty problems. Bits of glass arranged to amuse children led to the discovery of the kaleidoscope. Goodyear discovered how to vulcanize rubber by forgetting, until it became red hot, a skillet containing a compound which he had before considered worthless. A ship-worm boring a piece of wood suggested to Sir Isambard Brunel the idea of a tunnel under the Thames at London. Tracks of extinct animals in the old red sandstone led Hugh Miller on and on until he became the greatest geologist of his time. Sir Walter Scott once saw a shepherd boy plodding sturdily along, and asked him to ride. This boy was George Kemp, who became so enthusiastic in his study of sculpture that he walked fifty miles and back to see a beautiful statue. He did not forget the kindness of Sir Walter, and, when the latter died, threw his soul into the design of the magnificent monument erected in Edinburgh to the memory of the author of "Waverley."

A poor boy applied for a situation at a bank in Paris, but was refused. As he left the door, he picked up a pin. The bank president saw this, called the boy back, and gave him a situation from which he rose until he became the greatest banker of Paris,—Laffitte.

A Massachusetts soldier in the Civil War observed a bird hulling rice, and shot it; taking its bill for a model, he invented a hulling machine which has revolutionized the rice business.

The eye is a perpetual camera imprinting upon the sensitive mental plates and packing away in the brain for future use every face, every tree, every plant, flower, hill, stream, mountain, every scene upon the street, in fact, everything which comes within its range. There is a phonograph in our natures which catches, however thoughtless and transient, every syllable we utter, and registers forever the slightest enunciation, and renders it immortal. These notes may appear a thousand years hence, reproduced in our descendants, in all their beautiful or terrible detail.

"Least of all seeds, greatest of all harvests," seems to be one of the great laws of nature. All life comes from microscopic beginnings. In nature there is nothing small. The microscope reveals as great a world below as the telescope above. All of nature's laws govern the smallest atoms, and a single drop of water is a miniature ocean.

The strength of a chain lies in its weakest link, however large and strong all the others may be. We are all inclined to be proud of our strong points, while we are sensitive and neglectful of our weaknesses. Yet it is our greatest weakness which measures our real strength.

A soldier who escapes the bullets of a thousand battles may die from the scratch of a pin, and many a ship has survived the shocks of icebergs and the storms of ocean only to founder in a smooth sea from holes made by tiny insects.

Small things become great when a great soul sees them. A single noble or heroic act of one man has sometimes elevated a nation. Many an honorable career has resulted from a kind word spoken in season or the warm grasp of a friendly hand.

> It is the little rift within the lute
> That by and by will make the music mute,
> And, ever widening, slowly silence all.— Tennyson
> "It was only a glad 'good-morning,'
> As she passed along the way,
> But it spread the morning's glory
> Over the livelong day."
> "Only a thought in passing—a smile, or encouraging word,
> Has lifted many a burden no other gift could have stirred."

The Salary You Do Not Find in Your Pay Envelope

The quality which you put into your work will determine the quality of your life. The habit of insisting upon the best of which you are capable, of always demanding of yourself the highest, never accepting the lowest or second best, no matter how small your remuneration, will make all the difference to you between failure and success.

"If the laborer gets no more than the wages his employer offers him, he is cheated; he cheats himself."

A boy or a man who works simply for his salary, and is actuated by no higher motive, is dishonest, and the one whom he most defrauds is himself. He is cheating himself, in the quality of his daily work, of that which all the after years, try as he may, can never give him back.

If I were allowed but one utterance on this subject, so vital to every young man starting on the journey of life, I would say: "Don't think too much of the amount of salary your employer gives you at the start. Think, rather, of the possible salary you can give yourself, in increasing your skill, in expanding your experience, in enlarging and ennobling yourself." A man's or a boy's work is material with which to build character and manhood. It is life's school for practical training of the faculties, stretching the mind, and strengthening and developing the intellect, not a mere mill for grinding out a salary of dollars and cents.

Bismarck was said to have really founded the German Empire when working for a small salary as secretary to the German legation in Russia; for in that position he absorbed the secrets of strategy and diplomacy which later were used so effectively for his country. He worked so assiduously, so efficiently, that Germany prized his services more than those of the ambassador himself. If Bismarck had earned only his salary, he might have remained a perpetual clerk, and Germany a tangle of petty states.

I have never known an employee to rise rapidly, or even to get beyond mediocrity, whose pay envelope was his goal, who could not see infinitely more in his work than what he found in the envelope on Saturday night. That is necessity; but the larger part of the real pay of a real man's work is outside of the pay envelope.

One part of this outside salary is the opportunity of the employee to absorb the secrets of his employer's success, and to learn from his mistakes, while he is being paid for learning his trade or profession. The other part, and the best of all, is the opportunity for growth, for development, for mental expansion; the opportunity to become a larger, broader, more efficient man.

The opportunity for growth in a disciplinary institution, where the practical faculties, the executive faculties, are brought into systematic, vigorous exercise at a definite time and for a definite number of hours, is an advantage beyond computation. There is no estimating the value of such training. It is the opportunity, my employee friend, that will help you to make a large man of yourself, which, perhaps, you could not possibly do without being employed in some kind of an institution which has the motive, the machinery, the patronage to give you the disciplining and training you need to bring out your strongest qualities. And instead of paying for the opportunity of unfolding and developing from a green, ignorant boy into a strong, level-headed, efficient man, you are paid!

The youth who is always haggling over the question of how many dollars and cents he will sell his services for, little realizes how he is cheating himself by not looking at the larger salary he can pay himself in increasing his skill, in expanding his experience, and in making himself a better, stronger, more useful man.

The few dollars he finds in his pay envelope are to this larger salary as the chips which fly from the sculptor's chisel are to the angel which he is trying to call out of the marble.

You can draw from the faithfulness of your work, from the grand spirit which you bring to it, the high purpose which emanates from you in its performance, a recompense so munificent that what your employer pays you will seem insignificant beside it. He pays you in dollars; you pay yourself in valuable experience, in fine training, in increased efficiency, in splendid discipline, in self-expression, in character building.

Then, too, the ideal employer gives those who work for him a great deal that is not found in the pay envelope. He gives them encouragement, sympathy. He inspires them with the possibility of doing something higher, better.

How small and narrow and really blind to his own interests must be the youth who can weigh a question of salary against all those privileges he receives in exchange for the meager services he is able to render his employer.

Do not fear that your employer will not recognize your merit and advance you as rapidly as you deserve. It he is looking for efficient employees,—and what employer is not?—it will be to his own interest to do so,—just as soon as it is profitable. W. Bourke Cockran, himself a remarkable example of success, says: "The man who brings to his occupation a loyal desire to do his best is certain to succeed. By doing the thing at hand surpassingly well, he shows that it would be profitable to employ him in some higher form of occupation, and, when there is profit in his promotion, he is pretty sure to secure it."

Do you think that kings of business like Andrew Carnegie, John Wanamaker, Robert C. Ogden, and other lesser powers in the commercial world would have attained their present commanding success had they hesitated and haggled about a dollar or two of salary when they began their life-work? If they had, they would now probably be working on comparatively small salaries for other people. It was not salary, but opportunity, that each wanted,—a chance to show what was in him, to absorb the secrets of the business. They were satisfied with a dollar or two apiece a week, hardly enough to live on, while they were learning the lessons that made them what they are to-day. No, the boys who rise in the world are not those who, at the start, split hairs about salaries.

Often we see bright boys who have worked, perhaps for years, on small salaries, suddenly jumping, as if by magic, into high and responsible positions. Why? Simply because, while their employers were paying them but a few dollars a week, they were paying themselves vastly more in the fine quality of their work, in the enthusiasm, determination, and high purpose they brought to their tasks, and in increased insight into business methods.

Colonel Robert C. Clowry, president of the Western Union Telegraph Company, worked without pay as a messenger boy for months for experience, which he regarded as worth infinitely more than salary—and scores of our most successful men have cheerfully done the same thing.

A millionaire merchant of New York told me the story of his rise. "I walked from my home in New England to New York," he said, "where I secured a place to sweep out a store for three dollars and a half a week. At the end of a year, I accepted an offer from the firm to remain for five years at a salary of seven dollars and a half a week. Long before this time had expired, however, I had a proposition from another large concern in New York to act as its foreign representative at a salary of three thousand dollars a year. I told the manager that I was then under contract, but that, when my time should be completed, I should be glad to talk with him in regard to his proposition." When his contract was nearly up, he was called into the office of the head of the house, and a new contract with him for a term of years at three thousand dollars a year was proposed. The young man told his employers that the manager of another house had offered him that amount a year or more before, but that he did not accept it because he wouldn't break his contract. They told him they would think the matter over and see what they could do for him. Incredible as it may seem, they notified him, a little later, that they were prepared to enter into a ten-year contract with him at ten thousand dollars a year, and the contract was closed. He told me that he and his wife lived on eight dollars a week in New York, during a large part of this time, and that, by saving and investments, they laid up $117,000. At the end of his contract, he was taken into the firm as a partner, and became a millionaire.

Suppose that this boy had listened to his associates, who probably said to him, many times: "What a fool you are, George, to work here overtime to do the things which others neglect! Why should you stay here nights and help pack goods, and all that sort of thing, when it is not expected of you?" Would he then have risen above them, leaving them in the ranks of perpetual employees? No, but the boy who walked one hundred miles to

New York to get a job saw in every opportunity a great occasion, for he could not tell when fate might be taking his measure for a larger place. The very first time he swept out the store, he felt within him the ability to become a great merchant, and he determined that he would be. He felt that the opportunity was the salary. The chance actually to do with his own hands the thing which he wanted to learn; to see the way in which princely merchants do business; to watch their methods; to absorb their processes; to make their secrets his own,—this was his salary, compared with which the three dollars and fifty cents looked contemptible. He put himself into training, always looking out for the main chance. He never allowed anything of importance to escape his attention. When he was not working, he was watching others, studying methods, and asking questions of everybody he came in contact with in the store, so eager was he to learn how everything was done. He told me that he did not go out of New York City for twelve years; that he preferred to study the store, and to absorb every bit of knowledge that he could, for he was bound some day to be a partner or to have a store of his own.

It is not difficult to see a proprietor in the boy who sweeps the store or waits on customers—if the qualities that make a proprietor are in him—by watching him work for a single day. You can tell by the spirit which he brings to his task whether there is in him the capacity for growth, expansion, enlargement; an ambition to rise, to be somebody, or an inclination to shirk, to do as little as possible for the largest amount of salary.

When you get a job, just think of yourself as actually starting out in business for yourself, as really working for yourself. Get as much salary as you can, but remember that that is a very small part of the consideration. You have actually gotten an opportunity to get right into the very heart of the great activities of a large concern, to get close to men who do things; an opportunity to absorb knowledge and valuable secrets on every hand; an opportunity to drink in, through your eyes and your ears, knowledge wherever you go in the establishment, knowledge that will be invaluable to you in the future.

Every hint and every suggestion which you can pick up, every bit of knowledge you can absorb, you should regard as a part of your future capital which will be worth more than money capital when you start out for yourself.

Just make up your mind that you are going to be a sponge in that institution and absorb every particle of information and knowledge possible.

Resolve that you will call upon all of your resourcefulness, your inventiveness, your ingenuity, to devise new and better ways of doing things; that you will be progressive, up-to-date; that you will enter into your work with a spirit of enthusiasm and a zest which know no bounds, and you will be surprised to see how quickly you will attract the attention of those above you.

This striving for excellence will make you grow. It will call out your resources, call out the best thing in you. The constant stretching of the mind over problems which interest you, which are to mean everything to you in the future, will help you expand into a broader, larger, more effective man.

If you work with this spirit, you will form a like habit of accuracy, of close observation; a habit of reading human nature; a habit of adjusting means to ends; a habit of thoroughness, of system; *a habit of putting your best into everything you do*, which means the ultimate attainment of your maximum efficiency. In other words, if you give your best to your employer, the best possible comes back to you in skill, training, shrewdness, acumen, and power.

Your employer may pinch you on salary, but he can not close your eyes and ears; he can not shut off your perceptive faculties; he can not keep you from absorbing the secrets of his business which may have been purchased by him at an enormous cost of toil and sacrifice and even of several failures.

On the other hand, it is impossible for you to rob your employer by clipping your hours, shirking your work, by carelessness or indifference, without robbing yourself of infinitely more, of capital which is worth vastly more than money capital—the chance to make a man of yourself, the chance to have a clean record behind you instead of a smirched one.

If you think you are being kept back, if you are working for too small a salary, if favoritism puts some one into a position above you which you have justly earned, never mind, no one can rob you of your greatest reward, the skill, the efficiency, the power you have gained, the consciousness of doing your level best, of giving the best thing in you to your employer, all of which advantages you will carry with you to your next position, whatever it may be.

Don't say to yourself, "I am not paid for doing this extra work; I do not get enough salary, anyway, and it is perfectly right for me to shirk when my employer is not in sight or to clip my hours when I can," for this means a loss of self-respect. You will never again have the same confidence in your ability to succeed; you will always be conscious that you have done a little, mean thing, and no amount of juggling with yourself can induce that inward monitor which says "right" to the well-done thing and "wrong" to the botched work, to alter its verdict in your favor. There is something within you that you cannot bribe; a divine sense of justice and right that can not be blindfolded. Nothing will ever compensate you for the loss of faith in yourself. You may still succeed when others have lost confidence in you, but never when you have lost confidence in yourself. If you do not respect yourself; if you do not believe in yourself, your career is at an end so far as its upward tendency is concerned.

Then again, an employee's reputation is his capital. In the absence of money capital, his reputation means everything. It not only follows him around from one employer to another, but it also follows him when he goes into business for himself, and is always either helping or hindering him, according to its nature.

Contrast the condition of a young man starting out for himself who has looked upon his position as a sacred trust, a great opportunity, backed, buttressed, and supported by a splendid past, an untarnished reputation—a reputation for being a dead-in-earnest hard worker, square, loyal, and true to his employer's interests—with that of another young man of equal ability starting out for himself, who has done just as little work for his salary as possible, and who has gone on the principle that the more he could get out of an employer—the more salary he could get with less effort—the shrewder, smarter man he was.

The very reputation of the first young man is splendid credit. He is backed up by the good opinion of everybody that knows him. People are afraid of the other: they can not trust him. He beat his employer, why should not he beat others? Everybody knows that he has not been honest at heart with his employer, not loyal or true. He must work all the harder to overcome the handicap of a bad reputation, a smirched record.

In other words, he is starting out in life with a heavy handicap, which, if it does not drag him down to failure, will make his burden infinitely greater, and success, even a purely commercial success, so much the harder to attain.

There is nothing like a good, solid, substantial reputation, a clean record, an untarnished past. It sticks to us through life, and is always helping us. We find it waiting at the bank when we try to borrow money, or at the jobber's when we ask for credit. It is always backing us up and helping us in all sorts of ways.

Young men are sometimes surprised at their rapid advancement. They can not understand it, because they do not realize the tremendous power of a clean name, of a good reputation which is backing them.

I know a young man who came to New York, got a position in a publishing house at fifteen dollars a week, and worked five years before he received thirty-five dollars a week.

The other employees and his friends called him a fool for staying at the office after hours and taking work home nights and holidays, for such a small salary; but he told them that the opportunity was what he was after, not the salary.

His work attracted the attention of a publisher who offered him sixty dollars a week, and very soon advanced him to seventy-five; but he carried with him to the new position the same habits of painstaking, hard work, never thinking of the salary, but *regarding the opportunity as everything*.

Employees sometimes think that they get no credit for trying to do more than they are paid for; but here is an instance of a young man who attracted the attention of others even outside of the firm he worked for, just because he was trying to earn a great deal more than he was paid for doing.

The result was, that in less than two years from the time he was receiving sixty dollars a week, he went to a third large publishing house at ten thousand dollars a year, and also with an interest in the business.

The salary is of very little importance to you in comparison with the reputation for integrity and efficiency you have left behind you and the experience you have gained while earning the salary. These are the great things.

In olden times boys had to give years of their time in order to learn a trade, and often would pay their employer for the opportunity. English boys used to think it was a great opportunity to be able to get into a good concern, with a chance to work without salary for years in order to learn their business or trade. Now the boy is paid for learning his trade.

Many employees may not think it is so very bad to clip their hours, to shirk at every opportunity, to sneak away and hide during business hours, to loiter when out on business for their employer, to go to their work in the morning all used up from dissipation; but often when they try to get another place their reputation has gone before them, and they are not wanted.

Others excuse themselves for poor work on the ground that their employer does not appreciate their services and is mean to them. A youth might just as well excuse himself for his boorish manners and ungentlemanly conduct on the ground that other people were mean and ungentlemanly to him.

My young friends, you have nothing to do with your employer's character or his method of doing things. You may not be able to make him do what is right, but you can do right yourself. You may not be able to make him a gentleman, but you can be one yourself; and you can not afford to ruin yourself and your whole future just because your employer is not what he ought to be. No matter how mean and stingy he may be, your opportunity for the time is with him, and it rests with you whether you will use it or abuse it, whether you will make of it a stepping-stone or a stumbling-block.

The fact is that your present position, your way of doing your work, is the key that will unlock the door above you. Slighted work, botched work, will never make a key to unlock the door to anything but failure and disgrace.

There is nothing else so valuable to you as an opportunity to build a name for yourself. Your reputation is the foundation for your future success, and if you slip rotten hours, and slighted, botched work into the foundation, your superstructure will topple. The foundation must be clean, solid, and firm.

The quality which you put into your work will determine the quality of your life. The habit of insisting upon the best of which you are capable, of always demanding of yourself the highest, never accepting the lowest or second best, no matter how small your remuneration, will make all the difference to you between mediocrity or failure, and success. If you bring to your work the spirit of an artist instead of an artisan, a burning zeal, an absorbing enthusiasm, these will take the drudgery out of it and make it a delight.

Take no chances of marring your reputation by the picayune and unworthy endeavor "to get square" with a stingy or mean employer. Never mind what kind of a man he is, resolve that you will approach your task in the spirit of a master, that whether he is a man of high ideals or not, you will be one. Remember that you are a sculptor and that every act is a chisel blow upon life's marble block. You can not afford to strike false blows which may mar the angel that sleeps in the stone. Whether it is beautiful or hideous, divine or brutal, the image you evolve from the block must stand as an expression of yourself, of your ideals. Those who do not care how they do their work, if they can only get through with it and get their salary for it, pay very dearly for their trifling; they cut very sorry figures in life. Regard your work as a great life school for the broadening, deepening, rounding into symmetry, harmony, beauty, of your God-given faculties, which are uncut diamonds sacredly intrusted to you for the polishing and bringing out of their hidden wealth and beauty. Look upon it as a man-builder, a character-builder, and not as a mere living-getter. Regard the living-getting, money-making part of your career as a mere incidental as compared with the man-making part of it.

The smallest people in the world are those who work for salary alone. The little money you get in your pay envelope is a pretty small, low motive for which to work. It may be necessary to secure your bread and butter, but you have something infinitely higher to satisfy than that; that is, your sense of the right; the demand in you to do your level best, to be a man, to do the square thing, the fair thing. These should speak so loud in you that the mere bread-and-butter question will be insignificant in comparison.

Many young employees, just because they do not get quite as much salary as they think they should, deliberately throw away all of the other, larger, grander remuneration possible for them outside of their pay envelope, for the sake of "getting square" with their employer. They deliberately adopt a shirking, do-as-little-as-possible policy, and instead of getting this larger, more important salary, which they can pay themselves, they prefer the consequent arrested development, and become small, narrow, inefficient, rutty men and women, with nothing large or magnanimous, nothing broad, noble, progressive in their nature. Their leadership faculties, their initiative, their planning ability, their ingenuity and resourcefulness, inventiveness, and all the qualities which make the leader, the large, full, complete man, remain undeveloped. While trying to "get square" with their employer, by giving him pinched service, they blight their own growth, strangle their own prospects, and go through life half men instead of full men—small, narrow, weak men, instead of the strong, grand, complete men they might be.

I have known employees actually to work harder in scheming, shirking, trying to keep from working hard in the performance of their duties, than they would have worked if they had tried to do their best, and had given the largest, the most liberal service possible to their employers. The hardest work in the world is that which is grudgingly done.

Start out with a tacit understanding with yourself that you will be a man, that you will express in your work the highest thing in you, the best thing in you. You can not afford to debase or demoralize yourself by bringing out your mean side, the lowest and most despicable thing in you.

Never mind whether your employer appreciates the high quality of your work or not, or thinks more of you for your conscientiousness, you will certainly think more of yourself after getting the approval of that still small voice within you which says "right" to the noble act. The effort always to do your best will enlarge your capacity for doing things, and will encourage you to push ahead toward larger triumphs.

Everywhere we see people who are haunted by the ghosts of half-finished jobs, the dishonest work done away back in their youth. These covered-up defects are always coming back to humiliate them later, to trip them up, and to bar their progress. The great failure army is full of people who have tried to get square with their employers for the small salary and lack of appreciation.

No one can respect himself or have that sublime faith in himself which makes for high achievement while he puts half-hearted, mean service into his work. The man who has not learned to fling his whole soul into his task, who has not learned the secret of taking the drudgery out of his work by putting the best of himself into it, has not learned the first principles of success or happiness. Let other people do the poor jobs, the botched work, if they will. Keep your standard up. It is a lofty ideal that redeems the life from the curse of commonness and imparts a touch of nobility to the personality.

No matter how small your salary, or how unappreciative your employer, bring the entire man to your task; be all there; fling your life into it with all the energy and enthusiasm you can muster. *Poor work injures your employer a little, but it may ruin you.* Be proud of your work and go to it every morning superbly equipped; go to it in the spirit of a master, of a conqueror. Determine to do your level best and never to demoralize yourself by doing your second best.

Conduct yourself in such a way that you can always look yourself in the face without wincing; then you will have a courage born of conviction, of personal nobility and integrity which have never been tarnished.

What your employer thinks of you, what the world thinks of you, is not half as important as what you think of yourself. Others are with you comparatively little through life. *You have to live with yourself day and night through your whole existence, and you can not afford to tie that divine thing in you to a scoundrel.*

Expect Great Things of Yourself

"Why," asked Mirabeau, "should we call ourselves men, unless it be to succeed in everything everywhere?" Nothing else will so nerve you to accomplish great things as to believe in your own greatness, in your own marvelous possibilities. Count that man an enemy who shakes your faith in yourself, in your ability to do the thing you have set your heart upon doing, for when your confidence is gone, your power is gone. Your achievement will never rise higher than your self-faith. It would be as reasonable for Napoleon to have expected to get his army over the Alps by sitting down and declaring that the undertaking was too great for him, as for you to hope to achieve anything significant in life while harboring grave doubts and fears as to your ability.

The miracles of civilization have been performed by men and women of great self-confidence, who had unwavering faith in their power to accomplish the tasks they undertook. The race would have been centuries behind what it is to-day had it not been for their grit, their determination, their persistence in finding and making real the thing they believed in and which the world often denounced as chimerical or impossible.

There is no law by which you can achieve success in anything without expecting it, demanding it, assuming it. There must be a strong, firm self-faith first, or the thing will never come. There is no room for chance in God's world of system and supreme order. Everything must have not only a cause, but a sufficient cause—a cause as large as the result. A stream can not rise higher than its source. A great success must have a great source in expectation, in self-confidence, and in persistent endeavor to attain it. No matter how great the ability, how large the genius, or how splendid the education, the achievement will never rise higher than the confidence. He can who thinks he can, and he can't who thinks he can't. This is an inexorable, indisputable law.

It does not matter what other people think of you, of your plans, or of your aims. No matter if they call you a visionary, a crank, or a dreamer; you must believe in yourself. You forsake yourself when you lose your confidence. Never allow anybody or any misfortune to shake your belief in yourself. You may lose your property, your health, your reputation, other people's confidence, even; but there is always hope for you so long as you keep a firm faith in yourself. If you never lose that, but keep pushing on, the world will, sooner or later, make way for you.

A soldier once took a message to Napoleon in such great haste that the horse he rode dropped dead before he delivered the paper. Napoleon dictated his answer and, handing it to the messenger, ordered him to mount his own horse and deliver it with all possible speed.

The messenger looked at the magnificent animal, with its superb trappings, and said, "Nay, General, but this is too gorgeous, too magnificent for a common soldier."

Napoleon said, "Nothing is too good or too magnificent for a French soldier."

The world is full of people like this poor French soldier, who think that what others have is too good for them; that it does not fit their humble condition; that they are not expected to have as good things as those who are "more favored." They do not realize how they weaken themselves by this mental attitude of self-depreciation or self-effacement. They do not claim enough, expect enough, or demand enough of or for themselves.

You will never become a giant if you only make a pygmy's claim for yourself; if you only expect small things of yourself. There is no law which can cause a pygmy's thinking to produce a giant. The statue follows the model. The model is the inward vision.

Most people have been educated to think that it was not intended they should have the best there is in the world; that the good and the beautiful things of life were not designed for them, but were reserved for those especially favored by fortune. They have grown up under this conviction of their inferiority, and of course they will be inferior until they claim superiority as their birthright. A vast number of men and women who are really capable of doing great things, do small things, live mediocre lives, because they do not expect or demand enough of themselves. They do not know how to call out their best.

One reason why the human race as a whole has not measured up to its possibilities, to its promise; one reason why we see everywhere splendid ability doing the work of mediocrity; is because people do not think half enough of themselves. *We do not realize our divinity; that we are a part of the great causation principle of the universe.*

We do not think highly enough of our superb birthright, nor comprehend to what heights of sublimity we were intended and expected to rise, nor to what extent we can really be masters of ourselves. We fail to see that we can control our own destiny: make ourselves do whatever is possible; make ourselves become whatever we long to be.

"If we choose to be no more than clods of clay," says Marie Corelli, "then we shall be used as clods of clay for braver feet to tread on."

The persistent thought that you are not as good as others, that you are a weak, ineffective being, will lower your whole standard of life and paralyze your ability.

A man who is self-reliant, positive, optimistic, and undertakes his work with the assurance of success, magnetizes conditions. He draws to himself the literal fulfilment of the promise, "For unto every one that hath shall be given, and he shall have abundance."

There is everything in assuming the part we wish to play, and playing it royally. If you are ambitious to do big things, you must make a large program for yourself, and assume the part it demands.

There is something in the atmosphere of the man who has a large and true estimate of himself, who believes that he is going to win out; something in his very appearance that wins half the battle before a blow is struck. Things get out of the way of the vigorous, affirmative man, which are always tripping the self-depreciating, negative man.

We often hear it said of a man, "Everything he undertakes succeeds," or "Everything he touches turns to gold." By the force of his character and the creative power of his thought, such a man wrings success from the most adverse circumstances. Confidence begets confidence. A man who carries in his very presence an air of victory, radiates assurance, and imparts to others confidence that he can do the thing he attempts. As time goes on, he is reenforced not only by the power of his own thought, but also by that of all who know him. His friends and acquaintances affirm and reaffirm his ability to succeed, and make each successive triumph easier of achievement than its predecessor. His self-poise, assurance, confidence, and ability increase in a direct ratio to the number of his achievements. As the savage Indian thought that the power of every enemy he conquered entered into himself, so in reality does every conquest in war, in peaceful industry, in commerce, in invention, in science, or in art add to the conqueror's power to do the next thing.

Set the mind toward the thing you would accomplish so resolutely, so definitely, and with such vigorous determination, and put so much grit into your resolution, that nothing on earth can turn you from your purpose until you attain it.

This very assertion of superiority, the assumption of power, the affirmation of belief in yourself, the mental attitude that claims success as an inalienable birthright, will strengthen the whole man and give power to a combination of faculties which doubt, fear, and a lack of confidence undermine.

Confidence is the Napoleon of the mental army. It doubles and trebles the power of all the other faculties. The whole mental army waits until confidence leads the way.

Even a race-horse can not win the prize after it has once lost confidence in itself. Courage, born of self-confidence, is the prod which brings out the last ounce of reserve force.

The reason why so many men fail is because they do not commit themselves with a determination to win at any cost. They do not have that superb confidence in themselves which never looks back; which burns all bridges behind it. There is just uncertainty enough as to whether they will succeed to take the edge off their effort, and it is just this little difference between doing pretty well and flinging all oneself, all his power, into his career, that makes the difference between mediocrity and a grand achievement.

If you doubt your ability to do what you set out to do; if you think that others are better fitted to do it than you; if you fear to let yourself out and take chances; if you lack boldness; if you have a timid, shrinking nature; if the negatives preponderate in your vocabulary; if you think that you lack positiveness, initiative, aggressiveness, ability; you can never win anything very great until you change your whole mental attitude and learn to have great faith in yourself. Fear, doubt, and timidity must be turned out of your mind.

Your own mental picture of yourself is a good measure of yourself and your possibilities. If there is no out-reach to your mind, no spirit of daring, no firm self-faith, you will never accomplish much.

A man's confidence measures the height of his possibilities. A stream can not rise higher than its fountain-head.

Power is largely a question of strong, vigorous, perpetual thinking along the line of the ambition, parallel with the aim—the great life purpose. Here is where power originates.

The deed must first live in the thought or it will never be a reality; and a strong, vigorous concept of the thing we want to do is a tremendous initial step. A thought that is timidly born will be timidly executed. There must be vigor of conception or an indifferent execution.

All the greatest achievements in the world began in longing—in dreamings and hopings which for a time were nursed in despair, with no light in sight. This longing kept the courage up and made self-sacrifice easier until the thing dreamed of—the mental vision—was realized.

"According to your faith be it unto you." Our faith is a very good measure of what we get out of life. The man of weak faith gets little; the man of mighty faith gets much.

The very intensity of your confidence in your ability to do the thing you attempt is definitely related to the degree of your achievement.

If we were to analyze the marvelous successes of many of our self-made men, we should find that when they first started out in active life they held the confident, vigorous, persistent thought of and belief in their ability to accomplish what they had undertaken. Their mental attitude was set so stubbornly toward their goal that the doubts and fears which dog and hinder and frighten the man who holds a low estimate of himself, who asks, demands, and expects but little, of or for himself, got out of their path, and the world made way for them.

We are very apt to think of men who have been unusually successful in any line as greatly favored by fortune; and we try to account for it in all sorts of ways but the right one. The fact is that their success represents their expectations of themselves—the sum of their creative, positive, habitual thinking. It is their mental attitude outpictured and made tangible in their environment. They have wrought—created—what they have and what they are out of their constructive thought and their unquenchable faith in themselves.

We must not only believe we can succeed, but *we must believe it with all our hearts.*

We must have a positive conviction that we can attain success.

No lukewarm energy or indifferent ambition ever accomplished anything. *There must be vigor in our expectation, in our faith, in our determination, in our endeavor. We must resolve with the energy that does things.*

Not only must the desire for the thing we long for be kept uppermost, but there must be strongly concentrated intensity of effort to attain our object.

As it is the fierceness of the heat that melts the iron ore and makes it possible to weld it or mold it into shape; as it is the intensity of the electrical force that dissolves the diamond—the hardest known substance; so *it is the concentrated aim, the invincible purpose*, that wins success. Nothing was ever accomplished by a half-hearted desire.

Many people make a very poor showing in life, because there is no vim, no vigor in their efforts. Their resolutions are spineless; there is no backbone in their endeavor—no grit in their ambition.

One must have that determination which never looks back and which knows no defeat; that resolution which burns all bridges behind it and is willing to risk everything upon the effort. When a man ceases to believe in himself—gives up the fight—you can not do much for him except to try to restore what he has lost—his self-faith—and to get out of his head the idea that there is a fate which tosses him hither and thither, a mysterious destiny which decides things whether he will or not. You can not do much with him until he comprehends that *he is bigger than any fate*; that he has within himself a power mightier than any force outside of him.

One reason why the careers of most of us are so pinched and narrow, is because we do not have a large faith in ourselves and in our power to accomplish. We are held back by too much caution. We are timid about venturing. We are not bold enough.

Whatever we long for, yearn for, struggle for, and hold persistently in the mind, we tend to become just in exact proportion to the intensity and persistence of the thought. *We think ourselves into smallness, into inferiority by thinking downward.* We ought to think upward, then we would reach the heights where superiority dwells. The man whose mind is set firmly toward achievement does not appropriate success, *he is success.*

Self-confidence is not egotism. It is knowledge, and it comes from the consciousness of possessing the ability requisite for what one undertakes. Civilization to-day rests upon self-confidence.

A firm self-faith helps a man to project himself with a force that is almost irresistible. A balancer, a doubter, has no projectile power. If he starts at all, he moves with uncertainty. There is no vigor in his initiative, no positiveness in his energy.

There is a great difference between a man who thinks that "perhaps" he can do, or who "will try" to do a thing, and a man who "knows" he can do it, who is "bound" to do it; who feels within himself a pulsating power, an irresistible force, equal to any emergency.

This difference between uncertainty and certainty, between vacillation and decision, between the man who wavers and the man who decides things, between "I hope to" and "I can," between "I'll try" and "I will"—this little difference measures the distance between weakness and power, between mediocrity and excellence, between commonness and superiority.

The man who does things must be able to project himself with a mighty force, to fling the whole weight of his being into his work, ever gathering momentum against the obstacles which confront him; every issue must be met wholly, unhesitatingly. He can not do this with a wavering, doubting, unstable mind.

The fact that a man believes implicitly that he can do what may seem impossible or very difficult to others, shows that there is something within him that makes him equal to the work he has undertaken.

Faith unites man with the Infinite, and no one can accomplish great things in life unless he works in oneness with the Infinite. When a man lives so near to the Supreme that the divine Presence is felt all the time, then he is in a position to express power.

There is nothing which will multiply one's ability like self-faith. It can make a one-talent man a success, while a ten-talent man without it would fail.

Faith walks on the mountain tops, hence its superior vision. It sees what is invisible to those who follow in the valleys.

It was the sustaining power of a mighty self-faith that enabled Columbus to bear the jeers and imputations of the Spanish cabinet; that sustained him when his sailors were in mutiny and he was at their mercy in a little vessel on an unknown sea; that enabled him to hold steadily to his purpose, entering in his diary day after day—"This day we sailed west, which was our course."

It was this self-faith which gave courage and determination to Fulton to attempt his first trip up the Hudson in the *Clermont*, before thousands of his fellow citizens, who had gathered to howl and jeer at his expected failure. He believed he could do the thing he attempted though the whole world was against him.

What miracles self-confidence has wrought! What impossible deeds it has helped to perform! It took Dewey past cannons, torpedoes, and mines to victory at Manila Bay; it carried Farragut, lashed to the rigging, past the defenses of the enemy in Mobile Bay; it led Nelson and Grant to victory; it has been the great tonic in the world of invention, discovery, and art; it has won a thousand triumphs in war and science which were deemed impossible by doubters and the faint-hearted.

Self-faith has been the miracle-worker of the ages. It has enabled the inventor and the discoverer to go on and on amidst troubles and trials which otherwise would have utterly disheartened them. It has held innumerable heroes to their tasks until the glorious deeds were accomplished.

The only inferiority in us is what we put into ourselves. If only we better understood our divinity we should all have this larger faith which is the distinction of the brave soul. We think ourselves into smallness. Were we to think upward we should reach the heights where superiority dwells.

Perhaps there is no other one thing which keeps so many people back as their low estimate of themselves. They are more handicapped by their limiting thought, by their foolish convictions of inefficiency, than by almost anything else, for *there is no power in the universe that can help a man do a thing when he thinks he can not do it*. Self-faith must lead the way. You can not go beyond the limits you set for yourself.

It is one of the most difficult things to a mortal to really believe in his own bigness, in his own grandeur; to believe that his yearnings and hungerings and aspirations for higher, nobler things have any basis in reality or any real, ultimate end. But they are, in fact, the signs of ability to match them, of power to make them real. They are the stirrings of the divinity within us; the call to something better, to go higher.

No man gets very far in the world or expresses great power until self-faith is born in him; until he catches a glimpse of his higher, nobler self; until he realizes that his ambition, his aspiration, are proofs of his ability to reach the ideal which haunts him. The Creator would not have mocked us with the yearning for infinite achievement without giving us the ability and the opportunity for realizing it, any more than he would have mocked the wild birds with an instinct to fly south in the winter without giving them a sunny South to match the instinct.

The cause of whatever comes to you in life is within you. There is where it is created. The thing you long for and work for comes to you because your thought has created it; because there is something inside you that attracts it. It comes because there is an affinity within you for it. *Your own comes to you; is always seeking you*.

Whenever you see a person who has been unusually successful in any field, remember that he has usually thought himself into his position; his mental attitude and energy have created it; what he stands for in his community has come from his attitude toward life, toward his fellow men, toward his vocation, toward himself. Above all else, it is the outcome of his self-faith, of his inward vision of himself; the result of his estimate of his powers and possibilities.

The men who have done the great things in the world have been profound believers in themselves.

If I could give the young people of America but one word of advice, it would be this—*"Believe in yourself with all your might."* That is, believe that your destiny is inside of you, that there is a power within you which, if awakened, aroused, developed, and matched with honest effort, will not only make a noble man or woman of you, but will also make you successful and happy.

All through the Bible we find emphasized the miracle-working power of faith. Faith in himself indicates that a man has a glimpse of forces within him which either annihilate the obstacles in the way, or make them seem insignificant in comparison with his ability to overcome them.

Faith opens the door that enables us to look into the soul's limitless possibilities and reveals such powers there, such unconquerable forces, that we are not only encouraged to go on, but feel a great consciousness of added power because we have touched omnipotence, and gotten a glimpse of the great source of things.

Faith is that something within us which does not guess, but knows. It knows because it sees what our coarser selves, our animal natures can not see. It is the prophet within us, the divine messenger appointed to accompany man through life to guide and direct and encourage him. It gives him a glimpse of his possibilities to keep him from losing heart, from quitting his upward life struggle.

Our faith knows because it sees what we can not see. It sees resources, powers, potencies which our doubts and fears veil from us. Faith is assured, is never afraid, because it sees the way out; sees the solution of its problem. It has dipped in the realms of our finer life our higher and diviner kingdom. All things are possible to him who has faith, because faith sees, recognizes the power that means accomplishment. If we had faith in God and in ourselves we could remove all mountains of difficulty, and our lives would be one triumphal march to the goal of our ambition.

If we had faith enough we could cure all our ills and accomplish the maximum of our possibilities.

Faith never fails; it is a miracle worker. It looks beyond all boundaries, transcends all limitations, penetrates all obstacles and sees the goal.

It is doubt and fear, timidity and cowardice, that hold us down and keep us in mediocrity—doing petty things when we are capable of sublime deeds.

If we had faith enough we should travel Godward infinitely faster than we do.

The time will come when every human being will have unbounded faith and will live the life triumphant. Then there will be no poverty in the world, no failures, and the discords of life will all vanish.

The Next Time You Think You Are a Failure

If you made a botch of last year, if you feel that it was a failure, that you floundered and blundered and did a lot of foolish things; if you were gullible, made imprudent investments, wasted your time and money, don't drag these ghosts along with you to handicap you and destroy your happiness all through the future.

Haven't you wasted enough energy worrying over what can not be helped? Don't let these things sap any more of your vitality, waste any more of your time or destroy any more of your happiness.

There is only one thing to do with bitter experiences, blunders and unfortunate mistakes, or with memories that worry us and which kill our efficiency, and that is to *forget them, bury them*!

To-day is a good time to "leave the low-vaulted past," to drop the yesterdays, to forget bitter memories.

Resolve that you will close the door on everything in the past that pains and can not help you. Free yourself from everything which handicaps you, keeps you back and makes you unhappy. Throw away all useless baggage, drop everything that is a drag, that hinders your progress.

Enter upon to-morrow with a clean slate and a free mind. Don't be mortgaged to the past, and never look back.

There is no use in castigating yourself for not having done better.

Form a habit of expelling from your mind thoughts or suggestions which call up unpleasant subjects or bitter memories, and which have a bad influence upon you.

Every one ought to make it a life-rule to wipe out from his memory everything that has been unpleasant, unfortunate. We ought to forget everything that has kept us back, has made us suffer, has been disagreeable, and never allow the hideous pictures of distressing conditions to enter our minds again. There is only one thing to do with a disagreeable, harmful experience, and that is—*forget it*!

There are many times in the life of a person who does things that are worth while when he gets terribly discouraged and thinks it easier to go back than to push on. But *there is no victory in retreating*. We should never leave any bridges unburned behind us, any way open for retreat to tempt our weakness, indecision or discouragement. If there is anything we ever feel grateful for, it is that we have had courage and pluck enough to push on, to keep going when things looked dark and when seemingly insurmountable obstacles confronted us.

Most people are their own worst enemies. We are all the time "queering" our life game by our vicious, tearing-down thoughts and unfortunate moods. Everything depends upon our courage, our faith in ourselves, in our holding a hopeful, optimistic outlook; and yet, whenever things go wrong with us, whenever we have a discouraging day or an unfortunate experience, a loss or any misfortune, we let the tearing-down thought, doubt, fear, despondency, like a bull in a china shop, tear through our mentalities, perhaps breaking up and destroying the work of years of building up, and we have to start all over again. We work and live like the frog in the well; we climb up only to fall back, and often lose all we gain.

One of the worst things that can ever happen to a person is to get it into his head that he was born unlucky and that the Fates are against him. There are no Fates, outside of our own mentality. We are our own Fates. We control our own destiny.

There is no fate or destiny which puts one man down and another up. "It is not in our stars, but in ourselves, that we are underlings." He only is beaten who admits it. The man is inferior who admits that he is inferior, who voluntarily takes an inferior position because he thinks the best things were intended for somebody else.

You will find that just in proportion as you increase your confidence in yourself by the affirmation of what you wish to be and to do, your ability will increase.

No matter what other people may think about your ability, never allow yourself to doubt that you can do or become what you long to. Increase your self-confidence in every possible way, and you can do this to a remarkable degree by the power of self-suggestion.

This form of suggestion—talking to oneself vigorously, earnestly—seems to arouse the sleeping forces in the subconscious self more effectually than thinking the same thing.

There is a force in words spoken aloud which is not stirred by going over the same words mentally. They sometimes arouse slumbering energies within us which thinking does not stir up—especially if we have not been trained to think deeply, to focus the mind closely. They make a more lasting impression upon the mind, just as words which pass through the eye from the printed page make a greater impression on the brain than we get by thinking the same words; as seeing objects of nature makes a more lasting impression upon the mind than thinking about them. A vividness, a certain force, accompanies the spoken word—especially if earnestly, vehemently uttered—which is not apparent to many in merely thinking about what the words express. If you repeat a firm resolve to yourself aloud, vigorously, even vehemently, you are more likely to carry it to reality than if you merely resolve in silence.

We become so accustomed to our silent thoughts that the voicing of them, the giving audible expression to our yearnings, makes a much deeper impression upon us.

The audible self-encouragement treatment may be used with marvelous results in correcting our weaknesses; overcoming our deficiencies.

Never allow yourself to think meanly, narrowly, poorly of yourself. Never regard yourself as weak, inefficient, diseased, but as perfect, complete, capable. Never even think of the possibility of going through life a failure or a partial failure. Failure and misery are not for the man who has seen the God-side of himself, who has been in touch with divinity. They are for those who have never discovered themselves and their God-like qualities.

Stoutly assert that there is a place for you in the world, and that you are going to fill it like a man. Train yourself to expect great things of yourself. Never admit, even by your manner, that you think you are destined to do little things all your life.

It is marvelous what mental strength can be developed by the perpetual affirmation of vigorous fitness, strength, power, efficiency; these are thoughts and ideals that make a strong man.

The way to get the best out of yourself is to put things right up to yourself, handle yourself without gloves, and talk to yourself as you would to a son of yours who has great ability but who is not using half of it.

When you go into an undertaking just say to yourself, "Now, this thing is right up to me. I've got to make good, to show the man in me or the coward. There is no backing out."

You will be surprised to see how quickly this sort of self-suggestion will brace you up and put new spirit in you.

I have a friend who has helped himself wonderfully by talking to himself about his conduct. When he feels that he is not doing all that he ought to, that he has made some foolish mistake or has failed to use good sense and good judgment in any transaction, when he feels that his stamina and ambition are deteriorating, he goes off alone to the country, to the woods if possible, and has a good heart-to-heart talk with himself something after this fashion:

"Now young man, you need a good talking-to, a bracing-up all along the line. You are going stale, your standards are dropping, your ideals are getting dull, and the worst of it all is that when you do a poor job, or are careless about your dress and indifferent in your manner, you do not feel as troubled as you used to. You are not making good. This lethargy, this inertia, this indifference will seriously cripple your career if you're not very careful. You are letting a lot of good chances slip by you, because you are not as progressive and up-to-date as you ought to be.

"In short, you are becoming lazy. You like to take things easy. Nobody ever amounts to much who lets his energies flag, his standards droop and his ambition ooze out. Now, I am going to keep right after you, young man, until you are doing yourself justice. This take-it-easy sort of policy will never land you at the goal you started for. You will have to watch yourself very closely or you will be left behind.

"You are capable of something much better than what you are doing. You must start out to-day with a firm resolution to make the returns from your work greater to-night than ever before. You must make this a red-letter day. Bestir yourself; get the cobwebs out of your head; brush off the brain ash. Think, think, think to some purpose! Do not mull and mope like this. You are only half-alive, man; get a move on you!"

This young man says that every morning when he finds his standards are down and he feels lazy and indifferent he "hauls himself over the coals," as he calls it, in order to force himself up to a higher standard and put himself in tune for the day. It is the very first thing he attends to.

He forces himself to do the most disagreeable tasks first, and does not allow himself to skip hard problems. "Now, don't be a coward," he says to himself. "If others have done this, you can do it."

By years of stern discipline of this kind he has done wonders with himself. He began as a poor boy living in the slums of New York with no one to take an interest in him, encourage or push him. Though he had little opportunity for schooling when he was a small boy, he has given himself a splendid education, mainly since he was twenty-one. I have never known any one else who carried on such a vigorous campaign in self-victory, self-development, self-training, self-culture as this young man has.

At first it may seem silly to you to be talking to yourself, but you will derive so much benefit from it that you will have recourse to it in remedying all your defects. There is no fault, however great or small, which will not succumb to persistent audible suggestion. For example, you may be naturally timid and shrink from meeting people; and you may distrust your own ability. If so, you will be greatly helped by assuring yourself in your daily self-talks that you are not timid; that, on the contrary, you are the embodiment of courage and bravery. Assure yourself that there is no reason why you should be timid, because there is nothing inferior or peculiar about you; that you are attractive and that you know how to act in the presence of others. Say to yourself that you are never again going to allow yourself to harbor any thoughts of self-depreciation or timidity or inferiority; that you are going to hold your head up and go about as though you were a king, a conqueror, instead of crawling about like a whipped cur; you are going to assert your manhood, your individuality.

If you lack initiative, stoutly affirm your ability to begin things, and to push them to a finish. And always put your resolve into action at the first opportunity.

You will be surprised to see how you can increase your courage, your confidence, and your ability, if you will be sincere with yourself and strong and persistent in your affirmations.

I know of nothing so helpful for the timid, those who lack faith in themselves, as the habit of constantly affirming their own importance, their own power, their own divinity. The trouble is that we do not think half enough of ourselves; do not accurately measure our ability; do not put the right estimate upon our possibilities. We berate ourselves, belittle, efface ourselves, because we do not see the larger, diviner man in us.

Try this experiment the very next time you get discouraged or think that you are a failure, that your work does not amount to much—turn about face. Resolve that you will go no further in that direction. Stop and face the other way, and *go* the other way. Every time you think you are a failure, it helps you to become one, for your thought is your life pattern and you can not get away from it. You can not get away from your ideals, the standard which you hold for yourself, and if you acknowledge in your thought that you are a failure, that you can't do anything worth while, that luck is against you, that you don't have the same opportunity that other people have—-your convictions will control the result.

There are thousands of people who have lost everything they valued in the world, all the material results of their lives' endeavor, and yet, because they possess stout hearts, unconquerable spirits, a determination to push ahead which knows no retreat, they are just as far from real failure as before their loss; and with such wealth they can never be poor.

A great many people fail to reach a success which matches their ability because they are victims of their moods, which repel people and repel business.

We avoid morose, gloomy people just as we avoid a picture which makes a disagreeable impression upon us.

Everywhere we see people with great ambitions doing very ordinary things, simply because there are so many days when they do not "feel like it" or when they are discouraged or "blue."

A man who is at the mercy of a capricious disposition can never be a leader, a power among men.

It is perfectly possible for a well-trained mind to completely rout the worst case of the "blues" in a few minutes; but the trouble with most of us is that instead of flinging open the mental blinds and letting in the sun of cheerfulness, hope, and optimism, we keep them closed and try to eject the darkness by main force.

The art of arts is learning how to clear the mind of its enemies—enemies of our comfort, happiness, and success. It is a great thing to learn to focus the mind upon the beautiful instead of the ugly, the true instead of the false, upon harmony instead of discord, life instead of death, health instead of disease. This is not always easy, but it is possible to everybody. It requires only skilful thinking, the forming of the right thought habits.

The best way to keep out darkness is to keep the life filled with light; to keep out discord, keep it filled with harmony; to shut out error, keep the mind filled with truth; to shut out ugliness, contemplate beauty and loveliness; to get rid of all that is sour and unwholesome, contemplate all that is sweet and wholesome. Opposite thoughts can not occupy the mind at the same time.

No matter whether you feel like it or not, just affirm that you *must* feel like it, that you *will* feel like it, that you *do* feel like it, that you are normal and that you are in a position to do your best. Say it deliberately, affirm it vigorously and it will come true.

The next time you get into trouble, or are discouraged and think you are a failure, just try the experiment of affirming vigorously, persistently, that all that is real *must* be good, for God made all that is, and whatever doesn't seem to be good is not like its creator and therefore can not be real. Persist in this affirmation. You will be surprised to see how unfortunate suggestions and adverse conditions will melt away before it.

The next time you feel the "blues" or a fit of depression coming on, just get by yourself—if possible after taking a good bath and dressing yourself becomingly—and give yourself a good talking-to. Talk to yourself in the same dead-in-earnest way that you would talk to your own child or a dear friend who was deep in the mire of despondency, suffering tortures from melancholy. Drive out the black, hideous pictures which haunt your mind. Sweep away all depressing thoughts, suggestions, all the rubbish that is troubling you. Let go of everything that is unpleasant; all the mistakes, all the disagreeable past; just rise up in arms against the enemies of your peace and happiness; summon all the force you can muster and drive them out. Resolve that no matter what happens you are going to be happy; that you are going to enjoy yourself.

When you look at it squarely, it is very foolish—almost criminal—to go about this beautiful world, crowded with splendid opportunities, and things to delight and cheer us, with a sad, dejected face, as though life had been a disappointment instead of a priceless boon. Just say to yourself, "I am a man and I am going to do the work of a man. It's right up to me and I am going to face the situation."

Do not let anybody or anything shake your faith that you can conquer all the enemies of your peace and happiness, and that you inherit an abundance of all that is good.

We should early form the habit of erasing from the mind all disagreeable, unhealthy, death-dealing thoughts. We should start out every morning with a clean slate. We should blot out from our mental gallery all discordant pictures and replace them with the harmonious, uplifting, life-giving ones.

The next time you feel jaded, discouraged, completely played out and "blue," you will probably find, if you look for the reason, that your condition is largely due to exhausted vitality, either from overwork, overeating, or violating in some way the laws of digestion, or from vicious habits of some kind.

The "blues" are often caused by exhausted nerve cells, due to overstraining work, long-continued excitement, or over-stimulated nerves from dissipation. This condition is caused by the clamoring of exhausted nerve cells for nourishment, rest, or recreation. Multitudes of people suffer from despondency and melancholy, as a result of a run-down condition physically, due to their irregular, vicious habits and a lack of refreshing sleep.

When you are feeling "blue" or discouraged, get as complete a change of environment as possible. Whatever you do, do not brood over your troubles or dwell upon the things which happen to annoy you at the time. Think the pleasantest, happiest things possible. Hold the most charitable, loving thoughts toward others. Make a strenuous effort to radiate joy and gladness to everybody about you. Say the kindest, pleasantest things. You will soon begin to feel a wonderful uplift; the shadows which darkened your mind will flee away, and the sun of joy will light up your whole being.

Stoutly, constantly, everlastingly affirm that you will become what your ambitions indicate as fitting and possible. Do not say, "I shall be a success sometime"; say, "I am a success. Success is my birthright." Do not say that you are going to be happy in the future. Say to yourself, "I was intended for happiness, made for it, and I am happy now."

If, however, you affirm, "I am health; I am prosperity; I am this or that," but do not believe it, you will not be helped by affirmation. *You must believe what you affirm and try to realize it.*

Assert your actual possession of the things you need; of the qualities you long to have. Force your mind toward your goal; hold it there steadily, persistently, for this is the mental state that creates. The negative mind, which doubts and wavers, creates nothing.

"I, myself, am good fortune," says Walt Whitman. If we could only realize that the very attitude of assuming that we are the real embodiment of the thing we long to be or to attain, that we possess the good things we long for, not that we possess all the qualities of good, but that we are these qualities—with the constant affirming, "I myself am good luck, good fortune; I am myself a part of the great creative, sustaining principle of the universe, because my real, divine self and my Father are one"—what a revolution would come to earth's toilers!

Stand for Something

The greatest thing that can be said of a man, no matter how much he has achieved, is that *he has kept his record clean.*

Why is it that, in spite of the ravages of time, the reputation of Lincoln grows larger and his character means more to the world every year? It is because he kept his record clean, and never prostituted his ability nor gambled with his reputation.

Where, in all history, is there an example of a man who was merely rich, no matter how great his wealth, who exerted such a power for good, who was such a living force in civilization, as was this poor backwoods boy? What a powerful illustration of the fact that *character* is the greatest force in the world!

A man assumes importance and becomes a power in the world just as soon as it is found that he stands for something; that he is not for sale; that he will not lease his manhood for salary, for any amount of money or for any influence or position; that he will not lend his name to anything which he can not indorse.

The trouble with so many men to-day is that they do not stand for anything outside their vocation. They may be well educated, well up in their specialties, may have a lot of expert knowledge, but they can not be depended upon. There is some flaw in them which takes the edge off their virtue. They may be fairly honest, but you cannot bank on them.

It is not difficult to find a lawyer or a physician who knows a good deal, who is eminent in his profession; but it is not so easy to find one who is a man before he is a lawyer or a physician; whose name is a synonym for all that is clean, reliable, solid, substantial. It is not difficult to find a good preacher; but it is not so easy to find a real man, sterling manhood, back of the sermon. It is easy to find successful merchants, but not so easy to find men who put character above merchandise. What the world wants is men who have principle underlying their expertness—principle under their law, their medicine, their business; men who stand for something outside of their offices and stores; who stand for something in their community; whose very presence carries weight.

Everywhere we see smart, clever, longheaded, shrewd men, but how comparatively rare it is to find one whose record is as clean as a hound's tooth; who will not swerve from the right; who would rather fail than be a party to a questionable transaction!

Everywhere we see business men putting the stumbling-blocks of deception and dishonest methods right across their own pathway, tripping themselves up while trying to deceive others.

We see men worth millions of dollars filled with terror; trembling lest investigations may uncover things which will damn them in the public estimation! We see them cowed before the law like whipped spaniels; catching at any straw that will save them from public disgrace!

What a terrible thing to live in the limelight of popular favor, to be envied as rich and powerful, to be esteemed as honorable and straightforward, and yet to be conscious all the time of not being what the world thinks we are; to live in constant terror of discovery, in fear that something may happen to unmask us and show us up in our true light! But nothing can happen to injure seriously the man who lives four-square to the world; who has nothing to cover up, nothing to hide from his fellows; who lives a transparent, clean life, with never a fear of disclosures. If all of his material possessions are swept away from him, he knows that he has a monument in the hearts of his countrymen, in the affection and admiration of the people, and that nothing can happen to harm his real self because he has kept his record clean.

Mr. Roosevelt early resolved that, let what would come, whether he succeeded in what he undertook or failed, whether he made friends or enemies, he would not take chances with his good name—he would part with everything else first; that he would never gamble with his reputation; that he would keep his record clean. His first ambition was to stand for something, to be a man. Before he was a politician or anything else the man must come first.

In his early career he had many opportunities to make a great deal of money by allying himself with crooked, sneaking, unscrupulous politicians. He had all sorts of opportunities for political graft. But crookedness never had any attraction for him. He refused to be a party to any political jobbery, any underhand business. He preferred to lose any position he was seeking, to let somebody else have it, if he must get smirched in the getting it. He would not touch a dollar, place, or preferment unless it came to him clean, with no trace of jobbery on it. Politicians who had an "ax to grind" knew it was no use to try to bribe him, or to influence him with promises of patronage, money, position, or power. Mr. Roosevelt knew perfectly well that he would make many mistakes and many enemies, but he resolved to carry himself in such a way that even his enemies should at least respect him for his honesty of purpose, and for his straightforward, "square-deal" methods. He resolved to keep his record clean, his name white, at all hazards. Everything else seemed unimportant in comparison.

In times like these the world especially needs such men as Mr. Roosevelt—men who hew close to the chalk-line of right and hold the line plumb to truth; men who do not pander to public favor; men who make duty and truth their goal and go straight to their mark, turning neither to the right nor to the left, though a paradise tempt them.

Who can ever estimate how much his influence has done toward purging politics and elevating the American ideal. He has changed the view-point of many statesmen and politicians. He has shown them a new and a better way. He has made many of them ashamed of the old methods of grafting and selfish greed. He has held up a new ideal, shown them that unselfish service to their country is infinitely nobler than an ambition for self-aggrandizement. American patriotism has a higher meaning to-day, because of the example of this great American. Many young politicians and statesmen have adopted cleaner methods and higher aims because of his influence. There is no doubt that tens of thousands of young men in this country are cleaner in their lives, and more honest and ambitious to be good citizens, because here is a man who always stands for the "square deal," for civic righteousness, for American manhood.

Every man ought to feel that there is something in him that bribery can not touch, that influence can not buy; something that is not for sale; something he would not sacrifice or tamper with for any price; something he would give his life for if necessary.

If a man stands for something worth while, compels recognition for himself alone, on account of his real worth, he is not dependent upon recommendations; upon fine clothes, a fine house, or a pull. He is his own best recommendation.

The young man who starts out with the resolution to make his character his capital, and to pledge his whole manhood for every obligation he enters into, will not be a failure, though he wins neither fame nor fortune. No man ever really does a great thing who loses his character in the process.

No substitute has ever yet been discovered for honesty. Multitudes of people have gone to the wall trying to find one. Our prisons are full of people who have attempted to substitute something else for it.

No man can really believe in himself when he is occupying a false position and wearing a mask; when the little monitor within him is constantly saying, "You know you are a fraud; you are not the man you pretend to be." The consciousness of not being genuine, not being what others think him to be, robs a man of power, honeycombs the character, and destroys self-respect and self-confidence.

When Lincoln was asked to take the wrong side of a case he said, "I could not do it. All the time while talking to that jury I should be thinking, 'Lincoln, you're a liar, you're a liar,' and I believe I should forget myself and say it out loud."

Character as capital is very much underestimated by a great number of young men. They seem to put more emphasis upon smartness, shrewdness, long-headedness, cunning, influence, a pull, than upon downright honesty and integrity of character. Yet why do scores of concerns pay enormous sums for the use of the name of a man who, perhaps, has been dead for half a century or more? It is because there is power in that name; because there is character in it; because it stands for something; because it represents reliability and square dealing. Think of what the name of Tiffany, of Park and Tilford, or any of the great names which stand in the commercial world as solid and immovable as the rock of Gibraltar, are worth!

Does it not seem strange that young men who know these facts should try to build up a business on a foundation of cunning, scheming, and trickery, instead of building on the solid rock of character, reliability, and manhood? Is it not remarkable that so many men should work so hard to establish a business on an unreliable, flimsy foundation, instead of building upon the solid masonry of honest goods, square dealing, reliability?

A name is worth everything until it is questioned; but when suspicion clings to it, it is worth nothing. There is nothing in this world that will take the place of character. There is no policy in the world, to say nothing of the right or wrong of it, that compares with honesty and square dealing.

In spite of, or because of, all the crookedness and dishonesty that is being uncovered, of all the scoundrels that are being unmasked, integrity is the biggest word in the business world to-day. There never was a time in all history when it was so big, and it is growing bigger. There never was a time when character meant so much in business; when it stood for so much everywhere as it does to-day.

There was a time when the man who was the shrewdest and sharpest and cunningest in taking advantage of others got the biggest salary; but to-day the man at the other end of the bargain is looming up as never before.

Nathan Straus, when asked the secret of the great success of his firm, said it was their treatment of the man at the other end of the bargain. He said they could not afford to make enemies; they could not afford to displease or to take advantage of customers, or to give them reason to think that they had been unfairly dealt with,—that, in the long run, the man who gave the squarest deal to the man at the other end of the bargain would get ahead fastest.

There are merchants who have made great fortunes, but who do not carry weight among their fellow men because they have dealt all their lives with inferiority. They have lived with shoddy and shams so long that the suggestion has been held in their minds until their whole standards of life have been lowered; their ideals have shrunken; their characters have partaken of the quality of their business.

Contrast these men with the men who stood for half a century or more at the head of solid houses, substantial institutions; men who have always stood for quality in everything; who have surrounded themselves not only with ability but with men and women of character.

We instinctively believe in character. We admire people who stand for something; who are centered in truth and honesty. It is not necessary that they agree with us. We admire them for their strength, the honesty of their opinions, the inflexibility of their principles.

The late Carl Schurz was a strong man and antagonized many people. He changed his political views very often; but even his worst enemies knew there was one thing he would never go back on, friends or no friends, party or no party—and that was his devotion to principle as he saw it. There was no parleying with his convictions. He could stand alone, if necessary, with all the world against him. His inconsistencies, his many changes in parties and politics, could not destroy the universal admiration for the man who stood for his convictions. Although he escaped from a German prison and fled his country, where he had been arrested on account of his revolutionary principles when but a mere youth, Emperor William the First had such a profound respect for his honesty of purpose and his strength of character that he invited him to return to Germany and visit him, gave him a public dinner, and paid him great tribute.

Who can estimate the influence of President Eliot in enriching and uplifting our national ideas and standards through the thousands of students who go out from Harvard University? The tremendous force and nobility of character of Phillips Brooks raised everyone who came within his influence to higher levels. His great earnestness in trying to lead people up to his lofty ideals swept everything before it. One could not help feeling while listening to him and watching him that *there* was a mighty triumph of character, a grand expression of superb manhood. Such men as these increase our faith in the race; in the possibilities of the grandeur of the coming man. We are prouder of our country because of such standards.

It is the ideal that determines the direction of the life. And what a grand sight, what an inspiration, are those men who sacrifice the dollar to the ideal!

The principles by which the problem of success is solved are right and justice, honesty and integrity; and just in proportion as a man deviates from these principles he falls short of solving his problem.

It is true that he may reach *something*. He may get money, but is that success? The thief gets money, but does he succeed? Is it any honester to steal by means of a long head than by means of a long arm? It is very much more dishonest, because the victim is deceived and then robbed—a double crime.

We often receive letters which read like this:

"I am getting a good salary; but I do not feel right about it, somehow. I can not still the voice within me that says, 'Wrong, wrong,' to what I am doing."

"Leave it, leave it," we always say to the writers of these letters. "Do not stay in a questionable occupation, no matter what inducement it offers. Its false light will land you on the rocks if you follow it. It is demoralizing to the mental faculties, paralyzing to the character, to do a thing which one's conscience forbids."

Tell the employer who expects you to do questionable things that you can not work for him unless you can put the trade-mark of your manhood, the stamp of your integrity, upon everything you do. Tell him that if the highest thing in you can not bring success, surely the lowest can not. You can not afford to sell the best thing in you, your honor, your manhood, to a dishonest man or a lying institution. You should regard even the suggestion that you might sell out for a consideration as an insult.

Resolve that you will not be paid for being something less than a man; that you will not lease your ability, your education, your inventiveness, your self-respect, for salary, to do a man's lying for him; either in writing advertisements, selling goods, or in any other capacity.

Resolve that, whatever your vocation, you are going to stand for something; that you are not going to be *merely* a lawyer, a physician, a merchant, a clerk, a farmer, a congressman, or a man who carries a big money-bag; but that you are going to be a *man* first, last, and all the time.

Nature's Little Bill

Though the mills of God grind slowly, yet they grind exceeding small;
Though with patience He stands waiting, with exactness grinds He all.— Frederick von Logau

Because sentence against an evil work is not executed speedily, therefore the heart of the sons of men is fully set in them to do evil.— Ecclesiastes

Man is a watch, wound up at first but never
Wound up again: once down he's down forever.— Herrick

Old age seizes upon an ill-spent youth like fire upon a rotten house.—South

Last Sunday a young man died here of extreme old age at twenty-five.—John Newton

If you will not hear Reason, she'll surely rap your knuckles.— Poor Richard's Sayings

"Oh! oh! ah!" exclaimed Franklin; "what have I done to merit these cruel sufferings?" "Many things," replied the Gout; "you have eaten and drunk too freely, and too much indulged those legs of yours in your indolence."

Nature seldom presents her bill on the day you violate her laws. But if you overdraw your account at her bank, and give her a mortgage on your body, be sure she will foreclose. She may loan you all you want; but, like Shylock, she will demand the last ounce of flesh. She rarely brings in her cancer bill before the victim is forty years old. She does not often annoy a man with her drink bill until he is past his prime, and then presents it in the form of Bright's disease, fatty degeneration of the heart, drunkard's liver, or some similar disease. What you pay the saloon keeper is but a small part of your score.

We often hear it said that the age of miracles is past. We marvel that a thief dying on the cross should appear that very day in Paradise; but behold how that bit of meat or vegetable on a Hawarden breakfast table is snatched from Death, transformed into thought, and on the following night shakes Parliament in the magnetism and oratory of a Gladstone. The age of miracles past, when three times a day right before our eyes Nature performs miracles greater even than raising the dead? Watch that crust of bread thrown into a cell in Bedford Jail and devoured by a poor, hungry tinker; cut, crushed, ground, driven by muscles, dissolved by acids and alkalies; absorbed and hurled into the mysterious red river of life. Scores of little factories along this strange stream, waiting for this crust, transmute it as it passes, as if by magic, here into a bone cell, there into gastric juice, here into bile, there into a nerve cell, yonder into a brain cell. We can not trace the processes by which this crust arrives at the muscle and acts, arrives at the brain and thinks. We can not see the manipulating hand which throws back and forth the shuttle which weaves Bunyan's destinies, nor can we trace the subtle alchemy which transforms this prison crust into the finest allegory in the world, the Pilgrim's Progress. But we do know that, unless we supply food when the stomach begs and clamors, brain and muscle can not continue to act; and we also know that unless the food is properly chosen, unless we eat it properly, unless we maintain good digestion by exercise of mind and body, it will not produce the speeches of a Gladstone or the allegories of a Bunyan.

Truly we are fearfully and wonderfully made. Imagine a cistern which would transform the foul sewage of a city into pure drinking water in a second's time, as the black venous blood, foul with the ashes of burned-up brain cells and débris of worn-out tissues, is transformed in the lungs, at every breath, into pure, bright, red blood. Each drop of blood from that magic stream of liquid life was compounded by a divine Chemist. In it float all our success and destiny. In it are the extensions and limits of our possibilities. In it are health and long life, or disease and premature death. In it are our hopes and our fears, our courage, our cowardice, our energy or lassitude, our strength or weakness, our success or failure. In it are susceptibilities of high or broad culture, or pinched or narrow faculties handed down from an uncultured ancestry. From it our bones and nerves, our muscles and brain, our comeliness or ugliness, all come. In it are locked up the elements of a vicious or a gentle life, the tendencies of a criminal or a saint. How important is it, then, that we should obey the laws of health, and thus maintain the purity and power of this our earthly River of Life!

"We hear a great deal about the 'vile body,'" said Spencer, "and many are encouraged by the phrase to transgress the laws of health. But Nature quietly suppresses those who treat thus disrespectfully one of her highest products, and leaves the world to be peopled by the descendants of those who are not so foolish."

Nature gives to him that hath. She shows him the contents of her vast storehouse, and bids him take all he wants and be welcome. But she will not let him keep for years what he does not use. Use or lose is her motto. Every atom we do not utilize this great economist snatches from us.

If you put your arm in a sling and do not use it, Nature will remove the muscle almost to the bone, and the arm will become useless, but in exact proportion to your efforts to use it again she will gradually restore what she took away. Put your mind in the sling of idleness, or inactivity, and in like manner she will remove your brain, even to imbecility. The blacksmith wants one powerful arm, and she gives it to him, but reduces the other. You can, if you will, send all the energy of your life into some one faculty, but all your other faculties will starve.

A young lady may wear tight corsets if she chooses, but Nature will remove the rose from her cheek and put pallor there. She will replace a clear complexion with muddy hues and sallow spots. She will take away the elastic step, the luster from the eye.

Don't expect to have health for nothing. Nothing in this world worth anything can be had for nothing. Health is the prize of a constant struggle.

Nature passes no act without affixing a penalty for its violation. Whenever she is outraged she will have her penalty, although it take a life.

A great surgeon stood before his class to perform a certain operation which the elaborate mechanism and minute knowledge of modern science had only recently made possible. With strong and gentle hand he did his work successfully so far as his part of the terrible business went; and then he turned to his pupils and said, "Two years ago a safe and simple operation might have cured this disease. Six years ago a wise way of life might have prevented it. We have done our best as the case now stands, but Nature will have her word to say. She does not always consent to the repeal of her capital sentences." Next day the patient died.

Apart from accidents, we hold our life largely at will. What business have seventy-five thousand physicians in the United States? It is our own fault that even one-tenth of them get a respectable living. What a commentary upon our modern American civilization that three hundred and fifty thousand people in this country die annually from absolutely preventable diseases! Seneca said, "The gods have given us a long life, but we have made it short." Few people know enough to become old. It is a rare thing for a person to die of old age. Only three or four out of a hundred die of anything like old age. But Nature evidently intended, by the wonderful mechanism of the human body, that we should live well up to a century.

Thomas Parr, of England, lived to the age of one hundred and fifty-two years. He was married when he was a hundred and twenty, and did not leave off work until he was a hundred and thirty. The great Dr. Harvey examined Parr's body, but found no cause of death except a change of living. Henry Jenkins, of Yorkshire, England, lived to be a hundred and sixty-nine, and would probably have lived longer had not the king brought him to London, where luxuries hastened his death. The court records of England show that he was a witness in a trial a hundred and forty years before his death. He swam across a rapid river when he was a hundred.

There is nothing we are more ignorant of than the physiology and chemistry of the human body. Not one person in a thousand can correctly locate important internal organs or describe their use in the animal economy.

What an insult to the Creator who fashioned them so wonderfully and fearfully in His own image, that the graduates from our high schools and even universities, and young women who "finish their education," become proficient in the languages, in music, in art, and have the culture of travel, but can not describe or locate the various organs or functions upon which their lives depend! "The time will come," says Frances Willard, "when it will be told as a relic of our primitive barbarism that children were taught the list of prepositions and the names of the rivers of Thibet, but were not taught the wonderful laws on which their own bodily happiness is based, and the humanities by which they could live in peace and goodwill with those about them." Nothing else is so important to man as the study and knowledge of himself, and yet he knows less of himself than he does of the beasts about him.

The human body is the great poem of the Great Author. Not to learn how to read it, to spell out its meaning, to appreciate its beauties, or to attempt to fathom its mysteries, is a disgrace to our civilization.

What a price mortals pay for their ignorance, let a dwarfed, half-developed, one-sided, short-lived nation answer.

"A brilliant intellect in a sickly body is like gold in a spent swimmer's pocket."

Often, from lack of exercise, one side of the brain gradually becomes paralyzed and deteriorates into imbecility. How intimately the functions of the nervous organs are united! The whole man mourns for a felon. The least swelling presses a nerve against a bone and causes one intense agony, and even a Napoleon becomes a child. A corn on the toe, an affection of the kidneys or of the liver, a boil anywhere on the body, or a carbuncle, may seriously affect the eyes and even the brain. The whole system is a network of nerves, of organs, of functions, which are so intimately joined, and related in such close sympathy, that an injury to one part is immediately felt in every other.

Nature takes note of all our transactions, physical, mental, or moral, and places every item promptly to our debit or credit.

"The gods are just, and of our pleasant vices Make instruments to scourge us."

It is a wonder that we live at all. We violate every law of our being, yet we expect to live to a ripe old age. What would you think of a man who, having an elegant watch delicately adjusted to heat and cold, should leave it on the sidewalk with cases open on a dusty or a rainy day, and yet expect it to keep good time? What would you think of a householder who should leave the doors and windows of his mansion open to thieves and tramps, to winds and dust and rain?

What are our bodies but timepieces made by an Infinite Hand, wound up to run a century, and so delicately adjusted to heat and cold that the temperature will not vary half a degree between the heat of summer and the cold of winter whether we live in the regions of eternal frost or under the burning sun of the tropics? A particle of dust or the slightest friction will throw this wonderful timepiece out of order, yet we often leave it exposed to all the corroding elements. We do not always keep open the twenty-five miles of ventilating pores in the skin by frequent bathing. We seldom lubricate the delicate wheels of the body with the oil of gladness. We expose it to dust and cinders, cold and draughts, and poisonous gases.

How careful we are to filter our water, air our beds, ventilate our sleeping-rooms, and analyze our milk! We shrink from contact with filth and disease. But we put paper colored with arsenic on our walls, and daily breathe its poisonous exhalations. We frequent theaters crowded with human beings, many of whom are uncleanly and diseased. We sit for hours and breathe in upon fourteen hundred square feet of lung tissue the heated, foul, and heavy air; carbonic acid gas from hundreds of gas burners, each consuming as much oxygen as six people; air filled with shreds of tissue expelled from diseased lungs; poisonous effluvia exhaled from the bodies of people who rarely bathe, from clothing seldom washed, fetid breaths, and skin disease in different stages of development. For hours we sit in this bath of poison, and wonder at our headache and lassitude next morning.

We pour a glass of ice water into a stomach busy in the delicate operation of digestion, ignorant or careless of the fact that it takes half an hour to recover from the shock and get the temperature back to ninety-eight degrees, so that the stomach can go on secreting gastric juice. Then down goes another glass of water with similar results.

We pour down alcohol which thickens the velvety lining of the stomach, and hardens the soft tissues, the thin sheaths of nerves, and the gray matter of the brain. We crowd meats, vegetables, pastry, confectionery, nuts, raisins, wines, fruits, etc., into one of the most delicately constructed organs of the body, and expect it to take care of its miscellaneous and incongruous load without a murmur.

After all these abuses we do not give the blood a chance to go to the stomach and help it out of its misery, but summon it to the brain and muscles, notwithstanding the fact that it is so important to have an extra supply to aid digestion that Nature has made the blood vessels of the alimentary canal large enough to contain several times the amount in the entire body.

Who ever saw a horse leave his oats and hay, when hungry, to wash them down with water? The dumb beasts can teach us some valuable lessons in eating and drinking. Nature mixes our gastric juice or pepsin and acids in just the right proportion to digest our food, and keep it at *exactly* the right temperature. If we dilute it, or lower its temperature by ice water, we diminish its solvent or digestive power, and dyspepsia is the natural result.

English factory children have received the commiseration of the world because they were scourged to work fourteen hours out of the twenty-four. But there is many a theoretical republican who is a harsher taskmaster to his stomach than this; who allows it no more resting time than he does his watch; who gives it no Sunday, no holiday, no vacation in any sense, and who seeks to make his heart beat faster for the sake of the exhilaration he can thus produce.

Although the heart weighs a little over half a pound, yet it pumps eighteen pounds of blood from itself, forcing it into every nook and corner of the entire body, back to itself in less than two minutes. This little organ, the most perfect engine in the world, does a daily work equal to lifting one hundred and twenty-four tons one foot high, and exerts one-third as much muscle power as does a stout man at hard labor. If the heart should expend its entire force lifting its own weight, it would raise itself nearly twenty thousand feet an hour, ten times as high as a pedestrian can lift himself in ascending a mountain. What folly, then, to goad this willing, hard-working slave to greater exertions by stimulants!

We must pay the penalty of our vocations. Beware of work that kills the workman. Those who prize long life should avoid all occupations which compel them to breathe impure air or deleterious gases, and especially those in which they are obliged to inhale dust and filings from steel and brass and iron, the dust in coal mines, and dust from threshing machines. Stone-cutters, miners, and steel grinders are short lived, the sharp particles of dust irritating and inflaming the tender lining of the lung cells. The knife and fork grinders in Manchester, England, rarely live beyond thirty-two years. Those who work in grain elevators and those who are compelled to breathe chemical poisons are short lived.

Deep breathing in dusty places sends the particles of dust into the upper and less used lobes of the lungs, and these become a constant irritant, until they finally excite an inflammation, which may end in consumption. All occupations in which arsenic is used shorten life.

Dr. William Ogle, who is authority upon this subject, says, "Of all the various influences that tend to produce differences of mortality in any community, none is more potent than the character of the prevailing occupations." Finding that clergymen and priests have the lowest death-rate, he represented it as one hundred, and by comparison found that the rate for inn and hotel servants was three hundred and ninety-seven; miners, three hundred and thirty-one; earthenware makers, three hundred and seventeen; file makers, three hundred; innkeepers, two hundred and seventy-four; gardeners, farmers, and agricultural laborers closely approximating the clerical standard. He gave as the causes of high mortality, first, working in a cramped or constrained attitude; second, exposure to the action of poisonous or irritating substances; third, excessive work, mental or physical; fourth, working in confined or foul air; fifth, the use of strong drink; sixth, differences in liability to fatal accidents; seventh, exposure to the inhalation of dust. The deaths of those engaged in alcoholic industries were as one thousand five hundred and twenty-one to one thousand of the average of all trades.

It is very important that occupations should be congenial. Whenever our work galls us, whenever we feel it to be a drudgery and uncongenial, the friction grinds life away at a terrible rate.

Health can be accumulated, invested, and made to yield its compound interest, and thus be doubled and redoubled. The capital of health may, indeed, be forfeited by one misdemeanor, as a rich man may sink all his property in one bad speculation; but it is as capable of being increased as any other kind of capital.

One is inclined to think with a recent writer that it looks as if the rich men kept out of the kingdom of heaven were also excluded from the kingdom of brains. In New York, Boston, Philadelphia, and Chicago are thousands of millionaires, some of them running through three or four generations of fortune; and yet, in all their ranks, there is seldom a man possessed of the higher intellectual qualities that flower in literature, eloquence, or statesmanship. Scarcely one of them has produced a book worth printing, a poem worth reading, or a speech worth listening to. They are struck with intellectual sterility. They go to college; they travel abroad; they hire the dearest masters; they keep libraries among their furniture; and some of them buy works of art. But, for all that, their brains wither under luxury, often by their own vices or tomfooleries, and mental barrenness is the result. He who violates Nature's law must suffer the penalty, though he have millions. The fruits of intellect do not grow among the indolent rich. They are usually out of the republic of brains. Work or starve is Nature's motto; starve mentally, starve morally, even if you are rich enough to prevent physical starvation.

How heavy a bill Nature collects of him in whom the sexual instinct has been permitted to taint the whole life with illicit thoughts and deeds, stultifying the intellect, deadening the sensibilities, dwarfing the soul!

"I waive the quantum of the sin,
The hazard of concealing;
But och, it hardens all within,
And petrifies the feeling."

The sense of fatigue is one of Nature's many signals of danger. All we accomplish by stimulating or crowding the body or mind when tired is worse than lost. Insomnia, and sometimes even insanity, is Nature's penalty for prolonged loss of sleep.

One of the worst tortures of the Inquisition was that of keeping victims from sleeping, often driving them to insanity or death. Melancholy follows insomnia; insanity, both. To keep us in a healthy condition, Nature takes us back to herself, puts us under the ether of sleep, and keeps us there nearly one-third of our lives, while she overhauls and repairs in secret our wonderful mechanism. She takes us back each night wasted and dusty from the day's work, broken, scarred, and injured in the great struggle of life. Each cell of the brain is reburnished and refreshed; all the ashes or waste from the combustion of the tissues is washed out into the blood stream, pumped to the lungs, and thrown out in the breath; and the body is returned in the morning as fresh and good as new. The American honey does not always pay for the sting.

Labor is the eternal condition on which the rich man gains an appetite for his dinner, and the poor man a dinner for his appetite; but the habit of constant, perpetual industry often becomes a disease.

In the Norse legend, Allfader was not allowed to drink from Mirmir's Spring, the fount of wisdom, until he had left his eye as a pledge. Scholars often leave their health, their happiness, their usefulness behind, in their great eagerness to drink deep draughts at wisdom's fountain. Professional men often sacrifice everything that is valuable in life for the sake of reputation, influence, and money. Business men sacrifice home, family, health, happiness, in the great struggle for money and power. The American prize, like the pearl in the oyster, is very attractive, but is too often the result of disease.

Charles Linnaeus, the great naturalist, so exhausted his brain by over-exertion that he could not recognize his own work, and even forgot his own name. Kirk White won the prize at Cambridge, but it cost him his life. He studied at night and forced his brain by stimulants and narcotics in his endeavor to pull through, but he died at twenty-four. Paley died at sixty-two of overwork. He was called "one of the sublimest spirits in the world."

President Timothy Dwight of Yale College nearly killed himself by overwork when a young man. When at Yale he studied nine hours, taught six hours a day, and took no exercise whatever. He could not be induced to stop until he became so nervous and irritable that he was unable to look at a book ten minutes a day. His mind gave way, and it was a long time before he fully recovered.

Imagine the surprise of the angels at the death of men and women in the early prime and vigor of life. Could we but read the notes of their autopsies we might say less of mysterious Providence at funerals. They would run somewhat as follows:—

Notes from the Angels' Autopsies

What, is it returned so soon?—a body framed for a century's use returned at thirty?—a temple which was twenty-eight years in building destroyed almost before it was completed? What have gray hairs, wrinkles, a bent form, and death to do with youth?

Has all this beauty perished like a bud just bursting into bloom, plucked by the grim destroyer? Has she fallen a victim to tight-lacing, over-excitement, and the gaiety and frivolity of fashionable life?

Here is an educated, refined woman who died of lung starvation. What a tax human beings pay for breathing impure air! Nature provides them with a tonic atmosphere, compounded by the divine Chemist, but they refuse to breathe it in its purity, and so must pay the penalty in shortened lives. They can live a long time without water, a longer time without food, clothing, or the so-called comforts of life; they can live without education or culture, but their lungs must have good, healthful air-food twenty-four thousand times a day if they would maintain health. Oh, that they would see, as we do, the intimate connection between bad air, bad morals, and a tendency to crime!

Here are the ruins of an idolized son and loving husband. Educated and refined, what infinite possibilities beckoned him onward at the beginning of his career! But the Devil's agent offered him imagination, sprightliness, wit, eloquence, bodily strength, and happiness in *eau de vie*, or "water of life," as he called it, at only fifteen cents a glass. The best of our company tried to dissuade him, but to no avail. The poor mortal closed his "bargain" with the dramseller, and what did he get? A hardened conscience, a ruined home, a diseased body, a muddled brain, a heartbroken wife, wretched children, disappointed friends, triumphant enemies, days of remorse, nights of anguish, an unwept deathbed, an unhonored grave. And only to think that he is only one of many thousands! "What fools these mortals be!"

Did he not see the destruction toward which he was rushing with all the feverish haste of slavish appetite? Ah, yes, but only when it was too late. In his clenched hand, as he lay dead, was found a crumpled paper containing the following, in lines barely legible so tremulous were the nerves of the writer: "Wife, children, and over forty thousand dollars all gone! I alone am responsible. All has gone down my throat. When I was twenty-one I had a fortune. I am not yet thirty-five years old. I have killed my beautiful wife, who died of a broken heart; have murdered our children with neglect. When this coin is gone I do not know how I can get my next meal. I shall die a drunken pauper. This is my last money, and my history. If this bill comes into the hands of any man who drinks, let him take warning from my life's ruin."

What a magnificent specimen of manhood this would have been if his life had been under the rule of reason, not passion! He dies of old age at forty, his hair is gray, his eyes are sunken, his complexion sodden, his body marked with the labels of his disease. A physique fit for a god, fashioned in the Creator's image, with infinite possibilities, a physiological hulk wrecked on passion's seas, and fit only for a danger signal to warn the race. What would parents think of a captain who would leave his son in charge of a ship without giving him any instructions or chart showing the rocks, reefs, and shoals? Do they not know that those who sleep in the ocean are but a handful compared with those who have foundered on passion's seas? Oh, the sins of silence which parents commit against those dearer to them than life itself! Youth can not understand the great solicitude of parents regarding their education, their associations, their welfare generally, and the mysterious silence in regard to their physical natures. An intelligent explanation, by all mothers to the daughters and by all fathers to the sons, of the mysteries of their physical lives, when at the right age, would revolutionize civilization.

This young clergyman killed himself trying to be popular. This student committed suicide by exhausting his brain in trying to lead his class. This young lawyer overdrew his account at Nature's bank, and she foreclosed by a stroke of paralysis.

This merchant died at thirty-five by his own hand. His life was slipping away without enjoyment. He had murdered his capacity for happiness, and dug his own spiritual grave while making preparations for enjoying life. This young society man died of nothing to do and dissipation, at thirty.

What a miserable farce the life of men and women seems to us! Time, which is so precious that even the Creator will not give a second moment until the first is gone, they throw away as though it were water. Opportunities which angels covet they fling away as of no consequence, and die failures, because they have "no chance in life." Life, which seems so precious to us, they spurn as if but a bauble. Scarcely a mortal returns to us who has not robbed himself of years of precious life. Scarcely a man returns to us dropping off in genuine old age, as autumn leaves drop in the forest.

Has life become so cheap that mortals thus throw it away?

Habit—The Servant,—the Master

Habit, if wisely and skilfully formed, becomes truly a second nature.— Bacon

Habit, with its iron sinews,
Clasps and leads us day by day.— Lamartine

The chain of habit coils itself around the heart like a serpent, to gnaw and stifle it.— Hazlitt

You can not, in any given case, by any sudden and single effort, will to be true, if the habit of your life has been insincerity.— F. W. Robertson

It is a beautiful provision in the mental and moral arrangement of our nature, that that which is performed as a duty may by frequent repetition, become a habit; and the habit of stern virtue, so repulsive to others, may hang around our neck like a wreath of flowers.— Paxton Hood

"When shall I begin to train my child?" asked a young mother of a learned physician.

"How old is the child?" inquired the doctor.

"Two years, sir."

"Then you have lost just two years," replied he, gravely.

"You must begin with his grandmother," said Oliver Wendell Holmes, when asked a similar question.

"At the mouth of the Mississippi," says Beecher, "how impossible would it be to stay its waters, and to separate from each other the drops from the various streams that have poured in on either side,—of the Red River, the Arkansas, the Ohio, and the Missouri,—or to sift, grain by grain the particles of sand that have been washed from the Alleghany, or the Rocky Mountains; yet how much more impossible would it be when character is the river, and habits are the side-streams!"

"We sow an act, we reap a habit; we sow a habit, we reap a character."

While correct habits depend largely on self-discipline, and often on self-denial, bad habits, like weeds, spring up, unaided and untrained, to choke the plants of virtue and as with Canada thistles, allowed to go to seed in a fair meadow, we may have "one day's seeding, ten years' weeding."

We seldom see much change in people after they get to be twenty-five or thirty years of age, except in going further in the way they have started; but it is a great comfort to think that, when one is young, it is almost as easy to acquire a good habit as a bad one, and that it is possible to be hardened in goodness as well as in evil.

Take good care of the first twenty years of your life, and you may hope that the last twenty will take good care of you.

A writer on the history of Staffordshire tells of an idiot who, living near a town clock, and always amusing himself by counting the hour of the day whenever the clock struck, continued to strike and count the hour correctly without its aid, when at one time it happened to be injured by an accident.

Dr. Johnson had acquired the habit of touching every post he passed in the street; and, if he missed one, he was uneasy, irritable, and nervous till he went back and touched the neglected post.

"Even thought is but a habit."

Heredity is a man's habit transmitted to his offspring.

A special study of hereditary drunkenness has been made by Professor Pellman of Bonn University, Germany. He thus traced the careers of children, grandchildren, and great-grandchildren in all parts of the present German Empire, until he was able to present tabulated biographies of the hundreds descended from some original drunkard. Notable among the persons described by Professor Pellman is Frau Ada Jurke, who was born in 1740, and was a drunkard, a thief, and a tramp for the last forty years of her life, which ended in 1800. Her descendants numbered 834, of whom 709 were traced in local records from youth to death. One hundred and six of the 709 were born out of wedlock. There were 144 beggars, and 62 more who lived from charity. Of the women, 181 led disreputable lives. There were in the family 76 convicts, 7 of whom were sentenced for murder. In a period of some seventy-five years, this one family rolled up a bill of costs in almshouses, prisons, and correctional institutions amounting to at least 5,000,000 marks, or about $1,250,000.

Isaac Watts had a habit of rhyming. His father grew weary of it, and set out to punish him, which made the boy cry out:—

"Pray, father, on me mercy take,
And I will no more verses make."

A minister had a bad habit of exaggeration, which seriously impaired his usefulness. His brethren came to expostulate. With extreme humiliation over this fault as they set it forth, he said, "Brethren, I have long mourned over this fault, and I have shed *barrels of tears* because of it." They gave him up as incorrigible.

Men carelessly or playfully get into habits of speech or act which become so natural that they speak or act as they do not intend, to their discomfiture. Professor Phelps told of some Andover students, who, for sport, interchanged the initial consonants of adjacent words. "But," said he, "retribution overtook them. On a certain morning, when one of them was leading the devotions, he prayed the Lord to 'have mercy on us, feak and weeble sinners.'" The habit had come to possess him.

Many speakers have undesirable habits of utterance or gesture. Some are continually applying the hand to some part of the face, the chin, the whiskers; some give the nose a peck with thumb and forefinger; others have the habit characterized as,—

"Washing the hands with invisible soap
In a bowl of invisible water."

"We are continually denying that we have habits which we have been practising all our lives," says Beecher. "Here is a man who has lived forty or fifty years; and a chance shot sentence or word lances him, and reveals to him a trait which he has always possessed, but which, until now, he had not the remotest idea that he possessed. For forty or fifty years he has been fooling himself about a matter as plain as the nose on his face."

Had the angels been consulted, whether to create man, with this principle introduced, that, *if a man did a thing once, if would be easier the second time, and at length would be done without effort*, they would have said, "Create!"

Remember that habit is an arrangement, a principle of human nature, which we must use to increase the efficiency and ease of our work in life.

"Make sobriety a habit, and intemperance will be hateful; make prudence a habit, and reckless profligacy will be as contrary to the course of nature in the child, or in the adult, as the most atrocious crimes are to any of us."

Out of hundreds of replies from successful men as to the probable cause of failure, "bad habits" was in almost every one.

How easy it is to be nobody; it is the simplest thing in the world to drift down the stream, into bad company, into the saloon; just a little beer, just a little gambling, just a little bad company, just a little killing of time, and the work is done.

New Orleans is from five to fifteen feet below high water in the Mississippi River. The only protection to the city from the river is the levee. In May, 1883, a small break was observed in the levee, and the water was running through. A few bags of sand or loads of dirt would have stopped the water at first; but it was neglected for a few hours, and the current became so strong that all efforts to stop it were fruitless. A reward of five hundred thousand dollars was offered to any man who would stop it; but it was too late—it could not be done.

Beware of "small sins" and "white lies."

A man of experience says: "There are four good habits,—punctuality, accuracy, steadiness, and dispatch. Without the first, time is wasted; without the second, mistakes the most hurtful to our own credit and interest, and those of others, may be committed; without the third, nothing can be well done; and without the fourth, opportunities of great advantage are lost, which it is impossible to recall."

Abraham Lincoln gained his clear precision of statement of propositions by practise, and Wendell Phillips his wonderful English diction by always thinking and conversing in excellent style.

"Family customs exercise a vast influence over the world. Children go forth from the parent-nest, spreading the habits they have imbibed over every phase of society. These can easily be traced to their sources."

"To be sure, this is only a trifle in itself; but, then, the manner in which I do every trifling thing is of very great consequence, because it is just in these little things that I am forming my business habits. I must see to it that I do not fail here, even if this is only a small task."

"A physical habit is like a tree grown crooked. You can not go to the orchard, and take hold of a tree grown thus, and straighten it, and say, 'Now keep straight!' and have it obey you. What can you do? You can drive down a stake, and bind the tree to it, bending it back a little, and scarifying the bark on one side. And if, after that, you bend it back a little more every month, keeping it taut through the season, and from season to season, at length you will succeed in making it permanently straight. You can straighten it, but you can not do it immediately; you must take one or two years for it."

Sir George Staunton visited a man in India who had committed murder; and in order not only to save his life, but what was of much greater consequence to him, his caste, he had submitted to a terrible penalty,—to sleep for seven years on a bed, the entire top of which was studded with iron points, as sharp as they could be without penetrating the flesh. Sir George saw him during the fifth year of his sentence. His skin then was like the hide of a rhinoceros; and he could sleep comfortably on his bed of thorns, and he said that at the end of the seven years he thought he should use the same bed from choice. What a vivid parable of a sinful life! Sin, at first a bed of thorns, after a time becomes comfortable through the deadening of moral sensibility.

When the suspension bridge over Niagara River was to be erected, the question was, how to get the cable over. With a favoring wind a kite was elevated, which alighted on the opposite shores. To its insignificant string a cord was attached, which was drawn over, then a rope, then a larger one, then a cable; finally the great bridge was completed, connecting the United States with Canada.

First across the gulf we cast
Kite-borne threads till lines are passed,
And habit builds the bridge at last.

"Launch your bark on the Niagara River," said John B. Gough; "it is bright, smooth, and beautiful, Down the stream you glide on your pleasure excursion. Suddenly some one cries out from the bank, 'Young men, ahoy!' 'What is it?'

"'The rapids are below you.' 'Ha! ha! we have heard of the rapids, but we are not such fools as to get there. If we go too fast, then we shall up with the helm, and steer to the shore. Then on, boys, don't be alarmed—there is no danger.'

"'Young men, ahoy there!' 'What is it?' 'The rapids are below you!' 'Ha! ha! we will laugh and quaff. What care we for the future? No man ever saw it. Sufficient for the day is the evil thereof. We will enjoy life while we may, will catch pleasure as it flies. There's time enough to steer out of danger.'

"'Young men, ahoy!' 'What is it?' 'Beware! Beware! The rapids are below you!'

"Now you see the water foaming all around. See how fast you pass that point! Up with the helm! Now turn! Pull hard! Quick, quick! Pull for your lives! Pull till the blood starts from the nostrils, and the veins stand like whip-cords upon the brow! Set the mast in the socket! hoist the sail—ah! ah! it is too late! Shrieking, cursing, howling, blaspheming, over you go.

"Thousands go over the rapids every year, through the power of habit, crying all the while, 'When I find out that it is injuring me, I will give it up!'"

A community is often surprised and shocked at some crime. The man was seen on the street yesterday, or in his store, but he showed no indication that he would commit such crime to-day. Yet the crime committed to-day is but a regular and natural sequence of what the man did yesterday and the day before. It was but a result of the fearful momentum of all his past habits.

A painter once wanted a picture of innocence, and drew from life the likeness of a child at prayer. The little suppliant was kneeling by his mother. The palms of his hands were reverently pressed together, and his mild blue eyes were upturned with the expression of devotion and peace. The portrait was much prized by the painter, who hung it up on his wall, and called it "Innocence." Years passed away, and the artist became an old man. Still the picture hung there. He had often thought of painting a counterpart,—the picture of guilt,—but had not found the opportunity. At last he effected his purpose by paying a visit to a neighboring jail. On the damp floor of his cell lay a wretched culprit heavily ironed. Wasted was his body, and hollow his eyes; vice was visible in his face. The painter succeeded admirably; and the portraits were hung side by side for "Innocence" and "Guilt." The two originals of the pictures were discovered to be one and the same person,—first, in the innocence of childhood! second, in the degradation of guilt and sin and evil habits.

Will-power can be so educated that it will focus the thought upon the bright side of things, upon objects which lift and elevate. Habits of contentment and goodness may be formed the same as any others.

Walking upon the quarter-deck of a vessel, though at first intolerably confining, becomes by custom so agreeable to a sailor that on shore he often hems himself within the same bounds. Lord Kames tells of a man who, having relinquished the sea for a country life, reared an artificial mount, with a level summit, resembling a quarter-deck not only in shape, but in size, where he generally walked. When Franklin was superintending the erection of some forts on the frontier, as a defense against the Indians, he slept at night in a blanket on a hard floor; and, on his first return to civilized life, he could hardly sleep in a bed. Captain Ross and his crew, having been accustomed, during their polar wanderings, to lie on the frozen snow or a bare rock, afterwards found the accommodations of a whaler too luxurious for them, and the captain exchanged his hammock for a chair.

Two sailors, who had been drinking, took a boat off to their ship. They rowed but made no progress; and presently each began to accuse the other of not working hard enough. Lustily they plied the oars, but after another hour's work still found themselves no farther advanced. By this time they had become tolerably sober; and one of them, looking over the side, said to the other, "Why, Tom, we haven't pulled the anchor up yet." And thus it is with those who are anchored to something of which they are not conscious, perhaps, but which impedes their efforts, even though they do their very best.

"A youth thoughtless, when all the happiness of his home forever depends on the chances or the passions of an hour!" exclaims Ruskin. "A youth thoughtless, when his every act is a foundation-stone of future conduct, and every imagination a fountain of life or death! Be thoughtless in any after years, rather than now,—though, indeed, there is only one place where a man may be nobly thoughtless,—his deathbed. No thinking should ever be left to be done there."

Sir James Paget tells us that a practised musician can play on the piano at the rate of twenty-four notes a second. For each note a nerve current must be transmitted from the brain to the fingers, and from the fingers to the brain. Each note requires three movements of a finger, the bending down and raising up, and at least one lateral, making no less than seventy-two motions in a second, each requiring a distinct effort of the will, and directed unerringly with a certain speed, and a certain force, to a certain place.

Some can do this easily, and be at the same time busily employed in intelligent conversation. Thus, by obeying the law of habit until repetition has formed a second nature, we are able to pass the technique of life almost wholly over to the nerve centers, leaving our minds free to act or enjoy.

All through our lives the brain is constantly educating different parts of the body to form habits which will work automatically from reflex action, and thus is delegated to the nervous system a large part of life's duties. This is nature's wonderful economy to release the brain from the drudgery of individual acts, and leave it free to command all its forces for higher service.

Man's life-work is a masterpiece or a botch, according as each little habit has been perfectly or carelessly formed.

It is said that if you invite one of the devil's children to your home the whole family will follow. So one bad habit seems to have a relationship with all the others. For instance, the one habit of negligence, slovenliness, makes it easier to form others equally bad, until the entire character is honeycombed by the invasion of a family of bad habits.

A man is often shocked when he suddenly discovers that he is considered a liar. He never dreamed of forming such a habit; but the little misrepresentations to gain some temporary end, had, before he was aware of it, made a beaten track in the nerve and brain tissue, until lying has become almost a physical necessity. He thinks he can easily overcome this habit, but he will not. He is bound to it with cords of steel; and only by painful, watchful, and careful repetition of the exact truth, with a special effort of the will-power at each act, can he form a counter trunk-line in the nerve and brain tissue. Society is often shocked by the criminal act of a man who has always been considered upright and true. But, if they could examine the habit-map in his nervous mechanism and brain, they would find the beginnings of a path leading directly to his deed, in the tiny repetitions of what he regarded as trivial acts. All expert and technical education is built upon the theory that these trunk-lines of habit become more and more sensitive to their accustomed stimuli, and respond more and more readily.

We are apt to overlook the physical basis of habit. Every repetition of an act makes us more likely to perform that act, and discovers in our wonderful mechanism a tendency to perpetual repetition, whose facility increases in exact proportion to the repetition. Finally the original act becomes voluntary from a natural reaction.

It is cruel to teach the vicious that they can, by mere force of will-power, turn "about face," and go in the other direction, without explaining to them the scientific process of character-building, through habit-formation. What we do to-day is practically what we did yesterday; and, in spite of resolutions, unless carried out in this scientific way, we shall repeat to-morrow what we have done to-day. How unfortunate that the science of habit-forming is not known by mothers, and taught in our schools, colleges, and universities! It is a science compared with which other departments of education sink into insignificance. The converted man is not always told that the great battle is yet before him; that he must persistently, painfully, prayerfully, and with all the will-power he possesses, break up the old habits, and lay counter lines which will lead to the temple of virtue. He is not told that, in spite of all his efforts, in some unguarded moment, some old switch may be left open, some old desire may flash along the line, and that, possibly before he is aware of it, he may find himself yielding to the old temptation which he had supposed to be conquered forever.

An old soldier was walking home with a beefsteak in one hand and a basket of eggs in the other, when some one yelled, "Halt! Attention!" Instantly the veteran came to a stand; and, as his arms took the position of "attention," eggs and meat went tumbling into the street, the accustomed nerves responding involuntarily to the old stimulus.

Paul evidently understood the force of habit. "I find, then," he declares, "the law, that to me who would do good, evil is present. For I delight in the law of God after the inward man; but I see a different law in my members, warring against the law in my mind, and bringing me into captivity, under the law of sin, which is in my members. O wretched man that I am! who shall deliver me from the body of this death!" He referred to the ancient custom of binding a murderer face to face with the dead body of his victim, until suffocated by its stench and dissolution.

"I would give a world, if I had it," said an unfortunate wretch, "to be a true man; yet in twenty-four hours I may be overcome and disgraced with a shilling's worth of sin."

"How shall I a habit break?"
As you did that habit make.
As you gathered, you must lose;
As you yielded, now refuse.
Thread by thread the strands we twist,
Till they bind us, neck and wrist;
Thread by thread the patient hand
Must untwine, ere free we stand;
As we builded, stone by stone,
We must toil unhelped, alone,
Till the wall is overthrown.

The Cigarette

We are so accustomed to the sight and smell of tobacco that we entirely overlook the fact that the tobacco of commerce in all its forms is the product of a poisonous weed. It is first a narcotic and then an irritant poison. It has its place in all toxicological classifications together with its proper antidotes.

Tobacco has not achieved its almost universal popularity without strong opposition. In England King James launched his famous "Counterblaste" against its use. In Turkey, where men and women are alike slaves to its fascination, tobacco was originally forbidden under severe penalties; the loss of the ears, the slitting of the nostrils and even death itself being penalties imposed for the infraction of the law forbidding the use of tobacco in any form. Since then pipes, cigars, snuff and chewing tobacco have become popularized and tobacco in some form or another is used by almost every nation. The last development in the form of tobacco using was the cigarette rolled between the fingers, and the worst form of the cigarette is the manufactured article sold in cheap packages and freely used by boys who in many cases have not reached their teens.

The manufactured American cigarette seems to be especially deadly in its effect. It is said to contain five and one-half per cent. of nicotine, or more than twice as much as the Cuban-made cigarette contains, and more than six times as much as is contained in the Turkish cigarette.

I am not going to quarrel with the use of tobacco in general by mature men. He who has come to man's estate is free to decide for himself whether he shall force a poison on his revolting stomach; for the nausea that follows the first use of tobacco is the stomach's attempt to eject the poison which has been absorbed from pipe, cigar, or cigarette. The grown man, too, is able to determine whether he wants to pay the tax which the use of tobacco levies upon his time, his health, his income and his prosperity. The most that can be said of the use of tobacco is that if habitual users of the narcotic weed are successful in life they must be successful in spite of the use of tobacco and not because of it; for it is opposed to both reason and common sense that the habitual use of a poison in any form should promote the development and exercise of the faculties whose energetic use is essential to success.

What I desire to do is to warn the boy, the growing youth, of the baneful influence of the cigarette on minds yet unformed, on bodies yet in process of development.

The danger of the cigarette to the growing boy lies first in the fact that it poisons the body. That it does not kill at the outset is due to the fact that the dose is small and so slowly increased that the body gradually accommodates itself to this poison as it does to strychnine, arsenic, opium, and other poisons. But all the time there is a slow but steady process of physical degeneration. The digestion is affected, the heart is overtaxed, liver and bowels are deranged in their functions, and as the poison spreads throughout the system there is a gradual physical deterioration which is marked alike in the countenance and in the carriage of the body. Any person who cares to do so may prove for himself the poisonous nature of nicotine which is derived from tobacco and taken into the system by those who chew or smoke.

Dr. J. J. Kellogg says: "A few months ago I had all the nicotine removed from a cigarette, making a solution of it. I injected half the quantity into a frog, with the effect that the frog died almost instantly. The rest was administered to another frog with like effect. Both frogs were full grown, and of average size. The conclusion is evident that a single cigarette contains poison enough to kill two frogs. A boy who smokes twenty cigarettes a day has inhaled enough poison to kill forty frogs. Why does the poison not kill the boy? It does tend to kill him. If not immediately, he is likely to die sooner or later of weak heart, Bright's disease, or some other malady which scientific physicians everywhere now recognize as a natural result of chronic nicotine poisoning."

A chemist, not long since, took the tobacco used in an average cigarette and soaked it in several teaspoonfuls of water and then injected a portion of it under the skin of a cat. The cat almost immediately went into convulsions, and died in fifteen minutes. Dogs have been killed with a single drop of nicotine.

A single drop of nicotine taken from a seasoned pipe, and applied to the tongue of a venomous snake has caused almost instant death.

A Western farmer tried to rear a brood of motherless chickens in his greenhouse. But the chickens did not thrive. They refused to eat; their skins became dry and harsh; their feathers were ruffled; they were feverish and drank constantly. Soon they began to die. As the temperature and general condition of the greenhouse seemed to be especially favorable to the rearing of chickens, the florist was puzzled to determine the cause of their sickness and death. After a careful study of the symptoms he found that the source of the trouble arose from the fumes of the tobacco stems burned in the greenhouse to destroy green flies and destructive plant parasites. Though the chickens had always been removed from the greenhouse during the tobacco fumigation and were not returned while any trace of smoke was apparent to the human senses, it was evident that the soil, air, and leaves of the plants retained enough of the poison to keep the chickens in a condition of semi-intoxication. The conditions were promptly changed, and the chickens removed to other quarters recovered rapidly and in a short time were healthy and lively though they were stunted in growth because of this temporary exposure to the effects of nicotine. The symptoms in the chickens were almost identical with the symptoms of nicotine poisoning in young boys, and the effects were relatively the same.

The most moderate use of the cigarette is injurious to the body and mind of the youth; excessive indulgence leads inevitably to insanity and death.

A young man died in a Minnesota state institution not long ago, who, five years before, had been one of the most promising young physicians of the West. "Still under thirty years at the time of his commitment to the institution," says the newspaper account of his story, "he had already made three discoveries in nervous diseases that had made him looked up to in his profession. But he smoked cigarettes,—smoked incessantly. For a long time the effects of the habit were not apparent on him. In fact, it was not until a patient died on the operating table under his hands, and the young doctor went to pieces, that it became known that he was a victim of the paper pipes. But then he had gone too far. He was a wreck in mind as well as in body, and he ended his days in a maniac's cell."

Another unfortunate victim of the cigarette was, not long ago, taken to the Brooklyn Hospital. He was a fireman on the railroad and was only twenty-one years old. He said he began smoking cigarettes when a mere boy. Before being taken to the hospital he smoked all night for weeks without sleep. When in the hospital he recognized none, but called loudly to everyone he saw to kill him. He would batter his head against the wall in the attempt to commit suicide. At length he was taken to the King's County Hospital in a strait jacket, where death soon relieved him of his sufferings.

Similar results are following the excessive use of cigarettes, every day and in all sections of the country.

"Died of heart failure" is the daily verdict on scores of those who drop down at the desk or in the street. Can not this sudden taking off, of apparently hale and sturdy men be related, oftentimes to the heart weakness caused by the excessive use of tobacco and particularly of cigarettes?

Excessive cigarette smoking increases the heart's action very materially, in some instances twenty-five or thirty beats a minute. Think of the enormous amount of extra work forced upon this delicate organ every twenty-four hours! The pulsations are not only greatly increased but also very materially weakened, so that the blood is not forced to every part of the system, and hence the tissues are not nourished as they would be by means of fewer but stronger, more vigorous pulsations.

The indulgence in cigarettes stunts the growth and retards physical development. An investigation of all the students who entered Yale University during nine years shows that the cigarette smokers were the inferiors, both in weight and lung capacity, of the non-smokers, although they averaged fifteen months older.

It has been said that the universal habit of smoking has made Germany "a spectacled nation." Tobacco greatly irritates the eyes, and injuriously affects the optic nerves. The eyes of boys who use cigarettes to excess grow dull and weak, and every feature shows the mark of the insidious poison. The face is pallid and haggard, the cheeks hollow, the skin drawn, there is a loss of frankness of expression, the eyes are shifty, the movements nervous and uncertain, and all this is but preliminary to the ultimate degradation and loss of self-respect which follow the victim of the cigarette habit, through years of misery and failure.

Side by side with physical deterioration there goes on a process of moral degeneration which robs the cigarette smoking boy of refinement, of manners. The moral depravity which follows cigarette habit is appalling. Lying, cheating, swearing, impurity, loss of courage and manhood, a complete dropping of life's standards, result from such indulgence.

Magistrate Crane, of New York City, says: "Ninety-nine out of a hundred boys between the ages of ten and seventeen years who come before me charged with crime have their fingers disfigured by yellow cigarette stains—I am not a crank on this subject, I do not care to pose as a reformer, but it is my opinion that cigarettes will do more than liquor to ruin boys. When you have arraigned before you boys hopelessly deaf through the excessive use of cigarettes, boys who have stolen their sisters' earnings, boys who absolutely refuse to work, who do nothing but gamble and steal, you can not help seeing that there is some direct cause, and a great deal of this boyhood crime, is, in my mind, easy to trace to the deadly cigarette. There is something in the poison of the cigarette that seems to get into the system of the boy and to destroy all moral fiber."

He gives the following probable course of a boy who begins to smoke cigarettes: "First, cigarettes. Second, beer and liquors. Third, craps—petty gambling. Fourth, horse-racing—gambling on a bigger scale. Fifth, larceny. Sixth, state prison."

Another New York City magistrate says: "Yesterday I had before me thirty-five boy prisoners. Thirty-three of them were confirmed cigarette smokers. To-day, from a reliable source, I have made the grewsome discovery that two of the largest cigarette manufacturers soak their product in a weak solution of opium. The fact that out of thirty-five prisoners thirty-three smoked cigarettes might seem to indicate some direct connection between cigarettes and crime. And when it is announced on authority that most cigarettes are doped with opium, this connection is not hard to understand. Opium is like whisky,—it creates an increasing appetite that grows with what it feeds upon. A growing boy who lets tobacco and opium get a hold upon his senses is never long in coming under the domination of whisky, too. Tobacco is the boy's easiest and most direct road to whisky. When opium is added, the young man's chance of resisting the combined forces and escaping physical, mental, and moral harm is slim, indeed."

I think the above statement regarding the use of opium by manufacturers is exaggerated. Yet we know that young men of great natural ability, everywhere, some of them in high positions, are constantly losing their grip, deteriorating, dropping back, losing their ambition, their push, their stamina, and their energy, because of the cigarette's deadly hold upon them.

Did you ever watch the gradual deterioration of the cigarette smoker, the gradual withdrawal of manliness and character, the fading out of purpose, the decline of ambition; the substitution of the beastly for the manly, the decline of the divine and the ascendency of the brute?

A very interesting study this, to watch the gradual withdrawal from the face of all that was manly and clean, and all that makes for success. We can see where purity left him and was gradually replaced by vulgarity, and where he began to be cursed by commonness.

We can see the point at which he could begin to do a bad job or a poor day's work without feeling troubled about it.

We can tell when he began to lose his great pride in his personal appearance, when he began to leave his room in the morning and to go to his work without being perfectly groomed. Only a little while before he would have been greatly mortified to have been seen by his employers and associates with slovenly dress; but now baggy trousers, unblackened shoes, soiled linen, frayed neck-tie do not trouble him.

He is not quite as conscientious about his work as he used to be. He can leave a half-finished job, and cut his hours and rob his employer a little here and there without being troubled seriously. He can write a slipshod letter. He isn't particular about his spelling, punctuation, or handwriting, as formerly. He doesn't mind a little deceit.

Vulgarity no longer shocks him. He does not blush at the unclean test. Womanhood is not as sacred to him as in his innocent days. He does not reverence women as formerly; and he finds himself laughing at the coarse jest and the common remarks about them among his associates, when once he would have resented and turned away in disgust.

Dr. Lewis Bremer, late physician at St. Vincent's Institute for the Insane says, "Basing my opinion upon my experience gained in private sanitariums and hospitals, I will broadly state that the boy who smokes cigarettes at seven will drink whisky at fourteen, take morphine at twenty-five, and wind up at thirty with cocaine and the rest of the narcotics."

The saddest effects of cigarette smoking are mental. The physical signs of deterioration have their mental correspondencies. Sir William Hamilton said: "There is nothing great in matter but man; there is nothing great in man but mind." The cigarette smoker takes man's distinguishing faculty and uncrowns it. He "puts an enemy in his mouth to steal away his brains."

Anything which impairs one's success capital, which cuts down his achievement and makes him a possible failure when he might have been a grand success, is a crime against him. Anything which benumbs the senses, deadens the sensibilities, dulls the mental faculties, and takes the edge off one's ability, is a deadly enemy, and there is nothing else which effects all this so quickly as the cigarette. It is said that within the past fifty years not a student at Harvard University who used tobacco has been graduated at the head of his class, although, on the average, five out of six use tobacco.

The symptoms of a cigarette victim resembles those of an opium eater. A gradual deadening, benumbing influence creeps all through the mental and moral faculties; the standards all drop to a lower level; the whole average of life is cut down, the victim loses that power of mental grasp, the grip of mind which he once had. In place of his former energy and vim and push, he is more and more inclined to take things easy and to slide along the line of the least resistance. He becomes less and less progressive. He dreams more and acts less. Hard work becomes more and more irksome and repulsive, until work seems drudgery to him.

Professor William McKeever, of the Kansas Agricultural College, in the course of his findings after an exhaustive study of "The Cigarette Smoking Boy" presents facts which are as appalling as they are undeniable:

"For the past eight years I have been tracing out the cigarette boy's biography and I have found that in practically all cases the lad began his smoking habit clandestinely and with little thought of its seriousness while the fond parents perhaps believed that their boy was too good to engage in such practise.

"I have tabulated reports of the condition of nearly 2,500 cigarette-smoking schoolboys, and in describing them physically my informants have repeatedly resorted to the use of such epithets as 'sallow,' 'sore-eyed,' 'puny,' 'squeaky-voiced,' 'sickly,' 'short-winded,' and 'extremely nervous.' In my tabulated reports it is shown that, out of a group of twenty-five cases of young college students, smokers, whose average age of beginning was 13, according to their own admissions they had suffered as follows: Sore throat, four; weak eyes, ten; pain in chest, eight; 'short wind,' twenty-one; stomach trouble, ten; pain in heart, nine. Ten of them appeared to be very sickly. The younger the boy, the worse the smoking hurts him in every way, for these lads almost invariably inhale the fumes; and that is the most injurious part of the practise."

Professor McKeever made hundreds of sphygmograph records of boys addicted to the smoking habit. Discussing what the records showed, he says:

"The injurious effects of smoking upon the boy's mental activities are very marked. Of the many hundreds of tabulated cases in my possession, several of the very youthful ones have been reduced almost to the condition of imbeciles. Out of 2,336 who were attending public school, only six were reported 'bright students.' A very few, perhaps ten, were 'average,' and all the remainder were 'poor' or 'worthless' as students. The average grades of fifty smokers and fifty non-smokers were computed from the records of one term's work done in the Kansas Agricultural college and the results favored the latter group with a difference of 17.5 per cent. The two groups represented the same class rank; that is, the same number of seniors, juniors, sophomores, and freshmen."

A thorough investigation of the effects of cigarette smoking on boys has been carried on in one of the San Francisco schools for many months. This investigation was ordered because a great many of the boys were inferior to the girls, both mentally and morally.

It was found that nearly three-fourths of the boys who smoked cigarettes had nervous disorders, while only one of those who did not smoke had any nervous symptoms. A great many of the cigarette smokers had defective hearing, while only one of those who did not smoke was so afflicted. A large percentage of the boys who smoked were defective in memory, while only one boy who did not smoke was so affected. A large portion of the boys who smoked were reported as low in deportment and morals, while only a very small percentage of those who did not smoke were similarly affected. It was found that the minds of many of the cigarette smokers could not comprehend or grasp ideas as quickly or firmly as those who did not smoke. Nearly all of the cigarette smokers were found to be untidy and unclean in their personal appearance, and a great many of them were truants; but among those who did not smoke not a single boy had been corrected for truancy. Most of the smokers ranked very low in their studies as compared with those who did not smoke. Seventy-nine per cent. of them failed of promotion, while the percentage of failure among those who did not smoke was exceedingly small.

Of twenty boy smokers who were under careful observation for several months, nineteen stood below the average of the class, while only two of those who did not smoke stood below. Seventeen out of the twenty were very poor workers and seemed absolutely incapable of close or continuous application to any of their studies.

Professor Wilkinson, principal of a leading high school, says, "I will not try to educate a boy with the cigarette habit. It is wasted time. The mental faculties of the boy who smokes cigarettes are blunted."

Another high school principal says, "Boys who smoke cigarettes are always backward in their studies; they are filthy in their personal habits, and coarse in their manners, they are hard to manage and dull in appearance."

It is apparent therefore that the cigarette habit disqualifies the student mentally, that it retards him in his studies, dwarfs his intellect, and leaves him far behind those of inferior mental equipment who do not indulge in the injurious use of tobacco in any form.

The mental, moral, and physical deterioration from the use of cigarettes, has been noted by corporations and employers of labor generally, until to-day the cigarette devotee finds himself barred from many positions that are open to those of inferior capabilities, who are not enslaved by the deadly habit.

Cigarette smoking is no longer simply a moral question. The great business world has taken it up as a deadly enemy of advancement, of achievement. Leading business firms all over the country have put the cigarette on the prohibited list. In Detroit alone, sixty-nine merchants have agreed not to employ the cigarette user. In Chicago, Montgomery Ward and Company, Hibbard, Spencer and Bartlett, and some of the other large concerns have prohibited cigarette smoking among all employees under eighteen years of age. Marshall Field and Company, and the Morgan and Wright Tire Company have this rule: "No cigarettes can be smoked by our employees." One of the questions on the application blanks at Wanamaker's reads: "Do you use tobacco or cigarettes?"

The superintendent of the Linden Street Railway, of St. Louis, says: "Under no circumstances will I hire a man who smokes cigarettes. He is as dangerous on the front of a motor as a man who drinks. In fact, he is more dangerous; his nerves are apt to give way at any moment. If I find a car running badly, I immediately begin to investigate to find if the man smokes cigarettes. Nine times out of ten he does, and then he goes, for good."

The late E. H. Harriman, head of the Union Pacific Railroad system, used to say that they "might as well go to a lunatic asylum for their employees as to hire cigarette smokers." The Union Pacific Railroad prohibits cigarette smoking among its employees.

The New York, New Haven, and Hartford, the Chicago, Rock Island, and Pacific, the Lehigh Valley, the Burlington, and many others of the leading railroad companies of this country have issued orders positively forbidding the use of cigarettes by employees while on duty.

Some time ago, twenty-five laborers working on a bridge were discharged by the roadmasters of the West Superior, Wisconsin Railroad because of cigarette smoking. The Pittsburg and Western Railroad which is part of the Baltimore and Ohio system, gave orders forbidding the use of cigarettes by its employees on passenger trains and also notified passengers that they must not smoke cigarettes in their coaches.

In the call issued for the competitive examination for messenger service in the Chicago Post-office, sometime since, seven hundred applicants were informed that only the best equipped boys were wanted for this service, and that under no circumstances would boys who smoked cigarettes be employed. Other post-offices have taken a similar stand.

If some one should present you with a most delicately adjusted chronometer,—one which would not vary a second in a year—do you think it would pay you to trifle with it, to open the case in the dust, to leave it out in the rain overnight, or to put in a drop of glue or a chemical which would ruin the delicacy of its adjustment so that it would no longer keep good time? Would you think it wise to take such chances?

But the Creator has given you a matchless machine, so delicately and wondrously made that it takes a quarter of a century to bring it to perfection, to complete growth, and yet you presume to trifle with it, to do all sorts of things which are infinitely worse than leaving your watch open out of doors overnight, or even in water.

The great object of the watch is to keep time. The supreme purpose of this marvelous piece of human machinery is power. The watch means nothing except time. If the human machinery does not produce power, it is of no use.

The merest trifle will prevent the watch from keeping time; but you think that you can put anything into your human machinery, that you can do all sorts of irrational things with it, and yet you expect it to produce power—to keep perfect time. It is important that the human machine shall be kept as responsive to the slightest impression or influence as possible, and the brain should be kept clear so that the thought may be sharp, biting, gripping, so that the whole mentality will act with efficiency. And yet you do not hesitate to saturate the delicate brain-cells with vile drinks, to poison them with nicotine, to harden them with smoke from the vilest of weeds. You expect the man to turn out as exquisite work, to do the most delicate things to retain his exquisite sense of ability notwithstanding the hardening, the benumbing influence of cigarette poisoning.

Let the boy or youth who is tempted to indulge in the first cigarette ask himself—Can I afford to take this enormous risk? Can I jeopardize my health, my strength, my future, my all, by indulging in a practise which has ruined tens of thousands of promising lives?

Let the youth who is tempted say, "No! I will wait until mind and body are developed, until I have reached man's estate before I will begin to use tobacco." Experience proves that those who reach a robust manhood are rarely willing to sacrifice health and happiness to the cigarette habit.

Many years ago an eminent physician and specialist in nervous diseases put himself on record as holding the firm belief that the evil effects of the use of tobacco were more lasting and far reaching than the injurious consequences that follow the excessive use of alcohol. Apart from affections of the throat and cancerous diseases of lips and tongue which frequently affect smokers there is a physical taint which is transmitted to offspring which handicaps the unfortunate infant "from its earliest breath."

The only salvation of the race, said this physician, lay in the fact that women did not smoke. If they too acquired the tobacco habit future generations would be stamped by the degeneracy and depravity which follow the use of tobacco as surely as they follow the use of alcohol.

In view of these facts the increase of cigarette smoking among women may well alarm those who have at heart the wellbeing of the rising generation. So rapidly has this habit spread that fashionable hotels and cafes are providing rooms for the especial use of those women who like to indulge in an after-dinner cigarette. A noted restaurant in New York recently added an annex to which ladies with their escorts might retire and smoke. We often see women smoking in New York hotels and restaurants.

Not long ago the writer was a guest at a dinner and to his surprise several ladies at the table lighted their cigarettes with as much composure as if it were the most natural thing in the world.

At a reception recently, I saw the granddaughter of one of America's greatest authors smoking cigarettes.

What a spectacle, to see a descendant so nearly removed from one of Nature's grandest noblemen, a princely gentleman, smoking! And I said to myself, "What would her grandfather think if he could see this?"

On a train running between London and Liverpool, a compartment especially reserved for women smokers has been provided. It is said that three American women were the cause of this innovation. The superintendent of one of our largest American railways says that he would not be surprised if the American roads were compelled to follow the lead of their English brethren.

It is not unreasonable to suppose that this addiction to the use of tobacco is in many cases inherited. A friend told me of a very charming young woman who was passionately devoted to tobacco. At a time when it was not usual for women to smoke in public her craving for a cigarette was so strong that she could not deny herself the indulgence. She said her father, a deacon in the church, had been an inveterate smoker, and her love of tobacco dated back to her earliest remembrance. Every woman should use the uttermost of her influence to discourage the use of the cigarette and enlist the girls as well as boys in her fight against the evil and injurious practise of cigarette smoking.

The Power of Purity

Blessed are the pure in heart for they shall see God.— Sermon on the Mount

*My strength is as the strength of ten
Because my heart is pure.— Tennyson*

Virtue alone raises us above hopes, fears, and chances.— Seneca

Even from the body's purity the mind Receives a secret sympathetic aid.— Thomson

Purity is a broad word with a deep meaning. It denotes far more than superficial cleanness. It goes below the surface of guarded speech and polite manners to the very heart of being. "Out of the heart are the issues of life." Make the fountain clean and the waters that flow from it will be pure and limpid. Make the heart clean and the life will be clean.

Purity is defined as "free from contact with that which weakens, impairs or pollutes." How forceful then is the converse of the definition: Impurity weakens, impairs, and pollutes. It weakens both mind and body. It impairs the health. It pollutes not only the thoughts but the conduct which inevitably has its beginning and its end in thought.

Innocence is the state of natural purity. It was the state of Adam and Eve in the Garden of Eden. When they sinned "they knew that they were naked." They lost innocence never to regain it. But purity may be attained. As an unclean garment may be washed, so the heart may be purified and made clean. Ghosts of past impurities still may dog us, but they are ghosts that may be laid with an imperative "Get thee behind me, Satan." They are like the lions that affrighted Bunyan's pilgrim—chained securely. They may roar and threaten, but they are powerless if we deny their power. The man who is striving for purity whole-heartedly is like one who sits safely in a guarded house. Old memories of evil things like specters may peer in at the windows and mow and gibber at him, but they can not touch him unless he gives them power, unless he unlocks the door of his heart and bids them enter.

As the lotus flower grows out of the mud, so may purity and beauty spring up from even the vilest past if we but will it so.

As purity is power so impurity is impotence, weakness, degeneracy. Many a man goes on in an impure career thinking himself secure, thinking his secret hidden. But impurity, like murder, will out. There was a noted pugilist who was unexpectedly defeated in a great ring battle. People said the fight was a "fake," that it was a "put up job." But those who knew said "impurity." He had lived an evil, debauched life for several years, and he went into the ring impaired in strength, weakened by his transgressions of the law of pure living. Purity is power; impurity is weakness.

There is a saying of Scripture which is absolutely scientific: "Be sure your sin will find you out." Note this; it is not that your sin will be found out, but *your* sin will find *you* out. Sin recoils on the sinner, and of all sins that surely find us out, the sins against purity are the most certain to bring retribution.

Young men do not think that listening to an off-color story, or anything that is vulgar, can injure them much, and, for fear of ridicule, they laugh when they hear anything of the kind, even when it is repulsive to them, and when they loathe it. It is a rare thing for a young man to express with emphasis his disapproval. To know life properly is to know the best in it, not the worst. No one ever yet was made stronger by his knowledge of impurity or experience in sin.

It is said that the mind's phonograph will faithfully reproduce a bad story even up to the point of death. Do not listen once. You can never get the stain entirely out of your life. Your character will absorb the poison. Impurity is especially fatal in its grip upon the young, because of the vividness of the youthful imagination and the facility with which insinuating suggestions enter the youthful thought.

Our court records show that a very large percentage of criminals began their downfall through the fatal contagion of impurity communicated from various associations.

Remember that you can not tell what may come to you in the future, what honor or promotion; and you can not afford to take chances upon having anything in your history which can come up to embarrass you or to keep you back. A thing which you now look upon as a bit of pleasure may come up in the future to hamper your progress. The thing you do to-day while trying to have a good time may come up to block your progress years afterwards.

I know men who have been thrust into positions of honor and public trust who would give anything in the world if they could blot out some of the unclean experiences of their youth. Things in their early history, which they had forgotten all about and which they never expected to hear from again, are raked up when they become candidates for office or positions of trust. These forgotten bits of so-called pleasure loom up in after-life as insurmountable bars across their pathway.

I know a very rich young man who thought he was just having a good time in his youth—sowing his wild oats—who would give a large part of his vast wealth to-day if he could blot out a few years of his folly.

It seems strange that men will work hard to build a reputation, and then throw it all away by some weakness in their character. How many men there are in this country with great brain power, men who are kings in their specialties, men who have worked like slaves to achieve their aims, whose reputations have been practically ruined by the flaw of impurity!

Character is a record of our thoughts and acts. That which we think about most, the ideals and motives uppermost in our mind, are constantly solidifying into character. What we are constantly thinking about, and aiming toward and trying to obtain becomes a permanent part of the life.

The man whose thoughts are low and impure, very quickly gives this bent and tendency to his character.

The character levels itself with the thought, whether high or low. No man can have a pure, clean character who does not habitually have pure, clean thoughts. The immoral man is invariably an impure thinker—whatever we harbor in the mind out-pictures itself in the body.

In Eastern countries the leper is compelled to cry, "Unclean, unclean," upon the approach of any one not so cursed. What a blessing to humanity if our modern moral lepers were compelled to cry, "Unclean, unclean," before they approach innocent victims with their deadly contagion!

About the vilest thing on earth is a human being whose character is so tainted with impurity that he leaves the slimy trail of the serpent wherever he goes.

There never was a more beautiful and pathetic prayer than that of the poor soiled, broken-hearted Psalmist in his hour of shame, "Create in me a clean heart." "Who shall ascend into the hill of the Lord, who shall stand in His holy place? He that hath clean hands and a pure heart." There are thousands of men who would cut off their right hands to-day to be free from the stain, the poison, of impurity.

There can be no lasting greatness without purity. Vice honeycombs the physical strength as well as destroys the moral fiber. Now and again some man of note topples with a crash to sudden ruin. Yet the cause of the moral collapse is not sudden. There has been a slow undermining of virtue going on probably for years; then, in an hour when honor, truth, or honesty is brought to a crucial test, the weakened character gives way and there is an appalling commercial or social crash which often finds an echo in the revolver shot of the suicide.

Tennyson shows the effect of Launcelot's guilty love for Guinevere, in the great knight's conscious loss of power. His wrongful passion indirectly brought about the death of fair Elaine. He himself at times shrank from puny men wont to go down before the shadow of his spear. Like a scarlet blot his sin stains all his greatness, and he muses on it remorsefully:

> "For what am I? What profits me my name
> Of greatest knight? I fought for it and have it.
> Pleasure to have it, none; to lose it pain;
> Now grown a part of me: but what use in it?
> To make men worse by making my sin known?

Or sin seem less, the sinner seeming great?"
Later when the knights of the Round Table joined in the search for the Holy Grail, that lost sacred vessel,
"The cup, the cup itself from which our Lord
Drank at the last sad supper with his own,"

Launcelot was overtaken by his sin and failed ignominiously. Only Galahad the Pure was permitted to see the cup unsurrounded by a blinding glory, a fearful splendor of watching eyes and guarding shapes.

No one is quite the same in his own estimation when he has been once guilty of contact with impurity. His self-respect has suffered a loss. Something has gone out of his life. His own good opinion of himself has suffered deterioration, and he can never face his life-task with quite the same confidence again. Somehow he feels that the world will know of his soul's debauch and judge him accordingly.

There is nothing which will mar a life more quickly than the consciousness of a soul-stain. The loss of self-respect, the loss of character, is irreparable.

We are beginning to find that there is an intimate connection between absolute purity *of one's thought and life and his good health, good thinking, and good work,* a very close connection between the moral faculties and the physical health; that nothing so exhausts vitality and vitiates the quality of work and ideals, so takes the edge off of one's ambition, dulls the brain and aspiration, as impurity of thought and life. It seems to blight all the faculties and to demoralize the whole man, so that his efficiency is very much lessened. He does not speak with the same authority. The air of the conqueror disappears from his manner. He does not think so clearly; he does not act with so great certainty, and his self-faith is lost, because confidence is based upon self-respect, and he can no longer respect himself when he does things which he would not respect in another.

The fact that his impure acts are done secretly makes no difference. No one can thoroughly respect himself when he does that which demoralizes him, which is unbecoming a gentleman, no matter whether other people know it or not. Impurity blights everything it touches.

It is not enough to be thought pure and clean and sound. One must actually *be* pure and clean and sound morally, or his self-respect is undermined.

Purity is power because it means integrity of thought, integrity of conduct. It means wholeness. The impure man can not be a great power, because he can not thoroughly believe in himself when conscious that he is rotten in any part of his nature. Impurity works like leaven, which affects everything in a man. The very consciousness that the impurity is working within him robs him of power.

Apart from the moral side of this question, let us show how these things affect one's success in life by sapping the energies, weakening the nature, lowering one's standards, blurring one's ideals, discouraging one's ambition, and lessening one's vitality and power.

In the last analysis of success, the mainspring of achievement must rest in the strength of one's vitality, for, without a stock of health equal to great emergencies and persistent longevity, even the greatest ambition is comparatively powerless. And there is nothing that will sap the life-forces so quickly as dissipation and impure living.

Is there anything truer than that "To be carnally minded is death?" If the thought is carnal, the body must correspond, must express it in some physical discord.

Nothing else will destroy the very foundations of vitality quicker than impurity of thought and animal self-indulgence. The ideals must be kept bright and the ambition clean-cut.

Purity of thought means that the mental processes are not clouded, muddy, or clogged by brain ash from a dissipated life, from violation of the laws of health. Pure thought comes from pure blood, and pure blood from a clean, sane life. Purity signifies a great deal besides freedom from sensual taint. It means saneness, purity, and quality.

It has been characteristic of great leaders, men whose greatness has stood the acid test of time, that they have been virtuous in conduct, pure in thought.

"I have such a rich story that I want to tell you," said an officer, who one evening came into the Union camp in a rollicking mood. "There are no ladies present, are there?"

General Grant, lifting his eyes from the paper which he was reading, and looking the officer squarely in the eye, said slowly and deliberately:

"No, but there are gentlemen present."

"A great trait of Grant's character," said George W. Childs, "was his purity. I never heard him express an impure thought, or make an indelicate allusion in any way or shape. There is nothing I ever heard him say that could not be repeated in the presence of women. If a man was brought up for an appointment, and it was shown that he was an immoral man, Grant would not appoint him, no matter how great the pressure brought to bear."

On one occasion, when Grant formed one of a dinner-party of Americans in a foreign city, conversation drifted into references to questionable affairs, when he suddenly rose and said, "Gentlemen, please excuse me, I will retire."

It is the glory of a man to have clean lips and a clean mind. It is the glory of a woman not to know evil, even in her thoughts.

Isaac Newton's most intimate friend in young manhood was a noted foreign chemist. They were constant associates until one day the Italian told an impure story, after which Newton never would associate with him.

"My extreme youth, when I took command of the army of Italy," said Napoleon, "rendered it necessary that I should evince great reserve of manners and the utmost severity of morals. This was indispensable to enable me to sustain authority over men so greatly my superiors in age and experience. I pursued a line of conduct in the highest degree irreproachable and exemplary. In spotless morality I was a Cato, and must have appeared such to all. I was a philosopher and a sage. My supremacy could be retained only by proving myself a better man than any other man in the army. Had I yielded to human weakness, I should have lost my power."

The military antagonist and conqueror of Napoleon, the Duke of Wellington, was a man of simple life and austere virtue. When he was laid to rest in the crypt of St. Paul's Cathedral, "in streaming London's central roar," the poet who wrote his funeral ode was able to say of him:

"Whatever record leap to light
He never shall be shamed."

The peril of impurity lies in the insidiousness of the poison. Just one taint of impurity, one glance at a lewd picture, one hearing of an unclean story may begin the fatal corruption of mind and heart.

"It is the little rift within the lute
That by and by will make the music mute,
The little rift within the lover's lute
Or little pitted speck in garnered fruit
That rotting inward slowly molders all."

When Bunyan's pilgrim was assailed by temptation he stopped his ears with his fingers and fled for his life. Let the young man who values himself, who sets store upon health and has ambition to succeed in his chosen career, be deaf to unclean speech and flee the companionship of those who think and speak uncleanness.

It is the experience of every man who has forsaken vice and turned his feet into the paths of virtue that evil memories will, in his holiest hours, leap upon him like a lion from ambush. Into the harmony of the hymn he sings memory will interpolate unbidden, the words of some sensual song. Pictures of his debauches, his past licentiousness, will fill his vision, and the unhappy victim can only beat upon his breast and cry, "Me miserable! Whither shall I flee?" This has been, through all time, the experience of the men that have sought sanctity in seclusion. The saints, the hermits in their caves, the monks in their cells, could never escape the obsessions of memory which with horrible realism and scorching vividness revived past scenes of sin.

A boy once showed to another a book of impure words and pictures. He to whom the book was shown had it in his hands only a few minutes. In after-life he held high office in the church, and years and years afterwards told a friend that he would give half he possessed had he never seen it, because its impure images, at the most holy times, would arise unbidden to his mind.

Physicians tell us that every particle of the body changes in a very few years; but no chemistry, human or divine, can entirely expunge from the mind a bad picture. Like the paintings buried for centuries in Pompeii, without the loss of tint or shade, these pictures are as brilliant in age as in youth.

Association begets assimilation. We can not mix with evil associations without being contaminated; can not touch pitch without being defiled. Impurity is especially fatal in its grip upon the young, because of the vividness of the youthful imagination and the facility with which insinuating suggestions enter the youthful thought.

Indelible and satanic is the taint of the evil suggestive power which a lewd, questionable picture or story leaves upon the mind. Nothing else more fatally mars the ideals of life and lowers the standard of manhood and womanhood.

To read writers whose lines express the utmost possible impurity so dexterously and cunningly that not a vulgar word is used, but rosy, glowing, suggestive language—authors who soften evil and show deformity with the tints of beauty—what is this but to take the feet out of the straight road into the guiltiest path of seduction?

Very few realize the power of a diseased imagination to ruin a precious life. Perhaps the defect began in a little speck of taint. No other faculty has such power to curse or bless mankind, to build up or tear down, to ennoble or debauch, to make happy or miserable, or has such power upon our destiny, as the imagination.

Many a ruined life began its downfall in the dry rot of a perverted imagination. How little we realize that by subtle, moral manufacture, repeated acts of the imagination weave themselves into a mighty tapestry, every figure and fancy of which will stand out in living colors in the character-web of our lives, to approve or condemn us.

In many cases where, for no apparent reason, one is making failure after failure, never reaching, even approximately, the position which was anticipated for him, if he would look frankly into his own heart, and searchingly at his own secret habits, he would find that which, hidden, like the worm at the heart of the rose, is destroying and making impossible all that ennobles, beautifies, and enriches life.

"I solemnly warn you," says Beecher, "against indulging a morbid imagination. In that busy and mischievous faculty begins the evil. Were it not for his airy imagination, man might stand his own master,—not overmatched by the worst part of himself. But ah! these summer reveries, these venturesome dreams, these fairy castles, builded for no good purposes,—they are haunted by impure spirits, who will fascinate, bewitch, and corrupt you. Blessed are the pure in heart. Blessed art thou, most favored of God, whose *Thoughts* are chastened; whose imagination will not breathe or fly in tainted air, and whose path hath been measured by the golden reed of purity."

To be pure in heart is the youth's first great commandment. Do not listen to men who tell you that "vice is a necessity." Nothing is a necessity that is wrong,—that debauches self-respect. "All wickedness is weakness." Vice and vigor have nothing in common. Purity is strength, health, power.

Do not imagine that impurity can be hidden! One may as well expect to have consumption or any other deadly disease, and to look and appear healthy, as to be impure in thought and mind, and to look and appear manly and noble souled. Character writes its record in the flesh.

"No, no, these are not trifles," said George Whitefield, when a friend asked why he was so particular to bathe frequently, and always have his linen scrupulously clean; "a minister must be without spot, even in his garments." Purity in a good man can not be carried too far.

There is a permanency in the stamp left by the sins resulting from impure thought that follows even to the grave. Diseases unnameable, the consequences of the Scarlet Sin, the following after the "strange woman," write their record in the very bones, literally fulfilling the Scripture statement—"Their sins shall lie down with their bones in the dust."

We often detect in the eye and in the manner the black leper spots of impurity long before the youth suspects they have ever been noticed. When there is a scar or a stain upon one's self-respect it is bound to appear on the surface sooner or later. What fearful blots and stains are left on the characters of those who have to fight for a lifetime to rid themselves of a blighting and contaminating influence, moral or physical!

Chemists tell us that scarlet is the only color which can not be bleached. There is no known chemical which can remove it. So, formerly, scarlet rags were made into blotting paper. When the sacred writer wished to emphasize the power of Divine forgiveness, of Divine love, he said: "Even though thy sins be as scarlet, they shall be made white as wool!" It certainly takes omnipotent power to expunge impurity from the mind. There is certainly one sin which only Divine power can bleach out of the character—the sin of impurity.

No man can think much of himself when he is conscious of impurity anywhere in his life. And the very knowledge that one is absolutely pure in his thought and clean in his life increases his self-respect and his self-faith wonderfully.

It is a terrible handicap to be conscious that, however much others may think of us, we are foul inside, that our thoughts are vile. It does not matter that our vicious acts are secret, we can not cover them.

Whatever we have thought or done will outpicture itself in the expression, in the bearing. It will be hung out upon the bulletin board of the face and manner for the world to read. We instinctively feel a person's reality; not what he pretends, but what he is, for we radiate our reality, which often contradicts our words.

There is only one panacea for impurity. Constant occupation and pure, high thinking are absolutely necessary to a clean life.

"I should be a poor counselor of young men," wrote a true friend of youth, "if I taught you that purity is possible only by isolation from the world. We do not want that sort of holiness which can thrive only in seclusion; we want that virile, manly purity which keeps itself unspotted from the world, even amid its worst debasements, just as the lily lifts its slender chalice of white and gold to heaven, untainted by the soil in which it grows, though that soil be the reservoir of death and putrefaction."

Impurity is the forfeiture of manliness. The true man must be untarnished. James went so far as to declare that this is just what religion is. "Pure religion and undefiled before God and the Father is this * * to keep himself unspotted from the world."

Every true man shrinks from uncleanness. He knows what it means. Impurity makes lofty friendships impossible. It robs all of life's intercourse of its freshness and its joyous innocence. It sullies all beauty. It does these things chiefly because it separates men from God and His vision. The best and holiest is barred to the stained man. Impurity makes it impossible for him to appreciate what is pure and fine, dulls his finer perceptions, and he is not given the place where only pure and fine things are.

There can be no such thing as an impure gentleman. The two words contradict each other. A gentleman must be pure. He need not have fine clothes. He may have had few advantages. But he must be pure and clean. And, if he have all outward grace and gift and be inwardly unclean, though he may call himself a gentleman, he is a liar and a lie.

O, young man, guard your heart-purity! Keep innocency! Never lose it; if it be gone, you have lost from the casket the most precious gift of God. The first purity of imagination, of thought, and of feeling, if soiled, can be cleansed by no fuller's soap. If a harp be broken, art may repair it; if a light be quenched, the flame may kindle it; but if a flower be crushed, what art can repair it? If an odor be wafted away, who can collect or bring it back?

Parents are, in many cases, responsible for the impurity of their children. Through a mistaken sense of delicacy, they allow the awakened, searching mind of the child to get information concerning its physical nature from the mind of some boy or girl no better taught than itself, and so conceive wholly wrong and harmful ideas concerning things of which it is vitally important that every human being should at the outset of life have clear and adequate ideas. Such silence, many times, is fatal, and always foolish, if not criminal.

"I have noticed," says William Acton, "that all patients who have confessed to me that they have practised vice, lamented that they were not, when children, made aware of its consequences; and I have been pressed over and over again to urge on parents, guardians, schoolmasters, and others interested in the education of youth, the necessity of giving to their charges some warning, some intimation, of their danger. To parents and guardians I offer my earnest advice that they should, by hearty sympathy and frank explanation, aid their charges in maintaining pure lives." What stronger breastplate than a heart untainted?

A prominent writer says: "If young persons poison their bodies and corrupt their minds with vicious courses, no lapse of time, after a reform, is likely to restore them to physical soundness and the soul purity of their earlier days."

There is one idea concerning purity which should never have been conceived, and, having been conceived, should be, once and forever, eternally exploded. It is that purity is different in the different sexes.

It would be loosening the foundations of virtue to countenance the notion that, because of a difference in sex, men are at liberty to set morality at defiance, and to do with impunity that which, if done by a woman, would stain her character for life. To maintain a pure and virtuous condition of society, therefore, man as well as woman must be virtuous and pure, both alike shunning all acts infringing on the heart, character, and conscience,—shunning them as poison, which, once imbibed, can never be entirely thrown out again.

Is there any reason why a man should have any license to drag his thoughts through the mud and filth any more than a woman? Is there any sex in principle? Isn't a stain a blot upon a boy's character just as bad as upon a girl's? If purity is so refining and elevating for one sex, why should it not be for the other?

It is incredible that a man should be socially ostracized for comparatively minor offenses, yet be rotten with immorality and be received into the best homes. But, if a woman makes the least false step in this direction, she is not only ostracized but treated with the utmost contempt, while the man who was the chief sinner in causing a woman's downfall, society will pardon.

To put it on the very lowest ground, I am certain that if young men knew and realized the fearful risks to health that they take by indulging in gross impurities they would put them by with a shudder of disgust and aversion. It may very easily happen—it very often actually does happen—that one single step from the path of purity clouds a man's whole life with misery and unspeakable suffering; and not only that, but even entails lifelong disease on children yet unborn.

To return to its Maker at the close of life the marvelous body which He gave us, scarred by a heedless life, with the heart rotten with impurity, the imagination filled with vicious images, the character honeycombed with vice, is a most ungrateful return for the priceless life of opportunity.

A mind retaining all the dew and freshness of innocence shrinks from the very idea of impurity, the very suggestion of it, as if it were sin to have even thought or heard of it, as if even the shadow of the evil would leave some soil on the unsullied whiteness of the virgin mind. "When modesty is once extinguished, it knows not a return."

The Habit of Happiness

The highest happiness must always come from the exercise of the best thing in us.

When you find happiness in anything but useful work, you will be the first man or woman to make the discovery.

If you take an inventory of yourself at the very outset of your career you will find that you think you are going to find happiness in things or in conditions. Most people think they are going to find the largest part of their happiness in money, what money will buy or what it will give them in the way of power, influence, comforts, luxuries. They think they are going to find a great deal of their happiness in marriage. How quickly they find that the best happiness they will ever know is that which must be limited to their own capacity for enjoyment, that their happiness can not come from anything outside of them but must be developed from within. Many people believe they are going to find much of their happiness in books, in travel, in leisure, in freedom from the thousand and one anxieties and cares and worries of business; but the moment they get in the position where they thought they would have freedom many other things come up in their minds and cut off much of the expected joy. When they get money and leisure they often find that they are growing selfish, which cuts off a lot of their happiness. No man able to work can be idle without feeling a sense of guilt at not doing his part in the world, for every time he sees the poor laboring people who are working for him, who are working everywhere, he is constantly reminded of his meanness in shifting upon others what he is able to do and ought to do himself. Idleness is the last place to look for happiness. Idleness is like a stagnant pool. The moment the water ceases to flow, to work, to do something, all sorts of vermin and hideous creatures develop in it. It becomes torpid and unhealthy giving out miasma and repulsive odors. In the same way work is the only thing that will keep the individual healthy and wholesome and clean. An idle brain very quickly breeds impurities.

The married man quickly learns that his domestic happiness depends upon what he himself contributes to the partnership, that he can not take out a great deal without putting a great deal in, for selfishness always reaps a mean, despicable harvest. It is only the generous giver who gets much. There is nothing which will so shrivel up a man; and contract his capacity for happiness as selfishness. It is always a fatal blighter, blaster, disappointer. We must give to get, we must be great before we can get great enjoyment; great in our motive, grand in our endeavor, sublime in our ideas.

It is impossible, absolutely unscientific, for a bad person to be truly happy; just as impossible as it would be for one to be comfortable while lying on a bed of nettles which are constantly pricking him. There is no way under heaven by which a person can be really happy without being good, clean, square, and true. This does not mean that a person is happy because he does not use tobacco, drink, gamble, use profane language or does not do other vicious things. Some of the meanest, narrowest, most contemptible people in the world do none of these things but they are uncharitable, jealous, envious, revengeful. They stab you in the back, slander you, cheat you. They may be cunning, underhanded, and yet have a fairly good standing in the church. No person can be really happy who has a small, narrow, bigoted, uncharitable mind or disposition. Generosity, charity, kindness are absolutely essential to real happiness. Deceitful people can not be happy; they can not respect themselves because they inwardly despise themselves for deceiving you. A person must be open minded, transparent, simple, in order to be really happy. A person who is always covering up something, trying to keep things from you, misleading you, deceiving you, can not get away from self-reproach, and hence can not be really happy.

Selfishness is a fatal enemy of happiness because no one ever does a really selfish thing without feeling really mean, without despising himself for it. I have never seen a strong young man sneak into a vacant seat in a car and allow an old man or woman with a package or a baby in her arms to stand, without looking as though he knew he had done a mean, selfish thing. There is a look of humiliation in his face. We are so constituted that we can not help condemning ourselves for our mean or selfish acts.

The liar is never really happy. He is always on nettles lest his deceit betray him. He never feels safe. Dishonesty in all its phases is fatal to happiness, for no dishonest person can get his self-approval. Without this no happiness is possible.

Before you can be really happy, my friend, you must be able to look back upon a well-spent past, a conscientious, unselfish past. If not, you will be haunted by demons which will destroy your happiness. If you have been mean and selfish, greedy and dishonest with your fellowmen, all sorts of horrible things will rise out of your money pile to terrify and to make your happiness impossible.

In other words, happiness is merely a result of the life work. It will partake of the exact quality of the motive which you have put into your life work. If these motives have been selfish, greedy, grasping, if cunning and dishonesty have dominated in your career, your happiness will be marred accordingly.

You can not complain of your happiness, because it is your own child, the product of your own brain, your own effort. It has been made up of your motives, colored by your life aim. It exactly corresponds to the cause which produced it.

There is the greatest difference in the world between the happiness which comes from a sweet, beautiful, unselfish, helpful, sympathetic, industrious, honorable career, and the mean satisfaction which may grow to be a part of your marked self if you have lived a selfish, grasping life.

What we call happiness is the harvest from our life sowing, our habitual thought-sowing, deed-doing. If we have sown selfish, envious, jealous, revengeful, hateful seeds, greedy, grasping seeds, we can not expect a golden happiness harvest like that which comes from a clean and unselfish, helpful sowing.

If our harvest is full of the rank, poisonous weeds of jealousy, envy, dishonesty, cunning, and cruelty, we have no one to blame but ourselves, for we sowed the seed which produced that sort of a harvest.

Somehow some people have an entirely wrong idea of what real happiness is. They seem to think it can be bought, can be had by influence, that it can be purchased by money; that if they have money they can get that wonderful, mysterious thing which they call happiness.

But happiness is a natural, faithful harvest from our sowing. It would be as impossible for selfish seed, greed seed to produce a harvest of contentment, of genuine satisfaction, of real joy, as for thistle seeds to produce a harvest of wheat or corn.

Whatever the quality of your enjoyment or happiness may be, you have patterned it by your life motive by the spirit in which you have worked, by the principles which have actuated you.

A pretty different harvest, I grant, many of us must face, marred with all sorts of hideous, poisonous weeds, but they are all the legitimate product of our sowing. No one can rob us of our harvest or change it very much. Every thought, every act, every motive, whether secret or public, is a seed which no power on earth can prevent going to its harvest of beauty or ugliness, honor or shame. Most people have an idea that happiness is something that can be manufactured. They do not realize that it can no more be manufactured than wheat or corn can be manufactured. It must be grown, and the harvest will be like the seed.

You, young man, make up your mind at the very outset of your career that whatever comes to you in life, that whether you succeed or fail, whether you have this or that, there is one thing you will have, and that is a happy, contented mind, that you will extract your happiness as you go along. You will not take the chances of picking up or developing the happy habit after you get rich, for then you may be too old.

Most people postpone their enjoyment until they are disappointed to find the power of enjoyment has largely gone by and that even if they had the means they could not get anything like as much real happiness out of it as they could have gotten as they went along when they were younger. Take no chances with your happiness, or the sort of a life that can produce it; whatever else you risk, do not risk this. Early form the happy habit, the habit of enjoyment every day, no matter what comes or does not come to you during the day. Pick crumbs of comfort out of your situation, no matter how unpleasant or disagreeable.

I know a man who, although poor, can manage to get more comfort out of a real tough, discouraging situation than any one else I have ever seen. I have often seen him when he did not have a dollar to his name, with a wife to support; yet he was always buoyant, happy, cheerful, consented. He would even make fun out of an embarrassing situation, see something ludicrous in his extreme poverty.

There have never been such conflicting estimates, such varying ideas, regarding any state of human condition as to what constitutes happiness. Many people think that it is purchasable with money, but many of the most restless, discontented, unhappy people in the world are rich. They have the means of purchasing what they *thought* would produce happiness, but the real thing eludes them. On the other hand, some of the poorest people in the world are happy. The fact is that there is no possible way of cornering or purchasing happiness for it is absolutely beyond the reach of money. It is true, we can purchase a few comforts and immunities from some annoyances and worries with money which we can not get without it. On the other hand, the great majority of people who have inherited money are positively injured by it, because it often stops their own development by taking away the motive for self-effort and self-reliance.

When people get money they often stop growing because they depend upon the money instead of relying upon their own inherent resources.

Rich people suffer from their indulgences more than poor ones suffer from their hardships.

A great many rich people die with liver and kidney troubles which are effected both by eating and drinking. The kidneys are very susceptible to the presence of alcohol. If rich people try to get greater enjoyment out of life than poor people by eating and drinking, they are likely very quickly to come to grief. If they try to seek it through the avenue of leisure they soon find that an idle brain is one of the most dangerous things in the world—nothing deteriorates faster. The mind was made for continual strong action, systematic, vigorous exercise, and this is possible only when some dominating aim and a great life purpose leads the way.

No person can be really healthful whose mind is not usefully and continually employed. So there is no possibility of finding real happiness in idleness if we are able to work. Nature brings a wonderful compensatory power to those who are crippled or sick or otherwise disabled from working, but there is no compensation for idleness in those who are able to work. Nature only gives us the use of faculties we employ. "Use or lose" is her motto, and when we cease to use a faculty or function it is gradually taken away from us, gradually shrivels and atrophies.

There is no satisfaction like that which comes from the steady, persistent, honest, conscientious pursuit of a noble aim. There are a multitude of evidences in man's very structure that his marvelous mechanism was intended for action, for constant exercise, and that idleness and stagnation always mean deterioration and death of power. No man can remain idle without shrinking, shrivelling, constantly becoming a less efficient man; for he can keep up only those faculties and powers which he constantly employs, and there is no other possible way. Nature puts her ban of deterioration and loss of power upon idleness. We see these victims everywhere shorn of power—weak, nerveless, backboneless, staminaless, gritless people, without forcefulness, mere nonentities because they have ceased working. Without work mental health is impossible and without health the fullest happiness is impossible.

It has been said that happiness is the most delusive thing that man pursues. Yet why need it be a blind search?

If we were to stop the first hundred people we meet on the street and ask them what in their experience has given them the most happiness, probably the answer of no two would be alike.

How interesting and instructive it would be to give a thousand dollars to each of these hundred people, and without their knowing it, follow them and see what they would do with the money,—what it would mean to them.

To some poor youth hungry for an education, with no opportunity to gain it, this money would mean a college education. Another would see in his money a more comfortable home for his aged parents. To another this money would suggest all sorts of dissipation. Some would see books and leisure for self-improvement, a trip abroad.

We all wear different colored glasses and no two see life with the same tint.

Some find their present happiness in coarse dissipation; others in a quiet nook with a book. Some find their greatest happiness in friends, in social intercourse; others seek happiness in roving over the earth, always thinking that the greatest enjoyment is in another day, in another place, a little further on, in the next room, or to-morrow, or in another country.

To many people, happiness is never where they are, but almost anywhere else.

Most people lose sight of the simplicity of happiness. They look for it in big, complicated things. Real happiness is perfectly simple. In fact, it is incompatible with complexity. Simplicity is its very essence.

I was dining recently with a particularly successful young man who is trying very hard to be happy, but he takes such a complicated, strenuous view of everything that his happiness is always flying from him. He drives everything so fiercely, his life is so vigorous, so complicated, that happiness can not find a home with him very long. Nor does he understand why. He has money, health; but he always has that restless far-away, absent-minded gaze into something beyond, and I do not think he is ever really very happy. His whole manner of living is extremely complex. He does not seem to know where to find happiness. He has evidently mistaken the very nature of happiness. He thinks it consists in making a great show, in having great possessions, in doing things which attract a great deal of attention; but *happiness would be strangled, suffocated in such an environment.* The essentials of real happiness are few, simple, and close at hand.

Happiness is made up of very simple ingredients. It flees from the complex life. It evades pomp and show. The heart would starve amid the greatest luxuries.

Simple joys and the treasures of the heart and mind make happiness.

Happiness has very little to do with material things. It is a mental state of mind. Real permanent happiness can not be found in mere temporary things, because its roots reach away down into eternal principles.

One of the most pathetic pictures in civilization is the great army of men and women searching the world over for happiness, as though it existed in things rather than in a state of mind.

The people who have spent years and a fortune trying to find it look as hungry and as lean of contentment and all that makes life desirable as when they started out. Chasing happiness all over the world is about as silly a business as any human being ever engaged in, for it was never yet found by any pursuer. Yet happiness is the simplest thing in the world. It is found in many a home with carpetless floors and pictureless walls. It knows neither rank, station, nor color, nor does it recognize wealth. It only demands that it live with a contented mind and pure heart. It will not live with ostentation; it flees from pretense; it loves the simple life; it insists upon a sweet, healthful, natural environment. It hates the forced and complicated and formal.

Real happiness flees from the things that pass away; it abides only in principle, permanency.

I have never seen a person who has lived a grasping, greedy, money-chasing life, who was not disappointed at what money has given him for his trouble.

It is only in giving, in helping, that we find our quest. Everywhere we go we see people who are disappointed, chagrined, shocked, to find that what they thought would be the angel of happiness turned out to be only a ghost.

All the misery and the crime of the world rest upon the failure of human beings to understand the principle that *no man can really be happy until he harmonizes with the best thing in him, with the divine, and not with the brute.* No one can be happy who tries to harmonize his life with his animal instincts. *The God (the good) in him is the only possible thing that can make him happy.*

Real happiness can not be bribed by anything sordid or low. Nothing mean or unworthy appeals to it. There is no affinity between them.

Founded upon principle, it is as scientific as the laws of mathematics, and he who works his problem correctly will get the happiness answer.

There is only one way to secure the correct answer to a mathematical problem; and that is to work in harmony with mathematical laws. It would not matter if half the world believed there was some other way to get the answer, it would never come until the law was followed with the utmost exactitude.

It does not matter that the great majority of the human race believe there is some other way of reaching the happiness goal. The fact that they are discontented, restless, and unhappy shows that they are not working their problem scientifically.

We are all conscious that there is another man inside of us, that there accompanies us through life a divine, silent messenger, that other, higher, better self, which speaks from the depths of our nature and which gives its consent, its "amen" to every right action, and condemns every wrong one.

Man is built upon the plan of honesty, of rectitude—the divine plan. When he perverts his nature by trying to express dishonesty, chicanery, and cunning, of course he can not be happy.

The very essence of happiness is honesty, sincerity, truthfulness. He who would have real happiness for his companion must be clean, straightforward, and sincere. The moment he departs from the right she will take wings and fly away.

It is just as impossible for a person to reach the normal state of harmony while he is practising selfish, grasping methods, as it is to produce harmony in an orchestra with instruments that are all jangled and out of tune. To be happy, we must be in tune with the infinite within us, in harmony with our better selves. There is no way to get around it.

There is no tonic like that which comes from doing things worth while. There is no happiness like that which comes from doing our level best every day, everywhere; no satisfaction like that which comes from stamping superiority, putting our royal trade-mark upon everything which goes through our hands.

Recently a rich young man was asked why he did not work. "I do not have to," he said. "Do not have to" has ruined more young men than almost anything else. The fact is, Nature never made any provision for the idle man. Vigorous activity is the law of life; it is the saving grace, the only thing that can keep a human being from retrograding. Activity along the line of one's highest ambition is the normal state of man, and he who tries to evade it pays the penalty in deterioration of faculty, in paralysis of efficiency. Do not flatter yourself that you can be really happy unless you are useful. Happiness and usefulness were born twins. To separate them is fatal.

It is as impossible for a human being to be happy who is habitually idle as it is for a fine chronometer to be normal when not running. The highest happiness is the feeling of wellbeing which comes to one who is actively employed doing what he was made to do, carrying out the great life-purpose patterned in his individual bent. The practical fulfilling of the life-purpose is to man what the actual running and keeping time are to the watch. Without action both are meaningless.

Man was made to do things. Nothing else can take the place of achievement in his life. Real happiness without achievement of some worthy aim is unthinkable. One of the greatest satisfactions in this world is the feeling of enlargement, of growth, of stretching upward and onward. No pleasure can surpass that which comes from the consciousness of feeling one's horizon of ignorance being pushed farther and farther away—of making headway in the world—of not only getting on, but also of getting up.

Happiness is incompatible with stagnation. A man must feel his expanding power lifting, tugging away at a lofty purpose, or he will miss the joy of living.

The discords, the bickerings, the divorces, the breaking up of rich homes, and the resorting to all sorts of silly devices by many rich people in their pursuit of happiness, prove that it does not dwell with them, that happiness does not abide with low ideals, with selfishness, idleness, and discord. It is a friend of harmony, of truth, of beauty, of affection, of simplicity.

Multitudes of men have made fortunes, but have murdered their capacity for enjoyment in the process. How often we hear the remark, "He has the money, but can not enjoy it."

A man can have no greater delusion than that he can spend the best years of his life coining all of his energies into dollars, neglecting his home, sacrificing friendships, self-improvement, and everything else that is really worth while, for money, and yet find happiness at the end!

The happiness habit is just as necessary to our best welfare as the work habit, or the honesty or square-dealing habit.

No one can do his best, his highest thing, who is not perfectly normal, and happiness is a fundamental necessity of our being. It is an indication of health, of sanity, of harmony. The opposite is a symptom of disease, of abnormality.

There are plenty of evidences in the human economy that we were intended for happiness, that it is our normal condition; that suffering, unhappiness, discontent, are absolutely foreign and abnormal to our natures.

There is no doubt that our life was intended to be one grand, sweet song. We are built upon the plan of harmony, and every form of discord is abnormal.

There is something wrong when any human being in this world, tuned to infinite harmonies and beauties that are unspeakable, is unhappy and discontented.

Put Beauty into Your Life

When the barbarians overran Greece, desecrated her temples, and destroyed her beautiful works of art, even their savageness was somewhat tamed by the sense of beauty which prevailed everywhere. They broke her beautiful statues, it is true; but the spirit of beauty refused to die, and it transformed the savage heart and awakened even in the barbarian a new power. From the apparent death of Grecian art Roman art was born. "Cyclops forging iron for Vulcan could not stand against Pericles forging thought for Greece." The barbarian's club which destroyed the Grecian statues was no match for the chisel of Phidias and Praxiteles.

"What is the best education?" some one asked Plato many centuries ago. "It is," he replied, "that which gives to the body and to the soul all the beauty and all the perfection of which they are capable."

The life that would be complete; that would be sweet and sane, as well as strong, must be ornamented, softened, and enriched by a love of the beautiful.

There is a lack in the make-up of a person who has no appreciation of beauty, who does not thrill before a great picture or an entrancing sunset, or a glimpse of beauty in nature.

Savages have no appreciation of beauty. They have a passion for adornment, but there is nothing to show that their esthetic faculties are developed. They merely obey their animal instincts and passions.

But as civilization advances ambition grows, wants multiply, and higher and higher faculties show themselves, until in the highest expression of civilization, we find aspiration and love of the beautiful most highly developed. We find it manifested on the person, in the home, in the environment.

The late Professor Charles Eliot Norton of Harvard University, one of the finest thinkers of his day, said that beauty has played an immense part in the development of the highest qualities in human beings; and that civilization could be measured by its architecture, sculpture, and painting.

What an infinite satisfaction comes from beginning early in life to cultivate our finer qualities, to develop finer sentiments, purer tastes, more delicate feelings, the love of the beautiful in all its varied forms of expression!

One can make no better investment than the cultivation of a taste for the beautiful, for it will bring rainbow hues and enduring joys to the whole life. It will not only greatly increase one's capacity for happiness, but also one's efficiency.

A remarkable instance of the elevating, refining influence of beauty has been demonstrated by a Chicago school-teacher, who fitted up in her school a "beauty corner" for her pupils. It was furnished with a stained glass window, a divan covered with an Oriental rug, and a few fine photographs and paintings, among which was a picture of the Sistine Madonna. Several other esthetic trifles, artistically arranged, completed the furnishings of the "beauty corner." The children took great delight in their little retreat, especially in the exquisite coloring of the stained glass window. Insensibly their conduct and demeanor were affected by the beautiful objects with which they daily associated. They became more gentle, more refined, more thoughtful and considerate. A young Italian boy, in particular, who had been incorrigible before the establishment of the "beauty corner," became, in a short time, so changed and softened that the teacher was astonished. One day she asked him what it was that made him so good lately. Pointing to the picture of the Sistine Madonna the boy said, "How can a feller do bad things when she's looking at him?"

Character is fed largely through the eye and ear. The thousand voices in nature of bird and insect and brook, the soughing of the wind through the trees, the scent of flower and meadow, the myriad tints in earth and sky, in ocean and forest, mountain and hill, are just as important for the development of a real man as the education he receives in the schools. If you take no beauty into your life through the eye or the ear to stimulate and develop your esthetic faculties, your nature will be hard, juiceless, and unattractive.

Beauty is a quality of divinity, and to live much with the beautiful is to live close to the divine. "The more we see of beauty everywhere; in nature, in life, in man and child, in work and rest, in the outward and the inward world, the more we see of God (good)."

There are many evidences in the New Testament that Christ was a great lover of the beautiful especially in nature. Was it not He who said: "Consider the lilies of the field; they toil not, neither do they spin; yet Solomon in all his glory was not arrayed like one of these"?

Back of the lily and the rose, back of the landscape, back of all beautiful things that enchant us, there must be a great lover of the beautiful and a great beauty-principle. Every star that twinkles in the sky, every flower, bids us look behind it for its source, points us to the great Author of the beautiful.

The love of beauty plays a very important part in the poised, symmetrical life. We little realize how much we are influenced by beautiful people and things. We may see them so often that they become common in our experience and fail to attract much of our conscious attention, but every beautiful picture, every sunset and bit of landscape, every beautiful face and form and flower, beauty in any form, wherever we encounter it, ennobles, refines and elevates character.

There is everything in keeping the soul and mind responsive to beauty. It is a great refreshener, recuperator, life-giver, health promoter.

Our American life tends to kill the finer sentiments; to discourage the development of charm and grace as well as beauty; it over-emphasizes the value of material things and under-estimates that of esthetic things, which are far more developed in countries where the dollar is not the God.

As long as we persist in sending all the sap and energy of our being into the money-making gland or faculty and letting the social faculty, the esthetic faculty, and all the finer, nobler faculties lie dormant, and even die, we certainly can not expect a well-rounded and symmetrical life, for only faculties that are used, brain cells that are exercised, grow; all others atrophy. If the finer instincts in man and the nobler qualities that live in the higher brain are under-developed, and the coarser instincts which dwell in the lower brain close to the brute faculties are over-developed, man must pay the penalty of animality and will lack appreciation of all that is finest and most beautiful in life.

"The vision that you hold in your mind, the ideal that is enthroned in your heart—this you will build your life by, this you will become." It is the quality of mind, of ideals, and not mere things, that make a man.

It is as essential to cultivate the esthetic faculties and the heart qualities as to cultivate what we call the intellect. The time will come when our children will be taught, both at home and in school, to consider beauty as a most precious gift, which must be preserved in purity, sweetness, and cleanliness, and regarded as a divine instrument of education.

There is no investment which will give such returns as the culture of the finer self, the development of the sense of the beautiful, the sublime, and the true; the development of qualities that are crushed out or strangled in the mere dollar-chaser.

There are a thousand evidences in us that we were intended for temples of beauty, of sweetness, of loveliness, of beautiful ideas, and not mere storehouses for vulgar things.

There is nothing which will pay so well as to train the finest and truest, the most beautiful qualities in us in order that we may see beauty everywhere and be able to extract sweetness from everything.

Everywhere we go there are a thousand things to educate the best there is in us. Every sunset, landscape, mountain, hill, and tree has secrets of charm and beauty waiting for us. In every patch of meadow or wheat, in every leaf and flower, the trained eye will see beauty which would ravish an angel. The cultured ear will find harmony in forest and field, melody in the babbling brook, and untold pleasure in all Nature's songs.

Whatever our vocation, we should resolve that we will not strangle all that is finest and noblest in us for the sake of the dollar, but that we will *put beauty into our life at every opportunity*.

Just in proportion to your love for the beautiful will you acquire its charms and develop its graces. The beauty thought, the beauty ideal, will outpicture themselves in the face and manner. If you are in love with beauty you will be an artist of some kind. Your profession may be to make the home beautiful and sweet, or you may work at a trade; but whatever your vocation, if you are in love with the beautiful, it will purify your taste, elevate and enrich your life, and make you an artist instead of a mere artisan.

There is no doubt that in the future beauty will play an infinitely greater part in civilized life than it has thus far. It is becoming commercialized everywhere. The trouble with us is that the tremendous material-prizes in this land of opportunity are so tempting that we have lost sight of the higher man. We have developed ourselves along the animal side of our nature; the greedy, grasping side. The great majority of us are still living in the basement of our beings. Now and then one rises to the drawing-room. Now and then one ascends to the upper stories and gets a glimpse of the life beautiful, the life worth while.

There is nothing on earth that will so slake the thirst of the soul as the beauty which expresses itself in sweetness and light.

An old traveling man relates that once when on a trip to the West he sat next to an elderly lady who every now and then would lean out of the open window and pour some thick salt—it seemed to him—from a bottle. When she had emptied the bottle she would refill it from a hand-bag.

A friend to whom this man related the incident told him he was acquainted with the lady, who was a great lover of flowers and an earnest follower of the precept: "Scatter your flowers as you go, for you may never travel the same road again." He said she added greatly to the beauty of the landscape along the railroads on which she traveled, by her custom of scattering flower seeds along the track as she rode. Many roads have thus been beautified and refreshed by this old lady's love of the beautiful and her effort to scatter beauty wherever she went.

If we would all cultivate a love of the beautiful and scatter beauty seeds as we go through life, what a paradise this earth would become!

What a splendid opportunity a vacation in the country offers to put beauty into the life; to cultivate the esthetic faculties, which in most people are wholly undeveloped and inactive! To some it is like going into God's great gallery of charm and beauty. They find in the landscape, the valley, the mountains, the fields, the meadows, the flowers, the streams, the brooks and the rivers, riches that no money can buy; beauties that would enchant the angels. But this beauty and glory can not be bought; they are only for those who can see them, appreciate them—who can read their message and respond to their affinity.

Have you never felt the marvelous power of beauty in nature? If not, you have missed one of the most exquisite joys in life. I was once going through the Yosemite Valley, and after riding one hundred miles in a stage-coach over rough mountain roads, I was so completely exhausted that it did not seem as though I could keep my seat until we traveled over the ten more miles which would bring us to our destination. But on looking down from the top of the mountain I caught a glimpse of the celebrated Yosemite Falls and the surrounding scenery, just as the sun broke through the clouds; and there was revealed a picture of such rare beauty and marvelous picturesqueness that every particle of fatigue, brain-fag, and muscle weariness departed in an instant. My whole soul thrilled with a winged sense of sublimity, grandeur, and beauty, which I had never experienced before, and which I never can forget. I felt a spiritual uplift which brought tears of joy to my eyes.

No one can contemplate the wonderful beauties of Nature and doubt that the Creator must have intended that man, made in His own image and likeness, should be equally beautiful.

Beauty of character, charm of manner, attractiveness and graciousness of expression, a godlike bearing, are our birthrights. Yet how ugly, stiff, coarse, and harsh in appearance and bearing many of us are! No one can afford to disregard his good looks or personal appearance.

But if we wish to beautify the outer, we must first beautify the inner, for every thought and every motion shapes the delicate tracings of our face for ugliness or beauty. Inharmonious and destructive attitudes of mind will warp and mar the most beautiful features.

Shakespeare says: "God has given you one face and you make yourselves another." The mind can make beauty or ugliness at will.

A sweet, noble disposition is absolutely essential to the highest form of beauty. It has transformed many a plain face. A bad temper, ill nature, jealousy, will ruin the most beautiful face ever created. After all, there is no beauty like that produced by a lovely character. Neither cosmetics, massage, nor drugs can remove the lines of prejudice, selfishness, envy, anxiety, mental vacillation that are the results of wrong thought habits.

Beauty is from within. If every human being would cultivate a gracious mentality, not only would what he expressed be artistically beautiful, but also his body. There would indeed be grace and charm, a superiority about him, which would be even greater than mere physical beauty.

We have all seen even very plain women who, because of the charm of their personality, impressed us as transcendently beautiful. The exquisite soul qualities expressed through the body transformed it into their likeness. A fine spirit speaking through the plainest body will make it beautiful.

Some one, speaking of Fanny Kemble, said: "Although she was very stout and short, and had a very red face, yet she impressed me as the supreme embodiment of majestic attributes. I never saw so commanding a personality in feminine form. Any type of mere physical beauty would have paled to insignificance by her side."

Antoine Berryer says truly: "There are no ugly women. There are only women who do not know how to look pretty."

The highest beauty—beauty that is far superior to mere regularity of feature or form—is within reach of everybody. It is perfectly possible for one, even with the homeliest face, to make herself beautiful by the habit of perpetually holding in mind the beauty thought, not the thought of mere superficial beauty, but that of heart beauty, soul beauty, and by the cultivation of a spirit of kindness, hopefulness, and unselfishness.

The basis of all real personal beauty is a kindly, helpful bearing and a desire to scatter sunshine and good cheer everywhere, and this, shining through the face, makes it beautiful. The longing and the effort to be beautiful in character can not fail to make the life beautiful, and since the outward is but an expression of the inward, a mere outpicturing on the body of the habitual thought and dominating motives, the face, the manners, and the bearing must follow the thought and become sweet and attractive. If you hold the beauty thought, the love thought, persistently in the mind, you will make such an impression of harmony and sweetness wherever you go that no one will notice any plainness or deformity of person.

There are girls who have dwelt upon what they consider their unfortunate plainness so long that they have seriously exaggerated it. They are not half so plain as they think they are; and, were it not for the fact that they have made themselves very sensitive and self-conscious on the subject, others would not notice it at all. In fact, if they could get rid of their sensitiveness and be natural, they could, with persistent effort, make up in sprightliness of thought, in cheerfulness of manner, in intelligence, and in cheery helpfulness, what they lack in grace and beauty of face.

We admire the beautiful face, the beautiful form, but we love the face illumined by a beautiful soul. We love it because it suggests the ideal of the possible perfect man or woman, the ideal which was the Creator's model.

It is not the outward form of our dearest friend, but our ideal of friendship which he arouses or suggests in us that stirs up and brings into exercise our love and admiration. The highest beauty does not exist in the actual. It is the ideal, possible beauty, which the person or object symbolizes or suggests, that gives us delight.

Everyone should endeavor to be beautiful and attractive; to be as complete a human being as possible. There is not a taint of vanity in the desire for the highest beauty.

The love of beauty that confines itself to mere external form, however, misses its deepest significance. Beauty of form, of coloring, of light and shade, of sound, make our world beautiful; yet the mind that is warped and twisted can not see all this infinite beauty. It is the indwelling spirit, the ideal in the soul, that makes all things beautiful; that inspires and lifts us above ourselves.

We love the outwardly beautiful, because we crave perfection, and we can not help admiring those persons and things that most nearly embody or measure up to our human ideal.

But a beautiful character will make beauty and poetry out of the prosiest environment, bring sunshine into the darkest home, and develop beauty and grace amid the ugliest surroundings.

What would become of us if it were not for the great souls who realize the divinity of life, who insist upon bringing out and emphasizing its poetry, its music, its harmony and beauty?

How sordid and common our lives would become but for these beauty-makers, these inspirers, these people who bring out all that is best and most attractive in every place, every situation and condition!

There is no accomplishment, no trait of character, no quality of mind, which will give greater satisfaction and pleasure or contribute more to one's welfare than an appreciation of the beautiful. How many people might be saved from wrong-doing, even from lives of crime, by the cultivation of the esthetic faculties in their childhood! A love of the truly beautiful would save children from things which encoarsen and brutalize their natures. It would shield them from a multitude of temptations.

Parents do not take sufficient pains to develop the love and appreciation of beauty in their children. They do not realize that in impressionable youth, everything about the home, even the pictures, the paper on the wall, affect the growing character. They should never lose an opportunity of letting their boys and girls see beautiful works of art, hear beautiful music; they should make a practise of reading to them or having them read very often some lofty poem, or inspirational passages from some great writer, that will fill their minds with thoughts of beauty, open their souls to the inflow of the Divine Mind, the Divine Love which encompasses us round about. The influences that moved our youth determine the character, the success and happiness of our whole lives.

Every soul is born responsive to the beautiful, but this instinctive love of beauty must be fostered through the eye and the mind must be cultivated, or it will die. The craving for beauty is as strong in a child of the slums as in a favorite of fortune. "The physical hunger of the poor, the yearning of their stomachs," says Jacob A. Riis, "is not half so bitter, or so little likely to be satisfied as their esthetic hunger, their starving for the beautiful."

Mr. Riis has often tried to take flowers from his Long Island home to the "poors" in Mulberry Street, New York. "But they never got there," he says. "Before I had gone half a block from the ferry I was held up by a shrieky mob of children who cried for the posies and would not let me go another step till I had given them one. And when they got it they ran, shielding the flower with the most jealous care, to some place where they could hide and gloat over their treasure. They came dragging big, fat babies and little weazened ones that they might get a share, and the babies' eyes grew round and big at the sight of the golden glory from the fields, the like of which had never come their way. The smaller the baby, and the poorer, the more wistful its look, and so my flowers went. Who could have said them no?

"I learned then what I had but vaguely understood before, that there is a hunger that is worse than that which starves the body and gets into the newspapers. All children love beauty and beautiful things. It is the spark of the divine nature that is in them and justifies itself! To that ideal their souls grow. When they cry out for it they are trying to tell us in the only way they can that if we let the slum starve the ideal, with its dirt and its ugliness and its hard-trodden mud where flowers were meant to grow, we are starving that which we little know. A man, a human, may grow a big body without a soul; but as a citizen, as a mother, he or she is worth nothing to the commonwealth. The mark they are going to leave upon it is the black smudge of the slum.

"So when in these latter days we invade that slum to make homes there and teach the mothers to make them beautiful; when we gather the children into kindergartens, hang pictures in the schools; when we build beautiful new schools and public buildings and let in the light, with grass and flower and bird, where darkness and foulness were before; when we teach the children to dance and play and enjoy themselves—alas! that it should ever be needed—we are trying to wipe off the smudge, and to lift the heavy mortgage which it put on the morrow, a much heavier one in the loss of citizenship than any community, even the republic, can long endure. We are paying arrears of debt which we incurred by our sad neglect, and we could be about no better business."

There are many poor children in the slums of New York, Mr. Millionaire, who could go into your drawing-room and carry away from its rich canvases, its costly furnishings, a vision of beauty which you never perceived in them because your esthetic faculties, your finer sensibilities, were early stifled by your selfish pursuit of the dollar.

The world is full of beautiful things, but the majority have not been trained to discern them. We can not see all the beauty that lies around us, because our eyes have not been trained to see it; our esthetic faculties have not been developed. We are like the lady who, standing with the great artist, Turner, before one of his wonderful landscapes, cried out in amazement: "Why, Mr. Turner, I can not see those things in nature that you have put in your picture."

"Don't you wish you could, madam?" he replied. Just think what rare treats we shut out of our lives in our mad, selfish, insane pursuit of the dollar! Do you not wish that you could see the marvels that Turner saw in a landscape, that Ruskin saw in a sunset? Do you not wish that you had put a little more beauty into your life instead of allowing your nature to become encoarsened, your esthetic faculties blinded and your finer instincts blighted by the pursuit of the coarser things of life, instead of developing your brute instincts of pushing, elbowing your way through the world for a few more dollars, in your effort to get something away from somebody else?

Fortunate is the person who has been educated to the perception of beauty; he possesses a heritage of which no reverses can rob him. Yet it is a heritage possible to all who will take the trouble to begin early in life to cultivate the finer qualities of the soul, the eye, and the heart. "I am a lover of untainted and immortal beauty," exclaims Emerson. "Oh, world, what pictures and what harmony are thine!"

A great scientist tells us that there is no natural object in the universe which, if seen as the Master sees it, coupled with all its infinite meaning, its utility and purpose, is not beautiful. Beauty is God's handwriting. Just as the most disgusting object, if put under a magnifying glass of sufficient power, would reveal beauties undreamed of, so even the most unlovely environment, the most cruel conditions, will, when viewed through the glass of a trained and disciplined mind, show something of the beautiful and the hopeful. A life that has been rightly trained will extract sweetness from everything; it will see beauty everywhere.

Situated as we are in a world of beauty and sublimity, we have no right to devote practically all of our energies and to sap all our life forces in the pursuit of selfish aims, in accumulating material wealth, in piling up dollars. It is our duty to treat life as a glory, not as a grind or a purely business transaction, dealing wholly with money and bread-and-butter questions. Wherever you are, put beauty into your life.

Education by Absorption

John Wanamaker was once asked to invest in an expedition to recover from the Spanish Main doubloons which for half a century had lain at the bottom of the sea in sunken frigates.

"Young men," he replied, "I know of a better expedition than this, right here. Near your own feet lie treasures untold; you can have them all by faithful study.

"Let us not be content to mine the most coal, to make the largest locomotives, to weave the largest quantities of carpets; but, amid the sounds of the pick, the blows of the hammer, the rattle of the looms, and the roar of the machinery, take care that the immortal mechanism of God's own hand—the mind—is still full-trained for the highest and noblest service."

The uneducated man is always placed at a great disadvantage. No matter how much natural ability one may have, if he is ignorant, he is discounted. It is not enough to possess ability, it must be made available by mental discipline.

We ought to be ashamed to remain in ignorance in a land where the blind, the deaf and dumb, and even cripples and invalids, manage to obtain a good education.

Many youths throw away little opportunities for self-culture because they cannot see great ones. They let the years slip by without any special effort at self-improvement, until they are shocked in middle life, or later, by waking up to the fact that they are still ignorant of what they ought to know.

Everywhere we go we see men and women, especially from twenty-five to forty years of age, who are cramped and seriously handicapped by the lack of early training. I often get letters from such people, asking if it is possible for them to educate themselves so late in life. Of course it is. There are so many good correspondence schools to-day, and institutions like Chautauqua, so many evening schools, lectures, books, libraries, and periodicals, that men and women who are determined to improve themselves have abundant opportunities to do so.

While you lament the lack of an early education and think it too late to begin, you may be sure that there are other young men and young women not very far from you who are making great strides in self-improvement, though they may not have half as good an opportunity for it as you have.

The first thing to do is to make a resolution, strong, vigorous, and determined, that you are going to be an educated man or woman; that you are not going to go through life humiliated by ignorance; that, if you have been deprived of early advantages, you are going to make up for their loss.

Resolve that you will no longer be handicapped and placed at a disadvantage for that which you can remedy.

You will find the whole world will change to you when you change your attitude toward it. You will be surprised to see how quickly you can very materially improve your mind after you have made a vigorous resolve to do so. Go about it with the same determination that you would to make money or to learn a trade. There is a divine hunger in every normal being for self-expansion, a yearning for growth or enlargement. Beware of stifling this craving of nature for self-unfoldment.

Man was made for growth. It is the object, the explanation, of his being. To have an ambition to grow larger and broader every day, to push the horizon of ignorance a little further away, to become a little richer in knowledge, a little wiser, and more of a man—that is an ambition worth while. It is not absolutely necessary that an education should be crowded into a few years of school life. The best-educated people are those who are always learning, always absorbing knowledge from every possible source and at every opportunity.

I know young people who have acquired a better education, a finer culture, through a habit of observation, or of carrying a book in the pocket to read at odd moments, or by taking courses in correspondence schools, than many who have gone through college. Youths who are quick to catch at new ideas, and who are in frequent contact with superior minds, not only often acquire a personal charm, but even, to a remarkable degree, develop mental power.

The world is a great university. From the cradle to the grave we are always in God's great kindergarten, where everything is trying to teach us its lesson; to give us its great secret. Some people are always at school, always storing up precious bits of knowledge. Everything has a lesson for them. It all depends upon the eye that can see, the mind that can appropriate.

Very few people ever learn how to use their eyes. They go through the world with a superficial glance at things; their eye pictures are so faint and so dim that details are lost and no strong impression is made on the mind. Yet the eye was intended for a great educator. The brain is a prisoner, never getting out to the outside world. It depends upon its five or six servants, the senses, to bring it material, and the larger part of it comes through the eye. The man who has learned the art of seeing things looks with his brain.

I know a father who is training his boy to develop his powers of observation. He will send him out upon a street with which he is not familiar for a certain length of time, and then question him on his return to see how many things he has observed. He sends him to the show windows of great stores, to museums and other public places to see how many of the objects he has seen the boy can recall and describe when he gets home. The father says that this practise develops in the boy a habit of *seeing* things, instead of merely *looking* at them.

When a new student went to the great naturalist, Professor Agassiz of Harvard, he would give him a fish and tell him to look it over for half an hour or an hour, and then describe to him what he saw. After the student thought he had told everything about the fish, the professor would say, "You have not really seen the fish yet. Look at it a while longer, and then tell me what you see." He would repeat this several times, until the student developed a capacity for observation.

If we go through life like an interrogation point, holding an alert, inquiring mind toward everything, we can acquire great mental wealth, wisdom which is beyond all material riches.

Ruskin's mind was enriched by the observation of birds, insects, beasts, trees, rivers, mountains, pictures of sunset and landscape, and by memories of the song of the lark and of the brook. His brain held thousands of pictures—of paintings, of architecture, of sculpture, a wealth of material which he reproduced as a joy for all time. Everything gave up its lesson, its secret, to his inquiring mind.

The habit of absorbing information of all kinds from others is of untold value. A man is weak and ineffective in proportion as he secludes himself from his kind. There is a constant stream of power, a current of forces running to and fro between individuals who come in contact with one another, if they have inquiring minds. We are all giving and taking perpetually when we associate together. The achiever to-day must keep in touch with the society around him; he must put his finger on the pulse of the great busy world and feel its throbbing life. He must be a part of it, or there will be some lack in his life.

A single talent which one can use effectively is worth more than ten talents imprisoned by ignorance. Education means that knowledge has been assimilated and become a part of the person. It is the ability to express the power within one, to give out what one knows, that measures efficiency and achievement. Pent-up knowledge is useless.

People who feel their lack of education, and who can afford the outlay, can make wonderful strides in a year by putting themselves under good tutors, who will direct their reading and study along different lines.

The danger of trying to educate oneself lies in desultory, disconnected, aimless studying which does not give anything like the benefit to be derived from the pursuit of a definite program for self-improvement. A person who wishes to educate himself at home should get some competent, well-trained person to lay out a plan for him, which can only be effectively done when the adviser knows the vocation, the tastes, and the needs of the would-be student. Anyone who aspires to an education, whether in country or city, can find someone to at least guide his studies; some teacher, clergyman, lawyer, or other educated person in the community to help him.

There is one special advantage in self-education,—you can adapt your studies to your own particular needs better than you could in school or college. Everyone who reaches middle life without an education should first read and study along the line of his own vocation, and then broaden himself as much as possible by reading on other lines.

One can take up, alone, many studies, such as history, English literature, rhetoric, drawing, mathematics, and can also acquire by oneself, almost as effectively as with a teacher, a reading knowledge of foreign languages.

The daily storing up of valuable information for use later in life, the reading of books that will inspire and stimulate to greater endeavor, the constant effort to try to improve oneself and one's condition in the world, are worth far more than a bank account to a youth.

How many girls there are in this country who feel crippled by the fact that they have not been able to go to college. And yet they have the time and the material close at hand for obtaining a splendid education, but they waste their talents and opportunities in frivolous amusements and things which do not count in forceful character-building.

It is not such a very great undertaking to get all the essentials of a college course at home, or at least a fair substitute for it. Every hour in which one focuses his mind vigorously upon his studies at home may be as beneficial as the same time spent in college.

Every well-ordered household ought to protect the time of those who desire to study at home. At a fixed hour every evening during the long winter there should be by common consent a quiet period for mental concentration, for what is worth while in mental discipline, a quiet hour uninterrupted by time-thief callers.

In thousands of homes where the members are devoted to each other, and should encourage and help each other along, it is made almost impossible for anyone to take up reading, studying, or any exercise for self-improvement. Perhaps someone is thoughtless and keeps interrupting the others so that they can not concentrate their minds; or those who have nothing in common with your aims or your earnest life drop in to spend an evening in idle chatter. They have no ideals outside of the bread-and-butter and amusement questions, and do not realize how they are hindering you.

There is constant temptation to waste one's evenings and it takes a stout ambition and a firm resolution to separate oneself from a jolly, fun-loving, and congenial family circle, or happy-hearted youthful callers, in order to try to rise above the common herd of unambitious persons who are content to slide along, totally ignorant of everything but the requirements of their particular vocations.

A habit of forcing yourself to fix your mind steadfastly and systematically upon certain studies, even if only for periods of a few minutes at a time, is, of itself, of the greatest value. This habit helps one to utilize the odds and ends of time which are unavailable to most people because they have never been trained to concentrate the mind at regular intervals.

A good understanding of the possibilities that live in spare moments is a great success asset.

The very reputation of always trying to improve yourself, of seizing every opportunity to fit yourself for something better, the reputation of being dead-in-earnest, determined to be somebody and to do something in the world, would be of untold assistance to you. People like to help those who are trying to help themselves. They will throw opportunities in their way. Such a reputation is the best kind of capital to start with.

One trouble with people who are smarting under the consciousness of deficient education is that they do not realize the immense value of utilizing spare minutes. Like many boys who will not save their pennies and small change because they can not see how a fortune could ever grow by the saving, they can not see how a little studying here and there each day will ever amount to a good substitute for a college education.

I know a young man who never even attended a high school, and yet educated himself so superbly that he has been offered a professorship in a college. Most of his knowledge was gained during his odds and ends of time, while working hard at his vocation. Spare time meant something to him.

The correspondence schools deserve very great credit for inducing hundreds of thousands of people, including clerks, mill operatives, and employees of all kinds, to take their courses, and thus save for study the odds and ends of time which otherwise would probably be thrown away. We have heard of some most remarkable instances of rapid advancement which these correspondence school students have made by reason of the improvement in their education. Many students have reaped a thousand per cent on their educational investment. It has saved them years of drudgery and has shortened wonderfully the road to their goal.

Wisdom will not open her doors to those who are not willing to pay the price in self-sacrifice, in hard work. Her jewels are too precious to scatter before the idle, the ambitionless.

The very resolution to redeem yourself from ignorance at any cost is the first great step toward gaining an education.

Charles Wagner once wrote to an American regarding his little boy, "May he know the price of the hours. God bless the rising boy who will do his best, for never losing a bit of the precious and God-given time."

There is untold wealth locked up in the long winter evenings and odd moments ahead of you. A great opportunity confronts you. What will you do with it?

The Power of Suggestion

When plate-glass windows first came into use, Rogers, the poet, took a severe cold by sitting with his back to what he supposed was an open window in a dining-room but which was really plate-glass. All the time he was eating he imagined he was taking cold, but he did not dare ask to have the window closed.

We little realize how much suggestion has to do with health. In innumerable instances people have been made seriously ill, sometimes fatally so, by others telling them how badly they looked, or suggesting that they had inherited some fatal disease.

A prominent New York business man recently told me of an experiment which the friends of a robust young man made upon him. It was arranged that, beginning in the morning, each one should tell him, when he came to work, that he was not looking well, and ask him what the trouble was. They were to say it in a way that would not arouse his suspicions, and note the result. At one o'clock this vigorous young man had been so influenced by the suggestion that he quit work and went home, saying that he was sick.

There have been many interesting experiments in the Paris hospitals upon patients in a hypnotic trance, wounds being inflicted by mental suggestion. While a cold poker was laid across their limbs, for example, the subjects were told that they were being seared with a red-hot iron, and immediately the flesh would have the appearance of being severely burned.

I have known patients to collapse completely at the sight of surgical instruments in the operating room. I have heard them say that they could actually feel the cutting of the knife long before they took the anesthetic.

Patients are often put to sleep by the injection into their arms of a weak solution of salt and water, which they are led to think is morphia. Every physician of large experience knows that he can relieve or produce pain simply by suggestion.

Many a physician sends patients to some famous resort not so much for the waters or the air as for the miracle which the complete change of thought effects.

Even quacks and charlatans are able, by stimulating the hope of those who are sick, to produce marvelous cures.

The mental attitude of the nurse has much to do with the recovery of a sick person. If she holds the constant suggestion that the patient will recover; if she stoutly affirms it, it will be a wonderful rallying help to the forces which make for life. If, on the other hand, she holds the conviction that he is going to die, she will communicate her belief, and this will consequently depress the patient.

We are under the influence of suggestion every moment of our waking lives. Everything we see, hear, feel, is a suggestion which produces a result corresponding to its own nature. Its subtle power seems to reach and affect the very springs of life.

The power of suggestion on expectant minds is often little less than miraculous. An invalid with a disappointed ambition, who thinks he has been robbed of his chances in life and who has suffered for years, becomes all wrought up over some new remedy which is advertised to do marvels. He is in such an expectant state of mind that he is willing to make almost any sacrifice to obtain the wonderful remedy; and when he receives it, he is in such a receptive mood that he responds quickly, and thinks it is the medicine which has worked the magic.

Faith in one's physician is a powerful curative suggestion. Many patients, especially those who are ignorant, believe that the physician holds the keys of life and death. They have such implicit confidence in him that what he tells them has powerful influence upon them for good or ill.

The possibilities of healing power in the affirmative suggestion that the patient is going to get well are tremendous. The coming physician will constantly reassure his patient verbally, often vehemently, that he is absolutely bound to recover; he will tell him that there is an omnipotent healing power within him, and that he gets a hint of this in the power which heals a wound, and which refreshes, renews, and recreates him during sleep.

It is almost impossible for a patient to get well while people are constantly reminding him how ill he looks. His will-power together with all his physical recuperative forces could not counteract the effect of the reiteration of the sick suggestion.

Many a sick-room is made a chamber of horrors because of the depressing suggestion which pervades it. Instead of being filled with sunshine, good cheer, and encouragement, it is often darkened, God's beautiful sunshine shut out; ventilation is poor; everybody has a sad, anxious face; medicine bottles and surgical apparatus are spread about; everything is calculated to engender disease rather than to encourage health and inspire hope. Why, there is enough depressing suggestion in such a place to make a perfectly well person ill!

What people need is encouragement, uplift, hope. Their natural resisting powers should be strengthened and developed. Instead of telling a friend in trouble, despair, or suffering that you feel very sorry for him, try to pull him out of his slough of despond, to arouse the latent recuperative, restorative energies within him. Picture to him his God image, his better self, which, because it is a part of the great immortal principle, is never sick and never out of harmony, can never be discordant or suffer.

Right suggestion would prevent a great majority of our divorces. Great infatuation for another has been overcome by suggestion in numerous instances. Many women have been thus cured of a foolish love for impossible men, as in the case of girls who have become completely infatuated with the husband of a friend. Fallen women have been entirely reclaimed, have been brought to see their better, finer, diviner selves through the power of suggestion.

The suggestion which comes from a sweet, beautiful, charming character is contagious and sometimes revolutionizes a whole neighborhood. We all know how the suggestion of heroic deeds, great records, has aroused the ambitions and stirred the energies of others to do likewise. Many a life has turned upon a few moments' conversation, upon a little encouragement, upon the suggestion of an inspiring book.

Many men who have made their impress upon history, who have left civilization a little higher, accomplished what they did largely because their ambition was aroused by suggestion; some book or some individual gave them the first glimpse of their possibility and enabled them to feel for the first time a thrill of the power within them.

The suggestion of inferiority is one of the most difficult to overcome. Who can ever estimate the damage to humanity and the lives wrecked through it! I know men whose whole careers have been practically ruined through the constant suggestion, while they were children, that they would never amount to anything.

This suggestion of inferiority has made them so timid and shy and so uncertain of themselves that they have never been able to assert their individuality.

I knew a college student whose rank in his class entitled him to the highest recognition, whose life was nearly ruined by suggestion; he overheard some of his classmates say that he had no more dignity than a goose, and always made a very poor appearance; that under no circumstances would they think of electing him as class orator, because he would make such an unfortunate impression upon an audience. He had unusual ability, but his extreme diffidence, timidity, shyness, made him appear awkward and sometimes almost foolish,—all of which he would undoubtedly have overgrown, had he not overheard the criticism of his classmates. He thought it meant that he was mentally inferior, and this belief kept him back ever after.

What a subtle power there is in the suggestion of the human voice! What emotions are aroused in us by its different modulations! How we laugh and cry, become indignant, revengeful, our feelings leaping from one extreme to the other, according to the passion-freighted or love-freighted words which reach our ear; how we sit spell-bound, with bated breath, before the great orator who is playing upon the emotions of his audience, as a musician plays upon the strings of his harp, now bringing out tears, now smiles, now pathos, now indignation! The power of his word-painting makes a wonderful impression. A thousand listeners respond to whatever he suggests.

The voice is a great betrayer of our feelings and emotions. It is tender when conveying love to our friends; cold, selfish, and without a particle of sympathy during business transactions when we are trying to get the best of a bargain.

How we are attracted by a gentle voice, and repulsed by one that is harsh! We all know how susceptible even dogs and horses are to the different modulations of the human voice. They know the tone of affection; they are reassured and respond to it. But they are stricken with fear and trembling at the profanity of the master's rage.

Some natures are powerfully affected by certain musical strains; they are immediately lifted out of the deepest depression and despondency into ecstasy. Nothing has touched them; they have just merely felt a sensation through the auditory nerve which aroused and awakened into activity certain brain cells and changed their whole mental attitude.

Music has a decided influence upon the blood pressure in the arteries, and upon the respiration. We all know how it soothes, refreshes, and rests us when jaded and worried. When its sweet harmonies fill the soul, all cares, worries, and anxieties fly away.

George Eliot, in "The Mill on the Floss," gives voice to what some of us have often, doubtless, felt, when under its magic spell. "Certain strains of music," she says, "affect me so strangely that I can never hear them without changing my whole attitude of mind for a time, and if the effect would last, I might be capable of heroism."

Latimer, Ridley, and hundreds of others went to the stake actually rejoicing, the spectators wondering at the smile of ineffable peace which illumined their faces above the fierce glare of the flames, at the hymns of praise and thanksgiving heard amid the roar of crackling fagots.

"No, we don't get sick," said an actor, "because we can't get sick. Patti and a few other stars could afford that luxury, but to the majority of us it is denied. It is a case of 'must' with us; and although there have been times when, had I been at home, or a private man, I could have taken to my bed with as good a right to be sick as any one ever had, I have not done so, and have worn off the attack through sheer necessity. It's no fiction that will power is the best of tonics, and theatrical people understand that they must keep a good stock of it always on hand."

A tight-rope walker was so ill with lumbago that he could scarcely move. But when he was advertised to appear, he summoned all his will power, and traversed the rope several times with a wheelbarrow, according to the program. When through he doubled up and had to be carried to his bed, "as stiff as a frozen frog."

Somewhere I have read a story of a poor fellow who went to hang himself, but finding by chance a pot of money, he flung away the rope and went hurriedly home. He who hid the gold, when he missed it, hanged himself with the rope which the other man had left. Success is a great tonic, and failure a great depressant.

The successful attainment of what the heart longs for, as a rule, improves health and happiness. Generally we not only find our treasure where our heart is, but our health also. Who has not noticed men of indifferent health, perhaps even invalids, and men who lacked energy and determination, suddenly become roused to a realization of unthought-of powers and unexpected health upon attaining some signal success? The same is sometimes true of persons in poor health who have suddenly been thrown into responsible positions by death of parents or relatives, or who, upon sudden loss of property, have been forced to do what they had thought impossible before.

An education is a health tonic. Delicate boys and girls, whom parents and friends thought entirely too slender to bear the strain, often improve in health in school and college. Other things equal, intelligent, cultured, educated people enjoy the best health. There is for the same reason a very intimate relation between health and morals. A house divided against itself can not stand. Intemperance, violation of chastity, and vice of all kinds are discordant notes in the human economy which tend to destroy the great harmony of life. The body is but a servant of the mind. A well-balanced, cultured, and well-disciplined intellect reacts very powerfully upon the physique, and tends to bring it into harmony with itself. On the other hand, a weak, vacillating, one-sided, unsteady, and ignorant mind will ultimately bring the body into sympathy with it. Every pure and uplifting thought, every noble aspiration for the good and the true, every longing of the heart for a higher and better life, every lofty purpose and unselfish endeavor, reacts upon the body, makes it stronger, more harmonious, and more beautiful.

"As a man thinketh in his heart, so is he." The body is molded and fashioned by the thought. If a young woman were to try to make herself beautiful, she would not begin by contemplating ugliness, or dwelling upon the monstrosities of vice, for their hideous images would be reproduced in her own face and manners. Nor would she try to make herself graceful by practising awkwardness. We can never gain health by contemplating disease any more than we can reach perfection by dwelling upon imperfection, or harmony through discord.

We should *keep a high ideal of health and harmony constantly before the mind*; and we should fight every discordant thought and every enemy of harmony as we would fight a temptation to crime. *Never affirm or repeat about your health what you do not wish to be true.* Do not dwell upon your ailments nor study your symptoms. Never allow yourself to think that you are not complete master of yourself. Stoutly affirm your own superiority over bodily ills, and do not acknowledge yourself the slave of an inferior power.

The mind has undoubted power to preserve and sustain physical youth and beauty, to keep the body strong and healthy, to renew life, and to preserve it from decay, many years longer than it does now. The longest lived men and women have, as a rule, been those who have attained great mental and moral development. They have lived in the upper region of a higher life, beyond the reach of much of the jar, the friction, and the discords which weaken and shatter most lives.

Many nervous diseases have been cured by music, while others have been greatly retarded in their development by it. Anything which keeps the mind off our troubles tends to restore harmony throughout the body.

It is a great thing to form a habit, acquire a reputation, of always talking up and never down, of seeing good things and never bad, of encouraging and never discouraging, and of always being optimistic about everything.

"Send forth loving, stainless, and happy thoughts, and blessings will flow into your hands; send forth hateful, impure, and unhappy thoughts, and curses will rain down upon you and fear and unrest will wait upon your pillow."

There is no one principle that is abused to-day in the business world more than the law of suggestion. Everywhere in this country we see the pathetic victims of those who make a business of overpowering and controlling weaker minds. Thus is suggestion carried even to the point of hypnotism as is illustrated by unscrupulous salesmen and promoters.

If a person steals the property of another he is imprisoned, but if he hypnotizes his victim by projecting his own strong trained thought into the innocent, untrained, unsuspecting victim's mind, overcomes his objections, and induces him voluntarily to buy the thing he does not want and can not afford to buy, perhaps impoverishing himself for years so that he and his family suffer for the necessities of life, no law can stop him. It would be better and should be considered less criminal for a man to go into a home and steal articles of value than to overpower the minds of the heads of poor families and hypnotize them into signing contracts for what they have really no right and are not able to buy.

Solicitors often command big salaries because of their wonderful personal magnetism and great powers of persuasion. The time will come when many of these "marvelous persuaders," with long heads cunningly trained, traveling about the country, hypnotizing their subjects and robbing them of their hard-earned money, will be regarded as criminals.

On the other hand, suggestion is used for practical good in business life.

It is now a common practise in many concerns to put in the hands of their employees inspiring books and to republish in pamphlet form special articles from magazines and periodicals which are calculated to stir the employees to new endeavor, to arouse them to greater action and make them more ambitious to do bigger things. Schools of salesmanship are using very extensively the psychology of business and are giving all sorts of illustrations which will spur men to greater efficiency.

The up-to-date merchant shows his knowledge of the power of suggestion for customers by his fascinating show-windows and display of merchandise.

The restaurant keeper knows the power of suggestion of delicious viands upon the appetite, and we often see tempting dishes and articles of food displayed in the window or in the restaurant where the eye will carry the magic suggestion to the brain.

A person who has been reared in luxury and refinement would be so affected by the suggestion of uncleanliness and disorderliness in a cheap Bowery eating-place that he would lose the keenest appetite. If, however, the same food, cooked in the same way, could be transferred to one of the luxurious Broadway restaurants and served upon delicate china and spotless linen with entrancing music, the entire condition would be reversed. The new suggestion would completely reverse the mental and physical conditions.

The suggestion of the ugly suspicions of a whole nation so overpowered Dreyfus during his trial that it completely neutralized his individuality, overbalanced his consciousness of innocence. His whole manner was that of a guilty person, so that many of his friends actually believed him guilty. After the verdict, in the presence of a vast throng which had gathered to see him publicly disgraced, when his buttons and other insignia of office were torn from his uniform, his sword taken from him and broken, and the people were hissing, jeering, and hurling all sorts of anathemas at him, no criminal could have exhibited more evidence of guilt. The radiations of the guilty suggestion from millions of people completely over-powered his own mentality, his individuality, and, although he was absolutely innocent, his appearance and manner gave every evidence of the treason he was accused of.

There is no suggestion so fatal, so insinuating, as that of impurity. Vast multitudes of people have fallen victims to this vicious, subtle, fatal poison.

Who can depict the tragedies which have been caused by immoral, impure suggestion conveyed to minds which were absolutely pure, which have never before felt the taint of contamination? The subtle poisoning infused through the system makes the entrance of the succeeding vicious suggestions easier and easier, until finally the whole moral system becomes saturated with the poison.

There is a wonderful illustration of the power of suggestion in the experience of what are called the Stigmatists. These nuns who for years concentrated all of their efforts in trying to live the life that Christ did, to enter into all of His sufferings, so completely concentrated all of their energies upon the Christ suffering, and so vividly pictured the wounds in their imaginations, that their thought really changed the chemical and physical structure of the tissues and they actually reproduced the nail marks in the hands and feet and the spear wound as in the side of the crucified Christ.

These nuns devoted their lives to this reproduction of the physical evidences of the crucifixion. The fixing of the mind for a long period of time upon the wounds of the hands, feet, and the side, were so vivid, so concentrated, that the picture was made real in their own flesh. In addition to the mental picturing, they kept constantly before them the physical picture of the crucified Christ, which made their mental picture all the more vivid and concentrated. The religious ecstasy was so intense that they could actually see Christ being crucified, and this mental attitude was outpictured in the flesh.

The Curse of Worry

This monster dogs us from the cradle to the grave. There is no occasion so sacred but it is there. Unbidden it comes to the wedding and the funeral alike. It is at every reception, every banquet; it occupies a seat at every table.

No human intellect can estimate the unutterable havoc and ruin wrought by worry. It has ever forced genius to do the work of mediocrity; it has caused more failures, more broken hearts, more blasted hopes, than any other one cause since the dawn of the world.

Did you ever hear of any good coming to any human being from worry? Did it ever help anybody to better his condition? Does it not always—everywhere—do just the opposite by impairing the health, exhausting the vitality, lessening efficiency?

What have not men done under the pressure of worry! They have plunged into all sorts of vice; have become drunkards, drug fiends; have sold their very souls in their efforts to escape this monster.

Think of the homes which it has broken up; the ambitions it has ruined; the hopes and prospects it has blighted! Think of the suicide victims of this demon! If there is any devil in existence, is it not worry, with all its attendant progeny of evils?

Yet, in spite of all the tragic evils that follow in its wake, a visitor from another world would get the impression that worry is one of our dearest, most helpful friends, so closely do we hug it to ourselves and so loath are we to part from it.

Is it not unaccountable that people who know perfectly well that success and happiness both depend on keeping themselves in condition to get the most possible out of their energies should harbor in their minds the enemy of this very success and happiness? Is it not strange that they should form this habit of anticipating evils that will probably never come, when they know that anxiety and fretting will not only rob them of peace of mind and strength and ability to do their work, but also of precious years of life?

No man can utilize his normal power who dissipates his nervous energy in useless anxiety. Nothing will sap one's vitality and blight one's ambition or detract from one's real power in the world more than the worrying habit.

Work kills no one, but worry has killed vast multitudes. It is not the doing things which injures us so much as the dreading to do them—not only performing them mentally over and over again, but anticipating something disagreeable in their performance.

Many of us approach an unpleasant task in much the same condition as a runner who begins his start such a long distance away that by the time he reaches his objective point—the ditch or the stream which is to test his agility—he is too exhausted to jump across. Worry not only saps vitality and wastes energy, but it also seriously affects the quality of one's work. It cuts down ability. A man can not get the highest quality of efficiency into his work when his mind is troubled. The mental faculties must have perfect freedom before they will give out their best. A troubled brain can not think clearly, vigorously, and logically. The attention can not be concentrated with anything like the same force when the brain cells are poisoned with anxiety as when they are fed by pure blood and are clean and unclouded. The blood of chronic worriers is vitiated with poisonous chemical substances and broken-down tissues, according to Professor Elmer Gates and other noted scientists, who have shown that the passions and the harmful emotions cause actual chemical changes in the secretions and generate poisonous substances in the body which are fatal to healthy growth and action.

One of the worst forms of worry is the brooding over failure. It blights the ambition, deadens the purpose and defeats the very object the worrier has in view.

Some people have the unfortunate habit of brooding over their past lives, castigating themselves for their shortcomings and mistakes, until their whole vision is turned backward instead of forward, and they see everything in a distorted light, because they are looking only on the shadow side.

The longer the unfortunate picture which has caused trouble remains in the mind, the more thoroughly it becomes imbedded there, and the more difficult it is to remove it.

Are we not convinced that a power beyond our control runs the universe, that every moment of worry detracts from our success capital and makes our failure more probable; that every bit of anxiety and fretfulness leaves its mark on the body, interrupts the harmony of our physical and mental well-being, and cripples efficiency, and that this condition is at war with our highest endeavor?

Is it not strange that people will persist in allowing little worries, petty vexations, and unnecessary frictions to grind life away at such a fearful rate that old age stares them in the face in middle life? Look at the women who are shriveled and shrunken and aged at thirty, not because of the hard work they have done, or the real troubles they have had, but because of habitual fretting, which has helped nobody, but has brought discord and unhappiness to their homes.

Somewhere I read of a worrying woman who made a list of possible unfortunate events and happenings which she felt sure would come to pass and be disastrous to her happiness and welfare. The list was lost, and to her amazement, when she recovered it, a long time afterwards, she found that not a single unfortunate prediction in the whole catalogue of disasters had been realized.

Is not this a good suggestion for worriers? Write down everything which you think is going to turn out badly, and then put the list aside. You will be surprised to see what a small percentage of the doleful things ever come to pass.

It is a pitiable thing to see vigorous men and women, who have inherited godlike qualities and who bear the impress of divinity, wearing anxious faces and filled with all sorts of fear and uncertainty, worrying about yesterday, to-day, to-morrow—everything imaginable.

"Fear runs like a baleful thread through the whole web of life from beginning to end," says Dr. Holcomb. "We are born into the atmosphere of fear and dread, and the mother who bore us had lived in the same atmosphere for weeks and months before we were born. We are afraid of our parents, afraid of our teachers, afraid of our playmates, afraid of ghosts, afraid of rules and regulations and punishments, afraid of the doctor, the dentist, the surgeon. Our adult life is a state of chronic anxiety, which is fear in a milder form. We are afraid of failure in business, afraid of disappointments and mistakes, afraid of enemies, open or concealed; afraid of poverty, afraid of public opinion, afraid of accidents, of sickness, of death, and unhappiness after death. Man is like a haunted animal from the cradle to the grave, the victim of real or imaginary fears, not only his own, but those reflected upon him from the superstitions, self-deceptions, sensory illusions, false beliefs, and concrete errors of the whole human race, past and present."

Most of us are foolish children, afraid of our shadows, so handicapped in a thousand ways that we can not get efficiency into our life work.

A man who is filled with fear is not a real man. He is a puppet, a mannikin, an apology of a man.

Quit fearing things that may never happen, just as you would quit any bad practise which has caused you suffering. Fill your mind with courage, hope, and confidence.

Do not wait until fear thoughts become intrenched in your mind and your imagination. Do not dwell upon them. Apply the antidote instantly, and the enemies will flee. There is no fear so great or intrenched so deeply in the mind that it can not be neutralized or entirely eradicated by its opposite. The opposite suggestion will kill it.

Once Dr. Chalmers was riding on a stage-coach beside the driver, and he noticed that John kept hitting the off leader a severe crack with his whip. When he asked him why he did this, John answered: "Away yonder there is a white stone; that off leader is afraid of that stone; so by the crack of my whip and the pain in his legs I want to get his mind off from it." Dr. Chalmers went home, elaborated the idea, and wrote "The Expulsive Power of a New Affection." You must drive out fear by putting a new idea into the mind.

Fear, in any of its expressions, like worry or anxiety, can not live an instant in your mind in the presence of the opposite thought, the image of courage, fearlessness, confidence, hope, self-assurance, self-reliance. Fear is a consciousness of weakness. It is only when you doubt your ability to cope with the thing you dread that fear is possible. Fear of disease, even, comes from a consciousness that you will not be able to successfully combat it.

During an epidemic of a dreaded contagious disease, people who are especially susceptible and full of fear become panic-stricken through the cumulative effect of hearing the subject talked about and discussed on every hand and the vivid pictures which come from reading the newspapers. Their minds (as in the case of yellow fever) become full of images of the disease, of its symptoms—black vomit, delirium,—and of death, mourning, and funerals.

If you never accomplish anything else in life, get rid of worry. There are no greater enemies of harmony than little anxieties and petty cares. Do not flies aggravate a nervous horse more than his work? Do not little naggings, constantly touching him with the whip, or jerking at the reins, fret and worry him much more than the labor of drawing the carriage?

It is the little pin-pricks, the petty annoyances of our everyday life, that mar our comfort and happiness and rob us of more strength than the great troubles which we nerve ourselves to meet. It is the perpetual scolding and fault-finding of an irritable man or woman which ruins the entire peace and happiness of many a home.

The most deplorable waste of energy in human life is caused by the fatal habit of anticipating evil, of fearing what the future has in store for us, and under no circumstances can the fear or worry be justified by the situation, for it is always an imaginary one, utterly groundless and without foundation.

What we fear is invariably something that has not yet happened. It does not exist; hence is not a reality. If you are actually suffering from a disease you have feared, then fear only aggravates every painful feature of your illness and makes its fatal issue more probable.

The fear habit shortens life, for it impairs all the physiological processes. Its power is shown by the fact that it actually changes the chemical composition of the secretions of the body. Fear victims not only age prematurely but they also die prematurely. All work done when one is suffering from a sense of fear or foreboding has little efficiency. Fear strangles originality, daring, boldness; it kills individuality, and weakens all the mental processes. Great things are never done under a sense of fear of some impending danger. Fear always indicates weakness, the presence of cowardice. What a slaughterer of years, what a sacrificer of happiness and ambitions, what a miner of careers this monster has been! The Bible says, "A broken spirit drieth the bones." It is well known that mental depression—melancholy—will check very materially the glandular secretions of the body and literally dry up the tissues.

Fear depresses normal mental action, and renders one incapable of acting wisely in an emergency, for no one can think clearly and act wisely when paralyzed by fear.

When a man becomes melancholy and discouraged about his affairs, when he is filled with fear that he is going to fail, and is haunted by the specter of poverty and a suffering family, before he realizes it, he attracts the very thing he dreads, and the prosperity is crushed out of his business. But he is a *mental* failure first.

If, instead of giving up to his fear, a man would *persist in keeping prosperity in his mind*, assume a hopeful, optimistic attitude, and would conduct his business in a systematic, economical, far-sighted manner, actual failure would be comparatively rare. But when a man becomes discouraged, when he loses heart and grip, and becomes panic-stricken and a victim of worry, he is not in a position to make the effort which is absolutely necessary to bring victory, and there is a shrinkage all along the line.

There is not a single redeeming feature about worry or any of its numerous progeny. It is always, everywhere, an unmitigated curse. Although there is no reality in fear, no truth behind it, yet everywhere we see people who are slaves to this monster of the imagination.

Take a Pleasant Thought to Bed with You

Shut off your mental steam when you quit work. Lock up your business when you lock up your office or factory at night. Don't drag it into your home to mar your evening or to distress your sleep.

You can not afford to allow the enemies of your peace and happiness to etch their black pictures deeper and deeper into your consciousness.

Many people lie down to sleep as the camels lie down in the desert, with their packs still on their backs. They do not seem to know how to lay down their burdens, and their minds go on working a large part of the night. If you are inclined to worry during the night, to keep your mental faculties on the strain, taut, it will be a good plan for you to have a bow in your bedroom and unstring it every night as a reminder that you should also unstring your mind so that it will not lose its springing power. The Indian knows enough to unstring his bow just as soon as he uses it so that it will not lose its resilience.

If a man who works hard all day uses his brain a large part of the night, doing his work over and over again, he gets up in the morning weary, jaded. Instead of having a clear, vigorous brain capable of powerfully focusing his mind, he approaches his work with all his standards down, and with about as much chance of winning as a race horse who has been driven all night before a contest would have. Not even a man with the will of a Napoleon could win out under such conditions.

It is of the utmost importance to stop the grinding, rasping process in the brain at night and to keep from wearing life away and wasting one's precious vitality.

Many people become slaves to night worry. They get into a chronic habit of thinking after they retire—especially of contemplating their troubles and trials,—and it is a very difficult habit to break.

It is fundamental to sound health to make it a rule never to discuss business troubles and things that vex and irritate one at night, especially just before retiring, for whatever is dominant in the mind when one falls asleep continues its influence on the nervous structure long into the night.

Some people age more at night than during the daytime, when, it would appear, if they must worry at all, the reverse ought to be true. When hard at work during the day they do not have much time to think of their ailments, their business troubles, their misfortunes. But when they retire, the whole brood of troubling thoughts and worry ghosts fill the mind with horrors. They grow older instead of younger, as they would under the influence of sound, refreshing sleep.

Mental discord saps vitality, lessens courage, shortens life. It does not pay to indulge in violent temper, corroding thoughts, mental discord in any form. Life is too short, too precious, to spend any part of it in such unprofitable, soul-racking, health-destroying business. The imagination is particularly active at night, and all unpleasant, disagreeable things seem a great deal worse then than in the day, because in the silence and darkness imagination magnifies everything. We have all dreamed of the evening's experience, after we went to sleep: perhaps it is the refrain of a song or the intense situation in a play which we live over again. This shows how powerful impressions are; how important it is never to retire to rest in a fit of temper, or in an ugly, unpleasant mood. We should get ourselves into mental harmony, should become serene and quiet before retiring, and, if possible, lie down smiling, no matter how long it may take to secure this condition. Never retire with a frown on your brow; with a perplexed, troubled, vexed expression. Smooth out the wrinkles; drive away all the enemies of your peace of mind, and never allow yourself to go to sleep with critical, cruel, jealous thoughts toward any one.

It is bad enough to feel inimical toward others when under severe provocation or in a hot temper, but you certainly can not afford deliberately to continue this state of mind after the provocation has ceased. The wear and tear upon your nervous system and your health takes too much out of you.

Be at peace with all the world at least once every twenty-four hours. You can not afford to allow the enemies of your happiness and your manhood or womanhood to etch their miserable images deeper and deeper into your life and character as you sleep.

Many of us with crotchety, sour dispositions and quick tempers sometimes have very hard work to be decent in our treatment of others. But we can, at least when we are alone, and away from the people who nettle and antagonize us, forget injuries, quit harboring unpleasant thoughts and hard feelings toward others.

It is a great thing to form a habit of forgetting and forgiving before going to sleep, of clearing the mind of all happiness and success enemies. If we have been impulsive, foolish, or wicked during the day in our treatment of others; if we have been holding a vicious, ugly, revengeful, jealous attitude toward others, it is a good time to wipe off the slate and start anew. It is a blessed thing to put into practise St. Paul's exhortation to the Ephesians: "Let not the sun go down upon your wrath."

If you wish to wake up feeling refreshed and renewed, you simply must retire in a happy, forgiving, cheerful mood. If you go to sleep in an ugly mood or while worrying or depressed, you will wake up tired, exhausted and with no elasticity or spring in your brain or buoyancy in your spirits, for the blood poisoned by worry, by discordant mood, is incapable of refreshing the brain.

If you have a grudge against another, forget it, wipe it out, erase it completely, and substitute a charitable love thought, a kindly, generous thought, before you fall asleep. If you make a habit of clearing the mind every night of its enemies, of driving them all out before you go to sleep, your slumber will be undisturbed by hideous dreams and you will rise refreshed, renewed.

Clean your mental house before retiring. Throw out everything that causes you pain, everything that is disagreeable, undesirable; all unkind thoughts of anger, hatred, jealousy, all selfish, uncharitable thoughts. Do not allow them to print their black hideous pictures upon your mind. And when you have let go of all the rubbish and have swept and dusted and garnished your mind, fill it full of the pleasantest, sweetest, happiest, most helpful, encouraging, uplifting thought-pictures possible.

An evening-happiness bath ought to be the custom in every home. A bath of love and good-will toward every living creature is more important than a water bath.

We should fall asleep in the most cheerful, the happiest possible frame of mind. Our minds should be filled with lofty thoughts—with thoughts of love and of helpfulness—thoughts which will continue to create that which is helpful and uplifting, which will renew the soul and help us to awake in the morning refreshed and in superb condition for the day's work.

If you have any difficulty in banishing unpleasant or torturing thoughts, force yourself to read some good, inspiring book—something that will smooth out your wrinkles and put you in a happy mood; something that will make you see the real grandeur and beauty of life; something that will make you feel ashamed of petty meannesses and narrow, uncharitable thoughts.

After a little practise, you will be surprised to see how quickly and completely you can change your whole mental attitude so that you will face life the right way before you fall asleep.

You will be surprised also to find how wonderfully serene, calm, refreshed, and rejuvenated you will be when you wake in the morning, and how much easier it will be to start right, and wear a smile that won't come off during the day, than it was when you went to bed in an ill-humored, worrying or ugly mood, or full of ungenerous, uncharitable thoughts.

Unless you tune your mind to harmony for sleep, there will be a constant strain upon the nervous system. Even if you do manage to go to sleep with a troubled mind, the brain keeps on working and you will wake up exhausted.

We should take special pains to erase the memory of all unfortunate experiences of the day, all domestic business or professional troubles and anxieties, in order to retire in a placid, peaceful, harmonious state of mind; not only because of the necessity of rising refreshed and invigorated in the morning, but because the character and the disposition are affected by the condition of the mind upon falling asleep. Mental discords not only prevent sound sleep but also leave in the blood poisonous waste from the chemical changes which in turn dulls and impairs the brain action.

Many business men suffer so much torture at night that some of them actually dread to retire because of the long, tedious, wakeful hours. Financial troubles are particularly exaggerated at night; and even many optimists suffer more or less from pessimism then.

Business men ought to know how to turn off brain power when they are not using it. They would not think of leaving or closing their factories at night without turning off the machinery power. Why should they then attempt to go to sleep without turning off their mental power? It is infinitely important to one's health to turn off mental power when not actually using it to produce something.

When you get through your regular day's work, why allow your precious energy to dribble away in little worries? Why carry your business home, take it to bed with you, and waste your life forces in ineffective thinking? Why permit a great leakage of mental energy and a waste of life-force? You must learn to shut off mental steam when you quit work.

Many men use up almost as much mental energy in the evening and in a restless night as during their actual work in the day.

Refresh, renew, rejuvenate yourself by play and pleasant recreation. Play as hard as you work; have a jolly good time, and then you will get that refreshing, invigorating sleep which gives an overplus of energy, a buoyancy of spirit which will make you eager to plunge into the next day's work.

No matter how tired or busy you are, or how late you retire, make it a rule never to go to sleep without erasing every unfortunate impression, every disagreeable experience, every unkind thought, every particle of envy, jealousy, and selfishness, from the mind. *Just imagine that the words "harmony," "good cheer," and "good will to every living creature" are written all over your sleeping room in letters of light.*

People who have learned the art of putting themselves into harmony with all the world before they retire, of never harboring a thought of jealousy, hatred, envy, revenge, or ill-will of any kind against any human being, get a great deal more out of sleep and retain their youth much longer and are much more efficient than those who have the habit of reviewing their disagreeable experiences and thinking about all their troubles and trials in the night.

Make it a rule to put the mind into harmony and a good-will attitude when retiring, and you will be surprised to see how much fresher, younger, stronger and more normal you will become.

I know people whose lives have been completely revolutionized by this experiment of putting themselves in tune before going to sleep. Formerly they were in the habit of retiring in a bad mood; tired, discouraged over anticipated evils and all sorts of worries and anxieties. They would worry over the bad things in their business, the unfortunate conditions in their affairs, and their mistakes, and would discuss their misfortunes at night with their wives. The result was that their minds were in an upset condition when they fell asleep, and these melancholy, black, ugly pictures, so exaggerated in awful vividness in the stillness, became etched deeper and deeper into their minds, and they awoke in the morning weary and exhausted, instead of feeling, as every one should, like a newly-made creature with fresh ambition and invigorated determination.

Form the habit of making a call upon the Great Within of you before retiring. Leave the message of up-lift, of self-betterment, self-enlargement, which you yearn for and long to realize but do not know how to bring about. Registering this call, this demand for something higher and nobler, in your subconsciousness, *putting it right up to yourself*, will work like a leaven during the night; and after a while all the building forces within you will help to unite in furthering your aim; in helping you to realize your vision.

There are marvelous possibilities for health building, success building, happiness building, in the preparation of the mind before going to sleep by impressing, declaring, picturing as vividly as possible our ideals of ourselves, what we would like to become and what we long to accomplish. You will be surprised to see how quickly that wonderful force in your subjective self will begin to shape the pattern, to copy the model which you thus give it. In these great interior creative, restorative forces lies the great secret of life. Blessed is he who findeth it.

The Conquest of Poverty

No one can become prosperous while he really expects or half expects to remain poor. We tend to get what we expect, and to expect nothing is to get nothing.

When every step you take is on the road to failure, how can you hope to arrive at the success goal?

Prosperity begins in the mind and is impossible while the mental attitude is hostile to it. It is fatal to work for one thing and to expect something else, because everything must be created mentally first and is bound to follow its mental pattern.

Most people do not face life in the right way. They neutralize a large part of their effort because their mental attitude does not correspond with their endeavor, so that while working for one thing they are really expecting something else. They discourage, drive away, the very thing they are pursuing by holding the wrong mental attitude towards it. They do not approach their work with that assurance of victory which attracts, which forces results, that determination and confidence which knows no defeat.

To be ambitious for wealth and yet always expecting to be poor, to be always doubting your ability to get what you long for, is like trying to reach East by traveling West. There is no philosophy which will help a man to succeed when he is always doubting his ability to do so, and thus attracting failure.

The man who would succeed must think success, must think upward. He must think progressively, creatively, constructively, inventively, and, above all, optimistically.

You will go in the direction in which you face. If you look towards poverty, towards lack, you will go that way. If, on the other hand, you turn squarely around and refuse to have anything to do with poverty,—to think it,—live it, or recognize it—you will then begin to make progress towards the goal of plenty.

As long as you radiate doubt and discouragement, you will be a failure. If you want to get away from poverty, you must keep your mind in a productive, creative condition. In order to do this you must think confident, cheerful, creative thoughts. The model must precede the statue. *You must see a new world before you can live in it.*

If the people who are down in the world, who are side-tracked, who believe that their opportunity has gone forever, that they can never get on their feet again, only knew the power of reversal of their thought, they could easily get a new start.

If you would attract good fortune you must get rid of doubt. As long as that stands between you and your ambition, it will be a bar that will cut you off. You must have faith. No man can make a fortune while he is convinced that he can't. The "I can't" philosophy has wrecked more careers than almost anything else. Confidence is the magic key that unlocks the door of supply.

I never knew a man to be successful who was always talking about business being bad. The habit of looking down, talking down, is fatal to advancement.

The Creator has bidden every man to look up, not down. He made him to climb, not to grovel. *There is no providence which keeps a man in poverty, or in painful or distressing circumstances.*

The Creator never put vast multitudes of people on this earth to scramble for a limited supply, as though He were not able to furnish enough for all. There is nothing in this world which men desire and struggle for, and that is good for them, of which there is not enough for everybody.

Take the thing we need most—food. We have not begun to scratch the possibilities of the food supply in America.

The State of Texas could supply food, home, and luxuries to every man, woman, and child on this continent. As for clothing, there is material enough in the country to clothe all its inhabitants in purple and fine linen. We have not begun yet to touch the possibilities of our clothing and dress supply. The same is true of all of the other necessities and luxuries. We are still on the outer surface of abundance, a surface covering kingly supplies for every individual on the globe.

When the whale ships in New Bedford Harbor and other ports were rotting in idleness, because the whale was becoming extinct, Americans became alarmed lest we should dwell in darkness; but the oil wells came to our rescue with abundant supply. And then, when we began to doubt that this source would last, Science gave us the electric light.

There is building material enough to give every person on the globe a mansion finer than any that a Vanderbilt or Rothschild possesses. It was intended that we should all be rich and happy; that we should have an abundance of all the good things the heart can crave. We should live in the realization that there is an abundance of power where our present power comes from, and that we can draw upon this great source for as much as we can use.

There is something wrong when the children of the King of kings go about like sheep hounded by a pack of wolves. There is something wrong when those who have inherited infinite supply are worrying about their daily bread; are dogged by fear and anxiety so that they can not take any peace; that their lives are one battle with want; that they are always under the harrow of worry, always anxious. There is something wrong when people are so worried and absorbed in making a living that they can not make a life.

We were made for happiness, to express joy and gladness, to be prosperous. The trouble with us is that we do not trust the law of infinite supply, but close our natures so that abundance cannot flow to us. In other words, we do not obey the law of attraction. We keep our minds so pinched and our faith in ourselves so small, so narrow, that we strangle the inflow of supply. Abundance follows a law as strict as that of mathematics. If we obey it, we get the flow; if we strangle it, we cut it off. The trouble is not in the supply; there is abundance awaiting everyone on the globe.

Prosperity begins in the mind, and is impossible with a mental attitude which is hostile to it. We can not attract opulence mentally by a poverty-stricken attitude which is driving away what we long for. It is fatal to work for one thing and to expect something else. No matter how much one may long for prosperity, a miserable, poverty-stricken, mental attitude will close all the avenues to it. The weaving of the web is bound to follow the pattern. Opulence and prosperity can not come in through poverty-thought and failure-thought channels. They must be created mentally first. We must think prosperity before we can come to it.

How many take it for granted that there are plenty of good things in this world for others, comforts, luxuries, fine houses, good clothes, opportunity for travel, leisure, but not for them! They settle down into the conviction that these things do not belong to them, but are for those in a very different class.

But why are you in a different class? Simply because you think yourself into another class; think yourself into inferiority; because you place limits for yourself. You put up bars between yourself and plenty. You cut off abundance, make the law of supply inoperative for you, by shutting your mind to it. *And by what law can you expect to get what you believe you can not get? By what philosophy can you obtain the good things of the world when you are thoroughly convinced that they are not for you?*

One of the greatest curses of the world is the belief in the necessity of poverty. Most people have a strong conviction that some must necessarily be poor; that they were made to be poor. But there was no poverty, no want, no lack, in the Creator's plan for man. There need not be a poor person on the planet. The earth is full of resources which we have scarcely yet touched. We have been poor in the very midst of abundance, simply because of our own blighting limiting thought.

We are discovering that thoughts are things, that they are incorporated into the life and form part of the character, and if we harbor the fear thought, the lack thought, if we are afraid of poverty, of coming to want, this poverty thought, fear thought incorporates itself in the very life texture and makes us the magnet to attract more poverty like itself.

It was not intended that we should have such a hard time getting a living, that we should just manage to squeeze along, to get together a few comforts, to spend about all of our time making a living instead of making a life. The life abundant, full, free, beautiful, was intended for us.

Let us put up a new image, a new ideal of plenty, of abundance. Have we not worshiped the God of poverty, of lack, of want, about long enough? Let us hold the thought that God is our great supply, that if we can keep in tune, in close touch with Him, so that we can feel our at-one-ness with Him, the great Source of all supply, abundance will flow to us and we shall never again know want.

There is nothing which the human race lacks so much as unquestioned, implicit confidence in the divine source of all supply. We ought to stand in the same relation to the Infinite Source as the child does to its parents. The child does not say, "I do not dare eat this food for fear that I may not get any more." It takes everything with absolute confidence and assurance that all its needs will be supplied, that there is plenty more where these things came from.

We do not have half good enough opinions of our possibilities; do not expect half enough of ourselves; we do not demand half enough, hence the meagerness, the stinginess of what we actually get. We do not demand the abundance which belongs to us, hence the leanness, the lack of fulness, the incompleteness of our lives. We do not demand royally enough. We are content with too little of the things worth while. *It was intended that we should live the abundant life*, that we should have plenty of everything that is good for us. No one was meant to live in poverty and wretchedness. *The lack of anything that is desirable is not natural to the constitution of any human being.*

Erase all the shadows, all the doubts and fears, and the suggestions of poverty and failure from your mind. When you have become master of your thought, when you have once learned to dominate your mind, you will find that things will begin to come your way. Discouragement, fear, doubt, lack of self-confidence, are the germs which have killed the prosperity and happiness of tens of thousands of people.

Every man must play the part of his ambition. If you are trying to be a successful man you must play the part. If you are trying to demonstrate opulence, you must play it, not weakly, but vigorously, grandly. You must feel opulent, you must think opulence, you must appear opulent. Your bearing must be filled with confidence. You must give the impression of your own assurance, that you are large enough to play your part and to play it superbly. Suppose the greatest actor living were to have a play written for him in which the leading part was to represent a man in the process of making a fortune—a great, vigorous, progressive character, who conquered by his very presence. Suppose this actor, in playing the part, were to dress like an unprosperous man, walk on the stage in a stooping, slouchy, slipshod manner, as though he had no ambition, no energy or life, as though he had no real faith that he could ever make money or be a success in business; suppose he went around the stage with an apologetic, shrinking, skulking manner, as much as to say, "Now, I do not believe that I can ever do this thing that I have attempted; it is too big for me. Other people have done it, but I never thought that I should ever be rich or prosperous. Somehow good things do not seem to be meant for me. I am just an ordinary man, I haven't had much experience and I haven't much confidence in myself, and it seems presumptuous for me to think I am ever going to be rich or have much influence in the world." What kind of an impression would he make upon the audience? Would he give confidence, would he radiate power or forcefulness, would he make people think that that kind of a weakling could create a fortune, could manipulate conditions which would produce money? Would not everybody say that the man was a failure? Would they not laugh at the idea of his conquering anything?

Poverty itself is not so bad as the poverty thought. It is the conviction that we are poor and must remain so that is fatal. It is the attitude of mind that is destructive, the facing toward poverty, and feeling so reconciled to it that one does not turn about face and struggle to get away from it with a determination which knows no retreat.

If we can conquer *inward poverty*, we can soon conquer poverty of outward things, for, when we change the mental attitude, the physical changes to correspond.

Holding the poverty thought, keeps us in touch with poverty-stricken, poverty-producing conditions; and the constant thinking of poverty, talking poverty, living poverty, makes us mentally poor. This is the worst kind of poverty.

We can not travel toward prosperity until the mental attitude faces prosperity. As long as we look toward despair, we shall never arrive at the harbor of delight.

The man who persists in holding his mental attitude toward poverty, or who is always thinking of his hard luck and failure to get on, can by no possibility go in the opposite direction, where the goal of prosperity lies.

There are multitudes of poor people in this country who are *half satisfied to remain in poverty*, and who have ceased to make a desperate struggle to rise out of it. They may work hard, but they have lost the hope, the expectation of getting an independence.

Many people keep themselves poor by fear of poverty, allowing themselves to dwell upon the possibility of coming to want, of not having enough to live upon, by allowing themselves to dwell upon conditions of poverty.

When you make up your mind that you are done with poverty forever; that you will have nothing more to do with it; that you are going to erase every trace of it from your dress, your personal appearance, your manner, your talk, your actions, your home; that you are going to show the world your real mettle; that you are no longer going to pass for a failure; that you have set your face persistently toward better things—a competence, an independence—and that nothing on earth can turn you from your resolution, you will be amazed to find what a reenforcing power will come to you, what an increase of confidence, reassurance, and self-respect.

Resolve with all the vigor you can muster that, since there are plenty of good things in the world for everybody, you are going to have your share, without injuring anybody else or keeping others back. It was intended that you should have a competence, an abundance. It is your birthright. You are success organized, and constructed for happiness, and you should resolve to reach your divine destiny.

A New Way of Bringing up Children

"Only a thought, but the work it wrought
Could never by tongue or pen be taught,
But it ran through a life like a thread of gold,
And the life bore fruit a hundredfold."

Not long ago there was on exhibition in New York a young horse which can do most marvelous things; and yet his trainer says that only five years ago he had a very bad disposition. He was fractious, and would kick and bite, but now instead of displaying his former viciousness, he is obedient, tractable, and affectionate. He can readily count and reckon up figures, can spell many words, and knows what they mean.

In fact this horse seems to be capable of learning almost anything. Five years of kindness have completely transformed the vicious yearling colt. He is very responsive to kindness, but one can do nothing with him by whipping or scolding him. His trainer says that in all the five years he has never touched him with a whip but once.

I know a mother of a large family of children who has never whipped but one of them, and that one only once.

When her first child was born people said she was too good-natured to bring up children, that she would spoil them, as she would not correct or discipline them, and would do nothing but love them. But this love has proved the great magnet which has held the family together in a marvelous way. Not one of those children has gone astray. They have all grown up manly and womanly, and love has been wonderfully developed in their natures. Their own affection responded to the mother's love and has become their strongest motive. To-day all her children look upon "Mother" as the grandest figure in the world. She has brought out the best in them because she saw the best in them. The worst did not need correcting or repressing, because the expulsive power of a stronger affection drove out of the nature or discouraged the development of vicious tendencies which, in the absence of a great love, might have become dominant and ruined the life.

Love is a healer, a life-giver, a balm for our hurts. All through the Bible are passages which show the power of love as a healer and life-lengthener. "With long life will I satisfy him," said the Psalmist, "because he hath set his love upon me."

When shall we learn that the great curative principle is love, that love heals because it is harmony? There can be no discord where it reigns. Love is serenity, is peace and happiness.

Love is the great disciplinarian, the supreme harmonizer, the true peacemaker. It is the great balm for all that blights happiness or breeds discontent, a sovereign panacea for malice, revenge, and all the brutal propensities. As cruelty melts before kindness, so the evil passions and their antidote in sweet charity and loving sympathy.

The mother is the supreme shaper of life and destiny.

Many a mother's love for her children has undoubtedly stayed the ravages of some fatal disease. Her conviction that she was necessary to them and her great love for them have braced her, and have enabled her to successfully cope with the enemies of her life for a long time.

One mother I know seems to have the magical art of curing nearly all the ills of her children by love. If any member of the family has any disagreeable experience, is injured or pained, hurt or unhappy, he immediately goes to the mother for the universal balm, which heals all troubles.

This mother has a way of drawing the troubled child out of discord into the zone of perpetual harmony. If he is swayed by jealousy, hatred, or anger, she applies the love solvent, the natural antidote for these passion poisons. She knows that scolding a child when he is already suffering more than he can bear is like trying to put out a fire with kerosene.

Our orphan asylums give pathetic illustration of how quickly the child mind matures and ages prematurely without the uplift and enrichment of the mother love, the mother sympathy,—parental protection and home influence.

It is well known that children who lose their parents and are adopted by their grandparents and live in the country, where they do not have an opportunity to mingle much with other children, adopt the manners and mature vocabulary of their elders, for they are very imitative, and become little men and women before they are out of their youth.

Think of a child reared in the contaminating atmosphere of the slums, where everything is dripping with suggestions of vulgarity and wickedness of every description! Think of his little mind being filled with profanity, obscenity, and filth of all kinds! Is it any wonder that he becomes so filled with vicious, criminal suggestions that he tends to become like his environment?

Contrast such a child with one that is brought up in an atmosphere of purity, refinement, and culture, and whose mind is always filled with noble, uplifting suggestions of the true, the beautiful, and the lovely. What a difference in the chances of these two children, and without any special effort or choice of their own! One mind is trained upward, towards the light, the other downward, towards darkness.

What chance has a child to lead a noble life when all his first impressionable years are saturated with the suggestion of evil, when jealousy and hatred, revenge, quarreling and bickering, all that is low and degrading, fill his ears and eyes?

How important it is that the child should only hear and see and be taught that which will make for beauty and for truth, for loveliness and grandeur of character!

We ought to have a great deal of charity for those whose early lives have been soaked in evil, criminal, impurity thoughts.

The minds of children are like the sensitive plates of a photographer, recording every thought or suggestion to which they are exposed. These early impressions make up the character and determine the future possibility.

If you would encourage your child and help him to make the most of himself, inject bright, hopeful, optimistic, unselfish pictures into his atmosphere. To stimulate and inspire his confidence and unselfishness means growth, success, and happiness for him in his future years, while the opposite practice may mean failure and misery.

It is of infinitely more importance to hold the right thought towards a child, the confident, successful, happy, optimistic thought, than to leave him a fortune without this. With his mind properly trained he could not fail, could not be unhappy, without reversing the whole formative process of his early life.

Keep the child's mind full of harmony, of truth, and there will be no room for discord, for error.

It is cruel constantly to remind children of their deficiencies or peculiarities. Sensitive children are often seriously injured by the suggestion of inferiority and the exaggeration of defects which might have been entirely overcome. This everlasting harping against the bad does not help the child half as much as keeping his little mind full of the good, the beautiful, and the true. The constant love suggestion, purity suggestion, nobility suggestion will so permeate the life after a while that there will be nothing to attract the opposite. It will be so full of sunshine, so full of beauty and love, that there will be little or no place for their opposites.

The child's self-confidence should be buttressed, braced, and encouraged in every possible way; not that he should be taught to overestimate his ability and his possibilities, but the idea that he is God's child, that he is heir to an Infinite inheritance, magnificent possibilities, should be instilled into the very marrow of his being.

A great many boys, especially those who are naturally sensitive, shy, and timid, are apt to suspect that they lack the ability which others have. It is characteristic of such youths that they distrust their own ability and are very easily discouraged or encouraged. It is a sin to shake or destroy a child's self-confidence, to reflect upon his ability or to suggest that he will never amount to much. These discouraging words, like initials cut in the sapling, grow wider and wider with the years, until they become great ugly scars in the man.

Most parents do not half realize how impressionable children are, and how easily they may be injured or ruined by discouragement or ridicule.

Children require a great deal of appreciation, praise, and encouragement. They live upon it. It is a great tonic to them. On the other hand, they wither very quickly under criticism, blame, or depreciation. Their sensitive natures can not stand it. It is the worst kind of policy to be constantly blaming, chiding them, and positively cruel, bordering on criminality even, to suggest to them that they are mentally deficient or peculiar, that they are stupid and dull, and that they will probably never amount to anything in the world.

How easy it is for a parent or teacher to ruin a child's constructive ability, to change a naturally, positive creative mind to a negative, non-producing one, by chilling the child's enthusiasm, by projecting into his plastic mind the idea that he is stupid, dull, lazy, a "blockhead" and good-for-nothing; that he will never amount to anything; that it is foolish for him to try to be much, because he has not the ability or physical stamina to enable him to accomplish what many others do. Such teaching would undermine the brightest intellect.

I have known of an extremely sensitive, timid boy who had a great deal of natural ability, but who developed very slowly, whose whole future was nearly ruined by his teacher and parents constantly telling him that he was stupid and dull, and that he probably never would amount to anything. A little praise, a little encouragement, would have made a superb man of this youth, because he had the material for the making of one. But he actually believed that he was not up to the ordinary mental standard; he was thoroughly convinced that he was mentally deficient, and this conviction never entirely left him.

We are beginning to discover that it is much easier to attract than to coerce. Praise and encouragement will do infinitely more for children than threats and punishment. The warm sunshine is more than a match for the cold, has infinitely more influence in developing the bud, the blossom, and the fruit than the wind and the tempest, which suppress what responds voluntarily to the genial influence of the sun's rays.

We all know how boys will work like troopers under the stimulus of encouragement and praise. Many parents and teachers know this, and how fatal the opposite policy is. But unfortunately a great majority do not appreciate the magic of praise and appreciation.

Pupils will do anything for a teacher who is always kind, considerate, and interested in them; but a cross, fractious, nagging one so arouses their antagonism that it often proves a fatal bar to their progress. There must be no obstruction, no ill-feeling between the teacher and the pupil, if the best results are to be obtained.

Many parents are very much distressed by the waywardness of their children; but this waywardness is often more imaginary than real. A large part of children's pranks and mischief is merely the outcome of exuberant youthful spirits, which must have an outlet, and if they are suppressed, their growth is fatally stunted. They are so full of life, energy, and so buoyant that they can not keep still. They *must* do *something*. Give them an outlet for their animal spirits. Love is the only power that can regulate and control them.

Do not try to make men of your boys or women of your girls. It is not natural. Love them. Make home just as happy a place as possible, and give them rein, freedom. Encourage them in their play, for they are now in their fun age. Many parents ruin the larger, completer, fuller development of their children by repressing them, destroying their childhood, their play days, by trying to make them adults. There is nothing sadder in American life than the child who has been robbed of its childhood.

Children are little animals, sometimes selfish, often cruel, due to the fact that some parts of their brain develop faster than others, so that their minds are temporarily thrown out of balance, sometimes even to cruel or criminal tendencies, but later the mind becomes more symmetrical and the vicious tendencies usually disappear. Their moral faculties and sense of responsibility unfold more slowly than other traits, and of course, they will do mischievous things; but it is a fatal mistake to be always suppressing them. They must give out their surplus energy in some way. Encourage them to romp. Play with them. It will keep you young, and will link them to you with hooks of steel. Do not be afraid of losing your dignity. If you make home the happiest, most cheerful place on earth for your children, if you love them enough, there is little danger of their becoming bad.

Thousands of parents by being so severe with their children, scolding and criticizing them and crushing their childhood, make them secretive and deceitful instead of open and transparent, and estrange them and drive them away from home.

A man ought to look back upon the home of his childhood as the Eden of his life, where love reigned, instead of as a place where a long-faced severity and harshness ruled, where he was suppressed and his fun-loving spirits snuffed out.

Every mother, whether she realizes it or not, is constantly using the power of suggestion in rearing her children, healing all their little hurts. She kisses the bumps and bruises and tells the child all is well again, and he is not only comforted, but really believes that the kiss and caress have magic to cure the injury. The mother is constantly antidoting and neutralizing the child's little troubles and discords by giving the opposite thought and applying the love-elixir.

It is possible, through the power of suggestion, to develop in children faculties upon which health, success, and happiness depend. Most of us know how dependent our efficiency is upon our moods, our courage, hope. If the cheerful, optimistic faculties were brought out and largely developed in childhood, it would change our whole outlook upon life, and we would not drag through years of half-heartedness, discouragement, and mental anguish, our steps dogged by fear, apprehension, anxiety, and disappointment.

One reason why we have such poor health is because we have been steeped in poor-health thought from infancy. We have been saturated with the idea that pain, physical suffering, and disease, are a part of life; necessary evils which can not be avoided. We have had it so instilled into us that robust health is the exception and could not be expected to be the rule that we have come to accept this unfortunate condition of things as a sort of fate from which we can not hope to get away.

The child hears so much sick talk, is cautioned so much about the dangers of catching all sorts of diseases, that he grows up with the conviction that physical discords, aches, pains, all discomfort and suffering, are a necessary part of his existence, that at any time disease is liable to overtake him and ruin his happiness and thwart his career.

Think of what the opposite training would do for the child; if he were taught that health is the ever-lasting fact and that disease is but the manifestation of the absence of harmony! Think what it would mean to him if he were trained to believe that abounding health, rich, full, complete, instead of sickness, that certainty instead of uncertainty were his birthright! Think what it would mean for him to *expect* this during all his growing years, instead of building into his consciousness the opposite, instead of being saturated with the sick thought and constantly being cautioned against disease and the danger of contracting it!

The child should be taught that God never created disease, and never intended that we should suffer; that we were made for abounding health and happiness, made for enjoyment not for pain—made to be happy, not miserable, to express harmony, not discord.

Children are extremely credulous. They are inclined to believe everything that an adult tells them, especially the nurse, the father and mother, and their older brothers and sisters. Even the things that are told them in jest they take very seriously; and their imaginations are so vivid and their little minds so impressionable that they magnify everything. They are often punished for telling falsehoods, when the fault is really due to their excessively active imagination.

Many ignorant or thoughtless parents and nurses constantly use fear as a means of governing children. They fill their little minds full of all sorts of fear stories and terror pictures which may mar their whole lives. They often buy soothing syrups and all sorts of sleeping potions to prevent the little ones from disturbing their rest at night, or to keep them quiet and from annoying them in the day time, and thus are liable to stunt their brain development.

Even if children were not seriously injured by fear, it would be wicked to frighten them, for it is wrong to deceive them. If there is anything in the world that is sacred to the parent or teacher, it is the unquestioned confidence of children.

I believe that the beginnings of deterioration in a great many people who go wrong could be traced to the forfeiting of the children's respect and confidence by the parents and teachers. We all know from experience that confidence once shaken is almost never entirely restored. Even when we forgive, we seldom forget; the suspicion often remains. There should never be any shadows between the child and his parents and teachers. He should always be treated with the utmost frankness, transparency, sincerity. The child's respect is worth everything to his parents. Nothing should induce them to violate it or to shake it. It should be regarded as a very sacred thing, a most precious possession.

Think of the shock which must come to a child when he grows up and discovers that those he has trusted implicitly and who seemed almost like gods to him have been deceiving him for years in all sorts of ways!

I have heard mothers say that they dreaded to have their children grow up and discover how they had deceived them all through their childhood; to have them discover that they had resorted to fear, superstition, and all sorts of deceits in order to govern or influence them.

Whenever you are tempted to deceive a child again, remember that the time will come when *he will understand*, and that he will receive a terrible shock when he discovers that you, up to whom he has looked with such implicit trust, such simple confidence, have deceived him.

Parents should remember that every distressing, blood-curdling story told to a child, every superstitious fear instilled into his young life, the mental attitude they bear towards him, the whole treatment they accord him, are making phonographic records in his nature which will be reproduced with scientific exactness in his future life.

Whatever you do, never punish a child when he is suffering with fear. It is a cruel thing to punish children the way most mothers and teachers do, anyway; but to punish a child when he is already quivering with terror is extremely distressing, and to whip a child when you are angry is brutal. Many children never quite forget or forgive a parent or teacher for this cruelty.

Parents, teachers, friends often put a serious stumbling-block in the way of a youth by suggesting that he ought to study for the ministry, or the law; to be a physician, an engineer, or enter some other profession or business for which he may be totally unfitted. I know a man whose career was nearly ruined by the suggestion of his grandmother when he was a child that she would educate him for the church, and that it was her wish for him to become a clergyman.

It was not that she saw in the little child any fitness for this holy office, but because *she wanted a clergyman in the family*, and she often reminded him that he must not disappoint her. The boy, who idolized his grandmother, pondered this thought until he became a young man. The idea possessed him so strongly that every time he tried to make a choice of a career the picture of a clergyman rushed first to his mind, and, although he could see no real reason why he should become a clergyman, the suggestion that he ought to worked like leaven in his nature and kept him from making any other choice until too late to enable him to succeed to any great extent.

I know a most brilliant and marvelously fascinating woman who is extremely ambitious to make a name for herself, but she is almost totally lacking in her ability to apply herself, even in the line where her talent is greatly marked. She seems to be abundantly endowed in every faculty and quality except this. Now, if her parents had known the secret of correcting mental deficiencies, building up weak faculties, this girl could have been so trained that she would probably have had a great career and made a world-wide name for herself.

I have in mind another woman, a most brilliant linguist, who speaks fluently seven languages. She is a most fascinating conversationalist and impresses one as having read everything, but, although in good health, she is an object of charity to-day, simply because she has never developed her practical faculties at all, and this because she was never trained to work, to depend upon herself even in little things when she was a child. She was fond of her books, was a most brilliant scholar, but never learned to be practical or to do anything herself. Her self-reliance and independence were never developed. All of her early friends predicted a brilliant future for her, but because of the very consciousness of possessing so many brilliant qualities and of the fact that she was flattered during all her student life and not obliged to depend upon herself for anything, she continued to exercise her strong scholarship faculties only, little dreaming that the neglect to develop her weaker ones would wreck her usefulness and her happiness.

It is not enough to possess ability. We must be able to use it effectively, and whatever interferes with its activity to that extent kills efficiency. There are many people who are very able in most qualities and yet their real work is seriously injured and often practically ruined, or they are thrown into the mediocre class, owing to some weakness or deficiency which might have been entirely remedied by cultivation and proper training in earlier life.

I know a man of superb ability in nearly every respect who is so timid and shy that he does not dare push himself forward or put himself in the position of greatest advantage, does not dare *begin* things. Consequently his whole life has been seriously handicapped.

If children could only be taught to develop a positive, creative mind, it would be of infinitely more value and importance to them than inheriting a fortune with a non-productive one. Youths should be taught that the most valuable thing to learn in life next to integrity is how to build their minds up to the highest possible producing point, the highest possible state of *creative efficiency*.

The most important part of the education of the future will be to increase the chances of success in life and lessen the danger of failure and the wrecking of one's career by building up weak and deficient faculties, correcting one-sided tendencies, so that the individual will become more level-headed, better balanced, and have a more symmetrical mind.

Many students leave school and college knowing a great deal, but without a bit of improvement in their self-confidence, their initiative ability. They are just as timid, shy, and self-depreciatory as before entering.

Now, what advantage is it to send a youth out into the world with a head full of knowledge but without the confidence or assurance to use it effectively, or the ability to grapple with life's problems with that vigor and efficiency which alone can bring success?

It is an unpardonable reflection upon a college which turns out youths who dare not say their souls are their own, who have not developed a vigorous self-confidence, assurance, and initiative. Hundreds of students are turned out of our colleges every year who would almost faint away if they were suddenly called upon to speak in public, to read a resolution, or even to put a motion.

The time will come when an education will enable a youth while upon his feet in public to express himself forcefully, to use the ability he has and summon his knowledge quickly. He will be so trained in self-control, in self-confidence, in level-headedness, that he will not be thrown off his guard in an emergency. The future education will mean that what the student knows will be *available*, that he can utilize it at will, that he will be trained to use it *efficiently*.

Many of our graduates leave college every year as weak and inefficient in many respects as when they began their education. What is education for if it is not to train the youth to be the master of his faculties, master of every situation, able to summon all of his reserves of knowledge and power at will?

A college graduate, timid, stammering, blushing, and confused, when suddenly called upon to use his knowledge whether in public or elsewhere, ought to be an unknown thing. Of what use is education which can not be summoned at will? Of what good are the reserves of learning which can not be marshaled quickly when we need them, which do not help one to be master of himself and the situation, whatever it may be?

The time will come when no child will be allowed to grow up without being taught to believe in himself, to have great confidence in his ability. This will be a most important part of his education, for if he believes in himself *enough*, he will not be likely to allow a single deficient faculty or weakness to wreck his career.

He should be reared in the conviction that he was sent into this world with a mission and that he is going to deliver it.

Every youth should be taught that it was intended he should fill a place in the world which no one else can fill; that he should expect to fill it, and train himself for it; taught that he was made in the Creator's image, that in the truth of his being he is divine, perfect, immortal, and that the image of God can not fail. He should be taught to think grandly of himself, to form a sublime estimate of his possibilities and of his future. This will increase his self-respect and self-development in well-proportioned living.

The Home as a School of Good Manners

Not long ago I visited a home where such exceptionally good breeding prevailed and such fine manners were practised by all the members of the family, that it made a great impression upon me.

This home is the most remarkable school of good manners, refinement, and culture generally, I have ever been in. The parents are bringing up their children to practise their best manners on all occasions. They do not know what company manners mean.

The boys have been taught to treat their sisters with as much deference as though they were stranger guests. The politeness, courtesy, and consideration which the members of this family show toward one another are most refreshing and beautiful. Coarseness, gruffness, lack of delicacy find no place there.

Both boys and girls have been trained from infancy to make themselves interesting, and to entertain and try to make others happy.

The entire family make it a rule to dress before dinner in the evening, just as they would if special company were expected.

Their table manners are specially marked. At table every one is supposed to be at his best, not to bring any grouch, or a long or sad face to it, but to contribute his best thought, his wittiest sayings, to the conversation. Every member of the family is expected to do his best to make the meal a really happy occasion. There is a sort of rivalry to see who can be the most entertaining, or contribute the spiciest bits of conversation. There is no indication of dyspepsia in this family, because every one is trained to laugh and be happy generally, and laughter is a fatal enemy of indigestion.

The etiquette of the table is also strictly observed. Every member of the family tries to do just the proper thing and always to be mindful of others' rights. Kindness seems to be practised for the joy of it, not for the sake of creating a good impression on friends or acquaintances. There is in this home an air of peculiar refinement which is very charming. The children are early taught to greet callers and guests cordially, heartily, in real Southern, hospitable fashion, and to make them feel that they are very welcome. They are taught to make every one feel comfortable and at home, so that there will be no sense of restraint.

As a result of this training the children have formed a habit of good behavior and are considered an acquisition to any gathering. They are not embarrassed by the awkward slips and breaks which are so mortifying to those who only wear their company manners on special occasions.

A stranger would almost think this home was a school of good breeding, and it is a real treat to visit these people. It is true the parents in this family have the advantage of generations of fine breeding and Southern hospitality back of them, which gives the children a great natural advantage. There is an atmosphere of chivalry and cordiality in this household which is really refreshing.

Many parents seem to expect that their children will pick up their good manners outside of the home, in school, or while visiting. This is a fatal mistake. Every home should be a school of good manners and good breeding. The children should be taught that there is nothing more important than the development of an interesting personality, an attractive presence, and an ability to entertain with grace and ease. They should be taught that the great object of life is to develop a superb personality, a noble manhood and womanhood.

There is no art like that of a beautiful behavior, a fine manner, no wealth greater than that of a pleasing personality.

Mother

"All that I am or hope to be," said Lincoln, after he had become President, "I owe to my angel mother."

"My mother was the making of me," said Thomas Edison, recently. "She was so true, so sure of me; and I felt that I had some one to live for; some one I must not disappoint."

"All that I have ever accomplished in life," declared Dwight L. Moody, the great evangelist, "I owe to my mother."

"To the man who has had a good mother, all women are sacred for her sake," said Jean Paul Richter.

The testimony of great men in acknowledgment of the boundless debt they owe to their mothers would make a record stretching from the dawn of history to to-day. Few men, indeed, become great who do not owe their greatness to a mother's love and inspiration.

How often we hear people in every walk of life say, "I never could have done this thing but for my mother. She believed in me, encouraged me when others saw nothing in me."

"A kiss from my mother made me a painter," said Benjamin West.

A distinguished man of to-day says: "I never could have reached my present position had I not known that my mother expected me to reach it. From a child she made me feel that this was the position she expected me to fill; and her faith spurred me on and gave me the power to attain it."

Everything that a man has and is he owes to his mother. From her he gets health, brain, encouragement, moral character, and all his chances of success.

"In the shadow of every great man's fame walks his mother," says Dorothy Dix. "She has paid the price of his success. She went down into the Valley of the Shadow to give him life, and every day for years and years thereafter she toiled incessantly to push him on toward his goal.

"She gave the labor of her hands for his support; she poured into him ambition when he grew discouraged; she supplemented his weakness with her strength; she filled him with her hope and faith when his own failed.

"At last he did the Big Thing, and people praised him, and acclaimed him, and nobody thought of the quiet, insignificant little woman in the background, who had been the real power behind the throne. Sometimes even the king himself forgets who was the kingmaker."

Many a man is enjoying a fame which is really due to a self-effacing, sacrificing mother. People hurrah for the governor, or mayor, or congressman, but the real secret of his success is often tucked away in that little unknown, unappreciated, unheralded mother. His education and his chance to rise may have been due to her sacrifices.

It is a strange fact that our mothers, the molders of the world, should get so little credit and should be so seldom mentioned among the world's achievers. The world sees only the successful son; the mother is but a round in the ladder upon which he has climbed. Her name or face is seldom seen in the papers; only her son is lauded and held up to our admiration. Yet it was that sweet, pathetic figure in the background that made his success possible.

The woman who merits the greatest fame is the woman who gives a brilliant mind to the world. The mothers of great men and women deserve just as much honor as the great men and women themselves, and they will receive it from the better understanding of the coming days.

"A wife may do much toward polishing up a man and boosting him up the ladder, but unless his mother first gave him the intellect to scintillate and the muscles to climb with, the wife labors in vain," continues Dorothy Dix, in the *Evening Journal*.

"You can not make a clod shine. You can not make a mollusk aspire. You must have the material to work with, to produce results.

"By the time a man is married his character is formed, and he changes very little. His mother has made him; and no matter how hard she tries, there is very little that his wife can do toward altering him.

"It is not the philosophies, the theories, the code of ethics that a man acquires in his older years that really influence him. It is the things that he learned at his mother's knee, the principles that she instilled in him in his very cradle, the taste and habits that she formed, the strength and courage that she breathed into him.

"It is the childish impressions that count. It is the memory of whispered prayers, of bedtime stories, of old ideals held unfalteringly before a boy's gaze; it is half-forgotten songs, and dim visions of heroes that a mother taught her child to worship, that make the very warp and woof of the soul.

"It is the pennies, that a mother teaches a boy to save and the self-denial that she inculcates in doing it, that form the real foundation of the fortune of the millionaire.

"It is the mother that loves books, and who gives her sons her love of learning, who bestows the great scholars, the writers, and orators, on the world.

"It is the mother that worships science, who turns the eyes of the child upon her breast up to the wonder of the stars, and who teaches the little toddler at her side to observe the marvel of beast, and bird, and flower, and all created things, whose sons become the great astronomers and naturalists, and biologists."

The very atmosphere that radiates from and surrounds the mother is the inspiration and constitutes the holy of holies of family life.

"In my mother's presence," said a prominent man, "I become for the time transformed into another person."

How many of us have felt the truth of this statement! How ashamed we feel when we meet her eyes, that we have ever harbored an unholy thought, or dishonorable suggestion! It seems impossible to do wrong while under that magic influence. What revengeful plans, what thoughts of hatred and jealousy, have been scattered to the four winds while in the mother's presence! Her children go out from communion with her resolved to be better men, nobler women, truer citizens.

"How many of us have stood and watched with admiration the returning victor of some petty battle, cheering until we were hoarse, exhausting ourselves with the vehemence of our enthusiasm," says a writer, "when right beside us, possibly touching our hand, was one greater than he? One whose battle has not been petty—whose conflict has not been of short duration, but has for us fought many a severe fight.

"When we had the scarlet fever or diphtheria and not one would come near us, who held the cup of cold water to our fever-parched lips? Who bent over us day and night and fought away with almost supernatural strength the greatest of all enemies—death? The world's greatest heroine—Mother! Who is it that each Sunday dinner-time chose the neck of the chicken that we might have the juicy wing or breast or leg? Who is it stays home from the concert, the social, the play, that we may go with the others and not be stinted for small change? Who is it crucifies her love of pretty clothes, her desire for good things, her longing for pleasure that we may have all these? Who is it? Mother!"

The greatest heroine in the world is the mother. No one else makes such sacrifices, or endures anything like the suffering that she uncomplainingly endures for her children.

What is the giving of one's life in battle or in a wreck at sea to save another, in comparison with the perpetual sacrifice of many mothers of a living death lasting for half a century or more? How the world's heroes dwindle in comparison with the mother heroine! There is no one in the average family, the value of whose services begins to compare with those of the mother, and yet there is no one who is more generally neglected or taken advantage of. She must remain at home evenings, and look after the children, when the others are out having a good time. Her cares never cease. She is responsible for the housework, for the preparation of meals; she has the children's clothes to make or mend, there is company to be entertained, darning to be done, and a score of little duties which must often be attended to at odd moments, snatched from her busy days, and she is often up working at night, long after every one else in the house is asleep.

No matter how loving or thoughtful the father may be, the heavier burdens, the greater anxieties, the weightier responsibilities of the home, of the children, usually fall on the mother. Indeed, the very virtues of the good mother are a constant temptation to the other members of the family, especially the selfish ones, to take advantage of her. They seem to take it for granted that they can put all their burdens on the patient, uncomplaining mother; that she will always do anything to help out, and to enable the children to have a good time; and in many homes, sad to say, the mother, just because of her goodness, is shamefully imposed upon and neglected. "Oh, mother won't mind, mother will stay at home." How often we hear remarks like this from thoughtless children!

It is always the poor mother on whom the burden falls; and the pathetic thing is that she rarely gets much credit or praise.

Many mothers in the poor and working classes practically sacrifice all that most people hold dearest in life for their children. They deliberately impair their health, wear themselves out, make all sorts of sacrifices, to send a worthless boy to college. They take in washing, go out house-cleaning, do the hardest and most menial work, in order to give their boys and girls an education and the benefit of priceless opportunities that they never had; yet, how often, they are rewarded only with total indifference and neglect!

Some time ago I heard of a young girl, beautiful, gay, full of spirit and vigor, who married and had four children. Her husband died penniless, and the mother made the most heroic efforts to educate the children. By dint of unremitting toil and unheard of sacrifices and privations she succeeded in sending the boys to college and the girls to a boarding-school. When they came home, pretty, refined girls and strong young men, abreast with all the new ideas and tastes of their times, she was a worn-out, commonplace old woman. They had their own pursuits and companions. She lingered unappreciated among them for two or three years, and then died, of some sudden failure of the brain. The shock of her fatal illness woke them to consciousness of the truth. They hung over her, as she lay prostrate, in an agony of grief. The oldest son, as he held her in his arms, cried: "You have been a good mother to us!" Her face brightened, her eyes kindled into a smile, and she whispered: "You never said so before, John." Then the light died out, and she was gone.

Many men spend more money on expensive caskets, flowers, and emblems of mourning than they ever spent on their poor, loving, self-sacrificing mothers for many years while alive. Men who, perhaps, never thought of carrying flowers to their mothers in life, pile them high on their coffins.

Who can ever depict the tragedies that have been enacted in the hearts of American mothers, who have suffered untold tortures from neglect, indifference, and lack of appreciation?

What a pathetic story of neglect many a mother's letters from her grown-up children could tell! A few scraggy lines, a few sentences now and then, hurriedly written and mailed—often to ease a troubled conscience—mere apologies for letters, which chill the mother heart.

I know men who owe their success in life to their mother; who have become prosperous and influential, because of the splendid training of the self-sacrificing mother, and whose education was secured at an inestimable cost to her, and yet they seldom think of carrying to her flowers, confectionery, or little delicacies, or of taking her to a place of amusement, or of giving her a vacation or bestowing upon her any of the little attentions and favors so dear to a woman's heart. They seem to think she is past the age for these things, that she no longer cares for them, that about all she expects is enough to eat and drink, and the simplest kind of raiment.

These men do not know the feminine heart which never changes in these respects, except to grow more appreciative of the little attentions, the little considerations, and thoughtful acts which meant so much to them in their younger days.

Not long ago I heard a mother, whose sufferings and sacrifices for her children during a long and trying struggle with poverty should have given her a monument, say, that she guessed she'd better go to an old ladies' home and end her days there. What a picture that was! An aged woman with white hair and a sweet, beautiful face; with a wonderful light in her eye; calm, serene, and patient, yet dignified, whose children, all of whom are married and successful, made her feel as if she were a burden! They live in luxurious homes, but have never offered to provide a home for the poor, old rheumatic mother, who for so many years slaved for them. They put their own homes, stocks, and other property in their wives' names, and while they pay the rent of their mother's meagerly furnished rooms and provide for her actual needs, they apparently never think what joy it would give her to own her own home, and to possess some pretty furnishings, and a few pictures.

In many cases men through thoughtlessness do not provide generously for their mothers even when well able to. They seem to think that a mother can live most anywhere, and most anyway; that if she has enough to supply her necessities she is satisfied. Just think, you prosperous business men, how you would feel if the conditions were reversed, if you were obliged to take the dependent, humiliating position of your mother!

Whatever else you are obliged to neglect, take no chances of giving your mother pain by neglecting her, and of thus making yourself miserable in the future.

The time may come when you will stand by her bedside, in her last sickness, or by her coffin, and wish that you had exchanged a little of your money for more visits and more attentions and more little presents to your mother; when you will wish that you had cultivated her more, even at the cost of making a little less money.

There is no one else in this world who can take your mother's place in your life. And there is no remorse like that which comes from the remembrance of ill-treating, abusing, or being unkind to one's mother. These things stand out with awful vividness and terrible clearness when the mother is gone forever from sight, and you have time to contrast your treatment with her long suffering, tenderness, and love, and her years of sacrifice for you.

One of the most painful things I have ever witnessed was the anguish of a son who had become wealthy and in his prosperity neglected the mother, whose sacrifices alone had made his success possible. He did not take the time to write to her more than twice a year, and then only brief letters. He was too busy to send a good long letter to the poor old lonely mother back in the country, who had risked her life and toiled and sacrificed for years for him! Finally, when he was summoned to her bedside in the country, in her last sickness, and realized that his mother had been for years without the ordinary comforts of life, while he had been living in luxury, he broke down completely. And while he did everything possible to alleviate her suffering, in the few last days that remained to her on earth, and gave her an imposing burial, what torture he must have suffered, at this pitiful picture of his mother who had sacrificed everything for him!

"The regrets for thoughtless acts and indifference to admonitions now felt and expressed by many living sons of dead mothers will, in time, be felt and expressed by the living sons of living mothers," says Richard L. Metcalfe, in the "Commoner." "The boys of to-day who do not understand the value of the mother's companionship will yet sing—with those who already know—this song of tribute and regret:

"'The hours I spent with thee, dear heart,
Are as a string of pearls to me;
I count them over, every one apart,
My rosary.
"'Each hour a pearl, each pearl a prayer,
To still a heart in absence wrung;
I tell each bead unto the end, and there
A cross is hung.
"'O memories that bless—and burn!
Oh mighty gain and bitter loss!
I kiss each bead and strive at last to learn
To kiss the cross,
Sweet heart,
To kiss the cross.'"

No man worthy of the name ever neglects or forgets his mother.

I have an acquaintance, of very poor parentage, who had a hard struggle to get a start in the world; but when he became prosperous and built his beautiful home, he finished a suite of rooms in it especially for his mother, furnished them with all conveniences and comforts possible, and insisted upon keeping a maid specially for her. Although she lives with her son's family, she is made to feel that this part of the great home is her own, and that she is as independent as though she lived in her own house. Every son should be ambitious to see his mother as well provided for as his wife.

Really great men have always reverenced and cared tenderly for their mothers. President McKinley provided in his will that, first of all, his mother should be made comfortable for life.

The first act of Garfield, after he was inaugurated President, was to kiss his aged mother, who sat near him, and who said this was the proudest and happiest moment of her life.

Ex-President Loubet of France, even after his elevation to the presidency, took great pride in visiting his mother, who was a humble market gardener in a little French village. A writer on one occasion, describing a meeting between this mother and her son, says: "Her noted son awaited her in the market-place, as she drove up in her little cart loaded with vegetables. Assisting his mother to alight, the French President gave her his arm and escorted her to her accustomed seat. Then holding over her a large umbrella, to shield her from the threatening weather, he seated himself at her side, and mother and son enjoyed a long talk together."

I once saw a splendid young college graduate introduce his poor, plainly dressed old mother to his classmates with as much pride and dignity as though she was a queen. Her form was bent, her hands were calloused, she was prematurely old, and much of this deterioration was caused by all sorts of drudgery to help her boy to pay his college expenses.

I have seen other college men whose mothers had made similar sacrifices, and who were ashamed to have them attend their graduating exercises, ashamed to introduce them to their classmates.

Think of the humiliation and suffering of the slave mother, who has given all the best of her life to a large family, battling with poverty in her efforts to dignify her little home, and to give her children an education, when she realizes that she is losing ground intellectually, yet has no time or strength for reading, or self-culture, no opportunity for broadening her mental outlook by traveling or mingling with the world! But this is nothing compared to the anguish she endures, when, after the flower of her youth is gone and there is nothing left of her but the ashes of a burned-out existence, the shreds of a former superb womanhood, she awakes to the consciousness that her children are ashamed of her ignorance and desire to keep her in the background.

From babyhood children should be taught to look up to, not down on their mother. For that reason she should never appear before them in slovenly raiment, nor conduct herself in any way that would lessen their respect. She should keep up her intellectual culture that they may not advance beyond her understanding and sympathies.

No matter how callous or ungrateful a son may be, no matter how low he may sink in vice or crime, he is always sure of his mother's love, always sure of one who will follow him even to his grave, if she is alive and can get there; of one who will cling to him when all others have fled.

It is forever true, as Kipling poignantly expresses it in his beautiful verses on "Mother Love":

"If I were hanged on highest hill,
Mother o' mine, O mother o' mine!
I know whose love would follow still,
Mother o' mine, O mother o' mine!
"If I were drowned in the deepest sea,
Mother o' mine, O mother o' mine!
I know whose tears would come down to me,
Mother o' mine, O mother o' mine!
"If I were cursed of body and soul,
Mother o' mine, O mother o' mine!
I know whose prayer's would make me whole!
Mother o' mine, O mother o' mine!"

One of the saddest sights I have ever seen was that of a poor, old, broken-down mother, whose life had been poured into her children, making a long journey to the penitentiary to visit her boy, who had been abandoned by everybody but herself. Poor old mother! It did not matter that he was a criminal, that he had disgraced his family, that everybody else had forsaken him, that he had been unkind to her—the mother's heart went out to him just the same. She did not see the hideous human wreck that crime had made. She saw only her darling boy, the child that God had given her, pure and innocent as in his childhood.

Oh, there is no other human love like this, which follows the child from the cradle to the grave, never once abandons, never once forsakes him, no matter how unfortunate or degenerate he may become.

"So your best girl is dead," sneeringly said a New York magistrate to a young man who was arrested for attempting suicide. "Who was she?" Without raising his eyes, the unfortunate victim burst into tears and replied, "She was my mother!" The smile vanished from the magistrate's face and, with tears in his eyes, he said, "Young man, go and try to be a good man, for your mother's sake." How little we realize what tragedy may be going on in the hearts of those whom we sneeringly condemn!

What movement set on foot in recent years, deserves heartier support than that for the establishment of a national Mothers' Day?

The day set apart as Mothers' Day by those who have inaugurated this movement is *the second Sunday in May*. Let us unite in doing all we can to make it a real Mothers' Day, by especially honoring our mothers; in the flesh, those of us who are so fortunate as to have our mothers with us; in the spirit, those who are not so fortunate.

If away from her, write a good, loving letter, or telephone or telegraph to the best mother who ever lived—your mother. Send her some flowers, an appropriate present; go and spend the day with her, or in some other way make her heart glad. Show her that you appreciate her, and that you give her credit for a large part of your success.

Let us do all we can to make up for past neglect of the little-known, half-appreciated, unheralded mothers who have had so little credit in the past, and are so seldom mentioned among the world's achievers, by openly, and especially in our hearts, paying our own mothers every tribute of honor, respect, devotion, and gratitude that love and a sense of duty can suggest. Let us acknowledge to the world the great debt we owe them by wearing, every one of us, boy and girl, man and woman, on Mothers' Day, a white carnation—the flower chosen as the symbol and emblem of motherhood.

Happily chosen emblem! What could more fittingly represent motherhood with its whiteness symbolizing purity; its lasting qualities, faithfulness; its fragrance, love; its wide field of growth, charity; its form, beauty!

What an impressive and beautiful tribute to motherhood it would be for a whole nation to unite one day in wearing its chosen emblem, and in song and speech, and other appropriate exercises, to honor its mothers!

Why So Many Married Women Deteriorate

A woman writes me: "You would laugh if you knew the time I have had in getting the dollar which I enclose for your inspiring magazine. I would get a pound less of butter, a bar less of soap. I never have a cent of my own. Do you think it wrong of me to deceive my husband in this way? I either have to do this or give up trying at all."

There are thousands of women who work harder than their husbands and really have more right to the money, who are obliged to practise all sorts of deceit in order to get enough to buy clothing and other things essential to decent living.

The difficulty of extracting money from an unwilling husband has been the beginning of thousands of tragedies. The majority of husbands are inclined to exert a censorship over their wives' expenditures. I have heard women say that they would go without necessary articles of clothing and other requirements just as long as possible and worry for days and weeks before they could summon courage to ask for money, because they dreaded a scene and the consequent discord in the home. Many women make it a rule never to ask for money, except when the husband is leaving the house and in a hurry to get away. The disagreeable scene is thus cut as short as possible, as he has not time then to go into all the details of his wife's alleged extravagances and find out what has become of every cent of the money given her on some similar previous occasion.

The average man does not begin to realize how it humiliates his wife to feel that she must ask him for fifty cents, a dollar, or five dollars every time she needs it, and to tell him just exactly what she is going to do with it, and then perhaps be met with a sharp reproof for her extravagance of foolish expenditures.

Men who are extremely kind and considerate with their wives in most things are often contemptibly mean regarding money matters. Many a man who is generous with his tips and buys expensive cigars and orders costly lunches for himself and friends at the club because he wants to be considered a "good fellow," will go home at night and bicker with his wife over the smallest expenditure, destroying the whole peace of the household, when perhaps she does not spend as much upon herself as he does for cigars and drink.

Why is it that men are so afraid to trust their wives with money when they trust them implicitly with everything else, especially as women are usually much more economical than men would be in managing the home and providing for the children? A large part of the friction in the average home centers around money matters and could be avoided by a simple, definite understanding between husband and wife, and a business arrangement of household finances. A regular advance to the wife for the household and a certain sum for personal use which she need not account for, would do more to bring about peace and harmony in the majority of homes than almost anything else.

To be a slave to the home, as many women are, and then to be obliged to assume the attitude of a beggar for every little bit of money she needs for herself, or to have to give an accounting for every cent she spends and tell her lord and master what she did with her last money before she can get any more, is positively degrading.

When the husband gets ready to regard his wife as an equal partner in the marriage firm instead of as an employee with one share in a million-dollar company, or as merely a housekeeper; when he is willing to regard his income as much his wife's as his own and not put her in the position of a beggar for every penny she gets; when he will grant her the same privileges he demands for himself; when he is willing to allow his wife to live her own life in her own way without trying to "boss" her, we shall have more true marriages, happier homes, a higher civilization.

Some one says that a man is never so happy as when he has a few dollars his wife knows nothing about. And there is a great deal of truth in it. Men who are perfectly honest with their wives about most things are often secretive about money matters. They hoodwink them regarding their incomes and especially about any ready cash they have on hand.

No matter how much the average man may think of his wife, or how considerate he may be in other matters, he rarely considers that she has the same right to his cash that he has, although he may be boasting to outsiders of her superior management in matters of economy. He feels that he is the natural guardian of the money, as he makes it; that he has a little more right to it than has his wife, and that he must protect it and dole it out to her.

What disagreeable experiences, unfortunate bickerings, misunderstandings and family prejudice could be avoided if newly-married women would insist upon having a certain proportion of the income set aside for the maintenance of the home and for their own personal needs, without the censorship of their husbands and without being obliged to give an itemized account of their expenditures!

It is a rare thing to find a man who does not waste ten times as much money on foolish things as does his wife, and yet he would make ten times the talk about his wife's one-tenth foolishness as his own ten-tenths.

On the other hand, thousands of women, starving for affection, protest against their husband's efforts to substitute money for it—to satisfy their cravings, their heart-hunger, with the things that money can buy.

It is an insult to womanhood to try to satisfy her nature with material things, while the affections are famishing for genuine sympathy and love, for social life, for contact with the great, throbbing world outside. Women do admire beautiful things; but there is something they admire infinitely more. Luxuries do not come first in any real woman's desires. She prefers poverty with love to luxury with an indifferent or loveless husband.

How gladly would these women whose affections are blighted by cold indifference or the unfaithfulness of their husbands, exchange their liberal allowance, their luxuries, for genuine sympathy and affection!

One of the most pathetic spectacles in American life is that of the faded, outgrown wife, standing helpless in the shadow of her husband's prosperity and power, having sacrificed her youth, beauty, and ambition—nearly everything that the feminine mind holds dear—to enable an indifferent, selfish, brutish husband to get a start in the world.

It does not matter that in her unselfish effort to help him she burned up much of her attractiveness over the cooking stove; that she lost more of it at the washtub, in scrubbing and cleaning, and rearing and caring for their children during the slavery of her early married life; it does not matter how much she suffered during those terrible years of poverty and privation. Just as soon as the selfish husband begins to get prosperous, finds that he is succeeding, feels his power, he often begins to be ashamed of the woman who has given up everything to make his success possible.

It is a sad thing to see any human being whose life is blighted by the lack of love; but it is doubly pathetic to see a woman who has given everything to the man she loved and who gets in return only her board and clothes and an allowance, great or small.

Some men seem to think that the precept, "Man does not live by bread alone," was not meant to include woman. They can not understand why she should not be happy and contented if she has a comfortable home and plenty to eat and wear. They would be surprised to learn that many a wife would gladly give up luxuries and live on bread and water, if she could only have her husband's sympathy in her aspirations, his help and encouragement in the unfolding of her stifled talents.

I know a very able, promising young man who says that if he had had a rich father he never would have developed his creative power; that his ambition would have been strangled; that it was the desperate struggle to make a place for himself in the world that developed the real man in him.

This young man married a poor girl who had managed by the hardest kind of work and sacrifice to pay her way through college. She had just begun to develop her power, to feel her wings, when her husband caged her in his home, took away her highest incentive for self-development. He said that a man who could not support a wife without her working had no business to marry. He dressed his wife like a queen; gave her horses and carriages and servants. But all the time he was discouraging her from developing her self-reliance, taking away all motives for cultivating her resourcefulness and originality.

At first the wife was very eager to work. Her ambition rebelled against the gilded chains by which she was bound. She was restless, nervous, and longed to use her powers to do something for herself and the world.

But her husband did not believe in a woman doing the things she wished to do. He wanted his wife to look pretty and fresh when he returned from his business at night; to keep young and to shine in society. He was proud of her beauty and vivacity. He thought he loved her, but it was a selfish love, for real love has a tender regard for a person's highest good, for that person's sake.

Gradually the glamour of society, the lethe of a luxurious life, paralyzed her ambition, which clamored less and less peremptorily for recognition, until at length she subsided into a life of almost total inaction.

Multitudes of women in this country to-day are vegetating in luxurious homes, listless, ambitionless, living narrow, superficial, rutty lives, because the spur of necessity has been taken away from them; because their husbands, who do not want them to work, have taken them out of an ambition-arousing environment.

But a life of leisure is not the only way of paralyzing the development of a wife's individuality. It can be done just as effectively by her becoming a slave of her family. I believe that the average wife is confined to her home a great deal too much.

Many women do not seem to have any existence outside of the little home orbit; do not have any special interests or pleasures to speak of apart from their husbands. They have been brought up to think that wives have very little purpose in life other than to be the slaves and playthings of their lords and masters, to bear and bring up children, and to keep meekly in the background.

The wife who wishes to hold her husband's affection, if he is ambitious, must continue to grow, must keep pace with him mentally. She must make a continual investment in self-improvement and in intellectual charm so that her mental growth will compensate for the gradual loss of physical charm. She must keep her husband's admiration, and if he is a progressive man he is not likely to admire a wife who stands still mentally. Admiration is a very important part of love.

You may be very sure that if you have an ambitious husband you must do something to keep up with him besides lounging, idling about the home, reading silly novels, dressing stylishly and waiting for him to return at night. If he sees that your sun rises and sets in him, that you have little interest outside, that you are not broadening and deepening your life in other ways by extending your interests, reaching out for self-enlargement, self-improvement, he will be disappointed in you, and this will be a great strain upon his love.

It is impossible for a girl who has had only a little schooling to appreciate the transforming power that comes from liberal education and broad culture. For the sake of her husband and children and her own peace of mind and satisfaction, she should try to improve herself in every possible way. Think of what it means to be able to surround one's home with an atmosphere of refinement, culture and superior intelligence! The quality of one's own ideals has a great deal to do with the quality of the ideals of one's family.

Even considered alone from the standpoint of self-protection, as a safeguard, a woman ought to get a liberal education; a college education, if possible. The conditions of home life in this country are such that it is very difficult for the wife to keep up with her husband's growth, to keep pace with him, because he is constantly in an ambition-arousing, stimulating environment. Unless she is unusually ambitious and has great power of application and concentration and plenty of leisure, she is likely to drop behind her husband.

As a rule, the husband has infinitely more to encourage and stimulate him than has the wife. Success itself is a tremendous tonic. The consciousness of perpetual triumph, of conquering things, is a great stimulus.

It is true that women have developed more admirable and loving qualities in their home life than have men; but during all these centuries, while women have been shut up in the home, men have been touching hands with the great, busy world, absorbing knowledge of human nature and broadening their minds by coming into contact with men and things. They have developed independence, stamina, strength, by being compelled to solve the larger, more practical problems of life.

The business man and the professional man are really in a perpetual school, a great practical university. The strenuous life, however dangerous, is essentially educative. The man has the incalculable advantage of a great variety of experiences and of freshness of view. He is continually coming in contact with new people, new things, being molded by a vast number of forces in the busy world which never touch the wife.

If women, equally with men, do not continue to grow and expand after marriage, how can we expect race improvement? Woman must ascend to higher, wider planes, or both man and woman must descend. "Male and female created He them." There is no separating them; they must rise or fall together.

"The woman's cause is man's; they rise or sink Together, dwarfed or godlike, bond or free."

Many a man has tired of his wife because she has not kept pace with him; because, instead of growing broader and keener as the years pass, she has become narrow. It never occurs to him that the fault may be wholly his own. In the early years of their married life he perhaps laughed at her "dreams," as he called her longings for self-improvement. He discouraged, if he did not actually oppose, every effort she made to grow to the full stature of her womanhood. His indifference or hostility quenched the hopes she had indulged before marriage. The bitterness of her disappointment crushed her spirit. She lost her buoyancy and enthusiasm and gradually sank to the level of a household drudge. And the husband wonders what has changed the joyous, high-spirited girl he married into the dull, apathetic woman who now performs her duties like an automaton.

There are to-day thousands of wives doing the work of ordinary housemaids, who, putting it on a low standard, are smothering ability to earn perhaps more money than the men who enslave them, if they only had an opportunity to unfold the powers which God has given them; but they have been brought up from infancy to believe that marriage is the only real career for a woman, that these longings and hungerings for self-expression are to be smothered, covered up by the larger duties of a wife and mother.

If the husbands could change places with their wives for a year, they would feel the contracting, narrowing influence in which the average wife lives. Their minds would soon cease to reach out, they would quickly feel the pinching, paralyzing effect of the monotonous existence, of doing the same things every day, year in and year out. The wives, on the other hand, would soon begin to broaden out. Their lives would become richer, fuller, more complete, from contact with the world, from the constant stretching of their minds over large problems.

I have heard men say that remaining in the home on Sundays or holidays just about uses them up; that it is infinitely harder and more trying than the same time spent in their occupations, and that while they love their children their incessant demands, the noise and confusion would drive them to drink if they had to bear it all the time. Strong men admit that they can not stand these little nerve-racking vexations of the home. Yet they wonder why the wife and mother is nervous, and seem to think that she can bear this sort of thing three hundred and sixty-five days in the year without going away and getting relief for a half-dozen days during the whole time. Few men would exchange places with their wives. Their hours are shorter, and when their day's work is done, it is done, while a wife and mother not only works all day, but is also likely to be called during the night. If any one is disturbed in the night by the children, it is the mother; rarely the father.

How long would men continue to conduct their business offices or factories with the primitive, senseless methods in vogue in the average kitchen to-day? Man puts all his inventiveness, his ingenuity, in improving methods, in facilitating his business and getting the drudgery out of his work in his office and factory, but the wife and mother still plods along in an ill-fitted kitchen and laundry. And yet our greatest modern inventor has said that the cares of the home could be reduced to a minimum and the servant problem solved if the perfectly practicable devices, for lightening household labor were adopted in the home!

"But," many of our men readers will say, "is there any profession in the world grander than that of home making? Can anything be more stimulating, more elevating, than home making and the rearing of children? How can such a vocation be narrowing or monotonous?"

Of course it is grand. There is nothing grander in the universe than the work of a true wife, a noble mother. But it would require the constitution of a Hercules, an infinitely greater patience than that of a Job, to endure such work with almost no change or outside variety, year in and year out, as many wives and mothers do, without breaking down.

The average man does not appreciate how almost devoid of incentives to broadmindedness, to many-sidedness, to liberal growth, the home life of many women is.

There is a disease called arrested development, in which the stature of the adult remains that of a child, all physical growth and expansion having stopped.

One of the most pitiable phases of American life and one of the most discouraging elements in our civilization is the suppressed wife who is struggling with arrested development after marriage.

I have known of beautiful young wives who went to their husbands with the same assurance of confidence and trust as to their hopes and ambitions with which a child would approach its mother, only to meet with a brutal rebuff for even venturing to have an ambition which did not directly enhance the husband's comfort or convenience in his home.

It is a strange fact that most men think that when a woman marries she goes to her new home with as rigid vows as the monks take on entering the monastery, or the nuns the convent, and they regard the suggestion of a career for her, which does not directly bear upon the home, as domestic treason.

There are some women, especially sensitive ones, who would never again tell their husbands of their hopes and aspirations after they had been laughed at and ridiculed a few times, but would be forever silent, even when the canker of bitter disappointment was consuming them.

Suppose a girl has the brains and the ability of a George Eliot and she marries a young business man who thinks that writing articles or books or devoting a large part of her time to music is all nonsense; that her place is at home, taking care of it and bringing up her children, and denies her the right to exercise her talent. How would he like to have the conditions reversed? It is true that woman is peculiarly fitted for the home, and every normal woman should have a home of her own, but her career should not be confined or limited to it any more than a man's. I do not see why she should not be allowed to live the life normal to her; why she should be denied the right of self-expression, any more than the man. And I regard that man as a tyrant who tries to cramp her in the natural expression of her ambition or sneers at, nags, and criticizes her for seeking to bring out, to unfold, the sacred thing which the Creator has given her. This is one of her inalienable rights which no man should dare interfere with. If he does, he deserves the unhappiness which is likely to come to his home.

A wife should neither be a drudge nor a dressed-up doll; she should develop herself by self-effort, just as her husband develops himself. She should not put herself in a position where her inventiveness, resourcefulness, and individuality will be paralyzed by lack of motive.

We hear a great deal about the disinclination of college girls to marry. If this is a fact, it is largely due to the unfairness of men. The more education girls get, the more they will hesitate to enter a condition of slavery, even under the beautiful guise of home.

Is it any wonder that so many girls refuse to marry, refuse to take chances of suppressing the best thing in them? Is it any wonder that they protest against putting themselves in a position where they will not be able to deliver to the world the sacred message which the Creator has given them?

I believe in marriage, but I do not believe in that marriage which paralyzes self-development, strangles ambition, discourages evolution and self-growth, and which takes away the life purpose.

To be continually haunted by the ghosts of strangled talents and smothered faculties prevents real contentment and happiness. Many a home has been made miserable, not because the husband was not kind and affectionate, not because there was not enough to eat and to wear, but because the wife was haunted with unrealized hopes and disappointed ambitions and expectations.

Is there anything more pitiful than such a stifled life with its crushed hopes? Is there anything sadder than to go through life conscious of talents and powers which we can not possibly develop; to feel that the best thing in us must be strangled for the want of opportunity, for the lack of appreciation even by those who love us best; to know that we can never by any possibility reach our highest expression, but must live a sordid life when under different conditions a higher would be possible?

A large part of the marital infelicity about which we hear so much comes from the husband's attempt to cramp his wife's ambition and to suppress her normal expression. A perversion of native instinct, a constant stifling of ambition, and the longing to express oneself naturally, gradually undermine the character and lead to discontentment and unhappiness. A mother who is cramped and repressed transmits the seeds of discontent and one-sided tendencies to her children.

The happiest marriages are those in which the right of husband and wife to develop broadly and naturally along individual lines has been recognized by each. The noblest and most helpful wives and mothers are those who develop their powers to their fullest capacity.

Woman is made to admire power, and she likes to put herself under the domination of a masterful man and rest in his protection. But it must be a *voluntary* obedience which comes from admiration of original force, of sturdy, rugged, masculine qualities.

The average man can not get away from the idea of his wife's service to him personally; that she is a sort of running mate, not supposed to win the race, but to help to pull him along so that *he* will win it. He can not understand why she should have an ambition which bears no direct relation to his comfort, his well-being, his getting on in the world.

The very suggestion of woman's inferiority, that she must stand in the man's shadow and not get ahead of him, that she does not have quite the same rights in anything that he has, the same property rights, the same suffrage rights; in other words, the whole suggestion of woman's inferiority, has been a criminal wrong to her. Many women who are advocating woman's suffrage perhaps would not use the ballot if they had it. Their fight is one for freedom to do as they please, to live their own lives in their own way. The greatest argument in the woman's suffrage movement is woman's protest against unfair, unjust treatment by men. Man's opposition to woman suffrage is merely a relic of the old-time domestic barbarism. It is but another expression of his determination to "boss" everybody and everything about him.

The time will come when men will be ashamed that they ever opposed woman's suffrage. Think of a man considering it right and just for his most ignorant workman to have an equal vote with himself on public matters and yet denying the right to his educated wife and daughters!

Thrift

"Mony a mickle makes a muckle."— Scotch Proverb

"A penny saved is a penny earned."— English Saying

"Beware of little extravagances; a small leak will sink a big ship."— Franklin

"No gain is more certain than that which proceeds from the economical use of what we have."— Latin Proverb

"Make all you can, save all you can, give all you can."— John Wesley

"All fortunes have their foundation laid in economy."—J. G. Holland

In the philosophy of thrift, the unit measure of prosperity is always the smallest of coins current. Thrift is measured not by the pound but by the penny, not by the dollar but by the cent. Thus any person in receipt of an income or salary however small finds it in his power to practise thrift and to lay the foundation of prosperity.

The word thrift in its origin means the grasping or holding fast the things that we have. It implies economy, carefulness, as opposed to waste and extravagance. It involves self-denial and frugal living for the time being, until the prosperity which grows out of thrift permits the more liberal indulgence of natural desires.

One of the primary elements of thrift is to spend less than you earn, to save something however small from the salary received, to lay aside at regular intervals when possible some part of the money earned or made, in provision for the future.

"Every boy should realize, in starting out, that he can never accumulate money unless he acquires the habit of saving," said Russell Sage. "Even if he can save only a few cents at the beginning, it is better than saving nothing at all; and he will find, as the months go on, that it becomes easier for him to lay by a part of his earnings. It is surprising how fast an account in a savings bank can be made to grow, and the boy who starts one and keeps it up stands a good chance of enjoying a prosperous old age. Some people who spend every cent of their income on their living expenses are always bewailing the fact that they have never become rich. They pick out some man who is known to have made a fortune and speak of him as being 'lucky.' There is practically no such thing as luck in business, and the boy who depends upon it to carry him through is very likely not to get through at all. The men who have made a success of their lives are men who started out right when they were boys. They studied while at school, and when they went to work, they didn't expect to be paid wages for loafing half the time. They weren't always on the lookout for an 'easy snap' and they forged ahead, not waiting always for the opportunities that never came, and bewailing the supposed fact that times are no longer what they used to be."

"A young man may have many friends," says Sir Thomas Lipton, "but he will find none so steadfast, so constant, so ready to respond to his wants, so capable of pushing him ahead, as a little leather-covered book, with the name of a bank on the cover. Saving is the first great principle of success. It creates independence, it gives a young man standing, it fills him with vigor, it stimulates him with proper energy; in fact, it brings to him the best part of any success,—happiness and contentment."

It is estimated that if a man will begin at twenty years of age to lay by twenty-six cents every working day, investing at seven per cent. compound interest, he will at seventy years of age have amassed thirty-two thousand dollars.

"Economy is wealth." This proverb has been repeated to most of us until we are either tired of it or careless of it, but it is well to remember that a saying becomes a proverb because of its truth and significance. Many a man has proved that if economy is not actual wealth, it is, in many cases, potentially so.

Professor Marshall, the noted English economist, estimates that $500,000,000 is spent annually by the British working classes for things that do nothing to make their lives nobler or happier. At a meeting of the British Association, the president, in an address to the economic section, expressed his belief that the simple item of food-waste alone would justify the above-mentioned estimate. One potent cause of waste to-day is that very many of the women do not know how to buy economically, and are neither passable cooks nor good housekeepers. Edward Atkinson estimated that in the United States the waste from bad cooking alone is over a hundred million dollars a year!

"Provided he has some ability and good sense to start with, is thrifty, honest, and economical," said Philip D. Armour, "there is no reason why any young man should not accumulate money and attain so-called success in life." When asked to what qualities he attributed his own success, Mr. Armour said: "I think that thrift and economy had much to do with it. I owe much to my mother's training and to a good line of Scotch ancestors, who have always been thrifty and economical."

"A young man should cultivate the habit of always saving something," said the late Marshall Field, "however small his income." It was by living up to this principle that Mr. Field became the richest and most successful merchant in the world. When asked by an interviewer, whom I sent to him on one occasion, what he considered the turning point in his career, he answered, "Saving the first five thousand dollars I ever had, when I might just as well have spent the modest salary I made. Possession of that sum, once I had it, gave me the ability to meet opportunities. That I consider the turning point."

The first savings prove the turning point in many a young man's career. But it is true that the lack of thrift is one of the greatest curses of modern civilization. Extravagance, ostentatious display, a desire to outshine others, is a vice of our age, and especially of our country. Some one has said that "investigation would place at the head of the list of the cause of poverty, wastefulness inherited from wasteful parents."

"If you know how to spend less than you get," said Franklin, "you have the philosopher's stone." The great trouble with many young people is that they do not acquire the saving habit at the start, and never find the "philosopher's stone." They don't learn to spend less than they get. If they learned that lesson in time, they would have little difficulty in making themselves independent. It is this first saving that counts.

John Jacob Astor said it cost him more to get the first thousand dollars than it did afterwards to get a hundred thousand; but if he had not saved the first thousand, he would have died poor.

"The first thing that a man should learn to do," says Andrew Carnegie, "is to save his money. By saving his money he promotes thrift,—the most valued of all habits. Thrift is the great fortune-maker. It draws the line between the savage and the civilized man. Thrift not only develops the fortune, but it develops, also, the man's character."

The savings bank is one of the greatest encouragements to thrift, because it pays a premium on deposits in the form of interest on savings. One of the greatest benefits ever extended by this government to its citizens is the opening of Postal Savings Banks where money can be deposited with absolute security against loss, because the Federal Government would have to fail before the bank could fail. The economies which enable a man to start a savings account are not usually pinching economies, not the stinting of the necessaries of life, but merely the foregoing of selfish pleasures and indulgences which not only drain the purse but sap the physical strength and undermine the health of brain and body.

The majority of people do not even try to practise self-control; are not willing to sacrifice present enjoyment, ease, for larger future good. They spend their money at the time for transient gratification, for the pleasure of the moment, with little thought for to-morrow, and then they envy others who are more successful, and wonder why they do not get on better themselves. They store up neither money nor knowledge for the future. The squirrels know that it will not always be summer. They store food for the winter, which their instinct tells them is coming; but multitudes of human beings store nothing, consume everything as they go along, so that when sickness or old age come, there is no reserve, nothing to fall back upon. They have sacrificed their future for the present.

The facility with which loose change slips away from these people is most insidious and unaccountable. I know young men who spend more for unnecessary things, what they call "incidentals"—cigars, drinks, all sorts of sweets, soda-water and nick-nacks of various kinds—than for their essentials, board, clothes, rooms. Then they wonder where all their money goes to, as they never keep any account of it, and rarely restrain a desire. They do not realize it when they fling out a nickel here and a dime there, pay a quarter for this and a quarter for that; but in a week it counts up, and in a year it amounts to a large sum.

"He never lays up a cent" is an expression which we hear every day regarding those who earn enough to enable them to save a competence.

A short time ago, a young man in New York complained to a friend of poverty and his inability to save money.

"How much do you spend for luxuries?" asked the friend.

"Luxuries!" answered the young man, "if by luxuries you mean cigars and a few drinks, I don't average,—including an occasional cigar or a glass of light wine for a friend,—over six dollars a week. Most of the boys spend more, but I make it a rule to be moderate in my expenditures."

"Ten years ago," declared the friend, "I was spending about the same every week for the same things, and paying thirty dollars a month for five inconvenient rooms up four flights of stairs. I had just married then, and one day I told my wife that I longed to have her in a place befitting her needs and refinement. 'John,' was her reply, 'If you love me well enough to give up two things which are not only useless, but extremely harmful to you, we can, for what those things alone cost, own a pretty home in ten years.'

"She sat down by me with a pencil and paper, and in less than five minutes had demonstrated that she was right. You dined with me in the suburbs the other day, and spoke of the beauty and convenience of our cottage. That cottage cost three thousand dollars, and every dollar of it was my former cigar and drink money. But I gained more than a happy wife and pretty home by saving; I gained self-control, better health, self-respect, a truer manhood, a more permanent happiness. I desire every young man who is trying to secure pleasure through smoking and drinking, whether moderately or immoderately, to make use of his judgment, and pencil and paper, and see if he is not forfeiting in a number of directions far more than he is gaining."

There is an impressive fact in the Gospel story of the Prodigal Son. The statement "he wasted his substance in riotous living" means more than that he wasted his funds. It implies that he wasted *himself*. And the most serious phase of all waste is not the waste of substance but the waste of self, of one's energy, capital, the lowering of morals, the undermining of character, the loss of self-respect which thrift encourages and promotes.

Thrift is not only one of the foundation-stones of a fortune, but also one of character. The habit of thrift improves the quality of the character.

The saving of money usually means the saving of a man. It means cutting off indulgences or avoiding vicious habits which are ruinous. It often means health in the place of dissipation. It often means a clear instead of a cloudy and muddled brain.

Furthermore, the saving habit indicates an ambition to get on and up in the world. It develops a spirit of independence, of self-reliance. A little bank account or an insurance policy indicates a desire to improve one's condition, to look up in life. It means hope, it means ambition, a determination to "make good."

People believe in the young man, who, without being mean or penurious, saves a part of his income. It is an indication of many sterling qualities. Business men naturally reason that if a young man is saving his money, he is also saving his energy, his vitality, from being wasted, that he is looking up in the world, and not down; that he is longheaded, wise; that he is determined not to sacrifice the larger gain of the future for the gratification of the hour.

A snug little bank account will add to your self-respect and self-confidence, because it shows that you have practicability, a little more independence. You can look the world in the face with a little more assurance, you can stand a little more erect and face the future with more confidence, if you know that there stands between yourself and want a little ready money or a safe investment of some kind.

The very consciousness that there is something back of you that will prove a barrier to the wolf which haunts so many human beings, and which is a terror and an efficiency destroyer to so many, will strengthen and buttress you at every point. It will relieve you from worry and anxiety about the future; it will unlock your faculties, release them from the restraint and suppression which uncertainty, fear, and doubt impose, and leave you free to do your best work.

Another great aid and incentive to thrift is the life insurance policy. "Primarily devised for the support of widows and orphans, life insurance practise has been developed so as to include the secure investment of surplus earnings in conjunction with the insurance of a sum payable at death."

I am a great believer in the efficiency of savings-banks as character builders; but life insurance has some greater advantages, especially in furnishing that imperious "must," that spur of necessity so important as a motive to most people.

People can put money into savings-banks when they get it, provided some stronger desire does not overcome the inclination; but they feel that they *must* pay their insurance premium.

Then again, money obtainable just by signing the name is so easily withdrawn for spending in all sorts of ways. This is one reason why I often recommend life insurance to young people as a means of saving. It has been of untold value as an object-lesson of the tremendous possibilities in acquiring the saving habit.

I believe that life insurance is doing a great deal to induce the habit of saving. When a young man on a salary or a definite income takes out an insurance policy he has a definite aim. He has made up his mind positively to save so much money every year from his income to pay his premium. Then it is easier for him to say "No," to the hundred-and-one alluring temptations to spend his money for this and that. He can say "No," then with emphasis, because he knows he must keep up his insurance.

An insurance policy has often changed the habits of an entire family from thriftlessness and spendthrift tendencies to thrift and order. The very fact that a certain amount must be saved from the income every week, or every month, or every year, has often developed the faculty of prudence and economy of the entire household. Everybody is cautioned to be careful because the premium must be paid. And oftentimes it is the first sign of a program or order,—system in the home.

The consciousness of a sacred obligation to make payments on that which means protection for those dear to you often shuts out a great deal of foolishness, and cuts out a lot of temptation to spend money for self-gratification and to cater to one's weak tendencies.

The life insurance policy has thus proved to be a character insurance as well, an insurance against silly expenditures, an insurance against one's own weak will power, or vicious, weak tendencies; a real protection against one's self, one's real enemy.

Among the sworn enemies of thrift may be named going into debt, borrowing money, keeping no itemized account of daily expenditures, and buying on the instalment plan. That great English preacher Spurgeon said that debt, dirt, and the devil made up the trinity of evil. And debt can discount the devil at any time for possibilities of present personal torment. The temptations to go into debt are increasing rapidly. On every hand in the cities one may read such advertisements as "We Trust You," "Your Credit is Good With Us," and with these statements come offers of clothing, furniture, and what not "on easy payments." But as the Irishman remarked after an experience with the instalment purchase of furniture: "Onaisy payments they sure are." As a matter of fact, the easy payments take all the ease and comfort out of life—they are easy only for the man who receives them.

Beware of the delusions of buying on the instalment plan. There are thousands of poor families in this country who buy organs and sets of books and encyclopedias, lightning rods, farming implements, and all sorts of things which they might get along without, because they can pay for them a little at a time. In this way, they keep themselves poor. They are always pinching, sacrificing, to save up for the agent when he comes around to collect.

All through the South there are poor homes of both colored and white families, where there are not sufficient cooking utensils and knives, forks, and spoons to enable the members to eat with comfort, and yet you will find expensive things in their homes which they have bought on the instalment plan, and which keep them poor for years trying to pay for them.

As far as borrowing money is concerned the bitter experience of countless men and women is crystallized in that old saying: "He that goes a borrowing goes a sorrowing." There is a world of safety for the man who follows Shakespeare's advice: "Neither a borrower nor a lender be."

It is sometimes said flippantly that "poverty is no disgrace but it's mighty uncomfortable." And yet poverty is often a real disgrace. People born to poverty may rise above it. People who have poverty thrust upon them may overcome it. In this great land of abundance and opportunity poverty is in most cases a disgrace and a reproach.

Dr. Johnson said to Boswell, "I admonish you avoid poverty, the temptation and worry it breeds." There is something humiliating in being poor. The very consciousness that we have *nothing to show for our endeavor* besides a little character and the little we have done, is anything but encouraging. Somehow, we feel that we have not amounted to much, and we know the world looks upon us in the same way if we have not managed to accumulate something. It is a reflection upon our business ability, upon our judgment, upon our industry. It is not so much for the money, as for what it means to have earned and saved money; it is the idea of thrift. If we have not been thrifty, if we have not saved anything, the world will look upon us as good for nothing, as partial failures, as either lazy, slipshod, or extravagant. They regard us as either not having been able to make money, or if we have, not being able to save it.

But let it be remembered that thrift is not parsimony not miserliness. It often means very liberal spending. It is a perpetual protest against putting the emphasis on the wrong thing.

No one should make the mistake of economizing to the extent of planting seeds, and then denying liberal nourishment to the plants that grow from them; of conducting business without advertising; or of saving a little extra expense by pinching on one's table or dress. "A dollar saved is a dollar earned," but a dollar spent well and liberally is often several dollars earned. A dollar saved is often very many dollars lost. The progressive, generous spirit, nowadays, will leave far behind the plodder that devotes time to adding pennies that could be given to making dollars.

The only value a dollar has is its buying power. "No matter how many times it has been spent, it is still good." Hoarded money is of no more use than gold so inaccessible in old Mother Earth that it will never feel the miner's pick. There is plenty in this world, if we keep it moving and keep moving after it. Imagine everybody in the world stingy, living on the principle of "We can do without that," or "Our grandfathers got along without such things, and I guess I can." What would become of our parks, grand buildings, electrical improvements; of music and art? What would become of labor that nurses a tree from a forest to a piano or a palace car? What would become of those dependent upon the finished work? What would happen, what panic would follow, if everybody turned stingy, is indefinable.

"So apportion your wants that your means may exceed them," says Bulwer. "With one hundred pounds a year I may need no man's help; I may at least have 'my crust of bread and liberty.' But with five thousand pounds a year, I may dread a ring at my bell; I may have my tyrannical master in servants whose wages I can not pay; my exile may be at the fiat of the first long-suffering man who enters judgement against me; for the flesh that lies nearest my heart, some Shylock may be dusting his scales and whetting his knife. Every man is needy who spends more than he has; no man is needy who spends less. I may so ill manage that, with five thousand a year, I purchase the worst evils of poverty,—terror and shame; I may so well manage my money that, with one hundred pounds a year, I purchase the best blessings of wealth,—safety and respect."

A College Education at Home

"Tumbling around in a library" was the phrase Oliver Wendell Holmes used in describing in part his felicities in boyhood. One of the most important things that wise students get out of their schooldays is a familiarity with books in various departments of learning. The ability to pick out from a library what is needed in life is of the greatest practical value. It is like a man selecting his tools for intellectual expansion and social service. "Men in every department of practical life," says President Hadley of Yale, "men in commerce, in transportation, or in manufactures—have told me that what they really wanted from our colleges was men who have this selective power of using books efficiently. The beginnings of this kind of knowledge are best learned in any home fairly well furnished with books."

Libraries are no longer a luxury, but a necessity. A home without books and periodicals and newspapers is like a house without windows. Children learn to read by being in the midst of books; they unconsciously absorb knowledge by handling them. No family can now afford to be without good reading.

Children who are well supplied with dictionaries, encyclopedias, histories, works of reference, and other useful books, will educate themselves unconsciously, and almost without expense, and will learn many things of their own accord in moments which would otherwise be wasted; and which, if learned in schools, academies, or colleges, would cost ten times as much as the expense of the books would be. Besides, homes are brightened and made attractive by good books, and children stay in such pleasant homes; while those whose education has been neglected are anxious to get away from home, and drift off and fall into all manner of snares and dangers.

It is astonishing how much a bright child will absorb from being brought up in the atmosphere of good books, being allowed to constantly use them, to handle them, to be familiar with their bindings and titles. It is a great thing for children to be brought up in the atmosphere of books.

Many people never make a mark on a book, never bend down a leaf, or underscore a choice passage. Their libraries are just as clean as the day they bought them, and, often, their minds are just about as clean of information. Don't be afraid to mark your books. Make notes in them. They will be all the more valuable. One who learns to use his books in early life, grows up with an increasing power for effective usefulness.

It is related that Henry Clay's mother furnished him with books by her own earnings at the washtub.

Wear threadbare clothes and patched shoes if necessary, but do not pinch or economize on books. If you can not give your children an academic education you can place within their reach a few good books which will lift them above their surroundings, into respectability and honor.

Is not one's early home the place where he should get his principal training for life? It is here we form habits which shape our careers, and which cling to us as long as we live. It is here that regular, persistent mental training should fix the life ever after.

I know of pitiable cases where ambitious boys and girls have longed to improve themselves, and yet were prevented from doing so by the pernicious habits prevailing in the home, where everybody else spent the evenings talking and joking, with no effort at self-improvement, no thought of higher ideals, no impulse to read anything better than a cheap, exciting story. The aspiring members of the family were teased and laughed at until they got discouraged and gave up the struggle.

If the younger ones do not want to read or study themselves, they will not let anybody else so inclined do so. Children are naturally mischievous, and like to tease. They are selfish, too, and can not understand why anyone else should want to go off by himself to read or study when they want him to play.

Were the self-improvement habit once well established in a home, it would become a delight. The young people would look forward to the study hour with as much anticipation as to playing.

Were it possible for every family that squanders precious time, to spend an evening in such a home, it would be an inspiration. A bright, alert, intelligent, harmonious atmosphere so pervades a self-improving home that one feels insensibly uplifted and stimulated to better things.

I know a New England family in which all the children and the father and mother, by mutual consent, set aside a portion of each evening for study or some form of self-culture. After dinner, they give themselves completely to recreation. They have a regular romp and play, and all the fun possible for an hour. Then when the time comes for study, the entire house becomes so still that you could hear a pin drop. Everyone is in his place reading, writing, studying, or engaged in some form of mental work. No one is allowed to speak or disturb anyone else. If any member of the family is indisposed, or for any reason does not feel like working, he must at least keep quiet and not disturb the others. There is perfect harmony and unity of purpose, an ideal condition for study. Everything that would scatter the efforts or cause the mind to wander, all interruptions that would break the continuity of thought, is carefully guarded against. More is gained in one hour of close, uninterrupted study, than in two or three broken by many interruptions, or weakened by mind wandering.

Sometimes the habits of a home are revolutionized by the influence of one resolute youth who declares himself, taking a stand and announcing that, as for himself, he does not propose to be a failure, that he is going to take no chances as to his future. The moment he does this, he stands out in strong contrast with the great mass of young people who are throwing away their opportunities and have not grit and stamina enough to do anything worth while.

The very reputation of always trying to improve yourself in every possible way, of being dead in earnest, will attract the attention of everybody who knows you, and you will get many a recommendation for promotion which never comes to those who make no special effort to climb upward.

There is a great deal of time wasted even in the busiest lives, which, if properly organized, might be used to advantage.

Many housewives who are so busy from morning to night that they really believe they have no time for reading books, magazines, or newspapers would be amazed to find how much they would have if they would more thoroughly systematize their work. Order is a great time saver, and we certainly ought to be able to so adjust our living plan that we can have a fair amount of time for self-improvement, for enlarging life. Yet many people think that their only opportunity for self-improvement depends upon the time left after everything else has been attended to.

What would a business man accomplish if he did not attend to important matters until he had time that was not needed for anything else? The good business man goes to his office in the morning and plunges right into the important work of the day. He knows perfectly well that if he attends to all the outside matters, all the details and little things that come up, sees everybody that wants to see him, and answers all the questions people want to ask, that it will be time to close his office before he gets to his main business.

Most of us manage somehow to find time for the things we love. If one is hungry for knowledge, if one yearns for self-improvement, if one has a taste for reading, he will make the opportunity.

Where the heart is, there is the treasure. Where the ambition is, there is time.

It takes not only resolution but also determination to set aside unessentials for essentials, things pleasant and agreeable to-day for the things that will prove best for us in the end. There is always temptation to sacrifice future good for present pleasure; to put off reading to a more convenient season, while we enjoy idle amusements or waste the time in gossip or frivolous conversation.

The greatest things of the world have been done by those who systematized their work, organized their time. Men who have left their mark on the world have appreciated the preciousness of time, regarding it as the great quarry.

If you want to develop a delightful form of enjoyment, to cultivate a new pleasure, a new sensation which you have never before experienced, begin to read good books, good periodicals, regularly every day. Do not tire yourself by trying to read a great deal at first. Read a little at a time, but read some every day, no matter how little. If you are faithful you will soon acquire a taste for reading—the reading habit; and it will, in time, give you infinite satisfaction, unalloyed pleasure.

In a gymnasium, one often sees lax, listless people, who, instead of pursuing a systematic course of training to develop all the muscles of the body, flit aimlessly from one thing to another, exercising with pulley-weights for a minute or two, taking up dumb-bells and throwing them down, swinging once or twice on parallel bars, and so frittering away time and strength. Far better it would be for such people to stay away from a gymnasium altogether, for their lack of purpose and continuity makes them lose rather than gain muscular energy. A man or woman who would gather strength from gymnastic exercise must set about it systematically and with a will. He must put mind and energy into the work, or else continue to have flabby muscles and an undeveloped body.

[Illustration: Julia Ward Howe]

The physical gymnasium differs only in kind from the mental one. Thoroughness and system are as necessary in one as in the other. It is not the tasters of books—not those who sip here and there, who take up one book after another, turn the leaves listlessly and hurry to the end,—who strengthen and develop the mind by reading.

To get the most from your reading you must read with a purpose. To sit down and pick up a book listlessly, with no aim except to pass away time, is demoralizing. It is much as if an employer were to hire a boy, and tell him he could start when he pleased in the morning, work when he felt like it, rest when he wanted to, and quit when he got tired!

Never go to a book you wish to read for a purpose, if you can possibly avoid it, with a tired, jaded mentality. If you do, you will get the same in kind from it. Go to it fresh, vigorous, and with active, never passive, faculties. This practise is a splendid and effective cure for mind-wandering, which afflicts so many people, and which is encouraged by the multiplicity of and facility of obtaining reading matter at the present day.

What can give greater satisfaction than reading with a purpose, and that consciousness of a broadening mind that follows it, and growth, of expansion, of enriching the life, the consciousness that we are pushing ignorance, bigotry, and whatever clouds the mind and hampers progress a little further away from us?

The kind of reading that counts, that makes mental fiber and stamina is that upon which the mind is concentrated; approaching a book with all one's soul intent upon its contents.

How few people ever learn to concentrate their attention. Most of us waste a vast amount of precious time dawdling and idling. We sit or stand over our work without thinking. Our minds are blank much of the time.

Passive reading is even more harmful in its effects than desultory reading. It no more strengthens the brain than sitting down in a gymnasium develops the body. The mind remains inactive, in a sort of indolent revery, wandering here and there, without focusing anywhere. Such reading takes the spring and snap out of the mental faculties, weakens the intellect, and makes the brain torpid and incapable of grappling with great principles and difficult problems.

What you get out of a book is not necessarily what the author puts into it, but what you bring to it. If the heart does not lead the head; if the thirst for knowledge, the hunger for a broader and deeper culture, are not the motives for reading, you will not get the most out of a book. But, if your thirsty soul drinks in the writer's thought as the parched soil absorbs rain, then your latent possibilities and the potency of your being, like delayed germs and seeds in the soil, will spring forth into new life.

When you read, read as Macaulay did, as Carlyle did, as Lincoln did—as did every great man who has profited by his reading—with your whole soul absorbed in what you read, with such intense concentration that you will be oblivious of everything else outside of your book.

"Reading furnishes us only with the materials of knowledge," said John Locke; "it is thinking that makes what we read ours."

In order to get the most out of books, the reader must be a thinker. The mere acquisition of facts is not the acquisition of power. To fill the mind with knowledge that can not be made available is like filling our houses with furniture and bric-à-brac until we have no room to move about.

Food does not become physical force, brain, or muscle until it has been thoroughly digested and assimilated, and has become an integral part of the blood, brain, and other tissues. Knowledge does not become power until digested and assimilated by the brain, until it has become a part of the mind itself.

If you wish to become intellectually strong, after reading with the closest attention, form this habit: frequently close your book and sit and think, or stand and walk and think—but think, contemplate, reflect. Turn what you have read over and over in your mind.

It is not yours until you have assimilated it by your thought. When you first read it, it belongs to the author. It is yours only when it becomes an integral part of you.

Many people have an idea that if they keep reading everlastingly, if they always have a book in their hands at every leisure moment, they will, of necessity, become full-rounded and well-educated.

But they might just as well expect to become athletes by eating at every opportunity. It is even more necessary to think than to read. Thinking, contemplating what we have read, is what digestion and assimilation are to the food.

Some of the biggest fools I know are always cramming themselves with knowledge. But they never think. When they get a few minutes' leisure they grab a book and go to reading. In other words, they are always eating intellectually, but never digesting their knowledge or assimilating it.

I know a young man who has formed such a habit of reading that he is almost never without a book, a magazine, or a paper. He is always reading at home, on the cars, at the railway stations, and he has acquired a vast amount of knowledge. He has a perfect passion for knowledge, and yet his mind seems to have been weakened by this perpetual brain stuffing.

By every reader let Milton's words be borne in mind:
"Who reads
Incessantly, and to his reading brings not
A spirit and judgment equal or superior, . . .
Uncertain and unsettled still remains,
Deep versed in books and shallow in himself,
Crude or intoxicate, collecting toys
And trifles for choice matters, worth a sponge,
As children gathering pebbles on the shore."

When Webster was a boy, books were scarce, and so precious that he never dreamed that they were to be read only once, but thought they ought to be committed to memory, or read and re-read until they became a part of his very life.

Elizabeth Barrett Browning says, "We err by reading too much, and out of proportion to what we think. I should be wiser, I am persuaded, if I had not read half as much; should have had stronger and better exercised faculties, and should stand higher in my own appreciation."

Those who live more quietly do not have so many distracting influences, and consequently think more deeply and reflect more than others. They do not read so much but they are better readers.

You should bring your mind to the reading of a book, or to the study of any subject, as you take an ax to the grindstone; not for what you get from the stone, but for the sharpening of the ax.

The greatest advantage of books does not always come from what we remember of them, but from their suggestiveness, their character-building power.

"It is not in the library, but in yourself," says Fr. Gregory, "in your self-respect and your consciousness of duty nobly done—that you are to find the 'Fountain of Youth,' the 'Elixir of Life,' and all the other things that tend to preserve life's freshness and bloom.

"It is a grand thing to read a good book—it is a grander thing to live a good life—and in the living of such life is generated the power that defies age and its decadence."

It is not the ability, the education, the knowledge that one has that makes the difference between men. The mere possession of knowledge is not always the possession of power; knowledge which has not become a part of yourself, knowledge which can not swing into line in an emergency is of little use, and will not save you at the critical moment.

To be effective, a man's education must become a part of himself as he goes along. All of it must be worked up into power. A little practical education that has become a part of one's being and is always available, will accomplish more in the world than knowledge far more extensive that can not be utilized.

No one better illustrates what books will do for a man, and what a thinker will do with his books, than Gladstone, who was always far greater than his career. He rose above Parliament, reached out beyond politics, and was always growing. He had a passion for intellectual expansion. His peculiar gifts undoubtedly fitted him for the church, or he would have made a good professor at Oxford or Cambridge. But, circumstances led him into the political arena, and he adapted himself readily to his environment. He was an all round well read man, who thought his way through libraries and through life.

One great benefit of a taste for reading, and access to the book world, is the service it renders as a diversion and a solace.

What a great thing to be able to get away from ourselves, to fly away from the harassing, humiliating, discouraging, depressing things about us, to go at will to a world of beauty, joy, and gladness!

If a person is discouraged or depressed by any great bereavement or suffering, the quickest and the most effective way of restoring the mind to its perfect balance, to its normal condition, is to immerse it in a sane atmosphere, an uplifting, encouraging, inspiring atmosphere, and the most good in the world is found in the best books. I have known people who were suffering under the most painful mental anguish, from losses and shocks which almost unbalanced their minds, to be completely revolutionized in their mental state by the suggestive power which came from becoming absorbed in a great book.

Everywhere we see rich old men sitting around the clubs, smoking, looking out of the windows, lounging around hotels, traveling about, uneasy, dissatisfied, not knowing what to do with themselves, because they had never prepared for this part of their lives. They put all their energy, ambition, everything into their vocation.

I know an old gentleman who has been an exceedingly active business man. He has kept his finger upon the pulse of events. He has known what has been going on in the world during his whole active career. And he is now as happy and as contented as a child in his retirement, because he has always been a great reader, a great lover of his kind.

People who keep their minds bent in one direction too long at a time soon lose their elasticity, their mental vigor, freshness, spontaneity.

If I were to quote Mr. Dooley, it would be:—"Reading is not thinking; reading is the next thing this side of going to bed for resting the mind."

To my own mind, however, I would rather cite that versatile Englishman, Lord Rosebery. In a speech at the opening of a Carnegie library at West Calder, Midlothian, he made a characteristic utterance upon the value of books, saying in substance:

"There is, however, one case in which books are certainly an end in themselves, and that is to refresh and to recruit after fatigue. When the object is to refresh and to exalt, to lose the cares of this world in the world of imagination, then the book is more than a means. It is an end in itself. It refreshes, exalts, and inspires the man. From any work, manual or intellectual, the man with a happy taste for books comes in tired and soured and falls into the arms of some great author, who raises him from the ground and takes him into a new heaven and a new earth, where he forgets his bruises and rests his limbs, and he returns to the world a fresh and happy man."

"Who," asks Professor Atkinson, "can overestimate the value of good books, those strips of thought, as Bacon so finely calls them, voyaging through seas of time, and carrying their precious freight so safely from generation to generation? Here are finest minds giving us the best wisdom of present and past ages; here are the intellects gifted far beyond ours, ready to give us the results of lifetimes of patient thought, imaginations open to the beauty of the universe."

The lover of good books can never be very lonely; and, no matter where he is, he can always find pleasant and profitable occupation and the best of society when he quits work.

Who can ever be grateful enough for the art of printing; grateful enough to the famous authors who have put their best thoughts where we can enjoy them at will? There are some advantages of intercourse with great minds through their books over meeting them in person. The best of them live in their books, while their disagreeable peculiarities, their idiosyncrasies, their objectionable traits are eliminated. In their books we find the authors at their best. Their thoughts are selected, winnowed in their books. Book friends are always at our service, never annoy us, rasp or nettle us. No matter how nervous, tired, or discouraged one may be, they are always soothing, stimulating, uplifting.

We may call up the greatest writer in the middle of the night when we can not sleep, and he is just as glad to see us as at any other time. We are not excluded from any nook or corner in the great literary world; we can visit the most celebrated people that ever lived without an appointment, without influence, without the necessity of dressing or of observing any rules of etiquette. We can drop in upon a Milton, a Shakespeare, an Emerson, a Longfellow, a Whittier without a moment's notice and receive the warmest welcome.

"You get into society, in the widest sense," says Geikie, "in a great library, with the huge advantage of needing no introductions, and not dreading repulses. From that great crowd you can choose what companions you please, for in the silent levees of the immortals there is no pride, but the highest is at the service of the lowest, with a grand humility. You may speak freely with any, without a thought of your inferiority; for books are perfectly well bred, and hurt no one's feelings by any discriminations."

"It is not the number of books," says Professor William Mathews, "which a young man reads that makes him intelligent and well informed, but the number of well-chosen ones that he has mastered, so that every valuable thought in them is a familiar friend."

It is only when books have been read and reread with ever deepening delight, that they are clasped to the heart, and become what Macaulay found them to be, the old friends who are never found with new faces, who are the same to us in our wealth and in our poverty, in our glory and in our obscurity. No one gets into the inmost heart of a beautiful poem, a great history, a book of delicate humor, or a volume of exquisite essays, by reading it once or twice. He must have its precious thoughts and illustrations stored in the treasure-house of memory, and brood over them in the hours of leisure.

"A book may be a perpetual companion. Friends come and go, but the book may beguile all experiences and enchant all hours."

"The first time," says Goldsmith, "that I read an excellent book, it is to me just as if I had gained a new friend; when I read over a book I have perused before, it resembles the meeting with an old one."

"No matter how poor I am," says William Ellery Channing, "no matter though the prosperous of my own time will not enter my obscure dwelling; if the sacred writers will enter and take up their abode under my roof—if Milton will cross my threshold to sing to me of Paradise; and Shakespeare to open to me the worlds of imagination and the workings of the human heart,—I shall not pine for want of intellectual companionship, though excluded from what is called the best society in the place where I live."

"Books," says Milton, "do preserve as in a violl, the purest efficacie and extraction of that living intellect that bred them. A good Booke is the pretious life-blood of a master spirit, imbalm'd and treasur'd up on purpose to a Life beyond Life."

"A book is good company," said Henry Ward Beecher. "It comes to your longing with full instruction, but pursues you never. It is not offended at your absent-mindedness, nor jealous if you turn to other pleasures, of leaf, or dress, or mineral, or even of books. It silently serves the soul without recompense, not even for the hire of love. And yet more noble, it seems to pass from itself, and to enter the memory, and to hover in a silvery transformation there, until the outward book is but a body and its soul and spirit are flown to you, and possess your memory like a spirit."

DISCRIMINATION IN READING

A few books well read, and an intelligent choice of those few,—these are the fundamentals for self-education by reading.

If only a few well chosen, it is better to avail yourself of choices others have already made—old books, the standard works tested by many generations of readers. If only a few, let them be books of highest character and established fame. Such books are easily found even in small public libraries.

For the purpose of this chapter, which is to aid in forming a taste for reading, there should be no confusion of choice by naming too many books of one author. If you read one and like it, you can easily find another.

It is a cardinal rule that if you do not like a book, do not read it. What another likes, you may not. Any book list is suggestive; it can be binding only on those who prize it. Like attracts like.

Did you ever think that the thing you are looking for is looking for you; that it is the very law of affinities to get together?

If you are coarse in your tastes, vicious in your tendencies, you do not have to work very hard to find coarse vicious books; they are seeking you by the very law of attraction.

One's taste for reading is much like his taste for food. Dull books are to be avoided, as one refuses food disagreeable to him; to someone else the book may not be dull, nor the food disagreeable. Whole nations may eat cabbage, or stale fish, while I like neither. Ultimately, therefore, every reader must make his own selection, and find the book that finds him. Any one not a random reader will soon select a short shelf of books that he may like better than a longer shelf that exactly suits some one else. Either will be a shelf of good books, neither a shelf of the best books, since if best for you or me, they may not be best for everybody.

A most learned man in India, in turning the leaves of a book, as he read, felt a little prick in his finger; a tiny snake dropped out and wriggled out of sight. The pundit's finger began to swell, then his arm; and in an hour, he was dead.

Who has not noticed in the home a snake in a book that has changed the character of a boy through its moral poison so that he was never quite the same again?

How well did Carlyle divide books into sheep and goats.

It is probable that the careers of the majority of criminals in our prisons to-day might have been vastly different if the character of their reading when young had been different; had it been up-lifting, wholesome, instead of degrading.

"Christian Endeavor" Clark read a notice conspicuously posted in a large city:—"All boys should read the wonderful story of the desperado brothers of the Western plains, whose strange and thrilling adventures of successful robbery and murder have never before been equaled. Price five cents." The next morning, Dr. Clark read in a newspaper of that city that seven boys had been arrested for burglary, and four stores broken into by the "gang." One of the ringleaders was only ten years old. At their trial, it appeared that each had invested five cents in the story of border crime. "Red-eyed Dick, the Terror of the Rockies," or some such story has poisoned many a lad's life. A seductive, demoralizing book destroys the ambition unless for vicious living. All that was sweet, beautiful, and wholesome in the character before seems to vanish, and everything changes after the reading of a single bad book. It has aroused the appetite for more forbidden pleasures, until it crowds out the desire for everything better, purer, healthier. Mental dissipation from this exciting literature, often dripping with suggestiveness of impurity, giving a passport to the prohibited; this is fatal to all soundness of mind.

A lad once showed to another a book full of words and pictures of impurity. He only had it in his hands a few moments. Later in life he held high office in the church, and years afterward told a friend that he would have given half he possessed had he never seen it.

Light, flashy stories, with no intention in them, seriously injured the mind of a brilliant young lady, I once knew. Like the drug fiend whose brain has been stupefied, her brain became completely demoralized by constant mental dissipation. Familiarity with the bad, ruins the taste for the good. Her ambition and ideas of life became completely changed. Her only enjoyment was the excitement of her imagination through vicious books.

Nothing else will more quickly injure a good mind than familiarity with the frivolous, the superficial. Even though they may not be actually vicious, the reading of books which are not true to life, which carry home no great lesson, teach no sane or healthful philosophy, but are merely written to excite the passions, to stimulate a morbid curiosity, will ruin the best of minds in a very short time. It tends to destroy the ideals and to ruin the taste for all good reading.

Read, read, read all you can. But never read a bad book or a poor book. Life is too short, time too precious, to spend it in reading anything but the best.

Any book is bad for you, the reading of which takes away your desire for a better one.

Many people still hold that it is a bad thing for the young to read works of fiction. They believe that young minds get a moral twist from reading that which they know is not true, the descriptions of mere imaginary heroes and heroines, and of things which never happened. Now, this is a very narrow, limited view of a big question. These people do not understand the office of the imagination; they do not realize that many of the fictitious heroes and heroines that live in our minds, even from childhood's days, are much more real in their influence on our lives than some of those that exist in flesh and blood.

Dickens' marvelous characters seem more real to us than any we have ever met. They have followed millions of people from childhood to old age, and influenced their whole lives for good. Many of us would look upon it as a great calamity to have these characters of fiction blotted out of our memory and their influence taken out of our lives.

Readers are sometimes so wrought up by a good work of fiction, their minds are raised to such a pitch of courage and daring, all their faculties so sharpened and braced, their whole nature so stimulated, that they can for the time being attempt and accomplish things which were impossible to them without the stimulus.

This, it seems to me, is one of the great values of fiction. If it is good and elevating, it is a splendid exercise of all the mental and moral faculties; it increases courage; it rouses enthusiasm; it sweeps the brain-ash off the mind, and actually strengthens its ability to grasp new principles and to grapple with the difficulties of life.

Many a discouraged soul has been refreshened, re-invigorated, has taken on new life by the reading of a good romance. I recall a bit of fiction, called "The Magic Story," which has helped thousands of discouraged souls, given them new hope, new life, when they were ready to give up the struggle.

The reading of good fiction is a splendid imagination exerciser and builder. It stimulates it by suggestions, powerfully increases its picturing capacity, and keeps it fresh and vigorous and wholesome, and a wholesome imagination plays a very great part in every sane and worthy life. It makes it possible for us to shut out the most disagreeable past, to shut out at will all hideous memories of our mistakes, failures, and misfortunes; it helps us to forget our trouble and sorrows, and to slip at will into a new, fresh world of our own making, a world which we can make as beautiful, as sublime, as we wish. The imagination is a wonderful substitute for wealth, luxuries, and for material things. No matter how poor we may be, or how unfortunate, we may be bedridden even, we can by its aid travel round the world, visit its greatest cities, and create the most beautiful things for ourselves.

Sir John Herschel tells an amusing anecdote illustrating the pleasure derived from a book, not assuredly of the first order. In a certain village the blacksmith had got hold of Richardson's novel "Pamela, or Virtue Rewarded," and used to sit on his anvil in the long summer evenings and read it aloud to a large and attentive audience. It is by no means a short book, but they fairly listened to it all. "At length, when the happy turn of fortune arrived, which brings the hero and heroine together, and sets them living long and happily according to the most approved rules, the congregation were so delighted as to raise a great shout, and, procuring the church keys, actually set the parish bells ringing."

"It all comes back to us now," said the brilliant editor of the "Interior" not long ago, "that winter evening in the old home. The curtains are down, the fire is sending out a cheerful warmth and the shaded lamps diffusing a well-tempered radiance. The lad of fifteen is bent over a borrowed volume of sea tales. For hours he reads on, oblivious of all surroundings, until parental attention is drawn toward him by the unusual silence. The boy is seen to be trembling from head to foot with suppressed excitement. A fatherly hand is laid upon the volume, closing it firmly, and the edict is spoken, 'No more novels for five years.' And the lad goes off to bed, half glad, half grieved, wondering whether he has found fetters or achieved freedom.

"In truth he had received both; for that indiscriminating command forbade to him during a formative period of his life works which would have kindled his imagination, enriched his fancy, and heightened his power of expression; but if it closed to him the Garden of Hesperides, it also saved him from a possible descent to the Inferno; it made heroes of history, not demigods of mythology, his companions, and reserved to maturer years those excursions in the literature of the imagination which may lead a young man up to heaven or as easily drag him down to hell.

"The boy who is permitted to saturate his mind with stories of 'battle, murder, and sudden death,' is fitting himself, as the records of our juvenile courts show, for the penitentiary or perhaps the gallows. No man can handle pitch without defilement. We may choose our books, but we can not choose their effects. We may plant the vine or sow the thistle, but we can not command what fruit each shall bear. We may loosely select our library, but by and by it will fit us close as a glove.

"There was never such a demand for fiction as now, and never larger opportunities for its usefulness. Nothing has such an attraction for life as life. But what the heart craves is not 'life as it is.' It is life as it ought to be. We want not the feeble but the forceful; not the commonplace but the transcendent. Nobody objects to the 'purpose novel' except those who object to the purpose. Dealing as it does in the hands of a great master, with the grandest passions, the most tender emotions, the divinest hopes, it can portray all these spiritual forces in their majestic sweep and uplift. And as a matter of history, we have seen the novel achieve in a single generation the task at which the homily had labored ineffectively for a hundred years. Realizing this, it is safe to say that there is not a theory of the philosopher, a hope of the reformer, or a prayer of the saint which does not eventually take form in a story. The novel has wings, while logic plods with a staff. In the hour it takes the metaphysician to define his premises, the story-teller has reached the goal—and after him tumbles the crowd tumultuous."

With the assistance of Rev. Dr. E. P. Tenney, I venture upon the following lists of books in various lines of reading:

Fiction

"The Arabian Nights Entertainment."

"Stories from the Arabian Nights" (Riverside School Library), contains many of the more famous stories. 50 c.

Irving Bachelder's [Transcriber's note: "Bacheller"?] "Eben Holden," is a good book. 400,000 copies were sold.

J. M. Barrie's "Little Minister," a story of Scottish life, is very bright reading.

Bunyan's "Pilgrim's Progress," is one of the most famous of allegories.

Cervantes' "Don Quixote" is so widely known that any well-read man should know it. Its humor never grows old.

Ralph Connor's three books,—"The Man from Glengarry," "Black Rock," and "The Sky Pilot,"—have sold 400,000 copies.

Of George W. Cable's books, "The Cavalier," and "Old Creole Days" are among the best.

Dinah Mulock Craik's "John Halifax, Gentleman," is of rare merit.

C. E. Craddock's (pseudonym), "In the Tennessee Mountains" is entertaining. A powerful story of mountain-life.

Of F. Marion Crawford's stories, among the best are "Mr. Isaacs" and "A Roman Singer."

Alexander Dumas' "Count of Monte Christo" [Transcriber's note: "Cristo"?] is a world-famous romance.

Of George Eliot, "Silas Marner" is the best of the short stories, and "Romola" the best of the long. "Adam Bede" ranks barely second to "Silas Marner."

Charlotte Bronte's "Jane Eyre" remains a classic among earlier English novels.

Edward Everett Hale's "Man without a Country" will be read as long as the American flag flies.

Hawthorne's "Mosses from an Old Manse" are stories of unique interest, and "The Scarlet Letter" is known to all well-read people.

Of Rudyard Kipling, read "Kim," and "The Man Who Would be King."

Pierre Loti's "Iceland Fisherman" is translated by A. F. de Koven. McClurg, $1.00.

S. Weir Mitchell's "Hugh Wynne" sold 125,000 copies.

Thomas Nelson Page's "Gordon Keith" sold 200,000 copies.

If you read only one of Walter Scott's novels, take "Ivanhoe," or "The Talisman." Five more of those most read are likely to follow.

Henryk Sienkiewicz's "Quo Vadis" is most notable.

Robert L. Stevenson's "Treasure Island," and "Doctor Jekyll and Mr. Hyde," and "The Merry Men and Other Tales," are fair examples of the charm and insight of this author.

He who reads Frank Stockton's "Rudder Grange" is likely to read more of this author's books.

Mrs. H. B. Stowe's "Uncle Tom's Cabin" is still one of the great stories of the world.

Of Mark Twain, "Huckleberry Finn," "The Innocents Abroad," and the "Story of Joan of Arc" are representative volumes.

Miss Warner's "Wide, Wide World" is unique in American fiction.

John Watson's "Beside the Bonnie Briar Bush," sold 200,000 copies in America.

Lew Wallace's "Ben Hur" is the greatest of scriptural romances.

Thirty-eight books by twenty-eight authors. It would have been easier to name a hundred authors and two hundred books.

I will add from "The Critic" a list whose sales have reached six figures:—

Books of Every-day Life
"David Harum," by Westcott	727,000
"Mrs. Wiggs of the Cabbage Patch," by Alice Hegan Rice	345,000
"The Virginian," by Owen Wister	250,000
"Lovey Mary," by Alice Hegan Rice	188,000
"The Birds' Christmas Carol," by Mrs. Wiggin	100,000
"The Story of Patsy," by Mrs. Wiggin	100,000
"The Leopard's Spots," by Thomas G. Dixon, Jr	125,000

Romantic
"Richard Carvel," by Winston Churchill	400,000
"The Crisis," by Winston Churchill	400,000
"Graustark," by G. B. McCutcheon	300,000
"The Eternal City," by Hall Caine	175,000
"Dorothy Vernon," by Charles Major	150,000
"The Manxman," by Hall Caine	113,000
"When Knighthood Was in Flower," by Charles Major	400,000
"To Have and to Hold," by Miss Johnston	300,000
"Audrey," by Miss Johnston	165,000
"The Helmet of Navarre," by Bertha Runkle	100,000

Reading a Spur to Ambition

The great use in reading is for self-discovery. Inspirational, character-making, life-shaping books are the main thing.

Cotton Mather's "Essay to Do Good" influenced the whole career of Benjamin Franklin.

There are books that have raised the ideals and materially influenced entire nations.

Who can estimate the value of books that spur ambition, that awaken slumbering possibilities?

Are we ambitious to associate with people who inspire us to nobler deeds? Let us then read uplifting books, which stir us to make the most of ourselves.

We all know how completely changed we sometimes are after reading a book which has taken a strong, vigorous hold upon us.

Thousands of people have found themselves through the reading of some book, which has opened the door within them and given them the first glimpse of their possibilities. I know men and women whose whole lives have been molded, the entire trend of their careers completely changed, uplifted beyond their dreams by the books they have read.

When Senator Petters of Alabama went to California on horseback in 1849, he took with him a Bible, Shakespeare, and Burns's poems. He said that those books read and thought about, on the great plains, forever after spoiled him for reading poorer books. "The silence, the solitude," he said, "and the strange flickering light of the camp fire, seemed to bring out the tremendous significance of those great books; and I treasure them to-day as my choicest possessions."

Marshall Field and other proprietors of the great business houses of Chicago petitioned the school authorities for improved instruction along moral lines, affirming that the boys needed religious ideas to make them more reliable in business affairs.

It has been said by President White of Cornell that,—"The great thing needed to be taught in this country is *truth, simple ethics, the distinction between right and wrong*. Stress should be laid upon *what is best in biography*, upon *noble deeds and sacrifices*, especially those which show that the greatest man is not the greatest orator, or the tricky politician. They are a curse; what we need is *noble men*. National loss comes as the penalty for frivolous boyhood and girlhood, that gains no moral stamina from wholesome books."

If youths learn to feed on the thoughts of the great men and women of all times, they will never again be satisfied with the common or low; they will never again be satisfied with mediocrity; they will aspire to something higher and nobler.

A day which is passed without treasuring up some good thought is not well spent. Every day is a leaf in the book of life. Do not waste a day any more than you would tear out leaves from the book of life.

The Bible, such manuals as "Daily Strength for Daily Needs," such books as Professor C. C. Everett's "Ethics for Young People"; Lucy Elliott Keeler's "If I Were a Girl Again"; "Beauty through Hygiene," by Dr. Emma F. Walker, such essays as Robert L. Stevenson's "Gentlemen" (in his "Familiar Studies of Men and Books") Munger's "On the Threshold"; John Ruskin's "Sesame and Lilies"—these are the books that make young men and maidens so trustworthy that the Marshall Fields and John Wanamakers want their aid in the conduct of great business concerns. Blessed are they who go much farther in later years, and who become familiar with those

"Olympian bards who sang
Divine ideas below,
Which always find us young
And always keep us so."

The readers who do not know the Concord philosopher Emerson, and the great names of antiquity, Marcus Aurelius, Epictetus and Plato, have yet great pleasures to come.

Aside from reading fiction, books of travel are of the best for mental diversion; then there are Nature Studies, and Science and Poetry,—all affording wholesome recreation, all of an uplifting character, and some of them opening up study specialties of the highest order, as in the great range of books classified as Natural Science.

The reading and study of poetry is much like the interest one takes in the beauties of natural scenery. Much of the best poetry is indeed a poetic interpretation of nature. Whittier and Longfellow and Bryant lead their readers to look on nature with new eyes, as Ruskin opened the eyes of Henry Ward Beecher.

A great deal of the best prose is in style and sentiment of a true poetic character, lacking only the metrical form. To become familiar with Tennyson and Shakespeare, and the brilliant catalogue of British poets is in itself a liberal education. Rolfe's Shakespeare is in handy volumes, and so edited as to be of most service. Palgrave's "Golden Treasury" of the best songs and lyrical poems in the English language was edited with the advice and collaboration of Tennyson. His "Children's Treasury" of lyrical poetry is most attractive. Emerson's Parnassus, and Whittier's "Three Centuries of Song" are excellent collections of the most famous poems of the ages.

Of Books of Travel, here are a dozen titles, where one might easily name twelve hundred:—

Edmondo de Amicis,—"Holland and Its People," and his "Constantinople."

Frank T. Bullen's "Cruise of the Cachelot Round the World After Sperm Wales."
J. M. Hoppin's "Old England."
Clifton Johnson, "Among English Hedgerows."
W. D. Howell's "Venetian Life"; "Italian Journeys."
Irving's "Sketch Book," and the "Alhambra."
Henry James, "Portraits of Places."
Arthur Smith's "Chinese Characteristics," and especially his "Village Life in China."

It would be impossible to list books more interesting and more useful than most fiction, which may be called Nature Studies.

I will name a few books that will certainly incite the reader to search for more:—

Ernest Ingersoll's "Book of the Ocean."
Professor E. S. Holder's "The Sciences," a reading book for children.
Jean Mace's "History of a Mouthful of Bread."
E. A. Martin's "Story of a Piece of Coal."
Professor Charles A. Young's "The Sun," revised edition 1895.
Serviss' "Astronomy with an Opera-Glass," "Pleasures of the Telescope," "The Skies and the Earth."
Thoreau's "Walden; or Life in the Woods."
Mrs. F. T. Parsons' (Smith) Dana. "According to Seasons"; talks about the flowers in the order of their appearance in the woods and fields. Describes wild flowers in order of blooming, with information about their haunts and habits. Also, by the same author, "How to Know the Wild Flowers". Describes briefly more than 400 varieties common east of Chicago, grouping them by color.
Seton-Thompson's "Wild Animals I have Known"; of which 100,000 copies have been sold.
F. A. Lucas' "Animals of the Past"
Bradford Towey's "Birds in the Bush," and "Everyday Birds."
President D. S. Jordan's "True Tales of Birds and Beasts."
D. L. Sharp's "A Watcher in the Woods."
W. H. Gibson's "Sharp Eyes."
M. W. Morley's "The Bee-people."

Never before was a practical substitute for a college education at home made so cheap, so easy, and so attractive. Knowledge of all kinds is placed before us in a most attractive and interesting manner. The best of the literature of the world is found to-day in thousands of American homes where fifty years ago it could only have been obtained by the rich.

What a shame it is that under such conditions as these an American should grow up ignorant, should be uneducated in the midst of such marvelous opportunities for self-improvement! Indeed, most of the best literature in every line to-day appears in the current periodicals, in the form of short articles. Many of our greatest writers spend a vast amount of time in the drudgery of travel and investigation in gathering material for these articles, and the magazine publishers pay thousands of dollars for what a reader can get for ten or fifteen cents. Thus the reader secures for a trifle in periodicals or books the results of months and often years of hard work and investigation of our greatest writers.

A New York millionaire,—a prince among merchants,—took me over his palatial residence on Fifth Avenue, every room of which was a triumph of the architect's, of the decorator's, and of the upholsterer's art. I was told that the decorations of a single sleeping-room had cost ten thousand dollars. On the walls were paintings secured at fabulous prices, and about the rooms were pieces of massive and costly furniture, and draperies representing a small fortune, and carpets on which it seemed almost sacrilege to tread covered the floors. But there was scarcely a book in the house. He had expended a fortune for physical pleasures, comforts, luxury, and display. It was pitiful to think of the physical surfeit and mental starvation of the children of such a home as that. When I went out, he told me that he came to the city a poor boy, with all his worldly possessions done up in a little red bandana. "I am a millionaire," he said, "but I want to tell you that I would give half I have to-day for a decent education."

Many a rich man has confessed to confidential friends and his own heart that he would give much of his wealth,—all, if necessary,—to see his son a manly man, free from the habits which abundance has formed and fostered till they have culminated in sin and degradation and perhaps crime; and has realized that, in all his ample provision, he has failed to provide that which might have saved his son and himself from loss and torture,—good books.

There is a wealth within the reach of the poorest mechanic and day-laborer in this country that kings in olden times could not possess, and that is the wealth of a well-read, cultured mind. In this newspaper age, this age of cheap books and periodicals, there is no excuse for ignorance, for a coarse, untrained mind. To-day no one is so handicapped, if he have health and the use of his faculties, that he can not possess himself of wealth that will enrich his whole life, and enable him to converse and mingle with the most cultured people. No one is so poor but that it is possible for him to lay hold of that which will broaden his mind, which will inform and improve him, and lift him out of the brute stage of existence into their god-like realm of knowledge.

"No entertainment is so cheap as reading," says Mary Wortley Montague; "nor any pleasure so lasting." Good books elevate the character, purify the taste, *take the attractiveness out of low pleasures*, and lift us upon a higher plane of thinking and living.

"A great part of what the British spend on books," says Sir John Lubbock, "they save in prisons and police."

It seems like a miracle that the poorest boy can converse freely with the greatest philosophers and scientists, statesmen, warriors, authors of all time with little expense, that the inmates of the humblest cabin may follow the stories of the nations, the epochs of history, the story of liberty, the romance of the world, and the course of human progress.

Have you just been to a well educated sharp-sighted employer to find work? You did not need to be at any trouble to tell him the names of the books you have read, because they have left their indelible mark upon your face and your speech. Your pinched, starved vocabulary, your lack of polish, your slang expressions, tell him of the trash you have given your precious time to. He knows that you have not rightly systemized your hours. He knows that thousands of young men and women whose lives are crowded to overflowing with routine work and duties, manage to find time to keep posted on what is going on in the world, and for systematic, useful reading.

Carlyle said that a collection of books is a university. What a pity that the thousands of ambitious, energetic men and women who missed their opportunities for an education at the school age, and feel crippled by their loss, fail to catch the significance of this, fail to realize the tremendous cumulative possibilities of that great life-improver that admirable substitute for a college or university education—reading.

"Of the things which man can do or make here below," it was said by the sage of Chelsea, "by far the most momentous, wonderful, and worthy, are the things we call Books! Those poor bits of rag-paper with black ink on them; from the Daily Newspaper to the sacred Hebrew Book, what have they not done, what are they not doing?"

President Schurmann of Cornell, points with pride to a few books in his library which he says he bought when a poor boy by going many a day without his dinner.

The great German Professor Oken was not ashamed to ask Professor Agassiz to dine with him on potatoes and salt, that he might save money for books.

King George III, used to say that lawyers do not know so much more law than other people; but they know better where to find it.

A practical working knowledge of how to find what is in the book world, relating to any given point, is worth a vast deal from a financial point of view. And by such knowledge, one forms first an acquaintance with books, then friendship.

"When I consider," says James Freeman Clarke, "what some books have done for the world, and what they are doing, how they keep up our hope, awaken new courage and faith, soothe pain, give an ideal of life to those whose homes are hard and cold, bind together distant ages and foreign lands, create new worlds of beauty, bring down truths from heaven,—I give eternal blessings for this gift."

For the benefit of the younger readers we give below a list of forty juveniles.

Aesop's "Fables."

Louise M. Alcott's "Little Women," "Little Men," which stood at the top of a list of books chosen in eleven thousand elementary class-rooms in New York.

T. B. Aldrich's "Story of a Bad Boy."
Anderson's "Fairy Tales."
Amelia E. Barr's "The Bow of Orange Ribbon," a book for girls.
"Black Beauty."
E. S. Brooks, "True Story of General Grant."
Bulfinch's "Children's Lives of Great Men," "Age of Chivalry," and "Age of Fable."
Bullen's "Log of a Sea Waif."
Burnett's "Little Lord Fauntleroy," and "Sara Crewe," the latter a book for girls.
Butterworth's "Zig-Zag Journeys."
Carleton Coffin's, "Boys' of '76."
Eva Lovett Carson's "The Making of a Girl."
Ralph Connor's "Gwen," a book for girls.
Louis Carroll's "Alice in Wonderland," and "Through the Looking Glass."
Dana's "Two Years Before the Mast."
"De Amicin's Cuore," which has sold 200,000 in Italy.
DeFoe's "Robinson Crusoe."
Mary Mapes Dodge, "Hans Brinker," or "The Silver Skates," "Life in Holland."
Eugene Field's "A Little Book of Profitable Tales." It has sold 200,000 copies.
Grimm's "Fairy Tales."
Habberton's "Helen's Babies."
E. E. Hale's "Boy Heroes."
Chandler Harris' "Little Mr. Thimblefinger and His Queer Country; What the Children Saw and Heard There." Fantastic tale interweaving negro animal stories and other Georgia folklore with modern inventions. "Mr. Rabbit At Home"; sequel to "Little Mr. Thimblefinger and His Queer Country." Animal stories told to children.
Charles Kingsley's "Water Babies."
Kipling's "Jungle Books," which have sold 175,000 copies.
Knox's "Boy Travelers."
Lanier's "Boy Froissart," and "Boy's King Arthur."
Edward Lear's "Nonsense Books."
Mabie's "Norse Stories."
Samuel's "From the Forecastle to the Cabin." The experiences of the author who ran away from home and shipped as cabin boy; points out dangers that beset a seafaring life.
Mrs. A. D. T. Whitney's "Faith Gartney's Girlhood."
Kate Douglas Wiggin's "Rebecca of Sunnybrook Farm."

Not long ago President Eliot of Harvard College aroused widespread controversy over his selection of a library of books, which might be contained on a five-foot shelf. We append his selections as indicative of the choice of a great scholar and educator.

The following sixteen titles may be had in Everyman's Library, cloth 350. net per volume; leather 70 c. net per volume:

President Eliot's Five-Foot Shelf
Benjamin Franklin's Autobiography.
Sir Thomas Browne's "Religio Medici."
"Confessions of St. Augustine."
Shelley's "The Cenci" (contained in volume two of the complete works).
Emerson's "English Traits," and "Representative Men."
Emerson's Essays.
Chaucer's "Canterbury Tales."
Bacon's Essays.
Walton's "Complete Angler."
Milton's Poems.
Goethe's "Faust."
Marlowe's "Dr. Faustus."
Marcus Aurelius' "Meditations."
Browning's "Blot on the Scutcheon" (contained in volume one of the poems).
Dante's "Divine Comedy."
Bunyan's "Pilgrim's Progress."
Thomas Á. Kempis' "Imitation of Christ."
Burns's "Tam O'Shanter."
Dryden's "Translation of the Aeneid."
Walton's Lives of Donne, and Herbert.
Ben Johnson's "Volpone."
Smith's "Wealth of Nations."
Plutarch's "Lives."
Letters of Pliny.
Cicero's Select Letters.
Plato's "Phaedrus."
Epictetus' Discourses.
Socrates' "Apology and Crito."
Beaumont and Fletcher's "Maid's Tragedy."
Milton's Tractate on Education.
Bacon's "New Atlantis."
Darwin's "Origin of Species."
Webster's "Duchess of Malfi."
Dryden's "All for Love."
Thomas Middleton's "The Changeling."
John Woolman's Journal.
"Arabian Nights."
Tennyson's "Becket."

Penn's "Fruits of Solitude."
Milton's "Areopagitica."
The following list of books is offered as suggestive of profitable lines of reading for all classes and tastes:
Books on Nature
Thoreau's, "Cape Cod," "Maine Woods," "Excursions."
Burroughs' "Ways of Nature," "Wake Robin," "Signs and Seasons," "Pepacton."
Jefferies' "Life of the Fields," "Wild Life in a Southern Country," and "Idylls of Field and Hedgerow."
Lubbock's "Beauties of Nature."
Maeterlinck's "Life of the Bee."
Thompson's "My Winter Garden."
Warner's "My Summer in a Garden."
Van Dyke's "Little Rivers," "Fisherman's Luck."
White's "The Forest."
Mrs. Wright's "Garden of a Commuter's Wife."
Wordsworth's and Bryant's Poems.
Novels Descriptive of American Life
Simms' "The Partisan."
Cooper's "The Spy."
Hawthorne's "The House of the Seven Gables."
Cable's "Old Creole Days," "The Grandissimes."
Howells' "The Rise of Silas Lapham."
Howells' "A Hazard of New Fortunes."
Eggleston's "A Hoosier Schoolmaster."
Bret Harte's "Luck of Roaring Camp and Other Stories."
Mary Hallock Foote's "The Led-Horse Claim."
Octave Thanet's "Heart of Toil," "Stories of a Western Town."
Wister's "The Virginian," "Lady Baltimore."
E. Hopkinson Smith's "The Fortune of Oliver Horn."
Thomas Nelson Page's "Short Stories," and "Red Rock."
Mrs. Delands' "Old Chester Tales."
J. L. Allen's "Flute and Violin," "The Choir Invisible."
Frank Norris' "The Octopus," "The Pit"
Garland's "Main Traveled Roads."
Miss Jewett's "Country of the Pointed Firs," "The Tory Lover."
Miss Wilkins' "New England Nun," "Pembroke."
Churchill's "The Crisis," "Coniston," "Mr. Crewe's Career."
Brander Matthews' "His Father's Son."
S. Weir Mitchell's "Hugh Wynne."
Fox's "The Little Shepherd of Kingdom Come."
Mrs. Wharton's "The House of Mirth."
Robert Grant's "Unleavened Bread."

Robert Herrick's "The Common Lot," "The Memoirs of an American Citizen."
Grace E. King's "Balcony Stories."
Books Which Interpret American Ideals
Emerson's Addresses and Essays.
Lowell's Essay on Democracy.
Lincoln's Inaugural Addresses.
Booker T. Washington's "Up from Slavery."
Jacob Riis' "The Making of An American."
Higginson's "The New World and the New Book."
Brander Matthews' "Introduction to American Literature."
Whittier's "Snow-Bound."
Louise Manley's "Southern Literature."
Thomas Nelson Page's "The Old South."
E. J. Turner's "The Rise of the New West"
Churchill's "The Crossing."
James Bryce's "American Commonwealth."
Some of the Best Biographies
"Life of Sir Walter Scott," Lockhart.
"Life of Frederick the Great," Carlyle.
"Alfred Lord Tennyson," by his son.
"Life and Letters of Thomas Henry Huxley," by his son.
Plutarch's "Lives."
"Lives of Seventy of the Most Eminent Painters, Sculptors and Architects," Vasari.
"Cicero and His Friends," Boissier.
"Life of Samuel Johnson," Boswell.
Autobiography of Leigh Hunt.
"Memoirs of My Life and Writings," Gibbon.
Autobiography of Martineau.
"Life of John Sterling," Carlyle.
"Life and Times of Goethe," Grimm.
"Life and Letters of Macaulay," Trevelyan.
"Life of Charles James Fox," Trevelyan.
"Life of Carlyle," Froude.
Benvenuto Cellini's Autobiography.
Boswell's "Johnson."
Trevelyan's "Life of Macaulay."
Carlyle's, "Frederick the Great."
Stanley's, "Thomas Arnold."
Hughes', "Alfred the Great."
Mrs. Kingsley's, "Charles Kingsley."
Lounsbury's, "Cooper."
Greenslet's, "Lowell," and "Aldrich."
Mims', "Sidney Lanier."

Wister's, "Seven Ages of Washington."
Grant's Autobiography.
Morley's, "Chatham."
Harrison's, "Cromwell."
W. Clark Russell's, "Nelson."
Morse's, "Benjamin Franklin."
Twenty-four American Biographies
"Abraham Lincoln," Schurz.
"Life of George Washington," Irving.
"Charles Eliot, Landscape Architect," Eliot.
"Nathaniel Hawthorne and His Wife," Hawthorne.
"Henry Wadsworth Longfellow," Higginson.
"James Russell Lowell," Greenslet.
"Life of Francis Parkman," Farnham.
"Edgar Alien Poe," Woodberry.
Autobiography of Joseph Jefferson.
"Walt Whitman," Perry.
"Life and Letters of Whittier," Pickard.
"James Russell Lowell and His Friends," Hale.
"George Washington," Wilson.
Autobiography of Benjamin Franklin.
"Story of My Life," Helen Keller.
"Autobiography of a Journalist," Stillman.
"Autobiography of Seventy Years," Hoar.
"Life of Thomas Bailey Aldrich," Greenslet.
"Life of Alice Freeman Palmer," Palmer.
"Personal Memoirs," Grant.
"Memoirs," Sherman.
"Memoirs of Ralph Waldo Emerson," Cabot.
"Sidney Lanier," Mims.
"Life of J. Fenimore Cooper," Lounsbury.

The books enumerated have been selected as examples of the best in their respective classes. Even those books of fiction chosen, primarily, for entertainment, are instructive and educational. Whether the reader's taste runs to history, biography, travel, nature study, or fiction, he may select any one of the books named in these respective classifications and be assured of possessing a volume worthy of reading and ownership.

It is the author's hope and desire that the list of books he has given, limited as it is, may prove of value to those seeking self-education, and that the books may encourage the disheartened, stimulate ambition, and serve as stepping stones to higher ideals and nobler purposes in life.

Why Some Succeed and Others Fail

Life's highway is strewn with failures, just as the sea bed is strewn with wrecks.

A large percentage of those who embark in commercial undertakings fail, according to the records of commercial agencies.

Why do men fail? Why do adventures into business, happily launched, terminate in disastrous wreck?

Why do the few succeed and the many fail? Some failures are relative and not absolute; a partial success is achieved; a success that goes limping along through life; but the goal of ambition is unreached, the heart's desire unattained.

There are so many elements that enter into business that it is impossible to more than indicate them. Health, natural aptitude, temperament, disposition, a right start and in the right place, hereditary traits, good judgment, common sense, level-headedness, etc., are all factors which enter into one's chance of success in life. The best we can do in one chapter is to hang out the red flag over the dangerous places; to chart the rocks and shoals, whereon multitudes of vessels, which left the port of youth with flying colors, favoring breezes and every promise of a successful voyage, have been wrecked and lost.

The lack of self-confidence and lack of faith in one's ideas in one's mission in life have caused innumerable failures.

People who don't get on and who don't know why, do not realize the power of trifles to mar a career, what little things are killing their business or injuring their profession; do not realize how little things injure their credit; such as the lack of promptness in paying bills, or meeting a note at the bank.

Many men fail because they thought they had the field and were in no danger from competition, so that the heads of the firm took it easy, or because some enterprising up-to-date, progressive young man came to town, and, before they realized it, took their trade away from them, because they got into a rut, and didn't keep up-to-date stock and an attractive store.

They don't realize what splendid salesmen, an attractive place of business, up-to-date methods, and courteous treatment of customers mean.

Men often fail because they do not realize that creeping paralysis, caused by dry rot, is gradually strangling their business. Many business men fail because they dare not look their business conditions in the face when things go wrong, and do not adopt heroic methods, but continue to use palliatives, until the conditions are beyond cure, even with a surgeon's knife.

Lots of men fail because they don't know how to get rid of deadwood in their establishment, or retain non-productive employees, who with slip-shod methods, and indifference drive away more business than the proprietors can bring in by advertising.

Many other men fail because they tried bluff in place of capital, and proper training, or because they didn't keep up with the times.

Lots of young people fail to get ahead and plod along in mediocrity because they never found their place. They are round pegs in square holes. Others are not capable of coping with antagonism. Favoritism of proprietors and managers has killed many a business. A multitude of men fail to get on because they take themselves too seriously. They deliver their goods in a hearse, employ surly, unaccommodating clerks. Bad business manners have killed many a business. Slave-driving methods, inability to get along with others, lack of system, defective organizing ability, have cut short many a career.

A great many men are ruined by "side-lines" things outside their regular vocation. Success depends upon efficiency, and efficiency is impossible without intense, persistent concentration. Many traveling men think that they can pick up a little extra money and increase their income by taking up some "side-line." But it is always the small man, never the big one, who has a "side-line." Many of these men remain small, and are never able to rise to a big salaried position because they split up their endeavor, dissipate their energy. "Side-lines" are dangerous because they divert the mind, scatter effort, and nothing great can be accomplished without *intense concentration*.

Many people are always driving success away from them by their antagonistic manner, and their pessimistic thought. *They work for one thing, but expect something else.* They don't realize that their mental attitude must correspond with their ambition; that if they are working hard to get on, they must expect prosperity, and not kill their prospects by their adverse mental attitude—their doubts and fears.

Lots of men are ruined by "a sure thing," an inside tip, buying stocks on other people's judgment.

Many people fail because they lose their grit after they fail, or when they get down, they don't know how to get up. Many are victims of their moods, slaves of despondency. Courage and an optimistic outlook upon life are imperative to the winner. Fear is fatal to success. Many a young man fails because he can not multiply himself in others, can not delegate his work, is lost in detail. Other men fail in an attempt to build up a big business; their minds are not trained to grasp large subjects, to generalize, to make combinations; they are not self-reliant, depending upon other people's judgment and advice.

Many a man who works hard himself, does not know how to handle men, and does not know how to use other people's brains.

Thousands of youths fail to get on because they never fall in love with their work. Work that is drudgery never succeeds.

Fifty years ago, a stable-boy cleaned the horses of a prosperous hotel proprietor, who drove into Denver for supplies. That boy became Governor of Colorado, and later the hotel-keeper, with shattered fortunes, was glad to accept a place as watchman at the hand of the former stable-boy.

Life is made up of such contrasts. Every successful man, in whatever degree and in whatever line, has, at every step of his life, been on seemingly equal terms with hundreds of his fellows who, later, reached no such measure of success as he. Every miserable failure has had at some time as many chances, and at least as much possibility of cultivating the same qualities, as the successful people have had at some time in their lives.

Since humble birth and handicaps of every sort and degree have not prevented success in the determined man; since want has often spurred to needed action and obstacles but train to higher leaping, why should men fail? What causes the failures and half-successes that make up the generality of mankind?

The answer is manifold, but its lesson is plain. As one writer has expressed it, "*Every mainspring of success is a mainspring of failure, when wound around the wrong way.*" Every opportunity for advancement, for climbing for success, is just as much an opportunity for failure. Every success quality can be turned to one's disadvantage through excessive development or wrong use. No matter how broad and strong the dike may be, if a little hole lets the water through, ruin and disaster are sure. Possession of almost all the success-qualities may be absolutely nullified by one or two faults or vices. Sometimes one or two masterful traits of character will carry a person to success, in spite of defects that are a serious clog.

The numerous failures who wish always to blame their misfortunes upon others, or upon external circumstances, find small comfort in statistics compiled by those who have investigated the subject. In analyzing the causes of business failure in a recent year *Bradstreet's* found that seven-tenths were due to faults of those failing, and only three-tenths to causes entirely beyond their control. Faults causing failure, with per cent. of failures caused by each, are given as follows: incompetence, 19 per cent.; inexperience, 7.8 per cent.; lack of capital, 30.3 per cent.; unwise granting of credit, 3.6 per cent.; speculation, 2.3 per cent. It may be explained that "lack of capital" really means attempting to do too much with inadequate capital. This is a purely commercial analysis of purely commercial success. Character delinquencies must be read between the lines.

Forty successful men were induced, not long ago, to answer in detail the question, "What, in your observation, are the chief causes of the failure in life of business or professional men?" The causes attributed by these representative men were as follows:

Bad habits; bad judgment; bad luck; bad associates; carelessness of details; constant assuming of unjustifiable risks; desire to become rich too fast; drinking; dishonest dealings; desire of retrenchment; dislike to say no at the proper time; disregard of the Golden Rule; drifting with the tide; expensive habits of life; extravagance: envy; failure to appreciate one's surroundings; failure to grasp one's opportunities; frequent changes from one business to another; fooling away of time in pursuit of a so-called good time, gambling; inattention; incompetent assistants; incompetency; indolence; jealousy. Lack of attention to business; of application; of adaptation; of ambition; of business methods; of capital; of conservatism; of close attention to business; of confidence in self; of careful accounting; of careful observation; of definite purpose; of discipline in early life; of discernment of character; of enterprise; of energy; of economy; of faithfulness; of faith in one's calling; of industry; of integrity; of judgment; of knowledge of business requirements; of manly character; of natural ability; of perseverance; of pure principles; of proper courtesy toward people; of purpose; of pluck; of promptness in meeting business engagements; of system. Late hours; living beyond one's income; leaving too much to one's employees; neglect of details; no inborn love for one's calling; over-confidence in the stability of existing conditions; procrastination; speculative mania; selfishness; self-indulgence in small vices; studying ease rather than vigilance; social demoralization; thoughtless marriages; trusting one's work to others; undesirable location; unwillingness to pay the price of success; unwillingness to bear early privations; waste; yielding too easily to discouragement.

Surely, here is material enough for a hundred sermons if one cared to preach them. Without attempting to discuss all these causes of failure, some few may be profitably examined.

No youth can hope to succeed who is timid, who lacks faith in himself, who has not the courage of his convictions, and who always seeks for certainty before he ventures. "Self-distrust is the cause of most of our failures," said one. "In the assurance of strength there is strength, and they are the weakest, however strong, who have no faith in themselves or their powers."

"The ruin which overtakes so many merchants," said another, "is due, not so much to their lack of business talent, as to their lack of business nerve. How many lovable persons we see in trade, endowed with brilliant capacities, but cursed with yielding dispositions—who are resolute in no business habits and fixed in no business principles—who are prone to follow the instincts of a weak good nature, against the ominous hints of a clear intelligence; now obliging this friend by indorsing an unsafe note, and then pleasing that neighbor by sharing his risk in a hopeless speculation, and who, after all the capital they have earned by their industry and sagacity has been sunk in benevolent attempts to assist blundering or plundering incapacity, are doomed, in their bankruptcy, to be the mark of bitter taunts from growling creditors and insolent pity from a gossiping public."

Scattering one's forces has killed many a man's success. Withdrawal of the best of yourself from the work to be done is sure to bring final disaster. Every particle of a man's energy, intellect, courage, and enthusiasm is needed to win success in one line. Draw off part of the supply of any one or all of these, and there is danger that what is left will not suffice. A little inattention to one's business at a critical point is quite sufficient to cause shipwreck. The pilot who pays attention to a pretty passenger is not likely to bring his ship to port. Attractive side issues, great schemes, and flattering promises of large rewards, too often lure the business or professional man from the safe path in which he may plod on to sure success. Many a man fails to become a great man, by splitting into several small ones, choosing to be a tolerable Jack-at-all-trades, rather than to be an unrivalled specialist.

Lack of thoroughness is another great cause of failure. The world is overcrowded with men, young and old, who remain stationary, filling minor positions, and drawing meager salaries, simply because they have never thought it worth while to achieve mastery in the pursuits they have chosen to follow.

Lack of education has caused many failures; if a man has success qualities in him, he will not long lack such education as is absolutely necessary to his success. He will walk fifty miles if necessary to borrow a book, like Lincoln. He will hang by one arm to a street lamp, and hold his book with the other, like a certain Glasgow boy. He will study between anvil blows, like Elihu Burritt; he will do some of the thousand things that other noble strugglers have done to fight against circumstances that would deprive them of what they hunger for.

"The five conditions of failure," said H. H. Vreeland, president of the Metropolitan Street Railway Company of New York, "may be roughly classified thus: first, laziness, and particularly mental laziness; second, lack of faith in the efficiency of work; third, reliance on the saving grace of luck; fourth, lack of courage, initiative and persistence: fifth, the belief that the young man's job affects his standing, instead of the young man's affecting the standing of his job."

Look where you will, ask of whom you will, and you will find that not circumstances, but personal qualities, defects and deficiencies, cause failures. This is strongly expressed by a wealthy manufacturer who said: "Nothing else influences a man's career in life so much as his disposition. He may have capacity, knowledge, social position, or money to back him at the start; but it is his disposition that will decide his place in the world at the end. Show me a man who is, according to popular prejudice, a victim of bad luck, and I will show you one who has some unfortunate, crooked twist of temperament that invites disaster, He is ill-tempered, or conceited, or trifling, or lacks enthusiasm."

There are some men whose failure to succeed in life is a problem to others, as well as to themselves. They are industrious, prudent, and economical; yet after a long life of striving, old age finds them still poor. They complain of ill luck, they say fate is against them. But the real truth is that their projects miscarry, because they mistake mere activity for energy. Confounding two things essentially different, they suppose that if they are always busy, they must of necessity be advancing their fortunes; forgetting that labor misdirected is but a waste of activity.

The worst of all foes to success is sheer, downright laziness. There is no polite synonym for laziness. Too many young men are afraid to work. They are lazy. They aim to find genteel occupations, so that they can dress well, and not soil their clothes, and handle things with the tips of their fingers. They do not like to get their shoulders under the wheel, and they prefer to give orders to others, or figure as masters, and let some one else do the drudgery. There is no place in this century for the lazy man. He will be pushed to the wall. Labor ever will be the inevitable price for everything that is valuable.

A metropolitan daily newspaper not long ago invited confessions by letter from those who felt that their lives had been failures. The newspaper agreed not to disclose the name or identity of any person making such a confession, and requested frank statements. Two questions were asked: "Has your life been a failure? Has your business been a failure?"

Some of the replies were pitiable in the extreme.

Some attributed their failures to a cruel fate which seemed to pursue them and thwart all their efforts, some to hereditary weaknesses, deformities, and taints, some to a husband or a wife, others to "inhospitable surroundings," and "cruel circumstances."

It is worthy of note that not one of these failures mentioned laziness as a cause.

Here are some of the reasons they did give:

"J. P. T." considered that his life was a failure from too much genius. He said he thought he could do anything, and therefore he couldn't wait to graduate from college, but left and began the practise of law, was principal of an academy, overworked himself, and had too many irons in the fire. He failed, he said, from dissipating his energies, and having too much confidence in men.

"Rutherford," said he had four chances to succeed in life, but lost them all. The first cause of his failure was lack of perseverance. He tired of the sameness and routine of his occupation. His second shortcoming was too great liberality, too much confidence in others. Third, economy was not in his dictionary. Fourth, "I had too much hope, even in the greatest extremities." Fifth, "I believed too much in friends and friendships. I couldn't read human nature, and did not make allowance enough for mistakes." Sixth, "I never struck my vocation." Seventh, "I had no one to care for, to spur me on to do something in the world. I am seventy years old, never drank, never had bad habits, always attended church. But I am as poor as when I started for myself."

"G. C. S." failed dismally. "My weakness was building air-castles. I had a burning desire to make a name in the world, and came to New York from the country. Rebuffed, discouraged, I drifted. I had no heart for work. I lacked ability and push, without which no life can be a success."

"Lacked ability and push."—Push *is* ability. Laziness is lack of push. Nothing can take the place of push. Push means industry and endurance and everlasting stick-to-it-ive-ness.

"A somewhat varied experience of men has led me, the longer I live," said a great man, "to set less value on mere cleverness; to attach more and more importance to industry and physical endurance."

Goethe said that industry is nine-tenths of genius, and Franklin that diligence is the mother of good luck. A thousand other tongues and pens have lauded work. Idleness and shiftlessness may be set down as causing a large part of the failures of the world.

On every side we see persons who started out with good educations and great promise, but who have gradually "gone to seed." Their early ambition oozed out, their early ideals gradually dropped to lower standards. Ambition is a spring that sets the apparatus going. All the parts may be perfect, but the lack of a spring is a fatal defect. Without wish to rise, desire to accomplish and to attain, no life will succeed largely.

"Chief among the causes which bring positive failure or a disappointing portion of half success to thousands of honest strugglers is vacillation," said Thomas B. Bryan.

Many a business man has made his fortune by promptly deciding at some nice juncture to expose himself to a considerable risk. Yet many failures are caused by ill-advised changes and causeless vacillation of purpose. The vacillating man, however strong in other respects, is always pushed aside in the race of life by the determined man, the decisive man, who knows what he wants to do and does it; even brains must give way to decision. One could almost say that no life ever failed that was steadfastly devoted to one aim, if that aim were not in itself unworthy.

I am a great believer in a college education, but a great many college graduates have made failures of their lives who might have succeeded had they not gone to college, because they depended upon theoretical, impractical knowledge to help them on, and were not willing to begin at the bottom after graduation.

On every hand we see men who did well in college, but who do very poorly in life. They stood high in their classes, were conscientious, hard workers, but somehow when they get out into life, they do not seem able to catch on. They are not practical. It would be hard to tell why they never get ahead, but there seems to be something lacking in their make-up, some screw loose somewhere. These brilliant graduates, but indifferently successful men, are often enigmas to themselves. They don't understand why they don't get on.

There is no doubt that ill-health is often the cause of failure, but this is often due to a wrong mental attitude, wrong thinking. The pessimistic, discouraged mental attitude is very injurious to good health. Worry, fear, anxiety, jealousy, extreme selfishness, poison the system, so that it does not perform its functions perfectly, and will cause much ill-health.

A complete reversal of the mental attitude would bring robust health to multitudes of those who suffer from "poor health." If people would only think right, and live right, ill-health would be very rare. A wrong mental attitude is the cause of a large part of physical weakness, disease, and suffering.

It has been said that the two chief factors of success are industry and health. But the history of human triumphs over difficulties shows that the sick, the crippled, the deformed, have often outrun the strong and hale to the goal of success, in spite of tremendous physical handicaps. Many such instances are cited in other chapters of this volume.

Where men have built an abiding success, industry and perseverance have proven the foundation stone? of their great achievements. Every man may lay this foundation and build on it for himself. Whatever a man's natural advantages may be, great or small, industry and perseverance are his, if he chooses. By the exercise of these qualities he may rise, as others have done, to success, if like Palissy he

"Labors and endures and waits
And what he can not find creates."

When Is Success a Failure?

When you are doing the lower while the higher is possible.

When you are not a cleaner, finer, larger man on account of your life-work.

When you live only to eat, drink, have a good time, and accumulate money.

When you do not carry a higher wealth in your character than in your pocketbook.

When your highest brain cells have been crowded out of business by greed.

When it has made conscience an accuser, and shut the sunlight out of your life.

When all sympathy has been crushed out by selfish devotion to your vocation.

When the attainment of your ambition has blighted the aspirations and crushed the hopes of others.

When you plead that you never had time to cultivate your friendships, politeness, or good manners.

When you have lost on your way your self-respect, your courage, your self-control, or any other quality of manhood.

When you do not overtop your vocation; when you are not greater as a man than as a lawyer, a merchant, a physician, or a scientist.

When you have lived a double life and practised double-dealing.

When it has made you a physical wreck—a victim of "nerves" and moods.

When the hunger for more money, more land, more houses and bonds has grown to be your dominant passion.

When it has dwarfed you mentally and morally, and robbed you of the spontaneity and enthusiasm of youth. When it has hardened you to the needs and sufferings of others, and made you a scorner of the poor and unfortunate.

When there is a dishonest or a deceitful dollar in your possession; when your fortune spells the ruin of widows and orphans, or the crushing of the opportunities of others.

When your absorption in your work has made you practically a stranger to your family.

When you go on the principle of getting all you can and giving as little as possible in return.

When your greed for money has darkened and cramped your wife's life, and deprived her of self-expression, of needed rest and recreation, or amusement of any kind.

When the nervous irritability engendered by constant work, without relaxation, has made you a brute in your home and a nuisance to those who work for you.

When you rob those who work for you of what is justly their due, and then pose as a philanthropist by contributing a small fraction of your unjust gains to some charity or to the endowment of some public institution.

Rich Without Money

Let others plead for pensions; I can be rich without money, by endeavoring to be superior to everything poor. I would have my services to my country unstained by any interested motive.— Lord Collingwood

I ought not to allow any man, because he has broad lands, to feel that he is rich in my presence. I ought to make him feel that I can do without his riches, that I can not be bought,—neither by comfort, neither by pride,—and although I be utterly penniless, and receiving bread from him, that he is the poor man beside me.— Emerson

He is richest who is content with the least, for content is the wealth of nature.— Socrates

My crown is in my heart, not on my head, Nor decked with diamonds and Indian stones, Nor to be seen: my crown is called content; A crown it is, that seldom kings enjoy.— Shakespeare

Many a man is rich without money. Thousands of men with nothing in their pockets are rich.

A man born with a good, sound constitution, a good stomach, a good heart and good limbs, and a pretty good head-piece is rich.

Good bones are better than gold, tough muscles than silver, and nerves that carry energy to every function are better than houses and land.

"Heart-life, soul-life, hope, joy, and love, are true riches," said Beecher.

Why should I scramble and struggle to get possession of a little portion of this earth? This is my world now; why should I envy others its mere legal possession? It belongs to him who can see it, enjoy it. I need not envy the so-called owners of estates in Boston or New York. They are merely taking care of my property and keeping it in excellent condition for me. For a few pennies for railroad fare whenever I wish I can see and possess the best of it all. It has cost me no effort, it gives me no care; yet the green grass, the shrubbery, and the statues on the lawns, the finer sculptures and the paintings within, are always ready for me whenever I feel a desire to look upon them. I do not wish to carry them home with me, for I could not give them half the care they now receive; besides, it would take too much of my valuable time, and I should be worrying continually lest they be spoiled or stolen. I have much of the wealth of the world now. It is all prepared for me without any pains on my part. All around me are working hard to get things that will please me, and competing to see who can give them the cheapest. The little that I pay for the use of libraries, railroads, galleries, parks, is less than it would cost to care for the least of all I use.

Life and landscape are mine, the stars and flowers, the sea and air, the birds and trees. What more do I want? All the ages have been working for me; all mankind are my servants. I am only required to feed and clothe myself, an easy task in this land of opportunity.

A millionaire pays a big fortune for a gallery of paintings, and some poor boy or girl comes in, with open mind and poetic fancy, and carries away a treasure of beauty which the owner never saw. A collector bought at public auction in London, for one hundred and fifty-seven guineas, an autograph of Shakespeare; but for nothing a schoolboy can read and absorb the riches of "Hamlet."

"Want is a growing giant whom the coat of Have was never large enough to cover." "A man may as soon fill a chest with grace, or a vessel with virtue," says Phillips Brooks, "as a heart with wealth."

Shall we seek happiness through the sense of taste or of touch? Shall we idolize our stomachs and our backs? Have we no higher missions, no nobler destinies? Shall we "disgrace the fair day by a pusillanimous preference of our bread to our freedom"?

What does your money say to you: what message does it bring to you? Does it say to you, "Eat, drink, and be merry, for to-morrow we die"? Does it bring a message of comfort, of education, of culture, of travel, of books, of an opportunity to help your fellow-men or is the message "More land, more thousands and millions"? What message does it bring you? Clothes for the naked, bread for the starving, schools for the ignorant, hospitals for the sick, asylums for the orphans, or of more for yourself and none for others? Is it a message of generosity or of meanness, breadth or narrowness? Does it speak to you of character? Does it mean a broader manhood, a larger aim, a nobler ambition, or does it cry, "More, more, more"?

Are you an animal loaded with ingots, or a man filled with a purpose? He is rich whose mind is rich, whose thought enriches the intellect of the world.

A sailor on a sinking vessel in the Caribbean Sea eagerly filled his pockets with Spanish dollars from a barrel on board while his companions, about to leave in the only boat, begged him to seek safety with them. But he could not leave the bright metal which he had so longed for and idolized, and when the vessel went down he was prevented by his very riches from reaching shore.

"Who is the richest of men?" asked Socrates. "He who is content with the least, for contentment is nature's riches."

In More's "Utopia" gold was despised. Criminals were forced to wear heavy chains of it, and to have rings of it in their ears; it was put to the vilest uses to keep up the scorn of it. Bad characters were compelled to wear gold head-bands. Diamonds and pearls were used to decorate infants, so that the youth would discard and despise them.

"Ah, if the rich were as rich as the poor fancy riches!" exclaims Emerson.

In excavating Pompeii a skeleton was found with the fingers clenched round a quantity of gold. A man of business in the town of Hull, England, when dying, pulled a bag of money from under his pillow, which he held between his clenched fingers with a grasp so firm as scarcely to relax under the agonies of death.

"Oh! blind and wanting wit to choose, Who house the chaff and burn the grain; Who hug the wealth ye cannot use, And lack the riches all may gain."

Poverty is the want of much, avarice the want of everything.

A poor man while scoffing at the wealthy for not enjoying themselves was met by a stranger who gave him a purse, in which he was always to find a ducat. As fast as he took one out another was to drop in, but he was not to begin to spend his fortune until he had thrown away the purse. He took ducat after ducat out, but continually procrastinated and put off the hour of enjoyment until he had got "a little more," and died at last counting his millions.

A beggar was once met by Fortune, who promised to fill his wallet with gold, as much as he might desire, on condition that whatever touched the ground should turn at once to dust. The beggar opened his wallet, asked for more and yet more, until the bag burst. The gold fell to the ground, and all was lost.

When the steamer *Central America* was about to sink, the stewardess, having collected all the gold she could from the staterooms, and tied it in her apron, jumped for the last boat leaving the steamer. She missed her aim, fell into the water and the gold carried her down head first.

Franklin said money never made a man happy yet; there is nothing in its nature to produce happiness. The more a man has, the more he wants. Instead of filling a vacuum, it makes one. A great bank account can never make a man rich. It is the mind that makes the body rich. No man is rich, however much money or land he may possess, who has a poor heart. If that is poor, he is poor indeed, though he own and rule kingdoms. He is rich or poor according to what he is, not according to what he has.

Some men are rich in health, in constant cheerfulness, in a mercurial temperament which floats them over troubles and trials enough to sink a shipload of ordinary men. Others are rich in disposition, family, and friends. There are some men so amiable that everybody loves them; so cheerful that they carry an atmosphere of jollity about them.

The human body is packed full of marvelous devices, of wonderful contrivances, of infinite possibilities for the happiness and enrichment of the individual. No physiologist, inventor, nor scientist has ever been able to point out a single improvement, even in the minutest detail, in the mechanism of the human body. No chemist has ever been able to suggest a superior combination in any one of the elements which make up the human structure.

One of the first great lessons of life is to learn the true estimate of values. As the youth starts out in his career all sorts of wares will be imposed upon him and all kinds of temptations will be used to induce him to buy. His success will depend very largely upon his ability to estimate properly, not the apparent but the real value of everything presented to him. Vulgar Wealth will flaunt her banner before his eyes, and claim supremacy over everything else. A thousand different schemes will be thrust into his face with their claims for superiority. Every occupation and vocation will present its charms and offer its inducements in turn. The youth who would succeed must not allow himself to be deceived by appearance, but must place the emphasis of life upon the right thing.

Raphael was rich without money. All doors opened to him, and he was more than welcome everywhere. His sweet spirit radiated sunshine wherever he went.

Henry Wilson, the sworn friend of the oppressed, whose one question, as to measures or acts, was ever "Is it right; will it do good?" was rich without money. So scrupulous had this Natick cobbler been not to make his exalted position a means of worldly gain, that when he came to be inaugurated as Vice-President of the country, he was obliged to borrow of his fellow-senator, Charles Sumner, one hundred dollars to meet the necessary expenses of the occasion.

Mozart, the great composer of the "Requiem," left barely enough money to bury him, but he has made the world richer.

A rich mind and noble spirit will cast over the humblest home a radiance of beauty which the upholsterer and decorator can never approach. Who would not prefer to be a millionaire of character, of contentment, rather than possess nothing but the vulgar coins of a Croesus? Whoever uplifts civilization, though he die penniless, is rich, and future generations will erect his monument.

An Asiatic traveler tells us that one day he found the bodies of two men laid upon the desert sand beside the carcass of a camel. They had evidently died from thirst, and yet around the waist of each was a large store of jewels of different kinds, which they had doubtless been crossing the desert to sell in the markets of Persia.

The man who has no money is poor, but one who has nothing but money is poorer. He only is rich who can enjoy without owning; he is poor who though he have millions is covetous. There are riches of intellect, and no man with an intellectual taste can be called poor. He is rich as well as brave who can face compulsory poverty and misfortune with cheerfulness and courage.

We can so educate the will power that it will focus the thoughts upon the bright side of things, and upon objects which elevate the soul, thus forming a habit of happiness and goodness which will make us rich. The habit of making the best of everything and of always looking on the bright side is a fortune in itself.

He is rich who values a good name above gold. Among the ancient Greeks and Romans honor was more sought after than wealth. Rome was imperial Rome no more when the imperial purple became an article of traffic.

Diogenes was captured by pirates and sold as a slave. His purchaser released him, giving him charge of his household and of the education of his children. Diogenes despised wealth and affectation, and lived in a tub. "Do you want anything?" asked Alexander the Great, greatly impressed by the abounding cheerfulness of the philosopher under such circumstances. "Yes," replied Diogenes, "I want you to stand out of my sunshine and not take from me what you can not give me." "Were I not Alexander," exclaimed the great conqueror, "I would be Diogenes."

"Do you know, sir," said a devotee of Mammon to John Bright, "that I am worth a million sterling?" "Yes," said the irritated but calm-spirited respondent, "I do; and I know that it is all you are worth."

What power can poverty have over a home where loving hearts are beating with a consciousness of untold riches of the head and heart?

St. Paul was never so great as when he occupied a prison cell under the streets of Rome; and Jesus Christ reached the height of His success when, smitten, spat upon, tormented, and crucified, He cried in agony, and yet with triumphant satisfaction, "It is finished."

Don't start out in life with a false standard; a truly great man makes official position and money and houses and estates look so tawdry, so mean and poor, that we feel like sinking out of sight with our cheap laurels and our gold.

One of the great lessons to teach in this century of sharp competition and the survival of the fittest is how to be rich without money and to learn how to live without success according to the popular standard.

In the poem, "The Changed Cross," a weary woman is represented as dreaming that she was led to a place where many crosses lay, crosses of divers shapes and sizes. The most beautiful one was set in jewels of gold. It was so tiny and exquisite that she changed her own plain cross for it, thinking she was fortunate in finding one so much lighter and lovelier. But soon her back began to ache under the glittering burden, and she changed it for another, very beautiful and entwined with flowers. But she soon found that underneath the flowers were piercing thorns which tore her flesh. At last she came to a very plain cross without jewels, without carving, and with only the word, "Love," inscribed upon it. She took this one up and it proved the easiest and best of all. She was amazed, however, to find that it was her old cross which she had discarded.

It is easy to see the jewels and the flowers in other people's crosses, but the thorns and heavy weight are known only to the bearers. How easy other people's burdens seem to us compared with our own! We do not realize the secret burdens which almost crush the heart, nor the years of weary waiting for delayed success—the aching hearts longing for sympathy, the hidden poverty, the suppressed emotion in other lives.

William Pitt, the Great Commoner, considered money as dirt beneath his feet compared with the public interest and public esteem. His hands were clean.

The object for which we strive tells the story of our lives. Men and women should be judged by the happiness they create in those around them. Noble deeds always enrich, but millions of mere dollars may impoverish. *Character is perpetual wealth*, and by the side of him who possesses it the millionaire who has it not seems a pauper.

Invest in yourself, and you will never be poor. Floods can not carry your wealth away, fire can not burn it, rust can not consume it.

"If a man empties his purse into his head," says Franklin, "no man can take it from him. An investment in knowledge always pays the best interest."

> Howe'er it be, it seems to me,
> 'Tis only noble to be good.
> Kind hearts are more than coronets,
> And simple faith than Norman blood.— Tennyson

Stories From Life
A Book for Young People

Preface

To make a life, as well as to make a living, is one of the supreme objects for which we must all struggle. The sooner we realize what this means, the greater and more worthy will be the life which we shall make.

In putting together the brief life stories and incidents from great lives which make up the pages of this little volume, the writer's object has been to show young people that, no matter how humble their birth or circumstances, they may make lives that will be held up as examples to future generations, even as these stories show how boys, handicapped by poverty and the most discouraging surroundings, yet succeeded so that they are held up as models to the boys of to-day.

No boy or girl can learn too early in life the value of time and the opportunities within reach of the humblest children of the twentieth century to enable them to make of themselves noble men and women.

The stories here presented do not claim to be more than mere outlines of the subjects chosen, enough to show what brave souls in the past, souls animated by loyalty to God and to their best selves, were able to accomplish in spite of obstacles of which the more fortunately born youths of to-day can have no conception.

It should never be forgotten, however, in the strivings of ambition, that, while every one should endeavor to raise himself to his highest power and to attain to as exalted and honorable a position as his abilities entitle him to, his first object should be to make a noble life.

The author wishes to acknowledge the assistance of Miss Margaret Connolly in the preparation of this volume.

O.S.M.

Table of Contents

To-Day	536
"The Mill Boy of the Slashes"	537
The Greek Slave Who Won the Olive Crown	539
Turning Points in the Life of a Hero:	541
The First Turning Point	541
A Born Leader	542
"Farragut Is the Man"	543
He Aimed High and Hit the Mark	544
The Evolution of a Violinist	545
The Lesson of the Teakettle	548
How the Art of Printing Was Discovered	550
Sea Fever and What it Led to	553
Gladstone Found Time to Be Kind	555
A Tribune of the People	556
The Might of Patience	559
The Inspiration of Gambetta	560
Andrew Jackson: the Boy Who "Never Would Give Up"	562
Sir Humphry Davy's Greatest Discovery, Michael Faraday	564
The Triumph of Canova	566
Franklin's Lesson on Time Value	568
From Store Boy to Millionaire	569
"I Will Paint or Die!"	572
The Call That Speaks in the Blood	574
Washington's Youthful Heroism	576
A Cow His Capital	577
The Boy Who Said "I Must"	579
The Hidden Treasure	582
Love Tamed the Lion	585
"There Is Room Enough at the Top"	586
The Uplift of a Slave Boy's Ideal	588
"To the First Robin"	590

The "Wizard" as an Editor 591
How Good Fortune Came to Pierre 593
"If I Rest, I Rust" 596
A Boy Who Knew Not Fear 597
How Stanley Found Livingstone 602
The Nestor of American Journalists 608
The Man with an Idea 610
"Bernard of the Tuileries" 612
How the "Learned Blacksmith" Found Time 616
The Legend of William Tell 617
"Westward Ho!" 624
Three Great American Songs and Their Authors 626
    The Star-spangled Banner 626
    America 630
    The Battle Hymn of the Republic 634
Training for Greatness 637
    Glimpses of Abraham Lincoln's Boyhood 637
    The Marble Waiteth 648

TO-DAY

For the structure that we raise,
Time is with materials filled;
Our to-days and yesterdays
Are the blocks with which we build.—Longfellow.

To-day! To-day! It is ours, with all its magic possibilities of being and doing. Yesterday, with its mistakes, misdeeds, lost opportunities, and failures, is gone forever. With the morrow we are not immediately concerned. It is but a promise yet to be fulfilled. Hidden behind the veil of the future, it may dimly beckon us, but it is yet a shadowy, unsubstantial vision, one that we, perhaps, never may realize. But to-day, the Here, the Now, that dawned upon us with the first hour of the morn, is a reality, a precious possession upon the right use of which may depend all our future of happiness and success, or of misery and failure; for

"This day we fashion Destiny, our web of Fate we spin."

Lest he should forget that Time's wings are swift and noiseless, and so rapidly bear our to-days to the Land of Yesterday, John Ruskin, philosopher, philanthropist, and tireless worker though he was, kept constantly before his eyes on his study table a large, handsome block of chalcedony, on which was graven the single word "To-day." Every moment of this noble life was enriched by the right use of each passing moment.

A successful merchant, whose name is well-known throughout our country, very tersely sums up the means by which true success may be attained. "It is just this," he says: "Do your best every day, whatever you have in hand."

This simple rule, if followed in sunshine and in storm, in days of sadness as well as days of gladness, will rear for the builder a Palace Beautiful more precious than pearls of great price, more enduring than time.

"The Mill Boy of the Slashes"

A picturesque, as well as pathetic figure, was Henry Clay, the little "Mill Boy of the Slashes," as he rode along on the old family horse to Mrs. Darricott's mill. Blue-eyed, rosy-cheeked, and bare-footed, clothed in coarse shirt and trousers, and a time-worn straw hat, he sat erect on the bare back of the horse, holding, with firm hand, the rope which did duty as a bridle. In front of him lay the precious sack, containing the grist which was to be ground into meal or flour, to feed the hungry mouths of the seven little boys and girls who, with the widowed mother, made up the Clay family.

It required a good deal of grist to feed so large a family, especially when hoecake was the staple food, and it was because of his frequent trips to the mill, across the swampy region called the "Slashes," that Henry was dubbed by the neighbors "The Mill Boy of the Slashes."

The lad was ambitious, however, and, very early in life, made up his mind that he would win for himself a more imposing title. He never dreamed of winning world-wide renown as an orator, or of exchanging his boyish sobriquet for "The Orator of Ashland." But he who forms high ideals in youth usually far outstrips his first ambition, and Henry had "hitched his wagon to a star."

This awkward country boy, who was so bashful, and so lacking in self-confidence that he hardly dared recite before his class in the log schoolhouse, **Determined to Become an Orator**.

Henry Clay, the brilliant lawyer and statesman, the American Demosthenes who could sway multitudes by his matchless oratory, once said, "In order to succeed a man must have a purpose fixed, then let his motto be **Victory or Death**." When Henry Clay, the poor country boy, son of an unknown Baptist minister, made up his mind to become an orator, he acted on this principle. No discouragement or obstacle was allowed to swerve him from his purpose. Since the death of his father, when the boy was but five years old, he had carried grist to the mill, chopped wood, followed the plow barefooted, clerked in a country store,—did everything that a loving son and brother could do to help win a subsistence for the family.

In the midst of poverty, hard work, and the most pitilessly unfavorable conditions, the youth clung to his resolve. He learned what he could at the country schoolhouse, during the time the duties of the farm permitted him to attend school. He committed speeches to memory, and recited them aloud, sometimes in the forest, sometimes while working in the cornfield, and frequently in a barn with a horse and an ox for his audience.

In his fifteenth year he left the grocery store where he had been clerking to take a position in the office of the clerk of the High Court of

Chancery. There he became interested in law, and by reading and study began at once to supplement the scanty education of his childhood. To such good purpose did he use his opportunities that in 1797, when only twenty years old, he was licensed by the judges of the court of appeals to practice law.

When he moved from Richmond to Lexington, Kentucky, the same year to begin practice for himself, he had no influential friends, no patrons, and not even the means to pay his board. Referring to this time years afterward, he said, "I remember how comfortable I thought I should be if I could make one hundred pounds Virginia money (less than five hundred dollars) per year; and with what delight I received the first fifteen-shilling fee."

Contrary to his expectations, the young lawyer had "immediately rushed into a lucrative practice." At the age of twenty-seven he was elected to the Kentucky legislature. Two years later he was sent to the United States Senate to fill out the remainder of the term of a senator who had withdrawn. In 1811 he was elected to Congress, and made Speaker of the national House of Representatives. He was afterward elected to the United States Senate in the regular way.

Both in Congress and in the Senate Clay always worked for what he believed to be the best interests of his country. Ambition, which so often causes men to turn aside from the paths of truth and honor, had no power to tempt him to do wrong. He was ambitious to be president, but would not sacrifice any of his convictions for the sake of being elected. Although he was nominated by his party three times, he never became president. It was when warned by a friend that if he persisted in a certain course of political conduct he would injure his prospects of being elected, that he made his famous statement, "I would rather be right than be president."

Clay has been described by one of his biographers as "a brilliant orator, an honest man, a charming gentleman, an ardent patriot, and a leader whose popularity was equaled only by that of Andrew Jackson."

Although born in a state in which wealth and ancient ancestry were highly rated, he was never ashamed of his birth or poverty. Once when taunted by the aristocratic John Randolph with his lowly origin, he proudly exclaimed, "I was born to no proud paternal estate. I inherited only infancy, ignorance, and indigence."

He was born in Hanover County, Virginia, on April 12, 1777, and died in Washington, June 29, 1852. With only the humble inheritance which he claimed—"infancy, ignorance, and indigence" —Henry Clay made himself a name that wealth and a long line of ancestry could never bestow.

The Greek Slave Who Won the Olive Crown

The teeming life of the streets has vanished; the voices of the children have died away into silence; the artisan has dropped his tools, the artist has laid aside his brush, the sculptor his chisel. Night has spread her wings over the scene. The queen city of Greece is wrapped in slumber.

But, in the midst of that hushed life, there is one who sleeps not, a worshiper at the shrine of art, who feels neither fatigue nor hardship, and fears not death itself in the pursuit of his object. With the fire of genius burning in his dark eyes, a youth works with feverish haste on a group of wondrous beauty.

But why is this master artist at work, in secret, in a cellar where the sun never shone, the daylight never entered? I will tell you. Creon, the inspired worker, the son of genius, is a slave, and the penalty of pursuing his art is death.

When the Athenian law debarring all but freemen from the exercise of art was enacted, Creon was at work trying to realize in marble the vision his soul had created. The beautiful group was growing into life under his magic touch when the cruel edict struck the chisel from his fingers.

"O ye gods!" groans the stricken youth, "why have ye deserted me, now, when my task is almost completed? I have thrown my soul, my very life, into this block of marble, and now—"

Cleone, the beautiful dark-haired sister of the sculptor, felt the blow as keenly as her brother, to whom she was utterly devoted. "O immortal Athene! my goddess, my patron, at whose shrine I have daily laid my offerings, be now my friend, the friend of my brother!" she prayed.

Then, with the light of a new-born resolve shining in her eyes, she turned to her brother, saying:—

"The thought of your brain shall live. Let us go to the cellar beneath our house. It is dark, but I will bring you light and food, and no one will discover our secret. You can there continue your work; the gods will be our allies."

It is the golden age of Pericles, the most brilliant epoch of Grecian art and dramatic literature.

The scene is one of the most memorable that has ever been enacted within the proud city of Athens.

In the Agora, the public assembly or market place, are gathered together the wisdom and wit, the genius and beauty, the glory and power, of all Greece.

Enthroned in regal state sits Pericles, president of the assembly, soldier, statesman, orator, ruler, and "sole master of Athens." By his side sits his beautiful partner, the learned and queenly Aspasia. Phidias, one of the greatest sculptors, if not the greatest the world has known, who "formed a new style characterized by sublimity and ideal beauty," is there. Near him is Sophocles, the greatest of the tragic poets. Yonder we catch a glimpse of a face and form that offers the most striking contrast to the manly beauty of the poet, but whose wisdom and virtue have brought Athens to his feet. It is the "father of philosophy," Socrates. With his arm linked in that of the philosopher, we see— but why prolong the list? All Greece has been bidden to Athens to view the works of art.

The works of the great masters are there. On every side paintings and statues, marvelous in detail, exquisite in finish, challenge the admiration of the crowd and the criticism of the rival artists and connoisseurs who throng the place. But even in the midst of masterpieces, one group of statuary so far surpasses all the others that it rivets the attention of the vast assembly.

"Who is the sculptor of this group?" demands Pericles. Envious artists look from one to the other with questioning eyes, but the question remains unanswered. No triumphant sculptor comes forward to claim the wondrous creation as the work of his brain and hand. Heralds, in thunder tones, repeat, "Who is the sculptor of this group?" No one can tell. It is a mystery. Is it the work of the gods? or—and, with bated breath, the question passes from lip to lip, "Can it have been fashioned by the hand of a slave?"

Suddenly a disturbance arises at the edge of the crowd. Loud voices are heard, and anon the trembling tones of a woman. Pushing their way through the concourse, two officers drag a shrinking girl, with dark, frightened eyes, to the feet of Pericles. "This woman," they cry, "knows the sculptor; we are sure of this; but she will not tell his name."

Neither threats nor pleading can unlock the lips of the brave girl. Not even when informed that the penalty of her conduct was death would she divulge her secret. "The law," says Pericles, "is imperative. Take the maid to the dungeon."

Creon, who, with his sister, had been among the first to find his way to the Agora that morning, rushed forward, and, flinging himself at the ruler's feet, cried "O Pericles! forgive and save the maid. She is my sister. I am the culprit. The group is the work of my hands, the hands of a slave."

An intense silence fell upon the multitude, and then went up a mighty shout,—"To the dungeon, to the dungeon with the slave."

"As I live, no!" said Pericles, rising. "Not to the dungeon, but to my side bring the youth. The highest purpose of the law should be the development of the beautiful. The gods decide by that group that there is something higher in Greece than an unjust law. To the sculptor who fashioned it give the victor's crown."

And then, amid the applause of all the people, Aspasia placed the crown of olives on the youth's brow, and tenderly kissed the devoted sister who had been the right hand of genius.

Turning Points in the Life of a Hero

The First Turning Point

David Farragut was acting as cabin boy to his father, who was on his way to New Orleans with the infant navy of the United States. The boy thought he had the qualities that make a man. "I could swear like an old salt," he says, "could drink as stiff a glass of grog as if I had doubled Cape Horn, and could smoke like a locomotive. I was great at cards, and was fond of gambling in every shape. At the close of dinner one day," he continues, "my father turned everybody out of the cabin, locked the door, and said to me, 'David, what do you mean to be?'

"'I mean to follow the sea,' I said.

"'Follow the sea!' exclaimed father, 'yes, be a poor, miserable, drunken sailor before the mast, kicked and cuffed about the world, and die in some fever hospital in a foreign clime!'

"'No, father,' I replied, 'I will tread the quarterdeck, and command as you do.'

"'No, David; no boy ever trod the quarterdeck with such principles as you have and such habits as you exhibit. You will have to change your whole course of life if you ever become a man.'

"My father left me and went on deck. I was stunned by the rebuke, and overwhelmed with mortification. 'A poor, miserable, drunken sailor before the mast, kicked and cuffed about the world, and die in some fever hospital!' 'That's my fate, is it? I'll change my life, and *I Will Change it at Once*. I will never utter another oath, never drink another drop of intoxicating liquor, never gamble,' and, as God is my witness," said the admiral, solemnly, "I have kept these three vows to this hour."

A Born Leader

The event which proved David Glasgow Farragut's qualities as a leader happened before he was thirteen.

He was with his adopted father, Captain Porter, on board the Essex, when war was declared with England in 1812. A number of prizes were captured by the Essex, and David was ordered by Captain Porter to take one of the captured vessels, with her commander as navigator, to Valparaiso. Although inwardly quailing before the violent-tempered old captain of the prize ship, of whom, as he afterward confessed, he was really "a little afraid," the boy assumed the command with a fearless air.

On giving his first order, that the "main topsail be filled away," the trouble began. The old captain, furious at hearing a command given aboard his vessel by a boy not yet in his teens, replied to the order, with an oath, that he would shoot any one who dared touch a rope without his orders. Having delivered this mandate, he rushed below for his pistols.

The situation was critical. If the young commander hesitated for a moment, or showed the least sign of submitting to be bullied, his authority would instantly have fallen from him. Boy as he was, David realized this, and, calling one of the crew to him, explained what had taken place, and repeated his order. With a hearty "Aye, aye, sir!" the sailor flew to the ropes, while the plucky midshipman called down to the captain that "if he came on deck with his pistols, he would be thrown overboard."

David's victory was complete. During the remainder of the voyage none dared dispute his authority. Indeed his coolness and promptitude had won for him the lasting admiration of the crew.

"FARRAGUT IS THE MAN"

The great turning point which placed Farragut at the head of the American navy was reached in 1861, when Virginia seceded from the Union, and he had to choose between the cause of the North and that of the South. He dearly loved his native South, and said, "God forbid that I should have to raise my hand against her," but he determined, come what would, to "stick to the flag."

So it came about that when, in order to secure the control of the Mississippi, the national government resolved upon the capture of New Orleans, Farragut was chosen to lead the undertaking. Several officers, noted for their loyalty, good judgment, and daring, were suggested, but the Secretary of the Navy said, "Farragut is the man."

The opportunity for which all his previous noble life and brilliant services had been a preparation came to him when he was sixty-one years old. The command laid upon him was "the certain capture of the city of New Orleans." "The department and the country," so ran his instructions, "require of you success. ... If successful, you open the way to the sea for the great West, never again to be closed. The rebellion will be riven in the center, and the flag, to which you have been so faithful, will recover its supremacy in every state."

On January 9, 1862, Farragut was appointed to the command of the western gulf blockading squadron. "On February 2," says the National Cyclopedia of American Biograph, "he sailed on the steam sloop Hartford from Hampton Roads, arriving at the appointed rendezvous, Ship Island, in sixteen days. His fleet, consisting of six war steamers, sixteen gunboats, twenty-one mortar vessels, under the command of Commodore David D. Porter, and five supply ships, was the largest that had ever sailed under the American flag. Yet the task assigned him, the passing of the forts below New Orleans, the capture of the city, and the opening of the Mississippi River through its entire length was one of difficulty unprecedented in the history of naval warfare."

Danger or death had no terror for the brave sailor. Before setting out on his hazardous enterprise, he said: "If I die in the attempt, it will only be what every officer has to expect. He who dies in doing his duty to his country, and at peace with his God, has played the drama of life to the best advantage."

The hero did not die. He fought and won the great battle, and thus executed the command laid upon him,—"the certain capture of the city of New Orleans." The victory was accomplished with the loss of but one ship, and 184 men killed and wounded,—"a feat in naval warfare," says his son and biographer, "which has no precedent, and which is still without a parallel, except the one furnished by Farragut himself, two years later, at Mobile."

He Aimed High and Hit the Mark

"Without vision the people perish"

Without a high ideal an individual never climbs. Keep your eyes on the mountain top, and, though you may stumble and fall many times in the ascent, though great bowlders, dense forests, and roaring torrents may often bar the way, look right on, never losing sight of the light which shines away up in the clear atmosphere of the mountain peak, and you will ultimately reach your goal.

When the late Horace Maynard, LL.D., entered Amherst College, he exposed himself to the ridicule and jibing questions of his fellow-students by placing over the door of his room a large square of white cardboard on which was inscribed in bold outlines the single letter "V." Disregarding comment and question, the young man applied himself to his work, ever keeping in mind the height to which he wished to climb, the first step toward which was signified by the mysterious "V."

Four years later, after receiving the compliments of professors and students on the way he had acquitted himself as valedictorian of his class, young Maynard called the attention of his fellow- graduates to the letter over his door. Then a light broke in upon them, and they cried out, "Is it possible that you had the valedictory in mind when you put that 'V' over your door?"

"Assuredly I had," was the emphatic reply.

On he climbed, from height to height, becoming successively professor of mathematics in the University of Tennessee, lawyer, member of Congress, attorney-general of Tennessee, United States minister to Constantinople, and, finally, postmaster-general.

Honorable ambition is the leaven that raises the whole mass of mankind. Ideals, visions, are the stepping-stones by which we rise to higher things.

"Still, through our paltry stir and strife,
Glows down the wished ideal,
And longing molds in clay what life
Carves in the marble real;
"To let the new life in, we know,
Desire must ope the portal,—
Perhaps the longing to be so
Helps make the soul immortal."

The Evolution of a Violinist

He was a famous artist whom kings and queens and emperors delighted to honor. The emperor of all the Russias had sent him an affectionate letter, written by his own hand; the empress, a magnificent emerald ring set with diamonds; the king of his own beloved Norway, who had listened reverently, standing with uncovered head, while he, the king of violinists, played before him, had bestowed upon him the Order of Vasa; the king of Copenhagen presented him with a gold snuffbox, encrusted with diamonds; while, at a public dinner given him by the students of Christiana, he was crowned with a laurel wreath. Not all the thousands who thronged to hear him in London could gain entrance to the concert hall, and in Liverpool he received four thousand dollars for one evening's performance.

Yet the homage of the great ones of the earth, the princely gifts bestowed upon him, the admiration of the thousands who hung entranced on every note breathed by his magic violin, gave less delight than the boy of fourteen experienced when he received from an old man, whose heart his playing had gladdened, the present of four pairs of doves, with a card suspended by a blue ribbon round the neck of one, bearing his own name, "Ole Bull."

The soul of little Ole Bull had always been attuned to melody, from the time when, a toddling boy of four, he had kissed with passionate delight the little yellow violin given him by his uncle. How happy he was, as he wandered alone through the meadows, listening with the inner ear of heaven-born genius to the great song of nature. The bluebells, the buttercups, and the blades of grass sang to him in low, sweet tones, unheard by duller ears. How he thrilled with delight when he touched the strings of the little red violin, purchased for him when he was eight years old. His father destined him for the church, and, feeling that music should form part of the education of a clergyman, he consented to the mother's proposition that the boy should take lessons on the violin.

Ole could not sleep for joy, that first night of ownership; and, when the house was wrapped in slumber, he got up and stole on tiptoe to the room where his treasure lay. The bow seemed to beckon to him, the pretty pearl screws to smile at him out of their red setting. "I pinched the strings just a little," he said. "It smiled at me ever more and more. I took up the bow and looked at it. It said to me it would be pleasant to try it across the strings. So I did try it just a very, very little, and it did sing to me so sweetly. At first I did play very soft. But presently I did begin a capriccio, which I like very much, and it did go ever louder and louder; and I forgot that it was midnight and that everybody was asleep. Presently I hear something crack; and the next minute I feel my father's whip across my shoulders. My little red violin dropped on the floor, and was broken. I weep much for it, but it did no good. They did have a doctor to it next day, but it never recovered its health."

He was given another violin, however, and, when only ten, he would wander into the fields and woods, and spend hours playing his own improvisations, echoing the song of the birds, the murmur of the brook, the thunder of the waterfall, the soughing of the wind among the trees, the roar of the storm.

But childhood's days are short. The years fly by. The little Ole is eighteen, a student in the University of Christiana, preparing for the ministry. His brother students beg him to play for a charitable association. He remembers his father's request that he yield not to his passion for music, but being urged for "sweet charity's sake," he consents.

The youth's struggle between the soul's imperative demand and the equally imperative parental dictate was pathetic. Meanwhile the position of musical director of the Philharmonic and Dramatic Societies becoming vacant, Ole was appointed to the office; and, seeing that it was useless to contend longer against the genius of his son, the disappointed father allowed him to accept the directorship.

When fairly launched on a musical career, his trials and disappointments began. Wishing to assure himself whether he had genius or not, he traveled five hundred miles to see and hear the celebrated Louis Spohr, who received the tremulous youth coldly, and gave him no encouragement. No matter, he would go to the city of art. In Paris he heard Berlioz and other great musicians. Entranced he listened, in his high seat at the top of the house, to the exquisite notes of Malibran.

His soul feasted on music, but his money was fast dwindling away, and the body could not be sustained by sweet sounds. But the poor unknown violinist, who was only another atom in the surging life of the great city, could earn nothing. He was on the verge of starvation, but he would not go back to Christiana. He must still struggle and study. He became ill of brain fever, and was tenderly nursed back to life by the granddaughter of his kind landlady, pretty little Felicie Villeminot, who afterward became his wife. He had drained the cup of poverty and disappointment to the dregs, but the tide was about to turn.

He was invited to play at a concert presided over by the Duke of Montebello, and this led to other profitable engagements. But the great opportunity of his life came to him in Bologna. The people had thronged to the opera house to hear Malibran. She had disappointed them, and they were in no mood to be lenient to the unknown violinist who had the temerity to try to fill her place.

He came on the stage. He bowed. He grew pale under the cold gaze of the thousands of unsympathetic eyes turned upon him. But the touch of his beloved violin gave him confidence. Lovingly, tenderly, he drew the bow across the strings. The coldly critical eyes no longer gazed at him.

The unsympathetic audience melted away. He and his violin were one and alone. In the hands of the great magician the instrument was more than human. It talked; it laughed; it wept; it controlled the moods of men as the wind controls the sea.

The audience scarcely breathed. Criticism was disarmed. Malibran was forgotten. The people were under the spell of the enchanter. Orpheus had come again. But suddenly the music ceased. The spell was broken. With a shock the audience returned to earth, and Ole Bull, restored to consciousness of his whereabouts by the storm of applause which shook the house, found himself famous forever.

His triumph was complete, but his work was not over, for the price of fame is ceaseless endeavor. But the turning point had been passed. He had seized the great opportunity for which his life had been a preparation, and it had placed him on the roll of the immortals.

The Lesson of the Teakettle

The teakettle was singing merrily over the fire; the good aunt was bustling round, on housewifely cares intent, and her little nephew sat dreamily gazing into the glowing blaze on the kitchen hearth.

Presently the teakettle ceased singing, and a column of steam came rushing from its pipe. The boy started to his feet, raised the lid from the kettle, and peered in at the bubbling, boiling water, with a look of intense interest. Then he rushed off for a teacup, and, holding it over the steam, eagerly watched the latter as it condensed and formed into tiny drops of water on the inside of the cup.

Returning from an upper room, whither her duties had called her, the thrifty aunt was shocked to find her nephew engaged in so profitless an occupation, and soundly scolded him for what she called his trifling. The good lady little dreamed that James Watt was even then unconsciously studying the germ of the science by which he "transformed the steam engine from a mere toy into the most wonderful instrument which human industry has ever had at its command."

This studious little Scottish lad, who, because too frail to go to school, had been taught at home, was very different from other boys. When only six or seven years old, he would lie for hours on the hearth, in the little cottage at Greenock, near Glasgow, where he was born in 1736, drawing geometrical figures with pieces of colored chalk. He loved, too, to gaze at the stars, and longed to solve their mysteries. But his favorite pastime was to burrow among the ropes and sails and tackles in his father's store, trying to find out how they were made and what purposes they served.

In spite of his limited advantages and frail health, at fifteen he was the wonder of the public school, which he had attended for two years. His favorite studies were mathematics and natural philosophy. He had also made good progress in chemistry, physiology, mineralogy, and botany, and, at the same time, had learned carpentry and acquired some skill as a worker in metals.

So studious and ambitious a youth scarcely needed the spur of poverty to induce him to make the most of his talents. The spur was there, however, and, at the age of eighteen, though delicate in health, he was obliged to go out and battle with the world.

Having first spent some time in Glasgow, learning how to make mathematical instruments, he determined to go to London, there to perfect himself in his trade.

Working early and late, and suffering frequently from cold and hunger, he broke down under the unequal strain, and was obliged to return to his parents for a time until health was regained.

Always struggling against great odds, he returned to Glasgow when his trade was mastered, and began to make mathematical instruments, for which, however, he found little sale. Then, to help eke out a living, he began to make and mend other instruments,—fiddles, guitars, and flutes,—and finally built an organ,—a very superior one, too,—with several additions of his own invention.

A commonplace incident enough it seemed, in the routine of his daily occupation, when, one morning, a model of Newcomen's engine was brought to him for repair, yet it marked the turning point in his career, which ultimately led from poverty and struggle to fame and affluence.

Watt's practiced eye at once perceived the defects in the Newcomen engine, which, although the best then in existence could not do much better or quicker work than horses. Filled with enthusiasm over the plans which he had conceived for the construction of a really powerful engine, he immediately set to work, and spent two months in an old cellar, working on a model. "My whole thoughts are bent on this machine," he wrote to a friend. "I can think of nothing else."

So absorbed had he become in his new work that the old business of making and mending instruments had declined. This was all the more unfortunate as he was no longer struggling for himself alone. He had fallen in love with, and married, his cousin, Margaret Miller, who brought him the greatest happiness of his life. The neglect of the only practical means of support he had reduced Watt and his family to the direst poverty. More than once his health failed, and often the brave spirit was almost broken, as when he exclaimed in heaviness of heart, "Of all the things in the world, there is nothing so foolish as inventing."

Five years had passed since the model of the Newcomen engine had been sent to him for repair before he succeeded in securing a patent on his own invention. Yet five more long years of bitter drudgery, clutched in the grip of poverty, debt, and sickness, did the brave inventor, sustained by the love and help of his noble wife, toil through. On his thirty-fifth birthday he said, "To-day I enter the thirty-fifth year of my life, and I think I have hardly yet done thirty-five pence worth of good in the world; but I cannot help it."

Poor Watt! He had traveled with bleeding feet along the same thorny path trod by the great inventors and benefactors of all ages. But, in spite of all obstacles, he persevered; and, after ten years of inconceivable labor and hardship, during which his beautiful wife died, he had a glorious triumph. His perfected steam engine was the wonder of the age. Sir James Mackintosh placed him "at the head of all inventors in all ages and nations." "I look upon him," said the poet Wordsworth, "considering both the magnitude and the universality of his genius, as, perhaps, the most extraordinary man that this country ever produced."

Wealthy beyond his desires,—for he cared not for wealth,—crowned with the laurel wreath of fame, honored by the civilized world as one of its greatest benefactors, the struggle over, the triumph achieved, on August 19, 1819, he lay down to rest.

How the Art of Printing Was Discovered

"Look, Grandfather; see what the letters have done!" exclaimed a delighted boy, as he picked up the piece of parchment in which Grandfather Coster had carried the bark letters cut from the trees in the grove, for the instruction and amusement of his little grandsons.

"See what the letters have done!" echoed the old man. "Bless me, what does the child mean?" and his eyes twinkled with pleasure, as he noted the astonishment and pleasure visible on the little face. "Let me see what it is that pleases thee so, Laurence," and he eagerly took the parchment from the boy's hand.

"Bless my soul!" cried the old man, after gazing spellbound upon it for some seconds. The track of the mysterious footprint in the sand excited no more surprise in the mind of Robinson Crusoe than Grandfather Coster felt at the sight which met his eyes. There, distinctly impressed upon the parchment, was a clear imprint of the bark letters; though, of course, they were reversed or turned about.

But you twentieth-century young folks who have your fill of story books, picture books, and reading matter of all kinds, are wondering, perhaps, what all this talk about bark letters and parchment and imprint of letters means.

To understand it, you must carry your imagination away back more than five centuries—quite a long journey of the mind, even for "grown-ups"—to a time when there were no printed books, and when very, very few of the rich and noble, and scarcely any of the so-called common people, could read. In those far-off days there were no public libraries, and no books except rare and expensive volumes, written by hand, mainly by monks in their quiet monasteries, on parchment or vellum.

In the quaint, drowsy, picturesque town of Haarlem, in Holland, with its narrow, irregular, grass-grown streets and many-gabled houses, the projecting upper stories of which almost meet, one particular house, which seems even older than any of the others, is pointed out to visitors as one of the most interesting sights of the ancient place. It was in this house that Laurence Coster, the father of the art of printing, the man—at least so runs the legend—who made it possible for the poorest and humblest to enjoy the inestimable luxury of books and reading, lived and loved and dreamed more than five hundred years ago.

Coster was warden of the little church which stood near his home, and his days flowed peacefully on, in a quiet, uneventful way, occupied with the duties of his office, and reading and study, for he was one of those who had mastered the art of reading. A diligent student, he had conned over and over, until he knew them by heart, the few manuscript volumes owned by the little church of which he was warden.

A lover of solitude, as well as student and dreamer, the church warden's favorite resort, when his duties left him at leisure, was a dense grove not far from the town. Thither he went when he wished to be free from all distraction, to think and dream over many things which would appear nonsensical to his sober, practical-minded neighbors. There he indulged in day dreams and poetic fancies; and once, when in a sentimental mood, he carved the initials of the lady of his love on one of the trees.

In time a fair young wife and children came, bringing new brightness and joy to the serious-minded warden. With ever increasing interests, he passed on from youth to middle life, and from middle life to old age. Then his son married, and again the patter of little feet filled the old home and made music in the ears of Grandfather Coster, whom the baby grandchildren almost worshiped.

To amuse the children, and to impart to them whatever knowledge he himself possessed, became the delight of his old age. Then the habit acquired in youth of carving letters in the bark of the trees served a very useful purpose in furthering his object. He still loved to take solitary walks, and many a quiet summer afternoon the familiar figure of the venerable churchwarden, in his seedy black cloak and sugar-loaf hat, might be seen wending its way along the banks of the River Spaaren to his favorite resort in the grove.

One day, while reclining on a mossy couch beneath a spreading beech tree, amusing himself by tearing strips of bark from the tree that shaded him, and carving letters with his knife, a happy thought entered his mind. "Why can I not," he mused within himself, "cut those letters out, carry them home, and, while using them as playthings, teach the little ones how to read?"

The plan worked admirably. Long practice had made the old man quite expert in fashioning the letters, and many hours of quiet happiness were spent in the grove in this pleasing occupation. One afternoon he succeeded in cutting some unusually fine specimens, and, chuckling to himself over the delight they would give the children, he wrapped them carefully, placing them side by side in an old piece of parchment which he happened to have in his pocket. The bark from which they had been cut being fresh and full of sap, and the letters being firmly pressed upon the parchment, the result was the series of "pictures" which delighted the child and gave to the world the first suggestion of a printing press.

And then a mighty thought flashed across the brain of the poor, humble, unknown churchwarden, a thought the realization of which was destined not only to make him famous for all time, but to revolutionize the whole world. The first dim suggestion came to him in this form, "By having a series of letters and impressing them over and over again on parchment, cannot books be printed instead of written, and so multiplied and cheapened as to be brought within the reach of all?"

The remainder of his life was given up to developing this great idea. He cut more letters from bark, and, covering the smooth surface with ink, pressed them upon parchment, thus getting a better impression, though still blurred and imperfect. He then cut letters from wood instead of bark, and managed to invent himself a better and thicker ink, which did not blur the page. Next, he cut letters from lead, and then from pewter. Every hour was absorbed in the work of making possible the art of printing. His simple-minded neighbors thought he had lost his mind, and some of the more superstitious spread the report that he was a sorcerer. But, like all other great discoverers, he heeded not annoyances or discouragements. Shutting himself away from the prying curiosity of the ignorant and superstitious, he plodded on, making steady, if slow, advance toward the realization of his dream.

"One day, while old Coster was thus busily at work," says George Makepeace Towle, "a sturdy German youth, with a knapsack slung across his back, trudged into Haarlem. By some chance this youth happened to hear how the churchwarden was at work upon a wild scheme to print books instead of writing them. With beating heart, the young man repaired to Coster's house and made all haste to knock at the churchwarden's humble door."

The "sturdy German youth" who knocked at Laurence Coster's door was Johann Gutenberg, the inventor of modern printing. Coster invited him to enter. Gutenberg accepted the invitation, and then stated the object of his visit. He desired to learn more about the work on which Coster was engaged. Delighted to have a visitor who was honestly interested in his work, the old man eagerly explained its details to the youth, and showed him some examples of his printing.

Gutenberg was much impressed by what he saw, but still more by the possibilities which he dimly foresaw in Coster's discovery. "But we can do much better than this," he said with the enthusiasm of youth. "Your printing is even slower than the writing of the monks. From this day forth I will work upon this problem, and not rest till I have solved it."

Johann Gutenberg kept his word. He never rested until he had given the art of printing to the world. But to Laurence Coster, in the first place, if legend speaks truth, we owe one of the greatest inventions that has ever blessed mankind.

Sea Fever and What it Led to

"Jim, you've too good a head on you to be a wood chopper or a canal driver," said the captain of the canal boat for whom young Garfield had engaged to drive horses along the towpath.

"Jim" had always loved books from the time when, seated on his father's knee, he had with his baby lips pronounced after him the name "Plutarch." Mr. Garfield had been reading "Plutarch's Lives," and was much astonished when, without hesitation or stammering, his little son distinctly pronounced the name of the Greek biographer. Turning to his wife, with a glow of love and pride, the fond father said, "Eliza, this boy will be a scholar some day."

Perhaps the near approach of death had clarified the father's vision, but when, soon after, the sorrowing wife was left a widow, with an indebted farm and four little children to care for, she saw little chance for the fulfillment of the prophecy.

Even in his babyhood the boy whose future greatness the father dimly felt had learned the lesson of self-reliance. The familiar words which so often fell from his lips—"I can do that"—enabled him to conquer difficulties before which stouter hearts than that of a little child might well have quailed.

The teaching of his good mother, that "God will bless all our efforts to do the best we can," became a part of the fiber of his being. "What will He do," asked the boy one day, "when we don't do the best we can?" "He will withhold His blessing; and that is the greatest calamity that could possibly happen to us," was the reply, which made a deep impression on the mind of the questioner.

In spite of almost constant toil, and very meager schooling,—only a few weeks each year,—James Garfield excelled all his companions in the log schoolhouse. Besides solving at home in the long winter evenings, by the light of the pine fire, all the knotty problems in Adams' Arithmetic—the terror of many a schoolboy—he found time to revel in the pages of "Robinson Crusoe" and "Josephus." The latter was his special favorite

Before he was fifteen, Garfield had successfully followed the occupations of farmer, wood chopper, and carpenter. No matter what his occupation was he always managed to find some time for reading.

He had recently read some of Marryat's novels, "Sindbad the Sailor," "The Pirate's Own Book," and others of a similar nature, which had smitten him with a virulent attack of sea fever. This is a mental disease which many robust, adventurous boys are apt to contract in their teens. Garfield felt that he must "sail the ocean blue." The glamour of the sea was upon him. Everything must give way before it. His mother, however, could not be induced to assent to his plans, and, after long pleading, would only compromise by agreeing that he might, if he could, secure a berth on one of the vessels navigating Lake Erie.

He was rudely repulsed by the owner of the first vessel to whom he applied, a brutal, drunken creature, who answered his request for employment with an oath and a rough "Get off this schooner in double quick, or I'll throw you into the dock." Garfield turned away in disgust, his ardor for the sea somewhat dampened by the man's appearance and behavior. In this mood he met his cousin, formerly a schoolmaster, then captain of a canal boat, with whom he at once engaged to drive his horses.

After a few months on the towpath, young Garfield contracted another kind of fever quite unlike that from which he had been suffering previously, and went home to be nursed out of it by his ever faithful mother.

During his convalescence he thought a great deal over his cousin's words,—"Jim, you've got too good a head on you to be a wood chopper or a canal driver." "He who wills to do anything will do it," he had learned from his mother's lips when a mere baby, and then and there he said in his heart, "I will be a scholar; I will go to college." And so, out of his sea fever and towpath experience was born the resolution that made the turning point in his career.

Action followed hot upon resolve. He lost no time in applying himself to the work of securing an education. Alternately chopping wood and carpentering, farming and teaching school, ringing bells and sweeping floors, he worked his way through seminary and college. His strong will and resolute purpose to make the most of himself not only enabled him to obtain an education, but raised him from the towpath to the presidential chair.

Gladstone Found Time to Be Kind

A kindly act is a kernel sown,
That will grow to a goodly tree,
Shedding its fruit when time has flown
Down the gulf of Eternity.— John Boyle O'Reilly

In the restless desire for acquisition,—acquisition of money, of power, or of fame,—there is danger of selfishness, self-absorption, closing the doors of our hearts against the demands of brotherly love, courtesy, and kindness.

"I cannot afford to help," say the poor in pocket; "all I have is too little for my own needs." "I should like to help others," says the ambitious student, whose every spare moment is crowded with some extra task, "but I have no money, and cannot afford to take the time from my studies to give sympathy or kind words to the suffering and the poor." Says the busy man of affairs: "I am willing to give money, but my time is too valuable to be spent in talking to sick people or shiftless, lazy ones. That sort of work is not in my line. I leave it to women and the charitable organizations."

The business man forgets, as do many of us, the truth expressed by Ruskin, that "a little thought and a little kindness are often worth more than a great deal of money." A few kind words, a little sympathy and encouragement have often brought sunshine and hope into the lives of men and women who were on the verge of despair.

The great demand is on people's hearts rather than on their purses. In the matter of kindness we can all afford to be generous whether we have money or not. The schoolboy may give it as freely as the millionaire. No one is so driven by work that he has not time, now and then, to say a kind word or do a kind deed that will help to brighten life for another. If the prime minister of England, William E. Gladstone, could find time to carry a bunch of flowers to a little sick crossing-sweeper, shall we not be ashamed to make for ourselves the excuse, "I haven't time to be kind"?

A Tribune of the People

Clad in a homespun tow shirt, shrunken, butternut-colored, linsey-woolsey pantaloons, battered straw hat, and much-mended jacket and shoes, with ten dollars in his pocket, and all his other worldly goods packed in the bundle he carried on his back, Horace Greeley, the future founder of the New York Tribune, started to seek his fortune in New York.

A newspaper had always been an object of interest and delight to the little delicate, tow-haired boy, and at the mature age of six he had made up his mind to be a printer. His love of reading was unusual in one so young. Before he was six he had read the Bible and "Pilgrim's Progress" through.

Like the children of all poor farmers, Horace was put to work as soon as he was able to do anything. But he made the most of the opportunities given him to attend school, and his love of reading; stimulated him to unusual efforts to procure books. By selling nuts and bundles of kindling wood at the village store, before he was ten he had earned enough money to buy a copy of Shakespeare and of Mrs. Hemans's poems. He borrowed every book that could be found within a radius of seven miles of his home, and by many readings he had made himself familiar with the score of old volumes in his log-cabin home.

Mrs. Sarah K. Bolton draws a pleasing picture of the farmer boy reading at night after the day's work on the farm was done. "He gathered a stock of pine knots," she says, "and, lighting one each night, lay down by the hearth and read, oblivious to all around him. The neighbors came and made their friendly visits, and ate apples and drank cider, as was the fashion, but the lad never noticed their coming or their going. When really forced to leave his precious books for bed, he would repeat the information he had learned, or the lessons for the next day to his brother, who usually, most ungraciously, fell asleep before the conversation was half completed."

"Ah!" said Zaccheus Greeley, Horace's father, when the boy one day, in a fit of abstraction, tried to yoke the "off" ox on the "near" side: "Ah! that boy will never know enough to get on in the world. He'll never know more than enough to come in when it rains!"

Yet this boy knew so much that when at fourteen he secured a place as printer in a newspaper office at East Poultney, Vermont, he was looked up to by his fellow-printers as equal in learning to the editor himself.

At first they tried to make merry at his expense, poking fun at his odd-looking garments, his uncouth appearance, and his pale, delicate face and almost white hair, which subsequently won for him the nickname of "Ghost." But when they saw that Horace was too good humored and too much in earnest with his work to be disturbed by their teasing, they gave it up. In a short time he became a general favorite, not only in the office, but in the town of Poultney, whose debating and literary societies soon recognized him as leader. Even the minister, the lawyer, and the schoolteachers looked up to the poor, retiring young printer, who was a veritable encyclopedia of knowledge, ready at all times to speak or to write an essay on any subject.

But the Poultney newspaper was obliged to suspend soon after Horace had learned his trade, and, penniless,—for every cent of his earnings beyond what furnished the bare necessaries of life had been sent home to his parents in the wilderness,—he faced the world once more.

After working in different small towns wherever he could get a "job," reading, studying, enlarging his knowledge all the time when not in the office, he made up his mind to go to New York, "to be somebody," as he put it.

When he stepped off the towboat at Whitehall, near the Battery, that sunny morning in August, 1831, with only the experience of a score of years in life, a stout heart, quick brain, nimble fingers, and an abiding faith in God as his capital, his prospects certainly were not very alluring.

"An overgrown, awkward, white-headed, forlorn-looking boy; a pack suspended on a staff over his right shoulder; his dress unrivaled in sylvan simplicity since the primitive fig leaves of Eden; the expression of his face presenting a strange union of wonder and apathy: his whole appearance gave you the impression of a runaway apprentice in desperate search of employment. Ignorant alike of the world and its ways, he seemed to the denizens of the city almost like a wanderer from another planet."

Such was the impression Horace Greeley made on a New Yorker on his first arrival in that city which was to be the scene of his future work and triumphs.

He tramped the streets all that day, Friday, and the next, looking for work, everywhere getting the same discouraging reply, "No, we don't want any one."

At last, when weary and disheartened, his ten dollars almost gone, he had decided to shake the dust of New York from his feet, the foreman of a printing office engaged him to do some work that most of the men in the office had refused to touch. The setting up of a Polyglot Testament, with involved marginal references, was something new for the supposed "green" hand from the country. But when the day was done, the young printer was no longer looked upon as "green" by his fellow-workers, for he had done more and better work than the oldest and most experienced hands who had tried the Testament.

But, oh, what hard work it was, beginning at six o'clock in the morning, and working long after the going down of the sun, by the light of a candle stuck in a bottle, to earn six dollars a week, most of which was sent to his dear ones at home.

After nearly ten years more of struggle and privation, Greeley entered upon the great work of his life—the founding and editing of the New York Tribune. He had very little money to start with, and even that little was borrowed. But he had courage, truth, honesty, a noble purpose, and rare ability and industry to supplement his small financial capital. He needed them all in the work he had undertaken, for he was handicapped not only by lack of means, but also by the opposition of some of the New York papers.

In spite of the adverse conditions he succeeded in establishing one of the greatest and most popular newspapers in the country. The Tribune became the champion of the oppressed, the guardian of justice, the defender of truth, a power for good in the land. Through his paper Greeley became a tribune of the people. No thought of making money hampered him in his work. Unselfishly he wrought as editor, writer, and lecturer for the good of his country and the uplifting of mankind. "He who by voice or pen," he said, "strikes his best blow at the impostures or vices whereby our race is debased and paralyzed, may close his eyes in death, consoled and cheered by the reflection that he has done what he could for the emancipation and elevation of his kind."

Well, then, might he rejoice in his life work, for his voice and pen had to the last been active in thus serving the race.

He died on November 29, 1872, at the age of sixty-one. So great a man had Horace Greeley, the poor New Hampshire farmer boy, become that the whole nation mourned for his death. The people felt that in him they had lost one of their best friends. A workman who attended his funeral expressed the feeling of his fellow-workmen all over the land when he said, "It is little enough to lose a day for Horace Greeley who spent many a day working for us." "I've come a hundred miles to be at the funeral of Horace Greeley," said a farmer.

The great tribune had deserved well of the people and of his country

The Might of Patience

Perhaps some would feel inclined to ridicule rather than applaud the patience of a poor Chinese woman who tried to make a needle from a rod of iron by rubbing it against a stone.

It is doubtful whether she succeeded or not, but, so the story runs, the sight of the worker plying her seemingly hopeless task, put new courage and determination into the heart of a young Chinese student, who, in deep despondency, stood watching her.

Because of repeated failures in his studies, ambition and hope had left him. Bitterly disappointed with himself, and despairing of ever accomplishing anything, the young man had thrown his books aside in disgust. Put to shame, however, by the lesson taught by the old woman, he gathered his scattered forces together, went to work with renewed ardor, and, wedding Patience and Energy, became, in time, one of the greatest scholars in China.

When you know you are on the right track, do not let any failures dim your vision or discourage you, for you cannot tell how close you may be to victory. Have patience and stick, stick, stick. It is eternally true that he

"Who steers right on Will gain, at length, however far, the port."

The Inspiration of Gambetta

"Try to come home a somebody!" Long after Leon Gambetta had left the old French town of Cahors, where he was born October 30, 1838, long after the gay and brilliant streets of Paris had become familiar to him, did the parting words of his idolized mother ring in his ears, "Try to come home a somebody!" Pinched for food and clothes, as he often was, while he studied early and late in his bare garret near the Sorbonne, the memory of that dear mother cheered and strengthened him.

He could still feel her tears and kisses on his cheek, and the tender clasp of her hand as she pressed into his the slender purse of money which she had saved to release him from the drudgery of an occupation he loathed, and to enable him to become a great lawyer in Paris. How well he remembered her delight in listening to him declaim the speeches of Thiers and Guizot from the pages of the National, which she had taught him to read when but a mere baby, and from which he imbibed his first lessons in republicanism,—lessons that he never afterward forgot.

Such deep root had they taken that he could not be induced to change his views by the fathers of the preparatory school at Monfaucon, whither he had been sent to be trained for the priesthood. Finally despairing of bringing the young radical to their way of thinking, the Monfaucon fathers sent him home to his parents. "You will never make a priest of him," they wrote; "he has a character that cannot be disciplined."

His father, an honest but narrow-minded Italian, whose ideas did not soar beyond his little bazaar and grocery store, was displeased with the boy, who was then only ten years old. He could not understand how one so young dared to think his own thoughts and hold his own opinions. The neighbors held up their hands in dismay, and prophesied, "He will end his days in the Bastile." His mother wept and blamed herself and the National as the cause of all the trouble.

How little the fond mother, the disappointed father, or the gloomily foreboding neighbors dreamt to what heights those early lessons they now so bitterly deplored were to lead!

When at sixteen Leon Gambetta returned from the Lyceum to which he had been sent on his return from the Monfaucon seminary, his wide reading and deep study had but intensified and broadened the radicalism of his childhood. He longed to go to Paris to study law, but his father insisted that he must now confine his thoughts to selling groceries and yards of ribbon and lace, as he expected his son to succeed him in the business.

Poor, foolish Joseph Gambetta! he would confine the young eagle in a barnyard. But the eagle pined and drooped in his cage, and then the loving mother—ah, those loving mothers, will their boys ever realize how much they owe them!—threw open the doors and gave him freedom, an opportunity to win fame and fortune in the great city of Paris.

And now what mattered it that his clothes were poor, that his food was scant, and that it was often bitterly cold in his little garret. If not for his own sake, he MUST for hers "come home a somebody."

The doors which led to a wider future were already opening. The professors at the Sorbonne appreciated his great intellect and originality. "You have a true vocation," said one. "Follow it. But go to the bar, where your voice, which is one in a thousand, will carry you on, study and intelligence aiding. The lecture room is a narrow theater. If you like, I will write to your father to tell him what my opinion of you is." And he wrote, "The best investment you ever made would be to spend what money you can divert from your business in helping your son to become an advocate."

To such good purpose did the young student use his time that within two years he won his diploma. Still too young to be admitted to the bar, he spent a year studying life in Paris, listening to the debates in the Corps Legislatif, reading and debating in the radical club which he had organized, making himself ready at every point for the great opportunity which gained him a national reputation and made him the idol of the masses.

In 1868 his masterly defense of Delescluze, the radical editor, against the prosecution of the Imperial government, brought the brilliant but hitherto unknown young lawyer prominently before the public. He lost his case, but won fame. Gambetta had waited eighteen months for his first brief, and five times eighteen months for his first great case. This case proved to be the initial step that led him from victory to victory, until, after the fall of Napoleon at Sedan, he became practically Dictator of France. He was, more than any one man, the maker of the French Republic, whose rights and liberties he ever defended, even at the risk of his life. He died December 31, 1882.

Well had he fulfilled the hopes and ambitions of his loving mother, well had he answered the pathetic appeal, "Try to come home a somebody."

Andrew Jackson: the Boy Who "Never Would Give Up"

"Sir, I am a prisoner of war, and demand to be treated as such," was the spirited reply of Andrew Jackson to a British officer who had commanded him to clean his boots.

This was characteristic of the future hero of New Orleans, and president of the United States, whose independent spirit rebelled at the insolent command of his captor.

The officer drew his sword to enforce obedience, but, nothing daunted, the youth, although then only fourteen, persisted in his refusal. He tried to parry the sword thrusts aimed at him, but did not escape without wounds on head and arm, the marks of which he carried to his grave.

Stubborn, self-willed, and always dominated by the desire to be a leader, Andrew Jackson was by no means a model boy. But his honesty, love of truth, indomitable will and courage, in spite of his many faults, led him to greatness.

He was born with fighting blood in his veins, and, like other eminent men who have risen to the White House, poor. His father, an Irish immigrant, died before his youngest son was born,—in 1767,—and life held for the boy more hard knocks than soft places. His mother, who was ambitious to make him a clergyman, tried to secure him some early advantages of schooling. Andrew, however, was not of a studious disposition, nor at all inclined to the ministry, and made little effort to profit by even the limited opportunities he had.

But despite all the disadvantages of environment and mental traits by which he was handicapped, he was bound by the force of certain other traits to be a winner in the battle of life. The quality to which his success is chiefly owing is revealed by the words of a school-fellow, who, in spite of Jackson's slender physique and lack of physical strength at that time, felt the force of his iron will. Speaking of their wrestling matches at school, this boy said, "I could throw him [Jackson] three times out of four, but he never would stay throwed. He was dead game and never would give up."

A boy who "never would stay throwed," and "never would give up" would succeed though the whole world tried to bar his progress.

When, at the age of fifteen, he found himself alone in the world, homeless and penniless, he adapted himself to anything he could find to do.

Worker in a saddler's shop, school-teacher, lawyer, merchant, judge of the Supreme Court, United States senator, soldier, leader, step by step the son of the poor Irish immigrant rose to the highest office to which his countrymen could elect him—the presidency of the United States.

Rash, headstrong, and narrow-minded, Andrew Jackson fell into many errors during his life, but, notwithstanding his shortcomings, he persistently tried to live up to his boyhood's motto, "Ask nothing but what is right—submit to nothing wrong."

Sir Humphry Davy's Greatest Discovery, Michael Faraday

He was only a little, barefooted errand boy, the son of a poor blacksmith. His school life ended in his thirteenth year. The extent of his education then was limited to a knowledge of the three "R's." As he trudged on his daily rounds, through the busy streets of London, delivering newspapers and books to the customers of his employer, there was little difference, outwardly, between him and scores of other boys who jostled one another in the narrow, crowded thoroughfares. But under the shabby jacket of Michael Faraday beat a heart braver and tenderer than the average; and, under the well-worn cap, a brain was throbbing that was destined to illuminate the world of science with a light that would never grow dim.

Less than any one else, perhaps, did the boy dream of future greatness. For a year he served his employer faithfully in his capacity of errand boy, and, in 1805, at the age of fourteen, was apprenticed to a bookseller for seven years, as was the custom in England, to learn the combined trades of bookbinding and book- selling.

The young journeyman had to exercise all his self-control to confine his attention to the outside of the books which passed through his hands. In his spare moments, however, he made himself familiar with the inside of many of them, eagerly devouring such works on science, electricity, chemistry, and natural philosophy, as came within his reach. He was especially delighted with an article on electricity, which he found in a volume of the "Encyclopedia Britannica," which had been given him to bind. He immediately began work on an electrical machine, from the very crudest materials, and, much to his delight, succeeded. It was a red-letter day in his young life when a kind-hearted customer, who had noticed his interest in scientific works, offered to take him to the Royal Institution, to attend a course of lectures to be given by the great Sir Humphry Davy. From this time on, his thoughts were constantly turned toward science. "Oh, if I could only help in some scientific work, no matter how humble!" was the daily cry of his soul. But not yet was his prayer to be granted. His mettle must be tried in the school of patience and drudgery. He must fulfill his contract with his master. For seven years he was faithful to his work, while his heart was elsewhere. And all that time, in the eagerness of his thirst for knowledge, he was imbibing facts which helped him to plan electrical achievements, the possibilities of which have not, to this day, been exhausted, —or even half realized. Like Franklin, he seemed to forecast the scientific future for ages.

At length he was free to follow his bent, and his mind turned at once to Sir Humphry Davy. With a beating heart, divided between hope and fear, he wrote to the great man, telling what he wished, and asking his aid. The scientist, remembering his own day of small things, wrote the youth, politely, that he was going out of town, but would see if he could, sometime, aid him. He also said that "science is a harsh mistress, and, in a pecuniary point of view, but poorly rewards those who devote themselves exclusively to her service."

This was not very encouraging, but the young votary of science was nothing daunted, and toiled at his uncongenial trade, with the added discomfort of an ill-tempered employer, giving all his evenings and odd moments to study and experiments.

Then came another red-letter day. He was growing depressed, and feared that Sir Humphry had forgotten his quasi-promise, when one evening a carriage stopped at the door, and out stepped an important-looking footman in livery, with a note from the famous scientist, requesting the young bookbinder to call on him on the following morning. At last had come the answer to the prayer of little Michael Faraday, as will come the answer to all who back their prayers with patient, persistent hard work, in spite of discouragement, disappointment, and failure. And when, on that never-to-be-forgotten morning, he was engaged by the great scientist at a salary of six dollars a week, with two rooms at the top of the house, to wash bottles, clean the instruments, move them to and from the lecture rooms, and make himself generally useful in the laboratory and out of it, no happier youth could be found in all London.

The door was open; not, indeed, wide, but sufficiently to allow this ardent disciple to work his way into the innermost shrine of the temple of science. Though it took years and years of plodding, incessant work and study, and a devotion to purpose with which nothing was allowed to interfere, it made Faraday, by virtue of his marvelous discoveries in electricity, electro-magnetism, and chemistry, a world benefactor, honored not only by his own country and sovereign, but by other rulers and leading nations of the earth, as one of the greatest chemists and natural philosophers of his time.

So great has been his value to the scientific world, that his theories are still a constant source of inspiration to the workers in those great professions allied to electricity and chemistry. No library is complete without his published works. What wonder that Davy called Faraday his greatest discovery!

The Triumph of Canova

The Villa d'Asola, the country residence of the Signor Falieri, was in a state of unusual excitement. Some of the most distinguished patricians of Venice had been bidden to a great banquet, which was to surpass in magnificence any entertainment ever before given, even by the wealthy and hospitable Signer Falieri.

The feast was ready, the guests were assembled, when word came from the confectioner, who had been charged to prepare the center ornament for the table, that he had spoiled the piece. Consternation reigned in the servants' hall. What was to be done? The steward, or head servant, was in despair. He was responsible for the table decorations, and the absence of the centerpiece would seriously mar the arrangements. He wrung his hands and gesticulated wildly. What should he do!

"If you will let me try, I think I can make something that will do." The speaker was a delicate, pale-faced boy, about twelve years old, who had been engaged to help in some of the minor details of preparation for the great event. "You!" exclaimed the steward, gazing in amazement at the modest, yet apparently audacious lad before him. "And who are you?" "I am Antonio Canova, the grandson of Pisano, the stonecutter." Desperately grasping at even the most forlorn hope, the perplexed servant gave the boy permission to try his hand at making a centerpiece.

Calling for some butter, with nimble fingers and the skill of a practiced sculptor, in a short time the little scullion molded the figure of a crouching lion. So perfect in proportion, so spirited and full of life in every detail, was this marvelous butter lion that it elicited a chorus of admiration from the delighted guests, who were eager to know who the great sculptor was who had deigned to expend his genius on such perishable material. Signor Falieri, unable to gratify their curiosity, sent for his head servant, who gave them the history of the centerpiece. Antonio was immediately summoned to the banquet hall, where he blushingly received the praises and congratulations of all present, and the promise of Signer Falieri to become his patron, and thus enable him to achieve fame as a sculptor.

Such, according to some biographers, was the turning point in the career of Antonio Canova, who, from a peasant lad, born in the little Venetian village of Possagno, rose to be the most illustrious sculptor of his age.

Whether or not the story be true, it is certain that when the boy was in his thirteenth year, Signer Falieri placed him in the studio of Toretto, a Venetian sculptor, then living near Asola. But it is equally certain that the fame which crowned Canova's manhood, the title of Marquis of Ischia, the decorations and honors so liberally bestowed upon him by the ruler of the Vatican, kings, princes, and emperors, were all the fruits of his ceaseless industry, high ideals, and unfailing enthusiasm.

The little Antonio began to draw almost as soon as he could hold a pencil, and the gown of the dear old grandmother who so tenderly loved him, and was so tenderly loved in return, often bore the marks of baby fingers fresh from modeling in clay.

Antonio's father having died when the child was but three years old, his grandfather, Pisano, hoped that he would succeed him as village stonecutter and sculptor. Delicate though the little fellow had been from birth, at nine years of age he was laboring, as far as his strength would permit, in Pisano's workshop. But in the evening, after the work of the day was done, with pencil or clay he tried to give expression to the poetic fancies he had imbibed from the ballads and legends of his native hills, crooned to him in infancy by his grandmother.

Under Toretto his genius developed so rapidly that the sculptor spoke of one of his creations as "a truly marvelous production." He was then only thirteen. Later we find him in Venice, studying and working with ever increasing zeal. Though Signor Falieri would have been only too glad to supply the youth's needs, he was too proud to be dependent on others. Speaking of this time, he says: "I labored for a mere pittance, but it was sufficient. It was the fruit of my own resolution, and, as I then flattered myself, the foretaste of more honorable rewards, for I never thought of wealth."

Too poor to hire a workshop or studio, through the kindness of the monks of St. Stefano, he was given a cell in a vacant monastery, and here, at the age of sixteen, he started business as a sculptor on his own account.

Before he was twenty, the youth had become a master of anatomy, which he declared was "the secret of the art," was thoroughly versed in literature, languages, history, poetry, mythology,— everything that could help to make him the greatest sculptor of his age,—and had, even then, produced works of surpassing merit.

Effort to do better was the motto of his life, and he never permitted a day to pass without making some advance in his profession. Though often too poor to buy the marble in which to embody his conceptions, he for many years lived up to a resolution made about this time, never to close his eyes at night without having produced some design.

What wonder that at twenty-five this noble youth, whose incessant toil had perfected genius, was the marvel of his age! What wonder that his famous group, Theseus vanquishing the Minotaur, elicited the enthusiastic admiration of the most noted art critics of Rome! What wonder that the little peasant boy, who had first opened his eyes, in 1757, in a mud cabin, closed them at last, in 1822, in a marble palace, crowned with all of fame and honor and wealth the world could give! But better still, he was loved and enshrined in the hearts of the people, as a friend of the poor, a patron of struggling merit, a man in whom nobility of character overtopped even the genius of the artist.

Franklin's Lesson on Time Value

Dost thou love life? Then, do not squander time, for that is the stuff life is made of!— Franklin

Franklin not only understood the value of time, but he put a price upon it that made others appreciate its worth.

A customer who came one day to his little bookstore in Philadelphia, not being satisfied with the price demanded by the clerk for the book he wished to purchase, asked for the proprietor. "Mr. Franklin is very busy just now in the press room," replied the clerk. The man, however, who had already spent an hour aimlessly turning over books, insisted on seeing him. In answer to the clerk's summons, Mr. Franklin hurried out from the newspaper establishment at the back of the store.

"What is the lowest price you can take for this book, sir?" asked the leisurely customer, holding up the volume. "One dollar and a quarter," was the prompt reply. "A dollar and a quarter! Why, your clerk asked me only a dollar just now." "True," said Franklin, "and I could have better afforded to take a dollar than to leave my work."

The man, who seemed to be in doubt as to whether Mr. Franklin was in earnest, said jokingly, "Well, come now, tell me your lowest price for this book." "One dollar and a half," was the grave reply. "A dollar and a half! Why, you just offered it for a dollar and a quarter." "Yes, and I could have better taken that price then than a dollar and a half now."

Without another word, the crestfallen purchaser laid the money on the counter and left the store. He had learned not only that he who squanders his own time is foolish, but that he who wastes the time of others is a thief.

From Store Boy to Millionaire

"But I am only nineteen years old, Mr. Riggs," and the speaker looked questioningly into the eyes of his companion, as if he doubted his seriousness in asking him to become a partner in his business.

Mr. Riggs was not joking, however, and he met George Peabody's perplexed gaze smilingly, as he replied: "That is no objection. If you are willing to go in with me and put your labor against my capital, I shall be well satisfied."

This was the turning point in a life which was to leave its impress on two of the world's greatest nations. And what were the experiences that led to it? They were utterly commonplace, and in some respects such as fall to the lot of many country boys to-day.

At eleven the lad was obliged to earn his own living. At that time (1806), his native town, Danvers, Massachusetts, presented few opportunities to the ambitious. He took the best that offered—a position as store boy in the village grocer's.

Four years of faithful work and constant effort at self-culture followed. He was now fifteen. His ambition was growing. He must seek a wider field. Another year passed, and then came the longed- for opening. Joyfully the youth set out for his brother's store, in Newburyport, Massachusetts. Here he felt he would have a better chance. But disappointment and disaster were lurking round the corner. Soon after he had taken up his new duties, the store was burned to the ground.

In the meantime, his father had died, and his mother, whom he idolized, needed his help more than ever. Penniless and out of work, but not disheartened, he immediately looked about for another position. Gladly he accepted an offer to work in his uncle's dry goods store in Georgetown, D.C., and here we find him, two years later, at the time when Mr. Riggs made his flattering proposition.

Did influence, a "pull," or financial considerations have anything to do with the merchant's choice of a partner? Nothing whatever. The young man had no money and no "pull," save what his character had made for him. His agreeable personality had won him many friends and his uncle much additional trade. His business qualities had gained him an enviable reputation. "His tact," says Sarah K. Bolton, "was unusual. He never wounded the feelings of a buyer of goods, never tried him with unnecessary talk, never seemed impatient, and was punctual to the minute."

That Mr. Riggs had made no mistake in choosing his partner, the rapid growth of his business conclusively proved. About a year after the partnership had been formed, the firm moved to Baltimore. So well did the business flourish in Baltimore that within seven years the partners had established branch houses in New York and Philadelphia. Finally Mr. Riggs decided to retire, and Peabody, who was then but thirty-five, found himself at the head of the business.

London, which he had visited several times, now attracted him. It offered great possibilities for banking. He went there, studied finance, established a banking business, and thenceforth made London his headquarters.

Wealth began to pour in upon him in a golden stream. But, although he had worked steadily for this, it was not for personal ends. He never married, and, to the end, lived simply and unostentatiously. Through the long years of patient work a great purpose had been shaping his life. Daily he had prayed that God might give him means wherewith to help his fellow-men. His prayer was being answered in overflowing measure.

Business interests constrained him to spend the latter half of his life in London; but absence only deepened his love for his own country. All that great wealth could do to advance the welfare and prestige of the United States was done by the millionaire philanthropist. But above all else, he tried to bring within the reach of poor children that which was denied himself,—a school education.

The Peabody Institute in his native town, with its free library and free course of lectures; the Institute, Academy of Music, and Art Gallery of Baltimore; the Museum of Natural History at Yale University; the Museum of Archaeology and Ethnology at Harvard University; the Peabody Academy of Science at Salem, Massachusetts, besides large contributions every year to libraries and other educational and philanthropic institutions all over the country, bear witness to his love for humanity.

Surpassing all this, however, was his establishment of the Peabody fund of three million dollars for the education of the freed slaves of the South, and for the equally needy poor of the white race.

An equal amount had been previously devoted to the better housing of the London poor. A dream almost too good to come true it seemed to the toilers in the great city's slums, when they found their filthy, unhealthy tenements replaced by clean, wholesome dwellings, well supplied with air and sunlight and all modern conveniences and comforts. London presented its generous benefactor with the freedom of the city; a bronze statue was erected in his honor, and Queen Victoria, who would fain have loaded him with titles and honors,—all of which he respectfully declined,—declared his act to be "wholly without parallel." A beautiful miniature portrait of her Majesty, which she caused to be specially made for him, and a letter written by her own hand, were the only gifts he would accept.

Gloriously had his great purpose been fulfilled. He who began life as a poor boy had given to the furtherance of education and for the benefit of the poor in various ways the sum of nine million dollars. The remaining four million dollars of his fortune was divided among his relatives.

England loved and honored him even as his own country did; and when he died in London, November 4, 1869, she offered him a resting place among her immortals in Westminster Abbey. His last wish, however, was fulfilled, and he was laid beside his mother in his native land.

His legacies to humanity are doing their splendid work to-day as they have done in the past, and as they will continue to do in the future, enabling multitudes of aspiring souls to reach heights which but for him they never could have attained. These words of his, too, spoken on the occasion of the dedication of his gift to Danvers,—its free Institute,—will serve for ages as a bugle call to all youths who are anxious to make the most of themselves, and, like him, to give of their best to the world:—

"Though Providence has granted me an unvaried and unusual success in the pursuit of fortune in other lands," he said, "I am still in heart the humble boy who left yonder unpretending dwelling many, very many years ago. ... There is not a youth within the sound of my voice whose early opportunities and advantages are not very much greater than were my own; and I have since achieved nothing that is impossible to the most humble boy among you. Bear in mind, that, to be truly great, it is not necessary that you should gain wealth and importance. Steadfast and undeviating truth, fearless and straightforward integrity, and an honor ever unsullied by an unworthy word or action, make their possessor greater than worldly success or prosperity. These qualities constitute greatness."

"I Will Paint or Die!"

"I will paint or die!" So stoutly resolved a poor, friendless boy, on a far-away Ohio farm, amid surroundings calculated to quench rather than to foster ambition. He knew not how his object was to be accomplished, for genius is never fettered by details. He only knew that he would be an artist. That settled it. He had never seen a work of art, or read or heard anything on the subject. It was his soul's voice alone that spoke, and "the soul's emphasis is always right."

Left an orphan at the age of eleven, the boy agreed to work on his uncle's farm for a term of five years for the munificent sum of ten dollars per annum, the total amount of which he was to receive at the end of the five years. The little fellow struggled bravely along with the laborious farm work, never for a moment losing sight of his ideal, and profiting as he could by the few months' schooling snatched from the duties of the farm during the winter.

Toward the close of his five years' service a great event happened. There came to the neighborhood an artist from Washington,—Mr. Uhl, whom he overheard by chance speaking on the subject of art. His words transformed the dream in the youth's soul to a living purpose, and it was then he resolved that he would "paint or die," and that he would go to Washington and study under Mr. Uhl.

On his release from the farm he started for Washington, with a coarse outfit packed away in a shabby little trunk, and a few dollars in his pocket. With the trustfulness of extreme youth, and in ignorance of a great world, he expected to get work that would enable him to live, and, at the same time, find leisure for the pursuit of his real life work. He immediately sought Mr. Uhl, who, with great generosity, offered to teach him without charge.

Then began the weary search for work in a large city already overcrowded with applicants. In his earnestness and eagerness the youth went from house to house asking for any kind of work "that would enable him to study art." But it was all in vain, and to save himself from starvation he was at length forced to accept the position of a day laborer, crushing stones for street paving. Yet he hoped to study painting when his day's work was done!

Mr. Uhl was at this time engaged in painting the portraits of Mrs. Frances Hodgson Burnett's sons. In the course of conversation with Mrs. Burnett, he spoke of the heroic struggle the youth was making. The author's heart was touched by the pathetic story. She at once wrote a check for one hundred dollars, and handed it to Mr. Uhl, for his protege. With that rare delicacy of feeling which marks all beautiful souls, Mrs. Burnett did not wish to embarrass the struggler by the necessity of thanking her. "Do not let him even write to me," she said to Mr. Uhl. "Simply say to him that I shall sail for Europe in a few days, and this is to give him a chance to work at the thing he cares for so much. It will at least give him a start."

In the throbbing life of the crowded city one heart beat high with hope and happiness that night. A youth lay awake until morning, too bewildered with gratitude and amazement to comprehend the meaning of the good fortune which had come to him. Who could his benefactor be?

Three years later, at the annual exhibition of Washington artists, Mrs. Burnett stood before a remarkably vivid portrait. Addressing the artist in charge of the exhibition, she said: "That seems to me very strong. It looks as if it must be a realistic likeness. Who did it?"

"I am so glad you like it. It was painted by your protege, Mrs. Burnett."

"My protege! My protege! Whom do you mean?"

"Why, the young man you saved from despair three years ago. Don't you remember young W____?"

"W____?" queried Mrs. Burnett.

"The young man whose story Mr. Uhl told you."

Mrs. Burnett then inquired if the portrait was for sale. When informed that the picture was an order and not for sale, she asked if there was anything else of Mr. W____'s on exhibition. She was conducted to a striking picture of a turbaned head, which was pointed out as another of Mr. W____'s works.

"How much does he ask for it?"

"A hundred and fifty dollars."

"Put 'sold' upon it, and when Mr. W____ comes, tell him his friend has bought his picture," said Mrs. Burnett.

On her return home Mrs. Burnett made out a check, which she inclosed in a letter to the young painter. It was mailed simultaneously with a letter from her protege, who had but just heard of her return from Europe, in which he begged her to accept, as a slight expression of his gratitude, the picture she had just purchased. The turbaned head now adorns the hall of Mrs. Burnett's house in Washington.

"I do not understand it even to-day," declares Mr. W____. "I knew nothing of Mrs. Burnett, nor she of me. Why did she do it? I only know that that hundred dollars was worth more to me then than fifty thousand in gold would be now. I lived upon it a whole year, and it put me on my feet."

Mr. W____ is a successful artist, now favorably known in his own country and in England for the strength and promise of his work.

The Call That Speaks in the Blood

Nature took the measure of little Tommy Edwards for a round hole, but his parents, teachers, and all with whom his childhood was cast, got it into their heads that Tommy was certainly intended for a square hole. So, with the best intentions in the world,—but oh, such woeful ignorance!—they tortured the poor little fellow and crippled him for life by trying to fit him to their pattern instead of that designed for him by the all-wise Mother.

Mother Nature called to Tommy to go into the woods and fields, to wade through the brooks, and make friends with all the living things she had placed there,—tadpoles, beetles, frogs, crabs, mice, rats, spiders, bugs,—everything that had life. Willingly, lovingly did the little lad obey, but only to be whipped and scolded by good Mother Edwards when he let loose in her kitchen the precious treasures which he had collected in his rambles.

It was provoking to have rats, mice, toads, bugs, and all sorts of creepy things sent sprawling over one's clean kitchen floor. But the pity of it was that Mrs. Edwards did not understand her boy, and thought the only cure for what she deemed his mischievous propensity as whipping. So Tommy was whipped and scolded, and scolded and whipped, which, however, did not in the least abate his love for Nature.

Driven to desperation, his mother bethought her of a plan. She would make the boy prisoner and see if this would tame him. With a stout rope she tied him by the leg to a table, and shut him in a room alone. But no sooner was the door closed than he dragged himself and the table to the fireplace, and, at the risk of setting himself and the house on fire, burned the rope which bound him, and made his escape into the woods to collect new specimens.

And yet his parents did not understand. It was time, however, to send him to school. They would see what the schoolmaster would do for him. But the schoolmaster was as blind as the parents, and Tommy's doom was sealed, when one morning, while the school was at prayers, a jackdaw poked its head out of his pocket and began to caw.

His next teacher misunderstood, whipped, and bore with him until one day nearly every boy in the school found a horse-leech wriggling up his leg, trying to suck his blood. This ended his second school experience.

He was given a third trial, but with no better results than before. Things went on in the usual way until a centipede was discovered in another boy's desk. Although in this case Tommy was innocent of any knowledge of the intruder, he was found guilty, whipped, and sent home with the message, "Go and tell your father to get you on board a man-of-war, as that is the best school for irreclaimables such as you."

His school life thus ended, he was apprenticed to a shoemaker, and thenceforth made his living at the bench. But every spare moment was given to the work which was meat and drink, life itself, to him.

In his manhood, to enable him to classify the minute and copious knowledge of birds, beasts, and insects which he had been gathering since childhood, with great labor and patience he learned how to read and write. Later, realizing how his lack of education hampered him, he endeavored to secure the means to enable him to study to better advantage, and sold for twenty pounds sterling a very large number of valuable specimens. He tried to get employment as a naturalist, and, but for his poor reading and writing, would have succeeded.

Poor little Scotch laddie! Had his parents or teachers understood him, he might have been as great a naturalist as Agassiz, and his life instead of being dwarfed and crippled, would have been a joy to himself and an incalculable benefit to the world.

Washington's Youthful Heroism

"No great deed is done
By falterers who ask for certainty."

"God will give you a reward," solemnly spoke the grateful mother, as she received from the arms of the brave youth the child he had risked his life to save. As if her lips were touched with the spirit of prophecy, she continued, "He will do great things for you in return for this day's work, and the blessings of thousands besides mine will attend you."

The ear of George Washington was ever open to the cry of distress; his sympathy and aid were ever at the service of those who needed them. One calm, sunny day, in the spring of 1750, he was dining with other surveyors in a forest in Virginia. Suddenly the stillness of the forest was startled by the piercing shriek of a woman. Washington instantly sprang to his feet and hurried to the woman's assistance.

"My boy, my boy,—oh, my poor boy is drowning, and they will not let me go," screamed the frantic mother, as she tried to escape from the detaining hands which withheld her from jumping into the rapids. "Oh, sir!" she implored, as she caught sight of the manly youth of eighteen, whose presence even then inspired confidence; "Oh, sir, you will surely do something for me!"

For an instant Washington measured the rocks and the whirling currents with a comprehensive look, and then, throwing off his coat, plunged into the roaring rapids where he had caught a glimpse of the drowning boy. With stout heart and steady hand he struggled against the seething mass of waters which threatened every moment to engulf or dash him to pieces against the sharp- pointed rocks which lay concealed beneath.

Three times he had almost succeeded in grasping the child's dress, when the force of the current drove him back. Then he gathered himself together for one last effort. Just as the child was about to escape him forever and be shot over the falls into the whirlpool below, he clutched him. The spectators on the bank cried out in horror. They gave both up for lost. But Washington seemed to lead a charmed life, and the cry of horror was changed to one of joy when, still holding the child, he emerged lower down from the vortex of waters.

Striking out for a low place in the bank, within a few minutes he reached the shore with his burden. Then amid the acclamations of those who had witnessed his heroism, and the blessings of the overjoyed mother, Washington placed the unconscious, but still living, child in her arms.

A Cow His Capital

A cow! Now, of all things in the world; of what use was a cow to an ambitious boy who wanted to go to college? Yet a cow, and nothing more, was the capital, the entire stock in trade, of an aspiring farmer boy who felt within him a call to another kind of life than that his father led.

This youth, who was yet in his teens, next to his father and mother, loved a book better than anything else in the world, and his great ambition was to go to college, to become a "scholar." Whether he followed the plow, or tossed hay under a burning July sun, or chopped wood, while his blood tingled from the combined effects of exercise and the keen December wind, his thoughts were ever fixed on the problem, "How can I go to college?"

His parents were poor, and, while they could give him a comfortable support as long as he worked on the farm with them, they could not afford to send him to college. But if they could not give him any material aid, they gave him all their sympathy, which kept the fire of his resolution burning at white heat.

There is some subtle communication between the mind and the spiritual forces of achievement which renders it impossible for one to think for any great length of time on a tangled problem, without a method for its untanglement being suggested. So, one evening, while driving the cows home to be milked, the thought flashed across the brain of the would-be student: "If I can't have anything else for capital, why can't I have a cow? I could do something with it, I am sure, and to college I *must* go, come what will." Courage is more than half the battle. Decision and Energy are its captains, and, when these three are united, victory is sure. The problem of going to college was already more than half solved.

Our youthful farmer did not let his thought grow cold. Hurrying at once to his father, he said, "If you will give me a cow, I shall feel free, with your permission, to go forth and see what I can do for myself in the world." The father, agreeing to the proposition, which seemed to him a practical one, replied heartily, "My son, you shall have the best milch cow I own."

Followed by the prayers and blessings of his parents, the youth started from home, driving his cow before him, his destination being a certain academy between seventy-five and one hundred miles distant.

Very soon he experienced the truth of the old adage that "Heaven helps those who help themselves." At the end of his first day's journey, when he sought a night's lodging for himself and accommodation for his cow in return for her milk, he met with unexpected kindness. The good people to whom he applied not only refused to take anything from him, but gave him bread to eat with his milk, and his cow a comfortable barn to lie in, with all the hay she could eat.

During the entire length of his journey, he met with equal kindness and consideration at the hands of all those with whom he came in contact; and, when he reached the academy, the principal and his wife were so pleased with his frank, modest, yet self- confident bearing, that they at once adopted himself and his cow into the family. He worked for his board, and the cow ungrudgingly gave her milk for the general good.

In due time the youth was graduated with honors from the academy. He was then ready to enter college, but had no money. The kind- hearted principal of the academy and his wife again came to his aid and helped him out of the difficulty by purchasing his cow. The money thus obtained enabled him to take the next step forward. He bade his good friends farewell, and the same year entered college. For four years he worked steadily with hand and brain. In spite of the hard work they were happy years, and at their close the persevering student had won, in addition to his classical degree, many new friends and well-wishers. His next step was to take a theological course in another institution. When he had finished the course, he was called to be principal of the academy to which honest ambition first led him with his cow.

Years afterward a learned professor of Hebrew, and the author of a scholarly "Commentary," cheered and encouraged many a struggling youth by relating the story of his own experiences from the time when he, a simple rustic, had started for college with naught but a cow as capital.

This story was first related to the writer by the late Frances E. Willard, who vouched for its truth.

The Boy Who Said "I Must"

Farther back than the memory of the grandfathers and grandmothers of some of my young readers can go, there lived in a historic town in Massachusetts a brave little lad who loved books and study more than toys or games, or play of any kind. The dearest wish of his heart was to be able to go to school every day, like more fortunate boys and girls, so that, when he should grow up to be a man, he might be well educated and fitted to do some grand work in the world. But his help was needed at home, and, young as he was, he began then to learn the lessons of unselfishness and duty. It was hard, wasn't it, for a little fellow only eight years old to have to leave off going to school and settle down to work on a farm? Many young folks at his age think they are very badly treated if they are not permitted to have some toy or story book, or other thing on which they have set their hearts; and older boys and girls, too, are apt to pout and frown if their whims are not gratified. But Theodore's parents were very poor, and could not even indulge his longing to go to school.

Did he give up his dreams of being a great man? Not a bit of it. He did not even cry or utter a complaint, but manfully resolved that he would do everything he could "to help father," and then, "when winter comes," he thought, "I shall be able to go to school again." Bravely the little fellow toiled through the beautiful springtide, though his wistful glances were often turned in the direction of the schoolhouse. But he resolutely bent to his work and renewed his resolve that he would be educated. As spring deepened into summer, the work on the farm grew harder and harder, but Theodore rejoiced that the flight of each season brought winter nearer.

At length autumn had vanished; the fruits of the spring and summer's toil had been gathered; the boy was free to go to his beloved studies again. And oh, how he reveled in the few books at his command in the village school! How eagerly he trudged across the fields, morning after morning, to the schoolhouse, where he always held first place in his class! Blustering winds and fierce snowstorms had no terrors for the ardent student. His only sorrow was that winter was all too short, and the days freighted with the happiness of regular study slipped all too quickly by. But the kind-hearted schoolmaster lent him books, so that, when spring came round again, and the boy had to go back to work, he could pore over them in his odd moments of relaxation. As he patiently plodded along, guiding the plow over the rough earth, he recited the lessons he had learned during the brief winter season, and after dinner, while the others rested awhile from their labors, Theodore eagerly turned the pages of one of his borrowed books, from which he drank in deep draughts of delight and knowledge. Early in the summer mornings, before the regular work began, and late in the evening, when the day's tasks had all been done, he read and re-read his treasured volumes until he knew them from cover to cover.

Then he was confronted with a difficulty. He had begun to study Latin, but found it impossible to get along without a dictionary. "What shall I do?" he thought; "there is no one from whom I can borrow a Latin dictionary, and I cannot ask father to buy me one, because he cannot afford it. But I MUST have it." That "must" settled the question. Three quarters of a century ago, book stores were few and books very costly. Boys and girls who have free access to libraries and reading rooms, and can buy the best works of great authors, sometimes for a few cents, can hardly imagine the difficulties which beset the little farmer boy in trying to get the book he wanted.

Did he get the dictionary? Oh, yes. You remember he had said, "I must." After thinking and thinking how he could get the money to buy it, a bright idea flashed across his mind. The bushes in the fields about the farm seemed waiting for some one to pick the ripe whortle-berries. "Why," thought he, "can't I gather and sell enough to buy my dictionary?" The next morning, before any one else in the farmhouse was astir, Theodore was moving rapidly through the bushes, picking, picking, picking, with unwearied fingers, the shining berries, every one of which was of greater value in his eyes than a penny would be to some of you.

At last, after picking and selling several bushels of ripe berries, he had enough money to buy the coveted dictionary. Oh, what a joy it was to possess a book that had been purchased with his own money! How it thrilled the boy and quickened his ambition to renewed efforts! "Well done, my boy! But, Theodore, I cannot afford to keep you there."

"Well, father," replied the youth, "but I am not going to study there; I shall study at home at odd times, and thus prepare myself for a final examination, which will give me a diploma."

Theodore had just returned from Boston, and was telling his delighted father how he had spent the holiday which he had asked for in the morning. Starting out early from the farm, so as to reach Boston before the intense heat of the August day had set in, he cheerfully tramped the ten miles that lay between his home in Lexington and Harvard College, where he presented himself as a candidate for admission; and when the examinations were over, Theodore had the joy of hearing his name announced in the list of successful students. The youth had reached the goal which the boy of eight had dimly seen. And now, if you would learn how he worked and taught in a country school in order to earn the money to spend two years in college, and how the young man became one of the most eminent preachers in America, you must read a complete biography of Theodore Parker, the hero of this little story.

The Hidden Treasure

Long, long ago, in the shadowy past, Ali Hafed dwelt on the shores of the River Indus, in the ancient land of the Hindus. His beautiful cottage, set in the midst of fruit and flower gardens, looked from the mountain side on which it stood over the broad expanse of the noble river. Rich meadows, waving fields of grain, and the herds and flocks contentedly grazing on the pasture lands, testified to the thrift and prosperity of Ali Hafed. The love of a beautiful wife and a large family of light-hearted boys and girls made his home an earthly paradise. Healthy, wealthy, contented, rich in love and friendship, his cup of happiness seemed full to overflowing.

Happy and contented, as we have seen, was the good Ali Hafed, when one evening a learned priest of Buddha, journeying along the banks of the Indus, stopped for rest and refreshment at his home, where all wayfarers were hospitably welcomed and treated as honored guests.

After the evening meal, the farmer and his family, with the priest in their midst, gathered around the fireside, the chilly mountain air of the late autumn making a fire desirable. The disciple of Buddha entertained his kind hosts with various legends and myths, and last of all with the story of the creation.

He told his wondering listeners how in the beginning the solid earth on which they lived was not solid at all, but a mere bank of fog. "The Great Spirit," said he, "thrust his finger into the bank of fog and began slowly describing a circle in its midst, increasing the speed gradually until the fog went whirling round his finger so rapidly that it was transformed into a glowing ball of fire. Then the Creative Spirit hurled the fiery ball from his hand, and it shot through the universe, burning its way through other banks of fog and condensing them into rain, which fell in great floods, cooling the surface of the immense ball. Flames then bursting from the interior through the cooled outer crust, threw up the hills and mountain ranges, and made the beautiful fertile valleys. In the flood of rain that followed this fiery upheaval, the substance that cooled very quickly formed granite, that which cooled less rapidly became copper, the next in degree cooled down into silver, and the last became gold. But the most beautiful substance of all, the diamond, was formed by the first beams of sunlight condensed on the earth's surface.

"A drop of sunlight the size of my thumb," said the priest, holding up his hand, "is worth more than mines of gold. With one such drop," he continued, turning to Ali Hafed, "you could buy many farms like yours; with a handful you could buy a province, and with a mine of diamonds you could purchase a whole kingdom."

The company parted for the night, and Ali Hafed went to bed, but not to sleep. All night long he tossed restlessly from side to side, thinking, planning, scheming how he could secure some diamonds. The demon of discontent had entered his soul, and the blessings and advantages which he possessed in such abundance seemed as by some malicious magic to have utterly vanished. Although his wife and children loved him as before; although his farm, his orchards, his flocks, and herds were as real and prosperous as they had ever been, yet the last words of the priest, which kept ringing in his ears, turned his content into vague longings and blinded him to all that had hitherto made him happy.

Before dawn next morning the farmer, full of his purpose, was astir. Rousing the priest, he eagerly inquired if he could direct him to a mine of diamonds.

"A mine of diamonds!" echoed the astonished priest. "What do you, who already have so much to be grateful for, want with diamonds?"

"I wish to be rich and place my children on thrones."

"All you have to do, then," said the Buddhist, "is to go and search until you find them."

"But where shall I go?" questioned the infatuated man.

"Go anywhere," was the vague reply; "north, south, east, or west,—anywhere."

"But how shall I know the place?" asked the farmer.

"When you find a river running over white sands between high mountain ranges, in these white sands you will find diamonds. There are many such rivers and many mines of diamonds waiting to be discovered. All you have to do is to start out and go somewhere—" and he waved his hand—"away, away!"

Ali Hafed's mind was full made up. "I will no longer," he thought, "remain on a wretched farm, toiling day in and day out for a mere subsistence, when acres of diamonds—untold wealth—may be had by him who is bold enough to seek them."

He sold his farm for less than half its value. Then, after putting his young family under the care of a neighbor, he set out on his quest.

With high hopes and the coveted diamond mines beckoning in the far distance, Ali Hafed began his wanderings. During the first few weeks his spirits did not flag, nor did his feet grow weary. On, and on, he tramped until he came to the Mountains of the Moon, beyond the bounds of Arabia. Weeks stretched into months, and the wanderer often looked regretfully in the direction of his once happy home. Still no gleam of waters glinting over white sands greeted his eyes. But on he went, into Egypt, through Palestine, and other eastern lands, always looking for the treasure he still hoped to find. At last, after years of fruitless search, during which he had wandered north and south, east and west, hope left him. All his money was spent. He was starving and almost naked, and the diamonds—which had lured him away from all that made life dear—where were they? Poor

Ali Hafed never knew. He died by the wayside, never dreaming that the wealth for which he had sacrificed happiness and life might have been his had he remained at home.

"Here is a diamond! here is a diamond! Has Ali Hafed returned?" shouted an excited voice.

The speaker, no other than our old acquaintance, the Buddhist priest, was standing in the same room where years before he had told poor Ali Hafed how the world was made, and where diamonds were to be found.

"No, Ali Hafed has not returned," quietly answered his successor. "Neither is that which you hold in your hand a diamond; it is but a pretty black pebble I picked up in my garden."

"I tell you," said the priest, excitedly, "this is a genuine diamond. I know one when I see it. Tell me how and where you found it?"

"One day," replied the farmer, slowly, "having led my camel into the garden to drink, I noticed, as he put his nose into the water, a sparkle of light coming from the white sand at the bottom of the clear stream. Stooping down, I picked up the black pebble you now hold, guided to it by that crystal eye in the center from which the light flashes so brilliantly."

"Why, thou simple one," cried the priest, "this is no common stone, but a gem of the purest water. Come, show me where thou didst find it."

Together they flew to the spot where the farmer had found the "pebble," and, turning over the white sands with eager fingers, they found, to their great delight, other stones even more valuable and beautiful than the first. Then they extended their search, and, so the Oriental story goes, "every shovelful of the old farm, as acre after acre was sifted over, revealed gems with which to decorate the crowns of emperors and moguls."

Love Tamed the Lion

I would not enter on my list of friends,
(Though graced with polished manners and fine sense,
Yet wanting sensibility), the man
Who needlessly sets foot upon a worm.— Cowper

"Nero!" Crushed, baffled, blinded, and, like Samson, shorn of his strength, prostrate in his cage lay the great tawny monarch of the forest. Heedless of the curious crowds passing to and fro, he seemed deaf as well as blind to everything going on around him. Perhaps he was dreaming of the jungle. Perhaps he was longing to roam the wilds once more in his native strength. Perhaps memories of a happy past even in captivity stirred him. Perhaps—But what is this? What change has come o'er the spirit of his dreams? No one has touched him. Apparently, nothing has happened to arouse him. Only a woman's voice, soft, caressing, full of love, has uttered the name, "Nero." But there was magic in the sound. In an instant the huge animal was on his feet. Quivering with emotion, he rushed to the side of the cage from whence the voice proceeded, and threw himself against the bars with such violence that he fell back half stunned. As he fell he uttered the peculiar note of welcome with which, in happier days, he was wont to greet his loved and long-lost mistress.

Touched with the devotion of her dumb friend, Rosa Bonheur—for it was she who had spoken—released from bondage the faithful animal whom, years before, she had bought from a keeper who declared him untamable.

"In order to secure the affections of wild animals," said the great-hearted painter, "you must love them," and by love she had subdued the ferocious beast whom even the lion-tamers had given up as hopeless.

When about to travel for two years, it being impossible to take her pet with her, Mademoiselle Bonheur sold him to the Jardin des Plantes in Paris, where she found him on her return, totally blind, owing, it is said, to the ill treatment of the attendant.

Grieved beyond measure at the condition of poor Nero, she had him removed to her chateau, where everything was done for his comfort that love could suggest. Often in her leisure moments, when she had laid aside her painting garb, the artist would have him taken to her studio, where she would play with and fondle the enormous creature as if he were a kitten. And there, at last, he died happily, his great paws clinging fondly to the mistress who loved him so well, his sightless eyes turned upon her to the end, as if beseeching that she would not again leave him.

"There Is Room Enough at the Top"

These words ere uttered many years ago by a youth who had no other means by which to reach the top than work and will. They have since become the watchword of every poor boy whose ambition is backed by energy and a determination to make the most possible of himself.

The occasion on which Daniel Webster first said "There is room enough at the top," marked the turning point in his life. Had he not been animated at that time by an ambition to make the most of his talents, he might have remained forever in obscurity.

His father and other friends had secured for him the position of Clerk of the Court of Common Pleas, of Hillsborough County, New Hampshire. Daniel was studying law in the office of Mr. Christopher Gore, a distinguished Boston lawyer, and was about ready for his admission to the bar. The position offered him was worth fifteen hundred dollars a year. This seemed a fortune to the struggling student. He lay awake the whole night following the day on which he had heard the good news, planning what he would do for his father and mother, his brother Ezekiel, and his sisters. Next morning he hurried to the office to tell Mr. Gore of his good fortune.

"Well, my young friend," said the lawyer, when Daniel had told his story, "the gentlemen have been very kind to you; I am glad of it. You must thank them for it. You will write immediately, of course."

Webster explained that, since he must go to New Hampshire immediately, it would hardly be worth while to write. He could thank his good friends in person.

"Why," said Mr. Gore in great astonishment, "you don't mean to accept it, surely!"

The youth's high spirits were damped at once by his senior's manner. "The bare idea of not accepting it," he says, "so astounded me that I should have been glad to have found any hole to have hid myself in."

"Well," said Mr. Gore, seeing the disappointment his words had caused, "you must decide for yourself; but come, sit down and let us talk it over. The office is worth fifteen hundred a year, you say. Well, it never will be any more. Ten to one, if they find out it is so much, the fees will be reduced. You are appointed now by friends; others may fill their places who are of different opinions, and who have friends of their own to provide for. You will lose your place; or, supposing you to retain it, what are you but a clerk for life? And your prospects as a lawyer are good enough to encourage you to go on. Go on, and finish your studies; you are poor enough, but there are greater evils than poverty; live on no man's favor; what bread you do eat, let it be the bread of independence; pursue your profession, make yourself useful to your friends and a little formidable to your enemies, and you have nothing to fear."

How fortunate Webster as to have at this point in his career so wise and far-seeing a friend! His father, who had made many sacrifices to educate his boys, saw in the proffered clerkship a great opening for his favorite, Daniel. He never dreamed of the future that was to make him one of America's greatest orators and statesmen. At first he could not believe that the position which he had worked so hard to obtain was to be rejected.

"Daniel, Daniel," he said sorrowfully, "don't you mean to take that office?"

"No, indeed, father," was the reply, "I hope I can do much better than that. I mean to use my tongue in the courts, not my pen; to be an actor, not a register of other men's acts. I hope yet, sir, to astonish your honor in your own court by my professional attainments."

Judge Webster made no attempt to conceal his disappointment. He even tried to discourage his son by reminding him that there were already more lawyers than the country needed.

It was in answer to this objection that Daniel used the famous and oft-quoted words,—"There is room enough at the top."

"Well, my son," said the fond but doubting father, "your mother has always said you would come to something or nothing. She was not sure which; I think you are now about settling that doubt for her."

It was very painful to Daniel to disappoint his father, but his purpose was fixed, and nothing now could change it. He knew he had turned his face in the right direction, and though when he commenced to practice law he earned only about five or six hundred dollars a year, he never regretted the decision he had made. He aimed high, and he had his reward.

It is true now and forever, as Lowell says, that—

"Not failure, but low aim, is crime."

The Uplift of a Slave Boy's Ideal

Invincible determination, and a right nature, are the levers that move the world.— Porter

Born a slave, with the feelings and possibilities of a man, but with no rights above the beast of the field, Fred Douglass gave the world one of the most notable examples of man's power over circumstances.

He had no knowledge of his father, whom he had never seen. He had only a dim recollection of his mother, from whom he had been separated at birth. The poor slave mother used to walk twelve miles when her day's work was done, in order to get an occasional glimpse of her child. Then she had to walk back to the plantation on which she labored, so as to be in time to begin to work at dawn next morning.

Under the brutal discipline of the "Aunt Katy" who had charge of the slaves who were still too young to labor in the fields, he early began to realize the hardships of his lot, and to rebel against the state of bondage into which he had been born.

Often hungry, and clothed in hottest summer and coldest winter alike, in a coarse tow linen shirt, scarcely reaching to the knees, without a bed to lie on or a blanket to cover him, his only protection, no matter how cold the night, was an old corn bag, into which he thrust himself, leaving his feet exposed at one end, and his head at the other.

When about seven years old, he was transferred to new owners in Baltimore, where his kind-hearted mistress, who did not know that in doing so she was breaking the law, taught him the alphabet. He thus got possession of the key which was to unlock his bonds, and, young as he was, he knew it. It did not matter that his master, when he learned what had been done, forbade his wife to give the boy further instructions. He had already tasted of the fruit of the tree of knowledge. The prohibition was useless. Neither threats nor stripes nor chains could hold the awakened soul in bondage.

With infinite pains and patience, and by stealth, he enlarged upon his knowledge of the alphabet. An old copy of "Webster's Spelling Book," cast aside by his young master, as his greatest treasure. With the aid of a few good-natured white boys, who sometimes played with him in the streets, he quickly mastered its contents. Then he cast about for further means to satisfy his mental craving. How difficult it was for the poor, despised slave to do this, we learn from his own pathetic words. "I have gathered," he says, "scattered pages of the Bible from the filthy street gutters, and washed and dried them, that, in moments of leisure, I might get a word or two of wisdom from them."

Think of that, boys and girls of the twentieth century, with your day schools and evening schools, libraries, colleges, and universities,—picking reading material from the gutter and mastering it by stealth! Yet this boy grew up to be the friend and co-worker of Garrison and Phillips, the eloquent spokesman of his race, the honored guest of distinguished peers and commoners of England, one of the noblest examples of a self-made man that the world has ever seen.

Under equal hardships he learned to write. The boy's wits, sharpened instead of blunted by repression, saw opportunities where more favored children could see none. He gave himself his first writing lesson in his master's shipyard, by copying from the various pieces of timber the letters with which they had been marked by the carpenters, to show the different parts of the ship for which they were intended. He copied from posters on fences, from old copy books, from anything and everything he could get hold of. He practiced his new art on pavements and rails, and entered into contests in letter making with white boys, in order to add to his knowledge. "With playmates for my teachers," he says, "fences and pavements for my copy books, and chalk for my pen and ink, I learned to write."

While being "broken in" to field labor under the lash of the overseer, chained and imprisoned for the crime of attempting to escape from slavery, the spirit of the youth never quailed. He believed in himself, in his God-given powers, and he was determined to use them in freeing himself and his race.

How well he succeeded in the stupendous task to which he set himself while yet groping in the black night of bondage, with no human power outside of his own indomitable will to help him, his life work attests in language more enduring than "storied urn" or written history. A roll call of the world's great moral heroes would be incomplete without the name of the slave-born Douglass, who came on the stage of life to play the leading role of the Moses of his race in one of the saddest and, at the same time, most glorious eras of American history.

He was born in Talbot County, Maryland. The exact date of his birth is not known; but he himself thought it was in February, 1817. He died in Washington, D.C., February 20, 1895.

"To the First Robin"

The air was keen and biting, and traces of snow still lingered on the ground and sparkled on the tree tops in the morning sun. But the happy, rosy-cheeked children, lately freed from the restraints of city life, who played in the old garden in Concord, Massachusetts, that bright spring morning many years ago, heeded not the biting wind or the lingering snow. As they raced up and down the paths, in and out among the trees, their cheeks took on a deeper glow, their eyes a brighter sparkle, while their shouts of merry laughter made the morning glad.

But stay, what is this? What has happened to check the laughter on their lips, and dim their bright eyes with tears? The little group, headed by Louisa, has suddenly come to a pause under a tree, where a wee robin, half dead with hunger and cold, has fallen from its perch.

"Poor, poor birdie!" exclaimed a chorus of pitying voices. "It is dead, poor little thing," said Anna. "No," said Louisa, the leader of the children in fun and works of mercy alike; "it is warm, and I can feel its heart beat." As she spoke, she gathered the tiny bundle of feathers to her bosom, and, heading the little procession, turned toward the house.

A warm nest was made for the foundling, and, with motherly care, the little Louisa May Alcott, then only eight years old, fed and nursed back to life the half-famished bird.

Before the feathered claimant on her mercy flew away to freedom, the future authoress, the "children's friend," who loved and pitied all helpless things, wrote her first poem, and called it "To the First Robin." It contained only these two stanzas:—

"Welcome, welcome, little stranger,
Fear no harm, and fear no danger,
We are glad to see you here,
For you sing, 'Sweet spring is near.'

"Now the white snow melts away,
Now the flowers blossom gay,
Come, dear bird, and build your nest,
For we love our robin best."

The "Wizard" as an Editor

Although he had only a few months' regular schooling, at ten Thomas Alva Edison had read and thought more than many youths of twenty. Gibbon's "Rome," Hume's "England," Sears's "History of the World," besides several books on chemistry,—a subject in which he was even then deeply interested,—were familiar friends. Yet he was not, by any means, a serious bookworm. On the contrary, he was as full of fun and mischief as any healthy boy of his age.

The little fellow's sunny face and pleasing manners made him a general favorite, and when circumstances forced him from the parent nest into the big bustling world at the age of twelve, he became the most popular train boy on the Grand Trunk Railroad in central Michigan, while his keen powers of observation and practical turn of mind made him the most successful. His ambition soared far beyond the selling of papers, song books, apples, and peanuts, and his business ability was such that he soon had three or four boys selling his wares on commission.

His interest in chemistry, however, had not abated, and his busy brain now urged him to try new fields. He exchanged some of his papers for retorts and other simple apparatus, bought a copy of Fiesenius's "Qualitative Analysis," and secured the use of an old baggage car as a laboratory. Here, surrounded by chemicals and experimenting apparatus, he spent some of the happiest hours of his life.

But even this was not a sufficient outlet for the energies of the budding inventor. Selling papers had naturally aroused his interest in printing and editing, and with Edison interest always manifested itself in action. In buying papers, he had, as usual, made use of his eyes, and, with the little knowledge of printing picked up in this way, he determined to start a printing press and edit a paper of his own.

He first purchased a quantity of old type from the Detroit Free Press. Then he put a printing press in the baggage car, which did duty as printing and editorial office as well as laboratory, and began his editorial labors. When the first copy of the Grand Trunk Herald was put on sale, it would be hard to find a happier boy than its owner was.

No matter that the youthful editor's "Associated Press" consisted of baggage men and brakemen, or that the literary matter contributed to the Grand Trunk Herald was chiefly railway gossip, with some general information of interest to passengers, the little three-cent sheet became very popular. Even the great London Times deigned to notice it, as the only journal in the world printed on a railway train.

But, successful as he was in his editorial venture, Edison's best love was given to chemistry and electricity, which latter subject he had begun to study with his usual ardor. And well it was for the world when the youth of sixteen gave up train and newspaper work, that no poverty, no difficulties, no ridicule, no "hard luck," none of the trials and obstacles he had to encounter in after life, had power to chill or discourage the genius of the master inventor of the nineteenth century.

How Good Fortune Came to Pierre

Many years ago, in a shabby room in one of the poorest streets of London, a little golden-haired boy sat singing, in his sweet, childish voice, by the bedside of his sick mother. Though faint from hunger and oppressed with loneliness, he manfully forced back the tears that kept welling up into his blue eyes, and, for his mother's sake, tried to look bright and cheerful. But it was hard to be brave and strong while his dear mother was suffering for lack of the delicacies which he longed to provide for her, but could not. He had not tasted food all day himself. How he could drive away the gaunt, hungry wolf, Famine, that had come to take up its abode with them, was the thought that haunted him as he tried to sing a little song he himself had composed. He left his place by the invalid, who, lulled by his singing, had fallen into a light sleep. As he looked listlessly out of the window, he noticed a man putting up a large poster, which bore, in staring yellow letters, the announcement that Madame M____, one of the greatest singers that ever lived, was to sing in public that night.

"Oh, if I could only go!" thought little Pierre, his love of music for the moment making him forgetful of aught else. Suddenly his face brightened, and the light of a great resolve shone in his eyes. "I will try it," he said to himself; and, running lightly to a little stand that stood at the opposite end of the room, with trembling hands he took from a tiny box a roll of paper. With a wistful, loving glance at the sleeper, he stole from the room and hurried out into the street.

"Who did you say is waiting for me?" asked Madame M___ of her servant; "I am already worn out with company."

"It is only a very pretty little boy with yellow curls, who said that if he can just see you, he is sure you will not be sorry, and he will not keep you a moment."

"Oh, well, let him come," said the great singer, with a kindly smile, "I can never refuse children."

Timidly the child entered the luxurious apartment, and, bowing before the beautiful, stately woman, he began rapidly, lest his courage should fail him: "I came to see you because my mother is very sick, and we are too poor to get food and medicine. I thought, perhaps, that if you would sing my little song at some of your grand concerts, maybe some publisher would buy it for a small sum, and so I could get food and medicine for my mother."

Taking the little roll of paper which the boy held in his hand, the warm-hearted singer lightly hummed the air. Then, turning toward him, she asked, in amazement: "Did you compose it? you, a child! And the words, too?" Without waiting for a reply, she added quickly, "Would you like to come to my concert this evening?" The boy's face became radiant with delight at the thought of hearing the famous songstress, but a vision of his sick mother, lying alone in the poor, cheerless room, flitted across his mind, and he answered, with a choking in his throat:—

"Oh, yes; I should so love to go, but I couldn't leave my mother."

"I will send somebody to take care of your mother for the evening, and here is a crown with which you may go and get food and medicine. Here is also one of my tickets. Come to-night; that will admit you to a seat near me."

Overcome with joy, the child could scarcely express his gratitude to the gracious being who seemed to him like an angel from heaven. As he went out again into the crowded street, he seemed to tread on air. He bought some fruit and other little delicacies to tempt his mother's appetite, and while spreading out the feast of good things before her astonished gaze, with tears in his eyes, he told her of the kindness of the beautiful lady.

An hour later, tingling with expectation, Pierre set out for the concert. How like fairyland it all seemed! The color, the dazzling lights, the flashing gems and glistening silks of the richly dressed ladies bewildered him. Ah! could it be possible that the great artist who had been so kind to him would sing his little song before this brilliant audience? At length she came on the stage, bowing right and left in answer to the enthusiastic welcome which greeted her appearance.

A pause of expectancy followed. The boy held his breath and gazed spellbound at the radiant vision on whom all eyes were riveted. The orchestra struck the first notes of a plaintive melody, and the glorious voice of the great singer filled the vast hall, as the words of the sad little song of the child composer floated on the air. It was so simple, so touching, so full of exquisite pathos, that many were in tears before it was finished.

And little Pierre? There he sat, scarcely daring to move or breathe, fearing that the flowers, the lights, the music, should vanish, and he should wake up to find it all a dream. He was aroused from his trance by the tremendous burst of applause that rang through the house as the last note trembled away into silence. He started up. It was no dream. The greatest singer in Europe had sung his little song before a fashionable London audience. Almost dazed with happiness, he never knew how he reached his poor home; and when he related the incidents of the evening, his mother's delight nearly equaled his own. Nor was this the end.

Next day they were startled by a visit from Madame M____. After gently greeting the sick woman, while her hand played with Pierre's golden curls, she said: "Your little boy, Madame, has brought you a fortune. I was offered this morning, by the best publisher in London, 300 pounds for his little song; and after he has realized a certain amount from the sale, little Pierre here is to share the profits. Madame, thank God that your son has a gift from heaven." The grateful tears of the invalid and her visitor mingled, while the child knelt by his mother's bedside and prayed

God to bless the kind lady who, in their time of sorrow and great need, had been to them as a savior.

The boy never forgot his noble benefactress, and years afterward, when the great singer lay dying, the beloved friend who smoothed her pillow and cheered and brightened her last moments—the rich, popular, and talented composer—was no other than our little Pierre.

"If I Rest, I Rust"

"The heights by great men reached and kept
Were not attained by sudden flight;
But they, while their companions slept,
Were toiling upward in the night."

The significant inscription found on an old key,—"If I rest, I rust,"—would be an excellent motto for those who are afflicted with the slightest taint of idleness. Even the industrious might adopt it with advantage to serve as a reminder that, if one allows his faculties to rest, like the iron in the unused key, they will soon show signs of rust, and, ultimately, cannot do the work required of them.

Those who would attain "The heights by great men reached and kept" must keep their faculties burnished by constant use, so that they will unlock the doors of knowledge, the gates that guard the entrances to the professions, to science, art, literature, agriculture,—every department of human endeavor.

Industry keeps bright the key that opens the treasury of achievement. If Hugh Miller, after toiling all day in a quarry, had devoted his evenings to rest and recreation, he would never have become a famous geologist. The celebrated mathematician, Edmund Stone, would never have published a mathematical dictionary, never have found the key to the science of mathematics, if he had given his spare moments, snatched from the duties of a gardener, to idleness. Had the little Scotch lad, Ferguson, allowed the busy brain to go to sleep while he tended sheep on the hillside, instead of calculating the position of the stars by the help of a string of beads, he would never have become a famous astronomer.

"Labor vanquishes all,"—not in constant, spasmodic, or ill-directed labor, but faithful, unremitting, daily effort toward a well-directed purpose. Just as truly as eternal vigilance is the price of liberty, so is eternal industry the price of noble and enduring success.

"Seize, then, the minutes as they pass; The woof of life is thought! Warm up the colors; let them glow With fire of fancy fraught."

A Boy Who Knew Not Fear

Richard Wagner, the great composer, weaves into one of his musical dramas a beautiful story about a youth named Siegfried, who did not know what fear was.

The story is a sort of fairy tale or myth,—something which has a deep meaning hidden in it, but which is not literally true.

We smile at the idea of a youth who never knew fear, who even as a little child had never been frightened by the imaginary terrors of night, the darkness of the forest, or the cries of the wild animals which inhabited it.

Yet it is actually true that there was born at Burnham Thorpe, Norfolk, England, on September 29, 1758, a boy who never knew what fear was. This boy's name was Horatio Nelson,—a name which his fearlessness, ambition, and patriotism made immortal.

Courage even to daring distinguished young Nelson from his boy companions. Many stories illustrating this quality are told of him.

On one occasion, when the future hero of England was but a mere child, while staying at his grandmother's, he wandered away from the house in search of birds' nests. When dinner time came and went and the boy did not return, his family became alarmed. They feared that he had been kidnapped by gypsies, or that some other mishap had befallen him. A thorough search was made for him in every direction. Just as the searchers were about to give up their quest, the truant was discovered sitting quietly by the side of a brook which he was unable to cross.

"I wonder, child," said his grandmother, "that hunger and fear did not drive you home."

"Fear! grand-mamma," exclaimed the boy; "I never saw fear. What is it?"

Horatio was a born leader, who never even in childhood shrank from a hazardous undertaking. This story of his school days shows how the spirit of leadership marked him before he had entered his teens.

In the garden attached to the boarding school at North Walsham, which he and his elder brother, William, attended, there grew a remarkably fine pear tree. The sight of this tree, loaded with fruit was, naturally, a very tempting one to the boys. The boldest among the older ones, however, dared not risk the consequences of helping themselves to the pears, which they knew were highly prized by the master of the school.

Horatio, who thought neither of the sin of stealing the schoolmaster's property, nor of the risk involved in the attempt, volunteered to secure the coveted pears.

He was let down in sheets from the bedroom window by his schoolmates, and, after gathering as much of the fruit as he could carry, returned with considerable difficulty. He then turned the pears over to the boys, not keeping one for himself.

"I only took them," he explained, "because the rest of you were afraid to venture."

The sense of honor of the future "Hero of the Nile" and of Trafalgar was as keen in boyhood as in later life.

One year, at the close of the Christmas holidays, he and his brother William set out on horseback to return to school. There had been a heavy fall of snow which made traveling very disagreeable, and William persuaded Horatio to go back home with him, saying that it was not safe to go on.

"If that be the case," said Rev. Mr. Nelson, the father of the boys, when the matter was explained to him, "you certainly shall not go; but make another attempt, and I will leave it to your honor. If the road is dangerous, you may return; but remember, boys, I leave it to your honor."

The snow was really deep enough to be made an excuse for not going on, and William was for returning home a second time. Horatio, however, would not be persuaded again. "We must go on," he said; "remember, brother, it was left to our honor."

When only twelve years old, young Nelson's ambition urged him to try his fortune at sea. His uncle, Captain Maurice Suckling, commanded the Raisonnable, a ship of sixty-four guns, and the boy thought it would be good fortune, indeed, if he could get an opportunity to serve under him. "Do, William," he said to his brother, "write to my father, and tell him that I should like to go to sea with Uncle Maurice."

On hearing of his son's wishes, Mr. Nelson at once wrote to Captain Suckling. The latter wrote back without delay: "What has poor Horatio done, who is so weak, that he, above all the rest, should be sent to rough it out at sea? But let him come, and the first time we go into action, a cannon ball may knock off his head and provide for him at once."

This was not very encouraging for a delicate boy of twelve. But Horatio was not daunted. His father took him to London, and there put him into the stage coach for Chatham, where the Raisonnable was lying at anchor.

He arrived at Chatham during the temporary absence of his uncle, so that there was no friendly voice to greet him when he went on board the big ship. Homesick and heartsick, he passed some of the most miserable days of his life on the Raisonnable. The officers treated the sailors with a harshness bordering on cruelty. This treatment, of course, increased the natural roughness of the sailors; and, altogether, the conditions were such that Horatio's opinion of the Royal Navy was sadly altered.

But in spite of the separation from his brother William, who had been his schoolmate and constant companion, and all his other loved ones, the hardships he had to endure as a sailor boy among rough officers and rougher men, and his physical weakness, his courage did not fail him. He stuck bravely to his determination to be a sailor.

Later, the lad went on a voyage to the West Indies, in a merchant ship commanded by Mr. John Rathbone. During this voyage, his anxiety to rise in his profession and his keen powers of observation, which were constantly exercised, combined to make him a practical sailor.

After his return from the West Indies, his love of adventure was excited by the news that two ships—the Racehorse and the Carcass—were being fitted out for a voyage of discovery to the North Pole. Through the influence of Captain Suckling, he secured an appointment as coxswain, under Captain Lutwidge, who was second in command of the expedition.

All went well with the Racehorse and the Carcass until they neared the Polar regions. Then they were becalmed, surrounded with ice, and wedged in so that they could not move.

Young as Nelson was, he was put in command of one of the boats sent out to try to find a passage to the open water. While engaged in this work he was instrumental in saving the crew of another of the boats which had been attacked by walruses.

His most notable adventure during this Polar cruise, however, was a fight with a bear.

One night he stole away from his ship with a companion in pursuit of a bear. A fog which had been rising when they left the Carcass soon enveloped them. Between three and four o'clock in the morning, when the weather began to clear, they were sighted by Captain Lutwidge and his officers, at some distance from the ship, in conflict with a huge bear. The boys, who had been missed soon after they set out on their adventure, were at once signaled to return. Nelson's companion urged him to obey the signal, and, though their ammunition had given out, he longed to continue the fight.

"Never mind," he cried excitedly; "do but let me get a blow at this fellow with the butt end of my musket, and we shall have him."

Captain Lutwidge, seeing the boy's danger,—he being separated from the bear only by a narrow chasm in the ice,—fired a gun. This frightened the bear away. Nelson then returned to face the consequences of his disobedience.

He was severely reprimanded by his captain for "conduct so unworthy of the office he filled." When asked what motive he had in hunting a bear, he replied, still trembling from the excitement of the encounter, "Sir, I wished to kill the bear that I might carry the skin to my father."

The expedition finally worked its way out of the ice and sailed for home.

Horatio's next voyage was to the East Indies, aboard the Seahorse, one of the vessels of a squadron under the command of Sir Edward Hughes. His attention to duty attracted the notice of his senior officer, on whose recommendation he was rated as a midshipman.

After eighteen months in the trying climate of India, the youth's health gave way, and he was sent home in the Dolphin. His physical weakness affected his spirits. Gloom fastened upon him, and for a time he was very despondent about his future.

"I felt impressed," he says, "with an idea that I should never rise in my profession. My mind was staggered with a view of the difficulties I had to surmount and the little interest I possessed. I could discover no means of reaching the object of my ambition. After a long and gloomy revery in which I almost wished myself overboard, a sudden flow of patriotism was kindled within me and presented my king and my country as my patrons. My mind exulted in the idea. 'Well, then,' I exclaimed, 'I will be a hero, and, confiding in Providence, I will brave every danger!'"

In that hour Nelson leaped from boyhood to manhood. Thenceforth the purpose of his life never changed. From that time, as he often said afterward, "a radiant orb was suspended in his mind's eye, which urged him onward to renown."

His health improved very much during the homeward voyage, and he was soon able to resume duty again.

At nineteen he was made second lieutenant of the Lowestoffe; and at twenty he was commander of the Badger. Before he was twenty- one, owing largely to his courage and presence of mind in face of every danger, and his enthusiasm in his profession, "he had gained that mark," says his biographer, Southey, "which brought all the honors of the service within his reach."

Pleasing in his address and conversation, always kind and thoughtful in his treatment of the men and boys under him, Nelson was the best-loved man in the British navy,—nay, in all England.

When he was appointed to the command of the Boreas, a ship of twenty-eight guns, then bound for the Leeward Islands, he had thirty midshipmen under him. When any of them, at first, showed any timidity about going up the masts, he would say, by way of encouragement, "I am going a race to the masthead, and beg that I may meet you there." And again he would say cheerfully, that "any person was to be pitied who could fancy there was any danger, or even anything disagreeable, in the attempt."

"Your Excellency must excuse me for bringing one of my midshipmen with me," he said to the governor of Barbados, who had invited him to dine. "I make it a rule to introduce them to all the good company I can, as they have few to look up to besides myself during the time they are at sea." Was it any wonder that his "middies" almost worshiped him?

This thoughtfulness in small matters is always characteristic of truly great, large-souled men. Another distinguishing mark of Nelson's greatness was that he ruled by love rather than fear.

When, at the age of forty-seven, he fell mortally wounded at the battle of Trafalgar, all England was plunged into grief. The crowning victory of his life had been won, but his country was inconsolable for the loss of the noblest of her naval heroes.

"The greatest sea victory that the world had ever known was won," says W. Clark Russell, "but at such a cost, that there was no man throughout the British fleet—there was no man indeed in all England—but would have welcomed defeat sooner than have paid the price of this wonderful conquest."

The last words of the hero who had won some of the greatest of England's sea fights were, "Thank God, I have done my duty."

How Stanley Found Livingstone

In the year 1866 David Livingstone, the great African explorer and missionary, started on his last journey to Africa. Three years passed away during which no word or sign from him had reached his friends. The whole civilized world became alarmed for his safety. It was feared that his interest in the savages in the interior of Africa had cost him his life.

Newspapers and clergymen in many lands were clamoring for a relief expedition to be sent out in search of him. Royal societies, scientific associations, and the British government were debating what steps should be taken to find him. But they were very slow in coming to any conclusion, and while they were weighing questions and discussing measures, an energetic American settled the matter offhand.

This was James Gordon Bennett, Jr., manager of the New York Herald and son of James Gordon Bennett, its editor and proprietor.

Mr. Bennett was in a position which brought him into contact with some of the cleverest and most enterprising young men of his day. From all those he knew he singled out Henry M. Stanley for the difficult and perilous task of finding Livingstone.

And who was this young man who was chosen to undertake a work which required the highest qualities of manhood to carry it to success?

Henry M. Stanley, whose baptismal name was John Rowlands, was born of poor parents in Wales, in 1840. Being left an orphan at the age of three, he was sent to the poorhouse in his native place. There he remained for ten years, and then shipped as a cabin boy in a vessel bound for America. Soon after his arrival in this country, he found employment in New Orleans with a merchant named Stanley. His intelligence, energy, and ambition won him so much favor with this gentleman that he adopted him as his son and gave him his name.

The elder Stanley died while Henry was still a youth. This threw him again upon his own resources, as he inherited nothing from his adopted father, who died without making a will. He next went to California to seek his fortune. He was not successful, however, and at twenty he was a soldier in the Civil War. When the war was over, he engaged himself as a correspondent to the New York Herald.

In this capacity he traveled extensively in the East, doing brilliant work for his paper. When England went to war with King Theodore of Abyssinia, he accompanied the English army to Abyssinia, and from thence wrote vivid descriptive letters to the Herald. The child whose early advantages were only such as a Welsh poorhouse afforded, was already, through his own unaided efforts, a leader in his profession. He was soon to become a leader in a larger sense.

At the time Mr. Bennett conceived the idea of sending an expedition in search of Livingstone, Stanley was in Spain. He had been sent there by the Herald to report the civil war then raging in that country. He thus describes the receipt of Mr. Bennett's message and the events immediately following:—

"I am in Madrid, fresh from the carnage at Valencia. At 10 A.M. Jacopo, at No.—Calle de la Cruz, hands me a telegram; on opening it I find it reads, 'Come to Paris on important business.' The telegram is from James Gordon Bennett, Jr., the young manager of the New York Herald.

"Down come my pictures from the walls of my apartments on the second floor; into my trunks go my books and souvenirs, my clothes are hastily collected, some half washed, some from the clothesline half dry, and after a couple of hours of hasty hard work my portmanteaus are strapped up and labeled for 'Paris.'"

It was late at night when Stanley arrived in Paris. "I went straight to the 'Grand Hotel,'" he says, "and knocked at the door of Mr. Bennett's room.

"'Come in,' I heard a voice say. Entering I found Mr. Bennett in bed.

"'Who are you?' he asked.

"'My name is Stanley,' I answered.

"'Ah, yes! sit down; I have important business on hand for you.

"'Where do you think Livingstone is?'

"'I really do not know, sir.'

"'Do you think he is alive?'

"'He may be, and he may not be,' I answered.

"'Well, I think he is alive, and that he can be found, and I am going to send you to find him.'

"'What!' said I, 'do you really think I can find Dr. Livingstone? Do you mean me to go to Central Africa?'

"'Yes, I mean that you shall go and find him wherever you may hear that he is … . Of course you will act according to your own plans and do what you think Best—*but Find Livingstone.*'"

The question of expense coming up, Mr. Bennett said: "Draw a thousand pounds now; and when you have gone through that, draw another thousand; and when that is spent, draw another thousand; and when you have finished that, draw another thousand, and so on; but, *Find Livingstone.*"

Stanley asked no questions, awaited no further instructions. The two men parted with a hearty hand clasp. "Good night, and God be with you," said Bennett.

"Good night, sir," returned Stanley. "What it is in the power of human nature to do I will do; and on such an errand as I go upon, God will be with me."

The young man immediately began the work of preparation for his great undertaking. This in itself was a task requiring more than ordinary judgment and foresight, but Stanley was equal to the occasion.

On January 6, 1871, he reached Zanzibar, an important native seaport on the east coast of Africa. Here the preparations for the journey were completed. Soon, with a train composed of one hundred and ninety men, twenty donkeys, and baggage amounting to about six tons, he started from this point for the interior of the continent.

Then began a journey the dangers and tediousness of which can hardly be described. Stanley and his men were often obliged to wade through swamps filled with alligators. Crawling on hands and knees, they forced their way through miles of tangled jungle, breathing in as they went the sickening odor of decaying vegetables. They were obliged to be continually on their guard against elephants, lions, hyenas, and other wild inhabitants of the jungle. Fierce as these were, however, they were no more to be dreaded than the savage tribes whom they sometimes encountered. Whenever they stopped to rest, they were tormented by flies, white ants, and reptiles, which crawled all over them.

For months they journeyed on under these conditions. The donkeys had died from drinking impure water, and some of the men had fallen victims to disease.

It was no wonder that the survivors of the expedition—all but Stanley—had grown disheartened. Half starved, wasted by sickness and hardships of all kinds, with bleeding feet and torn clothes, some of them became mutinous. Stanley's skill as a leader was taxed to the utmost. Alternately coaxing the faint-hearted and punishing the insubordinate, he continued to lead them on almost in spite of themselves.

So far they had heard nothing of Livingstone, nor had they any clew as to the direction in which they should go. There was no ray of light or hope to cheer them on their way, yet Stanley never for a moment thought of giving up the search.

Once, amid the terrors of the jungle, surrounded by savages and wild animals, with supplies almost exhausted, and the remnant of his followers in a despairing condition, the young explorer came near being discouraged.

But he would not give way to any feeling that might lessen his chances of success, and it was at this crisis he wrote in his journal:

"No living man shall stop me—only death can prevent me. But death—not even this; I shall not die—I will not die—I cannot die! Something tells me I shall find him and—write it larger— **Find Him, Find Him!** Even the words are inspiring."

Soon after this a caravan passed and gave the expedition news which renewed hope: A white man, old, white haired, and sick, had just arrived at Ujiji.

Stanley and his followers pushed on until they came in sight of Ujiji. Then the order was given to "unfurl the flags and load the guns." Immediately the Stars and Stripes and the flag of Zanzibar were thrown to the breeze, and the report of fifty guns awakened the echoes. The noise startled the inhabitants of Ujiji. They came running in the direction of the sounds, and soon the expedition was surrounded by a crowd of friendly black men, who cried loudly, "*Yambo, Yambo, Bana!*" which signifies welcome.

"At this grand moment," says Stanley, "we do not think of the hundreds of miles we have marched, of the hundreds of hills that we have ascended and descended, of the many forests we have traversed, of the jungle and thickets that annoyed us, of the fervid salt plains that blistered our feet, of the hot suns that scorched us, nor the dangers and difficulties now happily surmounted.

"At last the sublime hour has arrived!—our dreams, our hopes and anticipations are now about to be realized! Our hearts and our feelings are with our eyes, as we peer into the palms and try to make out in which hut or house lives the white man with the gray beard we heard about on the Malagarazi."

When the uproar had ceased, a voice was heard saluting the leader of the expedition in English—"Good morning, sir."

"Startled at hearing this greeting in the midst of such a crowd of black people," says Stanley, "I turn sharply round in search of the man, and see him at my side, with the blackest of faces, but animated and joyous—a man dressed in a long white shirt, with a turban of American sheeting around his head, and I ask, 'Who the mischief are you?'

"'I am Susi, the servant of Dr. Livingstone,' said he, smiling, and showing a gleaming row of teeth.

"'What! Is Dr. Livingstone here?'

"'Yes, sir.'

"'In this village?'

"'Yes, sir.'

"'Are you sure?'

"'Sure, sure, sir. Why, I leave him just now.'

"'Susi, run, and tell the Doctor I am coming.'"

Susi ran like a madman to deliver the message. Stanley and his men followed more slowly. Soon they were gazing into the eyes of the man for news of whom the whole civilized world was waiting.

"My heart beat fast," says Stanley, "but I must not let my face betray my emotions, lest it shall detract from the dignity of a white man appearing under such extraordinary circumstances."

The young explorer longed to leap and shout for joy, but he controlled himself, and instead of embracing Livingstone as he would have liked to do, he grasped his hand, exclaiming, "I thank God, Doctor, that I have been permitted to see you."

"I feel grateful that I am here to welcome you," was the gentle reply.

All the dangers through which they had passed, all the privations they had endured were forgotten in the joy of this meeting. Doctor Livingstone's years of toil and suspense, during which he had heard nothing from the outside world; Stanley's awful experiences in the jungle, the fact that both men had almost exhausted their supplies; the terrors of open and hidden dangers from men and beasts, sickness, hope deferred, all were, for the moment, pushed out of mind. Later, each recounted his story to the other.

After a period of rest, the two joined forces and together explored and made plans for the future. Stanley tried to induce Livingstone to return with him. But in vain; the great missionary explorer would not lay down his work. He persevered, literally until death.

At last the hour of parting came. With the greatest reluctance Stanley gave his men the order, "Right about face." With a silent farewell, a grasp of the hands, and a look into each other's eyes which said more than words, the old man and the young man parted forever.

Livingstone's life work was almost done. Stanley was the man on whose shoulders his mantle was to fall. The great work he had accomplished in finding Livingstone was the beginning of his career as an African explorer.

After the death of Livingstone, Stanley determined to take up the explorer's unfinished work.

In 1874 he left England at the head of an expedition fitted out by the London Daily Telegraph and the New York Herald, and penetrated into the very heart of Africa.

He crossed the continent from shore to shore, overcoming on his march dangers and difficulties compared with which those encountered on his first journey sank into insignificance. He afterward gave an account of this expedition in his book entitled, "Darkest Africa."

Stanley had successfully accomplished one of the great works of the world. He had opened the way for commerce and Christianity into the vast interior of Africa, which, prior to his discoveries, had been marked on the map by a blank space, signifying that it was an unexplored and unknown country.

On his return the successful explorer found himself famous. Princes and scientific societies vied with one another in honoring him. King Edward VII of England, who was then Prince of Wales, sent him his personal congratulations; Humbert, the king of Italy, sent him his portrait; the khedive of Egypt decorated him with the grand commandership of the Order of the Medjidie; the Geographical Societies of London, Paris, Italy, and Marseilles sent him their gold medals; while in Berlin, Vienna, and many other large European cities, he was elected an honorary member of their most learned and most distinguished associations.

What pleased the explorer most of all, though, was the honor paid him by America. "The government of the United States," he says, "has crowned my success with its official approval, and the unanimous vote of thanks passed in both houses of the legislature has made me proud for life of the expedition and its achievements."

Honored to-day as the greatest explorer of his age, and esteemed alike for his scholarship and the immense services he has rendered mankind, Sir Henry Morton Stanley, the once friendless orphan lad whose only home was a Welsh poorhouse, may well be proud of the career he has carved out for himself.

The Nestor of American Journalists

"I heard that a neighbor three miles off, had borrowed from a still more distant neighbor, a book of great interest. I started off, barefoot, in the snow, to obtain the treasure. There were spots of bare ground, upon which I would stop to warm my feet. And there were also, along the road, occasional lengths of log fence from which the snow had melted, and upon which it was a luxury to walk. The book was at home, and the good people consented, upon my promise that it should be neither torn nor soiled, to lend it to me. In returning with the prize, I was too happy to think of the snow on my naked feet."

This little incident, related by Thurlow Weed himself, is a sample of the means by which he gained that knowledge and power which made him not only the "Nestor of American Journalists," but rendered him famous in national affairs as the "American Warwick" or "The King Maker."

There were no long happy years of schooling for this child of the "common people," whose father was a struggling teamster and farmer; no prelude of careless, laughing childhood before the stern duties of life began.

Thurlow Weed was born at Catskill, Greene County, New York, in 1797, a period in the history of our republic when there were very few educational opportunities for the children of the poor. "I cannot ascertain," he says, "how much schooling I got at Catskill, probably less than a year, certainly not a year and a half, and this was when I was not more than five or six years old."

At an early age Thurlow learned to bend circumstances to his will and, ground by poverty, shut in by limitations as he was, even while contributing by his earning to the slender resources of the family, he gathered knowledge and pleasure where many would have found but thorns and bitterness.

How simply he tells his story, as though his hardships and struggles were of no account, and how clearly the narrative mirrors the brave little fellow of ten!

"My first employment," he says, "was in sugar making, an occupation to which I became much attached. I now look with great pleasure upon the days and nights passed in the sap-bush. The want of shoes (which, as the snow was deep, was no small privation) was the only drawback upon my happiness. I used, however, to tie pieces of an old rag carpet around my feet, and got along pretty well, chopping wood and gathering up sap."

During this period he traveled, barefoot, to borrow books, wherever they could be found among the neighboring farmers. With his body in the sugar house, and his head thrust out of doors, "where the fat pine was blazing," the young enthusiast devoured with breathless interest a

"History of the French Revolution," and the few other well-worn volumes which had been loaned him.

Later, after he left the farm, we see the future journalist working successively as cabin boy and deck hand on a Hudson River steamboat, and cheerfully sending home the few dollars he earned. While employed in this capacity, he earned his first "quarter" in New York by carrying a trunk for one of the passengers from the boat to a hotel on Broad Street.

But his boyish ambition was to be a journalist, and, after a year of seafaring life, he found his niche in the office of a small weekly newspaper, the Lynx, published at Onondaga Hollow, New York.

So, at fourteen, owing to his indomitable will and perseverance, which conquered the most formidable obstacles, Thurlow Weed started on the career in which, despite the rugged road he still had to travel, he built up a noble character and won international fame.

The Man with an Idea

It is February, 1492. A poor man, with gray hair, disheartened and dejected, is going out of the gate from the beautiful Alhambra, in Granada, on a mule. Ever since he was a boy, he has been haunted with the idea that the earth is round. He has believed that the pieces of carved wood, picked up four hundred miles at sea, and the bodies of two men, unlike any other human beings known, found on the shores of Portugal, have drifted from unknown lands in the west. But his last hope of obtaining aid for a voyage of discovery has failed. King John of Portugal, under pretense of helping him, has secretly sent out an expedition of his own. His friends have abandoned him; he has begged bread; has drawn maps to keep him from starving, and lost his wife; his friends have called him crazy, and have forsaken him. The council of wise men, called by Ferdinand and Isabella, ridicule his theory of reaching the east by sailing west. "But the sun and moon are round," replies Columbus, "why not the earth?" "If the earth is a ball, what holds it up?" the wise men ask. "What holds the sun and moon up?" Columbus replies.

A learned doctor asks, "How can men walk with their heads hanging down, and their feet up, like flies on a ceiling?" "How can trees grow with their roots in the air?" "The water would run out of the ponds, and we should fall off," says another. "The doctrine is contrary to the Bible, which says, 'The heavens are stretched out like a tent.'" "Of course it is flat; it is rank heresy to say it is round."

He has waited seven long years. He has had his last interview, hoping to get assistance from Ferdinand and Isabella after they drive the Moors out of Spain. Isabella was almost persuaded, but finally refused. He is now old, his last hope has fled; the ambition of his life has failed. He hears a voice calling him. He looks back and sees an old friend pursuing him on a horse, and beckoning him to come back. He saw Columbus turn away from the Alhambra, disheartened, and he hastens to the queen and tells her what a great thing it would be, at a trifling expense, if what the sailor believes should prove true. "It shall be done," Isabella replies. "I will pledge my jewels to raise the money; call him back." Columbus turns back, and with him turns the world.

Three frail vessels, little larger than fishing boats, the Santa Maria, the Pinta, and the Nina, set sail from Palos, August 3, 1492, for an unknown land, upon untried seas; the sailors would not volunteer, but were forced to go by the king. Friends ridiculed them for following a crazy man to certain destruction, for they believed the sea beyond the Canaries was boiling hot. "What if the earth is round?" they said, "and you sail down the other side, how can you get back again? Can ships sail up hill?"

Only three days out, the Pinto's signal of distress is flying; she has broken her rudder. September 8 they discover a broken mast covered with seaweed floating in the sea. Terror seizes the sailors, but Columbus calms their fears with pictures of gold and precious stones of India. September 13, two hundred miles west of the Canaries, Columbus is horrified to find that the compass, his only guide, is failing him, and no longer points to the north star. No one had yet dreamed that the earth turns on its axis. The sailors are ready for mutiny, but Columbus tells them the north star is not exactly in the north. October 1 they are two thousand three hundred miles from land, though Columbus tells the sailors one thousand seven hundred. Columbus discovers a bush in the sea, with berries on it, and soon they see birds and a piece of carved wood. At sunset, the crew kneel upon the deck and chant the vesper hymn. It is sixty-seven days since they left Palos, and they have sailed nearly three thousand miles, only changing their course once. At ten o'clock at night they see a light ahead, but it vanishes. Two o'clock in the morning, October 12, Roderigo de Friana, on watch at the masthead of the Pinta, shouts, "Land! land! land!" The sailors are wild with joy, and throw themselves on their knees before Columbus, and ask forgiveness. They reach the shore, and the hero of the world's greatest expedition unfolds the flag of Spain and takes possession of the new world. Perhaps no greater honor was ever paid man than Columbus received on his return to Ferdinand and Isabella. Yet, after his second visit to the land he discovered, he was taken back to Spain in chains, and finally died in poverty and neglect; while a pickle dealer of Seville, who had never risen above second mate, on a fishing vessel, Amerigo Vespucci, gave his name to the new world. Amerigo's name was put on an old chart or sketch to indicate the point of land where he landed, five years after Columbus discovered the country, and this crept into print by accident.

"Bernard of the Tuileries"

Opposite the entrance to the Sevres Museum in the old town of Sevres, in France, stands a handsome bronze statue of Bernard Palissy, the potter. Within the museum are some exquisite pieces of pottery known as "Palissy ware." They are specimens of the art of Palissy, who spent the best years of his life toiling to discover the mode of making white enamel.

The story of his trials and sufferings in seeking to learn the secret, and of his final triumph over all difficulties, is an inspiring one.

Born in the south of France, as far back as the year 1509, Bernard Palissy did not differ much from an intelligent, high-spirited American boy of the twentieth century. His parents were poor, and he had few of the advantages within the reach of the humblest child in the United States to-day. In spite of poverty, he as cheerful, light hearted, and happy in his great love for nature, which distinguished him all through life. The forest was his playground, his companions the birds, insects, and other living things that made their home there.

From the first, Nature was his chief teacher. It was from her, and her alone, he learned the lessons that in after years made him famous both as a potter and a scientist. The habit of observation seemed natural to him, for without suggestions from books or older heads, his eyes and ears noticed all that the nature student of our day is drilled into observing.

The free, outdoor life of the forest helped to give the boy the strength of mind and body which afterward enabled him, in spite of the most discouraging conditions, to pursue his ideal. He was taught how to read and write, and from his father learned how to paint on glass. From him he also learned the names and some of the properties of the minerals employed in painting glass. All the knowledge that in after years made him an artist, a scientist, and a writer, was the result of his unaided study of nature. To books he was indebted for only the smallest part of what he knew.

Happy and hopeful, sunshiny of face and disposition, Bernard grew from childhood to youth. Then, when he was about eighteen, there came into his heart a longing to try his fortune in the great world which lay beyond his forest home. Like most country-bred boys of his age, he felt that he had grown too large for the parent nest and must try his wings elsewhere. In his case there was, indeed, little to induce an ambitious boy to stay at home. The trade of glass painting, which in previous years had been a profitable one, had at that time fallen somewhat out of favor, and there was not enough work to keep father and son busy.

When he shouldered his scanty wallet and bade farewell to father and mother, and the few friends and neighbors he knew in the straggling forest hamlet, Bernard Palissy closed the first chapter of his life. The second was a long period of travel and self- education.

He wandered through the forest of Ardennes, making observations and collecting specimens of minerals, plants, reptiles, and insects. He spent some years in the upper Pyrenees, at Tarbes. From Antwerp in the east he bent his steps to Brest, in the most westerly part of Brittany, and from Montpellier to Nismes he traveled across France. During his wanderings he supported himself by painting on glass, portrait painting (which he practiced after a fashion), surveying, and planning sites for houses and gardens. In copying or inventing patterns for painted windows, he had acquired a knowledge of geometry and considerable skill in the use of a rule and compass. His love of knowledge for its own sake made him follow up the study of geometry, as far as he could pursue it, and hence his skill as a surveyor.

At this time young Palissy had no other object in life than to learn. His eager, inquiring mind was ever on the alert. Wherever his travels led him, he sought information of men and nature, always finding the latter his chief instructor. He painted and planned that he might live to probe her secrets. But the time was fast approaching when a new interest should come into his life and overshadow all others.

After ten or twelve years of travel, he married and settled in Saintes where he pursued, as his services were required, the work of glass painter and surveyor. Before long he grew dissatisfied with the dull routine of his daily life. He felt that he ought to do more than make a living for his wife and children. There were two babies now to be cared for as well as his wife, and he could not shoulder his wallet, as in the careless days of his boyhood, and wander away in search of knowledge or fortune.

About this time an event happened which changed his whole life. He was shown a beautiful cup of Italian manufacture. I give in his own words a description of the cup, and the effect the sight of it had on him. "An earthen cup," he says, "turned and enameled with so much beauty, that from that time I entered into controversy with my own thoughts, recalling to mind several suggestions that some people had made to me in fun, when I was painting portraits. Then, seeing that these were falling out of request in the country where I dwelt, and that glass painting was also little patronized, I began to think that if I should discover how to make enamels, I could make earthen vessels and other things very prettily, because God has gifted me with some knowledge of drawing."

His ambition was fired at once. A definite purpose formed itself in his mind. He knew nothing whatever of pottery. No man in France knew the secret of enameling, which made the Italian cup so beautiful, and Palissy had not the means to go to Italy, where he probably could have learned it. He resolved to study the nature and properties of clays, and not to rest until he had discovered the secret of the white enamel. Delightful visions filled his imagination. He thought within himself that he would become the prince of potters, and would provide his wife and children with all the luxuries that money could buy. "Thereafter," he wrote, "regardless of the fact that I had no knowledge of clays, I began to seek for the enamels as a man gropes in the dark."

Palissy was a young man when he began his search for the enamel; he was past middle life when his labors were finally rewarded. Groping like a man in the dark, as he himself said, he experimented for years with clays and chemicals, but with small success. He built with his own hands a furnace at the back of his little cottage in which to carry on his experiments. At first his enthusiasm inspired his wife and neighbors with the belief that he would succeed in his efforts. But time went on, and as one experiment after another failed or was only partially successful, one and all lost faith in him. He had no friend or helper to buoy him up under his many disappointments. Even his wife reproached him for neglecting his regular work and reducing herself and her children to poverty and want, while he wasted his time and strength in chasing a dream. His neighbors jeered at him as a madman, one who put his plain duty aside for the gratification of what seemed to their dull minds merely a whim. His poor wife could hardly be blamed for reproaching him. She could neither understand nor sympathize with his hopes and fears, while she knew that if he followed his trade, he could at least save his family from want. It was a trying time for both of them. But who ever heard tell of an artist, inventor, discoverer, or genius of any kind being deterred by poverty, abuse, ridicule, or obstacles of any kind from the pursuit of an ideal!

After many painful efforts, the poor glass painter had succeeded in producing a substance which he believed to be white enamel. He spread it on a number of earthenware pots which he had made, and placed them in his furnace. The extremities to which he was reduced to supply heat to the furnace are set forth in his own words: "Having," he says, "covered the new pieces with the said enamel, I put them into the furnace, still keeping the fire at its height; but thereupon occurred to me a new misfortune which caused great mortification, namely, that the wood having failed me, I was forced to burn the palings which maintained the boundaries of my garden; which being burnt also, I was forced to burn the tables and the flooring of my house, to cause the melting of the second composition. I suffered an anguish that I cannot speak, for I was quite exhausted and dried up by the heat of the furnace. Further, to console me, I was the object of mockery; and even those from whom solace was due ran crying through the town that I was burning my floors, and in this way my credit was taken from me, and I was regarded as a madman.

"Others said that I was laboring to make false money, which was a scandal under which I pined away, and slipped with bowed head through the streets like a man put to shame. No one gave me consolation, but, on the contrary, men jested at me, saying, 'It was right for him to die of hunger, seeing that he had left off following his trade!' All these things assailed my ears when I passed through the street; but for all that, there still remained some hope which encouraged and sustained me, inasmuch as the last trials had turned out tolerably well; and thereafter I thought that I knew enough to get my own living, although I was far enough from that (as you shall hear afterward)."

This latest experiment filled him with joy, for he had at last discovered the secret of the enamel. But there was yet much to be learned, and several years more of extreme poverty and suffering had to be endured before his labors were rewarded with complete success. But it came at last in overflowing measure, as it almost invariably does to those who are willing to work and suffer privation and persevere to the end.

His work as a potter brought Palissy fame and riches. At the invitation of Catherine de' Medici, wife of King Henry II of France, he removed to Paris. He established a workshop in the vicinity of the royal Palace of the Tuileries, and was thereafter known as "Bernard of the Tuileries." He was employed by the king and queen and some of the greatest nobles of France to embellish their palaces and gardens with the products of his beautiful art.

Notwithstanding his lack of schooling, Bernard Palissy was one of the most learned men of his day. He founded a Museum of Natural History, wrote valuable books on natural science, and for several years delivered lectures on the same subject. His lectures were attended by the most advanced scholars of Paris, who were astonished at the extent and accuracy of his knowledge of nature. But he was as modest as he was wise and good, and when people wondered at his learning, he would reply with the most unaffected simplicity, "I have had no other book than the sky and the earth, known to all."

No more touching story of success, in spite of great difficulties, than Bernard Palissy's has been written. It is bad to think that after the terrible trials which he endured for the sake of his art, his last years also should have been clouded by misfortune. During the civil war which raged in France between the Huguenots and the Catholics, he was, on account of his religious views, imprisoned in the Bastile, where he died in 1589, at the age of eighty.

How the "Learned Blacksmith" Found Time

"The loss of an hour," says the philosopher, Leibnitz, "is the loss of a part of life." This is a truth that has been appreciated by most men who have risen to distinction,—who have been world benefactors. The lives of those great moral heroes put to shame the laggard youth of to-day, who so often grumbles: "I have no time. If I didn't have to work all day, I could accomplish something. I could read and educate myself. But if a fellow has to grub away ten or twelve hours out of the twenty-four, what time is left to do anything for one's self?"

How much spare time had Elihu Burritt, "the youngest of many brethren," as he himself quaintly puts it, born in a humble home in New Britain, Connecticut, reared amid toil and poverty? Yet, during his father's long illness, and after his death, when Elihu was but a lad in his teens, with the family partially dependent upon the work of his hands, he found time,—if only a few moments,—at the end of a fourteen-hour day of labor, for his books.

While working at his trade as a blacksmith, he solved problems in arithmetic and algebra while his irons were heating. Over the forge also appeared a Latin grammar and a Greek lexicon; and, while with sturdy blows the ambitious youth of sixteen shaped the iron on the anvil, he fixed in his mind conjugations and declensions.

How did this man, born nearly a century ago, possessing none of the advantages within reach of the poorest and humblest boy of to- day, become one of the brightest ornaments in the world of letters, a leader in the reform movements of his generation?

Apparently no more talented than his nine brothers and sisters, by improving every opportunity he could wring from a youth of unremitting toil, his love for knowledge grew with what it fed upon, and carried him to undreamed-of heights. In palaces and council halls, the words of the "Learned Blacksmith" were listened to with the closest attention and deference.

Read the life of Elihu Burritt, and you will be ashamed to grumble that you have no time—no chance for self-improvement.

The Legend of William Tell

"Ye crags and peaks, I'm with you once again! I hold to you the hands you first beheld, to show they still are free. Methinks I hear a spirit in your echoes answer me, and bid your tenant welcome to his home again! O sacred forms, how proud you look! how high you lift your heads into the sky! how huge you are, how mighty, and how free! Ye are the things that tower, that shine; whose smile makes glad—whose frown is terrible; whose forms, robed or unrobed, do all the impress wear of awe divine. Ye guards of liberty, I'm with you once again! I call to you with all my voice! I hold my hands to you to show they still are free. I rush to you as though I could embrace you!"

What schoolboy or schoolgirl is not familiar with those stirring lines from "William Tell's Address to His Native Mountains," by J. M. Knowles? And the story of William Tell,—is it not dear to every heart that loves liberty? Though modern history declares it to be purely mythical, its popularity remains unaffected. It will live forever in the traditions of Switzerland, dear to the hearts of her people as their native mountains, and even more full of interest to the stranger than authentic history.

"His image [Tell's]," says Lamartine, "with those of his wife and children, are inseparably connected with the majestic, rural, and smiling landscapes of Helvetia, the modern Arcadia of Europe. As often as the traveler visits these peculiar regions; as often as the unconquered summits of Mont Blanc, St. Gothard, and the Rigi, present themselves to his eyes in the vast firmament as the ever- enduring symbols of liberty; whenever the lake of the Four Cantons presents a vessel wavering on the blue surface of its waters; whenever the cascade bursts in thunder from the heights of the Splugen, and shivers itself upon the rocks like tyranny against free hearts; whenever the ruins of an Austrian fortress darken with the remains of frowning walls the round eminences of Uri or Claris; and whenever a calm sunbeam gilds on the declivity of a village the green velvet of the meadows where the herds are feeding to the tinkling of bells and the echo of the Ranz des Vaches—so often the imagination traces in all these varied scenes the hat on the summit of the pole—the archer condemned to aim at the apple placed on the head of his own child—the mark hurled to the ground, transfixed by the unerring arrow—the father chained to the bottom of the boat, subduing night, the storm, and his own indignation, to save his executioner—and finally, the outraged husband, threatened with the loss of all he holds most dear, yielding to the impulse of nature, and in his turn striking the murderer with a deathblow."

The story which tradition hands down as the origin of the freedom of Switzerland dates back to the beginning of the fourteenth century. At that time Switzerland was under the sovereignty of the emperor of Germany, who ruled over Central Europe. Count Rudolph of Hapsburg, a Swiss by birth, who had been elected to the imperial throne in 1273, made some efforts to save his countrymen from the oppression of a foreign yoke. His son, Albert, Archduke of Austria, who succeeded him in 1298, inherited none of his sympathies for Switzerland. On his accession to the throne Albert resolved to curtail the liberties still enjoyed by the inhabitants of some of the cantons, and to bend the whole of the Swiss people to his will.

The mountaineers of the cantons of Schwytz, Uri, and Unterwalden recognized no authority but that of the emperor; while the peasants of the neighboring valleys were at the mercy of local tyrants—the great nobles and their allies.

In order to carry out his project of subjecting all to the same yoke, Albert of Austria appointed governors to rule over the semi- free provinces or cantons. These governors, who bore the official title of Bailiffs of the Emperor, exercised absolute authority over the people. Men, women, and children were at their mercy, and were treated as mere chattels—the property of their rulers. Insult and outrage were heaped upon them until their lives became almost unendurable.

An instance of the manner in which these petty tyrants used their authority is related of the bailiff Landenberg, who ruled over Unterwalden.

For some trumped-up offense of which a young peasant, named Arnold of Melcthal, was accused, his oxen were confiscated by Landenberg. The deputy sent to seize the animals, which Landenberg really coveted for his own, said sneeringly to Arnold, "If peasants wish for bread, they must draw the plow themselves." Roused to fury by this taunt, Arnold attempted to resist the seizure of his property, and in so doing broke an arm of one of the deputy's men. He then fled to the mountains; but he could not hide himself from the vengeance of Landenberg. The peasant's aged father was arrested by order of the bailiff, and his eyes put out in punishment for his son's offense. "That puncture," says an old chronicler, "went so deep into many a heart that numbers resolved to die rather than leave it unrequited."

But the crudest and most vindictive of the Austrian or German bailiffs, as they were interchangeably called, was one Hermann Gessler. He had built himself a fortress, which he called "Uri's Restraint," and there he felt secure from all attacks.

This man was the terror of the whole district. His name was a synonym for all that was base, brutal, and tyrannical. Neither the property, the lives, nor the honor of the people were respected by him. His hatred and contempt for the peasants were so great that the least semblance of prosperity among them aroused his ire.

One day while riding with an armed escort through the canton of Schwytz, he noticed a comfortable-looking dwelling which was being built by one Werner Stauffacher. Turning to his followers, he cried, "Is it not shameful that miserable serfs like these should be permitted to build such houses when huts would be too good for them?" "Let this be finished," said his chief attendant; "we shall then sculpture over the gate the arms of the emperor, and a little time will show whether the builder has the audacity to dispute possession with us." The answer pleased Gessler, who replied, "Thou art right," and, planning future vengeance, he passed on with his escort.

The wife of Stauffacher, who had been standing near the new building, but concealed from Gessler and his men, heard the conversation, and reported it to her husband. The latter, filled with indignation, without uttering a word, arose and started for the home of his father-in-law, Walter Furst, in the village of Attinghaussen.

On his arrival Staffaucher was cordially welcomed by his father-in-law, who placed refreshments before him, and waited for him to explain the object of his visit. Pushing aside the food, he said, "I have made a vow never again to taste wine or swallow meat until we cease to be slaves." Stauffacher then related what had happened. Furst's anger was kindled by the recital. Both men were roused to such a pitch that they resolved, then and there, to free themselves and their countrymen from the chains which bound them, or die in the attempt. They conversed far into the night, making plans for the gaining of national independence. Then they sought out in his hiding-place Arnold of Melchthal, the young peasant whom Landenberg had so cruelly persecuted. In him they found, as they expected, an ardent supporter of their plans.

The three conspirators, Stauffacher, Furst, and Melchthal, represented different cantons; one belonging to Schwytz, another to Uri, and the third to Unterwalden. They hoped to form a league and unite the three cantons against the power of Austria. In pursuance of their plans, each pledged himself to select from among the most persecuted and the most daring in their respective cantons ten others to join them in the cause of liberty.

On the night of November 7, or 17 (the date is variously given), in the year 1307, the confederates met together in a secluded mountain spot called Rutli. There they bound themselves by an oath, the terms of which embodied their purpose: "We swear in the presence of God, before whom kings and people are equal, to live or die for our fellow-countrymen; to undertake and sustain all in common; neither to suffer injustice nor to commit injury; to respect the rights and property of the Count of Hapsburg; to do no violence to the imperial bailiffs, but to put an end to their tyranny." They fixed upon January 1, 1308, as the day for a general uprising.

Events were gradually shaping themselves for the appearance of William Tell on the scene. Up to this time his name does not appear in the annals of his country. The bold peasant of Uri was so little prominent among his countrymen that, according to some versions of the legend, although a son-in-law of Walter Furst, he had not been chosen among the thirty conspirators summoned to the meeting at Rutli. This, however, is contradicted by another, which asserts that he was "one of the oath-bound men of Rutli."

The various divergences in the different versions of the legend do not affect its main features, on which all the chroniclers are agreed. It was the crowning insult to his country which indisputably brought Tell into prominence and made his name forever famous.

Gessler's hatred of the people daily increased, and was constantly showing itself in every form of petty tyranny that a mean and wicked nature could devise. He noticed the growing discontent among the peasantry, but instead of trying to allay it, he determined to humiliate them still more. For this purpose he had a pole, surmounted by the ducal cap of Austria, erected in the market square of the village of Altdorf, and issued a command that all who passed it should bow before the symbol of imperial rule. Guards were placed by the pole with orders to make prisoners of all who refused to pay homage to the ducal cap.

William Tell, a bold hunter and skillful boatman of Uri, passing by one day, with his little son, Walter, refused to bend his knee before the symbol of foreign oppression. He was seized at once by the guards and carried before the bailiff.

There is considerable contradiction at this point as to whether Tell was at once carried before the bailiff or bound to the pole, where he remained, guarded by the soldiers, until the bailiff, returning the same day from a hunting expedition, appeared upon the scene. Schiller, in his drama of "William Tell," adopts the latter version of the story.

According to the drama, Tell is represented as being bound to the pole. In a short time he is surrounded by friends and neighbors. Among them are his father-in-law, Walter Furst, Werner Stauffacher, and Arnold of Melchthal. They advance to rescue the prisoner. The guards cry in a loud voice: "Revolt! Rebellion! Treason! Sedition! Help! Protect the agents of the law!"

Gessler and his party hear the cries, and rush to the support of the guards. Gessler cries in a loud authoritative voice: "Wherefore is this assembly of people? Who called for help? What does all this mean? I demand to know the cause of this!"

Then, addressing himself particularly to one of the guards and pointing to Tell, he says: "Stand forward! Who art thou, and why dost thou hold that man a prisoner?"

"Most mighty lord," replies the guard, "I am one of your soldiers placed here as a sentinel over that hat. I seized this man in the act of disobedience, for refusing to salute it. I was about to carry him to prison in compliance with your orders, and the populace were preparing to rescue him by force."

After questioning Tell, whose answers are not satisfactory, the bailiff pronounces sentence upon him. The sentence is that he shall shoot at an apple placed on the head of his little son, Walter, and if he fails to hit the mark he shall die.

"My lord," cries the agonized parent; "what horrible command is this you lay upon me? What! aim at a mark placed on the head of my dear child? No, no, it is impossible that such a thought could enter your imagination. In the name of the God of mercy, you cannot seriously impose that trial on a father."

"Thou shalt aim at an apple placed on the head of thy son. I will and I command it," repeats the tyrant.

"I! William Tell! aim with my own crossbow at the head of my own offspring! I would rather die a thousand deaths."

"Thou shall shoot, or assuredly thou diest with thy son!"

"Become the murderer of my child! My lord, you have no son—you cannot have the feelings of a father's heart!"

Gessler's friends interfere in behalf of the unhappy father, and plead for mercy. But all appeal is in vain. The tyrant is determined on carrying out his sentence.

The father and son are placed at a distance of eighty paces apart. An apple is placed on the boy's head, and the father is commanded to hit the mark. He hesitates and trembles.

"Why dost thou hesitate?" questions his persecutor. "Thou hast deserved death, and I could compel thee to undergo the punishment; but in my clemency I place thy fate in thy own skillful hands. He who is the master of his destiny cannot complain that his sentence is a severe one. Thou art proud of thy steady eye and unerring aim; now, hunter, is the moment to prove thy skill. The object is worthy of thee—the prize is worth contending for. To strike the center of a target is an ordinary achievement; but the true master of his art is he who is always certain, and whose heart, hand, and eye are firm and steady under every trial."

At length Tell nerves himself for the ordeal, raises his bow, and takes aim at the target on his son's head. Before firing, however, he concealed a second arrow under his vest. His movement did not escape Gessler's notice.

The marksman fires. The apple falls from his boy's head, cleft in twain by the arrow.

Even Gessler is loud in his admiration of Tell's skill. "By heaven," he cries, "he has clove the apple exactly in the center. Let us do justice; it is indeed a masterpiece of skill."

Tell's friends congratulate him. He is about to set out for his home with the child who has been saved to him from the very jaws of death as it were. But Gessler stays him.

"Thou hast concealed a second arrow in thy bosom," he says, sternly addressing Tell. "What didst thou intend to do with it?" Tell replies that such is the custom of all hunters.

Gessler is not satisfied and urges him to confess his real motive. "Speak truly and frankly," he says; "say what thou wilt, I promise thee thy life. To what purpose didst thou destine the second arrow?"

Tell can no longer restrain his indignation, and, fixing his eyes steadily on Gessler, he answers "Well then, my lord, since you assure my life, I will speak the truth without reserve. If I had struck my beloved child, with the second arrow I would have transpierced thy heart. Assuredly that time I should not have missed my mark."

"Villain!" exclaims Gessler, "I have promised thee life upon my knightly word; I will keep my pledge. But since I know thee now, and thy rebellious heart, I will remove thee to a place where thou shalt never more behold the light of sun or moon. Thus only shall I be sheltered from thy arrows."

He orders the guards to seize and bind Tell, saying, "I will myself at once conduct him to Kussnacht."

The fortress of Kussnacht was situated on the summit of Mount Rigi between Lake Lucerne, or the Lake of the Four Cantons as it is sometimes called, and Lake Zug. It was reached by crossing Lake Lucerne.

The prisoner was placed bound in the bottom of a boat, and with his guards, the rowers, an inexperienced pilot, and Gessler in command, the boat was headed for Kussnacht.

When about halfway across the lake a sudden and violent storm overwhelmed the party. They were in peril of their lives. The rowers and pilot were panic-stricken, and powerless in face of the danger that threatened them.

Tell's fame as a boatman was as widespread as that of his skill as an archer. The rowers cried aloud in their terror that he was the only man in Switzerland that could save them from death. Gessler immediately commanded him to be released from his bonds and given the helm.

Tell succeeded in guiding the vessel to the shore. Then seizing his bow and arrows, which his captors had thrown beside him, he sprang ashore at a point known as "Tell's Leap." The boat, rebounding, after he leaped from it was again driven out on the lake before any of the remainder of its occupants could effect a landing. After a time, however, the fury of the storm abated, and they reached the shore in safety.

In the meantime Tell had concealed himself in a defile in the mountain through which Gessler would have to pass on his way to Kussnacht. There he lay in wait for his persecutor who followed in hot pursuit.

Vowing vengeance as he went, Gessler declared that if the fugitive did not give himself up to justice, every day that passed by should cost him the life of his wife or one of his children. While the tyrant was yet speaking, an arrow shot by an unerring hand pierced his heart. Tell had taken vengeance into his own hands.

The death of Gessler was the signal for a general uprising. The oath-bound men of Rutli saw that this was their great opportunity. They called to their countrymen to follow them to freedom or death.

Gessler's crowning act of tyranny—his inhuman punishment of Tell—had roused the spirit of rebellion in the hearts of even the meekest and most submissive of the peasants. Gladly, then, did they respond to the call of the leaders of the insurrection.

The legend says that on New Year's Eve, 1308, Stauffacher, with a chosen band of followers, climbed the mountain which led to Landenberg's fortress castle of Rotzberg. There they were assisted by an inmate of the castle, a young girl whose lover was among the rebels. She threw a rope out of one of the windows of the castle, and by it her countrymen climbed one after another into the castle. They seized the bailiff, Landenberg, and confined him in one of the dungeons of his own castle. Next day the conspirators were reinforced by another party who gained entrance to the castle by means of a clever ruse. Landenberg and his men were given their freedom by the peasants on condition that they would quit Switzerland forever.

The castle of Uri was attacked and taken possession of by Walter Furst and William Tell, while other strongholds were captured by Arnold of Melchthal and his associates.

Bonfires blazed all over the country. The dawn of Switzerland's freedom had appeared. The reign of tyranny was doomed. William Tell was the hero of the hour, and ever since his name has been enshrined in the hearts of his countrymen as the watchword of their liberties. Even to this day, as history tells us, the Swiss peasant cherishes the belief that "Tell and the three men of Rutli are asleep in the mountains, but will awake to the rescue of their land should tyranny ever again enchain it."

Lamartine, to whose story of William Tell the writer is indebted, commenting on the legend says: "The artlessness of this history resembles a poem; it is a pastoral song in which a single drop of blood is mingled with the dew upon a leaf or a tuft of grass. Providence seems thus to delight in providing for every free community, as the founder of their independence, a fabulous or actual hero, conformable to the local situation, manners, and character of each particular race. To a rustic, pastoral people, like the Swiss, is given for their liberator a noble peasant; to a proud, aspiring race, such as the Americans, an honest soldier. Two distinct symbols, standing erect by the cradles of the two modern liberties of the world to personify their opposite natures: on the one hand Tell, with his arrow and the apple; on the other, Washington, with his sword and the law."

"Westward Ho!"

When the current serves, the unseen monitor that directs our affairs bids us step aboard our craft, and, with hand firmly grasping the helm, steer boldly for the distant goal.

Philip D. Armour, the open-handed, large-hearted merchant prince, who has left a standing memorial to his benevolence in the Armour Institute at Chicago, heard the call to put to sea when in his teens.

It came during the gold fever, which raged with such intensity from 1849 to 1851, when the wildest stories were afloat of the treasures that were daily being dug out of the earth in California. The brain of the sturdy youth, whose Scotch and Puritan blood tingled for some broader field than the village store and his father's farm in Stockbridge, New York, was haunted by the tales of adventure and fortune wafted across the continent from the new El Dorado. "I brooded over the difference," he says, "between tossing hay in the hot sun and digging gold by handfuls, until, one day, I threw down the pitchfork, went to the house, and told mother that I had quit that kind of work."

Armour was nineteen years old when he determined to seek his fortune in California. His determination once formed, he lost no time in carrying it out. As much of the journey across the plains was to be made on foot, he first provided himself with a pair of stout boots. Then he packed his extra clothing in an old carpetbag, and with a light heart bade his family good-by.

He had induced a young friend, Calvin Gilbert, to accompany him in his search for fortune. The two youths joined the motley crowd of adventurers who were flocking from all quarters to the Land of Promise, and set out on their journey.

Tramping over the plains, crossing rivers in tow-boats and ferryboats, and riding in trains and on wagons when they could, the adventurers, after many weary months, reached their destination. During the journey young Armour became sick, but was tenderly nursed back to health by his companion.

"I had scarcely any money when I arrived at the gold fields," said Armour, "but I struck right out and found a place where I could dig, and in a little time I struck pay dirt."

He entered into partnership with a Mr. Croarkin, and, with characteristic energy, kept digging and taking his turn at the rude housekeeping in the shanty which he and his partner shared. "Croarkin would cook one week," he says, "and I the next, and we would have a clean-up Sunday morning We baked our own bread, and kept a few hens, too, which supplied us with fresh eggs."

The young gold hunter, however, did not find nuggets as "plentiful as blackberries," but he found within himself that which led him to a bonanza far exceeding his wildest dreams of "finds" in the gold fields.

He discovered his business ability; he learned how to economize, how to rely upon himself, even to the extent of baking his own bread.

Three Great American Songs and Their Authors

The Star-Spangled Banner

"Poetry and music," says Sir John Lubbock, "unite in song. From the earliest ages song has been the sweet companion of labor. The rude chant of the boatman floats upon the water, the shepherd sings upon the hill, the milkmaid in the dairy, the plowman in the field. Every trade, every occupation, every act and scene of life, has long had its own especial music. The bride went to her marriage, the laborer to his work, the old man to his last long rest, each with appropriate and immemorial music."

It is strange that Lubbock did not mention specifically the power of music in inspiring the soldier as he marches to the defense of his country, or in arousing the spirit of patriotism and kindling the love of country, whether in peace or war, in every bosom. "Let me make the songs of a country," Fletcher of Saltoun has well said, "and I care not who makes its laws."

Not to know the words and the air of the national anthem or chief patriotic songs of one's country is considered little less than a disgrace. To know something of their authors and the occasion which inspired them, or the conditions under which they were composed, gives additional interest to the songs themselves.

Francis Scott Key, author of "The Star-spangled Banner," one of the, if not the most, popular of our national songs, was born in Frederick County, Maryland, on August 1, 1779. He was the son of John Ross Key, an officer in the Revolutionary army.

Young Key's early education was carried on under the direction of his father. Later he became a student in St. John's College, from which institution he was graduated in his nineteenth year. Immediately after his graduation he began to study law under his uncle, Philip Barton Key, one of the ablest lawyers of his time. He was admitted to the bar in 1801, and commenced to practice in Fredericktown, Maryland, where he won the reputation of an eloquent advocate. After a few years' practice in Fredericktown, he removed to Washington, where he was appointed district attorney for the District of Columbia.

Young Key was as widely known and admired as a writer of hymns and ballads as he was as a lawyer of promise. But the production of the popular national anthem which crowned him with immortality has so overshadowed the rest of his life work that we remember him only as its author.

The occasion which inspired "The Star-spangled Banner" must always be memorable in the annals of our country. The war with the British had been about two years in progress, when, in August, 1814, a British fleet arrived in the Chesapeake, and an army under General Ross landed about forty miles from the city of Washington.

The army took possession of Washington, burnt the capitol, the President's residence, and other public buildings, and then sailed around by the sea to attack Baltimore. The fleet was to bombard Fort McHenry, while the land forces were to attack the city.

The commanding officers of the fleet and land army, Admiral Cockburn and General Ross, made their headquarters in Upper Marlboro, Maryland, at the house of Dr. William Beanes, whom they held as their prisoner.

Francis Scott Key, who was a warm friend of Dr. Beanes, went to President Madison in order to enlist his aid in securing the release of Beanes. The president furnished Key with a vessel, and instructed John L. Skinner, agent for the exchange of prisoners, to accompany him under a flag of truce to the British fleet.

The British commander agreed to release Dr. Beanes, but would not permit Key and his party to return then, lest they should carry back important information to the American side. He boastingly declared, however, that the defense could hold out only a few hours, and that Baltimore would then be in the hands of the British.

Skinner and Key were sent on board the Surprise, which was under the command of Admiral Cockburn's son. But after a short time they were allowed to return to their own vessel, and from its deck they saw the American flag waving over Fort McHenry and witnessed the bombardment.

All through the night the furious attack of the British continued. The roar of cannon and the bursting of shells was incessant. It is said that as many as fifteen hundred shells were hurled at the fort.

Shortly before daybreak the firing ceased. Key and his companions waited in painful suspense to know the result. In the intense silence that followed the cannonading, each one asked himself if the flag of his country was still waving on high, or if it had been hauled down to give place to that of England. They strained their eyes in the direction of Baltimore, but the darkness revealed nothing.

At last day dawned, and to their delight the little party saw the American flag still floating over Fort McHenry. Key's heart was stirred to its depths, and in a glow of patriotic enthusiasm he immediately wrote down a rough draft of "The Star-spangled Banner."

On his arrival in Baltimore he perfected the first copy of the song, and gave it to Captain Benjamin Eades, of the 27th Baltimore Regiment, saying that he wished it to be sung to the air of "Anacreon in Heaven." Eades had it put in type, and took the first proof to a famous old tavern near the Holliday Street Theater, a favorite resort of actors and literary people of that day. The verses were read to the company assembled there, and Frederick Durang, an actor, was asked to sing them to the air designated by the author. Durang, mounting a chair, sang as requested. The song was enthusiastically received. From that moment it became the great popular favorite that it has ever since been, and that it will continue to be as long as the American republic exists.

Key died in Baltimore on January 11, 1843. A monument was erected to his memory by the munificence of James Lick, a Californian millionaire. The sculptor to whom the work was intrusted was the celebrated W. W. Story, who completed it in 1887. The monument, which is fifty-one feet high, stands in Golden Gate Park, San Francisco. It is built of travertine, in the form of a double arch, under which a bronze statue of Key is seated. A bronze figure, representing America with an unfolded flag, supports the arch.

On the occasion of the unveiling of this statue, the New York Home Journal contained an appreciative criticism of Key as a poet, and the following estimate of his greatest production.

"The poetry of the 'Star-spangled Banner' has touches of delicacy for which one looks in vain in most national odes, and is as near a true poem as any national ode ever was. The picture of the 'dawn's early light' and the tricolor, half concealed, half disclosed, amid the mists that wreathed the battle-sounding Patapsco, is a true poetic concept.

"The 'Star-spangled Banner' has the peculiar merit of not being a tocsin song, like the 'Marseillaise.' Indeed, there is not a restful, soothing, or even humane sentiment in all that stormy shout. It is the scream of oppressed humanity against its oppressor, presaging a more than quid pro quo; and it fitly prefigured the sight of that long file of tumbrils bearing to the Place de la Revolution the fairest scions of French aristocracy. On the other hand, 'God Save the King,' in its original, has one or two lines as grotesque as 'Yankee Doodle' itself; yet we have paraphrased it in 'America,' and made it a hymn meet for all our churches. But the 'Star-spangled Banner' combines dignity and beauty, and it would be hard to find a line of it that could be improved upon."

Over the simple grave of Francis Scott Key, in Frederick, Maryland, there is no other monument than the "star-spangled banner." In storm and in sunshine, in summer and in winter, its folds ever float over the resting place of the man who has immortalized it in verse. No other memorial could so fitly commemorate the life and death of this simple, dignified, patriotic American.

"A sweet, noble life," says a recent writer, "was that of the author of our favorite national hymn—a life of ideal refinement, piety, scholarly gentleness. Little did he think that his voice would be the storm song, the victor shout, of conquering America to resound down and down the ages!"

The Star-Spangled Banner

Oh! say, can you see, by the dawn's early light,
What so proudly we hailed at the twilight's last gleaming?
Whose broad stripes and bright stars through the perilous fight,
O'er the rampart we watched, were so gallantly streaming,
And the rocket's red glare, the bombs bursting in air,

Gave proof through the night that our flag was still there,
Oh! say, does that star-spangled banner yet wave
O'er the land of the free and the home of the brave?
On the shore, dimly seen through the mists of the deep,
Where the foe's haughty host in dread silence reposes,
What is that which the breeze, o'er the towering steep,
As it fitfully blows, half conceals, half discloses?
Now it catches the gleam of the morning's first beam,
In full glory reflected now shines on the stream,
'Tis the star-spangled banner' oh, long may it wave
O'er the land of the free and the home of the brave!

And where is that band, who so vauntingly swore
That the havoc of war and the battle's confusion
A home and a country should leave us no more?
Their blood has washed out their foul footsteps' pollution.
No refuge could save the hireling and slave,
From the terror of death and the gloom of the grave,
And the star spangled banner in triumph shall wave
O'er the land of the free and the home of the brave!
Oh! thus be it ever, when freemen shall stand
Between their loved homes and the war's desolation,
Blest with victory and peace, may the heaven rescued land
Praise the power that has made and preserved us a nation.
Then conquer we must, for our cause it is just,
And this be our motto, "In God is our trust"
And the star-spangled banner in triumph shall wave
O'er the land of the free and the home of the brave!

America

"And there's a nice youngster of excellent pith;
Fate tried to conceal him by naming him Smith!
But he shouted a song for the brave and the free—
Just read on his medal, 'My Country of Thee.'"

In these lines of his famous Reunion Poem, "The Boys," Dr. Oliver Wendell Holmes commemorated his old friend and college-mate, Dr. Samuel Francis Smith, author of "America."

Samuel Francis Smith was born in Boston, Massachusetts, on October 21, 1808. He attended the Latin School in his native city, and it is said that when only twelve years old he could "talk Latin." He entered Harvard College, Cambridge, Massachusetts, in 1825, and graduated in the famous class of 1829, of which Dr. Oliver Wendell Holmes, James Freeman Clarke, William E. Channing, and other celebrated Americans were members.

Dr. Smith, like so many other noted men, "worked his way through college." He did this principally by coaching other students, and by making translations from the German "Conversations-Lexicon" for the "American Cyclopedia."

After graduating from Harvard, he immediately entered Andover Theological Seminary. Three years later, in 1832, he wrote, among others, his most famous hymn, "America," of which the "National Cyclopedia of American Biography" says, "It has found its way wherever an American heart beats or the English language is spoken, and has probably proved useful in stirring the patriotic spirit of the American people."

Dr. Smith himself often said that he had heard "America" sung "halfway round the world, under the earth in the caverns of Manitou, Colorado, and almost above the earth near the top of Pike's Peak."

The hymn, as every child knows, is sung to the air of the national anthem of England,—"God Save the King." The author came upon it in a book of German music, and by it was inspired to write the words of "America," a work which he accomplished in half an hour. Many years after, referring to its impromptu composition, he wrote: "If I had anticipated the future of it, doubtless I should have taken more pains with it. Such as it is, I am glad to have contributed this mite to the cause of American freedom."

In a magazine article, written several years ago, Mr. Herbert Heywood gave an interesting account of an interview with Dr. Smith, who told him the story of the writing of the hymn himself.

"'I wrote "America,"' he said, 'when I was a theological student at Andover, during my last year there. In February, 1832, I was poring over a German book of patriotic songs which Lowell Mason, of Boston, had sent me to translate, when I came upon one with a tune of great majesty. I hummed it over, and was struck with the ease with which the accompanying German words fell into the music. I saw it was a patriotic song, and while I was thinking of translating it, I felt an impulse to write an American patriotic hymn. I reached my hand for a bit of waste paper, and, taking my quill pen, wrote the four verses in half an hour. I sent it with some translations of the German songs to Lowell Mason, and the next thing I knew of it I was told it had been sung by the Sunday-school children at Park Street Church, Boston, at the following Fourth of July celebration. The house where I was living at the time was on the Andover turnpike, a little north of the seminary building. I have been in the house since I left it in September, 1832, but never went into my old room.'" This room is now visited by patriotic Americans from every part of the country.

Two years after "America" was written, Dr. Smith became pastor of the First Baptist Church in Waterville, Maine, and also professor of modern languages in Waterville College, which is now known as Colby University. His great industry and zeal, both as a clergyman and student and teacher of languages, enabled him to perform the duties of both positions successfully. He was a noted linguist, and could read books in fifteen different languages. He could converse in most of the modern European tongues, and at eighty-six was engaged in studying Russian.

In 1842 Dr. Smith was made pastor of the First Baptist Church, Newton Center, Massachusetts, where he made his home for the rest of his life.

"When he died, in November, 1895," says Mr. Heywood, "he was living in the old brown frame-house at Newton Center, Massachusetts, which had been his home for over fifty years. It stood back from the street, on the brow of a hill sloping gently to a valley on the north. Pine trees were in the front and rear, and the sun, from his rising to his setting, smiled upon that abode of simple greatness. The house was faded and worn by wind and weather, and was in perfect harmony with its surroundings— the brown grass sod that peeped from under the snow, the dull-colored, leafless elms, and the gray, worn stone steps leading up from the street.

"An air of gentle refinement pervaded the interior, and every room spoke of its inmate. But perhaps the library was best loved of all by Dr. Smith, for here it was that his work went on. Here, beside a sunny bay window, stood his work table, and his high-backed, old-fashioned chair, with black, rounded arms. All about the room were ranged his bookcases, and an old, tall clock marked the flight of time that was so kind to the old man. His figure was short, his shoulders slightly bowed, and around his full, ruddy face, that beamed with kindness, was a fringe of white hair and beard."

Dr. Smith resigned his pastorate of the Newton church in 1854, and became editorial secretary of the American Baptist Missionary Union. In

1875 he went abroad for the first time, and spent a year in European travel. Five years later he went to India and the Burmese empire. During his travels he visited Christian missionary stations in France, Spain, Italy, Austria, Turkey, Greece, Sweden, Denmark, Burmah, India, and Ceylon.

The latter years of his life were devoted almost entirely to literary work. He wrote numerous poems which were published in magazines and newspapers, but never collected in book form. His hymns, numbering over one hundred, are sung by various Christian denominations. "The Morning Light is Breaking" is a popular favorite. Among his other published works are "Missionary Sketches," "Rambles in Mission Fields," a "History of Newton," and a "Life of Rev. Joseph Grafton." Besides his original hymns, he translated many from other languages, and wrote numerous magazine articles and sketches during his long and busy life.

Dr. Smith's vitality and enthusiasm remained with him to the last. A great-grandfather when he died in his eighty-seventh year, he was an inspiration to the younger generations growing up around him. He was at work almost to the moment of his death, and still actively planning for the future.

His great national hymn, if he had left nothing else, will keep his memory green forever in the hearts of his countrymen. It is even more popular to-day, after seventy-one years have elapsed, than it was when first sung in Park Street Church by the Sunday-school children of Boston. Its patriotic ring, rather than its literary merit, renders it sweet to the ear of every American. Wherever it is sung, the feeble treble of age will join as enthusiastically as the joyous note of youth in lendering the inspiring strains of

America

My country, 'tis of thee,
Sweet land of liberty,
Of thee I sing,
Land where my fathers died,
Land of the pilgrim's pride,
From every mountain side,
Let freedom ring.

My native country, thee,
Land of the noble, free,
Thy name I love;
I love thy rocks and rills,
Thy woods and templed hills,—
My heart with rapture thrills,
Like that above.

Let music swell the breeze,
And ring from all the trees
Sweet freedom's song;
Let mortal tongues awake,
Let all that breathe partake,
Let rocks their silence break,
The sound prolong.
Our fathers' God, to Thee,
Author of Liberty,
To Thee we sing;
Long may our land be bright
With freedom's holy light,—
Protect us by thy might,
Great God, our King.

The Battle Hymn of the Republic

"No single influence," says United States Senator George F. Hoar of Massachusetts, "has had so much to do with shaping the destiny of a nation—as nothing more surely expresses national character—than what is known as the national anthem."

There is some difference of opinion as to which of our patriotic hymns or songs is distinctively the national anthem of America. Senator Hoar seems to have made up his mind in favor of "The Battle Hymn of the Republic." Writing of its author, Julia Ward Howe, in 1903, he said: "We waited eighty years for our American national anthem. At last God inspired an illustrious and noble woman to utter in undying verse the thought which we hope is forever to animate the soldier of the republic:—

"'In the beauty of the lilies Christ was born across the sea With a glory in His bosom that transfigures you and me; As He died to make men holy, let us die to make men free, While God is marching on.'"

Mrs. Julia Ward Howe is as widely known for her learning and literary and poetic achievements as she is for her work as a philanthropist and reformer.

She was born in New York City, in a stately mansion near the Bowling Green, on May 27, 1819. From her birth she was fortunate in possessing the advantages that wealth and high social position bestow. Her father, Samuel Ward, the descendant of an old colonial family, was a member of a leading banking firm of New York. Her mother, Julia Cutter Ward, was a most charming and accomplished woman. She died very young, however, while her little daughter Julia was still a child. Mr. Ward was a man of advanced ideas, and was determined that his daughters should have, as far as possible, the same educational advantages as his sons.

Of course, in those early days there were no separate colleges for women, and they would not be admitted to men's colleges. It was impossible for Mr. Ward to overcome these difficulties wholly, but he did the next best thing he could for his girls. He engaged as their tutor the learned Dr. Joseph Green Cogswell, and instructed him to put them through the full curriculum of Harvard College.

On her entrance into society the "little Miss Ward," as Julia had been called from her childhood, at once became a leader of the cultured and fashionable circle in which she moved. In her father's home she met the most distinguished American men of letters of that time. The liberal education which she had received made the young girl feel perfectly at her ease in such society. In addition to other accomplishments, she was mistress of several ancient and modern languages, and a musical amateur of great promise.

In 1843 Miss Ward was married to Dr. Samuel G. Howe, director of the Institute for the Blind in South Boston, Massachusetts. Immediately after their marriage Dr. and Mrs. Howe went to Europe, where they traveled for some time. The home which they established in Boston on their return became a center for the refined and literary society of Boston and its environment. Mrs. Howe's grace, learning, and accomplishments made her a charming hostess and fit mistress of such a home.

Her literary talent was developed at a very early age. One of her friends has humorously said that "Mrs. Howe wrote leading articles from her cradle." However this may be, it is undoubtedly true that at seventeen she contributed valuable articles to a leading New York magazine. In 1854 she published her first volume of poems, "Passion Flowers." Other volumes, including collections of her later poems, books of travel, and a biography of Margaret Fuller, were afterward published. For more than half a century she has been a constant contributor to the leading magazines of the country.

Since 1869 Mrs. Howe has been a leader in the movement for woman's suffrage, and both by lecturing and writing has supported every effort put forth for the educational and general advancement of her sex.

Although in her eightieth year when the writer conversed with her a few years ago, Mrs. Howe was then full of youthful enthusiasm, and her interest in the great movements of the world was as keen as ever. Age had in no way lessened her intellectual vigor. Surrounded by her children and grandchildren, and one great- grandchild, she recently celebrated her eighty-fourth birthday.

The story of "The Battle Hymn of the Republic" has been left to the last, not because it is the least important, but, on the contrary, because it is one of the most important works of her life. Certain it is that the "Battle Hymn" will live and thrill the hearts of Americans centuries after its author has passed on to the other life.

The hymn was written in Washington, in November, 1861, the first year of our Civil War. Dr. and Mrs. Howe were visiting friends in that city. During their stay, they went one day with a party to see a review of Union troops. The review, however, was interrupted by a movement of the Confederate forces which were besieging the city. On their return, the carriage in which Mrs. Howe and her friends were seated was surrounded by soldiers. Stirred by the scene and the occasion, she began to sing "John Brown," to the delight of the soldiers, who heartily joined in the refrain.

At the close of the song Mrs. Howe expressed to her friends the strong desire she felt to write some words which might be sung to this stirring tune. But she added that she feared she would never be able to do so.

"That night," says her daughter, Maude Howe Eliot, "she went to sleep full of thoughts of battle, and awoke before dawn the next morning to find the desired verses immediately present to her mind. She sprang from her bed, and in the dim gray light found a pen and paper, whereon she wrote, scarcely seeing them, the lines of the poem. Returning to her couch, she was soon asleep, but not until she had said to herself, 'I like this better than anything I have ever written before.'"

The Battle Hymn of the Republic

Mine eyes have seen the glory of the coming of the Lord:
He is trampling out the vintage where the grapes of wrath are stored;
He hath loosed the fateful lightning of His terrible swift sword:
His truth is marching on.

I have seen Him in the watch fires of a hundred circling camps;
They have builded Him an altar in the evening dews and damps;
I can read His righteous sentence by the dim and flaring lamps;
His day is marching on.

I have read a fiery gospel, writ in burnished rows of steel:
"As ye deal with my contemners, so with you my grace shall deal;
Let the Hero born of woman crush the serpent with his heel,
Since God is marching on."

He has sounded forth the trumpet that shall never call retreat;
He is sifting out the hearts of men before His judgment seat:
Oh! be swift, my soul, to answer Him! be jubilant, my feet!
Our God is marching on.

In the beauty of the lilies Christ was born across the sea,
With a glory in His bosom that transfigures you and me:
As he died to make men holy, let us die to make men free,
While God is marching on.

Training for Greatness

Glimpses of Abraham Lincoln's Boyhood

In pronouncing a eulogy on Henry Clay, Lincoln said: "His example teaches us that one can scarcely be so poor but that, if he will, he can acquire sufficient education to get through the world respectably."

Endowed as he was with all the qualities that make a man truly great, Lincoln's own life teaches above all other things the lesson he drew from that of Henry Clay. Is there in all the length and breadth of the United States to-day a boy so poor as to envy Abraham Lincoln the chances of his boyhood? The story of his life has been told so often that nothing new can be said about him. Yet every fresh reading of the story fills the reader anew with wonder and admiration at what was accomplished by the poor backwoods boy.

Let your mind separate itself from all the marvels of the twentieth century. Think of a time when railroads and telegraph wires, telephones, great ocean steamers, lighting by gas and electricity, daily newspapers (except in a few centers), great circulating libraries, and the hundreds of conveniences which are necessities to the people of to-day, were unknown. Even the very rich at the beginning of the nineteenth century could not buy the advantages that are free to the poorest boy at the beginning of the twentieth century. When Lincoln was a boy, thorns were used for pins; cork covered with cloth or bits of bone served as buttons; crusts of rye bread were used by the poor as substitutes for coffee, and dried leaves of certain herbs for tea.

Abraham Lincoln was born on February 12, 1809, in a log cabin in Hardin County, now La Rue County, Kentucky. His father, Thomas Lincoln, was not remarkable either for thrift or industry. He was tall, well built, and muscular, expert with his rifle, and a noted hunter, but he did not possess the qualities necessary to make a successful pioneer farmer. The character of the mother of Abraham, may best be gathered from his own words: "All that I am or hope to be," he said when president of the United States, "I owe to my angel mother. Blessings on her memory!"

It was at her knee he learned his first lessons from the Bible. With his sister Sarah, a girl two years his senior, he listened with wonder and delight to the Bible stories, fairy tales, and legends with which the gentle mother entertained and instructed them when the labors of the day were done.

When Abraham was about four years old, the family moved from the farm on Nolin Creek to another about fifteen miles distant. There the first great event in his life took place. He went to school. Primitive as was the log-cabin schoolhouse, and elementary as were the acquirements of his first schoolmaster, it was a wonderful experience for the boy, and one that he never forgot.

In 1816 Thomas Lincoln again decided to make a change. He was enticed by stories that came to him from Indiana to try his fortunes there.

So, once more the little family "pulled up stakes" and moved on to the place selected by the father in Spencer County, about a mile and a half from Gentryville. It was a long, toilsome journey through the forest, from the old home in Kentucky to the new one in Indiana. In some places they had to clear their way through the tangled thickets as they journeyed along. The stock of provisions they carried with them was supplemented by game snared or shot in the forest and fish caught in the river. These they cooked over the wood fire, kindled by means of tinder and flint. The interlaced branches of trees and the sky made the roof of their bedchamber by night, and pine twigs their bed.

When the travelers arrived at their destination, there was no time for rest after their journey. Some sort of shelter had to be provided at once for their accommodation. They hastily put up a "half-faced camp"—a sort of rude tent, with an opening on one side. The framework of the tent was of upright posts, crossed by thin slabs, cut from the trees they felled. The open side, or entrance, was covered with "pelts," or half-dressed skins of wild animals. There was no ruder dwelling in the wilds of Indiana, and no poorer family among the settlers than the new adventurers from Kentucky. They were reduced to the most primitive makeshifts in order to eke out a living. There was no lack of food, however, for the woods were full of game of all kinds, both feathered and furred, and the streams and rivers abounded with fish. But the home lacked everything in the way of comfort or convenience.

Abraham, who was then in his eighth year, has been described as a tall, ungainly, fast-growing, long-legged lad, clad in the garb of the frontier. This consisted of a shirt of linsey-woolsey, a coarse homespun material made of linen and wool, a pair of home- made moccasins, deerskin leggings or breeches, and a hunting shirt of the same material. This costume was completed by a coonskin cap, the tail of the animal being left to hang down the wearer's back as an ornament.

This sturdy lad, who was born to a life of unremitting toil, was already doing a man's work. From the time he was four years old, away back on the Kentucky farm, he had contributed his share to the family labors. Picking berries, dropping seeds, and doing other simple tasks suited to his strength, he had thus early begun his apprenticeship to toil. In putting up the "half-faced" camp, he was his father's principal helper. Afterward, when they built a more, substantial cabin to take the place of the camp, he learned to handle an ax, a maul, and a wedge. He helped to fell trees, fashion logs, split rails, and do other important work in building the one-roomed cabin, which was to be the permanent home of the family. He assisted also in making the rough tables and chairs and the one rude bedstead or bed frame which constituted the principal furniture of the cabin. In his childhood Abraham did not enjoy the luxury of sleeping on a bedstead. His bed was simply a heap of dry leaves, which occupied a corner of the loft over the cabin. He climbed to it every night by a stepladder, or rather a number of pegs driven into the wall.

Rough and poor and full of hardship as his life was, Lincoln was by no means a sad or unhappy boy. On the contrary, he was full of fun and boyish pranks. His life in the open air, the vigorous exercise of every muscle which necessity forced upon him, the tonic of the forests which he breathed from his infancy, his interest in every living and growing thing about him,—all helped to make him unusually strong, healthy, buoyant, and rich in animal spirits.

The first great sorrow of his life came to him in the death of his dearly loved mother in 1818. The boy mourned for her as few children mourn even for the most loving parent. Day after day he went from the home made desolate by her death to weep on her grave under the near-by trees.

There were no churches in the Indiana wilderness, and the visits of wandering ministers of religion to the scattered settlements were few and far between. Little Abraham was grieved that no funeral service had been held over his dead mother. He felt that it was in some sense a lack of respect to her. He thought a great deal about the matter, and finally wrote a letter to a minister named Elkins, whom the family had known in Kentucky. Several months after the receipt of the letter Parson Elkins came to Indiana. On the Sabbath morning after his arrival, in the presence of friends who had come long distances to assist, he read the funeral service over the grave of Mrs. Lincoln. He also spoke in touching words of the tender Christian mother who lay buried there. This simple service greatly comforted the heart of the lonely boy.

Some time after Thomas Lincoln brought a new mother to his children from Kentucky. This was Mrs. Sally Bush Johnston, a young widow, who had been a girlhood friend of Nancy Hanks. She had three children,—John, Sarah, and Matilda Johnston,—who accompanied her to Indiana. The second Mrs. Lincoln brought a stock of household goods and furniture with her from Kentucky, and with the help of these made so many improvements in the rude log cabin that her stepchildren regarded her as a sort of magician or wonder worker. She was a good mother to them, intelligent, kind, and loving.

He was ten years old at this time, and had been to school but little. Indeed, he says himself that he only went to school "by littles," and that all his schooling "did not amount to more than a year." But he had learned to read when he was a mere baby at his mother's knee; and to a boy who loved knowledge as he did, this furnished the key to a broad education. His love of reading amounted to a passion. The books he had access to when a boy were very few; but they were good ones, and he knew them literally from cover to cover. They were the Bible, "Robinson Crusoe," "Pilgrim's Progress," a "History of the United States," and Weems's "Life of Washington." Some of these were borrowed, among them the "Life of

Washington," of which Abraham afterward became the happy owner. The story of how he became its owner has often been told.

The book had been loaned to him by a neighbor, a well-to-do farmer named Crawford. After reading from it late into the night by the light of pine knots, Abraham carried it to his bedroom in the loft. He placed it in a crack between the logs over his bed of dry leaves, so that he could reach to it as soon as the first streaks of dawn penetrated through the chinks in the log cabin. Unfortunately, it rained heavily during the night, and when he took down the precious volume in the morning, he found it badly damaged, all soddened and stained by the rain. He was much distressed, and hurried to the owner of the book as soon as possible to explain the mishap.

"I'm real sorry, Mr. Crawford," he said, in concluding his explanation, "and want to fix it up with you somehow, if you can tell me any way, for I ain't got the money to pay for it with."

"Well," said Mr. Crawford, "being as it's you, Abe, I won't be hard on you. Come over and shuck corn three days, and the book's yours."

The boy was delighted with the result of what at first had seemed a great misfortune. Verily, his sorrow was turned into joy. What! Shuck corn only three days and become owner of the book that told all about his greatest hero! What an unexpected piece of good fortune!

Lincoln's reading had revealed to him a world beyond his home in the wilderness. Slowly it dawned upon him that one day he might find his place in that great world, and he resolved to prepare himself with all his might for whatever the future might hold.

"I don't intend to delve, grub, shuck corn, split rails, and the like always," he told Mrs. Crawford after he had finished reading the "Life of Washington." "I'm going to fit myself for a profession."

"Why, what do you want to be now?" asked Mrs. Crawford, in surprise.

"Oh, I'll be president," said the boy, with a smile.

"You'd make a pretty president, with all your tricks and jokes, now wouldn't you?" said Mrs. Crawford.

"Oh, I'll study and get ready," was the reply, "and then maybe the chance will come."

If the life of George Washington, who had all the advantages of culture and training that his time afforded, was an inspiration to Lincoln, the poor hard-working backwoods boy, what should the life of Lincoln be to boys of to-day? Here is a further glimpse of the way in which he prepared himself to be president of the United States. The quotation is from Ida M. Tarbell's "Life of Lincoln."

"Every lull in his daily labor he used for reading, rarely going to his work without a book. When plowing or cultivating the rough fields of Spencer County, he found frequently a half hour for reading, for at the end of every long row the horse was allowed to rest, and Lincoln had his book out and was perched on stump or fence, almost as soon as the plow had come to a standstill. One of the few people left in Gentryville who still remembers Lincoln, Captain John Lamar, tells to this day of riding to mill with his father, and seeing, as they drove along, a boy sitting on the top rail of an old-fashioned, stake-and-rider worm fence, reading so intently that he did not notice their approach. His father, turning to him, said: 'John, look at that boy yonder, and mark my words, he will make a smart man out of himself. I may not see it, but you'll see if my words don't come true.' 'That boy was Abraham Lincoln,' adds Mr. Lamar, impressively."

Lincoln's father was illiterate, and had no sympathy with his son's efforts to educate himself. Fortunately for him, however, his stepmother helped and encouraged him in every way possible. Shortly before her death she said to a biographer of Lincoln: "I induced my husband to permit Abe to read and study at home, as well as at school. At first he was not easily reconciled to it, but finally he too seemed willing to encourage him to a certain extent. Abe was a dutiful son to me always, and we took particular care when he was reading not to disturb him,—would let him read on and on till he quit of his own accord."

Lincoln fully appreciated his stepmother's sympathy and love for him, and returned them in equal measure. It added greatly to his enjoyment of his reading and studies to have some one to whom he could talk about them, and in after life he always gratefully remembered what his second mother did for him in those early days of toil and effort.

If there was a book to be borrowed anywhere in his neighborhood, he was sure to hear about it and borrow it if possible. He said himself that he "read through every book he had ever heard of in that county for a circuit of fifty miles."

And how he read! Boys who have books and magazines and papers in abundance in their homes, besides having thousands of volumes to choose from in great city libraries, can have no idea of what a book meant to this boy in the wilderness. He devoured every one that came into his hands as a man famishing from hunger devours a crust of bread. He read and re-read it until he had made the contents his own.

"From everything he read," says Miss Tarbell, "he made long extracts, with his turkey-buzzard pen and brier-root ink. When he had no paper he would write on a board, and thus preserve his selections until he secured a copybook. The wooden fire shovel was his usual slate, and on its back he ciphered with a charred stick, shaving it off when it had become too grimy for use. The logs and boards in his vicinity he covered with his figures and quotations. By night he read and worked as long as there was light, and he kept a book in the crack of the logs in his loft to have it at hand at peep of day. When acting as ferryman on the Ohio in his nineteenth year, anxious, no doubt, to get through the books of the house where he boarded before he left the place, he read every night until midnight."

His stepmother said: "He read everything he could lay his hands on, and when he came across a passage that struck him, he would write it down on boards if he had no paper, and keep it by him until he could get paper. Then he would copy it, look at it, commit it to memory, and repeat it."

His thoroughness in mastering everything he undertook to study was a habit acquired in childhood. How he acquired this habit he tells himself. "Among my earliest recollections I remember how, when a mere child," he says, "I used to get irritated when anybody talked to me in a way I could not understand. I do not think I ever got angry at anything else in my life; but that always disturbed my temper, and has ever since. I can remember going to my little bedroom, after hearing the neighbors talk of an evening with my father, and spending no small part of the night walking up and down and trying to make out what was the exact meaning of some of their—to me—dark sayings.

"I could not sleep, although I tried to, when I got on such a hunt for an idea until I had caught it; and when I thought I had got it, I was not satisfied until I had repeated it over and over; until I had put it in language plain enough, as I thought, for any boy I knew to comprehend. This was a kind of passion with me, and it has stuck by me; for I am never easy now when I am handling a thought, till I have bounded it north and bounded it south and bounded it east and bounded it west."

With all his hard study, reading, and thinking, Lincoln was not a bookworm, nor a dull companion to the humble, unschooled people among whom his youth was spent. On the contrary, although he was looked up to as one whose acquirements in "book learning" had raised him far above every one in his neighborhood, he was the most popular youth in all the country round. No "husking bee," or "house raising" or merry-making of any kind was complete if Abraham was not present. He was witty, ready of speech, a good story-teller, and had stored his memory with a fund of humorous anecdotes, which he always used to good purpose and with great effect. He had committed to memory, and could recite all the poetry in the various school readers used at that time in the log- cabin schoolhouse. He could make rhymes himself, and even make impromptu speeches that excited the admiration of his hearers. He was the best wrestler, jumper, runner, and the strongest of all his young companions. Even when a mere youth he could lift as much as three full-grown men; and, "if you heard him fellin' trees in a clearin'," said his cousin, Dennis Hanks, "you would say there was three men at work by the way the trees fell. His ax would flash and bite into a sugar tree or sycamore, and down it would come."

His kindness and tenderness of heart were as great as his strength and agility. He loved all God's creatures, and cruelty to any of them always aroused his indignation. Only once did he ever attempt to kill any of the game in the woods, which the family considered necessary for their subsistence. He refers to this occasion in an autobiography, written by him in the third person, in the year 1860.

"A few days before the completion of his eighth year," he says, "in the absence of his father, a flock of wild turkeys approached the new log cabin; and Abraham, with a rifle gun, standing inside, shot through a crack and killed one of them. He has never since pulled the trigger on any larger game."

Any suffering thing, whether it was animal, man, woman, or child, was sure of his sympathy and aid. Although he never touched intoxicating drinks himself, he pitied those who lost manhood by their use. One night on his way home from a husking bee or house raising, he found an unfortunate man lying on the roadside overcome with drink. If the man were allowed to remain there, he would freeze to death. Lincoln raised him from the ground and carried him a long distance to the nearest house, where he remained with him during the night. The man was his firm friend ever after.

Women admired him for his courtesy and rough gallantry, as well as for his strength and kindness of heart; and he, in his turn, reverenced women, as every noble, strong man does. This big, bony, tall, awkward young fellow, who at eighteen measured six feet four, was as ready to care for a baby in the absence of its mother as he was to tell a good story or to fell a tree. Was it any wonder that he was popular with all kinds of people?

His stepmother says of him: "Abe was a good boy, and I can say what scarcely one woman—a mother—can say in a thousand; Abe never gave me a cross word or look, and never refused in fact or appearance to do anything I requested him. I never gave him a cross word in all my life. His mind and mine—what little I had— seemed to run together. He was here after he was elected president. He was a dutiful son to me always. I think he loved me truly. I had a son, John, who was raised with Abe. Both were good boys; but I must say, both now being dead, that Abe was the best boy I ever saw or expect to see."

Wherever he went, or whatever he did, he studied men and things, and gathered knowledge as much by observation as from books and whatever news-papers or other publications he could get hold of. He used to go regularly to the leading store in Gentryville, to read a Louisville paper, taken by the proprietor of the store, Mr. Jones. He discussed its contents, and exchanged views with the farmers who made the store their place of meeting. His love of oratory was great. When the courts were in session in Boonville, a town fifteen miles distant from his home, whenever he could spare a day, he used to walk there in the morning and back at night, to hear the lawyers argue cases and make speeches. By this time Abraham himself could make an impromptu speech on any subject with which he was at all familiar, good enough to win the applause of the Indiana farmers.

So, his boyhood days, rough, hard-working days, but not devoid of fun and recreation, passed. Abraham did not love work any more than other country boys of his age, but he never shirked his tasks. Whether it was plowing, splitting rails, felling trees, doing chores, reaping, threshing, or any of the multitude of things to be done on a farm, the work was always well done. Sometimes, to make a diversion, when he was working as a "hired hand," he would stop to tell some of his funny stories, or to make a stump speech before his fellow-workers, who would all crowd round him to listen; but he would more than make up for the time thus spent by the increased energy with which he afterward worked. Doubtless the other laborers, too, were refreshed and stimulated to greater effort by the recreation he afforded them and the inspiration of his example.

Thomas Lincoln had learned carpentry and cabinet making in his youth, and taught the rudiments of these trades to his son; so that in addition to his skill and efficiency in all the work that falls to the lot of a pioneer backwoods farmer, Abraham added the accomplishment of being a fairly good carpenter. He worked at these trades with his father whenever the opportunity offered. When he was not working for his family, he was hired out to the neighboring farmers. His highest wage was twenty-five cents a day, which he always handed over to his father.

Lincoln got his first glimpse of the world beyond Indiana when he worked for several months as a ferryman and boatman on the Ohio River, at Anderson Creek. He saw the steamers and vessels of all kinds sailing up and down the Ohio, laden with produce and merchandise, on their way to and from western and southern towns. He came in contact with different kinds of people from different states, and thus his views of the world and its people became a little more extended, and his longing to be somebody and to do something worth while in the world waxed stronger daily.

His work as a ferryman showed him that there were other ways of making a little money than by hiring out to the neighbors at twenty-five cents a day. He resolved to take some of the farm produce to New Orleans and sell it there. This project led to the unexpected earning of a dollar, which added strength to his purpose to prepare himself to take the part of a man in the world outside of Indiana. Let him tell in his own words, as he related the story to Mr. Seward years afterward, how he earned the dollar:—

"Seward," he said, "did you ever hear how I earned my first dollar?"

"No," said Mr. Seward.

"Well," replied he, "I was about eighteen years of age, and belonged, as you know, to what they call down south the 'scrubs'; people who do not own land and slaves are nobodies there; but we had succeeded in raising, chiefly by my labor, sufficient produce, as I thought, to justify me in taking it down the river to sell. After much persuasion I had got the consent of my mother to go, and had constructed a flatboat large enough to take the few barrels of things we had gathered to New Orleans. A steamer was going down the river. We have, you know, no wharves on the western streams, and the custom was, if passengers were at any of the landings, they were to go out in a boat, the steamer stopping and taking them on board. I was contemplating my new boat, and wondering whether I could make it stronger or improve it in any part, when two men with trunks came down to the shore in carriages, and looking at the different boats singled out mine, and asked, 'Who owns this?' I answered modestly, 'I do.' 'Will you,' said one of them, 'take us and our trunks to the steamer?' 'Certainly,' said I. I was very glad to have the chance of earning something, and supposed that each of them would give me a couple of bits. The trunks were put in my boat, the passengers seated themselves on them, and I sculled them out to the steamer. They got on board, and I lifted the trunks and put them on the deck. The steamer was about to put on steam again, when I called out, 'You have forgotten to pay me.' Each of them took from his pocket a silver half-dollar and threw it on the bottom of my boat. I could scarcely believe my eyes as I picked up the money. You may think it was a very little thing, and in these days it seems to me like a trifle, but it was a most important incident in my life. I could scarcely credit that I, the poor boy, had earned a dollar in less than a day; that by honest work I had earned a dollar. I was a more hopeful and thoughtful boy from that time."

In March, 1828, Lincoln was employed by one of the leading men of Gentryville to take a load of produce down the Mississippi River to New Orleans. For this service he was paid eight dollars a month and his rations.

This visit to New Orleans was a great event in his life. It showed him the life of a busy cosmopolitan city, which was a perfect wonderland to him. Everything he saw aroused his astonishment and interest, and served to educate him for the larger life on which he was to enter later.

The next important event in the history of the Lincoln family was their removal from Indiana to Illinois in 1830. The farm in Indiana had not prospered as they hoped it would,—hence the removal to new ground in Illinois. Abraham drove the team of oxen which carried their household goods from the old home to their new abiding place near Decatur, in Macon County, Illinois. Driving over the muddy, ill-made roads with a heavily laden team was hard and slow work, and the journey occupied a fortnight. When they arrived at their destination, Lincoln again helped to build a log cabin for the family home. With his stepbrother he also, as he said himself, "made sufficient of rails to fence ten acres of ground, and raised a crop of sown corn upon it the same year."

In that same year, 1830, he reached his majority. It was time for him to be about his own business. He had worked patiently and cheerfully since he was able to hold an ax in his hands for his own and the family's maintenance. They could now get along without him, and he felt that the time had come for him to develop himself for larger duties.

He left the log cabin, penniless, without even a good suit of clothes. The first work he did when he became his own master was to supply this latter deficiency. For a certain Mrs. Millet he "split four hundred rails for every yard of brown jeans, dyed with white walnut bark, necessary to make a pair of trousers."

For nearly a year he continued to work as a rail splitter and farm "hand." Then he was hired by a Mr. Denton Offut to take a flatboat loaded with goods from Sangamon town to New Orleans. So well pleased was Mr. Offut with the way in which Lincoln executed his commission that on his return he engaged him to take charge of a mill and store at New Salem.

There, as in every other place in which he had resided, he became the popular favorite. His kindness of heart, his good humor, his skill as a story teller, his strength, his courtesy, manliness, and honesty were such as to win all hearts. He would allow no man to use profane language before women. A boorish fellow who insisted on doing so in the store on one occasion, in spite of Lincoln's protests, found this out to his cost. Lincoln had politely requested him not to use such language before ladies, but the man persisted in doing so. When the women left the store, he became violently angry and began to abuse Lincoln. He wanted to pick a quarrel with him. Seeing this Lincoln said, "Well, if you must be whipped, I suppose I may as well whip you as any other man," and taking the man out of the store he gave him a well-merited chastisement. Strange to say, he became Lincoln's friend after this, and remained so to the end of his life.

His scrupulous honesty won for him in the New Salem community the title of "Honest Abe," a title which is still affectionately applied to him. On one occasion, having by mistake overcharged a customer six and a quarter cents, he walked three miles after the store was closed in order to restore the customer's money. At another time, in weighing tea for a woman, he used a quarter-pound instead of a half-pound weight. When he went to use the scales again, he discovered his mistake, and promptly walked a long distance to deliver the remainder of the tea.

Lincoln's determination to improve himself continued to be the leading object of his life. He said once to his fellow-clerk in the store, "I have talked with great men, and I do not see how they differ from others." His observation had taught him that the great difference in men's positions was not due so much to one having more talents or being more highly gifted than another, but rather to the way in which one cultivated his talent or talents and another neglected his.

Up to this time he had not made a study of grammar, but he realized that if he were to speak in public he must learn to speak grammatically. He had no grammar, and did not know where to get one. In this dilemma he consulted the schoolmaster of New Salem, who told him where and from whom he could borrow a copy of Kirkham's Grammar. The place named was six miles from New Salem. But that was nothing to a youth so hungry for an education as Lincoln. He immediately started for the residence of the fortunate people who owned a copy of Kirkham's Grammar. The book was loaned to him without hesitation. In a short time its contents were mastered, the student studying at night by the light of shavings burned in the village cooper's shop. "Well," said Lincoln to Greene, his fellow-clerk, when he had turned over the last page of the grammar, "if that's what they call a science, I think I'll go at another." The conquering of one thing after another, the thorough mastery of whatever he undertook to do, made the next thing easier of accomplishment than it would otherwise have been. In order to practice debating he used to walk seven or eight miles to debating clubs. No labor or trouble seemed too great to him if by it he could increase his knowledge or add to his acquirements. No matter how hard or exhausting his work, whether it was rail splitting, plowing, lumbering, boating, or store keeping, he studied and read every spare minute, and often until late at night.

But this sketch has already exceeded the limits of Lincoln's boyhood, for he had reached his twenty-second year while in the store in New Salem. How he was made captain of a company raised to fight against the Indians, how he kept store for himself, learned surveying, was elected a member of the Illinois legislature, studied law, and was admitted to the bar in Springfield, and how he finally became president of the United States,—all this belongs to a later chapter of his life.

Lincoln's rise from the poorest of log cabins to the White House, to be president of the greatest republic in the world, is one of the most inspiring stories in American biography. Yet he was not a genius, unless a determination to make the most of one's self and to persist in spite of all hardships, discouragements, and hindrances, be genius. He made himself what he was—one of the noblest, greatest, and best of men—by sheer dint of hard work and the cultivation of the talents that had been given him. No fortunate chances, no influential friends, no rare opportunities played a part in his life. Alone and unaided he made, by the grace of God, the great career which will forever challenge the admiration of mankind.

The Marble Waiteth

The Statue

The marble waits, immaculate and rude;
Beside it stands the sculptor, lost in dreams.
With vague, chaotic forms his vision teems.
Fair shapes pursue him, only to elude
And mock his eager fancy. Lines of grace
And heavenly beauty vanish, and, behold!
Out through the Parian luster, pure and cold,
Glares the wild horror of a devil's face.
The clay is ready for the modeling.
The marble waits: how beautiful, how pure,
That gleaming substance, and it shall endure,
When dynasty and empire, throne and king
Have crumbled back to dust. Well may you pause,
Oh, sculptor-artist! and, before that mute,
Unshapen surface, stand irresolute!
Awful, indeed, are art's unchanging laws.
The thing you fashion out of senseless clay,
Transformed to marble, shall outlive your fame;
And, when no more is known your race, or name,
Men shall be moved by what you mold to-day.
We all are sculptors. By each act and thought,
We form the model. Time, the artisan,
Stands, with his chisel, fashioning the Man,
And stroke by stroke the masterpiece is wrought.
Angel or demon? Choose, and do not err!
For time but follows as you shape the mold,
And finishes in marble, stern and cold,
That statue of the soul, the character.
By wordless blessing, or by silent curse,
By act and motive,—so do you define
The image which time copies, line by line,
For the great gallery of the Universe. —Ella Wheeler Wilcox

At the gateway of a new year, emerging from the gay carelessness of childhood, stand troops of buoyant, eager-eyed youths and maidens, gazing down the vista of the future with glad expectancy.

Fancy spreads upon her canvas radiant pictures of the joys and triumphs which await them in the unborn years. In their unclouded springtime there is no place for the specters of doubt and fear which too often overshadow the autumn of life.

In this formative period, the soul is unsoiled by warfare with the world. It lies, like a block of pure, uncut Parian marble, ready to be fashioned into—what?

Its possibilities are limitless. You are the sculptor. An unseen hand places in yours the mallet and the chisel, and a voice whispers: "The marble waiteth. What will you do with it?"

In this same block the angel and the demon lie sleeping. Which will you call into life? Blows of some sort you must strike. The marble cannot be left uncut. From its crudity some shape must be evolved. Shall it be one of beauty, or of deformity; an angel, or a devil? Will you shape it into a statue of beauty which will enchant the world, or will you call out a hideous image which will demoralize every beholder?

What are your ideals, as you stand facing the dawn of this new year with the promise and responsibility of the new life on which you have entered, awaiting you? Upon them depends the form which the rough block shall take. Every stroke of the chisel is guided by the ideal behind the blow.

Look at this easy-going, pleasure-loving youth who takes up the mallet and smites the chisel with careless, thoughtless blows. His mind is filled with images of low, sensual pleasures; the passing enjoyment of the hour is everything to him; his work, the future, nothing. He carries in his heart, perhaps, the bestial motto of the glutton, "Eat, drink, and be merry, for to-morrow we die;" or the flippant maxim of the gay worldling, "A short life and a merry one; the foam of the chalice for me;" forgetting that beneath the foam are the bitter dregs, which, be he ever so unwilling, he must swallow, not to-day, nor yet to-morrow,—perhaps not this year nor next; but sometime, as surely as the reaping follows the sowing, will the bitter draught follow the foaming glass of unlawful pleasure.

As the years go by, and youth merges into manhood, the sculptor's hand becomes more unsteady. One false blow follows another in rapid succession. The formless marble takes on distorted outlines. Its whiteness has long since become spotted. The sculptor, with blurred vision and shattered nerves, still strikes with aimless hand, carving deep gashes, adding a crooked line here, another there, soiling and marring until no trace of the virgin purity of the block of marble which was given him remains. It has become so grimy, so demoniacally fantastic in its outlines, that the beholder turns from it with a shudder.

Not far off we see another youth at work on a block of marble, similar in every detail to the first. The tools with which he plies his labor differ in no wise from those of the worker we have been following.

The glory of the morning shines upon the marble. Glowing with enthusiasm, the light of a high purpose illuminating his face, the sculptor, with steady hand and eye, begins to work out his ideal. The vision that flits before him is so beautiful that he almost fears the cunning of his hand will be unequal to fashioning it from the rigid mass before him. Patiently he measures each blow of the mallet. With infinite care he chisels each line and curve. Every stroke is true.

Months stretch into years, and still we find the sculptor at work. Time has given greater precision to his touch, and the skill of the youth, strengthened by noble aspirations and right effort, has become positive genius in the man. If he has not attained the ideal that haunted him, he has created a form so beautiful in its clear-cut outlines, so imposing in the majesty of its purity and strength, that the beholder involuntarily bows before it.

The Marble Waiteth. What Will You Do with It?

www.ingramcontent.com/pod-product-compliance
Lightning Source LLC
Chambersburg PA
CBHW022044160426
43198CB00008B/123